Social Interaction

READINGS IN SOCIOLOGY

FOURTH EDITION

Social Interaction

READINGS IN SOCIOLOGY

FOURTH EDITION

Edited by CANDACE CLARK
Montclair State College
HOWARD ROBBOY
Trenton State College

St. Martin's Press *New York*

To Our Parents
and to Larry W. DeBord

Acquisitions Editor: Louise H. Waller
Project management: Chad Colburn, Publication Services
Cover design: Jeheber and Peace, Inc.

Library of Congress Catalog Card Number: 90-63538

Manufactured in the United States of America.
65432
fedcba

For information, write:
St. Martin's Press, Inc.
175 Fifth Avenue
New York, New York 10010

ISBN: 0-312-05665-6

Preface

THE FOURTH EDITION OF *SOCIAL INTERACTION* BRINGS NEW, OFTEN PATH-BREAKING articles to the ranks of classics, such as William Foote Whyte's study of "corner boys," Erving Goffman's analysis of self-presentations in everyday life, and D. L. Rosenhan's look inside a mental hospital.

We have remained loyal to two themes that cross-cut the previous editions. First, the majority of our selections come from the symbolic interactionist school of sociological theory and research. Second, we have purposefully chosen, for all sections of the book, articles that recognize women's role in society and articles written by women sociologists. Further, we sought materials that were readable yet substantive and insightful—more than mere journalistic illustrations of concepts introduced in sociology texts.

Our goal is to engage both sociology students and their professors. We hope students will find that these articles strike familiar chords and offer ideas, concepts, and theories that help them make sense of their social worlds. We hope faculty members will also be excited by the new material and excited again by the old. We still feel the fascination of sociology after more than twenty years in the field, and we hope this book conveys that fascination and inspires it in others.

In preparing this edition of *Social Interaction,* we relied on many people. Our editors at St. Martin's Press—first Don Reisman, then Joanne Daniels and Randi Israelow, and later Louise Waller—were supportive and helpful. Also, a team of sociologists assisted us by reviewing each article in the fourth edition and suggesting deletions and additions. They are Richard Adams, UCLA; Robert Avery, University of Pittsburgh; Brian Berry, Rochester Institute of Technology; David Borgen, Boston University; William Brennan, St. Louis University; Marvin Bressler, Princeton University; Thomas Burns, University of Maryland; Timothy Curry, Ohio State; Arlene Kaplan Daniels, Northwestern University; Alan Davidson, University of Connecticut; Sanford Dornbusch, Stanford University; Saul Feinman, University of Wyoming; Peter Freund, Montclair State College; Kenneth Gardner, Ball State University; Glenn Goodwin, Pitzer College; Cecil Greek, Central State University; Kathleen Grove, University of San Diego; James House, University of Michigan at Ann Arbor; Sandra Hugaley, Emory University; Mark Hutter, Glassboro State College; James William Jordan, Longwood College; Marie Lewis, University of Arizona; Judith Little, Humboldt State University; George Lowe, Texas Tech University; David Maines, Wayne State University; Trudy Matheny, University of South Carolina; Richard Mitchell, Oregon State University; Robert Newby, Central Michigan University; Arthur Scott, Providence College; Donald Trow, SUNY Binghampton; Steven Worden, University of Arkansas; Eric Wright, Indiana University at Bloomington; Josephine Yelder, Pepperdine University; M. Ruggie, Barnard College; Michael Klausner, University of Pittsburgh; Roslyn Bologh, St. John's University; Diane Sachs, Rhodes College; Regina Kenen, Trenton State University; Kathleen Daly, Yale University; Robert P. Stuckert, Berea College; Elizabeth Watson, University of Redlands; S. Varmette, Southern Connecticut State University; Christian Ritter, Kent State University; Andrew Twaddle, University of Missouri at Columbia; Buford Farris, St. Louis University; Earl N. Nance, Rock Valley College; Theo Majka, University of Dayton; Robert H. West, Temple University; A. Pilkinston, California Polytechnic State University; Ray R. Canning, University of Utah; and C. Thomas Behler, Moravian College.

We also want to thank the many previous users of this book who on their own initiative have offered suggestions, comments, and praise. They have made the fourth edition possible.

Candace Clark
Howard Robboy

Contents

Correlation Chart for Social *Interaction* and Standard Sociology Texts

Part (Part No.)	Coser et al. 3/e *Introduction to Sociology* HBJ (1991)	Eitzen & Zinn Baca 4/e *Understanding Society* A&B (1988)	Hess et al. 4/e *Sociology* Macmillan (1991)	Kornblum *Sôciety in Changing World* Holt (1991)	Landis 7/e *Sociology* Wadsworth (1989)	Light et al. 5/e *Sociology* Knopf (1989)	Macionis 3/e *Sociology* Prentice-Hall (1991)	Persell 3/e *Understanding Society* Harper (1990)	Popenoe 8/e *Sociology* Prentice-Hall (1991)	Robertson 3/e *Sociology* Worth (1987)	Schaefer 3/e *Sociology* McGraw-Hill (1989)	Smelser 4/e *Sociology* Prentice-Hall (1991)	Shepard 4/e *Sociology* West (1989)	Stark 3/e *Sociology* Wadsworth (1989)	Thio 2/e *Sociology* Harper (1989)	Tischler et al. *Introduction to Sociology* Holt (1988)	VanderZanden *The Social Experience* Random House (1988)
INTRODUCTION (I)	1	1	1,2	1	1,15	1	1	1	1	1,2	1	1	1,2	1	1	1	1
CULTURE (II)	3	5	3	4	3	4	3	3	3	3	3	2	4	2,5	3	3	2
TRANSMISSION OF CULTURE: SOCIALIZATION (III)	5	6	5	6	2	5,6	5,6	5	6	5	4	4	6	6	6	4	3
INTERACTION IN EVERYDAY LIFE (IV)	4	3	5	7	2	3	4	4	4,5	6	5	5	5	3	4	5	3
SOCIAL ORGANIZATIONS: LIFE IN GROUPS (V)	6	2,4	4	3,7	4	8	7	4,6	7	7	6	3,6	7	4	5	6	4

INEQUALITIES: CLASS, RACE, GENDER (VI)	7,9, 10	9,10, 11,12	7,8, 9	8,12, 13,14	5,6	6,10, 11,12 13,14	9,10, 11,12, 13,14	9,10, 11,14	9,10, 11,12, 13	10, 11, 12	8,9 10,11, 12	9,10, 11,12	9,10, 11	9,10, 11,12	9,10, 11,12	8,9, 10,11	6,7, 8,9, 10,11
DEVIANCE,CONFORMITY, SOCIAL CONTROL (VII)	8	7,8	6	9	14	7	8	7	8	8	7	7	8	7,8	7	7 15	5
INTERACTION IN INSTI-TUTIONAL CONTEXTS: FAMILY (VIIIA)	11	15	10	15	7	16	15	14	14	15	13	13	13	13	13	12	9
INTERACTION IN INSTI-TUTIONAL CONTEXTS: EDUCATION (VIIIB)	13	16	12	17	8	17	16	15	15	14	16	14	16	16	14	14	10
INTERACTION IN INSTI-TUTIONAL CONTEXTS: WORK, ECONOMICS (VIIIC)	16	13	11	18	10	15	19	13	17	17	15	16	16	16	17	16	–
INTERACTION IN INSTI-TUTIONAL CONTEXTS: HEALTH, ILLNESS (VIIID)	14	–	15	–	–	19	20	18	–	16	17	–	–	–	18	–	10
INTERACTION IN INSTI-TUTIONAL CONTEXTS: RELIGION (VIIIE)	15	17	13	16	9	18	17	16	16	15	14	15	14	14	15	13	10
SOCIAL AND CULTURAL CHANGE (IX)	17,18	4	19,20	10,11	12,13	21,22	22,23	19	21,22	19,20, 21,22	20	19,20	17,20	17,19, 21	23	20,21	12

Part I. Introduction

THE SOCIOLOGICAL PERSPECTIVE

As participants in the give and take, ebb and flow of human interaction, we take much of our social experience for granted. We move from group to group—family, friends, strangers; in classrooms, in stores, in the workplace—unconcerned with the amazing complexity of human activity. We pay as little attention to what goes on beneath the surface of social activity as we do to the inner workings of the telephone or the automobile.

But the electronics technician and the automobile mechanic know that inside the telephone or under the hood of the car lies intricate machinery. In much the same way, the student of sociology learns to peer beneath the veneer of conventional understanding to look systematically at the patterns and the processes of our daily lives and the shared meanings and symbols that make the "social dance" possible. Sociology is, then, a unique way of viewing the human world. It is the study of the complexities of social life and interaction that we normally take for granted.

In this volume we have collected readings from articles and books that we, our colleagues, and especially our students have found to be exciting and challenging explorations beneath the surface of social life. The readings analyze human relationships taking place in small groups and huge bureaucracies. They report on investigations set in private homes, public offices, and street corner shops. They also consider important social processes—cooperation, conflict, socialization, and social change.

In the first selection, Peter Berger welcomes us to the sociological perspective. He examines the special meanings to sociology of the terms *society* and *social*. *Society,* according to Berger, can be defined as "a large complex of human relationships," "a system of interaction." A society does not necessarily comprise large numbers of interacting people; rather, a society is any relatively self-contained, autonomous system. The term *social* as used by sociologists refers to actions oriented toward others. Thus *social interaction* refers to those aspects of all types of human behavior that involve an awareness of other human beings.

Furthermore, Berger delineates four major sociological themes, or motifs. When used together, these motifs allow us to view the world through sociological "lenses," thereby gaining insight into the workings of the social world. The first theme is that of debunking many myths that people hold about their societies. Social scientists cannot be so naive as to accept at face value the common explanations of how things work. They must question these very explanations and try to understand how they are produced. They must gather evidence to determine whether or not they are accurate.

The second motif that Berger describes is that of paying attention to aspects of the social world that would be considered unrespectable by many middle-class members of society. Only by looking at criminals, the poor, minorities, and the like can we gain a complete picture of our world. "Respectable" citizens often describe the world in ways that protect and justify their own behavior. Also, their experiences with the system are not the same as the experiences of the "unrespectable." We need both viewpoints. For instance, a presidential commission studying the causes of widespread rioting in the mid-1960s included testimony of city officials *and* interviews with the residents of poor neighborhoods where rioting occurred. Their conclusion was that, contrary to the officials' views, societal racism (in which the officials themselves played a part) was responsible for the conditions that sparked the violence. In another vein, sociologists who have attempted to understand the failure of our prison system to rehabilitate criminals have paid as much attention to the prisoners' descriptions of prison life and how it affects them as to the statements of guards and wardens.

Third, sociologists must always keep in mind the relativity of social values and beliefs. By this we mean that standards of "right" and "wrong" as well as opinions and even "knowledge," can be understood fully only within the context of a given society at a given point in time. What is considered appropriate behavior or truth or evil in one society at one historical moment may be considered inappropriate behavior or falsehood or good in another. Values are, therefore, relative to the society under study, rather than being absolute or universal. Sociologists will not be able to understand what a value or belief means to those who hold it unless they maintain awareness of the principle of relativity.

Fourth, Berger discusses the cosmopolitan motif in sociological thought. What he means here is that, rather than being oriented strictly toward local issues and concerns, sociologists have generally been oriented toward other lands, other peoples, other ways of life and world views.

Of course, these four motifs are interrelated and mutually reinforcing. They are the essence of the "sociological imagination." As you read Berger's explanations of them, and the articles that follow, you too will start to view human interaction from the sociological perspective.

Herbert Blumer, author of the second reading, was a prominent theorist in the *symbolic interactionist* school of thought in sociology. Symbolic interactionists, rather than studying entire societies at the macrosocial level, focus primarily on microsocial events and processes. They want to discover how participants in human groups define or "construct" their social worlds—how they make sense of the activities, settings, and situations that constitute their everyday lives. Symbolic interactionists also examine the workings of social processes, such as training new members to take on the group's world view or creating and maintaining group cohesion as well as power differences (microhierarchies).

Blumer's point in "Society as Symbolic Interaction" is a fundamental one: when people interact, they use symbols to indicate to themselves the meanings of their own and each other's actions. Further, group actions involve the fitting together of individual lines of action. Thus society—group action—*is* symbolic interaction.

Most of the selections in this book have been shaped by the symbolic interactionist perspective. They focus on the microsocial level, the arenas in which people encounter each other face to face. These microlevel studies can also tell us a great deal about macrosocial issues such as how societies survive, how they are stratified, and the like.

HOW SOCIOLOGISTS GATHER DATA

As Berger notes, the sociologist works by making "inquisitive intrusions" beyond the facades of social life. Above all, sociology is an *empirical* study of human interaction, which means that it rests on research and observation of people working, relaxing, learning, thinking about their concerns—in short, how they are living their lives—rather than on prior assumptions or hunches about how society works.

Research takes many forms for sociologists, but all forms involve searching for evidence that will help us discover the abstract patterns operating beneath the facades. These forms include the survey, in which a series of predetermined questions is put to a large sample of people. A survey can be very short and focused—as with Gallup polls of voters' intentions—or longer and more encompassing—as with studies of life-styles, aspirations, attitudes, and the like.

Participant observation is another commonly used method of getting information about social behavior. The researcher actually becomes involved as a member of the group or situation under study in order to gain clearer insights into the meanings that people give to their behavior and to absorb more of the flavor of the lives of those under study.

With intensive interviews, sociologists begin with a brief, open-ended interview schedule that allows them to delve and probe into the life situations of those chosen for research. At the same time respondents can answer in their own words and explain their answers in detail.

The classical experiment is seldom used in sociology, because many human characteristics and patterns of behavior cannot be dictated or altered by the researcher. In a true experiment, the researcher must begin with at least two groups—the *experimental* group and the *control* group—that are identical in all ways considered relevant for the study. The experimental group must then be manipulated by the experimenter; that is, some "treatment," such as an educational program, a frightening film, or additional income, must be administered to the experimental group only. Any changes found within this group are then compared with developments within the control group. If the groups were in fact identical to begin with, and if the experimental group changed more than the control group, we then infer that the treatment caused those changes. In reality, it is often difficult to say that two groups were identical. Furthermore, many of the factors that we might expect to cause differences in people's lives—for instance, being born poor or black—cannot easily or ethically be introduced by the experimenter as treatments. Thus we rely often on other research methods, such as the survey or participant observation. With these methods, we can look at existing differences among people (whether they are poor or well-off, for example) to see if these differences are related to other factors (such as whether they can afford to attend college).

Using unobtrusive measures involves looking for traces of human actions and interactions without having to deal directly with those people under study. For example, one way of getting evidence about drinking patterns without asking people how much they drink is to observe the number of empty bottles thrown away. Researchers have determined which museum exhibits are the more popular by counting noseprints that accumulate on the glass enclosures of the exhibits. Documentary evidence of how people feel and act can be found in magazine stories, advertisements, newspaper editorials, telephone directories, and the like.

All the methods listed here except unobtrusive measures are reactive. By this we mean that the researcher must interact with those being studied, and the researcher's mere presence may cause others to react in ways that are not typical or completely truthful. Research involving humans is, therefore, necessarily subject to unique problems that chemists and physicists do not face. The research encounter itself is a type of interaction, and that interaction is based on informal, unwritten rules for how to act as, say, an "interviewer" and an "interviewee." Of course, this fact may cause us to question the validity, or accuracy, of research findings. No research method or technique is perfect, and we should be aware of likely flaws of various methods so that we can become critical consumers of information.

RECURRING THEMES

This section introduces several themes that will recur again and again. First, as we noted earlier, societal members are generally unaware of the patterned regularities and processes of beliefs and behavior that exist in their society. Second, when members of a society attempt to make sense of their social world, creating explanations for various events and phenomena, their explanations are often wrong. This is so because they do not have the time, the inclination, or the expertise to gather information appropriate for making valid observations and interpretations. Thus myths continue to exist in abundance.

A third theme that you will encounter here many times is the importance of social interaction for determining how we define the world, what we think of ourselves, and how we behave. By learning the symbols of our culture from those with whom we interact, we come to share in a common understanding of reality. Despite the fact that we in the United States have learned to think of ourselves as unique individuals who exercise "free will" to determine our own thoughts and behavior, in reality our interactions with others in various settings and situations are constantly constraining and limiting our thoughts, our actions, and even our emotions. All you need to do to convince yourself of the validity of this point is to imagine what your thoughts, values, opinions, emotions, and actions would be if you had been born in a different society—say, in Japan, in Iraq, or in Argentina. All these societies allow for some personal discretion in thought and behavior; but at the same time, all have definitions of reality, values, symbolic universes, and mechanisms of social control that shape those who happen to be born there (or who migrate there) at almost every turn. The very alternatives available to us are limited in number. And our choices among these alternatives are influenced by others with whom we interact, from parents to teachers to co-workers to police.

SOCIOLOGY AS A FORM OF CONSCIOUSNESS

Peter L. Berger

. . . Sociology is neither a timeless nor a necessary undertaking of the human mind. If this is conceded, the question logically arises as to the timely factors that made it a necessity to specific men. Perhaps, indeed, no intellectual enterprise is timeless or necessary. But religion, for instance, has been well-nigh universal in provoking intensive mental preoccupation throughout human history, while thoughts designed to solve the economic problems of exisitence have been a necessity in most human cultures. Certainly this does not mean that theology or economics . . . are universally present phenomena of the mind, but we are at least on safe ground if we say that there always seems to have been human thought directed towards the problems that now constitute the subject matter of these disciplines. Not even this much, however, can be said of sociology. It presents itself rather as a peculiarly modern and Western cogitation. And, as we shall try to argue [here], it is constituted by a peculiarly modern form of consciousness.

The peculiarity of sociological perspective becomes clear with some reflection concerning the meaning of the term "society," a term that refers to the object *par excellence* of the discipline. Like most terms used by sociologists, this one is derived from common usage, where its meaning is imprecise. Sometimes it means a particular band of people (as in "Society for the Prevention of Cruelty to Animals"), sometimes only those people endowed with great prestige or privilege (as in "Boston society ladies"), and on other occasions it is simply used to denote company of any sort (for example, "he greatly suffered in those years for lack of society"). There are other, less frequent meanings as well. The sociologist uses the term in a more precise sense, though, of course, there are differences in usage within the discipline itself. The sociologist thinks of "society" as denoting a large complex of human relationships, or to put it in more technical language, as referring to a system of interaction. The word "large" is difficult to specify quantitatively in this context. The sociologist may speak of a "society" including millions of human beings (say, "American society"), but he may also use the term to refer to a numerically much smaller collectivity (say, "the society of sophomores on this campus"). Two people chatting on a street corner will hardly constitute a "society," but three people stranded on an island certainly will. The applicability of the concept, then, cannot be decided on quantitative grounds alone. It rather applies when a complex of relationships is sufficiently succinct to be analyzed by itself, understood as an autonomous entity, set against others of the same kind.

The adjective "social" must be similarly sharpened for sociological use. In common speech it may denote, once more, a number of different things—the informal quality of a certain gathering ("this is a social meeting—let's not discuss business"), an altruistic attitude on somebody's part ("he had a strong social concern in his job"), or, more generally, anything derived from contact with other people ("a social disease"). The sociologist will use the term more narrowly and more precisely to refer to the quality of interaction, interrelationship, mutuality. Thus two men chatting on a street corner do not constitute a "society," but what transpires between them is certainly "social." "Society" consists of a complex of such "social" events. As to the exact definition of the "social," it is difficult to improve on Max Weber's definition of a "social" situation as one in which people orient their actions towards one another. The web of meanings, expectations and conduct resulting from mutual orientation is the stuff of sociological analysis.

Yet this refinement of terminology is not enough to show up the distinctiveness of the sociological angle of vision. We may get close by comparing the latter with the perspective of other disciplines concerned with human actions. The economist, for example, is concerned with the analyses of processes that occur in society and that can be described as social. These processes have to do with the basic problem of economic activity—the allocation of scarce goods and services within a society. The economist will be concerned with these processes in terms of the way in which they carry out, or fail to carry out, this function. The sociologist, in looking at the same processes, will naturally have to take into consideration their economic purpose. But his distinctive interest is not necessarily related to this purpose as such. He will be interested in a variety of human relationships and interactions that may occur here and that may be quite irrelevant to the economic goals in question. Thus economic activity involves relationships of power, prestige, prejudice, or even play that can be analyzed with only marginal reference to the properly economic function of the activity.

The sociologist finds his subject matter present in all human activities, but not all aspects of these activities constitute this subject matter. Social interaction is not some specialized sector of what men do with each other. It is rather a certain aspect of all these doings. Another way of putting this is by saying that the sociologist carries on a special sort of abstraction. The social, as an object of inquiry, is not a segregated field of human activity. Rather (to borrow a phrase from Lutheran sacramental theology) it is present "in, with, and under" many different fields of such activity. The sociologist does not look at phenomena that nobody else is aware of. But he looks at the same phenomena in a different way.

As a further example we could take the perspective of the lawyer. Here we actually find a point of view much broader in scope than that of the economist. Almost any human activity can, at one time or another, fall within the province of the lawyer. This, indeed, is the fascination of the law. Again, we find here a very special procedure of abstraction. From the immense wealth and variety of human deportment the lawyer selects those aspects that are pertinent (or, as he would say, "material") to his very particular frame of reference. As anyone who has ever been involved in a lawsuit well knows, the criteria of what is relevant or irrelevant legally will often greatly surprise the principals in the case in question. This need not concern us here. We would rather observe that the legal frame of reference consists of a number of carefully defined models of human activity. Thus we have clear models of obligation, responsibility or wrongdoing. Definite conditions have to prevail before any empirical act can be subsumed under one of these headings, and these conditions are laid down by statutes or precedent. When these conditions are not met, the act in question is legally irrelevant. The expertise of the lawyer consists of knowing the rules by which these models are constructed. He knows, within his frame of reference, when a business contract is binding, when the driver of an automobile may be held to be negligent, or when rape has taken place.

The sociologist may look at these same phenomena, but his frame of reference will be quite different. Most importantly, his perspective on these phenomena cannot be derived from statutes or precedent. His interest in the human relationships occurring in a business transaction has no bearing on the legal validity of contracts signed, just as sociologically interesting deviance in sexual behavior may not be capable of being subsumed under some particular legal heading. From the lawyer's point of view, the sociologist's inquiry is extraneous to the legal frame of reference. One might say that, with reference to the conceptual edifice of the law, the sociologist's activity is subterranean in character. The lawyer is concerned with what may be called the official conception of the situation. The sociologist often deals with very unofficial conceptions indeed. For the lawyer the essential thing to understand is how the law looks upon a certain type of criminal. For the sociologist it is equally important to see how the criminal looks at the law.

To ask sociological questions, then, presupposes that one is interested in looking some distance beyond the commonly accepted or officially defined goals of human actions. It presupposes a certain awareness that human events have different levels of meaning, some of which are hidden from the consciousness of everyday life. It may even presuppose a measure of suspicion about the way in which human events are offically interpreted by the authorities, be they political, juridical, or religious in character. If one is willing to go as far as that, it would seem evident that not all historical circumstances are equally favorable for the development of sociological perspective.

It would appear plausible, in consequence, that sociological thought would have the best chance to develop in historical circumstances marked by severe jolts to the self-conception, especially the official and authoritative and generally accepted self-conception, of a culture. It is only in such circumstances that perceptive men are likely to be motivated to think beyond the assertions of this self-conception and, as a result, question the authorities. . . . It was with the disintegration of [Christendom and feudalism and the emergence of urban, industrial states] that the underlying frame of "society" came into view—that is, a world of motives and forces that could not be understood in terms of the official interpretations of social reality. Sociological perspective can then be understood in terms of such phrases as "seeing through" "looking behind" very much as such phrases would be employed in common speech—"seeing through his game," "looking behind the scenes"—in other words, "being up on all the tricks."

We will not be far off if we see sociological thought as part of what Nietzsche called "the art of mistrust." Now, it would be a gross oversimplification to think that this art has existed only in modern times. "Seeing through" things is probably a pretty general function of intelligence, even in very primitive societies. The American anthropologist Paul Radin has provided us with a vivid description of the skeptic as a human type in primitive culture. We also have evidence from civilizations other than that of the modern West, bearing witness to forms of consciousness that could well be called protosociological. We could point, for instance, to Herodotus or to Ibn-Khaldun. There are even texts from ancient Egypt envincing a profound disenchantment with a political and social order that has acquired the reputation of having been one of the most cohesive in human history. However, with the beginning of the modern era in the West this form of consciousness intensifies, becomes concentrated and systematized, marks the thought of an increasing number of perceptive men. This is not the place to discuss in detail the prehistory of sociological thought . . . . Suffice it to stress once more that sociological thought marks the fruition of a number of intellectual developments that have a very specific location in modern Western history.

Let us return instead to the proposition that sociological perspective involves a process of "seeing through" the facades of social structures.

We could think of this in terms of a common experience of people living in large cities. One of the fascinations of a large city is the immense variety of human activities taking place behind the seemingly anonymous and endlessly undifferentiated rows of houses. A person who lives in such a city will time and again experience surprise or even shock as he discovers the strange pursuits that some men engage in quite unobtrusively in houses that, from the outside, look like all the others on a certain street. Having had this experience once or twice, one will repeatedly find oneself walking down a street, perhaps late in the evening, and wondering what may be going on under the bright lights showing through a line of drawn curtains. An ordinary family engaged in pleasant talk with guests? A scene of desperation amid illness or death? Or a scene of debauched pleasures? Perhaps a strange cult or a dangerous conspiracy? The facades of the houses cannot tell us, proclaiming nothing but an architectural conformity to the tastes of some group or class that may not even inhabit the street any longer. The social mysteries lie behind the facades. The wish to penetrate to these mysteries is [analogous] to sociological curiosity. In some cities that are suddenly struck by calamity this wish may be abruptly realized. Those who have experienced wartime bombings know of the sudden encounters with unsuspected (and sometimes unimaginable) fellow tenants in the air-raid shelter of one's apartment building. Or they can recollect the startling morning sight of a house hit by a bomb during the night, neatly sliced in half, the facade torn away and the previously hidden interior mercilessly revealed in the daylight. But in most cities that one may normally live in, the facades must be penetrated by one's own inquisitive intrusions. Similarly, there are historical situations in which the facades of society are violently torn apart and all but the most incurious are forced to see that there was a reality behind the facades all along. Usually this does not happen and the facades continue to confront us with seemingly rocklike permanence. The perception of the reality behind the facades then demands a considerable intellectual effort.

A few examples of the way in which sociology "looks behind" the facades of social structures might serve to make our argument clearer. Take, for instance, the political organization of a community. If one wants to find out how a modern American city is governed, it is very easy to get the official information about this subject. The city will have a charter, operating under the laws of the state. With some advice from informed individuals, one may look up various statutes that define the constitution of the city. Thus one may find out that this particular community has a city-manager form of administration, or that party affiliations do not appear on the ballot in municipal elections, or that the city government participates in a regional water district. In similar fashion, with the help of some newspaper reading, one may find out the offically recognized political problems of the community. One may read that the city plans to annex a certain suburban area, or that there has been a change in the zoning ordinances to facilitate industrial development in another area, or even that one of the members of the city council has been accused of using his office for personal gain. All such matters still occur on the, as it were, visible, official or public level of political life. However, it would be an exceedingly naive person who would believe that this kind of information gives him a rounded picture of the political reality of that community. The sociologist will want to know above all the constituency of the "informal power structure" (as it has been called by Floyd Hunter, an American sociologist interested in such studies), which is a configuration of men and their power that cannot be found in any statutes, and probably cannot be read about in the newspapers. The political scientist or the legal expert might find it very interesting to compare the city charter with the constitutions of other similar communities. The sociologist will be far more concerned with discovering the way in which powerful vested interests influence or even control the actions of officials elected under the charter. These vested interests will not be found in city hall, but rather in executive suites of corporations that may not even be located in that community, in the private mansions of a handful of powerful men, perhaps in the offices of certain labor unions or even, in some instances, in the headquarters of criminal organizations. When the sociologist concerns himself with power, he will "look behind" the official mechanisms that are supposed to regulate power in the community. This does not necessarily mean that he will regard the official mechanisms as totally ineffective or their legal definition as totally illusionary. But at the very least he will insist that there is another level of reality to be investigated in the particular system of power. In some cases he might conclude that to look for real power in the publicly recognized places is quite delusional.

• • •

Or take an example from economic life. The personnel manager of an industrial plant will take delight in preparing brightly colored charts that show the table of organization that is supposed to administer the production process. Every man has his place, every person in the organization knows from whom he receives his orders and to whom he must transmit them, every work team has its assigned role in the great drama of production. In reality things rarely work this way—and every good personnel manager knows this. Superimposed on the official blueprint of the organization is a much subtler, much less visible network of human groups, with their loyalties, prejudices, antipathies and (most important) codes of behavior. Industrial sociology is full of data on the operations of this informal network, which always exists in varying degrees of accommodation and conflict with the official system. Very much the same coexistence of formal and informal organization are to be found wherever large numbers of men work together or live together under a system of discipline—military organizations, prisons, hospitals, schools, going back to the mysterious leagues that children form among themselves and that their parents only rarely discern. Once more, the sociologist will seek to penetrate the smoke screen of the official versions of reality (those of the foreman, the officer, the teacher) and try to grasp the signals that come from the "underworld" (those of the worker, the enlisted man, the schoolboy).

Let us take one further example. In Western countries, and especially in America, it is assumed that men and women marry because they are in love. There is a broadly based popular mythology about the character of love as a violent, irresistable emotion that strikes where it will, a mystery that is the goal of most young people and often of the not-so-young as well. As soon as one investigates, however, which people actually marry each other, one finds that the lightning-shaft of Cupid seems to be guided rather strongly within very definite channels of class, income, education, racial and religious background. If one then investigates a little further into the behavior that is engaged in prior to marriage under the rather misleading euphemism of "courtship," one finds channels of interaction that are often rigid to the point of ritual. The suspicion begins to dawn on one that, most of the time, it is not so much the emotion of love that creates a certain kind of relationship, but carefully predefined and often planned relationships eventually generate the desired emotion. In other words, when certain conditions are met or have been constructed, one allows oneself "to fall in love." The sociologist investigating our patterns of "courtship" and marriage soon discovers a complex web of motives related in many ways to the entire institutional structure within which an individual lives his life—class, career, economic ambition, aspirations of power and prestige. The miracle of love now begins to look somewhat synthetic. Again, this need not mean in any given instance that the sociologist will declare the romantic interpretation to be an illusion. But once more, he will look beyond the immediately given and publicly approved interpretations. Contemplating a couple that in its turn is contemplating the moon, the sociologist need not feel constrained to deny the emotional impact of the scene thus illuminated. But he will observe the machinery that went into the construction of the scene in its nonlunar aspects—the status index of the automobile from which the contemplation occurs, the canons of taste and tactics that determine the costume of the contemplators, the many ways in which language and demeanor place them socially, thus the social location and intentionality of the entire enterprise.

It may have become clear at this point that the problems that will interest the sociologist are not necessarily what other people may call "problems." The way in which public officials and newspapers (and, alas, some college textbooks on sociology) speak about "social problems" serves to obscure this fact. People commonly speak of a "social problem" when something in society does not work the way it is supposed to according to the official interpretations. They then expect the sociologist to study the "problem" as they have defined it and perhaps even to come up with a "solution" that will take care of the matter to their own satisfaction. It is important, against this sort of expectation, to understand that a sociological problem is something quite different from a "social problem" in this sense. For example, it is naive to concentrate on crime as a "problem" because the law-enforcement agencies so define it, or on divorce because that is a "problem" to the moralists of marriage. Even more clearly, the "problem" of the foreman to get his men to work efficiently or of the line officer to get his troops to charge the enemy more enthusiastically need not be problematic at all to the sociologist (leaving out of consideration for the moment the probable fact that the sociologist asked to study such "problems" is employed by the corporation or the army). *The sociological problem is always the understanding of what goes on here in terms of social interaction.* Thus the sociological problem is not so much why some things "go wrong" from the viewpoint of the authorities and the management of the social scene, but *how the whole system works in the first place,* what are its presuppositions and by what means it is held together. The fundamental sociological problem is not crime but the law, not divorce but marriage, not racial discrimination but racially defined stratification, not revolution but government.

This point can be explicated further by an example. Take a settlement house in a lower-class district trying to wean away teen-agers from the publicly disapproved activities of a juvenile gang. The frame of reference within which social workers and police officers define the "problems" of this situation is constituted by the world of middle-class, respectable, publicly approved values. It is a "problem" if teen-agers drive around in stolen automobiles, and it is a "solution" if instead they will play group games in the settlement house. But if one changes the frame of reference and looks at the situation from the viewpoint of the leaders of the juvenile gang, the "problems" are defined in reverse order. It is a "problem" for the solidarity of the gang if its members are seduced away from those activities that lend prestige to the gang within its own social world, and it would be a "solution" if the social workers went way the hell back uptown where they came from. What is a "problem" to one social system is the normal routine of things to the other system, and vice versa. Loyalty and disloyalty, solidarity and deviance, are defined in contradictory terms by the representatives of the two systems. Now, the sociologist may, in terms of his own values, regard the world of middle-class respectability as more desirable and therefore want to come to the assistance of the settlement house, which is its missionary outpost *in partibus infidelium.* This, however, does not justify the identification of the director's headaches with what are "problems" sociologically. The "problems" that the sociologist will want to solve concern an understanding of the entire social situation, the values and modes of action in *both* systems, and the way in which the two systems coexist in space and time. Indeed, this very ability to look at a situation from the vantage points of competing systems of interpretation is, as we shall see more clearly later on, one of the hallmarks of sociological consciousness.

We could contend, then, that there is a *debunking* motif inherent in sociological consciousness. The sociologist will be driven time and again, by the very logic of his discipline, to debunk [or show that myths are not true regarding] the social systems he is studying. This unmasking tendency need not necessarily be due to the sociologist's temperament or inclinations. Indeed, it may happen that the sociologist, who as an individual may be of a conciliatory disposition and quite disinclined to disturb the comfortable assumptions on which he rests his own social existence, is nevertheless compelled by what he is doing to fly in the face of what those around him take for granted. In other words, we would contend that the roots of the debunking motif in sociology are not psychological but methodological. The sociological frame of reference, with its built-in procedure of looking for levels of reality other than those given in the official interpretations of society, carries with it a logical imperative to *unmask the pretensions* and the propaganda by which men cloak their actions with each other. This unmasking imperative is one of the characteristics of sociology particularly at home in the temper of the modern era.

• • •

The debunking tendency of sociology is implicit in all sociological theories that emphasize the autonomous character of social processes. For instance, Émile Durkheim, the founder of the most important school in French sociology, emphasized that society was a reality . . . that could not be reduced to psychological or other factors on different levels of analysis. . . . This is perhaps most sharply revealed in his well-known study of suicide, in the work of that title, where individual intentions of those who commit suicide are completely left out of the analysis in favor of statistics concerning various social characteristics of these individuals. In the Durkheimian perspective, to live in society means to exist under the domination of society's logic. Very often men act by this logic without knowing it. To discover this inner dynamic of society, therefore, the sociologist must frequently disregard the answers that the social actors themselves would give to his questions and look for explanations that are hidden from their own awareness. This essentially Durkheimian approach has been carried over into the theoretical approach now called functionalism. In functional analysis society is analyzed in terms of its own workings as a system, workings that are often obscure or opaque to those acting within the system. The contemporary American sociologist Robert Merton has expressed this approach well in his concepts of "manifest" and "latent" functions. The former are the conscious and deliberate functions of social processes, the latter the unconscious and unintended ones. Thus the "manifest" function of antigambling legislation may be to suppress gambling, its "latent" function to create an illegal empire for the gambling syndicates. Or Christian missons in parts of Africa "manifestly" tried to convert Africans to Christianity, "latently" helped to destroy the indigenous tribal cultures and thus provided an important impetus towards rapid social transformation. Or the control of the Communist Party over all sectors of social life in Russia "manifestly" was to assure the continued dominance of the revolutionary ethos, "latently" created a new class of comfortable bureaucrats uncannily bourgeois in its aspirations and increasingly disinclined toward the self-denial of Bolshevik dedication. Or the "manifest" function of many voluntary associations in America is sociability and public service, the "latent" function to attach status [indicators] to those permitted to belong to such associations.

• • •

It has been suggested above that sociological consciousness is likely to arise when the commonly accepted or authoritatively stated interpretations of society become shaky. As we have already said, there is a good case for thinking of the origins of sociology in France (the mother country of the discipline) in terms of an effort to cope intellectually with the consequences of the French Revolution, not only of the one great cataclysm of 1789 but of what De Tocqueville called the continuing Revolution of the nineteenth century. In the French case it is not difficult to perceive sociology against the background of the rapid transformations of modern society, the collapse of facades, the deflation of old creeds and the upsurge of frightening new forces on the social scene. In Germany, the other European country in which an important sociological movement arose in the nineteenth century, the matter has a rather different appearance. If one may quote Marx . . . , the Germans had a tendency to carry on in professors' studies the revolutions that the French performed on the barricades. At least one of these academic roots of revolution, perhaps the most important one, may be sought in the broadly based movement of thought that came to be called "historicism." This is not the place to go into the full story of this movement. Suffice it to say that it represents an attempt to deal philosophically with the overwhelming sense of the *relativity of all values in history.* [The term "relativity of values" refers to the fact that events and objects considered "good" or "bad" in one society may not be valued in the same way in other societies. Values are, thus, relative to the society in question at a given time.] This awareness of relativity was an almost necessary outcome of the immense accumulation of German historical scholarship in every conceivable field. Sociological thought was at least partly grounded in the need to bring order and intelligibility to the impression of chaos that this array of historical knowledge made on some observers. Needless to stress, however, the society of the German sociologist was changing all around him just as was that of his French colleague, as Germany rushed towards industrial power and nationhood in the second half of the nineteenth century. We shall not pursue these questions though. If we turn to America, the country in which sociology came to receive its most widespread acceptance, we find once more a different set of circumstances, though again against a background of rapid and profound social change. In looking at this American development we can detect another motif of sociology, closely related to that of debunking but not identical with it—its fascination with the *unrespectable* view of society.

In at least every Western society it is possible to distinguish between respectable and unrespectable sectors. In that respect American society is not in a unique position. But American respectability has a particularly pervasive quality about it. This may be ascribed in part, perhaps, to the lingering aftereffects of the Puritan way of life. More probably it has to do with the predominant role played by the bourgeoisie [or middle class] in shaping American culture. Be this as it may in terms of historical causation, it is not difficult to look at social phenomena in America and place them readily in one of these two sectors. We can perceive the official, respectable America represented symbolically by the Chamber of Commerce, the churches, the schools and other centers of civic ritual. But facing this world of respectability is an "other America," present in every town of any size, an America that has other symbols and that speaks another language. This language is probably the safest indentification tag. It is the language of the poolroom and the poker game, of bars and brothels and army barracks. But it is also the language that breaks out with a sigh of relief between two salesmen having a drink in the parlor car as their train races past clean little Midwestern villages on a Sunday morning, with clean little villagers trooping into the whitewashed sanctuaries. It is the language that is suppressed in the company of ladies and clergymen, owing its life mainly to oral transmission from one generation of Huckleberry Finns to another (though in recent years the language has found literary deposition in some books designed to thrill ladies and clergymen). The "other America" that speaks this language can be found wherever people are excluded, or exclude themselves, from the world of middle-class propriety. We can find it in those sections of the working class that have not yet proceeded too far on the road of *embourgeoisement,* in slums, shantytowns, and those parts of cities that urban sociologists have called "areas of transition." We find it expressed powerfully in the world of the American Negro. We also come on it in the subworlds of those who have, for one reason or another, withdrawn voluntarily from Main Street and Madison Avenue—in the worlds of hipsters, homosexuals, hoboes and other "marginal men," those worlds that are kept safely out of sight on the streets where the nice people live, work and amuse themselves....

American sociology, accepted early in both academic circles and by those concerned with welfare activities, was from the beginning associated with the "official America," with the world of policy makers in community and nation. Sociology today retains this respectable affiliation in university, business and government. The appellation hardly induces eyebrows to be raised, except the eyebrows of such Southern racists sufficiently literate to have read the footnotes of the desegregation decision of 1954. However, we would contend that there has been an important undercurrent in American sociology, relating it to that "other America" of dirty language and disenchanted attitudes, that state of mind that refuses to be impressed, moved or befuddled by the official ideologies.

This unrespectable perspective on the American scene can be seen most clearly in the figure of Thorstein Veblen, one of the early important sociologists in America. His biography itself constitutes an exercise in marginality: a difficult, querulous character; born on a Norwegian farm on the Wisconsin frontier; acquiring English as a foreign language; involved all his life with morally and politically suspect individuals; an academic migrant; an inveterate seducer of . . . women. The perspective on America gained from this angle of vision can be found in the unmasking satire that runs like a purple thread through Veblen's work, most famously in his *Theory of the Leisure Class,* that merciless look from the underside at the pretensions of the American [newly rich]. Veblen's view of society can be understood most easily as a series of non-Rotarian insights—his understanding of "conspicuous consumption" as against the middle-class enthusiasm for the "finer things," his analysis of economic processes in terms of manipulation and waste as against the American productivity ethos, his understanding of the machinations of real estate speculation as against the American community ideology, most bitterly his description of academic life (in *The Higher Learning in America*) in terms of fraud and flatulence as against the American cult of education. We are not associating ourselves here with a certain neo-Veblenism that has become fashionable with some younger American sociologists, nor arguing that Veblen was a giant in the development of the field. We are only pointing to his irreverent curiosity and clear-sightedness as marks of a perspective coming from those places in the culture in which one gets up to shave about noon on Sundays. Nor are we arguing that clear-sightedness is a general trait of unrespectability. Stupidity and sluggishness of thought are probably distributed quite fairly throughout the social spectrum. But where there is intelligence and where it manages to free itself from the goggles of respectability, we can expect a clearer view of society than in those cases where the oratorical imagery is taken for real life.

A number of developments in empirical studies in American sociology furnish evidence of this same fascination with the unrespectable view of society. For example, looking back at the powerful development of urban studies undertaken at the University of Chicago in the 1920s we are struck by the apparently irresistible attraction to the seamier sides of city life upon these researchers. The advice to his students of Robert Park, the most important figure in this development, to the effect that they should get their hands dirty with research often enough meant quite literally an intense interest in all the things that North Shore residents would call "dirty." We sense in many of these studies the excitement of discovering the picaresque undersides of the metropolis—studies of slum life, of the melancholy world of rooming houses, of Skid Row, of the worlds of crime and prostitution. One of the offshoots of this so-called "Chicago school" has been the sociological study of occupations, due very largely to the pioneering work of Everett Hughes and his students. Here also we find a fascination with every possible world in which human beings live and make a living, not only with the worlds of respectable occupations, but with those of the taxi driver, the apartment-house janitor, the professional boxer or the jazz musician. The same tendency can be discovered in the course of American community studies following in the wake of the famous *Middletown* studies of Robert and Helen Lynd. Inevitably these studies had to bypass the official versions of community life, to look at the social reality of the community not only from the perspective of city hall but also from that of the city jail. Such sociological procedure is *ipso facto* a refutation of the respectable presupposition that only certain views of the world are to be taken seriously.

We would not want to give an exaggerated impression of the effect of such investigations on the consciousness of sociologists. We are well aware of the elements of muckraking and romanticism inherent in some of this. We also know that many sociologists participate as fully in the respectable [outlook] as all the other PTA members on their block. Nevertheless, we would maintain that sociological consciousness predisposes one towards an awareness which already carries within itself the seeds of intellectual unrespectability. In the second *Middletown* study the Lynds have given a classic analysis of the mind of middle-class America in their series of "of course statements"—that is, statements that represent a consensus so strong that the answer to any question concerning them will habitually be prefaced with the words "Of course!" "Is our economy one of free enterprise?" "Of course!" "Are all our important decisions arrived at through the democratic process?"

"Of course!" "Is monogamy the natural form of marriage?" "Of course!" The sociologist, however conservative and conformist he may be in his private life, knows that there are serious questions to be raised about every one of these "of course statements." In this knowledge alone he is brought to the threshold of unrespectability.

This unrespectability motif of sociological consciousness need not imply a revolutionary attitude. We would even go further than that and express the opinion that sociological understanding is inimical to revolutionary ideologies, not because it has some sort of conservative bias, but because it sees not only through the illusions of the present *status quo* but also through the illusionary expectations concerning possible futures, such expectations being the customary spiritual nourishment of the revolutionary. This nonrevolutionary and moderating soberness of sociology we would value quite highly. More regrettable, from the viewpoint of one's values, is the fact that sociological understanding by itself does not necessarily lead to a greater tolerance with respect to the foibles of mankind. It is possible to view social reality with compassion or with cynicism, both attitudes being compatible with clear-sightedness. But whether he can bring himself to human sympathy with the phenomena he is studying or not, the sociologist will in some measure be detached from the taken-for-granted postures of his society. Unrespectability, whatever its ramifications in the emotions and the will, must remain a constant possibility in the sociologist's mind. It may be segregated from the rest of his life, overlaid by the routine mental states of everyday existence, even denied ideologically. Total respectability of thought, however, will invariably mean the death of sociology. This is one of the reasons why genuine sociology disappears promptly from the scene in totalitarian countries, as is well illustrated in the instance of Nazi Germany. By implication, sociological understanding is always potentially dangerous to the minds of policemen and other guardians of public order, since it will always tend to [question the universality of] the claim to absolute rightness upon which such minds like to rest.

Before concluding this chapter, we would look once more on this phenomenon of *relativization* that we have already touched upon a few times. We would now say explicitly that sociology is so much in tune with the temper of the modern era, precisely because it represents the consciousness of a world in which values have been radically relativized. This relativization has become so much a part of our everyday imagination that it is difficult for us to grasp fully how closed and absolutely binding the world views of other cultures have been and some places still are. . . . For the traditional mind one is what one is, where one is, and cannot even imagine how one could be anything different. The modern mind, by contrast, is mobile, participates vicariously in the lives of others differently located from oneself, easily imagines itself changing occupation or residence. Thus [a sociologist working in the contemporary Middle East] found that some of the illiterate respondents to his questionnaires could only respond with laughter to the question as to what they would do if they were in the position of their rulers and would not even consider the question as to the circumstances under which they would be willing to leave their native village. Another way of putting this would be to say that traditional societies assign definite and permanent identities to their members. In modern society identity itself is uncertain and in flux. One does not really know what is expected of one as a ruler, as a parent, as a cultivated person, or as one who is sexually normal. Typically, one then requires various experts to tell one. The book club editor tells us what culture is, the interior designer what taste we ought to have, and the psychoanalyst who we are. To live in modern society means to live at the center of a kaleidoscope of everchanging roles.

Again, we must forgo the temptation of enlarging on this point, since it would take us rather far afield from our argument into a general discussion of the social psychology of modern existence. We would rather stress the intellectual aspect of this situation, since it is in that aspect that we would see an important dimension of sociological consciousness. *The unprecedented rate of geographical and social mobility in modern society means that one becomes exposed to an unprecedented variety of ways of looking at the world.* The insights into other cultures that one might gather by travel are brought into one's own living room through the mass media. Someone once defined urbane sophistication as being the capacity to remain quite unperturbed upon seeing in front of one's house a man dressed in a turban and a loincloth, a snake coiled around his neck, beating a tom-tom as he leads a leashed tiger down the street. No doubt there are degrees to such sophistication, but a measure of it is acquired by every child who watches television. No doubt also this sophistication is commonly only superficial and does not extend to any real grappling with alternate ways of life. Nevertheless, the immensely broadened possibility of travel, in person and through the imagination, implies at least potentially the awareness that one's own culture, including its basic values, is relative in space and time. Social mobility, that is, the movement from one social stratum to another, augments this relativizing effect. Wherever industrialization occurs, a new dynamism is injected into the social system. Masses of people begin to change their social position, in groups or as individuals. And usually this change is in an "upward" direction. With this movement an individual's biography often involves a considerable journey not only through a variety of social groups but through the intellectual universes that are, so to speak, attached to these groups. Thus the Baptist mail clerk who used to read the *Reader's Digest* becomes an Epsicopalian junior executive who reads *The New Yorker,* or the faculty wife whose husband becomes department chairman may graduate from the best-seller list to Proust or Kafka.

In view of this overall fluidity of world views in modern society it should not surprise us that our age has been characterized as one of conversion. Nor should it be surprising that intellectuals especially have been prone to change their world views radically and with amazing frequency. The intellectual attraction of strongly presented, theoretically closed systems of thought such as Catholicism or Communism has been frequently commented upon. Psychoanalysis, in all its forms, can be understood as an institutionalized mechanism of conversion, in which the individual changes not only his view of himself but of the world in general. The popularity of a multitude of new cults and creeds, presented in different degrees of intellectual refinement depending upon the educational level of their clientele, is another manifestation of this proneness to conversion of our contemporaries. It almost seems as if modern man, and especially modern educated man, is in a perpetual state of doubt about the nature of himself and of the universe in which he lives. In other words, the awareness of relativity, which probably in all ages of history has been the possession of a small group of intellectuals, today appears as a broad cultural fact reaching far down into the lower reaches of the social system.

We do not want to give the impression that this sense of relativity and the resulting proneness to change one's entire [world view] are manifestations of intellectual or emotional immaturity. Certainly one should not take with too much seriousness some representatives of this pattern. Nevertheless, we would contend that an essentially similar pattern becomes almost a destiny in even the most serious intellectual enterprises. It is impossible to exist with full awareness in the modern world without realizing that moral, political, and philosophical commitments are relative, that, in Pascal's words, what is truth on one side of the Pyrenees is error on the other. Intensive occupation with the more fully elaborated meaning systems available in our time gives one a truly frightening understanding of the way in which these systems can provide a total interpretation of reality, within which will be included an interpretation of the alternate systems and of the ways of passing from one system to another. Catholicism may have a theory of Communism, but Communism returns the compliment and will produce a theory on Catholicism. To the Catholic thinker the Communist lives in a dark world of materialist delusion about the real meaning of life. To the Communist his Catholic adversary is helplessly caught in the "false consciousness" of a bourgeois mentality. To the psychoanalyst both Catholic and Communist may simply be acting out on the intellectual level the unconscious impulses that really move them. And psychoanalysis may be to the Catholic an escape from the reality of sin and to the Communist an avoidance of the realities of society. This means that the individual's choice of viewpoint will determine the way in which he looks back upon his own biography. American prisoners of war "brainwashed" by the Chinese Communists completely changed their viewpoints on social and political matters. To those that returned to America this change represented a sort of illness brought on by outward pressure, as a convalescent may look back on a delirious dream. But to their former captors this changed consciousness represents a brief glimmer of true understanding between long periods of ignorance. And to those prisoners who decided not to return, their conversion may still appear as the decisive passage from darkness to light.

Instead of speaking of conversion (a term with religiously charged connotations) we would prefer to use the more neutral term of *"alternation"* to describe this phenomenon. The intellectual situation just described brings with it the possibility that an individual may alternate back and forth between logically contradictory meaning systems. Each time, the meaning system he enters provides him with an interpretation of his existence and of his world, including in this interpretation an explanation of the meaning system he has abandoned. Also, the meaning system provides him with tools to combat his own doubts. Catholic confessional discipline, Communist "autocriticism" and the psychoanalytic techniques of coping with "resistance" all fulfill the same purpose of preventing alternation out of the particular meaning system, allowing the individual to interpret his own doubts in terms derived from the system itself, thus keeping him within it. On lower levels of sophistication there will also be various means employed to cut off questions that might threaten the individual's allegiance to the system, means that one can see at work in the dialectical acrobatics of even such relatively unsophisticated groups as Jehovah's Witnesses or Black Muslims.

If one resists the temptation, however, to accept such [narrow world views], and is willing to face squarely the experience of relativity brought on by the phenomenon of alternation, then one comes into possession of yet another crucial dimension of sociological consciousness—the awareness that not only identities but ideas are relative to specific social locations. . . . Suffice it to say here that this relativizing motif is another of the fundamental driving forces of the sociological enterprise.

In this chapter we have tried to outline the dimensions of sociological consciousness through the analysis of three motifs—those of debunking, unrespectability and relativizing. To these three we would, finally, add a fourth one, much less far-reaching in its implications but useful in rounding out our picture—the *cosmopolitan* motif. Going back to very ancient times, it was in cities that there developed an openness to the world, to other ways of thinking and acting. Whether we think of Athens or Alexandria, of medieval Paris or Renaissance Florence, or of the turbulent urban centers of modern history, we can identify a certain cosmopolitan consciousness that was especially characteristic of city culture. The individual, then, who is not only urban but urbane is one who, however passionately he may be attached to his own city, roams through the whole wide world in his intellectual voyages. His mind, if not his body and his emotions, is at home wherever there are other men who think. We would submit that sociological consciousness is marked by the same cosmopolitanism. This is why a narrow parochialism in its focus of interest is always a danger signal for the sociological venture (a danger signal that, unfortunately, we would hoist over quite a few sociological studies in America today). The sociological perspective is a broad, open, emancipated vista on human life. The sociologist, at his best, is a man with a taste for other lands, inwardly open to the measureless richness of human possibilities, eager for new horizons and new worlds of human meaning. It probably requires no additional elaboration to make the point that this type of man can play a particularly useful part in the course of events today.

Review Questions

1. Briefly summarize the four major sociological themes, or motifs, that Berger sets forth.
   a. debunking
   b. unrespectability
   c. cultural relativism
   d. cosmopolitanism
2. How would the "sociological consciousness" lead you to study the power structure of a city that is a gambling center (e.g., Atlantic City, New Jersey, or Las Vegas, Nevada)? How would your approach differ from the economist's approach or the lawyer's approach?
3. Berger claims that most of us are unaware of the patterned regularities in the phenomenon of love. What are our myths about love? What are some of the patterned regularities that show our myths to be partly or entirely false?
4. Why is it important to understand that a "sociological problem" is quite different from a "social problem"?

SOCIETY AS SYMBOLIC INTERACTION

Herbert Blumer

A VIEW OF HUMAN SOCIETY AS SYMBOLIC INTERACTION HAS BEEN FOLLOWED MORE than it has been formulated. Partial, usually fragmentary, statements of it are to be found in the writings of a number of eminent scholars, some inside the field of sociology and some outside. Among the former we may note such scholars as Charles Horton Cooley, W. I. Thomas, Robert E. Park, E. W. Burgess, Florian Znaniecki, Ellsworth Faris, and James Mickel Williams. Among those outside the discipline we may note William James, John Dewey, and George Herbert Mead. None of these scholars, in my judgment, has presented a systematic statement of the nature of human group life from the standpoint of symbolic interaction. Mead stands out among all of them in laying bare the fundamental premises of the approach, yet he did little to develop its methodological implications for sociological study. Students who seek to depict the position of symbolic interaction may easily give different pictures of it. What I have to present should be regarded as my personal version. My aim is to present the basic premises of the point of view and to develop their methodological consequences for the study of human group life.

The term "symbolic interaction" refers, of course, to the peculiar and distinctive character of interaction as it takes place between human beings. The peculiarity consists in the fact that human beings interpret or "define" each other's actions instead of merely reacting to each other's actions. Their "response" is not made directly to the actions of one another but instead is based on the meaning which they attach to such actions. Thus, human interaction is mediated by the use of symbols, by interpretation, or by ascertaining the meaning of one another's actions. . . .

The simple recognition that human beings interpret each other's actions as the means of acting toward one another has permeated the thought and writings of many scholars of human conduct and of human group life. Yet few of them have endeavored to analyze what such interpretation implies about the nature of the human being or about

SOURCE: "Symbolic Interaction" by Herbert Blumer. Rose, Arnold M. (editor), *Human Behavior and Social Processes*. Copyright ©1962 by Houghton-Mifflin. Used with permission.

the nature of human association. They are usually content with a mere recognition that "interpretation" should be caught by the student, or with a simple realization that symbols, such as cultural norms or values, must be introduced into their analyses. Only G. H. Mead, in my judgment, has sought to think through what the act of interpretation implies for an understanding of the human being, human action, and human association. The essentials of his analysis are so penetrating and profound and so important for an understanding of human group life that I wish to spell them out, even though briefly.

The key feature in Mead's analysis is that the human being has a self. This idea should not be cast aside as esoteric or glossed over as something that is obvious and hence not worthy of attention. In declaring that the human being has a self, Mead had in mind chiefly that the human being can be the object of his own actions. He can act toward himself as he might act toward others. Each of us is familiar with actions of this sort in which the human being gets angry with himself, rebuffs himself, takes pride in himself, argues with himself, tries to bolster his own courage, tells himself that he should "do this" or not "do that," sets goals for himself, makes compromises with himself, and plans what he is going to do. That the human being acts toward himself in these and countless other ways is a matter of easy empirical observation. To recognize that the human being can act toward himself is no mystical conjuration.

Mead regards this ability of the human being to act toward himself as the central mechanism with which the human being faces and deals with his world. This mechanism enables the human being to make indication to himself of things in his surroundings and thus to guide his actions by what he notes. Anything of which a human being is conscious is something which he is indicating to himself—the ticking of a clock, a knock at the door, the appearance of a friend, the remark made by a companion, a recognition that he has a task to perform, or the realization that he has a cold. Conversely, anything of which he is not conscious is, *ipso facto,* something which he is not indicating to himself. The conscious life of the human being, from the time that he awakens until he falls asleep, is a continual flow of self-indications—notations of the things with which he deals and takes into account. We are given, then, a picture of the human being as an organism which confronts its world with a mechanism of making indications to itself. This is the mechanism that is involved in interpreting the actions of others. To interpret the actions of another is to point out to oneself that the action has this or that meaning or character.

Now, according to Mead, the significance of making indications to oneself is of paramount importance. The importance lies along two lines. First, to indicate something is to extricate it from its setting, to hold it apart, to give it a meaning or, in Mead's language, to make it into an object. An object—that is to say, anything that an individual indicates to himself—is different from a stimulus; instead of having an intrinsic character which acts on the individual and which can be identified apart from the individual, its character or meaning is conferred on it by the individual. The object is a product of the individual's disposition to act instead of being an antecedent stimulus which evokes the act. Instead of the individual being surrounded by an environment of pre-existing objects which play upon him and call forth his behavior, the proper picture is that he constructs his objects on the basis of his on-going activity. In any of his countless acts—whether minor, like dressing himself, or major, like organizing himself for a professional career—the individual is designating different objects to himself, giving them meaning, judging their suitability to his action, and making decisions on the basis of the judgment. This is what is meant by interpretation or acting on the basis of symbols.

The second important implication of the fact that the human being makes indications to himself is that his action is constructed or built up instead of being a mere release. Whatever the action in which he is engaged, the human individual proceeds by pointing out to himself the divergent things which have to be taken into account in the course of his action. He has to note what he wants to do and how he is to do it; he has to point out to himself the various conditions which may be instrumental to his action and those which may obstruct his action; he has to take account of the demands, the expectations, the prohibitions, and the threats as they may arise in the situation in which he is acting. His action is built up step by step through a process of such self-indication. The human individual pieces together and guides his action by taking account of different things and interpreting their significance for his prospective action. There is no instance of conscious action of which this is not true.

The process of constructing action through making indications to oneself cannot be swallowed up in any of the conventional psychological categories. This process is distinct from and different from what is spoken of as the "ego"—just as it is different from any other conception which conceives of the self in terms of composition or organization. Self-indication is a moving communicative process in which the individual notes things, assesses them, gives them a meaning, and decides to act on the basis of the meaning. The human being stands over against the world, or against "alters," with such a process and not with a mere ego. Further, the process of self-indication cannot be subsumed under the forces, whether from the outside or inside, which are presumed to play upon the individual to produce his behavior. Environmental pressures, external stimuli, organic drives, wishes, attitudes, feelings, ideas, and their like do not cover or explain the process of self-indication. The process of self-indication stands over against them in that the individual points out to himself and interprets the appearance or expression of such things, noting a given social demand that is made on him, recognizing a command, observing that he is hungry, realizing that he wishes to buy something, aware that he has a given feeling, conscious that he dislikes eating with someone he despises, or aware that he is thinking of doing some given thing. By virtue of indicating such things to himself, he places himself over against them and is able to act back against them, accepting them, rejecting them, or transforming them in accordance with how he defines or interprets them. His behavior, accordingly, is not a result of such things as environmental pressures, stimuli, motives, attitudes, and ideas but arises instead from how he interprets and handles these things in the action which he is constructing. The process of self-indication by means of which human action is formed cannot be accounted for by factors which precede the act. The process of self-indication exists in its own right and must be accepted and studied as such. It is through this process that the human being constructs his conscious action.

Now Mead recognizes that the formation of action by the individual through a process of self-indication always takes place in a social context. Since this matter is so vital to an understanding of symbolic interaction it needs to be explained carefully. Fundamentally, group action takes the form of a fitting together of individual lines of action. Each individual aligns his action to the action of others by ascertaining what they are doing or what they intend to do—that is, by getting the meaning of their acts. For Mead, this is done by the individual "taking the role" of others—either the role of a specific person or the role of a group (Mead's "generalized other"). In taking such roles the individual seeks to ascertain the intention or direction of the acts of others. He forms and aligns his own action on the basis of such interpretation of the acts of others. This is the fundamental way in which group action takes place in human society.

The foregoing are the essential features, as I see them, in Mead's analysis of the bases of symbolic interaction. They presuppose the following: that human society is made up of individuals who have selves (that is, make indications to themselves); that individual action is a construction and not a release, being built up by the individual through noting and interpreting features of the situations in which he acts; that group or collective action consists of the aligning of individual actions, brought about by the individuals' interpreting or taking into account each other's actions. . . . [T]he three premises can be easily verified empirically. I know of no instance of human group action to which the three premises do not apply. The reader is challenged to find or think of a single instance which they do not fit.

Review Questions

1. In trying to clarify the term "society," Blumer says that society *is* symbolic interaction. What does he mean?

2. Blumer bases his explanation of society on George Herbert Mead's concept of the self. He argues that each person can act toward him or herself and make interpretations or "indications to self." Why is this fact important for understanding human societies?

3. Group action, according to Blumer, involves fitting together individual lines of action. How does this process occur?

Suggested Readings: Introduction

Berger, Peter L. *Invitation to Sociology: A Humanist Perspective.* Garden City, N.Y.: Anchor Books, 1963.

——, and Hansfried Kellner. *Sociology Reinterpreted: An Essay on Method and Vocation.* Garden City, N.Y.: Anchor Books, 1981.

Collins, Randall. *Sociological Insight: An Introduction to Non-Obvious Sociology.* New York: Oxford University Press, 1982.

Mills, C. Wright. *The Sociological Imagination.* New York: Oxford University Press, 1959.

Simmel, Georg. "The Problem of Sociology," trans. Albion W. Small, *The American Journal of Sociology* 15(1909): 290–316.

Part II. Culture

A PRIMARY REASON FOR THE COMPLEXITY OF SOCIAL INTERACTION IS THAT OUR species has no instinctive patterns of behavior. While we do have biological drives and needs, we have no instincts that force us to meet these needs in patterned ways. Unlike other species, humans must create and learn their own ways of coping with the environment, which includes their fellow beings. Such strategies for coping and interacting are, to a large extent, shared with others. They make up a way of life, or *culture.* A culture comprises all the objects, ideas, beliefs, norms, and values of a group of people—and the meanings that the group applies to its cultural elements. From the culture, we learn what to define as good and bad, which animals to consider suitable for food and which to consider inedible, and how to make love, make war, and make money.

Cultures vary a great deal, according to both time and place. The way people earn their living, rear children, and clean their homes in Bolivia, for instance, is different from the way people in Iceland or even in Mexico carry out these tasks. But all cultures are alike in that they are *ethnocentric* (culture-centered). That is, the members of every society come to believe that their culture is best and natural and that societies that do things differently are inferior. Imagine that you are traveling in the Far East. There you learn that it is a common practice for people to eat dog meat—but because you have learned not to consider the dog as a source of food, you are likely to react very negatively. In India, you might consider it strange that people your own age marry partners selected by their parents. Upon questioning, you discover that the mates hadn't met until the wedding day. Your immediate reaction may be that the American way is superior. But why? Because it is the way that you know. Of course, current American dating practices are seen as strange and unnatural by people from India.

As we go through our daily routines we are usually unaware of the influence that culture has on human behavior. We eat with knives and forks, believe that one type of car is better than another, make assumptions about "human nature," pay bills printed by computers, and fall in love—oblivious of the fact that such behavior is *not* typical of people in every other society.

It is relatively easy to recognize the influence of culture by examining societies other than our own. When we read of the eating of dog meat or arranged marriages, we become aware that people's behavior depends upon the culture in which they are reared. It is more difficult, though, for us to step outside our own society to analyze the elements of American culture and to see their effects on *us*. When we do, however, we reduce the tendency to assume that other cultures are peculiar and wrong, and that ours is normal and good.

In a classic article, "Body Ritual Among the Nacirema," the anthropologist Horace Miner helps us to stand apart from our culture and observe it in a more objective light. Miner originally wrote this article as a spoof on ethnocentric American anthropologists; the portion that is reprinted here humorously and imaginatively induces us to view components of our daily routines from a new, and quite different, perspective. Miner's description is valuable just because it makes us realize how odd our behavior might seem to someone from another culture. We are so used to doing things in certain ways that we are often unaware of much of our own behavior and fail to consider that alternative behavior patterns (called *functional alternatives*) exist.

The next selection in Part II brings the concept of culture close to all of us. In "Sympathy and Culture," Candace Clark analyzes an emotion that most of us feel at one time or another. By contrasting the American system for giving and receiving sympathy with an extremely unsympathetic society, she points out that this emotion is shaped and guided by cultural "feeling rules." She argues that a person in our society must follow rules of respectability and rules of reciprocity in order to receive sympathy. Although her focus is on sympathy, her analysis implies that the many other emotions a person experiences—love, disdain, awe, jealously, and more—are also shaped by the forces of culture.

Ruth Horowitz's research on a Mexican-American community in Chicago introduces the theme of subcultural variation. A subculture is a somewhat unique way of life that exists within a larger culture. Members of a subsociety such as an ethnic, religious, occupational, or even a deviant group are affected both by the larger culture and by their subculture. In "Honor on 32nd Street," Horowitz describes the social world of a neighborhood composed of recent immigrants from Mexico. These people have brought with them a centuries-old, patriarchal way of life passed down from one generation of the family to the next. In the Mexican way of life, honor—one's standing in the eyes of the community—plays a very important role. And one's honor depends on how well one's actions and persona bring credit to the family. A person's identity, therefore, is tied to both family and honor. In the modern-day United States, on the other hand, how much an individual contributes to the family reputation has become less important than it once was. Nowadays our values stress *individual* success, achievement, and expression, while the concept of family honor has diminished.

Horowitz shows what happens when the traditional Mexican culture meets North American culture head on. The residents of 32nd Street are often torn between two cultural prescriptions for how to act and who to be. Conflict between generations is especially acute. As you will see, resolving cultural dilemmas is not an easy process. Of course, what Horowitz describes for Mexican-Americans has general significance for other immigrant groups and other types of subcultures as well.

BODY RITUAL AMONG THE NACIREMA

Horace Miner

THE ANTHROPOLOGIST HAS BECOME SO FAMILIAR WITH THE DIVERSITY OF WAYS IN which different peoples behave in similar situations that he is not apt to be surprised by even the most exotic customs. In fact, if all of the logically possible combinations of behavior have not been found somewhere in the world, he is apt to suspect that they must be present in some yet undescribed tribe. This point has, in fact, been expressed with respect to clan organization by Murdock (1949:71). In this light, the magical beliefs and practices of the Nacirema present such unusual aspects that it seems desirable to describe them as an example of the extremes to which human behavior can go.

Professor Linton first brought the ritual of the Nacirema to the attention of anthropologists years ago (1936:326), but the culture of this people is still very poorly understood. They are a North American group living in the territory between the Canadian Cree, the Yaqui and Tarahumare of Mexico, and the Carib and Arawak of the Antilles. Little is known of their origin, although tradition states that they came from the east. According to Nacirema mythology, their nation was originated by a cultural hero, Notgnihsaw, who is otherwise known for two great feats of strength—the throwing of a piece of wampum across the river Pa-To-Mac and the chopping down of a cherry tree in which the Spirit of Truth resided.

Nacirema culture is characterized by a highly developed market economy which has evolved in a rich natural habitat. While much of the people's time is devoted to economical pursuits, a large part of the fruits of these labors and a considerable portion of the day are spent in ritual activity. The focus of this activity is the human body, the appearance and health of which loom as a dominant concern in the ethos of the people. While such a concern is certainly not unusual, its ceremonial aspects and associated philosophy are unique.

The fundamental belief underlying the whole system appears to be that the human body is ugly and that its natural tendency is to debility

SOURCE: Horace Miner, "Body Ritual Among the Nacirema." Reproduced by permission of the American Anthropological Association and the author, from *The American Anthropologist* 58:3 June (1956). Not for further reproduction.

and disease. Incarcerated in such a body, man's only hope is to avert these characteristics through the use of the powerful influences of ritual and ceremony. Every household has one or more shrines devoted to this purpose. The more powerful individuals in the society have several shrines in their houses and, in fact, the opulence of a house is often referred to in terms of the number of such ritual centers it possesses. Most houses are of wattle and daub construction, but the shrine rooms of the more wealthy are walled with stone. Poorer families imitate the rich by applying pottery plaques to their shrine walls.

While each family has at least one such shrine, the rituals associated with it are not family ceremonies but are private and secret. The rites are normally only discussed with children, and then only during the period when they are being initiated into these mysteries. I was able, however, to establish sufficient rapport with the natives to examine these shrines and to have the rituals described to me.

The focal point of the shrine is a box or chest which is built into the wall. In this chest are kept the many charms and magical potions without which no native believes he could live. These preparations are secured from a variety of specialized practitioners. The most powerful of these are the medicine men, whose assistance must be rewarded with substantial gifts. However, the medicine men do not provide the curative potions for their clients, but decide what the ingredients should be and then write them down in an ancient and secret language. This writing is understood only by the medicine men and by the herbalists who, for another gift, provide the required charm.

The charm is not disposed of after it has served its purpose, but is placed in the charm-box of the household shrine. As these magical materials are specific for certain ills, and the real or imagined maladies of the people are many, the charm-box is usually full to overflowing. The magical packets are so numerous that people forget what their purposes were and fear to use them again. While the natives are very vague on this point, we can only assume that the idea in retaining all the old magical materials is that their presence in the charm-box, before which the body rituals are conducted, will in some way protect the worshipper.

Beneath the charm-box is a small font. Each day every member of the family, in succession, enters the shrine room, bows his head before the charm-box, mingles different sorts of holy water in the font, and proceeds with a brief rite of ablution. The holy waters are secured from the Water Temple of the community, where the priests conduct elaborate ceremonies to make the liquid ritually pure.

In the hierarchy of magical practitioners, and below the medicine men in prestige, are specialists whose designation is best translated "holy-mouth-men." The Nacirema have an almost pathological horror of and fascination with the mouth, the condition of which is believed to have a supernatural influence on all social relationships. Were it not for the rituals of the mouth, they believe that their teeth would fall out, their gums bleed, their jaws shrink, their friends desert them, and their lovers reject them. They also believe that a strong relationship exists between oral and moral characteristics. For example, there is a ritual ablution of the mouth for children which is supposed to improve their moral fiber.

The daily body ritual performed by everyone includes a mouth-rite. Despite the fact that these people are so punctilious about care of the mouth, this rite involves a practice which strikes the uninitiated stranger as revolting. It was reported to me that the ritual consists of inserting a small bundle of hog hairs into the mouth, along with certain magical powders, and then moving the bundle in a highly formalized series of gestures.

In addition to the private mouth-rite, the people seek out a holy-mouth-man once or twice a year. These practitioners have an impressive set of paraphernalia, consisting of a variety of augers, awls, probes, and prods. The use of these objects in the exorcism of the evils of the mouth involves almost unbelievable ritual torture of the client. The holy-mouth-man opens the client's mouth and, using the above mentioned tools, enlarges any holes which decay may have created in the teeth. Magical materials are put into these holes. If there are no naturally occurring holes in the teeth, large sections of one or more teeth are gouged out so that the supernatural substance can be applied. In the client's view, the purpose of these ministrations is to arrest decay and to draw friends. The extremely sacred and traditional character of the rite is evident in the fact that the natives return to the holy-mouth-men year after year, despite the fact that their teeth continue to decay.

It is to be hoped that, when a thorough study of the Nacirema is made, there will be careful inquiry into the personality structure of these people. One has but to watch the gleam in the eye of a holy-mouth-man, as he jabs an awl into an exposed nerve, to suspect that a certain amount of sadism is involved. If this can be established, a very interesting pattern emerges, for most of the population shows definite masochistic tendencies. It was to these that Professor Linton referred in discussing a distinctive part of the daily body ritual which is performed only by men. This part of the rite involves scraping and lacerating the surface of the face with a sharp instrument. Special women's rites are performed only four times during each lunar month, but what they lack in frequency is made up in barbarity. As part of this ceremony, women bake their heads in small ovens for about an hour. The theoretically interesting point is that what seems to be a preponderantly masochistic people have developed sadistic specialists.

The medicine men have an imposing temple, or *latipso*, in every community of any size. The more elaborate ceremonies required to treat very sick patients can only be performed at this temple. These ceremonies involve not only the thaumaturge [or miracle worker] but a permanent group of vestal maidens who move sedately about the temple chambers in distinctive costume and headdress.

The *latipso* ceremonies are so harsh that it is phenomenal that a fair proportion of the really sick natives who enter the temple ever recover. Small children whose indoctrination is still incomplete have been known to resist attempts to take them to the temple because "that is where you go to die." Despite this fact, sick adults are not only willing but eager to undergo the protracted ritual purification, if they can afford to do so. No matter how ill the supplicant or how grave the emergency, the guardians of many temples will not admit a client if he cannot give a rich gift to the custodian. Even after one has gained admission and survived the ceremonies, the guardians will not permit the neophyte to leave until he makes still another gift.

The supplicant entering the temple is first stripped of all his or her clothes. In everyday life the Nacirema avoids exposure of his body and its natural functions. Bathing and excretory acts are performed only in the secrecy of the household shrine, where they are ritualized as part of the body-rites. Psychological shock results from the fact that body secrecy is suddenly lost upon entry into the *latipso*. A man, whose own wife has never seen him in an excretory act, suddenly finds himself naked and assisted by a vestal maiden while he performs his natural functions into a sacred vessel. This sort of ceremonial treatment is necessitated by the fact that the excreta are used by a diviner to ascertain the course and nature of the client's sickness. Female clients, on the other hand, find their naked bodies are subjected to the scrutiny, manipulation and prodding of the medicine man.

Few supplicants in the temple are well enough to do anything but lie on their hard beds. The daily ceremonies, like the rites of the holy-mouth-men, involve discomfort and torture. With ritual precision, the vestals awaken their miserable charges each dawn and roll them about on their beds of pain while performing ablutions, in the formal movements of which the maidens are highly trained. At other times they insert magic wands in the supplicant's mouth or force him to eat substances which are supposed to be healing. From time to time the medicine men come to their clients and jab magically treated needles into their flesh. The fact that these temple ceremonies may not cure, and may even kill the neophyte, in no way decreases the people's faith in the medicine men.

There remains one other kind of practitioner, known as a "listener." This witch-doctor has the power to exorcise the devils that lodge in the heads of people who have been bewitched. The Nacirema believe that parents bewitch their own children. Mothers are particularly suspected of putting a curse on children while teaching them the secret body rituals. The counter-magic of the witch-doctor is unusual in its lack of ritual. The patient simply tells the "listener" all his troubles and fears, beginning with the earliest difficulties he can remember. The memory displayed by the Nacirema in these exorcism sessions is truly remarkable. It is not uncommon for the patient to bemoan the rejection he felt upon being weaned as a babe, and a few individuals even see their troubles going back to the traumatic effects of their own birth.

In conclusion, mention must be made of certain practices which have their base in native esthetics but which depend upon the pervasive aversion to the natural body and its functions. There are ritual fasts to make fat people thin and ceremonial feasts to make thin people fat. Still other rites are used to make women's breasts larger if they are small, and smaller if they are large. General dissatisfaction with breast shape is symbolized in the fact that the ideal form is virtually outside the range of human variation. A few women afflicted with almost inhuman hypermammary development are so idolized that they make a handsome living by simply going from village to village and permitting the natives to stare at them for a fee.

Reference has already been made to the fact that excretory functions are ritualized, routinized, and relegated to secrecy. Natural reproductive functions are similarly distorted. Intercourse is taboo as a topic and scheduled as an act. Efforts are made to avoid pregnancy by the use of magical materials or by limiting intercourse to certain phases of the moon. Conception is actually very infrequent. When pregnant, women dress so as to hide their condition. Parturition takes place in secret, without friends or relatives to assist, and the majority of women do not nurse their infants.

• • •

REFERENCES

Linton, Ralph
1936 *The Study of Man*. New York, D. Appleton-Century Co.

Murdock, George P.
1949 *Social Structure*. New York, The Macmillan Co.

Review Questions

1. Using Miner's style of analysis, describe dating and courtship among the Nacirema.
2. Miner's article on the Nacirema was intended to point out the ethnocentrism of American anthropologists and sociologists. How does it do this?
3. Give examples of the sociological concepts *values*, *beliefs*, and *norms* from Miner's article.

CULTURE AND SYMPATHY

Candace Clark

INTRODUCTION

WHEN HUMANS PRODUCE CULTURE, THEY CREATE MORE THAN HOUSES, POTS and pans, and family and work arrangements. They also create rules to guide and shape people's actions, perceptions, and even their emotions. Emotions—such as love, hate, shame, pride, awe, gratitude, and sympathy—are social. They are social because they often have other human beings as their objects. Further, they cause us to form attachments, create boundaries between "us" and "them," and follow social norms and laws, all of which in turn helps create the social order. And emotions are social because they are socially defined and bounded: what to feel, when to feel it, and if and how to show feelings—all these are subject to feeling rules. When we study emotions, we can see just how far culture can permeate inside us.

This article focuses on the emotion of sympathy in American society. Before looking at our own culture, though, let us consider a remarkably unsympathetic group—the Ik, or "Mountain People," of central Africa, described by anthropologist Colin Turnbull (1972). After World War II, central African governments turned the former Ik hunting areas into a protected wildlife park and relocated the Ik from their low-lying homelands to unfamiliar hilly territory. Drought and hunting restrictions brought famine. As the Ik, once a gentle and kindhearted people, edged toward starvation and extinction, their friendship and caring for one another faded. They developed a set of norms that promoted self-concern and forbade sympathy for others. Their motto seemed to be: "Who knows what the other is feeling? In each you only know your own feeling" (Turnbull, p. 253). Not knowing another's feelings meant not having to care. Some cooperative activities did continue among the Ik, or we would not even call them a society. But cooperation was guided strictly by principles of impersonal exchange; people aided others in order to obligate them.

SOURCE: Candace Clark: "Culture and Sympathy" Reproduced by permission of the author and the *American Journal of Sociology* 92:3 (1987).

Consider the following specifics of Ik life. The Ik thought one-sided giving of food, water, assistance, or even sentiment to anyone, family member or foe, was a waste. The feeble and the frail were objects, not of pity and care, but of scorn, sniggering, and humor. "Anyone falling down was good for a laugh . . . particularly if he was old or weak or blind" (p. 113). Ik parents banished their children from their round stick-and-thatch houses at about age three; the children survived only if they found begrudging acceptance, by no means a given, among bands of their age-mates. Note the case of Adupa:

> The best game of all . . . was teasing poor little Adupa [who] was a little mad . . . [because she] . . . did not go and jump on other people's play houses, and she lavished enormous care on hers. . . . That of course made it all the more jump-on-able. . . . [W]hen Adupa pulled herself from the ruins of her house, crying, [the other children] beat her over the head and danced around her. (pp. 113–114)

Ik children were not the only ones to treat Adupa heartlessly. She eventually starved to death when her parents purposely trapped her inside the hut.

Indeed, others' misery provided about the only source of Ik humor that Turnbull could find. In his words, "[m]isfortune of others was their greatest joy" (p. 260). For instance, around the evening fire:

> [M]en would watch a child with eager anticipation as it crawled toward the fire, then burst into gay and happy laughter as it plunged a skinny hand into the coals. Such times were the few times when parental affection showed itself; a mother would glow with pleasure to hear such joy occasioned by her offspring, and pull it tenderly out of the fire. (p. 112)

Turnbull begged his readers not to call the Ik primitive, savage, and inhuman. The fact that a human society could develop such extreme, far-reaching unsympathetic norms as the Ik did, Turnbull points out, is testimony to the force of culture. These norms eventually gripped Turnbull himself.

> The unpleasantness of [the mountain trek] was somewhat alleviated by Atum's [my chief informant's] suffering on the way up the stony trail. Several times he slipped, which made Lojieri and me laugh. . . . [I]t was a pleasure to move rapidly ahead and leave Atum gasping behind so that we could be sitting up on the [village's sitting place] when he finally appeared and laugh at his discomfort. . . . [Later, in my compound] when I heard Atum wheezing [a greeting] I kept silent and wondered what I would eat for dinner. (p. 216)

When Turnbull found himself adopting the Ik's world view and practices, it worried him. It also impressed upon him the phenomenal power of group norms to shape the very kinds of feelings and behavior many Westerners are wont to see as most "natural" and "human."

In contrast to the Ik, present-day Americans hold (ideally, at least) that some sympathy is a good, even a noble or saintly thing. Of course, we can better afford the time, energy, and money a gift of sympathy may require. At the same time, Americans are not indiscriminately sympathetic. A variety of feeling rules guide and shape our concern for others.

DATA SOURCES

To study sympathy giving, I first sought expressions of sympathy in greeting cards, newspaper and television reports, advice columns, etiquette books, song lyrics, and literature. . . .

A second source of data is the ethnographic materials produced by generations of sociologists studying victims, the downtrodden, the bereaved, the sick, and other underdogs (Becker 1967) and potential sympathizees. These materials yield information on how people make claims to sympathy and how sympathy gatekeepers respond.

I also involved myself as a participant observer (sometimes more as participant, others more as observer) of sympathy interactions in natural settings (e.g., hospitals, funeral homes, offices, etc.) over a period of two years. Field notes from these observations were especially useful in analyzing sympathy margin and etiquette.

A fourth source of data is a survey of northern New Jersey residents (hereafter designated "respondents"). Student interviewers presented vignettes depicting three plights to a cross section of adult nonstudents. The 877 respondents were predominantly white Catholics, ranged in age from 18 to 77, and came mostly from the working and middle classes. In one of the vignettes, a hurricane has damaged a family's house; in another, a women is brutally beaten by a man she "met in passing in a bar"; in the third, a young couple's marriage is jeopardized by one spouse's problems with alcohol. Respondents were asked to read one of these vignettes, to indicate the degree of sympathy they felt for the character(s) (from "extremely sorry" to "somewhat sorry" to "not sorry at all"), and to describe what aspects of the story had affected their responses. . . .

Finally, four trained male and female interviewers and I conducted intensive interviews with 12 men and 13 women (hereafter termed "interviewees") between the ages of 25 and 80 living in northern New Jersey. Three interviewees were Jewish; the remainder were almost evenly divided between Protestants and Catholics. Their occupations ranged from blue-collar (e.g., technician, waitress) to middle-class (secretary, teacher, radio announcer) to upper-middle-class (psychologist, stockbroker). Three were black, two Hispanic, and 20 white. All marital statuses were represented. The interview schedule asked people to describe specific cases in which they had given, not given, received, rejected, expected, feigned, and "worked on" (Hochschild 1983, pp. 35–55) sympathy. They were also asked to describe their "inner feelings" about these cases.

• • •

THE CONCEPT OF SYMPATHY MARGIN

In life, as in the literature that socializes us, to receive sympathy one must be a "sympathetic character." But what constitutes a sympathetic character? Part of the answer has to do with one's social statuses, and my data suggest that another part is related to relationships built up over time and involving considerable reciprocity. Jacqueline Wiseman (1979), in her analysis of the plight of skid row men and of the agents of social control who deal with them, points to a concept that helps us to understand how sympathy and compassion come about. That concept is "social margin," that is ". . . the amount of *leeway* a given individual has in making errors on the job, buying on credit, or stepping on the toes of significant others without suffering such serious penalties as being fired, denied credit, or losing friends and family. . . . A person with margin can get help" (1979, p. 223). Wiseman claims that respectability, especially in work and family careers, must be maintained to acquire margin (Wiseman 1979, p. 224).

Wiseman's insights have general utility in explaining interaction in the emotional economy of everyday life. One's moral worth and network ties affect how many emotional commodities, including "units" of sympathy and compassion, can be claimed from others and that others feel they owe. Social margin thus includes sympathy margin. Margin (social and otherwise) must be *ascribed by others*. Since we all interact with a variety of others, we may speak of people as having many margins of variable widths—one with each specific other in one's network.

In keeping with Wiseman's terminology, I have drawn a banking analogy with sympathy flow. Each group member has, I maintain, what amounts to an "account" of "sympathy credits" (similar to Goffman's concept of social credits [Wiseman 1979, p. 325] and Hollander's concept of deviance credits [1958]) held for him or her by each other group member. A certain number of sympathy credits are automatically on deposit in each of the sympathy accounts of the ordinary group member, available for cashing in when they are needed. They are a right of group membership.[1]

The right to sentiment.—Simply put, group members are expected to feel some sympathy toward each other. How much sympathy (how many credits) each member can claim from each other member varies, but there is some minimum, albeit an unspecifiable and unquantifiable one. In general, people involved in "close" or "deep" relationships have an obligation to create wider sympathy margins for each other than do acquaintances or secondary group members (Coser 1982). More sympathy is due per occasion, more *genuine* sympathy is due, and it is due in a wider range of circumstances. We may, for example, feel sympathy for strangers or even enemies in what are considered disastrous or freak circumstances (being pushed under a subway car or being subjected to an earthquake or a terrorist attack), yet our friends and loved ones can call out, and count on, our sympathies for their minor problems as well as for their disasters. Also, credit is more freely given to an intimate than to an acquaintance, even before accounts have been settled.

The right to empathy.—Furthermore, there is an obligation to be empathic and to search for evidence that group members, especially intimates, have problems that merit sympathy (see Locker 1981, p. 62). When Goffman (1983, p. 13) discusses the role of "knowership," he recognizes this point, noting that in close relationships, one is supposed to keep the friend's biography in mind, ask questions about how issues in that person's life have been resolved, refer to his or her past illnesses, and the like. Focusing conversation on each other's biographies enhances communication and empathy between "knowers."

The right to display.—Abundant evidence also exists to show that group members are obligated to *display* sympathy appropriate to the person and the plight. Sometimes words of sympathy are expected, sometimes nonverbal messages and kid glove treatment. Some problems call for "off-the-rack" sentiments available in greeting cards.[2]

Sudnow's (1967) study of hospital staff provides examples of the display norms expected of those dealing face to face with bereaved family members. Physicians giving "bad news" to relatives "cannot, like the telegram deliverer, merely present the news and leave the scene, but must evidence some degree of general concern and responsibility" (p. 129). The relative has the right to cry, moan, scream out, in other words, "to suspend his concern for normally enforceable requirements of . . . composure" (p. 136) on hearing of the death. He or she also has the right to indicate when interaction may proceed after the period of "carrying on" (p. 142). The staff member has the obligation to defer to the other, to present him- or herself solemnly, with appropriate tone of voice, facial expression, and the like.

Among my own interviewees, a 40-year-old professional woman, in reporting her reaction to a friend's illness, said: "I can remember saying to myself, 'Now, this is a shock, and you haven't taken it in yet, but you'd better *look* serious.'" Another woman, a 36-year-old waitress and college student, in noting violations of display norms, said: "My children were shocked to see [distant relatives] laughing and drinking at *their grandma's* funeral. In fact, so was I!" Interestingly enough, when my interviewees merely began to think, in the interview situation, about their reactions to others' plights, they frequently adopted the facial expressions, postures, and tones of voice appropriate to sympathy display—erasing smiles, knitting eyebrows, sitting up straighter, and speaking in "concerned" tones.

Changes in Sympathy Margin

A given sympathy account or margin held by a specific other does not always remain constant. It is continually negotiated and may be increased, decreased, replenished, or used up entirely. Beyond the number of sympathy credits automatically "on account" in one's margins, a group member can earn credits, for example, by investing sympathy, help, and concern in others. The nature of the relationship between the two parties may also change as the sympathy margins of one or both change. Investing in another usually implies (whether as a consequence or a cause) a greater degree of intimacy between the parties.

Sympathy credits can also be cashed in. Claiming or accepting sympathy reduces one's margins, and one should draw against accounts that are solvent. The sick person who does not try to get well, like the skid row man who does not try to reform, may soon find his or her sympathy accounts depleted or even overdrawn (Parsons 1951; Wiseman, 1979, p. 223). The number of sympathy credits is limited.

Of course, it is possible to overdraw one's accounts with some people in one's network but not with others. One might, for instance, try to claim equal amounts of sympathy from an acquaintance and from an intimate and find that the former claim is not honored while the latter is. Further, a given sympathy account sometimes depends on the total amount of sympathy a person is receiving. Thus, as several interviewees stated, co-workers may believe that married people will get sympathy from their spouses and, consequently, offer little themselves. My observations show that the members of a network often know each other and discuss among themselves how much sympathy a given member has claimed and how much others have given. The accounts held by some of these people are small because they believe that others are offering "enough." Accounts were drained completely in several cases involving prolonged periods of unemployment, divorce, extended illness, series of mishaps, and claims felt to be exaggerated. The potential sympathizee had to find new networks of significant others—open new accounts—when sympathy was still desired.

To be ascribed sympathy margins by others, one must have dealt properly with sympathy in the past. That is, sympathy margins are affected by one's sympathy biography—previous adherence to the protocols or etiquette for owing, giving, claiming, and accepting sympathy per se. I will now present the rules of sympathy etiquette that my research has uncovered.

SYMPATHY ETIQUETTE: RULES FOR SYMPATHIZEES

Rule 1: Do Not Make False Claims to Sympathy

The foremost rule of sympathy etiquette is not to falsely manipulate others' sympathy by pretending to need it, by exaggerating claims, or by courting disaster with the intent of calling out emotions in others. In short, one should not claim another's sympathy needlessly.

Aesop provides an interesting illustrative case, the familiar tale of the boy who cried wolf. The boy's first few cries were heeded, but in each case no concrete evidence of the wolf's visit could be found. He was given some margin by others, but eventually his sympathy accounts disappeared. When the wolf actually threatened, the boy was judged to be lying and undeserving of sympathy.

A person who engages in any of the above practices, and who is caught out, erodes bases for trust. All of his or her claims may be called into question. Sympathy accounts may be closed. Others will find themselves not making efforts to empathize, not feeling sympathy sentiments, and/or not feeling obligations to display sympathy in otherwise sympathy-worthy situations. A young working-class man explained his reactions to a co-worker's claims: "I can't take the time to sort out which things she claims are real. Now everything she says is suspect to me."

My interviewees were, on the whole, quite concerned about violations of this rule.[3] They reported feeling "taken advantage of," "betrayed," and "conned" when other people played on their sympathies for their own gain. A psychologist in her 50s said of her sister:

> Amy's a disaster area! *But* . . . she makes her own problems. She calls collect from Hawaii to tell me that her husband is selling the house out from under them. She wants me to say, "Poor Amy!" I have to say to her, "He can't do that unless you sign the papers too." But she won't think or do anything for herself. . . . She makes things bad for herself to get sympathy. . . . I used to feel sorry for her, but now I try to avoid her.

Another interviewee, a 37-year-old real estate agent, spoke heatedly of a man who had got his friend's parents to feel sorry for him because his wife divorced him. The friend's parents were quite sympathetic. They rented him a house cheaply and then sold it to him for half the market value. The interviewee complained: "He just used the [former landlords], and I could never help him out again knowing what he's like."

What is at issue here is a breach of public trust, a loss of faith that others will play by the rules. Despite the fact that we know to expect cynical and manipulative performances in everyday encounters, it comes as a shock when our expectations are realized and cannot be overlooked or explained away—when the fictions that make interaction easier are shattered. The tags "untrustworthy" and "con artist" are affixed to those who mishandle others' emotions as well as to those who abuse their money or property. One with such a reputation will have little sympathy margin.

Rule 2: Do Not Claim Too Much Sympathy

Even when legitimate grounds exist, do not claim "too much" sympathy "too often" or for "too long." That is, one should not overdraw one's sympathy accounts. The person who does so risks receiving sympathy displays with less sentiment than would be forthcoming otherwise, displays without sentiment, or, worse, no displays at all.

Although the point of Aesop's story was that pretenses to sympathy are interpersonally dangerous, I contend that even if there had actually been an unlimited number of wolves, the boy could not have hoped to receive unlimited sympathy. In our terminology here, the boy had cashed in his sympathy credits. After his first few claims were honored, he had already received his sympathy allotment and depleted his sympathy accounts.

There is a variety of ways to ask for too much sympathy. First, one can ask too much for a particular problem. One's own plight may seem dire, but others may have perceived it as low in sympathy-worthiness. For example:

> Every time I see her, I think, "Here we go again!" She's like a broken record. "Sam did this to me; Sam didn't do that for me." I'm sorry, but a lot of us have been through divorces and survived. She's gone completely overboard. [Field notes, teacher in his 30s]

And:

> She looks like she's about 30. I mean, what does she want? Why should I feel sorry for her just because she's having her fortieth birthday? [Field notes, 45-year-old woman]

Second, one can ask for too much for a particular other's present situation. People who have their own problems are, to some extent, exempt from the obligation to feel or display sympathy to others—especially to others in less serious plights. These comments of a survey respondent, a Hispanic custodian in her 50s, show that she applied this "rule for breaking rules" to herself: "Why should I feel sorry for those people in that story [about hurricane damage]? I've got no job, and my husband died."

Third, in specific encounters and relationships, claims to sympathy may be considered excessive, as panhandlers regularly discover. Fourth, one can ask for too much sympathy for a particular setting. For instance, a claim that would be honored at lunch may not be honored in the office.

Finally, sympathy may be claimed over too long a period of time—a point that merits further comment.

The estimated duration of a problem is related to the size of one's sympathy accounts in a curvilinear fashion. Problems of either very short or very long duration will engender less, or less consistent, sympathy than intermediate-range problems. Problems that are over quickly, such as a painful medical test lasting only a few moments, elicit minimal sympathy because these situations are not "worth" much. Long-term problems, while they may be worth more sympathy, may call for greater emotional expenditures than others can or will put forth. For instance, those who grieve too long (Wood 1975) or who cannot recover from a divorce or disaster in a timely fashion may find their margins diminished. Chronic illness—arthritis, for example—may thus be awarded less sympathy than an intermediate-range, acute illness, such as pneumonia (see, e.g., Strauss et al. 1982, p. 256).[4]

Regardless of one's misfortune, then, claiming and accepting sympathy can seriously diminish others' capacity to sympathize. George Eliot speaks of physical limits on how much sympathy can be felt or displayed:

> If we had a keen vision and feeling of all ordinary human life, it would be like hearing the grass grow and the squirrel's heart beat, and we should die of that roar which lies on the other side of silence. [(1872) 1981, p. 191]

Wiseman concurs:

> Charity and compassion are not available in unlimited supply, the Bible notwithstanding. Like so many other strong emotions, compassion cannot be called forth on every possible occasion without exhausing the giver. [1979, p. 242]

Sympathy recipients are expected to be sensitive to the sacrifices of sympathizers. If they are not, they may diminish others' willingness to sympathize. For both physical and cultural reasons, then, there appears to be a maximum amount of sympathy that an individual may claim from a specific other in a given period.

Those I observed and interviewed recognized these limits on others' sympathy. Several noted that, if they had recently received sympathy, help, time off from work, and the like, they were reluctant even to mention new problems that cropped up soon after. As one man, a carpenter in his 50s, put it,

> That month when I had three deaths in the family and my car broke down and my mother-in-law needed constant care and the kids were sick, well, it was too unbelievable. I was embarrassed to even tell people what was happening. I didn't bring up all the details.

An interviewee in her 30s, who had experienced surgery, a death in the family, and job problems, stated,

> I had to deal with it jokingly. I'd list all the terrible things and laugh. There were just too many things all at once.

She takes care to protect her significant others, thereby protecting her sympathy margins as well.

The other side of this sympathy rule is that, if one does *not* claim very much sympathy or help very often, one may be, in commonsense terms, "due for" it. Note the case of Mr. F, cited by Locker (1981). He is a stoic who has very rarely claimed sympathy and attention for illness and who is thought by his wife to deserve some:

> . . . he had very bad flu, it's the first time he's been ill since we've been married, and I couldn't get the doctor to come and see him. OK, so everybody has flu, but he had a high temperature. . . . I felt that if Dr. M. [their former physician] and his old receptionist had been there . . . they would have thought: Mr. F never ever comes near us, he must really not be well, or even if he's not . . . we owe him a visit. [p. 108]

Many of us, like Mr. F, may store up sympathy credits by being competent, functioning group members. (That we can go too far with this practice is the subject of rule 3 below.)

Corollary 2a: Do not accept sympathy too readily.—In addition to not needing too much sympathy, one should not appear to want it too much. One should not expect, take for granted, or demand sympathy but, rather, underplay problems and count blessings.

Giving expressions of strength, independence, and bravery helps one avoid being perceived as self-pitying or as enjoying others' displays of sympathy. The oft-repeated question, "How are you bearing up?" implies that one should be trying to bear up. The appropriate response, "I'm okay," or "Pretty well." One's tone of voice, energy level, and other nonverbal cues may indicate otherwise—for instance, one may exhibit what a character of Henry James's called "the droop of the misunderstood" (James [1881] 1963, p. 192). But verbal expressions of bravery are expected. One interviewee pointed out that she often catalogs her misfortunes and problems for others but expressly declines sympathy: "I guess I'm conveying that I *could* ask for their sympathy, but I'm not. I'm being brave" (young typist).

Underplaying problems is quite common, as Sudnow also found in his (1967) research on dying and the bereaved. "Persons are engaged, so it seems, in the continual de-emphasis of their feelings of loss, out of respect for the difficulties of interaction facing those less intimately involved in the death than themselves" (p. 140). For instance, sympathy phone calls which Sudnow managed to overhear included remarks initiated by the bereaved about the concerns of the sympathizer: "How are your children these days?" (p. 137). Underplaying represents, first, significant emotion work undertaken to align feelings with the norms of various interactional settings and, second, a meaningful gesture to the nonbereaved.

On those occasions when people do not "keep a stiff upper lip," sympathy is, in effect, claimed. And, of course, claims diminish margins. An interviewee, a medical researcher in his 40s, reacted to a sympathy-demanding co-worker as follows: "I always tell people to watch out for Josh. He can be quite a leech if you let him. His problems are endless. You just have to keep your distance." The "greedy" sympathizee is shunned.

The victim of circumstances is also commonly expected to focus on other good luck or blessings that are thought to compensate for the present bad luck. Hurricane victims, interviewed by network newscasters in the fall of 1984, lived up to this expectation. Indeed, none whose interviews were aired failed to strike a positive note. For example: "It could have been worse" (middle-aged woman). "At least we're still alive" (middle-aged man). "We'll just start rebuilding and try to forget all this" (elderly man).

My survey respondents reacting to the vignette about hurricane victims echoed this theme: "I feel sorry, but at least they've got each other and no one was killed" (housewife in her 50s). "Sometimes a disaster like this draws people together. They're fortunate because they'll probably be closer now" (young secretary).

One typical get well card from Hallmark makes the count-your-blessings norm explicit. It attempts to convince the "unlucky" sufferer that he or she is really "lucky."

CHEER UP!
Things Could Be Worse!
Suppose you had a SNEEZING FIT
Or you maybe had the GOUT,
Suppose your ARCHES all FELL IN
Or all your HAIR FELL OUT—

. . . .

You're really lucky when you think
Of what it MIGHT HAVE BEEN—
But just the same, here's hoping
You will SOON BE WELL AGAIN!

Other cards, presumably for a male audience, exhort the hospitalized person to pay attention to the nurses rather than to the pain and danger.

To summarize this corollary, one who eagerly and openly accepts sympathy is an embarrassment because she or he is not meeting the role obligations of the sympathizee. Each of us has a right to some sympathy, but interactional strategies that explicitly call for these rights to be honored will diminish sympathy margins rapidly. The resulting sentiment is usually less sincere, and display, if there is any, may be empty.

Rule 3: Claim Some Sympathy

Prescriptions of bravery notwithstanding, to keep sympathy margins viable one should claim and accept some sympathy from others when circumstances are appropriate. This sympathy rule is perhaps less obvious than the others. Taken together with rule 2, it suggests that there is some optimal amount of sympathy to claim. The self-reliant—who remain independent, pay cash, and do not develop credit ratings by borrowing and repaying—may not have sympathy accounts in times of need. Paradoxically, those who have histories of never crying wolf may find no one heeding their legitimate cries. This rule is most clearly applicable in relationships involving intimates or equals, but it operates to some extent for nonintimates, subordinates, and superiors as well.

Just as the act of claiming sympathy has a variety of meanings, so, too, does not claiming or accepting sympathy. In general, one who never claims or accepts sympathy from another over a period of time in a stable relationship may simply come to be defined as an inactive member of the interaction network. (This definition results especially, but not only, when one gives little sympathy to others as well.) Nonaccepters are of the group but not in it. When roles have solidified and become habitual, an out-of-character claim for sympathy may not "compute."

As my interviewees indicated, a number of signals may be sent if one does not, from time to time, claim and accept some sympathy. One may appear too lofty or too self-possessed. In the former case, one is unworthy of sympathy; in the latter, not in need. Or, like rate-buster's, one's fortune is too good or the ability to cope too expert compared with that of the average person. The following case shows that highly competent people who rarely claim sympathy can easily find themselves defined as not needing sympathy, as not having the problems, worries, or stage fright common among the less able:

> I was so surprised—shocked—at the reaction of my colleagues last week. I had to give a big presentation that lasted two days. I've done shorter ones before, but this was frightening. I found myself getting nervous and tried to talk to my friends about it. They just said, "Oh, you'll do okay. You always do." Not an ounce of sympathy! And these were "near" friends, too, not just people I know.

Although this young editor gives sympathy to others, she rarely finds the need to claim it. The event she describes led her to recognize that she had no sympathy accounts with her co-workers. She reported that she intends to change their perceptions of her by letting them know more about her insecurities—that is, by claiming some sympathy.

My interviewees also attributed such meanings to not accepting sympathy as the unwillingness to incur obligations, the unwillingness to allow others to discharge their obligations, and the unwillingness to admit others into backstage regions where problems and vulnerabilities are apparent. Finally, nonclaimers may give the impression that they feel too "lowly" to expect others' attention and sympathy.

Rule 3 shows that, as a particular sympathy exchange unfolds, group boundaries are created. Insiders and outsiders, intimates and nonintimates are defined. At the same time, group structure—the system of power and status relationships—is affected.

To begin with, A's claim and B's subsequent gift of sympathy create (1) a bond of "knowership" (Goffman 1983, p. 13) or intimacy between them and (2) trust on the part of the sympathizee. Further, the direction of the exchange crystallizes the statuses and roles of those in the relationship along a *superordinate-subordinate* dimension. Mutual exchanges of sympathy commonly symbolize equality, whereas one-way gifts of sympathy usually signify inequality.

If one both gives and receives sympathy, one is a friend, intimate, or peer. Former acquaintances who have not been particularly close may find their relationship taking on a more intimate cast, once sympathy has been exchanged.

On the other hand, the person who gives without claiming or accepting sympathy in return does not allow recipients a chance to discharge their obligations. Rather than enhancing equality, these situations engender the "parent-child" relationship between donor and recipient that Mead (1962, p. 367) saw as the essential form of sympathy. And the "parent" may be rightly or wrongly perceived as not requiring or needing sympathy for him- or herself. Furthermore, the state of owing engendered in the "child" (recipient) may be so uncomfortable as to cause resentment against the donor, providing justification for not returning sympathy or actually interfering with feeling it.

To recap, there appears to be an optimal amount of sympathy to claim and/or receive (depending on the relative power and authority of the actor and the desired closeness of the relationship), if one wants to keep accounts open. Claiming too little, as well as claiming too much, may diminish margins.

Rule 4: Reciprocate to Others for the Gift of Sympathy

A final rule for maintaining an adequate supply of sympathy credits is that one must reciprocate. Depending in part on one's position vis-à-vis the donor, one may be expected to repay the gift of sympathy with gratitude, deference, and esteem, or to pay back sympathy. Whether conscious of the fact or not, people usually expect returns when they give sympathy.

This sympathy rule illustrates the part played by norms of reciprocity and exchange in negotiating sympathy encounters and sympathy margins. Commonsense beliefs tell us that sympathy can be misspent, and we often exhort one another not to "waste your pity" on those who do not appreciate its value. McCall contends, "When someone has expended . . . scarce resources . . . in establishing a relationship, he cannot afford to throw them away without realizing substantial returns" (1970, p. 8). If, on the other hand, recipients "regularly discharge their obligations, they prove themselves worthy of further credit" (Blau 1964, p. 98).

As Lévi-Strauss (1969, p. 54) points out, returns for social "gifts" do not have to accrue to the original donor to be considered valuable. Returns to family members, friends, and even to charities or the community at large may serve to erase obligations. For instance, if A receives sympathy from B, A can discharge the debt by showing gratitude to B's spouse or by giving sympathy to B's children should they experience problems. But a recipient who never makes a good-faith effort to show appreciation to the group may come to be ignored.

The minimal and most immediate type of return expected for sympathy is gratitude. Paying gratitude for sympathy signifies that one is in, and acknowledges being in, a position of need. She or he is "one-down" or "one-less-up." First, the recipient is in trouble, ailing, or otherwise not able to function in usual social roles, or the sympathy would not be needed. Second, he or she has "burdened" the sympathizer because of these difficulties. Third, the recipient knows that the sympathizer well could have "believed in a just world" and offered blame rather than sympathy. To refuse to pay gratitude can imply, then, a refusal to recognize the state of need, a refusal to accept the sympathy and well-wishes of other group members, or an expectation that sympathy is a right involving no obligations. Any of these signals can create a gap between the sympathizee and the sympathetic other, who may feel (to use my interviewees' words) "used," "taken for granted," or "unappreciated." On the other hand, showing gratitude, even minimally with a nod or a look, can serve to cement ties. In the Outer Hebrides of Scotland and some rural communities in the United States, a gratitude column in which recipients of sympathy visits and flowers publicly give acknowledgments and thanks is a regular feature of weekly newspapers. Some potential sympathizees—students, skid row residents, low-income crime victims—may even be required to display gratitude before they receive sympathy (see Wiseman 1979, p. 243).

The type of gratitude expected in return for sympathy varies with the relative social standings of donor and recipient. Those whom I observed and interviewed rarely mentioned receiving sympathy from a subordinate but noted receiving it from "personages." They remembered and remarked baskets of fruit sent by company presidents at times of bereavement and cards sent to former pet owners by veterinarians (even though such cards were routinely signed and mailed by secretaries). Gifts of sympathy given by superiors (especially when the superior is frugal with such gifts) are imbued with greater value than the same gift from an equal or an inferior. For this reason, as Schwartz (1967) argues, the returns appropriate for a gift from a superior differ from the returns appropriate for peers. What is owed a superior is gratitude cum deference. Deference is a weightier and dearer commodity than gratitude. Deferential behavior implies that one is inferior to the recipient in a fundamental and perhaps permanent way, grateful for the valuable gift from the superior, and unable to repay the debt with an equally valuable gift. A lack of deference and gratitude is often seen as arrogance, and arrogance can diminish sympathy margin (see, e.g., Chambliss 1973; Wiseman 1979, p. 72).

Sympathizees must not only show gratitude and deference, they must show them even when the sympathy displays they have received are crude, inept, hurtful, or unwanted. Sudnow's research on bereavement suggests that "offers of sympathy must be accepted without invitation" (1967, p. 156). In some of his cases, an open-door policy existed that allowed anyone to enter the house of the bereaved to offer sympathy, whether it was timely or not. Moreover, the awkwardness often felt by sympathizers may result in bungled communications, empty phrases ("I just don't know what to say"), jocular attempts to cheer up the victim that actually induce tears or horror, and the like. Another common mode of sympathizing is the recitation of the sympathizer's own problems ("I know just how you feel, because the same thing has happened to me and I . . . "). This sort of communication is intended, one may assume, to refocus the sympathizee's attention and to indicate that one is not alone in misfortune. (A sympathy recipient may feel compelled to listen to or even to elicit such remarks, thereby switching roles with the sympathizer.) The sympathizee must put up with all of the above types of communications, because the mere fact of expressing some sympathy is thought to indicate that the sympathizer means well.

Beyond gratitude, another important type of return is sympathy itself. Paying back past awards replenishes sympathy credits, a fact that I infer from contrary evidence:

> He's having a hard time, but I'm keeping my distance. . . . I gave him a lot of sympathy . . . but he didn't even notice when I needed it. [25-year-old man, teacher]

> I was by her side at her mother's funeral. Where was she when my brothers died? I don't count her as part of the family any more. [Retired secretary, age 70]

Although these people feel that their past investments entitle them to sympathy, there is no FDIC to guarantee emotional returns. The people who failed to repay debts when an occasion arose risked and got closed accounts.

Rules for repaying sympathy with sympathy, like those for paying gratitude, are contingent on power relations. For example, repaying a superior with sympathy (an equal return) may be considered an insult; gratitude is often preferred. The peer or intimate is more likely to receive sympathy for sympathy.

In general, then, [American] sympathizers expect recognition of their gifts of sympathy, and sympathizees acknowledge the fact that they incur debts when they accept such gifts. The rules do not specify commensurate returns in every case, because it is hard to measure how much has been received (and is therefore owed) and because people may want to maintain rather than erode power differences. On the whole, though, most people do not receive much more sympathy than they repay with their gratitude or their own sympathy. Margins not replenished soon become overdrawn. The Ik, on the other hand, establish no sympathy margins at all.

NOTES

1. Of course, as we will see in rule 2, some degree of exemption from sympathizing is allowed if one has one's own troubles.

2. The greeting card industry—which sells Americans 7 billion cards per year (McGough 1986)—both reflects and influences display norms. Sympathy cards marketed for those sympathizing with the bereaved are grave and solemn in tone (they usually are white or gray); often have no pictures or pictures of flowers (as appropriate symbols of sympathy); and use a vocabulary of deep, sincere, or heartfelt concern, caring, and understanding. Sympathy cards that are "suitable for business settings" usually offer only "sympathy" or "condolences." Get well cards, in contrast are often humorous, sexy, or cheery (cheer is the most commonly used word in nonhumorous cards). They picture flowers, animals, bugs, people in beds, and hospital personnel. One exception is the type of card labeled "suitable for serious illness," which still may mention cheer but does not suggest that the recipient "get well quick." More specialized cards are also available for those who have lost pets and for those who are remembering the anniversary of the loss of a loved one. Finally, the new "coping cards" offer comfort, commiseration, and, often, license to eat chocolates to people who are "down" or "blue." The underlying theme of all these cards, a theme explicitly stated in many, is that the sender is connected to the recipient, despite the temporary separation, figurative or literal, required by the plight. The fact that such cards are purchased and sent is evidence of sympathy-display norms.

3. A small number did admit admiration for others' creative abilities in evoking sympathy to get out of school, work, or family obligations.

4. Partly for this reason, many elderly people find their sympathy margins with younger people smaller than they expect, especially when they have few resources to offer in social exchanges (Dowd 1980). Furthermore, rules for claim-

ing sympathy may be more permissive in subcultures of the elderly than in the larger society (Jay Livingston 1986, personal communication).

REFERENCES

Becker, Howard S.
1967 "Whose Side Are We On?" *Social Problems* 14:239–47.

Blau, Peter M.
1964 *Exchange and Power in Social Life.* New York: Wiley.

Chambliss, William J.
1973 "The Saints and the Roughnecks." *Society* 11: 24–31.

Coser, Rose Laub
1982 "The American Family: Changing Patterns of Social Control." Pp. 187–203 in *Social Control: Views from the Social Sciences,* edited by Jack P. Gibbs. Beverly Hills, Calif: Sage.

Dowd, James J.
1980 "Aging as Exchange: A Preface to Theory." Pp. 103–21 in *Aging, the Individual, and Society,* edited by Jill S. Quadagno. New York: St. Martin's.

Eliot, George (Mary Ann Evans Cross) (1872)
1981 *Middlemarch: A Study of Provincial Life.* New York: New American Library.

Goffman, Erving
1983 "The Interactional Order." *American Sociological Review* 48: 1–17.

Hochschild, Arlie Russell
1979 "Emotion Work, Feeling Rules, and Social Structure." *American Journal of Sociology* 85: 551–75.

Hollander, Edwin P.
1958 "Conformity, Status, and Idiosyncrasy Credit." *Psychology Review* 65: 117–27.

James, Henry (1881)
1963 *The Portrait of a Lady.* New York: Penguin.

Lévi-Strauss, Claude
1969 *The Elementary Structures of Kinship.* Boston: Beacon.

Locker, David
1981 *Symptoms and Illness: The Cognitive Organization of Disorder.* London: Tavistock.

McCall, George, J., ed.
1970 *Social Relationships.* Chicago: Aldine.

McGough, Robert
1986 "Pansies Are Green." *Forbes* 137: 89–92.

Mead, George Herbert (1934)
1962 *Mind, Self, and Society: From the Standpoint of a Social Behaviorist,* edited by Charles W. Morris. Chicago: University of Chicago Press.

Parsons, Talcott
1951 *The Social System.* Glencoe, Ill.: Free Press.

Schwartz, Barry
1967 "The Social Psychology of the Gift." *American Journal of Sociology* 73: 1–11.

Strauss, Anselm, Shizuko Fagerhaugh, Barbara Suczek, and Carolyn Wiener
1982 "Sentimental Work in the Technological Hospital." *Sociology of Health and Illness* 4: 254–78.

Sudnow, David
1967 *Passing On: The Social Organization of Dying.* Englewood Cliffs, N.J.: Prentice-Hall.

Turnbull, Colin
1972 *The Mountain People.* New York: Simon & Schuster.

Wiseman, Jacqueline P.
1979 *Stations of the Lost: The Treatment of Skid Row Alcoholics,* 2d ed. Chicago: University of Chicago Press.

Wood, Juanita
1975 "The Structure of Concern: The Ministry in Death-Related Situations." *Urban Life* 4: 369–84.

Review Questions

1. Sympathy giving follows certain rules in the United States. Why is this fact evidence that cultural factors guide our emotions?
2. What does the norm of reciprocity have to do with sympathy in our society?
3. Clark argues that Rule 2 (do not claim too much sympathy) and Rule 3 (claim some sympathy) appear to be contradictory. Why are they *not* really contradictory?
4. How can sympathy margins change? What do changes in margins indicate about a person's group ties?

HONOR ON 32ND STREET: FAMILY AND IDENTITY IN A MEXICAN-AMERICAN COMMUNITY

Ruth Horowitz

THREE MONTHS PRIOR TO ANA'S COTILLION, OR *QUINCECAÑERA* (FIFTEENTH BIRTHday celebration), everything appeared to be ready. Sponsors to pay for almost all aspects of the religious ceremony and the party afterward had been found. Relatives, *compadres* (godparents), and friends had been enlisted to help: an uncle was paying for the food, an aunt was paying for the liquor, a grandmother was buying her dress, baptismal godparents were buying the cake, and two of their daughters were going to "stand up" (serve as an attendant) for the church procession. Other relatives and friends were enlisted as godparents to pay for the flowers, a *cojín* (pillow) to kneel on in the church, a *diadema* (diadem or tiara), the bands, the photographs, and several other incidentals. As Ana had chosen to have the dinner and dance in the gym of the local community center, she did not have to rent a hall. An order for two hundred invitations had been placed at the engravers with the names of all the attendants printed on an inserted sheet.

In addition to finding enough relatives and friends of the family to pay for the affair, Ana had found the requisite fourteen young couples, *damas* (women) and *chambelaones* (men), to stand up in matching dresses and tuxedos. This is frequently a difficult task, as each of the young women has to buy her own dress . . . which Ana, like most celebrants, picked out of a catalog of bridesmaid dresses. The cost of the rented tuxedo is often $40. A cotillion is an expense for everyone. Ana had already stood up for two of the young women, who were returning the favor, and she was scheduled to participate in four more. Finding fourteen couples who could afford and would agree to stand up for the affair was difficult. In addition, she wanted to exclude from the males any potential troublemakers. As it was, two of the young women

SOURCE: From *Honor and the American Dream: Culture and Identity in a Chicano Community*, Ruth Horowitz. Copyright 1983 by Rutgers, the State University. Reprinted with the permission of Rutgers University Press.

were standing up with their brothers, who were in different gangs, and another's escort was in a rival gang, but none [was] known as [a troublemaker] at parties.

Problems began several weeks before the affair. An aunt's family dropped out, claiming they could not afford to pay for the band because they had to attend the funeral of a relative in Mexico. Excuses such as this are common, but the day was rescued when Ana's mother agreed to try to pay for the band herself.

One week prior to the cotillion Ana discovered that her mother had hired only a Mexican *ranchera* (Mexican country music) band and not a rock group. Ana did not want a cotillion without a rock group, and a local band was finally located forty-eight hours before the party. Then one of the couples decided that they could not afford to pay for the clothes and dropped out. Another couple broke up and an escort had to be found on short notice. While anxious about having only thirteen couples, Ana claimed it was better than seven or eight, as some had. Her problems were not over. An aunt informed her mother that she had seen Ana kissing her boyfriend, and her mother threatened to cancel the event because she did not want to endure the questions about Ana's virginity that public knowledge of her activities might engender. If the affair had been cancelled, the strength of the family network might have been questioned.

A cotillion is a public affirmation both of a young woman's virginity and of her kin's ability to work together to pay for such an event. Not all fifteen year olds have cotillions. Many families cannot afford them. Moreover, rumors often claim that a young woman holding a cotillion is trying to prove that she is still a virgin when she no longer is one. On the other hand, failing to have a cotillion is frequently considered a good indication that the young woman is no longer a virgin and may even be pregnant.

The evening before the affair required major organization, as beans and rice had to be prepared for two to three hundred guests and the gym had to be decorated. Retiring at two in the morning, everyone was awake by six. Clothes had to be ironed for her six brothers and sisters, and both Ana and her older sister had to buy shoes the day of the affair. Her family congratulated themselves for having chosen to buy fried chicken rather than spending the considerable effort to cook the more traditional *mole* (a spicy baked chicken in sauce), though a few guests later commented on its absence.

Ana marched down the church aisle in her long white dress and veil on the arm of her uncle, following the thirteen couples and the new godparents. As she knelt with her boyfriend before the priest, Ana and the others resembled a wedding party. She did not kiss him but quietly left her flowers at a side altar and prayed there to the Virgin Mary. Her mother was pleased that seventy-five guests attended the church ceremony and that close to two hundred attended the party, many of whom brought presents. Wandering around the room while the photographer took pictures, one could hear compliments about the open bar, the dresses Ana had chosen, and the Mexican band.

Several of the members of the Lions gang arrived after dinner, having learned of the party from their member Ten Pen, whose sister stood up for Ana. On their best behavior and wearing their good clothes, they sat quietly drinking and, when the rock band played slow tunes, got up to dance. No incidents occurred, unlike several weeks before, when a groom fought at his own wedding and was arrested when the fight continued outside the hall. Ana's cotillion was dubbed a success by all. After the party, the photographs were admired over and over.

This event symbolizes much of what is valued in the Chicano family: the close, interdependent family network and the family's success in finances, in containing the sexual activities of the daughter so that she not only remains a virgin but is perceived as such, and in following the proper forms of social interaction. Expectations based on symbols of the expanded family, male domination, virginity, motherhood, and formalism determine the meanings of social relationships within and outside the family. The family relationships should be strong, the males should be dominant, the unmarried women must remain virgins, and the married women should center their lives around motherhood. Courtesy toward and respect for others, particularly elders, is expected of everyone. . . .

. . . On 32nd Street the move from other areas of the United States or from Mexico has not greatly altered traditional arrangements. The worlds of the men and the women remain largely segregated and traditionally oriented yet interdependent. This is attributable to a number of factors: relatives often came together or followed one another; close networks were expanded to include *compadres* (children's godparents), who were often friends and/or neighbors; and the cultural symbols that give meaning to social relationships were frequently stronger than many of the forces of change. It is situations where the circumstances (ecological, social, or economic) have changed that highlight the strengths and weakness of the collective expectations. What *should* be done may become unclear, be revised, or be reaffirmed. Let us look at these dilemmas and the evolving solutions.

A COHESIVE FAMILY

The kinship network on 32nd Street can best be termed an "expanded family". . . . While many relatives of varying generations tend to live nearby and interact continuously, each household is comprised of a nuclear family unit. A similar structure is found throughout the Chicano population regardless of social class and is the expected standard for families. In Mexico, particularly among the urban poor, the ties of kinship have been augmented to include *compadres* (fictive kin) through treating the godparents of the children as part of the expanded family network. While there is some indication that the importance of fictive kin as an extension of family relationships is lessening in some areas of the United States today, in other communities it remains important. On 32nd Street, the relationship between the godparents of a child's baptism and the child's parents remains particularly important for many families. *Padrinos* (godfathers) and *madrinas* (godmothers) are remembered on mother's and father's day and celebrate birthdays and many holidays with their godchildren. The interaction among generations and the closeness among age groups serve in part to maintain cultural continuity. . . .

The expanded family is the normative familial form for all classes, whether or not it includes fictive kin in the United States as in Mexico. An important aspect of the expanded family network is one of continuous exchanges that are not governed by laws of supply and demand. Not only is the relationship with friends who have engaged in these exchanges strengthened by being named *compadres,* but the mutual obligations further strengthen the relationship of the entire expanded family unit both as a symbol of their cohesiveness and because they need each other. . . . On 32nd Street the exchange of economic and personal services is frequently necessary for survival. Exchanges of money and individual skills are frequently made among kin and fictive kin. Turning for help to outside agencies such as public welfare or a public employment agency is regarded as a failure of a family's solidarity and worth. Ana's mother, for example, feared a public disgrace for the family when an aunt's family could not assist by paying for the band at the cotillion.

Having a large, close family that can be augmented by *compadres* who can and will readily help in time of need is very highly valued. Being seen as a cohesive family transcends economic success. In such a family on 32nd Street and in other Chicano communities, members lend each other money, locate a car mechanic, and help out in innumerable other situations. "We can hardly keep track of all the money that goes around between us anymore. We just assume it's about equal," a young couple declared while discussing the state of their finances and their families' aid.

Much tension and weight are placed on the family relationship, which sometimes cannot support the demands made on it. At times these demands may lead to conflicts. With the lack of economic resources available to a nuclear family unit, its financial situation can easily become overextended, as when Ana's uncle dropped out, leaving her mother with additional expenses that were more than she could afford. This situation strained the family's relationship for several months until Ana's uncle was again able to help them. Economic pressures can disrupt the ongoing flow of resources and social relationships.

• • •

Those families who do not have relatives or *compadres* on whom to rely must turn to public welfare in time of financial problems or must ask for support, thereby publicly acknowledging their humiliation. The neighborhood is attuned to such events, and news of them is quickly shared. One of the members of the Lions gang frequently attempted to invite himself to dinner at other homes. The other gang members often refused and laughed at his attempts, ridiculing him for his inability to obtain readily a meal from the usual sources—relatives. While eating at relatives' homes is common, no one *asks* to do so; relatives or *compadres* are expected to offer meals to anyone at their homes at mealtime. A person who can survive without money for a long period by going from relative to relative is viewed as having a cohesive family. A responsible individual does make some attempt to reciprocate, though no accounting is kept and the help received may not be reciprocated for a long period of time. However, even within the family, overdependence can lead to tension, as there is little money to go around.

Compadres and relatives usually make up an emotional and social support group. Women move freely back and forth between homes—cooking together, talking, taking care of one another's children, shopping, and going out together for entertainment. They have frequent Tupperware, makeup, toy, and clothes demonstrations at relatives' or *compadres'* homes. . . .

Holidays, birthdays, and other special occasions are usually celebrated with *compadres*, relatives, and their children. A special dinner is prepared, and people eat in several shifts if no table is large enough to accommodate all the guests. Attending a Thanksgiving dinner, which includes not only turkey and sweet potatoes but rice, beans, and chili sauce, at the Mendoza home with two sets of *compadres* (each of the three families had seven children, then all below seventeen years old), guests ate in three or four shifts. The children played and ran in and out, while the women discussed problems of child rearing in the kitchen and then joined the men to dance to Latin music.

• • •

The strong network of intergenerational relationships provides a means by which traditions can be readily passed on. Few child-rearing manuals are used, and intergenerational aid encourages traditional practices. Young girls spend time helping their mothers and learning the mothering role. Girls frequently take on household responsibilities and care for their younger siblings before becoming mothers themselves. At ten or twelve, girls frequently are party to discussions among their mothers' friends and between their mothers and grandmothers about family life and relationships. The intergenerational interaction and the strong emotional support these relationships provide are a solid basis for the maintenance of traditional sex role relationships within the family, upon which the code of honor is based.

MANHOOD

Manhood is expressed through independence, personal strength, control over situations, and domination. This image of manhood, particularly in relationship to femininity, has been traced by some scholars to the culture of Spain, where the desire for precedence in interpersonal relationships and authority over the family are important symbols of manliness. Others trace it to the culture of the Aztecs, where women were expected to be subordinate and submissive to men, while a third group argues that male domination was a result of colonialism. Though the traditional symbols of manhood have not changed substantially in the transition to 32nd Street and have significant implications for men's relationships as fathers, husbands, sons, and brothers, male domination as worked out within the family does not weaken the critical position of the mother.

The role of the Mexican father/husband has been described as one of domination and control over his wife and daughters. Studies of Mexican towns demonstrate that men are seen as people who cannot be "gotten around." Fathers are seen as rigid, closed, and distant. Sons become independent at an early age. Some of these descriptions are similar to those of relationships for fathers and husbands in the 32nd Street community while others are not. The symbols of manhood articulate many of the salient meanings of social relationships within the family. The father/husband, as the dominant member of the household, must maintain the honor of his wife and daughters. To dishonor them reflects not only on them but also on his ability to maintain his self-respect as an independent and dominant individual. He alone must be responsible for supporting his family and must not publicly appear to become dependent on a working wife. The husband/father as the family head and the son as an independent young man both expect to be served by the women in the household and to come and go as they please. Sara, an eighteen year old, explained:

> My brother, he comes rushing in and sits down at the table expecting a hot dinner no matter what time it is, just like my father. . . . You know he gets it every time and we have to make it.

No one found it extraordinary that one wife, who worked an early shift (7:00 A.M. to 3:00 P.M.), was expected to prepare dinner for her husband, who finished his shift at 11 P.M. and arrived home to eat at 4:00 A.M., after several hours of drinking. If she was asleep he woke her, and she had to cook and still get their seven children ready for school and be at work by 7:00 A.M. A spotless house was also expected and provided.

Though the men can demand and usually receive services (cooking, cleaning, and so forth) of the women when they want, the men are dependent on the women to provide these services. Men are taught that cooking, washing clothes, and cleaning are women's and *not* men's work. . . . A man who does "woman's work" must be unable to find a woman to do that work, and therefore less than a man, or must be unduly controlled by his woman. This male dependence actually gives a woman a significant source of power.

Husbands

While a husband may have extramarital affairs, he should not publicly flaunt them because it would demonstrate lack of respect for his wife. In one family with seven children the mother caught her husband three times with the same fifteen-year-old woman. The oldest son beat his father. "It was OK, my mother doesn't like him either. He tricks [goes out with other women] on her all the time." This man could barely support his family, making the situation worse for him. His wife frequently said she would leave him but she never did. Though this is not typical, similar situations exist.

• • •

While not all husbands have girlfriends, many wives believe that as long as their men come home to them, husbands should be allowed to do what they want. Christina, a friend of Margie's, claimed . . .

> You can't control what a man does and you got to accept him the way he is. Men are free spirits and as long as they come home to you, why should you worry? If you bring in some money and you cook, clean, sew, and are ready for them, why should they leave? Margie made a mistake that night at their party. She shouldn't have left when they had that fight, because she should have known that Dino would just stay there with one of his girlfriends. She holds him in too tight.

While wives may not like the fact that their husbands leave them home, many believe men must be free to roam.

As the person who must maintain his dominance and control the household, the husband is responsible for supporting the family without the help of his wife. Given the poorly paid jobs available, the wages of a working wife or daughter frequently become an economic necessity. Over 40 percent of the community women work, though many of them have working husbands or fathers (Schensul, 1972).

Within this cultural context, men are caught in what appears to be an unresolvable dilemma. A working wife is a public indication that the husband is unable to support his family and therefore lacks control in the family and dominance over his wife, who could become economically independent. But the alternatives to an employed wife are few and not much better. A hungry and poorly clothed family does not enhance a man's reputation, nor does depending on support from the expanded family for any length of time without reciprocation. Caught in this dilemma, many husbands prefer to let their wives work and explain their actions within the traditional cultural context. By stating that they are still in control, that they *let* their wives work, and then only to pay for incidental expenses while the men remain the main breadwinners, their actions are legitimized. For example, while two men in their thirties were sitting in a bar discussing whether wives should work, one said to the other, "I would never let my wife work while I got this good job, but a lot of guys are getting laid off now and my wife didn't get bad money before we got married." The second responded, "I got her working now 'cause we need a new washer and dryer to help her out. Now she has to go to the laundromat." Both men criticized another man whose wife was working though he had a well-paying job and the couple had a "good home." Only if a man explains that he is still in control is a working wife considered legitimate. . . .

Fathers and Sons

A son, like any man, is expected to be independent and dominant in any social relationship with women. In the family this means he should come and go as he pleases, as his father does. Staying near home is not regarded as proper. One eleven year old who always remained on his front steps was told by his father to "go hang somewhere else." What he does outside with his peers is seen largely as his own business. Some parents do not know that their sons are gang members and may know little of their sons' lives outside the home, to the point of not recognizing their "street names." One gang member told me to tell his parents that I met him in a settlement house because they did not know he was a Lion. Should a son begin to jeopardize his job potential by getting into too much trouble, his parents are faced with a dilemma. To interfere is to question his autonomy and threaten his manhood. Paradoxically, a father who refuses to control his son's behavior fails to fulfill his role as dominant family member. A situation of normative ambiguity exists: if he interferes, he violates his son's independence; if he does not, he demonstrates his lack of control. There is no higher order of rules to resolve this striking moral incongruity. Each situation must be negotiated.

• • •

Felipe at fifteen was rarely punished, though he was often absent from school. He was a man, according to his father, and should be granted independence outside the home. The father felt that he had no authority over his sons and could not tell them how to organize their lives. Only inside the walls of his home did he feel he had a right to control his sons' activities. If Felipe talked back to his father or mother, or came in noisy and drunk, then his father felt he had a right to act. As a man, he had a right to maintain order in his home; otherwise, he felt he had no say. Another father felt similarly about his son. After trying for a long time to encourage his son to continue his education, the father decided that he could not use punishment to force his sixteen-year-old son to attend school.

> I know my son is real smart, his teachers told me that many times, but he and his friends leave school every day before they finish. He says its boring. He's a good artist—I told him he could go to art school but he says the teachers are all fags [homosexuals]. He has to finish school to get anywhere, but I can't force him. He's a man.

Other fathers put their sons in military schools or send them to Mexico, resolving the dilemma. The father remains in control and the son retains some independence by living away from home.

This dilemma is a triggering situation in that either solution carries implications for the parents' (largely the father's) identity in the eyes of their sons and other people in the community. If the father tries to control his son's activities, he will become known as a strict disciplinarian who is denying his son's independence. Community members will see him as someone who takes the American dream seriously but may be making his son into less of a man. If he leaves his son on his own, the son may perceive his father as distant and tough but allowing him to pursue his activities as he sees fit, as an independent man. In that case, community residents may see the father as helping to develop an independent, honorable man but failing to maintain his own manhood by losing control over his son's activities.

• • •

VIRGINITY

The Virgin Mother is among the most salient religious symbols in Mexico. She is more important than the adult Christ in many Mexican religious ceremonies. For example, *el día de la Virgen de Guadalupe* (December 12) is an important celebration both in Mexico and on 32nd Street, when even men who rarely attend church go to mass. In Mexico City women walk on their knees the several miles from the downtown to the Virgin in Guadalupe's shrine. The sexual purity of women—the faithfulness of a wife to her husband or the virginity of an unmarried woman—is symbolized by the Virgin Mother. The honor of a man is besmirched if a daughter is not a virgin at marriage or a wife is unfaithful. His honor is inexorably tied to that of his family. In Mexican villages, the role of an honorable woman, both as a mother and as a daughter, is that of a *mujer abnegada*, a self-sacrificing, dutiful woman (Diaz, 1966: 78). While the symbol of the Virgin Mother is used in evaluating women's relationships on 32nd Street, some expectations have changed from those of the traditional Mexican village.

According to Mexican tradition, maintaining a young woman's public image as a virgin requires that she be accompanied on social occasions by a chaperone (usually an older or younger relative). On 32nd Street, chaperonage of unmarried women has largely been eliminated. . . . The result is that everyone is aware that most women can escape the watchful eyes of their kin. Consequently, maintenance both of a woman's virginity or faithfulness and of community perception of that state are difficult. . . .

Brothers and other relatives act as unofficial chaperones for young women. They will often stop young women from drinking, watch their sisters if they are with young men, or tell all their friends to stay away. For example, at a party sixteen-year-old Sara asked me:

> Please tell me if you see my brother because I can't drink with him around, he'll beat me. Me and my sisters are not supposed to drink, he doesn't like that. You know when we go to dances on the north side, we got to sneak 'cause if he ever found out he would follow us around and we'd never get to go anywhere.

The importance that parents give to a daughter's identity as a virgin [cannot be overestimated]. . . . [Thus p]arents are faced with what seems to many an unresolvable dilemma. If they follow the traditional honor-based code and refuse to allow their daughter to go out unsupervised, then her virginity remains publicly unquestioned and the honor of her family is upheld. . . . Freedom heightens the risk of the daughter losing her virginity or being perceived as having lost it. But if they closely supervise her activities, they risk alienating her. Again a situation of normative ambiguity exists and the resolution must be situationally negotiated between parents and their daughters.

The parental dilemma is exacerbated by the expectation that men will take what they can from women. Men are defined as dominant and women defined as submissive; consequently, only male relatives can be trusted with women. One father succinctly expressed these views:

> You know what all men are after. . . . It's natural for them to go out and get it anyway they can. I don't trust any of the young punks around here. They

take it and run. There are too many unmarried pregnant girls around here. The young girls don't know how to handle themselves.

• • •

Some families are able to retain strict control over their daughters. Lana, for example, must ask permission to sit in front of her house and rarely is allowed to go anywhere. . . . Another mother timed her daughter's return from school every day; it took eight minutes to walk home and if her daughter was not home within twelve minutes after the last bell, the mother went out looking for her. While this case is extreme, other families only allow their daughters to attend parties or dances under the supervision of a mature older relative. Most of the young women, however, have enough freedom to do what they want during the hours they are permitted outside the house. Many skip school to attend parties or be alone with their boyfriends.

Unable to resolve the dilemma with their parents, many young women marry in order to leave home. Marriage is one of the few culturally legitimate means for young women to leave home and still maintain their honor and that of their families.

• • •

MOTHERHOOD

Motherhood is the most culturally acceptable identity available to women. The role of independent career woman is not culturally acceptable. Women must be either wives, sisters, or mothers to men. Motherhood is seen not as a last resort but rather as a highly honored role. The Mexican image of the Virgin Mother, loving and dependable, the person with whom the child satisfies desires for nurturing and acceptance, is the 32nd Street model of motherhood. Motherhood is the basis of the strongest bonds of blood ties. These bonds are much stronger than those of husbands and wives or fathers and children.

The husband-wife bond is based on procreation and expression of love but little on companionship. The expectation that men will dominate in all situations makes it difficult to develop companionable relationships between men and women even in marriage, as sociability usually develops between equals. (Moreover, any time a man and a woman who are not related through blood ties are together, it is expected that they will become sexually involved, because men dominate women and, lacking equality and the possibility of friendship, the only reason they would be together is as sexual partners.) Most socializing occurs in single-sex groups, and the expanded family network fulfills companionship functions. But children's ties with their mothers are natural and lifelong: they never become distant with age, as do ties with their fathers, who discipline and control them. While the dynamics of the father-child interaction is in part determined by the child's willingness to obey him and demonstrate respect for him, mothering places no such conditions on the parent-child relationship.

Loyalty and support for his mother was demonstrated by a young man who had become addicted to heroin and entered a methadone program only after stealing from his mother:

> I used to steal all the time from my brothers and sisters and went through my old man's coat pockets many times . . . even stole his watch once and pawned it, but you know when I took some bread [money] from my old lady, then I knew I had to do something. Taking from your old lady's real bad.

The mother remains the central and most stable feature in a son's life. He depends on her for nurture and emotional support and she on him for support and the ultimate protection of her honor. As a son his honor is dependent on hers; any aspersion cast on her honor reflects on his own.

• • •

The traditional expectation that a woman's unique role is to be a mother with many children creates a conflict for those young women who have interests outside the home. Some reject motherhood. One nineteen-year-old college student, the eldest of seven, despised the traditional female role of daughter and mother:

> I had to change diapers for my three youngest brothers and sisters. They were such a mess and were so much trouble. I hate them for it. I wish my mother didn't have them. What did she need so many kids for anyway? It would have been a lot better without the last two. They were always crying and wanting attention . . . comb their hair, wash them, feed them, change their diapers, and put them to sleep. . . . They're my mother's kids. She should be responsible for them. I'm not their mother . . . if my mother gets married again and has another kid I'll die. One time I told her I wasn't going to have any kids. She really got angry and said God will punish me. It was up to Him, not me. She didn't speak to me for a week. I'm not going to have any kids. They're just trouble.

• • •

The[se] views . . . are not generally accepted and often considered immoral. They violate all expectations of femininity and the family. Though it is becoming more common for young women to desire to limit family size, in part because of the expense of bringing up children, older people and many younger ones see this not only as tampering with "God's will" but also as comparing things that cannot be compared: economics and family. . . . For most, social and economic success are not valued above motherhood. Problems arise only for those young women who are beginning to strive for success in the wider society. . . .

CHIVALRY AND RESPECT

Chivalry and etiquette are not regarded as critical for most of American society today, . . . but the precise form of social relationships remains important for the residents of 32nd Street. The formalities of social interaction are essential in an honor-based subculture, where even the slightest word or movement may be seen as placing a person in a demeaning situation. . . .

. . . On 32nd Street swearing is not tolerated in the home by either females or males. Swearing often results in a slap or a belt across the seat, administered by a mother, father, or older sister or brother. Nor is insolence or rudeness tolerated in the home. Doors must be closed nicely. An older person must be greeted and taken leave of with a courtesy that would please Emily Post.

• • •

Not only do formal interactions help youths to maintain order between generations, between the sexes, and between men, but youths who successfully employ the rules of etiquette at home are well received by all adults, while those who demonstrate a lack of manners within the home are denigrated by the community regardless of behavior outside the home. Those who know when to use their manners are those who gain the respect of others, even among gang members. Consequently, the use of common rules of etiquette not only demonstrates respect for others and channels behavior but is also highly valued by others in the community.

It is clear what the important symbols of family life are: solidarity, male domination, virginity, motherhood, and respect. In the context of an urban community within a highly industrialized and educated society, some of the expectations derived from these symbols become distorted, are ambiguous, or are in conflict. While some of the problematic situations can be resolved within the traditional culture, for other situations all solutions seem less than perfect.

• • •

The cohesive family with its strong network of relatives and *compadres* provides economic supports to help deal with financial realities, emotional supports to deal with normative ambiguity and conflict, and social supports and mechanisms to maintain the traditional symbols of sex role relationships and nearly traditional behavior patterns. . . .

Youths are caught between the traditional model of social relationships and the Chicago urban reality: the streets, the school, the media, and the job scene. With the freedom they take or are given, the youths are faced with many dilemmas as they venture beyond the confines of the communal and familial order. . . .

REFERENCES

Schensul, Steven.
1972. "Action Research in a Chicano Community," paper presented at the American Anthropological Association annual meetings, Toronto.

Diaz, May N.
1966. *Tonalá: Conservatism, Authority and Responsibility in a Mexican Town.* Berkeley: University of California Press.

Review Questions

1. What is the "expanded family" that characterizes the residents of 32nd Street, and how does it serve to maintain cultural continuity?
2. In the traditional Mexican culture, how do the rules for gaining honor differ between men and women?
3. What evidence does Horowitz give that the residents of 32nd Street experience conflict between the Mexican and North American cultures? How are cultural dilemmas resolved?

Suggested Readings: Culture

Berger, Peter L., and Thomas Luckmann. *The Social Construction of Reality: A Treatise in the Sociology of Knowledge.* Garden City, N.Y.: Anchor Books, 1967.

Greenblat, Cathy Stein, and John H. Gagnon. "Temporary Strangers: Travel and Tourism from a Sociological Perspective," *Sociological Perspectives* 26 (Jan. 1983): 89–110.

Hall, Edward T. *The Silent Language.* Garden City, N.Y.: Anchor Books, 1959.

Gans, Herbert. *Popular Culture and High Culture.* New York: Basic Books, 1974.
Kephart, Williams. *Extraordinary Groups.* 3rd ed. New York: St. Martin's Press, 1986.
Moffat, Michael. *Coming of Age in New Jersey.* New Brunswick, N.J.: Rutgers University Press, 1989.
Moore, MacDonald Smith. *Yankee Blues: Musical Culture and American Identity.* Bloomington, Ind.: Indiana University Press, 1985.
Reed, John Shelton. *One South: An Ethnic Approach to Regional Culture.* Baton Rouge: Louisiana State University Press, 1982.
Sutton-Smith, Brian. *Toys as Culture.* New York: Gardner, 1986.
Swidler, Ann. "Culture in Action—Symbols and Strategies," *American Sociological Review* 51(1986): 273–86.

Part III. Transmission of Culture: Socialization

THE HUMAN INFANT IS NOT BORN KNOWING WHAT TO EAT, WHAT TO VALUE, HOW TO communicate, or what to believe about the social world or its own self. It is born with curiosity and, according to developmental psychologists, a need to "make sense" out of the events and objects it encounters. The infant interacts with others in its social milieu, searching for category systems, meanings, and rules. At the same time, other members of the child's social world attempt to mold, to instruct, to reward and punish, to explain the culture's symbols and ways of classifying experience. This two-way process of learning and teaching culture by and to new members, called *socialization,* enables the child to become a part of its society, to interact relatively smoothly with others, and to share in the culture's common stock of symbols, norms, and knowledge.

Moreover, through the socialization process, the child develops a *self-concept.* By this term we mean the sum of all cognitions or thoughts one holds about oneself. The self-concept is composed of what are sometimes called "identity elements" that are more or less organized into "subidentities" corresponding to societal statuses or categories. The child must learn the *categories* in which to think about itself—for example, son, friend, female, driver, consumer, farmer, and so on—as well as learning *how to evaluate* its performance, relative to others, in these roles. Our self-concepts are, then, learned by observing others and their reactions to us, as Charles Horton Cooley's term, "looking-glass self," implies.

In turn, our behavior is affected by our self-concepts; we often act in ways that are consistent with the images of ourselves that we developed through interaction in our society. Sociologists say that the individual has *internalized* the culture once the societal categories and standards for evaluation are learned and applied to oneself. In other words, the individual comes to rely less on the input of others and to reward and punish him- or herself—by feeling guilt, pride, or shame—for behaving according to the rules of the culture.

The articles in this section illustrate a number of aspects of the socialization process. One of the most far-reaching categorizations in American culture is the one based on sex. No other social status has such an impact on the behavior of societal members. Children are socialized from infancy onward to the *social roles,* or scripts, attached to the statuses "male" and "female."

The first article, by Janet Lever, looks in depth at how children's gender socialization comes about. Lever spent hundreds of hours observing children at play. In "Sex Differences in the Games Children Play," she shows us that boys' play activities are organized and structured differently from the activities that occupy girls. Furthermore, the structure of play sends important messages to the players. "Boys' games" teach players to be assertive, to compete, to be good team members, and to protect their own rights. "Girls' play" teaches nurturing, role playing, getting along with others, and protecting others' rights. The formal and informal rules of boys' and girls' games and play activities, according to Lever, have effects that may last long beyond childhood.

Sex roles are expectations that are important in almost all aspects of one's life. Of course, there are many other roles that must be learned, some of which are quite specific, like occupational roles. In advanced technological societies, socialization to occupational roles most often begins in schools. But—as graduates of medical schools, truck-driving schools, and police academies can all attest—conditions on the job and expectations of co-workers play a major part in socialization to an occupation. Schools teach ideal norms, while the physician in the emergency room, the driver on the interstate highway, and police on the street must learn the "ropes," or the actual norms, to survive. We thus speak of socialization as occurring both formally and informally. In "New Cops on the Street: Learning Normal Force," Jennifer Hunt describes how rookie police officers are socialized, both formally (in the academy) and informally (on the streets), as to when and how to use force on suspects.

The selection by Donileen Loseke and Spencer Cahill deals with the problems that a group of budding social workers faced when they entered their first field placements. What they had not learned in their college courses was how to establish a "way of being" that could signal to others and to themselves that they were "real" social workers. More than learning techniques and rules, then, these neophytes had to learn how to construct proper identities.

Loseke and Cahill argue that becoming socialized to occupational identities was more difficult for social-work students than it would be for those entering older, more established professions with clear identity symbols, such as medicine. In other words, it is easier to establish "who you are" and "what you are" if you are in the process of becoming a physician than if you are in the process of becoming a social worker. Since our economy is in flux—becoming less production oriented and more service oriented—new occupations are emerging. Thus, it seems likely that the problems that social-work students face will also characterize a large number of people who will be entering other new occupations.

As police academy graduates and neophyte social workers move along in their careers, they will undergo socialization to even more roles. Police officers may become sergeants, captains, or police chiefs. Social workers may become supervisors or agency heads. Likewise, all of us moving through occupational and life-cycle stages will be socialized repeatedly to the new roles we are to enact. Consider in your own case the process of learning the ins and outs of the role of the "high school student" and then the "college student." Indeed, according to evidence collected by sociologists, as we age, we are socialized to the role of "the dying."

SEX DIFFERENCES IN THE GAMES CHILDREN PLAY

Janet Lever

CHILDREN'S SOCIALIZATION IS ASSUMED TO HAVE CONSEQUENCES FOR their adult lives. When sex differences in socialization are considered, a chief concern is the extent to which one group (men) is advantaged over another (women). Assuming that girls' socialization equips them less well for occupational careers than boys', the question becomes, "what is it about socialization that has this effect?" Typically, the answers have focused on institutional agents, primarily the family but also the school, and on the values, attitudes, and bodies of knowledge imparted by them.

In this [article][1], I take a different tack. I examine the peer group as the *agent* of socialization, children's play as the *activity* of socialization, and role skills as the *product* of socialization. Despite the importance attributed to peers during adolescence, the peer group and playtime have been relatively neglected in the study of child development. Perhaps social scientists have ignored the subject because they feel that sex differences in the preferred activities of children are obvious. Or maybe no one pauses to reflect upon the consequences of children's leisure activities because of the general tendency to view play as trivial. Yet it is during play that we have an opportunity to observe the development of precisely those role skills that are crucial for success in modern society.

Mead and Piaget are the foremost authorities who have recognized the social value of play and game participation. Mead (1934) suggests that the game experience is important as a situation in which the child can develop a sense of "self as object" and learn the complex role-playing skills relevant to later life. Mead illustrates his point by referring to the boys' games of baseball, but he does not tell us how girls, who are less familiar with team play, learn these critical lessons. Piaget (1965), through a close study of the game of marbles, meticulously explains how children develop moral values while they play rule-bounded games.[2]

He mentions almost as an afterthought that he did not find a single girls' game that has as elaborate an organization of rules as the boys' game of marbles. If we believe that games can be rich learning environments, then we must give serious attention to the differential exposure of boys and girls to certain types of play.[3] The research question then becomes: Are there sex differences in the organization of children's playtime activities?

METHODOLOGY

I used a variety of methods to gather as much data as possible in one year, 1972. Some 181 fifth-grade children, aged 10 and 11, were studied. Half were from a suburban school and the other half from two city schools in Connecticut. The entire fifth grade of each school was included in the study. I selected three schools whose student populations were predominately white and middle-class—a choice made deliberately because I believe that race and class distinctions would only confound the picture at this stage of exploratory research.

Four techniques of data collection were employed: observation of schoolyards, semi-structured interviews, written questionnaires, and a diary record of playtime activities. The diary was a simple instrument used to document where the children had actually spent their time for the period of one week. Each morning I entered the classrooms and had the children fill out a short form on which they described *what* they had done the previous day after school, *whom* they did it with, *where* the activity took place, and *how long* it had lasted. Half the diaries were collected in the winter and half in the spring. Over two thousand diary entries were recorded. The questionnaire, designed to elicit how children spend their time away from school, was also administered by me inside the classroom. I conducted semi-structured interviews with one-third of the sample. Some were done in order to help me design the questionnaire and diary; others were done later to help me interpret the results. I gathered the observational data while watching children's play activity during recess, physical education classes, and after school.[4]

THE DISTRIBUTION OF PLAY IN SPACE AND TIME

Children spend an extraordinary proportion of their day at play. For this reason alone the subject is worthy of serious investigation. Boys and girls alike spent only 24% of their free time (i.e., outside school) activities engaged in *non-play.* The activities most frequently mentioned were household chores, doing homework, and going to religious services.[5]

Another 24% of the activities listed in the diaries were neither "play" nor "non-play," but rather *vicarious pastimes.* The most important pastime, by far, was watching TV. Again, virtually no sex differences were found; both boys and girls watched TV from 15 to 20 hours per week. However, there were strong differences in the types of shows preferred by each sex. Generally speaking, girls preferred family-oriented situation comedies and boys preferred adventure shows.

Looking now at the 52% of the activities representing *real play,* we see that the differences between boys and girls become clear and strong. Following are six differences I observed:

First, boys play outdoors far more than girls. Many of the preferred activities of girls—like playing with Barbie dolls or board games—are best played indoors. Many of the boys' preferred activities—like team sports or fantasy games like "War"—have to be played outdoors. According to the diaries, 40% of the girls compared with 15% of the boys spent less than one-quarter of their playtime outdoors. This sex difference has several important implications. Girls, playing indoors, are necessarily restricted in body movement and vocal expressions. Boys, playing outdoors, move in larger, more open spaces and go farther away from the home, which, undoubtedly, is part of their greater independence training. We can think of girls' indoor games (usually played behind closed doors) as *private* affairs whereas boys' outdoor games are *public* and open to surveillance.

Second, even though boys and girls spent the same amount of their playtime alone (approximately 20%), when they were involved in social play, *boys more often played in larger groups.* This second sex difference is related to the first, for indoor environments place structural limitations on the maximum number of participants that can join in play. But this finding is also independent of the first point, for, according to the diary data, girls played in smaller groups even when they were outdoors. The nature of boys' games is such that a larger number of participants is required for proper play. For example, team sports require a larger number of players than activities like tag, hopscotch, or jumprope. On the questionnaire, 72% of the boys compared with 52% of the girls reported that their neighborhood games usually include four or more persons. Diary and observational data ran in the same direction, although the sex differences reflected were slightly weaker.[6]

Third, boys' play occurs in more age-heterogeneous groups. Children between ages 8 and 12 prefer to play in sex-segregated and age-homogeneous groups. But if boys' games require a larger number of participants, the limited availability of their age-peers necessitates allowing some younger children to join the game. The implicit understanding is that "you're better off with a little kid in the outfield than no one at all."

For example, I witnessed numerous ice hockey games where ages ranged from 9 to 15 or 16. The youngest children tried their best to keep up with the older ones or dropped out. They learned to accept their bruises, stifle their frustrations, or not be invited to play again. The very few times I observed girls in age-mixed play was at summer camp when the 10–12-year-olds used much younger children of 5 and 6 as "live dolls," leading them in circle songs like "ring around the rosy" or versions of tag like "duck, duck, goose." Here the oldest girls had to play on the level of the youngest instead of vice versa. The implications of this female play pattern for learning child care/nurturance skills are so obvious as to require little comment.[7]

Fourth, girls more often play in predominately male games than boys play in girls' games. We would expect more girls to be included in boys' games in accordance with the same principle: "you're better off with even a girl in the outfield than no one at all." Besides, there are theoretical reasons to make this prediction. It is believed that girls are punished neither as early nor as severely for sex-inappropriate behavior (Lynn, 1966).

The evidence for this proposition is mixed. In each of the three schools, there were one or two girls who were skilled enough to be included as regular members of the boys' basketball or baseball teams. On the other hand, there were many occasions when boys were seen playing girls' games like hopscotch or jumprope too. They did this without being censured, for they entered the game in the role of "buffoon" or "tease"—there to interrupt and annoy the girls and not be taken as serious participants. This is a clear example of what Goffman (1961) calls "role distance." The point to be made here is that girls playing boys' games had to do so as serious participants and suffered the consequence of being labeled a "tomboy," whereas the boys had a convenient protective device available to soften the consequences of sex-inappropriate play behavior.

Fifth, boys play competitive games more often than girls. For the purposes of analysis, a distinction was made between play and games.[8] *Play* was defined as a *cooperative* interaction that has no explicit goal, no end point, and no winners. To the contrary, formal *games* are *competitive* interactions, governed by a set body of rules, and aimed at achieving an explicit, known goal (e.g., baskets, touchdowns). Formal games have a predetermined end point (e.g., when one opponent reaches so many points, or at the end of the ninth inning) that is simultaneous with the declaration of a winner. Some activities may be organized as either play or game. For instance, just riding bikes is play whereas racing bikes is a game. Sixty-five percent of the play activities boys reported in their diaries were formal games, compared with 35% of the girls' activities.

In other words, *girls played more* than boys and *boys gamed more* than girls. Boys' greater involvement in team sports accounts for much of the strength of this sex difference in competitiveness, as well as the other sex differences described. But team sports constituted only 30% of the boys' play activities; if they were excluded from the analysis, the sex differences reported above would be weakened but by no means would they disappear. For example, eliminating team sports for both sexes, 54% of the boys' activities and 30% of the girls' activities are competitively structured. That is to say, if there were no team sports, we would still find important differences in the nature of the games boys and girls play.

Sixth, boys' games last longer than girls' games. According to the diary data, it was found that 72% of all boys' activities lasted longer than 60 minutes while only 43% of the girls' play activities did so. This finding was supported by recess observations. Boys' games lasting the entire period of 25 minutes were common, but in a whole year in the field, I did not observe a single girls' activity that lasted longer than 15 minutes.

There are several possible explanations for this sex difference. The most obvious is that the *ceiling of skill*[9] is higher in boys' games. A group of eight-year-olds find the game of baseball fun and challenging, and those same boys at twelve years of age can play the game and enjoy it just as much because the requisite skills have been developing all along; thus, the element of challenge remains. By contrast, girls who could play the games of jumprope and tag in the first grade are still playing them in the fifth grade but find them "boring" now. To be sure, they are better jumpers and runners, but the ceiling of skill was reached long ago. Moreover, girls' games have less structured potential for surprise, such as stealing bases or bunting as in the game of baseball. In short, it is likely that boys find their games more challenging and, therefore, have a longer span of attention.

Even when girls play games with a high ceiling of skill, the games often end shortly after they begin because the players have not developed the motor skills necessary to keep the action exciting. Some girls I watched could not catch or throw a volleyball. The one spontaneous girls' sports game I observed—a game of kickball—ended after fifteen minutes because the fielders had not succeeded in getting a single player out, and they were both frustrated and bored.

Another reason that boys' games continued for a longer period of time than girls' games is because boys could resolve their disputes more effectively. During the course of this study, boys were seen quarreling all the time, but not once was a game terminated because of a quarrel, and no game was interrupted for more than seven minutes. In the gravest debates, the final word was always to "repeat the play," generally followed by a chorus of "cheater's proof." The P.E. teacher in one school noted that his boys seemed to enjoy the legal debates every bit as much as the game itself. Even players who were marginal because of lesser skills or size took equal part in these recurring squabbles. Learning to deal with disputes may have been facilitated by the model set by the older boys during the age-mixed play referred to earlier.[10] Piaget argues that children learn respect for rules by playing rule-bounded games; Kohlberg (1964) adds that these lessons are greatest where there are areas of ambiguity and the players experience dissonance.

If Kohlberg is right, the moral lessons inherent in girls' play are fewer since there are almost no areas of ambiguity comparable to a player sliding into first base. Traditional girls' games like jumprope and hopscotch are *turn-taking* games where the nature of the competition is *indirect* (that is, there is preordained action: first my turn, then your turn, finally we compare achievements). "Hogging" is impossible when participation is determined by turn-taking; nor can personal fouls occur when competition is indirect. These turn-taking games do not contain contingent rules of strategy as in sports games; rather they are regulated by invariable rules of procedure. Given the structure of girls' games, disputes are not likely to occur. Thus, girls gain little experience in the judicial process. This lack of experience shows dramatically when they do play games where rule interpretation and adjudication are important. Most girls interviewed claimed that when a quarrel begins, the game breaks up, and little effort is made to resolve the problem. As I observed almost no examples of self-organized sports games, let me quote one interviewee, the captain of the girls' after-school soccer team, for a description of what occurs:

> Girls' soccer is pretty bad because most of the girls don't show up every time. We have to keep changing our teams to make them even. Then pretty soon we start arguing over whether something was fair or not. And then some girls quit and go home if they don't get their way. Sometimes calling them "babies" helps to get them to stay and play a while longer.

Other girls concurred, and some complained that their friends could not resolve the basic issues of choosing up sides, deciding who is to be captain, which team will start, and sometimes not even what game to play!

The most striking example of boys' greater consciousness and experience with rules was witnessed in a gym class when the teacher introduced a game called "newcombe," a variation on volleyball. The principal rule was that the ball had to be passed three times before it could be returned to the other side of the net. Although this game was new to both the boys and the girls, the boys did not once forget the "3-pass" rule, yet the girls forgot it on over half the volleys that first day.

DISCUSSION

Even though barriers still exist, many forms of discrimination against women are beginning to be eliminated. Some social scientists have oriented their research to answer the question: If we succeed in ending all forms of discrimination on the basis of sex, is there anything about the way we raise our daughters that will present obstacles to their pursuance of any occupational choice, including the professions and higher levels of business administration? The answers have been in the affirmative; the focus has been on personality and motivation. Some have examined aspects of childhood socialization that produce dependent, passive, obedient personalities in girls (Bronfenbrenner, 1961; Kagan, 1964). Others have stressed aspects of training that limit girls' motivation for success in the occupational world (Horner, 1972).

My own observations, however, lead me to stress a rather different theme, namely, that the differences in leisure patterns of boys and girls lead to the development of particular *social skills* and capacities. These skills, in turn, are important for the performance of different adult roles. Specifically, I suggest that boys' games may help prepare their players for successful performance in a wide range of work settings in modern society. In contrast, girls' games may help prepare their players for the private sphere of the home and their future roles as wives and mothers.

Boys' games provide many valuable lessons. The evidence presented here suggests that boys' games further independence training, encourage the development of organizational skills necessary to coordinate the activities of a numerous and diverse group of persons, and offer experience in rule-bounded events and the adjudication of disputes. Mead offered us the insight that team sports teach young children to play a role at the same time as they take into account the roles of other players.

Furthermore, boys' experience in controlled and socially approved competitive situations may improve their ability to deal with interpersonal competition in a forthright manner. And experience in situations demanding interdependence between teammates should help boys incorporate more general cooperative skills, as well as giving some team members (especially the older boys during age-mixed play) very specific training in leadership skills. The social and organizational skills learned in large play groups may generalize to non-play situations.

On the other hand, girls' games may provide a training ground for the development of delicate socio-emotional skills. We have seen that girls' play occurs in small, intimate groups, most often the dyad. It occurs in private places and often involves mimicking primary human relationships instead of playing formal games. Their age-mixed play is the type that helps girls to develop nurturance skills. Finally, girls' play, to a large extent, is spontaneous and free of structure and rules; its organization is cooperative more often than competitive.

The qualitative data collected through interviews and observation present a more convincing picture of girls' early friendships as a training ground for their later heterosexual courtship relations. The girls in this study claimed to feel more comfortable in pairs, less so in a triad, and least comfortable in groups of four or more. Most girls interviewed said they had a single "best" friend with whom they played nearly every day. They learn to know that person and her moods so well that through non-verbal cues alone, a girl understands whether her playmate is hurt, sad, happy, bored, and so on. There is usually an open show of affection between these little girls—both physically in the form of hand-holding and verbally through "love notes" that reaffirm how special each is to the other. Sharing secrets binds the union together, and "telling" the secrets to outsiders is symbolic of the "break-up." Such friendships may vary from two weeks to two years or more in duration. These girls experience the heartbreak of serial monogamy long before heterosexual dating begins some three to six years later.

Simmel's (1950:123) reflections on the dyad explain the precarious nature of these special relationships and why the larger play groups of boys are more stable:

> The dyad has a different relation to each of its two elements than have larger groups to their members. . . . The social structure here rests immediately on the other of the two, and the secession of either would destroy the whole. The dyad, therefore, does not attain that super-personal life which the individual feels to be independent of himself.

There can be no shift from the person to the role, let alone from the role to the collectivity, for the dyadic relationship is characterized by the *unique* interaction between two individuals. A girl engaged in pastimes with one of a series of "best friends" may be gaining training appropriate for the later dating experiences where sensitivity skills are called for, but she is less likely than her sports-oriented brother to learn organizationally relevant skills. Returning to Meadian terms, boys develop the ability to take the role of the *generalized other,* whereas girls develop empathy to take the role of the *particular other.*

To be sure, boys also have strong friendships, and the interpersonal skills they learn through their games are many. But these interpersonal skills are more instrumental than expressive. A boy and his best friend often find themselves on opposing teams. They must learn ways to resolve disputes so that the quarrels do not become so heated that they rupture friendships. Boys must learn to "depersonalize the attack." Not only do they learn to compete against friends, they also learn to cooperate with teammates whom they may or may not like personally. Such interpersonal skills have obvious value in an organizational milieu. Boys learn to share the limelight, for they are told that team goals must be put ahead of opportunities for self-glorification. The lessons in emotional discipline are repeated daily: boys must restrain their energy, temper, and frustration for the cohesiveness of the group. Self-control, rather than self-expression, is valued highly. Good-natured participation in any activity the majority elects to pursue is expected from all. In other words, boys must develop the social skills of "gregariousness" and "amiability"—social skills which Riesman (1961) claims are more closely linked to modern organizational life than are technical skills. . . .

. . . [T]he world of play and game activity may be a major force in the development and perpetuation of differential abilities between the sexes—differences that reinforce the preparation of girls for traditional socio-emotional roles. It might be wise to review educational policy with these thoughts in mind. Perhaps we should support a broadening of physical education programs for girls to include learning opportunities now found primarily in boys' play activities. Since deeply ingrained patterns are slow to change, alternate opportunities might be developed in non-play situations—for example, encouraging teachers to design group projects in which girls can gain experience in specialization of labor, coordination of roles, and interdependence of effort. At the same time, males have roles as husbands and fathers as well as occupational roles. A fully considered social policy will have to assess the extent to which emphasis on large-scale, organized sports for boys means systematic underexposure to activities in which delicate socio-emotional skills are learned.

Children's play patterns are part of that vast behavioral repertoire passed on from generation to generation. American parents have always encouraged their boys to play contact team sports because they believe the "male nature" requires rough and tumble action, and organized competition is the best outlet for this surplus energy. Parents believe their girls are frail and less aggressive, and therefore do not enjoy serious competition; rather, they believe girls feel their maternal instincts early and prefer playing with dolls and reconstructing scenarios of the home. But parents give little thought to the structural components of those games and to the lessons inherent in each type of play. Yet it is perfectly clear that if the very different organization of children's play has *any* impact on the performance of adult roles, that influence must be a conservative one, serving to protect the traditional sex-role divisions within our society.

NOTES

1. This paper is drawn from my Ph.D. dissertation (Lever, 1974). The research was supported by an N. I. M. H. Fellowship. I would like to thank Stanton Wheeler, Louis W. Goodman, and R. Stephen Warner for their advice and encouragement throughout this project.

2. Sometimes the word "rule" is used to refer to game norms or customs. Here the term "rule-bounded" is used in the narrower sense and refers to games in which the rules are known to all players before the game begins and remain reasonably constant from one game situation to the next and in which the infraction of those rules carries penalties (Eifermann, 1972).

3. Among others who have recognized the importance of play are Huizinga, 1955; Moore and Anderson, 1969; and Stone, 1965.

4. Further details on data collection can be found in Lever, 1974. As a contribution to the folklore of strategies of field research, I should mention that I sat in my car near a schoolyard every lunch hour for a month before formally beginning this study. I doubt a male researcher could have lasted three days before being questioned.

5. It should be said that the distinction between play and work for children is even fuzzier than it is for adults. A child walking to school appears to us only to be walking, but she may be involved in a private game like avoiding stepping on cracks; or, the newspaper boy making his deliveries appears to be working, which he is, yet simultaneously he may be immersed in a game of target practice with each shot at our doors. Some things we adults consider work—like cooking and baking—the children clearly defined as play, and were so categorized in my study, while there was no doubt that boys and girls alike saw making beds and washing dishes as work.

6. One of the important features of using different measure is that one gets a feel for what different measures produce. In this study, the children's statements of what they *usually* do and what they *prefer* to do (i.e., the questionnaire and interview data) showed the strongest sex differences. My own observation of what children did in the arena of the public schoolyard reflected differences of intermediate strength. The diary data—i.e., what children *actually* do when away from the eyes of parents, teachers, and peers of the opposite sex—showed the weakest differences. In other words, the diary data were furthest from the cultural stereotypes of what boys and girls *ought to be doing.* Nevertheless, sex differences reported in the diaries are often strong.

7. The opportunity for age-mixed play is different for fifth-grade boys and girls. While boys' sports continue to be of interest through the teens and beyond, girls have already dropped out of the game culture by the time they reach age 13 or 14. Psychologists who have noted an earlier decline in girls' participation in schoolyard play believe it is due to girls' earlier maturation rate and superior verbal skills. The accepted argument is that girls are able to exchange games for conversation earlier and with more satisfaction (Eifermann, 1968:76). Leaving aside the empirical question of differential skills, I suggest a reversal in the causal model. Based on evidence presented in this paper, we can conclude that our culture is deficient in non-sports games that are sufficiently sophisticated and challenging for older girls, thereby forcing them to drop out of playground activity. Development of verbal skills may be seen as a consequence, rather than a cause, of this pattern.

8. This distinction is consistent with that made by G. H. Mead (1934), as well as the classificatory schemes of contemporary observers of play and games (Sutton-Smith *et al.*, 1963).

9. Csikszentmihalyi and Bennett (1971) coined this term.

10. Wheeler (1966:60) points out the advantages of being part of a system with *serial* rather than disjunctive socialization. In this case, it means that when older boys permit younger ones to join them in their games, they in effect teach their juniors a great deal about the setting, not only in terms of the requisite physical skills but the social ones as well. In this context, such lessons are more often due to sheer exposure than to self-conscious instruction.

REFERENCES

Bronfenbrenner, Urie
1961 "The changing American child: a speculative analysis." *Merrill-Palmer Quarterly* 7:73–83, 89.

Csikszentmihalyi, M. and S. Bennett
1971 "An exploratory model of play." *American Anthropologist,* 73:45–58.

Eifermann, Rivka
1968 "School children's games." U.S. Office of Education, Bureau of Research. (Mimeographed Report.)
1972 "Free social play: a guide to directed playing." Unpublished paper.

Goffman, Erving
1961 *Encounters.* Indianapolis: Bobbs-Merrill Co.

Horner, Matina
1972 "Toward an understanding of achievement-related conflicts in women." *Journal of Social Issues,* 28:157–175.

Huizinga, Johan
1955 *Homo Ludens: A Study of the Play-Element in Culture.* Boston: Beacon Press.

Kagan, Jerome
1964 "Acquisition and significance of sex typing and sex-role identification." Pp. 137–167 in M. L. Hoffmann and L. W. Hoffmann (eds.), *Review of Child Development Research,* Vol. I, New York: Russell Sage Foundation.

Kohlberg, Lawrence
1964 "Development of moral character and moral ideology." Pp. 383–431 in M. L. Hoffmann and L. W. Hoffmann (eds.), *Review of Child Development Research,* Vol. I. New York: Russell Sage Foundation.

Lever, Janet
1974 *Games Children Play: Sex Differences and the Development of Role Skills.* Unpublished Ph.D. dissertation. Department of Sociology. Yale University.

Lynn, David B.
1966 "The process of learning parental and sex-role identification." *Journal of Marriage and the Family,* 28:466–470.

Mead, George Herbert
1934 "Play, the game and the generalized other." Pp. 152–164 in *Mind, Self and Society.* Chicago: University of Chicago Press.

Moore, O. K. and A. R. Anderson
1969 "Some principles for the design of clarifying educational environments." Pp. 571–613 in David A. Goslin (ed.) *Handbook of Socialization Theory and Research.* Chicago: Rand McNally.

Piaget, Jean
1965 *The Moral Judgment of the Child.* New York: Free Press.

Riesman, David
1961 *The Lonely Crowd.* New Haven: Yale University Press.

Simmel, Georg
1950 *The Sociology of Georg Simmel.* Trans. and ed. by Kurt H. Wolff, New York: Free Press.

Stone, Gregory P.
1965 "The play of little children," *Quest* 4:23–31.

Sutton-Smith, B., B. G. Rosenberg, and E. F. Morgan, Jr.
1963 "Development of sex differences in play choices during preadolescence." *Child Development* 34:119–126.

Wheeler, Stanton
1966 "The structure of formally organized socialization settings." Pp. 53–116 in Orville G. Brim, Jr., and Stanton Wheeler (eds.) *Socialization After Childhood.* New York: John Wiley and Sons.

Review Questions

1. In what ways are the play activities of the boys and girls in this study alike?
2. What are the six differences between boys' and girls' activities that Lever found?
3. What kinds of roles and skills do boys' activities ignore or discourage?
4. What kinds of roles and skills do girls' activities ignore or discourage?

NEW COPS ON THE STREET: LEARNING NORMAL FORCE

Jennifer Hunt

THE POLICE ARE REQUIRED TO HANDLE A VARIETY OF PEACE-KEEPING AND LAW enforcement tasks including settling disputes, removing drunks from the street, aiding the sick, controlling crowds, and pursuing criminals. What unifies these diverse activities is the possibility that their resolution might require the use of force. Indeed, the capacity to use force stands at the core of the police mandate (Bittner, 1980).

• • •

The following research[1] . . . explores how police themselves classify and evaluate acts of force as either legal, normal, or excessive. Legal force is that coercion necessary to subdue, control, and restrain suspects in order to take them into custody. Although force not accountable in legal terms is technically labelled excessive by the courts and the public, the police perceive many forms of illegal force as normal. Normal force involves coercive acts that specific "cops" on specific occasions formulate as necessary, appropriate, reasonable, or understandable, although not always legitimated or admired. . . .

Most officers are expected to use both legal and normal force as a matter of course in policing the streets. In contrast, excessive force or brutality exceeds even working police notions of normal force. These are acts of coercion that cannot be explained by the routine police accounting practices ordinarily used to justify or excuse force. These are acts of coercion that cannot be explained by the routine police accounting practices ordinarily used to justify or excuse force. Brutality is viewed as illegal, illegitimate, and often immoral violence, but the police draw the lines in extremely different ways and at different points than do either the court system or the public.

These processes of assessing and accounting for the use of force, with special reference to the critical distinction between normal and excessive force as drawn by the police, will be explored [here]. The study begins by examining how rookie police learn on the street to

SOURCE: Jennifer Hunt: Excerpts from "Police Accounts of Normal Force," *Urban Life*, Vol. 13, No. 4 (Sage Publications, January 1985). Reprinted by permission of Sage Publications.

use and account for force in a manner that contradicts what they were taught at the academy. It . . . is based on approximately eighteen months of participant observation in a major urban police department referred to as the Metro City P.D. I attended the police academy with male and female recruits and later rode with individual officers in one-person cars on evening and night shifts in high crime districts. . . .[2]

LEARNING TO USE NORMAL FORCE

• • •

In the formal world of the police academy, the recruit learns to account for force by reference to legality. He or she is issued the regulation instruments and trained to use them to subdue, control, and restrain a suspect. If threatened with great bodily harm, the officer learns that he can justifiably use deadly force and fire his revolver. Yet the recruit is taught that he cannot use baton, jack, or gun unnecessarily to torture, maim, or kill a suspect.

When recruits leave the formal world of the academy and are assigned to patrol a district, they are introduced to an informal world in which police recognize normal as well as legal and brutal force. Through observation and instruction, rookies gradually learn to apply force and account for its use in terms familiar to the street cop. First, rookies learn to adjust their arsenals to conform to street standards. They are encouraged to buy the more powerful weapons worn by veteran colleagues as these colleagues point out the inadequacy of a wooden baton or compare their convoy jacks to vibrators. They quickly discover that their department-issued equipment marks them as new recruits. At any rate, within a few weeks, most rookies have dispensed with the wooden baton and convoy jack and substituted them with the more powerful plastic nightstick and flat headed slapjack.[3]

Through experience and informal instruction, the rookie also learns the street use of these weapons. In school, for example, recruits are taught to avoid hitting a person on the head or neck because it could cause lethal damage. On the street, in contrast, police conclude that they must hit wherever it causes the most damage in order to incapacitate the suspect before they themselves are harmed. New officers also learn that they will earn the respect of their veteran co-workers not by observing legal niceties in using force, but by being "aggressive" and using whatever force is necessary in a given situation.

Peer approval helps neutralize the guilt and confusion that rookies often experience when they begin to use force to assert their authority. One female officer, for example, learned she was the object of a brutality suit while listening to the news on television. At first, she felt so mortified that she hesitated to go to work and face her peers. In fact, male colleagues greeted her with a standing ovation and commented, "You can use our urinal now." In their view, any aggressive police officer regularly using normal force might eventually face a brutality suit or civilian complaint. Such accusations confirm the officer's status as a "street cop" rather than an "inside man" who doesn't engage in "real police work."[4]

Whereas male rookies are assumed to be competent dispensers of force unless proven otherwise, women are believed to be physically weak, naturally passive, and emotionally vulnerable.[5] Women officers are assumed to be reluctant to use physical force and are viewed as incompetent "street cops" until they prove otherwise. As a result, women rookies encounter special problems in learning to use normal force in the process of becoming recognized as "real street cops." It becomes crucial for women officers to create or exploit opportunities to display their physical abilities in order to overcome sexual bias and obtain full acceptance from co-workers. As a result, women rookies are encouraged informally to act more aggressively and to display more machismo than male rookies. Consider the following incident where a young female officer reflects upon her use of force during a domestic disturbance:

> And when I get there, if goddamn, there isn't a disturbance going on. So Tom comes, the guy that I went to back up. The male talks to him. I take the female and talk to her. And the drunk (cop) comes and the sergeant comes and another guy comes. So while we think we have everything settled, and we have the guy calmed down, he turns around and says to his sister, no less, that's who it is, "Give me the keys to my car!" And with that, she rips them out of her pocket and throws them at him. Now, he goes nuts. He goes into a Kung fu stance and says he's gonna kill her. The drunk cop says, "Yo, knock it off!" and goes to grab him and the guy punches him. So Mike (the drunk cop) goes down. Tommy goes to grab him and is wrestling with him. And all the cops are trying to get in there. So I ran in with my stick and I stick the guy in the head. But I just missed Tommy's face and opened him (the suspect) up. So all of a sudden everybody's grabbin' him and I'm realizing that if we get him down, he won't hurt anybody. So I pushed the sergeant out of the way and I got my stick under the guy's legs and I pulled his legs out from under him and I yelled, "Tommy, take him down." I pulled his legs and he went down and I sat on him. . . .
>
> So, when I [finally] get my cuffs, we cuff him. And we're sitting there talking. And Tommy, he has no regard for me whatsoever. . . . The guy's opened up and he bled all over Tommy's shirt. And I turned around and said, "Tommy, look at your shirt. There's blood all over your shirt." He said, "Who the hell almost clobbered me?" I said, "I'm sorry Tom, that was me." He said, "You're the one that opened him up?" And I said, "Yeh. I'm sorry, I didn't mean to get so close to you." . . .
>
> So when the sergeant came out he said, "And you, what do you mean telling me to get outta the way." . . . And I said, "I didn't want you to get hurt

> . . . and I was afraid he was gonna kick one of you." And he says, "I still can't believe you pushed me outta your way. You were like a little dynamo." And I found after that I got respect from the sergeant. He doesn't realize it but he treated me differently after that.

Her colleagues' reactions provided informal instruction in the use of normal force, confirming that her actions under these circumstances were reasonable and even praiseworthy.

For a street cop, it is often a graver error to use too little force and develop a "shaky" reputation than it is to use too much force and be told to calm down. Thus officers, particularly rookies, who do not back up their partners in appropriate ways or who hesitate to use force in circumstances where it is deemed necessary are informally instructed regarding their aberrant ways. If the problematic incident is relatively insignificant and his general reputation is good, a rookie who "freezes" one time is given a second chance before becoming generally known as an untrustworthy partner. However, such incidents become the subject of degrading gossip, gossip that pressures the officer either to use force as expected or risk isolation. Such talk also informs rookies about the general boundaries of legal and normal force.

For example, a female rookie was accused of "freezing" in an incident that came to be referred to as a "Mexican standoff." A pedestrian had complained that "something funny is going on in the drugstore." The officer walked into the pharmacy where she found an armed man committing a robbery. Although he turned his weapon on her when she entered the premises, she still pulled out her gun and pointed it at him. When he ordered her to drop it, claiming that his partner was behind her with a revolver at her head, she refused and told him to drop his.[6] He refused, and the stalemate continued until a sergeant entered the drugstore and ordered the suspect to drop his gun.

Initially, the female officer thought she had acted appropriately and even heroically. She soon discovered, however, that her hesitation to shoot had brought into question her competence with some of her fellow officers. Although many veterans claimed that "she had a lotta balls" to take her gun out at all when the suspect already had a gun on her, most contended "she shoulda shot him." Other policemen confirmed that she committed a "rookie mistake"; she had failed to notice a "lookout" standing outside the store and hence had been unprepared for an armed confrontation. Her sergeant and lieutenant, moreover, even insisted that she had acted in a cowardly manner, despite her reputation as a "gung-ho cop," and cited the incident as evidence of the general inadequacy of policewomen.

In the weeks that followed, this officer became increasingly depressed and angry. She was particularly outraged when she learned that she would not receive a commendation, although such awards were commonly made for "gun pinches" of this nature. Several months later, the officer vehemently expressed the wish that she had killed the suspect and vowed that next time she would "shoot first and ask questions later." The negative sanctions of supervisors and colleagues clearly encouraged her to adopt an attitude favorable to using force with less restraint in future situations.

Reprimand, gossip, and avoidance constitute the primary means by which police try to change or control the behavior of co-workers perceived as unreliable or cowardly. Formal accusations, however, are discouraged regardless of the seriousness of the misconduct. One male rookie, for example, earned a reputation for cowardice after he allegedly had to be "dragged" out of the car during an "assist officer." Even then, he apparently refused to help the officers in trouble. Although no formal charges were filed, everyone in the district was warned to avoid working with this officer.

Indeed, to initiate formal charges against a co-worker may discredit the accuser. In one incident a male rookie, although discouraged by veteran officers and even his district captain, filed charges of cowardice against a female rookie. The rookie gained the support of two supervisors and succeeded in having the case heard before the Board of Inquiry. During the trial he claimed the woman officer failed to aid him in arresting a man who presented physical resistance and had a knife on his person. In rebuttal, the woman testified that she perceived no need to participate in a physical confrontation because she saw no knife and the policeman was hitting the suspect. In spite of conflicting testimony, she was found guilty of "Neglect of Duty." Although most veterans thought the woman was "flaky" and doubted her competence, they also felt the male rookie had exaggerated his story. Moreover, they were outraged that he filed formal charges, and he quickly found himself ostracized.

At the same time that male and female rookies are commended for using force under appropriate circumstances, they are reprimanded if their participation in force is viewed as excessive or inappropriate. In this way, rookies are instructed that although many acts of coercion are accepted and even demanded, not everything goes. They thereby learn to distinguish between normal and brutal force. In the following incident, for example, a policewoman describes how she instructed a less experienced officer that her behavior was unreasonable and should be checked. Here, the new officer is chastised for misreading interactional cues and overreacting to minor affronts when treating a "crazy person" involved in a minor dispute as if he were a serious felon.[7]

> . . . [W]hen I first heard about it (another fight) I'd wondered if Mary had provoked it any because we'd gone on a disturbance and it was a drunk black guy who called to complain that the kid who lived upstairs keeps walking

> through his apartment. The kid to me looks wacky. He's talking crazy. He's saying they shoulda sent men. What are you women going to do. Going on and on. And to me it was a bullshit job. But Mary turns around and says, "We don't have to take that from him. Let's lock him up." I said, "Mary forget it." And the kid has numchuck sticks on him and when he turned his back . . . he had them in his back pocket. So, as he's pulling away saying you're scared, like a little kid, I turned around and said, "I've got your sticks." And I go away. Mary . . . was so disappointed in me . . . like I'd turned chicken on her. So I tried to explain to her, I said, "Mary, all we have is disorderly conduct. That's a summary offense. That's bullshit." I said, "Did you want to get hurt for a summary offense?" I said, "The guy was drunk who called to complain. It wasn't even a legit complaint." I said, "It's just . . . You've got to use discretion. If you think I'm chicken think of the times when a 'man with a gun' comes over the air and I'm the first car there." I said, "When it's worth it, I'll do anything. When it's not worth it, I'll back off." And I think she tries to temper herself some because Collette and her, they finally had a talk about why they hated each other. And Collette said to her, "I think you're too physical. I think you look for fights." And I think maybe Mary hearing it twice, once from me and once from Collette, might start to think that maybe she does provoke. . . .

In summary, when rookies leave the academy, they begin to familiarize themselves with street weapons and to gain some sense of what kinds of behavior constitute too little or too much force. They also begin to develop an understanding of street standards for using and judging appropriate and necessary force. By listening to and observing colleagues at work and by experiencing a variety of problematic interactions with the public, newcomers become cognizant of the occasions and circumstances in which to use various degrees and kinds of force. But at the same time, they are learning not only when and how to use force, but also a series of accounting practices to justify and to legitimate as "normal" (and sometimes to condemn) these acts of coercion. Normal force is thus the product of the police officers' accounting practices for describing what happened in ways that prefigure or anticipate the conclusion that it was in some sense justified or excusable and hence "normal."

• • •

EXCESSIVE FORCE AND PEER RESPONSES

Although police routinely excuse and justify many incidents where they or their co-workers have used extreme force against a citizen or suspect, this does not mean that on any and every occasion the officer using such force is exonerated. Indeed, the concept of normal force is useful because it suggests that there are specific circumstances under which police officers will not condone the use of force by themselves or colleagues as reasonable and acceptable. Thus, officer-recognized conceptions of normal force are subject to restrictions of the following kinds:

1. Police recognize and honor some rough equation between the behavior of the suspect and the harmfulness of the force to which it is subject. There are limits, therefore, to the degree of force that is acceptable in particular circumstances. In [one] incident, for example, an officer remarked on his fear when a [rude drunk], a "symbolic assailant" (Skolnick, 1975: 45), was mistakenly subject to more force than he "deserved" and almost killed.

• • •

2. Although it is considered normal and natural to become emotional and angry in highly charged, taut encounters, officers nonetheless prefer to minimize the harmful consequences of the use of force. As a result, officers usually acknowledge that emotional reactions that might lead to extreme force should be controlled and limited by co-workers if at all possible. In [one case involving a male officer and a female suspect], for example, [the] officer justified the use of force as a legitimate means to regain situational control when physically challenged. Nonetheless, he expressed gratitude to his partner for stopping him from doing serious harm when he "snapped out" and lost control.

• • •

3. Similarly, even in cases where suspects are seen as deserving some violent punishment, this force should not be used randomly and without control. Thus, . . . an officer who "snapped out" and began to beat a child abuser clearly regarded his partner's attempt to stop the beating as reasonable.

• • •

Learning . . . restrictions on the use of normal force and . . . informal practices of peer control are important processes in the socialization of newcomers. This socialization proceeds both through ongoing observation and experience and, on occasion, through explicit instruction. For example, one veteran officer advised a rookie, "The only reason to go in on a pursuit is not to get the perpetrator but to pull the cop who gets there first offa the guy before he kills him."

It is against this background that patrol officers identify excessive force and the existence of violence-prone peers. Some officers become known for recurrently committing acts of coercion that exceed working notions of normal force and that cannot be excused or justified with routine accounting practices. In contrast to the officer who makes a "rookie mistake" and uses excessive force from inexperience, the brutal cop does not honor the practices of normal force. Such an officer is also not effectively held in check by routine means of peer control. As a result, more drastic measures must be taken to prevent him from endangering the public and his colleagues.

One rookie gained a reputation for brutality from frequent involvement in "unnecessary" fights. One such incident was particularly noteworthy: Answering a call on a demented male with a weapon, he came upon a large man pacing the sidewalk carrying a lead pipe. The officer got out of the patrol car and yelled in a belligerent tone of voice, "What the fuck are you doing, creep?" At this point "the creep" attacked the officer and tried to take away his gun. A policewoman arrived on the scene, joined the fight, called an assist, and rescued the patrolman. Although no one was hurt, colleagues felt the incident was provoked by the officer who aggressively approached a known crazy person who should have been assumed to be unpredictable and nonresponsible.

When colleagues first began to doubt this officer's competence, he was informally instructed to moderate his behavior by veteran and even rookie partners. When his behavior persisted, confrontations with fellow officers became explosive. When peers were unable to check his behavior, complaints were made to superiors. Officially, colleagues indicated they did not want to work with him because of "personality problems." Informally, however, supervisors were informed of the nature of his provocative and dangerous behavior. The sergeant responded by putting the rookie in a wagon with a responsible partner whom he thought might succeed in controlling him. When this strategy proved unsuccessful, he was eventually transferred to the subway unit. Such transfers to "punishment districts," isolated posts, "inside units," or the subway are typical means of handling police officers deemed dangerous and out of control.

As this discussion indicates, the internal control of an exceptionally or inappropriately violent police officer is largely informal. With the exception of civilian complaints and brutality suits, the behavior of such officers rarely becomes the subject of formal police documents. However, their reputations are often well-known throughout the department and the rumors about their indiscretions educate rookies about how the line between normal force and brutality is drawn among working police officers.

It takes more than one incident of excessively violent behavior for a police officer to attain a brutal reputation. The violent officer is usually involved in numerous acts of aggressive behavior that are not accountable as normal force either because of their frequency or because of their substance. However, once identified as "brutal," a "head beater," and so on, an officer's use of force will be condemned by peers in circumstances in which competent officers would be given the benefit of the doubt. For example, one officer gained national notoriety during a federal investigation into a suspicious shooting. Allegedly, a local resident had thrown an axe at the patrol wagon. According to available accounts, the police pursued the suspect inside a house, and the officer in question shot him in the head. Although witnesses claimed the victim was unarmed, the officer stated that he fired in self-defense. The suspect reportedly attacked him with a metal pipe. This policeman had an established reputation for being "good with his hands," and many colleagues assumed he had brutally shot an unarmed man in the aftermath of a pursuit.[8]

CONCLUSION

The organization of policework reflects a poignant moral dilemma: for a variety of reasons, society mandates to the police the right to use force but provides little direction as to its proper use in specific, "real life" situations. Thus, the police, as officers of the law, must be prepared to use force under circumstances in which its rationale is often morally, legally, and practically ambiguous. This fact explains some otherwise puzzling aspects of police training and socialization.

The police academy provides a semblance of socialization for its recruits by teaching formal rules for using force. It is a semblance of socialization because it treats the use of force as capable of rationalization within the moral and legal conventions of the civilian world. The academy also, paradoxically, trains recruits in the use of tools of violence with potential for going far beyond the limitations of action imposed by those conventions. Consequently, the full socialization of a police officer takes place outside the academy as the officer moves from its idealizations to the practicalities of the street. This movement involves several phases: (1) a decisive, practical separation from the formal world established within the academy; (2) the cultivation of a working distinction between what is formally permissible and what is practically and informally required of the "street cop"; and (3) the demonstration of competence in using and accounting for routine street practices that are morally and legally problematic for those not working the street.

The original dilemma surrounding the use of force persists throughout the socialization process, but is increasingly dealt with by employing accounts provided by the police community that reduce and neutralize the moral tension. The experienced "street cop" becomes an expert at using techniques of neutralization (Sykes and Matza, 1957) to characterize the use of force on the streets, at judging its use by others and at evaluating the necessity for using force by standards those techniques provide. Use of these techniques also reinforces the radical separation of the formal and informal worlds of policework, duplicating within the context of the organization itself the distinction between members and outsiders. This ["second training"] guarantees that members will be able to distinguish between those who can and cannot be trusted to use force and to understand the conditions under which its use is "reasonable."

NOTES

1. I am deeply indebted for both substantive and editorial assistance to Michael Brown and Robert M. Emerson. I would also like to thank Peter Manning, Bill DiFazio, Jim Birch, and Marie DeMay Della Guardia for their comments on an earlier draft of this article.

2. The female officers described in this research were among the first 100 women assigned to the ranks of uniformed patrol as a result of a discrimination suit filed by the Justice Department and a policewoman plaintiff. Nonetheless masculine pronouns are generally used to refer to the police in this article, because the Metro P.D. remained dominated by men numerically, in style and in tone.

My fieldwork experience is discussed in detail in Hunt, 1984.

3. Some officers also substitute a large heavy duty flashlight for the nightstick. If used correctly, the flashlight can inflict more damage than the baton and is less likely to break when applied to the head or other parts of the body.

4. For a discussion of the cultural distinction between "inside men" who handle desk and administrative tasks and "real cops" who work outside on the street, see Hunt (1984).

5. As the Metro City Police Commissioner commented in an interview: "In general, they (women) are physically weaker than males. . . . I believe they would be inclined to let their emotions all too frequently overrule their good judgment . . . there are periods in their life when they are psychologically unbalanced because of physical problems that are occurring within them."

6. The woman officer later explained that she did not obey the suspect's command because she saw no reflection of the partner in the suspect's glasses and therefore assumed he was lying.

7. Patrol officers do not view demented people as responsible for their acts and therefore do not hold them strictly culpable when they challenge an officer's authority (see Van Maanen, 1978: 231). In dealing with such persons, coercion other than that narrowly required for control and self-protection tends to be viewed as inappropriate and unjustifiable.

8. The suspect was known to other officers from prior encounters as a slightly demented cop antagonizer. Consequently, the officer's actions appeared completely unnecessary because he was not dealing with an unpredictable stranger. The suspect's neighbors depicted him as a mentally disturbed person who was deathly afraid of the police because he had been a frequent target of harassment.

REFERENCES

Bittner, E.

1980 *The Functions of the Police in Modern Society.* Cambridge, MA: Oelgeschlager, Gunn & Hain.

Hunt, J.
1984 "The development of rapport throughout the negotiation of gender in field work among police." *Human Organization* 43:283–96.

Skolnick, J.
1975 *Justice Without Trial.* New York: John Wiley.

Sykes, G. M. and D. Matza
1957 "Techniques of neutralization: A theory of delinquency." *Amer. Soc. Rev.* 22:664–70.

Van Maanen, J.
1978 "The asshole," in P. K. Manning and J. Van Maanen (eds.) *Policing: A View From the Street.* Santa Monica, CA: Goodyear.

Review Questions

1. In the police academy studied by Hunt, rookies learned both how to use tools of force and rules for when to use them. Describe these tools and rules.
2. Which of the rules taught in the academy turned out not to be followed on the street?
3. How did the rookies get their "second training" in how much force to use? What kinds of sanctions were used?
4. What were the consequences for the officers of using too little force?
5. What were the consequences for the officers of using too much force?

ACTORS IN SEARCH OF A CHARACTER

Donileen R. Loseke and Spencer E. Cahill

PROFESSIONAL SOCIALIZATION INVOLVES SOMEWHAT MORE THAN THE ACQUISITION of specialized knowledge and the internalization of professional values. . . . [Neophytes] must dramatically convince both others and themselves that they possess the expertise and the personal qualities that are the defining characteristics of occupational incumbents' official image of themselves. The result of this process might best be described as a "conversion" to a new view of self (Haas and Shaffir 1977).

Although neophytes' attempts to realize an occupational identity are seldom pursued without trauma and perils, they no doubt face qualitatively different challenges depending on the particular occupational identity to which they aspire. This article analyzes student social workers' attempts to realize the identity of "social worker" and contrasts their experiences to those of medical students. . . .

DRAMATURGICAL BACKGROUND

Since the emergence of social work as a paid occupation in the early 1900s, there has been considerable debate over whether this occupation qualifies as a profession. . . . [S]ocial workers have had little success in restricting access to social work practice to those who hold degrees from . . . accredited programs of study. . . . [They] have never effectively claimed a distinctive area of expertise or practice. . . . [P]racticing social workers are employed by a wide variety of both public and private organizations, they serve clientele as different as public–school students and prison inmates, and they are engaged in such diverse activities as individual counseling, community organizing, and public policy planning. . . . In other words, practicing social workers do not share common educational backgrounds, distinct world views, set of skills, type of clientele or similar occupational environments. . . . Indeed, even the *Encyclopedia of Social Work* fails to provide a definition of its topic. . . . [Moreover,]

SOURCE: Loseke, Donileen R. and Spencer E. Cahill, "Actors in Search of a Character: Student Social Workers' Quest for Professional Identity." *Symbolic Interaction,* vol. 9, no. 2 (Fall, 1986). Reprinted by permission of JAI Press.

when given a choice, most individuals say that they would prefer to discuss their problems with someone other than a social worker (Condie et al. 1978). In brief, unlike those who are preparing for careers in the more established professions, neophyte social workers must attempt to realize an occupational identity that is neither clearly defined nor generally respected.

This study draws upon the experiences of undergraduate student interns in social work. . . . [I]t is based on interviews and essays written by a 14-member senior class in an accredited BSW program at a small, private liberal arts college. . . . Like other accredited BSW programs, the particular program in which these students were enrolled required senior students to participate in an internship program for which they received academic credit, the so-called field practicum. . . .

According to social work educators, the field practicum is the most important component of social work education. It is this experience that is supposed to complete the process whereby students are transformed into the type of persons social work practitioners are expected to be. . . . [T]he field instructor—a practicing social worker—is expected to do more than help students acquire technical skills. His/her primary responsibility is to "purge" the student of those beliefs, feelings, and patterns of behavior that are inconsistent with social workers' official image of themselves and thereby transform the student into a professional social worker. . . .

[E]ach of the students on which this study is focused was required to work . . . at an assigned agency without pay. . . . The 12 agencies to which these 14 students were assigned . . . reflected the diversity of stages on which practicing social workers typically perform their occupational identity. These included a hospital, an elementary school, a medium-security prison, a psychiatric halfway house, a juvenile detention center, a home for the elderly, community outreach programs and counseling centers. . . . [T]hey were engaged in such diverse activities as community organizing, client advocacy, educational testing, dispute mediation, and various types of "counseling." They also served a variety of different types of clients such as the elderly, single mothers, public–school students, prisoners, hospital patients, and so-called drug and alcohol abusers.

The diversity of stages, parts, and audiences encountered by these students produced two immediate consequences. First, the common identity of "social work student" that they had developed over the course of their prior academic training quickly dissolved during the field practicum. In contrast to student doctors who tend to accumulate similar experiences in the course of their professional socialization, these student social workers found that their individual experiences were too dissimilar to sustain a common identity. . . . Second, many students complained that the characteristics of their particular field assignments did not provide them with opportunities to realize the identity of social worker. For example, one student described her work as a community organizer as similar to arranging a church social, and since "anyone can do that," she maintained that it was not social work. Another who worked with involuntary clients maintained that because social work depended on "open lines of communication with clients," she too was not engaged in actual social work. . . .

. . . [T]he students in this study also found that their prior academic training was of little use to them in their capacity as neophyte social workers.

> I think I'm still realizing that both the content and process that I've learned are totally unrelated to both the process and content of being good at the field placement.

Even the few students who found their prior coursework of some use could not draw direct guidance from it.

> I'm sure I'm using things that come from the textbooks but if someone asked me to write it down, take from my classes, put into words what I'm using, I don't think I could.

In any case, these neophyte social workers found that their prior academic training was not a source of clear guidelines upon which they could draw in their attempts to realize the identity of social worker. Of course, in this respect, neophyte social workers are similar to those who embark on careers in the more established professions. . . . Social work students, however, would probably find more support than law or medical students for their evaluation of the practical utility of their academic training. . . . [E]ven practicing social workers question the necessity of formal academic preparation for this career (Clearfield 1977). . . . [Additionally,] in comparison to law and medical students, social work students are provided with few opportunities to convince others and thereby themselves that they are being transformed into the types of persons occupational incumbents are expected to be. Their first notable opportunity to do so is often provided by the fieldwork practicum during which they are expected to enact the identity of social worker.

Neophyte social workers must also attempt to realize the occupational identity to which they aspire without the benefit of unambiguous symbols of that identity. Unlike doctors, there is no standard uniform for social workers. Some of the students in this study attempted to dress "professionally," whereas others imitated the costumes of their clients. Needless to say, neither strategy served to display effectively the distinctive identity of social worker. Moreover, in contrast to medical students, these social work students did not possess a distinctive occupational dialect that served to display the specific identity that they were attempting to realize. Although many of these students used such expressions as "reflective listening," "processing information through my channels," and "targeting," these and similar expressions are also used by members of other "helping professions" as well as by a growing segment of the lay public. Indeed, there are apparently no symbols such as white laboratory coats, stethoscopes, or a distinctive occupational dialect through which the identity of social worker can be unambiguously announced.

• • •

In the course of the field practicum, these neophyte social workers also discovered that they could not evaluate the effectiveness of their identity portrayals on the basis of audiences' reactions to their occupational performances. Although they had been warned that social work was a "low status" profession, they now confronted the reality underlying that abstraction. For example, students often complained about the treatment of social workers by other "professionals" such as teachers, corrections officers, psychologists, and doctors.

> Sometimes I feel she is the low man on the totem pole as a social worker. . . . What she says is not taken as seriously as I would like.

> They call social work something for liberal-minded, bleeding hearts. . . . They're always wary of new people who come in under the heading of social work.

> They blame the social workers for what's happening, but the problem isn't there.

Like veteran social workers (Clearfield 1977), these neophytes attributed such lack of regard for their chosen occupation to ignorance and prejudice. Nevertheless, they become painfully aware that social workers' official image of themselves was not always shared by those with whom they worked.

For social workers, though, clients are the most crucial audience for their occupational performances. According to their official image of themselves, a social worker's claim to a professional status rests on an uncommon ability to "help" clients in myriad ways. By implication, thankful clients can provide a practicing social worker with convincing evidence that he/she has successfully realized the identity of social worker despite negative reviews from his/her coworkers. These neophyte social workers found, however, that such convincing evidence was often difficult to obtain.

> At times, I question what [we're] doing because sometimes people can't really be helped or it takes so long. It's very discouraging.

> Some of these people really don't recognize their problems, really have no interest in dealing with it, no interest in wellness.

In brief, unlike medical students who rehearse their occupational identity in front of relatively receptive client audiences (Haas and Shaffir 1982b), these students rehearsed the identity of social worker in front of audiences who were reluctant to applaud *any* performance of that identity.

Although neophyte social workers do not have the benefit of clear directorial cues, a distinctive set of identifying symbols, or receptive audiences for their occupational performances, these dramaturgical handicaps merely reflect a more fundamental problem involved in realizing the identity of social worker. Indeed, the students on which this study is focused did not believe that realization of that identity depended on receptive audiences, displays of identifying symbols, or the enactment of a specific, predefined part. From their points of view, a certain constellation of personal qualities was the defining characteristic of an "authentic" social worker.

THE SOCIAL WORKER AS CHARACTER TYPE

When asked to describe the veteran social workers whom they admired, these students described such model social workers as emotionally controlled, hard-working, "nice persons," "extremely personable," having an "incredible respect for the people who come in there," and "caring—there's a real warmth." . . . [T]he image of social workers to which these students subscribed was not one of their own creation, as one student clearly revealed.

> In the coursework we always read about what a social worker is and I've found (my field instructor) to be just that.

In other words, accredited programs of study in social work apparently transmit an image of the authentic social worker as a recognizable character type.

• • •

[However,] on the basis of their observations of practicing social workers, the students in this study . . . conclude[d] that social work education was neither sufficient nor necessary to produce the type of personal character that social workers are expected to possess. For example, some students complained that practitioners who held social work degrees were more competitive than social workers should be. Other students were shocked by the apparent cynicism of such practitioners.

> He said that he will start to not like someone before he'd met them, and I said 'but that's not what you're taught as a social worker, you know. Your values are lost.' And, he said 'well, yeah,' and they laugh about it.

In addition, these students also learned that some of those who were identified by their job titles as "social workers" did not hold social work degrees, and, as one student noted, those without such a degree are sometimes the "best" social workers. . . .

Many of these students also implicitly recognized that the configuration of personal qualities that they considered the defining characteristic of "authentic" social workers is not unique to those who claim such an identity. . . . This was apparent in some students' responses to the question: "What is a social worker?"

> A person who is going to aid you in doing something you don't know how to do, someone to sound off to, someone to bail you out because you're freaked out, or just a friend.
>
> Working with people and if you do that you can take on anything, work in any role. A mother is a social worker. She has to be.
>
> If you're teaching and caring about people and seeing them as whole beings, you're doing more than teaching. You're doing social work.

As these comments suggest, at least some students seemed to believe that caring teachers, loving mothers, and good friends possess the same constellation of personal qualities that is the defining characteristic of an authentic social worker.

As an apparent consequence of their belief that such a configuration of personal qualities is neither unique to social workers nor a product of social work education, these students seemed to conclude that the defining characteristics of an authentic social worker were not acquired but developed "naturally." For example, in the course of describing a practicing social worker whom she admired, one student observed that perhaps "it's just her personality." Another characterized her field instructor's commitment to her occupation as "just her thing." These students apparently believed that the character of the ideal-typical social worker simply evolved.

In any case, these students did not believe that they could simply enact such a character. This was apparent in their responses to the question: "What makes a good social worker?"

> [D]eveloping a self which can only come from within. . . . Such a professional self includes a set of skills, a style of presentation and an integration of one's native personality.
>
> The little things, by that I mean inside you. How much you're willing to give . . . of what you feel.

In other words, unlike neophyte doctors who self-consciously manage impressions in their attempts to realize the occupational identity to which they aspire (Haas and Shaffir 1977, 1982b), these students did not believe that they could realize the identity of social worker by doing so.

IN SEARCH OF THE CHARACTER

. . . [T]hese students believed that realization of the occupational identity to which they aspired required management of the feelings from which behavioral expressions follow.

> Before I can help others I must understand and be able to control the way I think, feel, communicate and relate to others.

In other words, these students believed that effective enactment of the identity of social worker required what Arlie Hochschild (1979, p. 558) has termed "depth-acting" rather than mere "surface-acting." They believed that such a person must be sincere; that is, he/she must not only perform his/her occupational role but must also believe in the impressions which that performance fosters (Goffman 1959, p. 18).

> A quality that I hope to continue to develop is a sincere interest in the people that I serve whether I like them personally or not. In my opinion, a social worker should care for the people that she works with in order to truly care if they are helped.

By implication, every time these social work students self-consciously managed their behavioral expressions, they were reminded that they had not yet been transformed into the kinds of persons they believed social workers should be.

In their capacity as neophyte social workers, however, they often resorted to surface-acting. Some admitted that they self-consciously had to conceal their anger toward clients.

> Several times the tone of a client's voice or the response gets me so angry that I really have to bite my tongue or I would say things in relation to how thankful they should feel.

Others admitted that they self-consciously had to conceal their sympathy for clients.

> I get frustrated with myself because sometimes I think "I don't blame you." Like, I don't say it. I don't put that attitude across, but it's frustrating because I feel hypocritical when I say to clients "now do this, do that."

In either case, their dependence on the self-conscious management of behavioral expressions was inconsistent with the image of the authentic social worker to which they subscribed.

Not surprisingly, few of these students identified themselves as social workers. For example, when asked if they considered themselves social workers, most of these neophytes said that they continued to think of themselves as students.

> I still identify myself as a student, as a person who's been put in this frustrating situation of supposing to be something which you're not really.

> I thought I was going to feel more like a professional. I still feel like a student . . . I'm still me. I haven't changed. Rats.

While some students did use specific job titles such as "community organizer," "corrections counselor," or "drug therapist" to refer to themselves, in each instance they contrasted such identities to that of social worker.

Although some of these students continued to believe that they would eventually realize the occupational identity to which they aspired, others feared that they would never do so.

> I don't know what it takes to make you feel part of the profession. . . . I don't know. I don't know if I ever will.

> I know that I'll never be a social worker. It's a process. I'll always be working on it.

It is clear that the realization of the identity of professional social worker remained an elusive goal for most of the students despite their sometimes valiant efforts to achieve that goal. They were truly actors in search of a character.

CONCLUSIONS

As the preceding case study illustrates, in at least one important respect neophyte social workers are engaged in a more difficult undertaking than are those who embark on careers in the more established professions. Student doctors can wrap themselves in a "cloak of competence" by adopting commonly recognized symbols of their chosen occupation, convince relatively receptive audiences of their authority over their role, and thereby convince themselves that they have realized the occupational identity to which they aspire. In contrast, neophyte social workers are not provided with commonly recognized symbols of their chosen occupation, and they seldom perform their occupational role in front of receptive audiences. Furthermore, neophyte social workers' academic training tends to convince them that the identity of social worker cannot be effectively enacted by self-consciously managing impressions.

• • •

Although Haas and Shaffir (1982a, p. 151) have observed that the biographical [individual] and historical [societal] processes of professionalization are "strikingly analogous," this case study indicates that these two processes are also reflexively related. The problem neophyte social workers encounter in their attempts to realize the identity of social worker reflect their chosen occupation's difficulties in gaining public recognition as a profession. . . . In other words, the history of an occupation supplies the resources with which recruits attempt to realize a distinctive and valued occupational identity, and their effectiveness in doing so shapes the occupation's future. Indeed, the relationship between the historical and biographical processes of professionalization "goes right to the heart of sociology" (Ritzer 1973, p. 62). History provides the resources out of which individuals must fashion their biographies, and in fashioning their biographies, individuals make history.

REFERENCES

Clearfield, Sidney
1977 "Professional Self-Image of the Social Worker: Implications for Social Work Education." *Journal of Education for Social Work* 23 (Winter):23–30.

Condie, C. David; Janet Hanson; Nanci Lang; Deanna Moss; and Rosalie Kane
1978 "How the Public Views Social Work." *Social Work* 23 (January): 47–53.

Goffman, Erving
1959 *The Presentation of Self in Everyday Life.* Garden City, NY: Doubleday.

Haas, Jack and William Shaffir
1977 "The Professionalization of Medical Students: Developing Competence and a Cloak of Competence." *Symbolic Interaction* 1 (Fall): 71–88.
1982a "Ritual Evaluation of Competence: The Hidden Curriculum of Professionalization in an Innovative Medical School Program." *Work and Occupations* 9 (May): 131–154.
1982b "Taking on the Role of Doctor: A Dramaturgical Analysis of Professionalization." *Symbolic Interaction* 5 (Fall): 187–203.

Hochschild, Arlie
1979 "Emotion Work, Feeling Rules and Social Structure." *American Journal of Sociology* 85 (November): 551–575.

Ritzer, George
1973 "Professionalism and the Individual." Pp. 59–73 in *The Professions and Their Prospects,* edited by Eliot Freidson. Beverly Hills: Sage.

Review Questions

1. When the student social workers left the classroom and entered their field placements, what problems did they encounter in developing appropriate identities as social workers?
2. What factors seem to help neophytes create occupational identities? What factors helped medical students become socialized to their new identities?

3. Based on Loseke and Cahill's data, is constructing an occupational identity as important a part of occupational socialization as acquiring technical skills?

Suggested Readings: Transmission of Culture: Socialization

Becker, Howard S. "Becoming a Marijuana User," *American Journal of Sociology* 59 (Nov. 1953):235–242.

Bem, Sandra L. and Daryl J. Bem. "Training the Woman to Know Her Place: The Power of a Nonconscious Ideology," in Michele Hoffnung Garskof, ed., *Roles Women Play: Readings Toward Liberation*. Belmont, Calif.: Brooks/Cole, 1971, pp. 84–96.

Clausen, John A. *Socialization and Society*. Boston: Little, Brown, 1968.

Denzin, Norman K. "Play, Games and Interaction: The Contexts of Childhood Socialization." *Sociological Quarterly* 16 (Autumn 1975): 458–478.

Dornbush, Sanford M. "The Military Academy as an Assimilating Institution," *Social Forces* 33 (May 1955):316–321.

Fine, Gary Alan. *With the Boys: Little League Baseball and Preadolescent Culture*. Chicago: University of Chicago Press, 1987.

Nelsen, Hart M. and Alice Kroliczak. "Parental Use of the Threat 'God Will Punish': Replication and Extension," *Journal of the Scientific Study of Religion* 23 (Sept. 1984): 267–277.

Spiro, Melford. *Children of the Kibbutz*, rev. ed. Cambridge, Mass: Harvard University Press, 1975.

Part IV. Interaction in Everyday Life

THE STUDY OF SOCIAL LIFE TAKES US INTO ALL KINDS OF ACTIVITIES AND settings. Even in situations where one might think that "nothing is happening here," sociologists see important elements and processes of social interaction. For one thing, social interaction is much more complicated than simply learning, through socialization, a set of cultural norms and roles and applying them in all situations with all people. Norms and roles are very often situationally tied, and we must try to determine the nature of the situation we are in, in order to behave more or less appropriately.

People are always, therefore, both *reading* and *giving off* cues from and to each other, communicating symbolically even though they may be unaware that they are doing so. When you walk through a lobby or enter a classroom before the class begins, it may seem that nothing is happening. But the others in that setting will begin to "define" who you are by assessing your clothing, appearance, gestures, props, tone of voice, facial expressions, and so on within the framework of meanings already learned from our culture. You will also pay attention to *their* clothing, appearance, and so on. The ways in which they act toward you (even if they decide to ignore you) depend on their perceptions of you, and your actions depend on your perceptions of them. None of us acts or reacts in the same way in all settings or situations. We try to figure out what the nature of the situation is and what behavior it calls for. We can rarely say, therefore, that nothing is happening, because we would be ignoring a great deal of mental work involved in social perception and evaluation, as well as various forms of behavior actually taking place.

Consider how differently you would act if a person with gray hair, carrying a briefcase, and speaking forcefully entered your classroom on the first day of the term than if a younger person in informal attire carrying notebooks and texts entered the same room. In the first instance, you would probably decide that the person was the professor; in the second case, you would think you were in the presence of another student. (You may learn though further interaction that you were wrong, but your initial impression is all you have to guide you for the moment.)

How might your own tone of voice, facial expressions, language, and behavior differ?

The process we are describing here is an important one for understanding interaction in everyday life. It was termed the "definition of the situation" by an early influential sociologist, W. I. Thomas. In 1923, Thomas outlined this process, contending that each of the participants in any social interaction must define for him or herself what kind of situation exists and what types of others are present, in order to call forth the culturally appropriate behaviors necessary to mesh with the other "actors" who are present. A situation is defined (as, say, a pleasant, informal encounter; a formal dance; or a no-nonsense workplace) by reading *cues* from the environment, including the other actors. In addition, the individual emits cues as to his or her social statuses, expectations, attitudes, and the like which are read by the others involved. Thus, a process of give-and-take occurs in which a more or less agreed upon definition of the situation is negotiated. This process is critical if interaction is to proceed.

W. I. Thomas is probably best remembered for his idea that one's own perception or definition of the situation—whether it is "accurate" or "inaccurate," shared by others or not—is of prime importance in determining one's own behavior, or line of action, in that situation. Thus, "a situation defined as real, is real in its consequences." Returning to our example of the persons entering your classroom, you would probably act toward the gray-haired person with the briefcase *as if* this person were the professor, even if your definition of the situation were inaccurate.

In this section of the book, we have collected four pieces which bear on one aspect or another of the process of defining situations as it affects ensuing interactions. First is an excerpt from *The Presentation of Self in Everyday Life,* a classic book by Erving Goffman. Goffman analyzes everyday interaction using what he terms the *dramaturgical approach.* This approach focuses on those aspects of the lives of everyday people that are similar to the behavior of stage actors and other dramatic performers. Thus, Goffman views *every* encounter between two or more people as an event that calls for each "actor" to present one or more of his or her social roles to the other(s), much as in a stage performance. Individuals are motivated to present (selected) information about themselves to others, a process called *impression management* by Goffman, in order to have some impact on the common definition of the situation. Sometimes we give honest and *sincere* performances, trying to convey accurate information about ourselves. At other times, we give *cynical* performances which we know to be false. Regardless of whether a performance is cynical or sincere, we may use a number of nonverbal means of communicating information about ourselves, including props (e.g., the physician's white coat), settings (furniture arrangements and the like), gestures (such as a shrug of the shoulders), tone of voice, and so on, in addition to strictly verbal cues. Goffman categorizes and describes these elements of impression management as well as showing the ubiquitous presence of self-presentation in everyday interaction.

Goffman's view might be disturbing to some of you. If we are all on stage, manipulating what others see and think about us, then we must wonder when we are our "real selves." Goffman does not answer this question directly but, rather, shows us how social actors may present different aspects of themselves to different groups of people. His point is that we have *many* "real selves." After all, don't you act differently with various groups of people? It is unlikely, for example, that you behave the same way in class as you do in the dorm or at your parents' home. (What would your family think if you raised your hand during dinner to ask a question?) Why does your behavior change as the people around you change? Try to list the numerous ways in which your behavior changes during an average week. The tone of your voice, your language, dress, and posture are only a few aspects of your presentation that vary as you present each of your numerous "selves." Think too of what would happen if you did *not* modify your behavior. And think of how important the question of self-presentation was to the social work students Loseke and Cahill studied.

The concepts of the definition of the situation, impression management, and identity are also central to the work of Edward Gross and Gregory Stone on "Embarrassment and the Analysis of Role Requirements," the second selection in this section. In order to interact with others in everyday life, they contend, individuals must be able to behave in ways that explain to others which role or roles they expect to perform—that is, to establish an "identity" by "presenting themselves." An identity exists when the individual's claims about who and what he or she is are accepted by the others in the situation. At this point, the individual is "located," and a definition of the situation is possible. The parties to the interaction have a fairly good idea not only of who and what each individual is, but also of what each individual can be expected to do in the "future," that is, as the interaction progresses. To summarize, then, in order to give co-actors an idea of what we will be doing in the (very near or not so near) future, we must establish identities. Gross and Stone go on to indicate that "poise," or the maintenance of a unified identity, is also required for interaction to begin and to continue.

The focus of this article is actually on the problems that arise when an individual cannot establish an identity that others agree to or when the individual fails to maintain poise. Various "slips," either within or beyond the control of the individual, may disrupt the definition of the situation and lead to embarrassment for that person and for the co-actors, causing interaction to cease. Indeed, the fact that embarrassment occurs was what led Gross and Stone to infer the necessity for establishing and maintaining identities and poise.

In the third article, "The Managed Heart," Arlie Russell Hochschild shifts our attention to how people align their self-presentations to conform with employers' expectations. Hochschild's research centers on the airline industry's expectations for flight attendants. She finds that managers and trainers delineate more than the specific tasks that flight attendants should accomplish, such as serving meals and giving safety instructions. In addition, they train flight attendants to control their own feelings and expressions in order to shape passengers' emotions, keeping them calm and happy. The airplane is to become the living room in which the attendant presents him- or herself as a host or hostess.

Yet every set of passengers includes a few who are unpleasant, obnoxious, or unruly. Hochschild shows that the attendant is often able to engage in "deep acting," actually controlling his or her inner feelings in order to fulfill the job requirement to keep smiling. Sometimes, however, the perpetual smile belies real feelings of frustration or hostility. What does this kind of self-presentation, this "emotional labor," cost the worker? To what degree do job demands impinge on the worker's internal senses and sentiments? Hochschild's respondents voiced concerns about forcing their false smiles and, over time, becoming divorced or alienated from their true feelings.

These concerns are not, of course, limited to flight attendants. A great number of jobs in the growing service sector of our economy—salesperson, hairdresser, teacher, nurse, shop owner, entertainer, and many more—require emotional labor to present the proper emotions to the public. We are just beginning to recognize this fact and to study its consequences for individuals and for society as a whole.

We started this section with the issue of how people present selves to each other in their everyday interactions. We considered what happens when someone fails to present a desired self as well as how people's self-presentations and identities are constrained by job requirements. In the final selection, Anselm Strauss examines how people's selves or identities—the core of what they are trying to present to others—change. What events and experiences lead to the statement: "I'm not the same person I used to be"? Meeting a goal or being betrayed—either of these can cause a reassessment and redefinition of oneself.

This excerpt from Strauss's book, *Mirrors and Masks: The Search for Identity,* makes several contributions to our understanding of interaction in everyday life. First, it offers a typology of the events that force people to adopt new identities and shed old ones. Second, it gives concrete illustrations of how people redefine situations, showing that our understandings of ourselves and our environments can and do alter radically at times. Third, it gives support to the important sociological insight that what seem to be "personal" experiences and changes are actually common among people who occupy similar positions in the social structure.

The four readings in this section should give you a good idea of how the sociological perspective can take us beyond our "common sense" interpretations of everyday encounters. The articles illustrate the complexities of seemingly simple and straightforward actions and interactions. Ordinarily people don't take the time to read and analyze the meanings that lie behind daily events, but these authors open our eyes to new ways of seeing and understanding them.

THE PRESENTATION OF SELF IN EVERYDAY LIFE

Erving Goffman

When an individual enters the presence of others, they commonly seek to acquire information about him or to bring into play information about him already possessed. They will be interested in his general socioeconomic status, his conception of self, his attitude toward them, his competence, his trustworthiness, etc. Although some of this information seems to be sought almost as an end in itself, there are usually quite practical reasons for acquiring it. Information about the individual helps to define the situation, enabling others to know in advance what he will expect of them and what they may expect of him. Informed in these ways, the others will know how best to act in order to call forth a desired response from him.

For those present, many sources of information become accessible and many carriers (or "sign-vehicles") become available for conveying this information. If unacquainted with the individual, observers can glean clues from his conduct and appearance which allow them to apply their previous experience with individuals roughly similar to the one before them or, more important, to apply untested stereotypes to him. They can also assume from past experience that only individuals of a particular kind are likely to be found in a given social setting. They can rely on what the individual says about himself or on documentary evidence he provides as to who and what he is. If they know, or know of, the individual by virtue of experience prior to the interaction, they can rely on assumptions as to the persistence and generality of psychological traits as a means of predicting his present and future behavior.

However, during the period in which the individual is in the immediate presence of the others, few events may occur which directly provide the others with the conclusive information they will need if they are to direct wisely their own activity. Many crucial facts lie beyond the time and place of interaction or lie concealed within it. For example, the "true" or "real" attitudes, beliefs, and emotions of the individual can be ascertained only indirectly, through his avowals or through what appears to be involuntary expressive behavior. Similarly, if the individual offers the others a product or service, they will often find that during the interaction there will be no time and place immediately available for eating the pudding that the proof can be found in. They will be forced to accept some events as conventional or natural signs of something not directly available to the senses. In Ichheiser's terms,[1] the individual will have to act so that he intentionally or unintentionally *expresses* himself, and the others will in turn have to be *impressed* in some way by him.

The expressiveness of the individual (and therefore his capacity to give impressions) appears to involve two radically different kinds of sign activity: the expression that he *gives,* and the expression that he *gives off.* The first involves verbal symbols or their substitutes which he uses admittedly and solely to convey the information that he and the others are known to attach to these symbols. This is communication in the traditional and narrow sense. The second involves a wide range of action that others can treat as symptomatic of the actor, the expectation being that the action was performed for reasons other than the information conveyed in this way. As we shall have to see, this distinction has an only initial validity. The individual does of course intentionally convey misinformation by means of both of these types of communication, the first involving deceit, the second feigning.

Taking communication in both its narrow and broad sense, one finds that when the individual is in the immediate presence of others, his activity will have a promissory character. The others are likely to find that they must accept the individual on faith, offering him a just return while he is present before them in exchange for something whose true value will not be established until after he has left their presence. (Of course, the others also live by inference in their dealings with the physical world, but it is only in the world of social interaction that the objects about which they make inferences will purposely facilitate and hinder this inferential process.) The security that they justifiably feel in making inferences about the individual will vary, of course, depending on such factors as the amount of information they already possess about him, but no amount of such past evidence can entirely obviate the necessity of acting on the basis of inferences. As William I. Thomas suggested:

> It is also highly important for us to realize that we do not as a matter of fact lead our lives, make our decisions, and reach our goals in everyday life either statistically or scientifically. We live by inference. I am, let us say, your guest. You do not know, you cannot determine scientifically, that I will not steal your money or your spoons. But inferentially I will not, and inferentially you have me as a guest.[2]

Let us now turn from the others to the point of view of the individual who presents himself before them. He may wish them to think highly of him, or to think that he thinks highly of them, or to perceive how in fact he feels toward them, or to obtain no clear-cut impression; he may wish to ensure sufficient harmony so that the interaction can be sustained, or to defraud, get rid of, confuse, mislead, antagonize, or insult them. Regardless of the particular objective which the individual has in mind and of his motive for having this objective, it will be in his interests to control the conduct of the others, especially their responsive treatment of him.[3] This control is achieved largely by influencing the definition of the situation which the others come to formulate, and he can influence this definition by expressing himself in such a way as to give them the kind of impression that will lead them to act voluntarily in accordance with his own plan. Thus, when an individual appears in the presence of others, there will usually be some reason for him to mobilize his activity so that it will convey an impression to others which it is in his interests to convey. Since a girl's dormitory mates will glean evidence of her popularity from the calls she receives on the phone, we can suspect that some girls will arrange for calls to be made, and Willard Waller's finding can be anticipated:

> It has been reported by many observers that a girl who is called to the telephone in the dormitories will often allow herself to be called several times, in order to give all the other girls ample opportunity to hear her paged.[4]

Of the two kinds of communication—expressions given and expressions given off—this report will be primarily concerned with the latter, with the more theatrical and contextual kind, the nonverbal, presumably unintentional kind, whether this communication be purposely engineered or not. As an example of what we must try to examine, I would like to cite at length a novelistic incident in which Preedy, a vacationing Englishman, makes his first appearance on the beach of his summer hotel in Spain:

> But in any case he took care to avoid catching anyone's eye. First of all, he had to make it clear to those potential companions of his holiday that they were of no concern to him whatsoever. He stared through them, round them, over them—eyes lost in space. The beach might have been empty. If by chance a ball was thrown his way, he looked surprised; then let a smile of amusement lighten his face (Kindly Preedy), looked around dazed to see that there *were* people on the beach, tossed it back with a smile to himself and not a smile *at* the people, and then resumed carelessly his nonchalant survey of space.
>
> But it was time to institute a little parade, the parade of the Ideal Preedy. By devious handlings he gave any who wanted to look a chance to see the title of his book—a Spanish translation of Homer, classic thus, but not daring, cosmopolitan too—and then gathered together his beachwrap and bag into a neat sand-resistant pile (Methodical and Sensible Preedy), rose slowly to

> stretch at ease his huge frame (Big-Cat Preedy), and tossed aside his sandals (Carefree Preedy, after all).
>
> The marriage of Preedy and the sea! There were alternate rituals. The first involved the stroll that turns into a run and a dive straight into the water, thereafter smoothing into a strong splashless crawl towards the horizon. But of course not really to the horizon. Quite suddenly he would turn on to his back and thrash great white splashes with his legs, somehow thus showing that he could have swum further had he wanted to, and then would stand up a quarter out of water for all to see who it was.
>
> The alternative course was simpler, it avoided the cold-water shock and it avoided the risk of appearing too high-spirited. The point was to appear to be so used to the sea, the Mediterranean, and this particular beach, that one might as well be in the sea as out of it. It involved a slow stroll down and into the edge of the water—not even noticing his toes were wet, land and water all the same to *him!*—with his eyes up at the sky gravely surveying portents, invisible to others, of the weather (Local Fisherman Preedy).[5]

The novelist means us to see that Preedy is improperly concerned with the extensive impressions he feels his sheer bodily action is giving off to those around him. We can malign Preedy further by assuming that he has acted merely in order to give a particular impression, that this is a false impression, and that the others present receive either no impression at all, or worse still, the impression that Preedy is affectedly trying to cause them to receive this particular impression. But the important point for us here is that the kind of impression Preedy thinks he is making is in fact the kind of impression that others correctly and incorrectly glean from someone in their midst.

I have said that when an individual appears before others his actions will influence the definition of the situation which they come to have. Sometimes the individual will act in a thoroughly calculating manner, expressing himself in a given way solely in order to give the kind of impression to others that is likely to evoke from them a specific response he is concerned to obtain. Sometimes the individual will be calculating in his activity but be relatively unaware that this is the case. Sometimes he will intentionally and consciously express himself in a particular way, but chiefly because the tradition of his group or social status require this kind of expression and not because of any particular response (other than vague acceptance or approval) that is likely to be evoked from those impressed by the expression. Sometimes the traditions of an individual's role will lead him to give a well-designed impression of a particular kind and yet he may be neither consciously nor unconsciously disposed to create such an impression. The others, in their turn, may be suitably impressed by the individual's efforts to convey something, or may misunderstand the situation and come to conclusions that are warranted neither by the individual's intent nor by the facts. In any case, insofar as the others act *as if* the individual had conveyed a particular impression, we may take a functional or pragmatic view and say that the individual has "effectively" projected a given definition of the situation and "effectively" fostered the understanding that a given state of affairs obtains.

There is one aspect of the others' response that bears special comment here. Knowing that the individual is likely to present himself in a light that is favorable to him, the others may divide what they witness into two parts: a part that is relatively easy for the individual to manipulate at will, being chiefly his verbal assertions, and a part in regard to which he seems to have little concern or control, being chiefly derived from the expressions he gives off. The others may then use what are considered to be the ungovernable aspects of his expressive behavior as a check upon the validity of what is conveyed by the governable aspects. In this a fundamental asymmetry is demonstrated in the communication process, the individual presumably being aware of only one stream of his communication, the witnesses of this stream and one other. For example, in Shetland Isle one crofter's [or farmer's] wife, in serving native dishes to a visitor from the mainland of Britain, would listen with a polite smile to his polite claims of liking what he was eating; at the same time she would take note of the rapidity with which the visitor lifted his fork or spoon to his mouth, the eagerness with which he passed food into his mouth, and the gusto expressed in chewing the food, using these signs as a check on the stated feelings of the eater. The same woman, in order to discover what one acquaintance (A) "actually" thought of another acquaintance (B), would wait until B was in the presence of A but engaged in conversation with still another person (C). She would then covertly examine the facial expressions of A as he regarded B in conversation with C. Not being in conversation with B, and not being directly observed by him, A would sometimes relax usual constraints and tactful deceptions, and freely express what he was "actually" feeling about B. This Shetlander, in short, would observe the unobserved behavior.

Now given the fact that others are likely to check up on the more controllable aspects of behavior by means of the less controllable, one can expect that sometimes the individual will try to exploit this very possibility, guiding the impression he makes through behavior felt to be reliably informing.[6] For example, in gaining admission to a tight social circle, the participant observer may not only wear an accepting look while listening to an informant, but may also be careful to wear the same look when observing the informant talking to others; observers of the observer will then not as easily discover where he actually stands. A specific illustration may be cited from Shetland Isle. When a neighbor dropped in to have a cup of tea, he would ordinarily wear at least a hint of an expectant warm smile as he passed through the door into the cottage. Since lack of physical obstructions outside the cottage and lack of light within it usually made it possible to observe the visitor unobserved as he approached the house, islanders sometimes took pleasure in watching the visitor drop whatever expression he was manifesting and replace it with a sociable one just before reaching the door. However, some visitors, in appreciating that this examination was occurring, would blindly adopt a social face a long distance from the house, thus ensuring the projection of a constant image.

This kind of control upon the part of the individual reinstates the symmetry of the communication process, and sets the stage for a kind of information game—a potentially infinite cycle of concealment, discovery, false revelation, and rediscovery. It should be added that since the others are likely to be relatively unsuspicious of the presumably unguided aspect of the individual's conduct, he can gain much by controlling it. The others of course may sense that the individual is manipulating the presumably spontaneous aspects of his behavior, and seek in this very act of manipulation some shading of conduct that the individual has not managed to control. This again provides a check upon the individual's behavior, this time his presumably uncalculated behavior, thus re-establishing the asymmetry of the communication process. Here I would like only to add the suggestion that the arts of piercing an individual's effort at calculated unintentionality seem better developed than our capacity to manipulate our own behavior, so that regardless of how many steps have occurred in the information game, the witness is likely to have the advantage over the actor, and the initial asymmetry of the communication process is likely to be retained.

When we allow that the individual projects a definition of the situation when he appears before others, we must also see that the others, however passive their role may seem to be, will themselves effectively project a definition of the situation by virtue of their response to the individual and by virtue of any lines of action they initiate to him. Ordinarily the definitions of the situation projected by the several different participants are sufficiently attuned to one another so that open contradiction will not occur. I do not mean that there will be the kind of consensus that arises when each individual present candidly expresses what he really feels and honestly agrees with the expressed feeling of the others present. This kind of harmony is an optimistic ideal and in any case not necessary for the smooth working of society. Rather, each participant is expected to suppress his immediate heartfelt feelings, conveying a view of the situation which he feels the others will be able to find at least temporarily acceptable. The maintenance of this surface of agreement, this veneer of consensus, is facilitated by each participant concealing [his] wants behind statements while asserting values to which everyone present feels obliged to give lip service. Further, there is usually a kind of division of definitional labor. Each participant is allowed to establish the tentative official ruling regarding matters which are vital to him but not immediately important to others, e.g., the rationalizations and justifications by which he accounts for his past activity. In exchange for this courtesy he remains silent or non-committal on matters important to others but not immediately important to him. We have then a kind of interactional *modus vivendi.* Together, the participants contribute to a single over-all definition of the situation which involves not so much a real argument as to what exists but rather a real agreement as to whose claims concerning what issues will be temporarily honored. Real agreement will also exist concerning the desirability of avoiding an open conflict of definitions of the situation.[7] I will refer to this level of agreement as a "working consensus." It is to be understood that the working consensus established in one interaction setting will be quite different in content from the working consensus established in a different type of setting. Thus, between two friends at lunch, a reciprocal show of affection, respect, and concern for the other is maintained. In service occupations, on the other hand, the specialist often maintains an image of disinterested involvement in the problem of the client, while the client responds with a show of respect for the competence and integrity of the specialist. Regardless of such differences in content, however, the general form of these working arrangements is the same.

In noting the tendency for a participant to accept the definitional claims made by the others present, we can appreciate the crucial importance of the information that the individual *initially* possesses or acquires concerning his fellow participants, for it is on the basis of this initial information that the individual starts to define the situation and starts to build up lines of responsive action. The individual's initial projection commits him to what he is proposing to be and requires him to drop all pretenses of being other things. As the interaction among the participants progresses, additions and modifications in this initial informational state will of course occur, but it is essential that these later developments be related without contradiction to, and even built up from, the initial positions taken by the several participants. It would seem that an individual can more easily make a choice as to what line of treatment to demand from and extend to the others present at the beginning of an encounter than he can alter the line of treatment that is being pursued once the interaction is underway.

In everyday life, of course, there is a clear understanding that first impressions are important. Thus, the work adjustment of those in service occupations will often hinge upon a capacity to seize and hold the initiative in the service relations, a capacity that will require subtle aggressiveness on the part of the server when he is of lower socioeconomic status than his client. W. F. Whyte suggests the waitress as an example:

> The first point that stands out is that the waitress who bears up under pressure does not simply respond to her customers. She acts with some skill to control her behavior. The first question to ask when we look at the customer relationship is, "Does the waitress get the jump on the customer, or does the customer get the jump on the waitress?" The skilled waitress realizes the crucial nature of this question....
>
> The skilled waitress tackles the customer with confidence and without hesitation. For example, she may find that a new customer has seated himself before she could clear off the dirty dishes and change the cloth. He is now leaning on the table studying the menu. She greets him, says, "May I change the cover, please?" and, without waiting for an answer, takes his menu away from him so that he moves back from the table, and she goes about her work. The relationship is handled politely but firmly, and there is never any question as to who is in charge.[8]

When the interaction that is initiated by "first impressions" is itself merely the initial interaction in an extended series of interactions involving the same participants, we speak of "getting off on the right foot" and feel that it is crucial that we do so. Thus, one learns that some teachers take the following view:

> You can't ever let them get the upper hand on you or you're through. So I start out tough. The first day I get a new class in, I let them know who's boss.... You've got to start off tough, then you can ease up as you go along. If you start out easy-going, when you try to be tough, they'll just look at you and laugh.[9]

Similarly, attendants in mental institutions may feel that if the new patient is sharply put in his place the first day on the ward and made to see who is boss, much future difficulty will be prevented.[10]

Given the fact that the individual effectively projects a definition of the situation when he enters the presence of others, we can assume that events may occur within the interaction which contradict, discredit, or otherwise throw doubt upon this projection. When these disruptive events occur, the interaction itself may come to a confused and embarrassed halt. Some of the assumptions upon which the responses of the participants had been predicated became untenable, and the participants find themselves lodged in an interaction for which the situation has been wrongly defined and is now no longer defined. At such moments the individual whose presentation has been discredited may feel ashamed while the others present may feel hostile, and all the participants may come to feel ill at ease, nonplussed, out of countenance, embarrassed, experiencing the kind of anomy that is generated when the minute social system of face-to-face interaction breaks down.

In stressing the fact that the initial definition of the situation projected by an individual tends to provide a plan for the cooperative activity that follows—in stressing this action point of view—we must not overlook the crucial fact that any projected definition of the situation also has a distinctive moral character. It is this moral character of projections that will chiefly concern us in this report. Society is organized on the principle that any individual who possesses certain social characteristics has a moral right to expect that others will value and treat him in an appropriate way. Connected with this principle is a second, namely that an individual who implicitly or explicitly signifies that he has certain social characteristics ought in fact to be what he claims he is. In consequence, when an individual projects a definition of the situation and thereby makes an implicit or explicit claim to be a person of a particular kind, he automatically exerts a moral demand upon the others, obliging them to value and treat him in the manner that persons of his kind have a right to expect. He also implicitly forgoes all claims to be things he does not appear to be[11] and hence forgoes the treatment that would be appropriate for such individuals. The others find, then, that the individual has informed them as to what is and as to what they *ought* to see as the "is."

One cannot judge the importance of definitional disruptions by the frequency with which they occur, for apparently they would occur more frequently were not constant precautions taken. We find that preventive practices are constantly employed to avoid these embarrassments and that corrective practices are constantly employed to compensate for discrediting occurrences that have not been successfully avoided. When the individual employs these strategies and tactics to protect his own projections, we may refer to them as "defensive practices"; when a participant employs them to save the definition of the situation projected by another, we speak of "protective practices" or "tact." Together, defensive and protective practices comprise the techniques employed to safeguard the impression fostered by an individual during his presence before others. It should be added that while we may be ready to see that no fostered impression would survive if defensive practices were not employed, we are less ready perhaps to see that few impressions could survive if those who received the impression did not exert tact in their reception of it.

In addition to the fact that precautions are taken to prevent disruption of projected definitions, we may also note that an intense interest in these disruptions comes to play a significant role in the social life of the group. Practical jokes and social games are played in which embarrassments which are to be taken unseriously are purposely engineered.[12] Fantasies are created in which devastating exposures occur. Anecdotes from the past—real, embroidered, or fictitious—are told and retold, detailing disruptions which occurred, almost occurred, or occurred and were admirably resolved. There seems to be no grouping which does not have a ready supply of these games, reveries, and cautionary tales, to be used as a source of humor, a catharsis for anxieties, and a sanction for inducing individuals to be modest in their claims and reasonable in their projected expectations. The individual may tell himself through dreams of getting into impossible positions. Families tell of the time a guest got his dates mixed and arrived when neither the house nor anyone in it was ready for him. Journalists tell of times when an all-too-meaningful misprint occurred, and the paper's assumption of objectivity or decorum was humorously discredited. Public servants tell of times a client ridiculously misunderstood form instructions, giving answers which implied an unanticipated and bizarre definition of the situation.[13] Seamen, whose home away from home is rigorously he-man, tell stories of coming back home and inadvertently asking mother to "pass the fucking butter."[14] Diplomats tell of the time a near-sighted queen asked a republican ambassador about the health of his king.[15]

To summarize, then, I assume that when an individual appears before others he will have many motives for trying to control the impression they receive of the situation.

NOTES

1. Gustav Ichheiser, "Misunderstandings in Human Relations," Supplement to *The American Journal of Sociology,* 55 (September 1949): 6–7.

2. Quoted in E. H. Volkart, editor, *Social Behavior and Personality,* Contributions of W. I. Thomas to Theory and Social Research (New York: Social Science Research Council, 1951), p. 5.

3. Here I owe much to an unpublished paper by Tom Burns of the University of Edinburgh. He presents the argument that in all interaction a basic underlying theme is the desire of each participant to guide and control the responses made by the others present. A similar argument has been advanced by Jay Haley in a recent unpublished paper, but in regard to a special kind of control, that having to do with the relationship of those involved in the interaction.

4. Willard Waller, "The Rating and Dating Complex," *American Sociological Review,* 2:730.

5. William Sansom, *A Contest of Ladies* (London: Hogarth, 1956), pp. 230–32.

6. The widely read and rather sound writings of Stephen Potter are concerned in part with signs that can be engineered to give a shrewd observer the apparently incidental cues he needs to discover concealed virtues the gamesman does not in fact possess.

7. An interaction can be purposely set up as a time and place for voicing differences in opinion, but in such cases participants must be careful to agree not to disagree on the proper tone of voice, vocabulary, and degree of seriousness in which all arguments are to be phrased, and upon the mutual respect which disagreeing participants must carefully continue to express toward one another. This debaters' or academic definition of the situation may also be invoked suddenly and judiciously as a way of translating a serious conflict of views into one that can be handled within a framework acceptable to all present.

8. W. F. Whyte, "When Workers and Customers Meet," Chap. VII, *Industry and Society,* ed. W. F. Whyte (New York: McGraw-Hill, 1946), pp. 132–33.

9. Teacher interview quoted by Howard S. Becker, "Social Class Variations in the Teacher-Pupil Relationship," *Journal of Educational Sociology,* 25: 459.

10. Harold Taxel, "Authority Structure in a Mental Hospital Ward" (unpublished Master's thesis, Department of Sociology, University of Chicago, 1953).

11. This role of the witness in limiting what it is the individual can be has been stressed by Existentialists, who see it as a basic threat to individual freedom. See Jean-Paul Sartre, *Being and Nothingness,* trans. by Hazel E. Barnes (New York: Philosophical Library, 1956), p. 365 ff.

12. Goffman, *op. cit.,* pp. 319–27.

13. Peter Blau, *Dynamics of Bureaucracy: A Study of Interpersonal Relationships in Two Government Agencies,* 2nd ed. (Chicago: University of Chicago Press, 1963).

14. Walter M. Beattie, Jr., "The Merchant Seaman" (unpublished M.A. Report, Department of Sociology, University of Chicago, 1950), p. 35.

15. Sir Frederick Ponsonby, *Recollections of Three Reigns* (New York: Dutton, 1952), p. 46.

Review Questions

1. Distinguish between the two types of sign activity discussed by Goffman: "expressions given" and "expressions given off."

2. Give examples of performances which are sincere and honest and performances which are cynical and dishonest. Do our norms require us to give cynical performances in some situations?

3. Using Goffman's dramaturgical approach, analyze the behavior of a person being interviewed for a job.

4. When disruptive events occur in interaction which cast doubt on one participant's definitions, how do other participants react?

EMBARRASSMENT AND THE ANALYSIS OF ROLE REQUIREMENTS

Edward Gross and Gregory P. Stone

. . . EMBARRASSMENT OCCURS WHENEVER SOME *CENTRAL* ASSUMPTION IN a transaction has been *unexpectedly* and unqualifiedly discredited for at least one participant. The result is that he is incapacitated for continued role performance.[1] Moreover, embarrassment is infectious. It may spread out, incapacitating others not previously incapacitated. It is destructive dis-ease. In the wreckage left by embarrassment lie the broken foundations of social transactions. By examining such ruins, the investigator can reconstruct the architecture they represent.

To explore this idea, recollections of embarrassment were expressly solicited from two groups of subjects: (1) approximately 800 students enrolled in introductory sociology courses; and (2) about 80 students enrolled in an evening extension class. Not solicited, but gratefully received, were many examples volunteered by colleagues and friends who had heard of our interest in the subject. Finally we drew upon many recollections of embarrassment we had experienced ourselves. Through these means at least one thousand specimens of embarrassment were secured.

We found that embarrassments frequently occurred in situations requiring continuous and coordinated role performance—speeches, ceremonies, processions, or working concerts. In such situations embarrassment is particularly noticeable because it is so devastating. Forgetting one's lines, forgetting the wedding ring, stumbling in a cafeteria line, or handing a colleague the wrong tool, when these things occur without qualification, bring the performance to an obviously premature and unexpected halt. At the same time, manifestations of the embarrassment—blushing, fumbling, stuttering, sweating[2]—coerce awareness of the social damage and the need for immediate repair. In some instances, the damage may be potentially so great that embarrassment cannot be allowed to spread among the role performers. The incapacity may be

SOURCE: Edward Gross and Gregory P. Stone, "Embarrassment and the Analysis of Role Requirements," *American Journal of Sociology*, 70 (July, 1964) pp. 1–15 (with deletions). Reprinted by permission of University of Chicago Press and the authors.

qualified, totally ignored, or pretended out of existence.[3] For example, a minister, noting the best man's frantic search for an absent wedding ring, whispers to him to ignore it, and all conspire to continue the drama with an imaginary ring. Such rescues are not always possible. Hence we suggest that every enduring social relation will provide means of preventing embarrassment, so that the entire transaction will not collapse when embarrassment occurs. A second general observation would take into account that some stages in the life cycle, for example, adolescence in our society, generate more frequent embarrassments than others. These are points to which we shall return.

To get at the content of embarrassment, we classified the instances in categories that remained as close to the specimens as possible. A total of seventy-four such categories were developed, some of which were forced choices between friends, public mistakes, exposure of false front, being caught in a cover story, misnaming, forgetting names, slips of the tongue, body exposure, invasions of others' back regions, uncontrollable laughter, drunkenness in the presence of sobriety (or vice versa), loss of visceral control, and the sudden recognition of wounds or other stigmata. Further inspection of these categories disclosed that most could be included in three general areas: (1) inappropriate identity; (2) loss of poise; (3) disturbance of the assumptions persons make about one another in social transactions.

Since embarrassment always incapacitates persons for role performance (to embarrass is, literally, to bar or stop), a close analysis of the conditions under which it occurs is especially fruitful in the revelation of the requirements *necessary* for role-playing, role-taking, role-making, and role performance in general. These role requirements are thus seen to include the establishment of identity, poise, and valid assumptions about one another among all the parties of a social transaction. We turn now to the analysis of those role requirements.

IDENTITY AND POISE

In every social transaction, selves must be established, defined, and accepted by the parties. Every person in the company of others is, in a sense, obligated to bring his best self forward to meet the selves of others also presumably best fitted to the occasion. When one is "not himself" in the presence of others who expect him to be just that, as in cases where his mood carries him away either by spontaneous seizure (uncontrollable laughter or tears) or by induced seizure (drunkenness), embarrassment ensues. Similarly, when one is "shown up" to other parties to the transaction by the exposure of unacceptable moral qualifications or inappropriate motives, embarrassment sets in all around. However, the concept, self, is a rather gross concept, and we wish to single out two phases that frequently provided focal points for embarrassment—identity and poise.[4]

Identity. Identity is the substantive dimension of the self.[5]

> Almost all writers using the term imply that identity establishes what and where the person is in social terms. It is not a substitute word for "self." Instead, when one has identity, he is *situated*—that is, cast in the shape of a social object by the acknowledgement of his participation or membership in social relations. One's identity is established when others *place* him as a social object by assigning the same words of identity that he appropriates for himself or *announces*. It is in the coincidence of placements and announcements that identity becomes a meaning of the self.

Moreover, . . . identity stands at the base of role. When inappropriate identities are established or appropriate identities are lost, role performance is impossible.

If identity *locates* the person in social terms, it follows that locations or spaces emerge as symbols of identity, since social relations are spatially distributed. Moreover, as Goffman has remarked,[6] there must be a certain coherence between one's personal appearance and the setting in which he appears. Otherwise embarrassment may ensue with the resulting incapacitation for role performance. Sexual identity is pervasively established by personal appearance, and a frequent source of embarrassment among our subjects was the presence of one sex in a setting reserved for the other. Both men and women reported inadvertent invasions of spaces set aside for the other sex with consequent embarrassment and humiliation. The implication of such inadvertent invasions is, of course, that one literally does not know where one is, that one literally has no identity in the situation, or that the identity one is putting forward is so absurd as to render the proposed role performance totally irrelevant. Everyone is embarrassed, and such manifestations as, for example, cries and screams, heighten the dis-ease. In such situations, laughter cannot be enjoined to reduce the seriousness of the unexpected collapse of the encounter, and only flight can insure that one will not be buried in the wreckage.

To establish *what* he is in social terms, each person assembles a set of apparent[7] symbols which he carries about as he moves from transaction to transaction. Such symbols include the shaping of the hair, painting of the face, clothing, cards of identity, other contents of wallets and purses, and sundry additional marks and ornaments. The items in the set must cohere, and the set must be complete. Taken together, these apparent symbols have been called *identity documents*,[8] in that they enable others to validate announced identities. Embarrassment often resulted when our subjects made personal appearances with either invalid or incomplete identity documents. It was embarrassing for many, for example, to announce their identities as customers at restaurants or stores, perform the customer role and then, when the crucial validation of this identity was requested—the payoff—to discover that the wallet had been left at home.

Because the social participation of men in American society is relatively more frequently caught up in the central structures, for example, the structure of work, than is the social participation of women who are relatively more immersed in interpersonal relations, the identities put forward by men are often *titles*; by women, often *names*. Except for very unusual titles,[9] such identities are shared, and their presentation has the consequence of bringing people together. Names, on the other hand, mark people off from one another. So it is that a frequent source of embarrassment for women in our society occurs when they appear together in precisely the same dress. Their identity documents are invalidated. The embarrassment may be minimized, however, if the space in which they make their personal appearance is large enough. In one instance, both women met the situation by spending an entire evening on different sides of the ballroom in which their embarrassing confrontation occurred, attempting to secure validation from social circles with minimal intersection, or, at least, where intersection was temporally attenuated. Men, on the other hand, will be embarrassed if their clothing does not resemble the dress of the other men present in public and official encounters. Except for "the old school tie" their neckties seem to serve as numbers on a uniform, marking each man off from every other. Out of uniform, their structural membership cannot be visibly established, and role performance is rendered extremely difficult, if not impossible.[10]

Not only are identities undocumented, they are also misplaced, as in misnaming or forgetting, or other incomplete placements. One relatively frequent source of embarrassment we categorized as "damaging someone's personal representation." This included cases of ethnically colored sneers in the presence of one who, in fact, belonged to the deprecated ethnic group but did not put that identity forward, or behind-the-back slurs about a woman who turned out to be the listener's wife. The victim of such misplacement, however inadvertent, will find it difficult to continue the transaction or to present the relevant identity to the perpetrators of the embarrassment in the future. The awkwardness is reflexive. Those who are responsible for the misplacement will experience the same difficulties and dis-ease.

Other sources of embarrassment anchored in identity suggest a basic characteristic of all human transactions, which, as Strauss puts it, are "carried on in thickly peopled and complexly imaged contexts."[11] One always brings to transactions more identities than are necessary for his role performance. As a consequence, two or more roles are usually performed at once by each participant.[12]

If we designate the relevant roles in transactions as *dominant roles*[13] then we may note that *adjunct roles*—a type of side involvement, as Goffman would have it,[14] or better, a type of side *activity*—are usually performed in parallel with dominant role performance. Specifically, a lecturer may smoke cigarettes or a pipe while carrying out the dominant performance, or one may carry on a heated conversation with a passenger while operating a motor vehicle. Moreover, symbols of *reserve identities* are often carried into social transactions. Ordinarily, they are concealed, as when a court judge wears his golfing clothes beneath his robes. Finally, symbols of abandoned or *relict identities* may persist in settings where they have no relevance for dominant role performances.[15] For example, photographs of the performer as an infant may be thrust into a transaction by a doting mother or wife, or one's newly constituted household may still contain the symbols of a previous marriage.

In these respects, the probability of avoiding embarrassment is a function of at least two factors: (1) the extent to which adjunct roles, reserve identities and relict identities are not incongruent with the dominant role performance;[16] and (2) the allocation of prime attention to the dominant role performance so that less attention is directed toward adjunct role performance, reserve identities, and relict identities. Thus the professor risks embarrassment should the performance of his sex role appear to be the main activity in transactions with female students where the professorial role is dominant—for example, if the student pulls her skirt over her knees with clearly more force than necessary. The judge may not enter the courtroom in a golf cap, nor may the husband dwell on the symbols of a past marriage in the presence of a new wife while entertaining guests in his home. Similarly, should adjunct role performance prove inept, as when the smoking lecturer ignites the contents of a wastebasket or the argumentative driver fails to observe the car in front in time to avert a collision, attention is diverted from the dominant role performance. Even without the golf cap, should the judge's robe be caught so that his golfing attire is suddenly revealed in the courtroom, the transactions of the court will be disturbed. Fetishistic devotion to the symbols of relict identities by bereaved persons is embarrassing even to well-meaning visitors.

However, the matter of avoiding incongruence and allocating attention appropriately among the several identities a performer brings to a transaction verges very closely on matters of poise, as we shall see. Matters of poise converge on the necessity of controlling representations of the self, and identity-symbols are important self-representations.

Personal poise. Presentation of the self in social transactions extends considerably beyond making the appropriate personal appearance. It includes the presentation of an entire situation. Components of situations, however, are often representations of self, and in this sense self and situation are two sides of the same coin. Personal poise refers to the performer's control over self and situation, and whatever disturbs that control, depriving the transaction, as we have said before, of any relevant future, is incapacitating and consequently embarrassing. . . .

First, *spaces* must be so arranged and maintained that they are role-enabling. This is sometimes difficult to control, since people appear in spaces that belong to others, over which they exercise no authority and for which they are not responsible. Students, invited to faculty parties where faculty members behave like faculty members, will "tighten up" to the extent that the students' role performance is seriously impeded. To avoid embarrassment, people will go to great lengths to insure their appearance in appropriate places, and to some to be deprived of access to a particular setting is to limit performance drastically. . . .

We have already touched upon problems presented by invasions of spaces, and little more need be said. Persons lose poise when they discover they are in places forbidden to them, for the proscription itself means they have no identity there and hence cannot act. They can do little except withdraw quickly. It is interesting that children are continually invading the territories of others—who can control the course of a sharply hit baseball?—and part of the process of socialization consists of indications of the importance of boundaries. . . .

Such considerations raise questions concerning both how boundaries are defined and how boundary violations may be prevented. Walls provide physical limits, but do not necessarily prevent communications from passing through.[17] Hence walls work best when there is also tacit agreement to ignore audible communication on the other side of the wall. Embarrassment frequently occurs when persons on one side of the wall learn that intimate matters have been communicated to persons on the other side. A common protective device is for the captive listeners to become very quiet so that their receipt of the communication will not be discovered by the unsuspecting intimates. When no physical boundaries are present, a group gathered in one section of a room may have developed a common mood which is bounded by a certain space that defines the limits of their engagement to one another. The entry of someone new may be followed by an embarrassed hush. It is not necessary that the group should have been talking about that person. Rather, since moods take time to build up, it will take time for the newcomer to "get with it" and it may not be worth the group's trouble to "fill him in." However unintentionally, he has destroyed a mood that took some effort to build up and he will suffer for it, if only by being stared at or by an obvious change of subject. In some cases, when the mood is partially sustained by alcohol, one can prepare the newcomer immediately for the mood by loud shouts that the group is "three drinks ahead" of him and by thrusting a drink into his hand without delay. So, too, a function of foyers, halls, anterooms, and other buffer zones or decompression chambers around settings is to prepare such newcomers and hence reduce the likelihood of their embarrassing both themselves and those inside. . . .

Next, every social transaction requires the manipulation of *equipment*. If props are ordinarily stationary during encounters, equipment is typically moved about, handled, or touched.[18] Equipment can range from *words* to *physical objects*, and a loss of control over such equipment is a frequent source of embarrassment. Here are included slips of the tongue, sudden dumbness when speech is called for, stalling cars in traffic, dropping bowling balls, spilling food, and tool failures. Equipment appearances that cast doubt on the adequacy of control are illustrated by the clanking motor, the match burning down to the fingers, tarnished silverware, or rusty work tools. Equipment sometimes extends beyond what is actually handled in the transaction to include the stage props. Indeed, items of equipment in disuse, reserve equipment, often become props—the Cadillac in the driveway or the silver service on the shelf—and there is a point at which the objects used or scheduled for use in a situation are both equipment and props. At one instant, the items of a table setting lie immobile as props; at the next, they are taken up and transformed into equipment. The close linkage of equipment and props may be responsible for the fact that *embarrassment* at times not only *infects* the participants in the transaction but the *objects* as well. For example, at a formal dinner, a speaker was discovered with his fly zipper undone. On being informed of this embarrassing oversight after he was reseated, he proceeded to make the requisite adjustment, unknowingly catching the table cloth in his trousers. When obliged to rise again at the close of the proceedings, he took the stage props with him and of course scattered the dinner tools about the setting in such a way that others were forced to doubt his control. His poise was lost in the situation. . . .

. . . [C]*lothing* must also be maintained, controlled, and coherently arranged. Its very appearance must communicate this. Torn clothing, frayed cuffs, stained neckties, and unpolished shoes are felt as embarrassing in situations where they are expected to be untorn, neat, clean, and polished. Clothing is of special importance since, as William James observed,[19] it is as much a part of the self as the body—a part of what he called the "material me." Moreover, since it is so close to the body, it conveys the impression of body maintenance, paradoxically, by concealing body-maintenance activities.[20] Hence, the double wrap—outer clothes and underclothes. Underclothes bear the marks of body maintenance and tonic state, and their unexpected exposure is a frequent source of embarrassment. The broken brassière strap sometimes produces a shift in appearance that few women (or men, for that matter) will fail to perceive as embarrassing.

... [T]he *body* must always be in a state of readiness to act, and its appearance must make this clear. Hence any evidence of unreadiness or clumsiness is embarrassing. Examples include loss of whole body control (stumbling, trembling, or fainting), loss of visceral control (flatulence, involuntary urination, or drooling), and the communication of other "signs of the animal." The actress who is photographed from her "bad side" loses poise, for it shakes the foundation on which her fame rests. So does the person who is embarrassed about pimples, warts, or missing limbs, as well as those embarrassed in his presence.

Ordinarily, persons will avoid recognizing such stigmata, turn their eyes away, and pretend them out of existence, but on occasion stigmata will obtrude upon the situation causing embarrassment all around. A case in point was a minor flirtation reported by one of our students. Seated in a library a short distance from a beautiful girl, the student began the requisite gestural invitation to a more intimate conversation. The girl turned, smiling, to acknowledge the bid, revealing an amputated left arm. Our student's gestural line was brought to a crashing halt. Embarrassed, he abandoned the role he was building even before the foundation was laid, pretending that his inviting gestures were directed toward some imaginary audience suggested by his reading. Such stigmata publicize body-maintenance activities, and, when they are established in social transactions, interfere with role performances. The pimples on the face of the job applicant cast doubt on his maturity, and, consequently, on his qualifications for any job requiring such maturity. . . .

MAINTENANCE OF CONFIDENCE

When identities have been validated and persons poised, interaction may begin. Its continuation, however, requires that a scaffolding be erected and that attention be given to preventing this scaffolding from collapsing. The scaffold develops as the relationship becomes stabilized. In time persons come to expect that the way they place the other is the way the other announces himself, and that poise will continue to be maintained. Persons now begin to count on these expectations and to have confidence in them. But at any time they may be violated. It was such violations of confidence that made up the greatest single source of embarrassment in our examples. Perhaps this is only an acknowledgment that the parties to every transaction must always maintain themselves *in role* to permit the requisite role-taking, or that identity-switching ought not be accomplished so abruptly that others are left floundering in the encounter as they grope for the new futures that the new identity implies.

This is all the more important in situations where roles are tightly linked together as in situations involving a division of labor. In one instance, a group of social scientists was presenting a progress report of research to a representative of the client subsidizing the research. The principal investigator's presentation was filled out by comments from the other researchers, his professional peers. Negatively critical comments were held to a bare minimum. Suddenly the principal investigator overstepped the bounds. He made a claim that they were well on the road to confirming a hypothesis which, if confirmed, would represent a major contribution. Actually, his colleagues (our informant was one of them) knew that they were very far indeed from confirming the hypothesis. They first sought to catch the leader's eye to look for a hidden message. Receiving none, they lowered their eyes to the table, bit their lips, and fell silent. In the presence of the client's representative, they felt they could not "call" their leader for that would be embarrassing, but they did seek him out immediately afterward for an explanation. The leader agreed that they were right, but said his claim was politic, that new data might well turn up, and that it was clearly too late to remedy the situation.

Careful examination of this case reveals a more basic reason for the researchers' hesitance to embarrass the leader before the client's representative. If their leader were revealed to be the kind of person who goes beyond the data (or to be a plain liar), serious questions could have been raised about the kind of men who willingly work with such a person. Thus they found themselves coerced into unwilling collusion. It was not simply that their jobs depended on continued satisfaction of the client. Rather they were unwilling to say to themselves and to the client's representative that they were the kind of researchers who would be party to a fraud. To embarrass the leader, then, would have meant embarrassing themselves by casting serious question upon their identities as researchers. Indeed, it was their desire to cling to their identities that led, not long afterward (and after several other similar experiences), to the breakup of the research team.

Just as, in time, an identity may be discredited, so too may poise be upset. Should this occur, each must be able to assume that the other will render assistance if he gets into such control trouble, and each must be secure in the knowledge that the assumption is tenable. Persons will be alert for incipient signs of such trouble—irrelevant attitudes—and attempt to avert the consequences. Goffman has provided many examples in his discussion of dramaturgical loyalty, discipline, and circumspection in the presentation of the self, pointing out protective practices that are employed, such as clearing one's throat before interrupting a conversation, knocking on doors before entering an occupied room, or begging the other's pardon before an intrusion.[21]

The danger that one's confidence in the other's continued identity or his ability to maintain his poise may be destroyed leads to the generation of a set of *performance norms*. These are social protections against embarrassment.[22] If persons adhere to them, the probability of embarrassment is reduced. We discovered two major performance norms.

First, *standards of role performance almost always allow for flexibility and tolerance*. One is rarely, if ever, totally in role (an exception might be highly ritualized performances where to acknowledge breaches of expectation is devastatingly embarrassing).[23] To illustrate, we expect one another to give attention to what is going on in our transactions, but the attention we anticipate is always *optimal*, never total. To lock the other person completely in one's glance and refuse to let go is very embarrassing. A rigid attention is coerced eventuating in a loss of poise. . . . Similarly, never to give one's attention to the other is role-incapacitating. If one focuses his gaze not on the other's eyes, but on his forehead, let us say, the encounter is visibly disturbed.[24] Norms allowing for flexibility and tolerance permit the parties to social transactions ordinarily to assume that they will not be held to rigid standards of conduct and that temporary lapses will be overlooked. . . .

The second performance norm was that of *giving the other fellow the benefit of the doubt*. For the transaction to go on at all, one has at least to give the other fellow a *chance* to play the role he seeks to play. Clearly, if everyone went around watching for chances to embarrass others, so many would be incapacitated for role performance that society would collapse. Such considerate behavior is probably characteristic of all human society, because of the dependence of social relations on role performance. A part of socialization, therefore, must deal with the prevention of embarrassment by the teaching of tact. People must learn not only not to embarrass others, but to ignore the lapses that can be embarrassing whenever they occur. In addition, people must learn to *cope* with embarrassment. Consequently, embarrassment will occasionally be deliberately perpetrated to ready people for role incapacitation when it occurs.

• • •

CONCLUSION

In this paper, we have inquired into the conditions necessary for role performance. Embarrassment has been employed as a sensitive indicator of those conditions, for that which embarrasses incapacitates role performance. Our data have led us to describe the conditions for role performance in terms of identity, poise, and sustained confidence in one another. When these become disturbed and discredited, role performance cannot continue. Consequently, provisions for the avoidance or prevention of embarrassment, or quick recovery from embarrassment when it does occur, are of key importance to any society or social transaction, and devices to insure the avoidance and minimization of embarrassment will be part of every persisting social relationship. . . .

NOTES

1. Not all incapacitated persons are always embarrassed or embarrassing, because others have come to expect their *incapacities* and are consequently prepared for them.

2. Erving Goffman, in "Embarrassment and Social Organization," *American Journal of Sociology*, LXII (November 1956), 264–71, describes these manifestations vividly.

3. A more general discussion of this phenomenon, under the rubric civil inattention, is provided in Erving Goffman, *Behavior in Public Places* (New York: Free Press of Glencoe, 1963), pp. 83–88 and *passim*.

4. Other dimensions of the self—value and mood—will be taken up in subsequent publications.

5. Gregory P. Stone, "Appearance and the Self," in Arnold Rose (ed.), *Human Behavior and Social Processes* (Boston: Houghton Mifflin, 1962), p. 93.

6. Erving Goffman, *The Presentation of Self in Everyday Life* (New York: Doubleday Anchor Books, 1959), p. 25.

7. We use the term "appearance" to designate that dimension of a social transaction given over to identifications of the participants. Apparent symbols are those symbols used to communicate such identifications. They are often nonverbal. Appearance seems, to us, a more useful term than Goffman's "front" (*ibid.*), which in everyday speech connotes misrepresentation.

8. Erving Goffman, *Stigma* (Englewood Cliffs, N.J.: Prentice-Hall, 1963), pp. 59–62. Goffman confines the concept to personal identity, but his own discussion extends it to include matters of social identity.

9. For example, the title, "honorary citizen of the United States," which was conferred on Winston Churchill, served the function of a name, since Churchill was the only living recipient of the title. Compare the titles, "professor," "manager," "punch-press operator," and the like.

10. The implication of the discussion is that structured activities are uniformed, while interpersonal activities emphasize individuation in dress. Erving Goffman suggests, in correspondence, that what may be reflected here is the company people keep in their transactions. The work of men in our society is ordinarily teamwork, and teams are uniformed, but housework performed by a wife is solitary work and does not require a uniformed appearance, though the "housedress" might be so regarded.

11. Anselm L. Strauss, *Mirrors and Masks* (Glencoe, Ill.: Free Press, 1959), p. 57.

12. This observation and the ensuing discussion constitute a contribution to and extension of present perspectives on role conflict. Most discussions conceive

of such conflict as internalized contradictory obligations. They do not consider simultaneous multiple-role performances. An exception is Everett C. Hughes' discussion of the Negro physician innocently summoned to attend a prejudiced emergency case in "Dilemmas and Contradictions in Status," *American Journal of Sociology*, L (March 1945), pp. 353–59.

13. We have rewritten this discussion to relate to Goffman's classification which came to our attention after we had prepared an earlier version of this article. Goffman distinguishes between what people do in transactions and what the situation calls for. He recognizes that people do many things at once in their encounters and distinguishes those activities that command most of their attention and energies from those which are less demanding of energy and time. Here, the distinction is made between *main* and *side involvements*. On the other hand, situations often call for multiple activities. Those which are central to the situation, Goffman speaks of as *dominant involvements*; others are called *subordinate involvements*. Dominant roles, therefore, are those that are central to the transactional situation—what the participants have come together to do (see Goffman, *Behavior in Public Places*, pp. 43–59).

14. Adjunct roles are one type of side involvement or activity. We focus on them because we are concerned here with identity difficulties. There are other side *activities* which are *not* necessarily adjunct *roles*, namely, sporadic nosepicking, scratching, coughing, sneezing, or stomach growling, which are relevant to matters of embarrassment, but not to the conceptualization of the problem in these terms. Of course, such activities, insofar as they are consistently proposed and anticipated, may become incorporated in the *personal role* (always an adjunct in official transactions), as in the case of Billy Gilbert, the fabulous sneezer.

15. This phenomenon provides the main theme and source of horror and mystery in Daphne du Maurier's now classic *Rebecca*.

16. Adjunct roles, reserve identities, and relict identities need not cohere with the dominant role; they simply must not clash so that the attention of participants in a transaction is not completely diverted from the dominant role performance.

17. See Erving Goffman, *Behavior in Public Places*, pp. 151–52.

18. Whether objects in a situation are meant to be moved, manipulated, or taken up provides an important differentiating dimension between equipment on the one hand and props (as well as clothing, to be discussed shortly) on the other. Equipment is meant to be moved, manipulated, or taken up *during* a social transaction whereas clothing and props are expected to remain unchanged during a social transaction but will be moved, manipulated, or taken up *between* social transactions. To change props, as in burning the portrait of an old girl friend (or to change clothes, as in taking off a necktie), signals a change in the situation. The special case of the strip-tease dancer is no exception, for her act transforms clothes into equipment. The reference above to the "stickiness" of props may now be seen as another way of describing the fact that they are not moved, manipulated, or taken up during transactions, but remain unchanged for the course of the transaction. Clothing is equally sticky but the object to which it sticks differs. Clothing sticks to the body; props stick to the settings.

19. William James, *Psychology* (New York: Henry Holt & Co., 1892), pp. 177–78.

20. A complete exposition of the body-maintenance function of clothing is set forth in an advertisement for Jockey briefs, entitled: "A Frank Discussion: What Wives Should Know about Male Support," *Good Housekeeping*, May, 1963, p. 237.

21. Goffman, *The Presentation of Self in Everyday Life*, pp. 212–33.

22. Implicit in Georg Simmel, *The Sociology of Georg Simmel*, trans. Kurt H. Wolff (Glencoe, Ill.: Free Press, 1950), p. 308.

23. See the discussion of "role distance" in Erving Goffman, *Encounters* (Indianapolis, Ind.: Bobbs-Merrill Co., 1961), pp. 105–52.

24. Here we are speaking of what Edward T. Hall calls the "gaze line." He points out there are cultural variations in this phenomenon. See his "A System for the Notation of Proxemic Behavior," *American Anthropologist*, LXV (October 1963), 1012–14.

Review Questions

1. Define the terms *identity* and *poise*. How do threats to identity and poise disrupt interaction?

2. How are spaces, props, equipment, and clothing used to validate identities and to maintain poise?

3. Distinguish between dominant roles, adjunct roles, reverse identities, and relict identities. How are these related to embarrassment?

4. Discuss the two "performance norms" described by Gross and Stone which protect against embarrassment. Give examples of these norms from your own experiences.

THE MANAGED HEART: COMMERCIALIZATION OF HUMAN FEELING

Arlie Russell Hochschild

WHEN RULES ABOUT HOW TO FEEL AND HOW TO EXPRESS FEELING ARE SET BY management, when workers have weaker rights to courtesy than customers do, when deep and surface acting* are forms of labor to be sold, and when private capacities for empathy and warmth are put to corporate uses, what happens to the way a person relates to her feelings or to her face? When worked-up warmth becomes an instrument of service work, what can a person learn about herself from her feelings? And when a worker abandons her work smile, what kind of tie remains between her smile and her self?

[This article examines such questions by focusing on how employers (in this case, the airline industry) require certain feelings and emotions of employees (flight attendants). Professor Hochschild's research techniques included observing and interviewing flight attendants, trainers, and supervisors at Delta Airlines in the late 1970s and early 1980s. During this period, deregulation of airline prices and a redistribution of routes were occurring. Before deregulation, airfares were fixed and service was a primary means for one airline to compete with another. After deregulation, price competition came about, fares went lower overall and varied among airlines, planes were fuller, and the clientele was less select and sophisticated. We will now see the efforts of the companies to get more and more "emotional labor" from flight attendants and the attendants' responses.]

• • •

* *Surface acting* refers to behavior that one feels to be false. *Deep acting* is acting that convinces oneself; it begins as an act and transforms one's own feelings [Eds.].

BEHIND THE SUPPLY OF ACTING: SELECTION

Even before an applicant for a flight attendant's job is interviewed, she is introduced to the rules of the game. Success will depend in part on whether she has a knack for perceiving the rules and taking them seriously. Applicants are urged to read a preinterview pamphlet before coming in. In the 1979–1980 *Airline Guide to Stewardess and Steward Careers*, there is a section called "The Interview." Under the subheading "Appearance," the manual suggests that facial expressions should be "sincere" and "unaffected." One should have a "modest but friendly smile" and be "generally alert, attentive, not overly aggressive, but not reticent either." Under "Mannerisms," subheading "Friendliness," it is suggested that a successful candidate must be "outgoing but not effusive," "enthusiastic with calm and poise," and "vivacious but not effervescent." As the manual continues: "Maintaining eye contact with the interviewer demonstrates sincerity and confidence, but don't overdo it. Avoid cold or continuous staring." Training, it seems, begins even before recruitment.

Like company manuals, recruiters sometimes offer advice on how to appear. Usually they presume that an applicant is planning to put on a front; the question is which one. In offering tips for success, recruiters often talked in a matter-of-fact way about acting, as though assuming that it is permissible if not quite honorable to feign. As one recruiter put it, "I had to advise a lot of people who were looking for jobs, and not just at Pan Am. . . . And I'd tell them the secret to getting a job is to imagine the kind of person the company wants to hire and then become that person during the interview. The hell with your theories of what you believe in, and what your integrity is, and all that other stuff. You can project all that when you've got the job."

• • •

Different companies favor different variations of the ideal type of sociability. Veteran employees talk about differences in company personality as matter-of-factly as they talk about differences in uniform or shoe style. United Airlines, the consensus has it, is "the girl-next-door," the neighborhood babysitter grown up. Pan Am is upper class, sophisticated, and slightly reserved in its graciousness. PSA is brassy, funloving, and sexy. Some flight attendants could see a connection between the personality they were supposed to project and the market segment the company wants to attract. One United worker explained: "United wants to appeal to Ma and Pa Kettle. So it wants Caucasian girls—not so beautiful that Ma feels fat, and not so plain that Pa feels unsatisfied. It's the Ma and Pa Kettle market that's growing, so that's why they use the girl-next-door image to appeal to that market. You know, the Friendly Skies. They offer reduced rates for wives and kids. They weed out busty women because they don't fit the image, as they see it."

Recruiters understood that they were looking for "a certain Delta personality," or "a Pan Am type." The general prerequisites were a capac ity to work with a team ("we don't look for chiefs, we want Indians"), interest in people, sensitivity, and emotional stamina. Trainers spoke somewhat remotely of studies that indicate that successful applicants often come from large families, had a father who enjoyed his work, and had done social volunteer work in school. Basically, however, recruiters look for someone who is smart but can also cope with being considered dumb, someone who is capable of giving emergency safety commands but can also handle people who can't take orders from a woman, and someone who is naturally empathic but can also resist the numbing effect of having that empathy engineered and continuously used by a company for its own purposes.

• • •

The trainees, it seemed to me, were also chosen for their ability to take stage directions about how to "project" an image. They were selected for being able to act well—that is, without showing the effort involved. They had to be able to appear at home on stage.

TRAINING

The training at Delta was arduous, to a degree that surprised the trainees and inspired their respect. Most days they sat at desks from 8:30 to 4:30 listening to lectures. They studied for daily exams in the evenings and went on practice flights on weekends. There were also morning speakers to be heard before classes began. One morning at 7:45 I was with 123 trainees in the Delta Stewardess Training Center to hear a talk from the Employee Representative, a flight attendant whose regular job was to communicate rank-and-file grievances to management and report back. Her role in the training process was different, however, and her talk concerned responsibilities to the company:

> Delta does not believe in meddling in the flight attendant's personal life. But it does want the flight attendant to uphold certain Delta standards of conduct. It asks of you first that you keep your finances in order. Don't let your checks bounce. Don't spend more than you have. Second, don't

> drink while in uniform or enter a bar. No drinking twenty-four hours before flight time. [If you break this rule] appropriate disciplinary action, up to and including dismissal, will be taken. While on line we don't want you to engage in personal pastimes such as knitting, reading, or sleeping. Do not accept gifts. Smoking is allowed if it is done while you are seated.

The speaker paused and an expectant hush fell across the room. Then, as if in reply to it, she concluded, looking around, "That's all." There was a general ripple of relieved laughter from the trainees: so that was *all* the company was going to say about their private lives.

Of course, it was by no means all the company was going to say. The training would soon stake out a series of company claims on private territories of self. First, however, the training prepared the trainees to accept these claims. It established their vulnerability to being fired and their dependence on the company. Recruits were reminded day after day that eager competitors could easily replace them. I heard trainers refer to their "someone-else-can-fill-your-seat" talk. As one trainee put it, "They stress that there are 5,000 girls out there wanting *your* job. If you don't measure up, you're out."

Adding to the sense of dispensability was a sense of fragile placement vis-à-vis the outside world. Recruits were housed at the airport, and during the four-week training period they were not allowed to go home or to sleep anywhere but in the dormitory. At the same time they were asked to adjust to the fact that for them, home was an idea without an immediate referent. Where would the recruit be living during the next months and years? Houston? Dallas? New Orleans? Chicago? New York? As one pilot advised: "Don't put down roots. You may be moved and then moved again until your seniority is established. Make sure you get along with your roommates in your apartment."

Somewhat humbled and displaced, the worker was now prepared to identify with Delta. . . . Training seemed to foster the sense that it was safe to feel dependent on the company. Temporarily rootless, the worker was encouraged to believe that this company of 36,000 employees operated as a "family." The head of the training center, a gentle, wise, authoritative figure in her fifties, appeared each morning in the auditorium; she was "mommy," the real authority on day-to-day problems. Her company superior, a slightly younger man, seemed to be "daddy." Other supervisors were introduced as concerned extensions of these initial training parents. (The vast majority of trainees were between nineteen and twenty-two years old.) As one speaker told the recruits: "Your supervisor is your friend. You can go to her and talk about anything, and I mean *anything*." The trainees were divided up into small groups; one class of 123 students (which included three males and nine blacks) was divided into four subgroups, each yielding the more intimate ties of solidarity that were to be the prototype of later bonds at work.

• • •

The company claim to emotion work was mainly insinuated by example. As living illustrations of the right kind of spirit for the job, trainers maintained a steady level of enthusiasm despite the long hours and arduous schedule. On Halloween, some teachers drew laughs by parading through the classroom dressed as pregnant, greedy, and drunk passengers. All the trainers were well liked. Through their continuous cheer they kept up a high morale for those whose job it would soon be to do the same for passengers. It worked all the better for seeming to be genuine.

Trainees must learn literally hundreds of regulations, memorize the location of safety equipment on four different airplanes, and receive instruction on passenger handling. In all their courses, they were constantly reminded that their own job security and the company's profit rode on a smiling face. A seat in a plane, they were told, "is our most perishable product—we have to keep winning our passengers back." How you do it is as important as what you do. There were many direct appeals to smile: "Really work on your smiles." "Your smile is your biggest asset—use it." In demonstrating how to deal with insistent smokers, with persons boarding the wrong plane, and with passengers who are sick or flirtatious or otherwise troublesome, a trainer held up a card that said "Relax and smile." By standing aside and laughing at the "relax and smile" training, trainers parried student resistance to it. They said, in effect, "It's incredible how much we have to smile, but there it is. We know that, but we're still doing it, and you should too."

HOME IN THE SKY

Beyond this, there were actual appeals to modify feeling states. The deepest appeal in the Delta training program was to the trainee's capacity to act as if the airplane cabin (where she works) were her home (where she doesn't work). Trainees were asked to think of a passenger *as if* he were a "personal guest in your living room." The workers' emotional memories of offering personal hospitality were called up and put to use. . . . As one recent graduate put it:

> You think how the new person resembles someone you know. *You see your sister's eyes in someone sitting at that seat.* That makes you want to put out

> for them. I like to think of the cabin as the living room of my own home. When someone drops in [at home], you may not know them, but you get something for them. You put that on a grand scale—thirty-six passengers per flight attendant—but *it's the same feeling.*

On the face of it, the analogy between home and airplane cabin unites different kinds of experiences and obscures what is different about them. It can unite the empathy of friend for friend with the empathy of worker for customer, because it assumes that empathy is the *same sort of feeling* in either case. Trainees wrote in their notebooks, "Adopt the passenger's point of view," and the understanding was that this could be done in the same way one adopts a friend's point of view. The analogy between home and cabin also joins the worker to her company; just as she naturally protects members of her own family, she will naturally defend the company. Impersonal relations are to be seen *as if* they were personal. Relations based on getting and giving money are to be seen *as if* they were relations free of money. The company brilliantly extends and uses its workers' basic human empathy, all the while maintaining that it is not interfering in their "personal" lives.

• • •

By the same token, the injunction to act "as if it were my home" obscured crucial differences between home and airplane cabin. Home is safe. Home does not crash. It is the flight attendant's task to convey a sense of relaxed, homey coziness while at the same time, at takeoff and landing, mentally rehearsing the emergency announcement, "Cigarettes out! Grab ankles! Heads down!" in the appropriate languages. Before takeoff, safety equipment is checked. At boarding, each attendant secretly picks out a passenger she can call on for help in an emergency evacuation. Yet in order to sustain the *if,* the flight attendant must shield guests from this unhomelike feature of the party. As one flight attendant mused:

> ...If we were going down, if we were going to make a ditching in water, the chances of our surviving are slim, even though we [the flight attendants] know exactly what to do. *But I think I would probably*—and I think I can say this for most of my fellow flight attendants—*be able to keep them from being too worried about it.* I mean my voice might quiver a little during the announcements, but somehow I feel we could get them to believe... the best.

Her brave defense of the "safe homey atmosphere" of the plane might keep order, but at the price of concealing the facts from passengers who might feel it their right to know what was coming.

Many flight attendants spoke of enjoying "work with people" and adopted the living room analogy as an aid in being as friendly as they wanted to be. . . . Others spoke of being frustrated when the analogy broke down, sometimes as the result of passenger impassivity. One flight attendant described a category of unresponsive passengers who kill the analogy unwittingly. She called them "teenage execs."

> Teenage execs are in their early to middle thirties. Up and coming people in large companies, computer people. They are very dehumanizing to flight attendants. You'll get to their row. You'll have a full cart of food. They will look up and then look down and keep on talking, so you have to interrupt them. They are demeaning . . . you could be R2–D2 [the robot in the film *Star Wars*]. They would like that better.

• • •

Despite the generous efforts of trainers and workers themselves to protect it, the living room analogy remains vulnerable on several sides. For one thing, trainees were urged to "*think* sales," not simply to act in such a way as to induce sales. Promoting sales was offered to the keepers of the living room analogy as a rationale for dozens of acts, down to apologizing for mistakes caused by passengers: "Even if it's their fault, it's very important that you don't blame the passengers. That can have a lot of impact. Imagine a businessman who rides Delta many times a year. Hundreds, maybe thousands of dollars ride on your courtesy. Don't get into a verbal war. It's not worth it. They are our lifeblood. As we say, the passenger isn't always right, but he's never wrong."

• • •

The cabin-to-home analogy is vulnerable from another side too. The flight attendant is asked to see the passenger as a potential friend, or as like one, and to be as understanding as one would be with a good friend. The *if* personalizes an impersonal relation. On the other hand, the student is warned, the reciprocity of real friendship is not part of the *if* friendship. The passenger has no obligation to return empathy or even courtesy. As one trainer commented: "If a passenger snaps at you and you didn't do anything wrong, just remember it's not you he is snapping at. It's your uniform, it's your role as a Delta flight attendant. Don't take it personally." The passenger, unlike a real friend or guest in a home, assumes a right to unsuppressed anger at irritations, having purchased that tacit right with the ticket.

• • •

It is when the going gets rough—when flights are crowded and planes are late, when babies bawl and smokers bicker noisily with nonsmokers, when the meals run out and the air conditioning fails—that maintaining the analogy to home, amid the Muzak and the drinks, becomes truly a monument to our human capacity to suppress feeling.

Under such conditions some passengers exercise the privilege of not suppressing their irritation; they become "irates." When that happens, back-up analogies are brought into service. In training, the recruit was told: "Basically, the passengers are just like children. They need attention. Sometimes first-time riders are real nervous. And some of the troublemakers really just want your attention." The passenger-as-child analogy was extended to cover sibling rivalry: "You can't play cards with just one passenger because the other passengers will get jealous." To think of unruly passengers as "just like children" is to widen tolerance of them. If their needs are like those of a child, those needs are supposed to come first. The worker's right to anger is correspondingly reduced; as an adult he must work to inhibit and suppress anger at children.

Should the analogy to children fail to induce the necessary deep acting, surface-acting strategies for handling the "irate" can be brought into play. Attendants were urged to "work" the passenger's name, as in "Yes, Mr. Jones, it's true the flight is delayed." This reminds the passenger that he is not anonymous, that there is at least some pretension to a personal relation and that some emotion management is owed. Again, workers were told to use terms of empathy. As one flight attendant, a veteran of fifteen years with United, recalled from her training: "Whatever happens, you're supposed to say, I know just how you feel. Lost your luggage? I know just how you feel. Late for a connection? I know just how you feel. Didn't get that steak you were counting on? I know just how you feel." Flight attendants report that such expressions of empathy are useful in convincing passengers that they have misplaced the blame and misaimed their anger.

• • •

Finally, the living room analogy is upheld by admitting that it sometimes falls down. In the Recurrent Training classes held each year for experienced flight attendants, most of the talk was about times when it feels like the party is over, or never began. In Initial Training, the focus was on the passenger's feeling; in Recurrent Training, it was on the flight attendant's feeling. In Initial Training, the focus was on the smile and the living room analogy; in Recurrent Training, it was on avoiding anger. As a Recurrent Training instructor explained: "Dealing with difficult passengers is part of the job. It makes us angry sometimes. And anger is part of stress. So that's why I'd like to talk to you about being angry. I'm not saying you should do this [work on your anger] for Delta Airlines. I'm not saying you should do it for the passengers. I'm saying do it for *yourselves*."

From the beginning of training, managing feeling was taken as the problem. The causes of anger were not acknowledged as part of the problem. Nor were the overall conditions of work—the crew size, the virtual exclusion of blacks and men, the required accommodation to sexism, the lack of investigation into the considerable medical problems of flight attendants, and the company's rigid antiunion position. These were treated as unalterable facts of life. The only question to be seriously discussed was "How do you rid yourself of anger?"

The first recommended strategy . . . is to focus on what the *other* person might be thinking and feeling: imagine a reason that excuses his or her behavior. If this fails, fall back on the thought "I can escape." One instructor suggested, "You can say to yourself, it's half an hour to go, now it's twenty-nine minutes, now it's twenty-eight." And when anger could not be completely dispelled by any means, workers and instructors traded tips on the least offensive ways of expressing it: "I chew on ice, just crunch my anger away." "I flush the toilet repeatedly." "I think about doing something mean, like pouring Ex-Lax into his coffee." In this way a semiprivate "we-girls" right to anger and frustration was shared, in the understanding that the official ax would fall on anyone who expressed her anger in a more consequential way.

Yet for those who must live under a taboo on anger, covert ways of expressing it will be found. One flight attendant recalled with a grin:

> There was one time when I finally decided that somebody had it coming. It was a woman who complained about absolutely everything. I told her in my prettiest voice, "We're doing our best for you. I'm sorry you aren't happy with the flight time. I'm sorry you aren't happy with our service." She went on and on about how terrible the food was, how bad the flight attendants were, how bad her seat was. Then she began yelling at me and my co-worker friend, who happened to be black. "You nigger bitch!" she said. Well, that did it. I told my friend not to waste her pain. This lady asked for one more Bloody Mary. I fixed the drink, put it on a tray, and when I got to her seat, my toe somehow found a piece of carpet and I tripped—and that Bloody Mary hit that white pants suit!

Despite the company's valiant efforts to help its public-service workers offer an atmosphere perfumed with cheer, there is the occasional escapee who launders her anger, disguises it in mock courtesy, and serves it up with flair. There remains the possibility of sweet revenge.

• • •

RESPONSES TO THE CONTRADICTION

The slowdown is a venerable tactic in the wars between industrial labor and management. Those whose work is to offer "personalized service" may also stage a slowdown, but in a necessarily different way. Since their job is to act upon a commercial stage, under managerial directors, their protest may take the form of rebelling against the costumes, the script, and the general choreography. . . .

For a decade now, flight attendants have quietly lodged a counterclaim to control over their own bodily appearance. Some crews, for example, staged "shoe-ins." ("Five of us at American just walked on the job in Famolares [low-heeled shoes] and the supervisor didn't say anything. After that we kept wearing them.") Others, individually or in groups, came to work wearing an extra piece of jewelry, a beard a trifle shaggier, a new permanent, or lighter makeup. . . . Sometimes, as in the case of body-weight regulations, the issue was taken to court. . . .

Workers have also—in varying degrees—reclaimed control of their own smiles, and their facial expressions in general. According to Webster's Dictionary, "to smile" is "to have or take on a facial expression showing pleasure, amusement, affection, friendliness, irony, derision, etc., and characterized by an upward curving of the corners of the mouth and a sparkling of the eyes." But in the flight attendant's work, smiling is separated from its usual function, which is to express a personal feeling, and attached to another one—expressing a company feeling. The company exhorts them to smile more, and "more sincerely," at an increasing number of passengers. The workers respond to the speed-up with a slowdown: they smile less broadly, with a quick release and no sparkle in the eyes, thus dimming the company's message to the people. It is a war of smiles.

• • •

The smile war has its veterans and its lore. I was told repeatedly, and with great relish, the story of one smile-fighter's victory, which goes like this. A young businessman said to a flight attendant, "Why aren't you smiling?" She put her tray back on the food cart, looked him in the eye, and said, "I'll tell you what. You smile first, then I'll smile." The businessman smiled at her. "Good," she replied. "Now freeze, and hold that for fifteen hours." Then she walked away. In one stroke, the heroine not only asserted a personal right to her facial expressions but also reversed the roles in the company script by placing the mask on a member of the audience. She challenged the company's right to imply, in its advertising, that passengers have a right to her smile. This passenger, of course, got more: an expression of her genuine feeling.

The slowdown has met resistance from all quarters and not least from passengers who "misunderstand." Because nonstop smiling had become customary before the speed-up occurred, the absence of a smile is now cause for concern. Some passengers simply feel cheated and consider unsmiling workers facial "loafers." Other passengers interpret the absence of a smile to indicate anger. As one worker put it: "When I don't smile, passengers assume I'm angry. But I'm not angry when I don't smile. I'm just not smiling."

• • •

The friction between company speed-up and worker slowdown extends beyond display to emotional labor. Many flight attendants recalled a personal breaking point. Here are three examples:

> I guess it was on a flight when a lady spat at me that I decided I'd had enough. I tried. God knows, I tried my damnedest. I went along with the program, I was being genuinely nice to people. But it didn't work. I reject what the company wants from me emotionally. The company wants me to bring the emotional part of me to work. I won't.

• • •

> The time I snapped was on a New York to Miami flight. On those flights, passengers want everything yesterday. There's a constant demand for free decks of cards. One woman fought for a free deck and groused when I told her we were all out. Finally I happened to see a deck under a seat, so I picked it up and brought it to her. She opened her purse and there were fifteen decks inside.

• • •

> I thought I'd heard them all. I had a lady tell me her doctor gave her a prescription for playing cards. I had a man ask me to tell the pilot to use the cockpit radio to reserve his Hertz car. I had a lady ask me if we gave enemas on board. But the time I finally cracked was when a lady just took her tea and threw it right on my arm. That was it.

Workers who refuse to perform emotional labor are said to "go into robot." They withhold deep acting and retreat to surface acting. They pretend to be showing feeling. Some who take this stance openly protest the need to conduct themselves in this way. "I'm not a robot," they say, meaning "I'll pretend, but I won't try to hide the fact that I'm pretending." Under the conditions of speed-up and slowdown, covering up a lack of genuine feeling is no longer considered necessary.

• • •

What is distinctive in the airline industry slowdown is the manner of protest and its locus. If a stage company were to protest against the director, the costume designer, and the author of a play, the protest would almost certainly take the form of a strike—a total refusal to act. In the airline industry the play goes on, but the costumes are gradually altered, the script is shortened little by little, and the style of acting itself is changed—at the edge of the lips, in the cheek muscles, and in the mental activities that regulate what a smile means.

The general effect of the speed-up on workers is stress. As one base manager at Delta frankly explained: "The job is getting harder, there's no question about it. We see more sick forms. We see more cases of situational depression. We see more alcoholism and drugs, more trouble sleeping and relaxing." The San Francisco base manager for United Airlines commented:

> I'd say it's since 1978, when we got the Greyhound passengers, that we've had more problems with drug and alcohol abuse, more absenteeism, more complaints generally.
>
> It's mainly our junior flight attendants and those on reserve—who never know when they will be called up—who have the most problems. The senior flight attendants can arrange to work with a friend in first class and avoid the Friendship Express altogether.

There are many specific sources of stress—notably, long shifts, disturbance in bodily rhythms, exposure to ozone, and continual social contact with a fairly high element of predictability. But there is also a general source of stress, a thread woven through the whole work experience: the task of managing an estrangement between self and feeling and between self and display.

Review Questions

1. Hochschild contends that service jobs require *emotional labor,* or work that puts other people in a certain emotional state. Explain and give examples of how flight attendants engage in emotional labor while they are presenting themselves to passengers.

2. How do flight attendants use "surface acting" and "deep acting" to manage their own emotions so they can do their emotional labor?

3. What other types of service workers do emotional labor, managing other people's emotions? In what cases is this type of labor explicitly called for in job descriptions? In what cases is it just assumed to be part of the job?

4. What does Hochschild's analysis add to Goffman's dramaturgical approach?

TURNING POINTS IN IDENTITY

Anselm Strauss

[IN TRANSFORMATIONS OF IDENTITIES, OR] COMING TO NEW TERMS, A PERSON becomes something other than [she or] he once was. [Such] shifts necessitate [and point up] new evaluations: of self and others, of events, acts, and objects. . . . [T]ransformation of perception is irreversible; once having changed, there is no going back. One can look back, but can evaluate only from the new status.

Some transformations of identity and perspective are planned, or at least fostered, by institutional representatives; others happen despite, rather than because of, such regulated anticipation; and yet other transformations take place outside the orbits of the more visible social structure. . . . As a way of introducing these several dimensions of personal change, I shall discuss . . . certain critical incidents that occur to force a person to recognize that "I am not the same as I was, as I used to be." . . . These critical incidents constitute turning points in the onward movement of personal careers.

TURNING POINTS

. . . [W]hat takes place at . . . turning points [is often] misalignment—surprise, shock, chagrin, anxiety, tension, bafflement, self-questioning—and also the need to try out the new self, to explore and validate the new and often exciting or fearful conceptions. Rather than discussing critical junctures in general, let us consider their typology. The list will not be a long one, but long enough to suggest the value both of its extension and of relating turning points to changes of identity.

A change in your relations with others is often so mundane, so gradual that it passes virtually unnoticed. Some incident is needed to bring home to you the extent of the shift. A *marker of progression*, or *retrogression*, is needed. When the incident occurs it is likely to strike with great impact, for it tells you: "Look! you have come way out to here! This is a milestone!" Recognition then necessitates new stances, new alignments.

SOURCE: Anselm Strauss. From "Turning Points in Identity," *Mirrors and Masks: Transformations of Identity*, The Sociology Press, pp. 93–100.

A striking example of the "milestone" is found in the autobiographies of many immigrants to America who later visited their native lands, only then realizing how little affinity they had retained, how identified they had become with America and Americans. Any return home, insofar as you have really left it, will signalize some sort of movement in identity. Some people literally go back home in an effort both to deny how far they have strayed and to prevent further defection.

Sometimes the path of development is foretold but is not believed, either because the one who forecasts is distrusted or because the prophecy cannot be understood. *Prophets* not only *point out new directions*: they *give you measuring rods* for calculating movement if you happen to traverse the paths prophesied. This is certainly one of the critical experiences in the psychology of conversion. For instance, a recruit to a religious sect, only partly convinced, is told what will happen when he [or she] tries to explain the new position to his [or her] old minister, attempts to sell pamphlets to the heathen, and so on, and lo! events turn out as predicted. The prediction will be in terms of a new vocabulary, hence when the vocabulary is shown to be workable the recruit is well on the road toward adopting it in part or *in toto*. The point holds for any kind of conversion—occupational, political, or what not. A novice is told by the old-timer, "Your clients will be of such and such sorts and you'll have such and such experiences with them." When the graph of experience is thus plotted and confirmed, then the person can recognize his [or her] own transformation.

Forecasting is often institutionalized in such a fashion that *public proclamation* is made: "Said candidate has followed the predicted and prescribed path of experience and has gotten to the desired point. Kneel, knight, and receive knighthood. Come to the platform and receive your diploma." When paths are institutionalized, candidates can easily mark their progress, note how far they have come, and how far they have yet to go. If there are the usual institutionalized acknowledgments of partial steps toward the goal, then these may constitute turning points in self-conception also. If the institutionalized steps are purely formalized, are no longer invested with meaning by the institution, or if the candidate believes them of no real significance, they will not, of course, be turning points for him [or her].

Private proclamation to a public audience is quite another matter. Having announced or avowed your position, it is not easy to beat a retreat. Often you find yourself in interpersonal situations climbing out on a limb, announcing a position, and then having to live up to it. In a more subtle sense, one often marks a recognition of self-change by announcement, but this announcement itself forces a stance facing forward since the way back, however tempting it may still look, is now blocked.

A related turning point—since ceremonial announcement often follows it—is *the meeting of a challenge*, either self-imposed or imposed by others. Any institution . . . possesses regularized means for testing and challenging its members. If you are closely identified with the institution, some tests will be crucial for your self-regard. If you pass them, everyone recognizes that you have met the challenge. However, some challenges, although they occur in institutional settings, are not themselves institutionalized. For instance every student nurse early in her training must face the situation of having a patient die in her arms. For some nurses this appears to be a turning point for self-conception: the test is passed and she—in her own eyes at least—has new status; she can now think of herself as more of a professional. Crucial tests are imposed by individuals on themselves; if they pass they have been psychologically baptized, so to speak, but if they fail then a new path must be taken, a new set of plans drawn up. Naturally, failure does not always result in immediate self-transformation, but may lead to more complete preparation until the test is definitely failed or passed.

One potent form of self-test is the deliberate *courting of temptation*. Failure to resist it is usually followed by new tests or by yielding altogether. The fuller meaning of temptation is this: you are withdrawing from an old psychological status and coming into a new, and in doing so something akin to the "withdrawal symptoms" of drug addiction occurs. When you are able to resist temptation then an advance is signalized; but when no longer even tempted, you are well aware of having progressed still further. Institutions find it easier to check upon the overt resistance of their members than upon their covert desires. Genuine conversion means the death of old desires. "Backsliding" signifies a failure to resist temptation; frequent backsliding results in a return to previous status or change to yet another.

A rather subtle type of transforming incident occurs when you have *played a strange but important role and unexpectedly handled it well*. Whether you had considered this an admirable or a despicable role does not matter. The point is that you never thought you could play it, never thought this potential "me" was in yourself. Unless you can discount your acts as "not me" or as motivated by something not under your control, you bear the responsibility or the credit for the performance. Cowardly and heroic roles are both likely to bring unexpected realignment in self-regard. But more usual, and more subtle, are those instances where you find yourself miraculously able to enact roles that you believed—at least as yet—beyond you. [All people] new to a job find [themselves], through no fault of [their] own, at some point taken by clients or fellow workers as of more advanced status than [they are]. . . . Once having carried off the disguise, you realize something new about yourself. The net result is likely to be that you wish to experiment with this new aspect of yourself. Conversely, there are roles previously viewed with suspicion, even despised, that you now find yourself enacting with unexpected success and pleasure. You must either wash your hands of it, actually or symbolically—as in *Macbeth*—or come to grips with this new aspect of yourself.

It is probable that some of the effect of experimental role-dramas is that the drama allows and forces [people] to play a range of roles [they] did not believe [themselves] capable of playing, or never conceived of playing; it brings [them] face to face with [their] potential as well as . . . actual selves. Sociable parties . . . by their very episodic and expressive nature, allow and further such exploration of roles. Similarly, some of the effect of psychiatric therapy seems to rest upon the skill of the psychiatrist in making patients face up to the full range of [their] acts, rather than repress awareness of them or blame them upon outside forces.

A critical experience with built-in ambivalence occurs when someone *surpasses the performance of [a role model]*, as when a student overtakes [a] beloved teacher, or a son exceeds his father's social position. When allegiance is very strong this awareness of overtaking the model may be crippling, and refuge is sought by drawing back from the abyss of departure. To be a success, one must surpass . . . models and depart from them. Departures are institutionalized in America by such mechanisms as myths of success, by the easy accessibility of higher social positions, and by the blessings of parents who in turn experience vicarious success through the performances of their offspring. Despite the institutionalized devices for reducing the strain of upward departure, ambivalence and stress undoubtedly persist even for many of our most successful climbers.

Another kind of transforming experience, one with shattering or sapping impact, is *betrayal*—by your heroes, in fact by anybody with whom you are closely "identified." Betrayal implicates you as well as [the other], in exceedingly subtle ways. Consider three varieties. When you have closely patterned yourself after a model, you have in effect "internalized" what you suppose are the model's values and motives. If the model abandons these, it leaves you with a grievous dilemma. Has the model gone over to the enemy?—then you may with wry smile redouble your efforts along the path [originally] laid out. . . . Or did the model lead you up an illusory path of values?—then with cynicism and self-hate you had better abandon your former self too. A different species of betrayal, involving search for atonement, is illustrated by the stunned . . . mother whose [child . . . becomes converted to another religious or political philosophy]. The cry here is always: "Where did I go wrong that my child, an extension of me, should go wrong?" A third variety of betrayal often goes by the name of "rejection"; that is, rejection of you after you had closely identified with the model. Here the beloved has symbolically announced that you and your values are not right, or at least are not wholly satisfying. [Children who] reject and drift away from immigrant parents illustrate this. Betrayal of this type consists, usually, of a series of incidents, rather than of a single traumatic event. During the course of day-to-day living, decisions are made whose full implications are not immediately apparent. People can go on deceiving themselves about paths that actually have been closed by those decisions. At the point when it becomes apparent that former possibilities are dead issues, the person stands at the crossroads. A severe instance of such a turning point occurs when one traps oneself into an occupation—much as a house painter might paint himself unthinkingly into a corner of the room—believing that he can always get out when he wants to. Jazz musicians who go commercial "just for a while" to make money may find eventually that the commercial style has caught them, that they can no longer play real jazz as it should be played. This kind of crossroad may not be traumatic, but nostalgically reminiscent, signifying then that the gratifications arising from past decisions are quite sufficient to make past possibilities only pleasantly lingering "maybes." Final recognition that they are really dead issues is then more of a ritualistic burial and is often manifested by a revisiting of old haunts—actually or symbolically.

A final type of critical experience that I shall discuss is akin to betrayal, but the agent of destruction is less personal. A [person] may realize that he [or she] has been *deceived*, not by any specific person but *by events in general*. If the deception strikes home severely, [one] may respond with self-hate. "Why did I not discover this before?"; with personalized resentment against someone, "Why did they not tell me?"; or with diffuse resentment against the world in general. An essential aspect of this critical experience is that a [person's] naming of self is disoriented. [One] is not what [one] thought [one] was. Self-classificatory disorientation, of course, can be mild. For instance, a Jewish boy, brought up in a moderately Orthodox home, discovered later that all Jews were not Orthodox, but that there were Reformed Jews (who made him feel not at all Jewish) and very Orthodox Jews (who made him feel not at all Jewish). Such discoveries come as shocks, but not necessarily as traumas. There is more anguish involved when a [person] finds that although he believed he possessed a comfortable dual identity, [black] and American, significant others are now challenging one of those identities. This is, or at least was, an unnerving experience for many Northern [blacks] who visited in the South, however much they may have read or been warned. This negation of a portion of identity may not provide much of a crisis if the person withdraws from his attackers, but if [one] stays, as some [blacks] have stayed in the South, [one] must make . . . peace with the challenging audience. A more crucial juncture in the maintenance of identity occurs when a person discovers that [a] chief self-referential term is completely erroneous. Cases in point are adopted children who do not discover until later years the fact of their adoption, and those occasional tragic cases of children who are raised as members of the opposite sex and eventually discover the mis-naming. Imagine also the destructive effects, compounded with guilt and self-hate, of discovering an actual identity with a group formerly reviled and despised, as for instance an anti-Semite discovering that he [or she] is partly Jewish.

Enough has been said about various types of turning points to suggest that these are points in development when an individual has to take stock, to reevaluate, revise, resee, and rejudge. Although stock-taking goes on within the single individual, it is obviously both a socialized and a socializing process. Moreover, the same kinds of incidents that precipitate the revision of identity are extremely likely to befall and to be equally significant to other persons of the same generation, occupation, and social class. This is equivalent to saying that insofar as experiences and interpretations are socially patterned, so also will be the development of personal identities. . . .

Review Questions

1. Strauss presents ten kinds of turning points in this article. Give examples from your own experience of each of them.

2. Strauss maintains that people in a similar social status, or social location, may face similar turning points. Discuss two such statuses and the turning points their occupants are likely to face.

3. Discuss the implications for people's self-concepts of living through turning points.

Suggested Readings: Interaction in Everyday Life

Becker, Ernest. *The Birth and Death of Meaning*. 2nd ed. New York: Free Press, 1971.

Cooley, Charles Horton. *Human Nature and the Social Order*. New York: Schocken Books, 1964.

Couch, Carl J. "From Hell to Utopia and Back to Hell: Charismatic Relationships," *Symbolic Interaction* 12 (1989):265–280.

Derber, Charles. *The Pursuit of Attention: Power and Individualism in Everyday Life*. New York: Oxford University Press, 1983.

Festinger, Leon, Henry W. Riecken, and Stanley Schacter. *When Prophecy Fails*. Minneapolis: University of Minnesota Press, 1956.

Goffman, Erving. *The Presentation of Self in Everyday Life*. Garden City, N.Y.: Anchor Books, 1959.

———. *Behavior in Public Places*. New York: Free Press, 1963.

Hewitt, John. *Dilemmas of the American Self*. Philadelphia: Temple University Press, 1990.

Lemert, Edwin. "Paranoia and the Dynamics of Exclusion," *Sociometry* 25 (1962):2–20.

Tannen, Deborah. *You Just Don't Understand: Men and Women in Conversation*. New York: Ballentine, 1990.

Part V. Social Organization: Life in Groups

ALTHOUGH A GREATER PROPORTION OF OUR INTERACTIONS OCCURS WITH strangers than was the case in agricultural societies of the past, most still occur within groups. All of the groups of which we are members—from the level of the primary group, to the secondary group, to the formal organization, to the society—are organized. What we mean by this is that each of these types of groups—even the small friendship group—develops a system of beliefs and norms, a division of labor, a method of ranking members, and a system of social-control techniques to ensure conformity to the group's goals and rules. Sociologists have paid attention to a number of elements of group organization: group size (primary groups usually being small, societies large), the ways in which norms are created (informally within primary groups, formally in secondary groups or large-scale organizations), the degree of intimacy among members (greater within the primary group than the secondary group), the method of determining leadership and power positions (informally in the primary group, usually formally in secondary groups and societies), and so on. They have also focused on the internal processes of both small and large groups such as communication, development of group cohesion, boundary maintenance, and facilitation of smooth interaction.

Of course, we are all members of many groups, of all types, simultaneously; and within large groups, smaller ones may be found. The expectations and demands of these groups may conflict at times, causing problems for the individual torn between competing claims. As societies themselves have become larger, more complex, more industrialized, and more interdependent, the number of claims on the individual have increased and, as a result, the very character of everyday life has changed.

The articles and excerpts presented in this part of our reader are intended to illustrate the patterning and constraining aspects of various levels of social organization, as well as the differences between types of groups in the kinds of behavior they call for. The *organization* of the small, intimate groups into which we are born (families); of the associations we join; of the formal organizations in which we work, study, and even play; and of the larger society, has important implications for our daily lives.

First, Lyn Lofland asks, What is the nature of human bonds in primary groups? What do people "do" for each other as they interact? She approaches this question from an ingenious angle: she looks at what is *missing* from the lives of people who have lost family members and friends through death. In "Loss and Human Connection," Lofland spells out the important aspects of relationships as seen through the eyes of those whose relationships have just ended. She discovers that people experiencing the loss of a significant other miss not only the other person but also one or more of the following: a role partner, help with everyday chores, linkages to the wider community, support for their self-concepts, support for comforting myths, confirmation of their views of reality, and possible futures.

Furthermore, Lofland discusses cultural and historical differences in *patterns* of connectedness. Here she points out that the way in which a society is organized influences the number and types of others to whom people are connected. In some societies, for instance, people tend to count on one type of person for, say, help with everyday chores and another type of person for confirmation of their views of reality. In contemporary American society, we tend to put our eggs in fewer baskets—to count on a smaller number of significant others to provide all the functions listed above—than is the case in many societies.

In the next selection, "Corner Boys," William Foote Whyte directs our attention to interaction in one type of primary group: the peer group. Whyte moved into a neighborhood where groups of young men spent much of their free time hanging around on the street. He spent more than three years as a participant observer studying these peer groups, and his research resulted in one of the best known and frequently cited works in sociology, *Street Corner Society*.

In this article by Whyte, he explains his research methods and a few of the research findings pertaining to group processes. He demonstrates, for example, the determinants of leadership among the corner boys. We are also shown how an individual's status within the group affects with whom he or she is likely to spend time. Further, there is the issue of who initiates and who receives more interaction. At the most general level, Whyte's research shows the powerful influence of the group upon individual behavior.

As you read this article, think of similar examples of group processes in your own social groups. To take one example, have you noticed that followers often must convince more powerful group members to introduce or implement their ideas rather than voicing them directly? Also, are you aware of the altruistic behavior of leaders? Do the leaders of your groups spend more time and money on followers than the reverse? That is, do leaders do favors for followers so they can call in their markers later? You should be able to illustrate from your own experience these and many other general principles of peer group behavior that Whyte sets forth.

The college classroom, a setting familiar to us all, is the situation which David Karp and William Yoels have chosen for study. The members of a classroom form a collectivity which is much less intimate and more formal than a primary group (although, to be sure, primary groups may exist *within* the classroom). Role relationships, as in other *secondary groups,* are segmental, which means that teacher and students interact within (usually) fairly narrow boundaries rather than becoming involved with each other in a more total way. The occupants of each of these reciprocal positions have expectations both for their own behavior and for the behavior of those in the reciprocal role. When these expectations differ, a kind of *role strain* may develop. Whose definition of the situation will win out? Can social processes arise to alleviate the strain?

The professor expects the students to be prepared for class—to have read and carefully considered the assigned material and, in class, to ask questions or make comments based on their reading. Ideally, much of the class period will be spent in a stimulating discussion that will involve most of the students.

Many of the students, on the other hand, prefer to take a passive role. They view their professor as an expert who will "feed" them his or her views on the subject at hand. Because they know that the professor expects them to have read the material thoroughly, perhaps with a greater commitment than they actually care to generate, they enter the classroom with a "presentation of self" that indicates a solid knowledge of the material. As long as they are not asked to discuss anything, an uneasy silence is maintained.

How is the issue of participation actually resolved? Fortunately, each class contains a few talkers. These individuals assume the responsibility of carrying on class discussion and thus take the pressure off both the "silent majority" and the professor. When the professor asks a question, it is almost always one of the group of "regulars" who responds. Although a regular talker in one class may not fulfill that role in another, someone will probably do so, easing the strain so that the class may proceed. Rarely will the teacher or the students place one another under such stress that their behavior will deviate from the relatively distant, formal attitude appropriate in secondary groups.

Formality and politeness may be top priority in the college classroom, but in the type of organization we call the *total institution,* they are not. A total institution is an organization with highly rigid rules and roles; one of its key features is that the lives of the clients or inmates are restricted and regimented 24 hours a day. Prisons, boarding schools, monasteries, hospitals, military bases, and nursing homes are all examples of the total institution, the type of group setting we will analyze in the final article in this section.

In order to study nursing home life, Andrea Fontana joined the janitorial staff of Sunny Hill convalescent center. He documents, in "Growing Old Between Walls," that client care took a backseat to the profit motive. The lowest level of staff—who maintained the highest levels of contact with the patients—did the least desirable, physically draining tasks and were paid poorly. Their work goals quickly came to be getting through the day, not meeting the needs and demands of the clients. Growing old in the care of workers like these is, for most people, dismal.

Membership in any group involves a certain loss of freedom, but being a member of the Sunny Hill community affords the client no autonomy at all over the basic activities that make up the day. It is ironic that those who directly control the timing and tenor of everyday activities are *not* the top administrators and medical professionals, but the people who do the "dirty work" for the management. In this case, the clients themselves *are* the dirty work.

LOSS AND HUMAN CONNECTION

Lyn H. Lofland

. . . THE ENDING—THROUGH DEATH, DESERTION, OR GEOGRAPHICAL SEPARAtion, for example—of a relationship defined by an actor as "significant" or "meaningful" is generally conceived of as a "loss" experience. In this essay,[1] I want to pursue the question: What is lost? Stated more positively, I want to ask what it is that humans *do* for one another? What links self to other, what is the nature of the social bond?

• • •

ATTACHMENT, GRIEF, AND LOSS

Humans are social animals. This rather simple, even simplistic, statement covers a multitude of complexities. Lift it up and we see such matters as these: that the human animal is slow to mature and thus stands in a relationship of need to older members of the species for a considerable period of time; that "humanness"—the capacities and characteristics of the species—is a social creation, forged from the biological clay by the group; that all human behavior is necessarily social; and that attachments—emotional linkages—to other humans occur. It is this latter "fact," as part of the complex of "socialness," that is of concern here. Humans do not simply live in proximity to one another. They link themselves to one another. They tie. They bond. They bind.

• • •

Attachment behavior . . . most certainly is a contributor to human pain. For the dark side of attachment is grief. . . .

. . . [W]hen some modern Westerners undergo the rupturing of a relationship they define as significant, they report experiencing a discomforting combination of physical and psychic symptoms, typically labeled grief.[2] I want to ask: For these persons, what is the cause of the pain? The simple answer, the breaking of an attachment, is satisfactory at one level. But I wish to delve more deeply. I wish to inquire into the nature of the attachment itself. I want to ask, with *what* do we attach ourselves to others? What, more specifically, are the ties that bind?

SOURCE: Lyn Lofland: "Loss and Human Connection," From W. Ickes and E. S. Knowles, eds., *Personalities, Roles and Social Behavior* (Springer-Verlag, 1982), pp. 219–242.

• • •

THREADS OF HUMAN CONNECTEDNESS

In this section, I will propose seven "threads of connectedness": seven kinds of ways that humans bond themselves to one another. The materials from which this formulation emerges are of four types: (1) intensive interviews with persons who had experienced an involuntary[3] relational loss; (2) published first-person accounts of a grief experience; (3) published case and interview data from scholarly investigations of the grief experience; and (4) unpublished letters of condolence, funeral memorializations, and personal anecdotes. Of these diverse materials, I continually asked the questions: What are these people saying about what it is that is missed? What do they say the "lost" person did for them? What is it they think they have lost?

Although the formulation that follows cannot be said to be built upon prior efforts to categorize types of relationships or types of interpersonal loss, it is nonetheless thoroughly informed by them. In 1967, for example, Warren Breed, noting that "loss" is a recurrent notion in the psychological and psychoanalytic literature on suicide causation, asks (as I do) "What is lost?" and answers: position, person, mutuality (Breed, 1967). Robert Weiss (1969) has proposed five categories of relational functions, each of which, he postulated, was for the most part provided by a different relationship: intimacy, social integration, opportunity for nurturant behavior, reassurance of worth, and assistance—with guidance added as a possible sixth function (see also Lopata, 1969).

But it is Samuel Wallace's (1973) ruminations about the meanings of his interview data on the bereavement experience of widows of suicides which most clearly herald the route taken herein:

> The loss . . . is not simply the loss of an *object;* a *relationship,* a *status,* a *way of being* are also lost when someone goes out of our lives. The "object" or person lost also takes with him or her that part of our self that they alone maintained—our self which was a son, our self which was a mother, our self which was a spouse. The loss of object and relationship also loses us a status, a position in the social universe. No longer are we married, have children, or are known as the lost one's friends. And within whatever status is lost lies an equally lost way of being.
>
> Bereavement, then, is social loss, of person, relationship, status, and way of being. The experience may be said to *vary* with our life's involvement with the person, relationship, status and way of being which is lost. (p. 231 [italics added])

Let us now examine each of the seven "connections" in turn. They are, as will be clear, both logically and empirically interrelated. But that interrelationship is not invariant. . . .

ROLE PARTNER

Much of the descriptive and analytic literature on loss and grief seems to touch on the role partner "thread of connectedness"—unsurprisingly, since it is one of the easiest to see and conceptualize, both for the actor and observer. Clearly, certain roles—certain organized and recurrent ways of being and acting—require for their realization, an "other." If the other is lost, so is the opportunity for playing the role. One cannot "be" daughter without mother, father without child, lover without lover, helper without helped, employee without employer, even enemy without enemy (see Lifton, 1973, pp. 45–46). It is primarily to this kind of loss that widows in Helena Lopata's study refer when they report that they are "lonely for the husband as [among other things] . . . a partner or companion in activities; an escort in couple-companionate interaction; 'someone' with whom to talk; 'someone' around whom work and time are organized . . ." (Lopata, 1973, p. 68; see also 1979, pp. 117–118). Similarly, a young male informant speaks of missing his deceased grandmother as a "playmate" and a young widow writes, in her diary, a letter to her dead husband about what their sons are missing.

> At times Keith is so frustrated; he misses you, Dwight, and needs you. He needs you as only an eight-year-old boy can need a father. I love him and try to show my love but that doesn't take your place. He needs that father and son shoulder-to-shoulder companionship and approval of work well done. But you knew he would need you! And Gary needs you; he needs you to help with all of his many building projects. He wants to build and create rockets, boats, hot rods.[4] (Beck, 1965, pp. 53–54)

Of course, most role partners, *qua* partners, are replaceable. The line of activity can be reactivated as part of one's continuing repertoire, although the speed or ease of replacement will vary according to the role itself and across time and space. And, when a single other serves as a partner in multiple roles, as in C. S. Lewis's (1961) description of his dead wife,

> She was my daughter and my mother, my pupil and my teacher, my subject and my sovereign; and always, holding all these in solution, my trusty comrade, friend, shipmate, fellow-soldier. (p. 39)

replacement, even substituting multiple others for the one, may become highly problematic. But until replacement occurs, the individual is in a condition of loss.

MUNDANE ASSISTANCE

People help one another. When the help is desired (it may not be, of course), the absence of the helper engenders a loss. The death of a neighbor may mean that one now has no one to look after pets and plants when one is away. The death of a work acquaintance may mean that one no longer has a ready source of job advice. . . . The death of a teenaged son may leave many household tasks undone, as this extract from the summary of an interview with a bereaved mother makes clear.

> She says that the entire family did not fully appreciate just how much he did in the way of helping tasks until he died. He was the kind of boy, she says, who did things without being asked—cleaning his room, emptying the trash, pruning the roses, mowing the lawn. On this past Christmas day, her two other children got up about 6 A.M. She asked them why, since they hadn't gotten up that early the year before. "Oh, yes, we did," they said, "but [the teenaged son] wouldn't let us come downstairs until 7:30."[5]

Or the death of a husband may eliminate a buffer in one's relations with others.

> Anytime the children do something wrong that goes against me, I start to think about him. They fly up against me, they never did when their father was here. They say things to hurt me, you know, and that's when I think about him. He would never have allowed them to talk to me that way. . . . (Wallace, 1973, p. 166)

It is important to recognize that removal of a helper may necessitate more than simply "picking up the slack" or finding substitute sources of aid. It may, as often in the illness or death of a spouse, necessitate learning a whole new set of skills, and as such, require the jettisoning of old "selves" or aspects of selves—yet another loss.

> A year ago, he was the boss, he managed this house completely, even the kids he controlled with the strictest discipline. I had to learn how to pay bills, I had never even written a check and I had to balance the checkbook, and oh, that was so hard to learn, everything that he used to do. Everything I did I used to ask him about first. I needed his advice, I depended on him so. He always knew the answers to everything. Then when he got sick, I had nobody, no one to take his place. *I had to learn how to live all over, to be a different person.* (Wallace, 1973, p. 39 [italics added]; see also Lopata, 1969, p. 253; Weiss, 1975, p. 97)

In fact, the literature on the experience of widowhood—as well as what little is available on widowers—suggests that a large element of the trauma engendered by the loss of a spouse in contemporary Western societies has to do with the loss of mundane assistance. People find themselves burdened with other aspects of the loss at the same time that they have to cope with such new matters as earning a living, balancing a checkbook, cooking, driving a car, making household repairs, cleaning house, and washing clothes. This has led some observers—quite independent of any feminist inclinations—to call for a reduction in sex-role specialization in the marital relationship (see, for example, Caine, 1974; Wedemeyer, 1974).

LINKAGES TO OTHERS

The considerable social isolation of men and women following the deaths of their spouses or the breakup of their marriages is reported frequently in the literature on "loneliness." As Lopata notes,

> Many wives enjoy company parties, golf, couple-companionate dinners, and such events, and will not engage in them after the husband dies or have them no longer available *since it was his presence which formed the connecting link in the first place.* (Lopata, 1969, p. 253 [italics added]; see also Lopata, 1979, p. 118; Weiss, 1975, pp. 52, 58)

But it is clearly not only in the multiple bondedness of a marital relationship that persons can serve this linking function for one another. Friends and acquaintances often involve one another in their larger individual friendship and acquaintance networks—person A meets and relates to persons C, D, and E primarily through the arrangements of person B. One informant told me of feeling absolutely devastated when a close friend moved to another city, importantly because, rather to her surprise, she discovered that she had "no friends of my own"—only acquaintances through the now absent friend. Of course, the secondary linkage that B has provided between A and C, D, and E may eventually become primary. But when it does not, then loss of B occasions the simultaneous loss of C, D, and E, as well.

THE CREATION AND MAINTENANCE OF SELF

. . . [I]n the loss of a single other, part or all of self is lost as well.

> When the loss has been sudden, large, and forced upon the attention, words implying mutilation and outrage tend to be used. One widow described her feelings on viewing the corpse of her husband: "It's as if my inside had been torn out and left a horrible wound there." A comparison is sometimes made to amputation: widows say that their husband has been "cut off," "as if half of myself was missing." In less violent terms, the loss of self is often referred to as a "gap"—"it's a great emptiness," "an unhappy void." (Parkes, 1972, p. 97)

. . . [S]ocial psychology . . . understands the self and its components importantly as the ongoing creation of the significant others who surround the actor.[6] . . . [R]eports of self loss are not viewed merely as description through analogy but as literal depiction. That aspect of self (or those multiple aspects) that was significantly and uniquely generated and/or sustained in interaction with the other is, quite literally, lost when the other is lost.

If one's desirability, for example, is proffered and affirmed only in interaction with a single other human, the death of that human is the death of that part of self. A widow remembers:

> Here I am so big and fat and sometimes I'd be reading and would look up and he'd be sitting there looking at me—and I'd say, "What are you thinking about?" And he would say, "Oh, I was just thinking how pretty you are." (Lopata, 1969, p. 252)

Another widow reports,

> I think he found me as a very strong person. And being able to handle almost anything. And I think I probably saw in him someone who needed me very much. Which my first husband obviously did not.... When someone needs you, you... just automatically respond to them.... And I needed to be needed. (Wallace, 1973, p. 27; see also Thomas, 1957, Chap. 4; McCabe, 1970)

Similarly, a woman writes of a recently deceased friend:

> But the main thing that welded me to her so strongly was that she thought so much of me. She didn't flatter; she just never seemed to suspect that I wasn't as witty or wise or talented or nice as she thought I was, so I tried never to let on. In our 13 years of friendship, there was nothing she thought I couldn't do, and there was, in turn, nothing I wouldn't have done for her. (Barthel, 1972, p. 56)

Even when there are multiple others in the actor's milieu who help to maintain some aspect of self, a particular individual may be viewed as pivotal, as especially crucial to the actor's conception of self. Speaking of a man, now deceased, who had been important to him in his boyhood, a male informant muses over what this person had meant to him.

> He believed in me. He gave of his self to me, in the sense that he gave me responsibility, trusted me with responsibility for his very body [during epileptic seizures], his very physical existence which I was very honored to have someone trust me that way. That was probably the most responsibility I'd ever been given. Let's say the most meaningful responsibility.

• • •

It might be argued, of course, that self-maintenance is not threatened by the death or other loss of a significant other because memory allows continued—if entirely internal—interaction. To some degree, and for some period of time, this may be true. But the author, C. S. Lewis, writing about his "grief" over the death of his wife, suggests that the continued evocation of the other through memory has serious limitations.

> Slowly, quietly, like snow-flakes—like the small flakes that come when it is going to snow all night—little flakes of me, my impressions, my selections, are settling down on the image of her. The real shape will be quite hidden

> in the end. Ten minutes—ten seconds—of the real H. would correct all of this. And yet, even if those ten seconds were allowed me, one second later the little flakes would begin to fall again. The rough, sharp, cleaning tang of her otherness is gone. (Lewis, 1961, p. 19)

SUPPORT FOR COMFORTING MYTHS

For many humans, living comfortably in a world beset by the possibility of sudden death, catastrophic illness, unforeseen financial difficulties—all the hazards of existence—would seem to be made possible by the embrace of myth, of comforting stories about possibilities, situations, eventualities, self, others. These are stories that the individual knows, quite rationally, to be impossible, but which are clung to nonetheless. Like aspects of self, the reality of which seem to reside in the eyes of others, some of these myths appear to depend for their continued viability on the presence, or at least existence, of other persons. If these persons disappear, so do the myths and all the comfort and protection they afford. A particularly articulate informant, who shared with me some entries in her private journal, writes of just such a loss.

> Bob, like Ann, was so intertwined with so many memories of Rocklane [her home town] and my growing up there, that he and the town are, in some sense, synonymous. Not that he was always there while I was growing up. I was 10 to 11 or 12 before I ever met him, and he was gone for a period between about 8th grade and second year high school. But the time he was there, he was so crucial, that especially during my adolescent years, I cannot think of Rocklane without a memory of him crowding in. When my folks moved, I felt a tie to the home town cut, but it was not until Bob's death that I felt the real sense of the break. He was dead. The years of my adolescence were really gone. The home town of my childhood was passed and could never be regained, because the person who had been so much a part of that time and that town was dead. *For the first time, really for the first time, I understood that I was growing older and that what was passed was forever, irremediably passed. It could never come again.* Of course, we always know this in our heads. I mean, one can't be alive without knowing it. But only with Bob's death did the full realization of this "fact of life" hit me with full force. I would never be 16 again, Rocklane would never again be for me the place it had been at 16. The people who peopled my memories of those years were gone; their older versions might still be around, but they were gone. The past was passed. It could not be reclaimed. [italics added]

The comfort from the myths seems not to reside in their sharpness or detail. Rather, they sit in the mind, shadowy, rather unsubstantial, off to the side, obliquely and intermittently viewed. Only when the myth is destroyed must its content be fully recognized.

• • •

It should be noted that the keystone of the myth may reside less in the person than in the relationship itself, as in the following interview extract in which a woman informant speaks of her separation from her husband.

> I had an almost mystical sense that no matter what I did, no matter how I behaved, no matter what, he'd be there, sticking to me, my assurance not only that I could "hold a man," but that somebody cared for me. Rather like a child feels with very loving parents. We'd had a lot of fights and threatened each other with divorce many times, but it was all unreal. He was my secure future, my "Linus blanket," which told me that the things that happened to other people, the terrible painful things, couldn't happen to me. (see also, Caine, 1974, p. 135; Weiss, 1975, p. 49)

REALITY MAINTENANCE

Peter Berger and Hansfried Kellner in "Marriage and the Construction of Reality" have written persuasively of the reality-validating character of marital and other intimate relationships.

> Every individual requires the ongoing validation of his world, including crucially the validation of his identity and place in this world, by those few who are his truly significant others. . . . Again, in the broad sense, all the actions of the significant others and even their simple presence serve this sustaining function. In everyday life, however, the principal method employed is speech. In this sense, it is proper to view the individual's relationship with his significant others as an ongoing conversation. As the latter occurs, it validates over and over again the fundamental definitions of reality once entered into, not, of course, so much by explicit articulation, but precisely by taking the definitions silently for granted and conversing about all conceivable matters on this taken-for-granted basis. (1964, pp. 4–5)

Certainly, the scholarly and popular literature on grief would appear to confirm these observations. . . . Colin Parkes has noted, for example, how the death of a husband alters the character of the world inhabited by the wife. "Even when words remain appropriate, their meaning changes—'the family' is no longer the same object it was, neither is 'home' or 'marriage'; even 'old age' now has a new meaning" (1972, p. 93). First-person accounts of the grief experience, as another example, typically contain references to feeling "odd," "strange," "peculiar," "out of touch with reality," "weird"—in fact, an "altered sensorium" is considered part of the normal symptomatology of grief (see references cited in Footnote 2).

But reality maintenance would appear to connect more than just intimates. As Berger and Kellner argue,

> This validation [of common-sense reality] . . . requires ongoing interaction with others who co-inhabit this same socially constructed world. In a broad

> sense, all the other co-inhabitants of the world serve a validating function. Every morning the newspaper boy validates the widest co-ordinates of my world and the mailman bears tangible validation of my own location within these co-ordinates. (1964, p. 4)

In this sense, the death or other loss of any noticed other in one's world threatens, however mildly, the validity of common-sense reality, and mass death may, as Robert Lifton (1967) has argued, destroy the survivor's very faith in the "connectedness of the world". . . .

THE MAINTENANCE OF POSSIBLE FUTURES

Finally, the materials here under analysis suggest that persons are connected to one another through the parts they play in one another's futures. To "lose" certain persons is to lose certain futures, certain quite realistic possibilities for action, the very possibility of which provides comfort and/or pleasure to the actor. C. S. Lewis, for example, found pain in the realization that

> Never, in any place or time, will she [his deceased wife] have her son on her knees, or bathe him, or tell him a story, or plan for his future, or see her grandchild. (1961, p. 24)

A widow spoke of watching

> this older couple—I think this gets to me quicker than anything—is to see an older couple walking along the street, you know, and I say to myself, "I'll never be there." (Wallace, 1973, p. 114)

And a woman whose son had been killed in an accident told me that her sense of loss seemed to revolve primarily around a sense of potential not realized. She felt that her son was on his way to manhood, that he was in the process of becoming an interesting person, not just a son, but someone of whom she could feel proud, whom she could enjoy, with whom she could be friends. It was this potential that had been stripped away. She had been cheated—deprived—of the person her son was in the process of becoming.

The future that is destroyed by the loss of the other may be broadly and generally conceived, as the foregoing interview extracts suggest. But very circumscribed and/or detailed scenarios may also be cherished and relinquished with pain—a "scene" that will bring a relationship right again, for example.

> When I heard, in a letter when I was in college, that he had died, I was very angry that no one had told me because I had felt this strong need to put things right between us. To come to an understanding. I don't know what kind of understanding. To have corrected any misunderstanding that might have been there. To tell him how much I appreciated all that he had cared for me. Which I never got to tell him. . . .

Or, a "place" in which a relationship is to be played out. A woman, separated from her husband, describes one such, now forfeited, location.

> Do you know what [the southern part of a state] is like? Well, up towards . . . we wanted to buy some land and build an A-frame and it's like, really hilly and forested and we had an area picked out where we wanted to buy some land there and we drew up this house that we wanted to build and there was room in it for two kids. . . . We called it the gingerbread house.

In sum, then, I am postulating that the "ties that bind," the "threads of connectedness" are of seven sorts. We are linked to others by the *roles* we play, by the *help* we receive, by the wider *network* of others made available to us, by the *selves* others create and sustain, by the comforting *myths* they allow us, by the *reality* they validate for us and by the *futures* they make possible. I make no claim that this listing is exhaustive, nor even that it is the most felicitous that could be conceived. I have, however, found it useful in thinking about varying patterns of connectedness and the possible relationship between such patterns and the grief experience. To those matters, let us now turn.

PATTERNS OF CONNECTEDNESS

• • •

Table 1 illustrates four different ways that a person (A) might distribute his or her "connections"—each of the seven variations in linking symbols between Person A and Person B, Person A and Person C, and so forth, standing for one of the seven links. Thus, in the first pattern, we conceive of a person who, in a network of others, manages to encompass all seven ties, but with a minimum of multiple bonding to any one person. That is, Person A in this pattern is tied to Person B as role partner and for mundane assistance, to Person C as a link to others, to Person D through reality and future maintenance and to Person E as a creator and maintainer of self and as a supporter of comforting myths. Pattern 2 imagines a person, also with a minimum of multiple bonding, but in this instance, lacking the full range of possible linkages. Here Person A is tied to B as a role partner, to C as a link to others, and as a creator and maintainer of self and to D through future maintenance; the other possible connections are simply missing. Pattern 3 postulates someone who is maximally multiply bonded to multiple others, while Pattern 4 illustrates maximal multiple bonding, but to a single other. The reader can imagine many other possible patterns and can complicate the picture enormously simply by varying, more than

Table 1. Patterns of Connectedness

1. Full range of connections, spread among multiple others

```
  ------------                                            ============
 A++++++++++++B        A: : : : : : : : : : : : :C        A. . . . . . . . . . . . .D
                         ############
                         ************
```

2. Limited connections, spread among multiple others

```
 A------------B        A: : : : : : : : : : : : :C        A. . . . . . . . . . . . .D
                       A############E
```

3. All connections to a single other, multiples of such others

```
  ************           ************           ************
  ------------           ------------           ------------
  : : : : : : : : : : : :   : : : : : : : : : : : :   : : : : : : : : : : : :
 A++++++++++++B         A++++++++++++C         A++++++++++++D
  ============           ============           ============
  . . . . . . . . . . . .   . . . . . . . . . . . .   . . . . . . . . . . . .
  ############           ############           ############
```

4. All connections linked to a single other

```
                         ************
                         ------------
                         : : : : : : : : : : : :
                        A++++++++++++B
                         ============
                         . . . . . . . . . . . .
                         ############
```

-----, role partner; +++++, mundane assistance; : : : : :, linkages to others; ### ##, creation and maintenance of self; * * * * *, support for comforting myths; =====, reality maintenance; . . . . . , maintenance of possible futures.

has been done here, the number of others to whom any given actor is linked.

There are additional "complications" which, in this brief essay, I will not address. For example, some linkages can themselves be compounded or intensified in a single relationship, as in many intimacies involving multiple role partnerships. Or, as another matter, I have throughout assumed the status of adult among relational participants. When it is a child, especially a very young child, who is at the receiving end of a set of connections, one would expect the "power" of any single tie to be intensified.

. . . We might ask, as one line of inquiry, whether there is *historical and cultural variation* in the *range, dominance and idealization* of [these] patterns. And, assuming such variation to be discovered, we might ask further whether or in what way it relates to possible differences in the emotional experience of grief, to observed differences in mourning practices and to other social psychological and/or structural diversities among human groups.

For example, might it be that "death demographics" are importantly linked to the dominant pattern or patterns or even range of patterns to be found in a given social order during a given period? That is, might it be that what appears to be, by modern standards, relative emotional coolness in the face of the death of presumed intimates among historic Westerners is best understood as a quite reasonable "spread" of connections (e.g., a preponderance of Patterns 1 and 2 over 3 and 4) under conditions of high mortality rates? When the demographer E. A. Wrigley reports that

> It was entirely in accord with the usage of that time [early 1600's in England], that the children's father, William, should have remarried so soon after the death of his first wife. Remarriages within a period of weeks rather than months were not uncommon. (1969, p. 83)

are we observing not an historically different social psychology, or even a greater . . . acceptance of death, but a different structural patterning of *connectedness?*

As another example, might observed cultural differences in mourning practices be linked to a group's typical patterning of linkages? Edmund Volkart postulated exactly such a connection nearly 25 years ago. . . .

> In his study of the Ifaluk people, [M. E.] Spiro was puzzled by some features of bereavement behavior there. When a family member died, the immediate survivors displayed considerable pain and distress . . . in accordance with local custom. However, as soon as the funeral was over, the bereaved were able to laugh, smile and behave in general as if they had suffered no loss or injury at all. Their "grief" seemed to disappear as if by magic, and this too was approved by custom. . . . In terms of the thesis being developed here, the bereavement behavior of the Ifaluk suggests that their family system is such as to develop selves that are initially less vulnerable in bereavement than are the selves we are accustomed to. . . . Another way of stating this is that in self-other relations among the Ifaluk, the other is not valued by the self as a unique and necessary personality. . . . [T]he roles of others [are] dispersed. . . . Multiple and interchangeable personnel performing the same functions for the individual provides the individual with many psychological anchors in his social environment; the death of any one person leaves the others and thus diminishes the loss (1976, pp. 247–249; for further discussions on cultural variation, see Anderson, 1965; Devereux, 1942; Levy, 1973; Lutz, 1986; Plath, 1968; Yamamoto, 1970. On historical variation, see L. H. Lofland, 1985; Rosenblatt, 1983; Stearns, 1986).

Taking the lead from Volkart, is it possible that there exists a dominance of and/or preference for some variant on Pattern 3 (which might be termed "the multiple intimates pattern") among contemporary Americans? . . . That is, might it be that Americans cannot substitute one "relational provision for another" because they believe that the only meaningful relationships—the only relationships that provide "emotional attachment"—are intimate ones? . . .

I have suggested that inquiry into historical and cultural variation in patterns of connectedness might be fruitful. Let me suggest further that inquiries into *experiential variation* might prove equally so. . . .

One such variant in the experience of death provides the focus of a goodly portion of the scholarly and first-person literature on grief—what might be called *devastating loss.* It is in reference to devastating loss that the literature, quite properly, speaks of survivors, for the language of its accompanying grief is the language of personal disaster.

Devastating loss may occur when there is a death involving a *solitary multibonded relationship.* If we imagine a continuum of connectedness based on numbers of persons involved, we can visualize at one end an actor who is linked in diverse ways (some multiple bonding, some single bonding, etc.) to a very large number of others. At the other end is a person who has literally placed all his or her eggs in one basket—all the linkages are to a single other person (Pattern 4, above). Now, this latter situation is probably empirically very infrequent, possibly nonexistent. Even if others are linked to us in no other ways, they are, as Berger and Kellner (1964) have pointed out, at least contributing to the validation of our commonsense reality. Nonetheless, close approximations of this extreme situation are anything but rare.

> Everything I did revolved around him. He was my whole world. [When he died] my heart was gone. My reason to live, everything.

And death involving such a relationship (or its approximation) is devastating because in one fell swoop all (or almost all) of the actor's "connections" are severed.

As numerous commentators have suggested, it may be that the very intense grief experience reported so frequently by widows and widowers in the contemporary United States and Britain . . . has importantly to do with a tendency for marital relationships to become solitary and multibonded. *A* significant other becomes *the most* significant other—permeating every corner of our lives.

• • •

Another sort of devastating loss results not from the removal of a single person in whom all connections are encompassed but from the simultaneous removal of all connections, that is, in circumstances of *mass death.* Of course, once again, we are dealing with a continuum.

The extreme case where every single known other in the actor's world is removed, is empirically rare. But, tragically, close approximations are less so. Robert Lifton's studies of the survivors of Hiroshima provides one of the most detailed records of this particular death experience (1967, 1976)—an experience that in its intensity and profundity seems almost to defy our capacity to understand it. . . .

I suggested at the beginning of this essay that my intent was to make a modest foray into that area of inquiry which sociologists would identify as involving the nature of the social bond. . . . I happen to believe, and I think others working in the areas of attachment, connection, grief, and loss would concur, that these areas provide one plausible route to the achievement of that goal (see also Lofland, 1985). Certainly we have a long way to go. As the reader has discovered, we are far from understanding even experiential variations in patterns of connection and loss, much less the historical and cultural structuring of connection and loss, and even less the relation between such patterning and structuring and the organization of social orders. To strive for such an understanding, however, as I hope I have made clear, is well worth the effort. Such an understanding should bring us closer to grasping that very social and socially connected animal that is ourself and that matrix of connectedness that is our social order and our home.

NOTES

1. I owe a great debt of gratitude to many informants, friends, and colleagues—all of whom must remain anonymous—who have shared so freely of personal mementos, anecdotes, memories, and musings about matters that for many of them are still sources of pain. I am grateful as well for the generosity of colleagues who read earlier drafts of this paper and who provided support and comments and/or criticisms. I wish to thank Kathy Charmaz, Candace Clark, Gary Hamilton, John Lofland, Victor Marshall, and Howard Robboy. I must admit, however, to having resisted dealing with a number of their more telling and well-taken criticisms. I trust this resistance will in no way threaten any of our "threads of connection."

2. Enumerations of the diverse but consistently reported "symptoms" of grief may be found in Charmaz, 1980; Clayton et al., 1968; Glick, Weiss, and Parkes, 1974; Hoyt, 1980-1981; Lindemann, 1944; Marris, 1958; Parkes, 1970, 1972; Stern, 1965.

3. I here emphasize *involuntary* severance on the presumption that situations of *voluntary* severance are likely to tell us more about frustrated expectations than about relational components. However, in his study of broken marriages, Robert Weiss (1975) found considerable evidence of "grieving" among the *instigators* of the separation/divorce. Clearly, a relationship, however unsatisfactory, is still a relationship, involving "connections," and is thus relevant to the

matters under consideration here. Nonetheless, I shall restrict my inquiry to instances of involuntary severance on the strategic grounds of "cleanliness."

4. One sees here a first example of the frequent empirical compounding of "ties"—in this instance, the tie of "role partner" between son and father is compounded by "mundane assistance" (see below).

5. Quotations not otherwise referenced are from my interviews.

6. I am here separating out "role" from self. . . . In my reading of the data, people are simply not talking about the same things when they speak of the loss of someone as role partner and when they speak of loss of self through loss of other. . . .

REFERENCES

Anderson, B. G.
1965 Bereavement as a subject of cross-cultural inquiry: An American sample. *Anthropological Quarterly,* 38, 181–200.

Barthel, J.
1972 I promise you, it will be all right. The dilemma of a friend's dying. *Life,* March 17.

Beck, F.
1965 *The Diary of a Widow.* Boston: Beacon Press.

Berger, P., and Kellner, H.
1964 Marriage and the construction of reality. *Diogenes,* 46, 1–24.

Breed, W.
1967 Suicide and loss in social interaction. In E. S. Shneidman (Ed.), *Essays in Self-destruction.* New York: Science House.

Caine, L.
1974 *Widow.* New York: William Morrow.

Charmaz, K. C.
1980 *The Social Reality of Death.* Reading, Mass.: Addison-Wesley.

Clayton, P., Desmarais, L., & Winokur, G.
1968 A study of normal bereavement. *American Journal of Psychiatry,* 125, 64–74.

Devereux, G.
1942 Social structure and the economy of affective bonds. *The Psychanalytic Review,* 29, 303–314.

Glick, I. O., Weiss, R. S., and Parkes, C. M.
1974 *The First Year of Bereavement.* New York: Wiley.

Hoyt, M. F.
1980–1981 Clinical notes regarding the experiences of "presences" in mourning. *Omega,* 11, 105–111.

Levy, R. I.
1973 *Tahitians: Mind and Experience in the Society Islands.* Chicago: University of Chicago Press.

Lewis, C. S.
1961 *A Grief Observed.* New York: Seabury Press.

Lifton, R. J.
1967 *Death in Life; Survivors of Hiroshima.* New York: Vintage.
1973 *Home from the War.* New York: Simon & Schuster.
1976 Psychological effects of the atomic bomb in Hiroshima: The theme of death. In R. Fulton (Ed.), *Death and Identity* (rev. ed.). Bowie, Md.: Charles Press Publishers (Originally published, 1963).

Lindemann, E.
1944 Symptomatology and management of acute grief. *American Journal of Psychiatry,* 101, 141–148.

Lofland, L. H.
1985 The social shaping of emotion: The case of grief. *Symbolic Interaction,* 8, 171–190.

Lopata, H. Z.
1969 Loneliness: Forms and components. *Social Problems, 17,* 248–261.
1973 *Widowhood in an American City.* Cambridge, Mass.: Schenkman.
1979 *Women as Widows: Support Systems.* New York: Elsevier.

Lutz, C.
1986 Depression and the translation of emotional worlds. In A. Kleinman and B. Good (Eds.), *Culture and Depression.* Berkeley: University of California Press.

McCabe, C.
1970 A sprig of rosemary. *San Francisco Chronicle,* May 5.

Marris, P.
1958 *Widows and Their Families.* London: Routledge & Kegan Paul.

Parkes, C. M.
1970 "Seeking" and "finding" a lost object: Evidence from recent studies of the reaction to bereavement. *Social Science and Medicine,* 4, 187–201.
1972 *Bereavement: Studies of Grief in Adult Life.* New York: International Universities Press.

Plath, D. W.
1968 Maintaining relations with kin: Social ties after death in Japan. In H. K. Geiger (Ed.), *Comparative Perspectives on Marriage and the Family.* Boston: Little, Brown.

Rosenblatt, P. C.
1983 *Bitter, Bitter Tears: 19th Century Diarists and the 20th Century Grief Theories.* Minneapolis: University of Minnesota Press.

Stearns, P. N.
1986 The problems of change in emotions research. Paper presented at the meetings of the American Sociological Association, New York, New York.

Stern, K., Williams, G., and Prados, M.
1965 Grief reactions in later life. In R. Fulton (Ed.), *Death and Identity.* New York: Wiley.

Thomas, C.
1957 *Leftover Life to Kill.* Boston: Little, Brown.

Volkart, E. H. (with collaboration of S. T. Michael).
1976 Bereavement and mental health. In R. Fulton (Ed.), *Death and Identity* (rev. ed.). Bowie, Md.: Charles Press. (Originally published, 1957).

Wallace, S. E.
1973 *After Suicide.* New York: Wiley.

Wedemeyer, D.
1974 "Widowers: They face unique problems which widows do not." *Sacramento Bee,* November 16.

Weiss, R. S.
1969 The fund of sociability. *Trans-action* (now, *Society*), July/August, 36–43.
1975 *Marital Separation.* New York: Basic Books.

Wrigley, E. A.
1969 *Population and History.* New York: McGraw-Hill.

Yamamoto, J.
1970 Cultural factors in loneliness, death and separation. *Medical Times, 98,* 177–183.

Review Questions

1. Provide examples from your own circle of family, friends, and acquaintances of the seven threads of connectedness that Lofland describes:
   a. role partner
   b. mundane assistance
   c. linkages to others
   d. creation and maintenance of self
   e. support for comforting myths
   f. reality maintenance
   g. maintenance of possible futures
2. How have you "distributed your connections"? That is, how many other people in your social world do you count on to provide you with

roles, mundane assistance, and the like? Which (if any) of the four patterns of connectedness best describes you?

3. Which of the four patterns of connectedness best characterizes American society today? Explain your answer.

4. In which of the four patterns of connectedness is devastating loss most likely to occur? Explain your answer.

CORNER BOYS: A STUDY OF CLIQUE BEHAVIOR

William Foote Whyte

THIS PAPER PRESENTS SOME OF THE RESULTS OF A STUDY OF LEADERSHIP IN informal groupings or gangs of corner boys in "Cornerville," a slum area of a large eastern city. The aim of the research was to develop methods whereby the position (rank or status) of the individual in his clique might be empirically determined; to study the bases of group cohesion and of the subordination and superordination of its members; and, finally, to work out means for determining the position of corner gangs in the social structure of the community.

• • •

While my subjects called themselves corner boys, they were all grown men, most of them in their twenties, and some in their thirties. . . . While some of the men I observed were engaged in illegal activities, I was not interested in crime as such; instead, I was interested in studying the nature of clique behavior, regardless of whether or not the clique was connected with criminal activity. . . . I made an intensive and detailed study of five gangs on the basis of personal observation, intimate acquaintance, and participation in their activities for an extended period of time. Throughout three-and-a-half years of research, I lived in Cornerville, not in a settlement house, but in tenements such as are inhabited by Cornerville people.

The population of the district is almost entirely of Italian extraction. Most of the corner boys belong to the second generation of immigrants. In general, they are men who have had little education beyond grammar school and who are unemployed, irregularly employed, or working steadily for small wages.

Their name arises from the nature of their social life. For them "the corner" is not necessarily at a street intersection. It is any part of the sidewalk which they take for their social headquarters, and it often includes a poolroom, barroom, funeral parlor, barbershop, or clubroom.

SOURCE: William F. Whyte: "Corner Boys: A Study of Clique Behavior," *American Journal of Sociology*, vol. 46 (March, 1941), pp. 647–664 (with deletions).

Here they may be found almost any afternoon or evening, talking and joking about sex, sports, personal relations, or politics in season. Other social activities either take place "on the corner" or are planned there.

HIERARCHY OF PERSONAL RELATIONS

The existence of a hierarchy of personal relations in these cliques is seldom explicitly recognized by the corner boys. Asked if they have a leader or boss, they invariably reply, "No, we're all equal." It is only through the observation of actions that the group structure becomes apparent. My problem was to apply methods which would produce an objective and reasonably exact picture of such structures.

In any group containing more than two people there are subdivisions to be observed. No member is equally friendly with all other members. In order to understand the behavior of the individual member it is necessary to place him not only in his group but also in his particular position in the subgroup.

My most complete study of groupings was made from observations in the rooms of the Cornerville Social and Athletic Club. This was a club of corner boys, which had a membership of about fifty and was divided primarily into two cliques, which had been relatively independent of each other before the formation of the club. There were, of course, subdivisions in each clique.

I sought to make a record of the groupings in which I found the members whenever I went into the club. While the men were moving around, I would be unable to retain their movements for my record, but on most occasions they would settle down in certain spatial arrangements. In the accompanying example (Figure 1) two were at a table playing checkers with one watching, four at another table playing whist and three more watching the game, and six talking together toward the back of the room. As I looked around the room, I would count the number of men present so that I should know later how many I should have to account for. Then I would say over to myself the names of the men in each grouping and try to fix in my mind their positions in relation to one another. In the course of an evening there might be a general reshuffling of positions. I would not be able to remember every movement, but I would try to observe with which members the movements began; and, when another spatial arrangement had developed, I would go through the same mental process as I had with the first. As soon as I got home from the club, I would draw a map or maps of the spatial positions I had observed and add any movements between positions which I recalled. The map (Figure 1) indicates the sort of data that came out of these observations.

Figure 1. The Cornerville S & A Club, February 29, 1940, 8–8:15 P.M.

Street

Checker game between 2 & 3, 1 watches

5, 7, 8, & 10 play whist
4, 6, & 9 watch

Conversation among 11, 12, 13, 14, 15, & 16

1 2 3 4 5 6 7 8 9 10 Observer 11 12 13 14 15 16

Legend

Direction in which chairs & couches face indicates direction in which men face.
Arrows indicate direction in which standing men face.
Dotted lines enclose those interacting.

In this case I have the following notes on movements of the members:

> Eleven walked over to One and pinched his cheek hard, went out of the club rooms, returned and pinched cheek again. One pretended to threaten Eleven with an ash tray. Eleven laughed and returned to seat on couch. I [the observer] asked Eleven about the purpose of the club meeting. He asked Ten and Ten explained. Eleven laughed and shrugged his shoulders. Sixteen, the janitor, served beer for the card players.

On the basis of a number of maps such as this it is not difficult to place most of the men in the clique and grouping within the clique to which they belong. I did not attempt to place all the men, because the club had a fluctuating membership and some of the men were available for observation for only a short time. There were, throughout the ten months of my observation, some thirty-odd members who were active most of the time. Events in the club could be explained largely in terms of the actions of these men; and, therefore, when I had placed them in relation to one another, I did not need to press further in this direction.

Positional map-making is simply an extension of the techniques of observation and recording which have been used in the past by social anthropologists and sociologists. All these techniques require practice before they can be effectively applied. While my first maps left out a number of men, later I was able to record accurately enough so that on most occasions I could account for every man present at a particular time; and on several occasions I was able to work out two maps giving different positional arrangements during the course of the same period of observation. Beyond two I did not attempt to go, and it was not necessary to do so because there would rarely be more than two positional arrangements in the course of an evening sufficiently different from one another to require additional maps.

While the data from such maps enable one to determine groupings, they do not reveal the position or rank of the men in the groupings. For this purpose other data are needed. In practice they may be gathered at the same time as the positional arrangements are observed.

As I conceive it, position in the informal group means power to influence the actions of the group. I concentrated my attention upon the origination of action, to observe who proposed an action, to whom he made the proposal, and the steps that followed up to the completion of the action. I was dealing with "pair events" and "set events," to use the terminology of Arensberg and Chapple.[1] A "pair event" is an event between two people. A "set event" is an event in which one person originates action for two or more others at the same time. In working out the relations between men in an informal group, this is an important distinction to bear in mind. I found that observations of pair events did not provide a safe guide for the ranking of the members of the pair. At times A would originate action for B, at other times B would originate action for A. In some cases there would be a predominance of originations in one direction; but on the whole the data did not support rankings based upon quantitative comparisons of the rates of origination of action in pair events. Qualitatively one could say that when A originated action for B he used a tone of voice and words which indicated that he held a superior position. To take the extreme case, it is not difficult to tell the difference between an order and a request, although both may originate action. It is not safe, however, to rely upon such qualitative differences. The observer may read into the situation his own impression of the relative positions of the men and thus lose the objective basis for his conclusions.

It is observation of set events which reveals the hierarchical basis of informal group organization. As defined by Arensberg and Chapple,

> a *set* is an aggregate of relations such that every individual related in the set is a member either (*a*) of a class of individuals who only originate action, or (*b*) of an intermediate class of individuals who at some time originate action and at another time terminate action, or (*c*) of a class of individuals who only terminate action.[2]

Study of corner-boy groups reveals that the members may, indeed, be divided and ranked upon this basis. Several examples will illustrate.

At the top of the Cornerville S. and A. Club (see Figure 2), we have Tony, Carlo, and Dom. They were the only ones who could originate action for the entire club. At the bottom were Dodo, Gus, Pop, Babe, Marco, and Bob, who never originated action in a set event involving anyone above their positions. Most of the members fell into the intermediate class. They terminated action on the part of the top men and originated action for the bottom men. Observations of the actions of the men of the intermediate class when neither top nor bottom men were present revealed that there were subdivisions or rankings within that class. This does not mean that the intermediate or bottom men never have any ideas as to what the club should do. It means that their ideas must go through the proper channels if they are to go into effect.

In one meeting of the Cornerville S. and A. Club, Dodo proposed that he be allowed to handle the sale of beer in the clubrooms in return for 75 percent of the profits. Tony spoke in favor of Dodo's suggestion but proposed giving him a somewhat smaller percentage. Dodo agreed. Then Carlo proposed to have Dodo handle the beer in quite a different way, and Tony agreed. Tony made the motion, and it was carried unanimously. In this case Dodo's proposal was carried through, after substantial modifications, upon the actions of Tony and Carlo.

In another meeting Dodo said that he had two motions to make: that the club's funds be deposited in a bank and that no officer be allowed to serve two consecutive terms. Tony was not present at this time. Dom, the president, said that only one motion should be made at a time and that, furthermore, Dodo should not make any motions until there had been opportunity for discussion. Dodo agreed. Dom then commented that it would be foolish to deposit the funds when the club had so little to deposit. Carlo expressed his agreement. The meeting passed on to other things without action upon the first motion and without even a word of discussion on the second one. In the same meeting Chris moved that a member must be in the club for a year before being allowed to hold office. Carlo said that it was a good idea, he seconded the motion, and it carried unanimously.

All my observations indicate that the idea for group action which is carried out must originate with the top man or be accepted by him so that he acts upon the group. A follower may originate action for a leader in a pair event, but he does not originate action for the leader and other

Figure 2. Informational Organization of the Cornerville S & A Club, February 1940

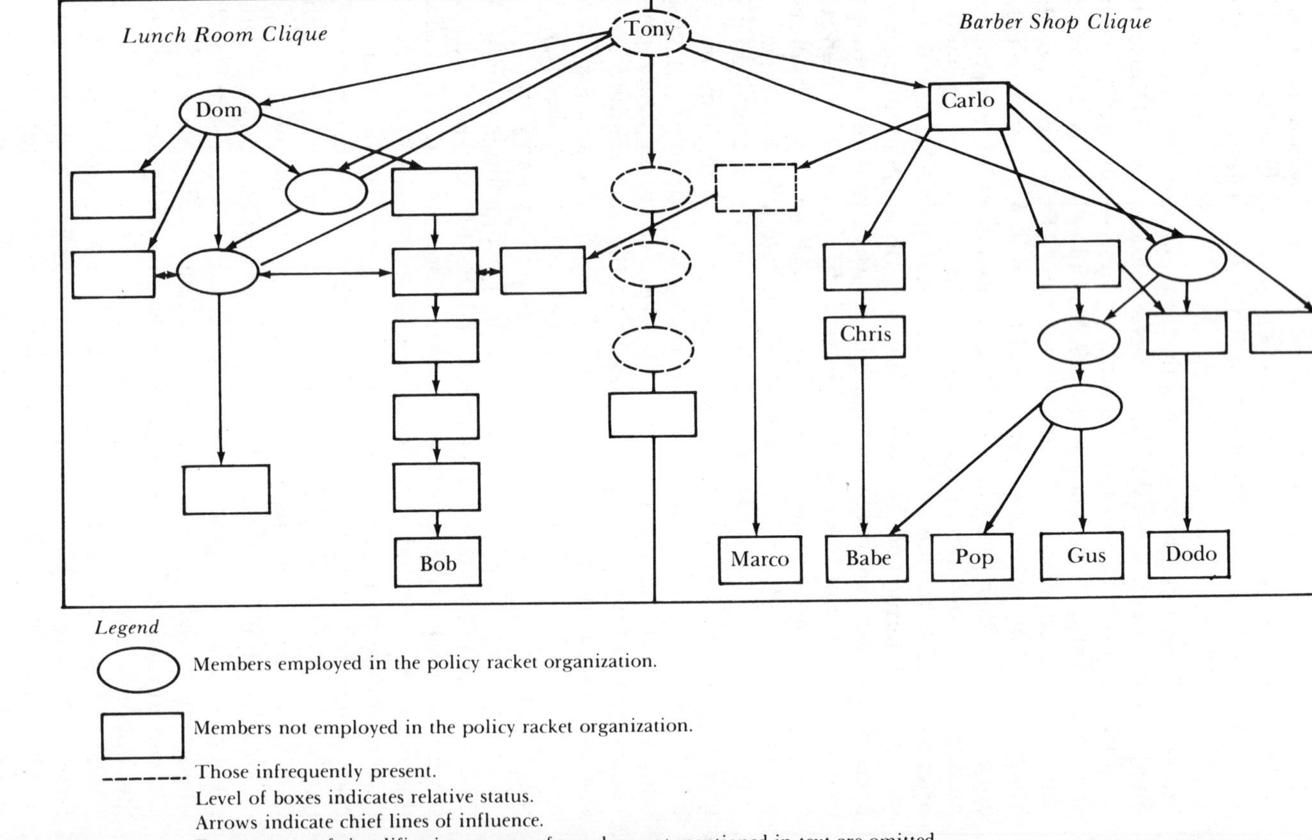

followers at the same time—that is, he does not originate action in a set event which includes the leader.

One may also observe that, when the leader originates action for the group, he does not act as if his followers were all of equal rank. Implicitly he takes the structure of the group into account. An example taken from the corner gang known as the "Millers" will illustrate this point. The Millers were a group of twenty corner boys, who were divided into two subgroups. Members of both subgroups frequently acted together; but, when two activities occupied the men at the same time, the division generally fell between the subgroups. Sam was the leader of the Millers. Joe was directly below him in one subgroup. Chichi led the other subgroup. Joe as well as Sam was in a position to originate action for Chichi and his subgroup.

It was customary for the Millers to go bowling every Saturday night. On this particular Saturday night Sam had no money, so he set out to persuade the boys to do something else. They followed his suggestion. Later Sam explained to me how he had been able to change the established social routine of the group. He said:

> I had to show the boys that it would be in their own interests to come with me—that each one of them would benefit. But I knew I only had to convince two of the fellows. If they start to do something, the other boys will say to themselves, "If Joe does it—or if Chichi does it—it must be a good thing for us too." I told Joe and Chichi what the idea was, and I got them to come with me. I didn't pay no attention to the others. When Joe and Chichi came, all the other boys came along too.

Another example from the Millers indicates what happens when the leader and the man next to him in rank disagree upon group policy. This is Sam talking again:

> One time we had a raffle to raise money to build a camp on Lake______ [on property lent them by a local businessman]. We had collected $54, and Joe and I were holding the money. . . . That week I knew Joe was playing pool, and he lost three or four dollars gambling. When Saturday came, I says to the boys, "Come on, we go out to Lake______. We're gonna build that camp on the hill. . . ." Right away Joe said, "If yuz are gonna build the camp on the hill, I don't come. I want it on the other side. . . ." All the time I knew he had lost the money, and he was only making up excuses so he wouldn't have to let anybody know. . . . Now the hill was really the place to build that camp. On the other side, the ground was swampy. That would have been a stupid place. . . . But I knew that if I tried to make them go through with it now, the group would split up into two cliques. Some would come with me, and some would go with Joe. . . . So I let the whole thing drop for a while. . . . After, I got Joe alone, and I says to him, "Joe, I know you lost some of that money, but that's all right. You can pay up when you have it and nobody will say nothin'. But Joe, you know we shouldn't have the camp on the other side of the hill because the land is no good there. We

should build it on the hill. . . ." So he said, "All right," and we got all the boys together, and we went out to build the camp.

Under ordinary circumstances the leader implicitly recognizes and helps to maintain the position of the man or men immediately below him, and the group functions smoothly. In this respect the informal organization is similar to the formal organization. If the executive in a factory attempts to pass over his immediate subordinates and gives orders directly to the men on the assembly line, he creates confusion. The customary channels must be used.

The social structures vary from group to group, but each one may be represented in some form of hierarchy. The members have clearly defined relations of subordination and superordination, and each group has a leader. Since we are concerned with informal organization, the Cornerville S. and A. members must be considered as two groups, with Carlo leading the barbershop boys, and Dom leading the lunchroom boys. Since Tony's position requires special consideration, he will be discussed later.

BASES OF GROUP STRUCTURE

Observation not only serves to provide a description of the group structure. It also reveals information upon the bases of structure and the factors differentiating between the positions of members. The clique structure arises out of the habitual association of the members over a long period of time. The nuclei of most gangs can be traced back to early boyhood years when living close together provided the first opportunities for social contacts. School years modified the original pattern somewhat, but I know of no corner gangs which arose through classroom or school-playground association. The gangs grew up "on the corner" and have remained there with remarkable persistence. In the course of years some groups have been broken up by the movement of families away from Cornerville, and the remaining members have merged with gangs on nearby corners; but frequently movement out of the district does not take the corner boy away from his corner. On any evening in Cornerville on almost any corner one finds corner boys who have come in from other parts of the city or from suburbs to be with their old friends. The residence of the corner boy may also change within the district, but nearly always he retains his allegiance to his original corner.

The leader of one group spoke to me in this way about corner boys:

Fellows around here don't know what to do except within a radius of about 300 yards. That's the truth, Bill. . . . They come home from work, hang on the corner, go up to eat, back on the corner, up (to) a show, and they come

> back to hang on the corner. If they're not on the corner, it's likely the boys there will know where you can find them. . . . Most of them stick to one corner. It's only rarely that a fellow will change his corner.

The stable composition of the group over a long period and the lack of social assurance felt by most of the members contribute toward producing a very high rate of social interaction within the group. *The structure to be observed is a product of past interactions.*

Out of these interactions there arises a system of mutual obligations which is fundamental to group cohesion. If the men are to carry on their activities as a unit, there are many occasions when they must do favors for one another. Frequently, one member must spend money to help another who does not have the money to participate in some of the group activities. This creates an obligation. If the situation is later reversed, the recipient is expected to help the man who gave him aid. The code of the corner boy requires him to help his friends when he can and to refrain from doing anything to harm them. When life in the group runs smoothly, the mutual obligations binding members to one another are not explicitly recognized. A corner boy, asked if he helped a fellow-member because of a sense of obligation, will reply, "No, I didn't have to do it. He's my friend. That's all." It is only when the relationship breaks down that the underlying obligations are brought to light. When two members of the group have a falling-out, their actions form a familiar pattern. One tells a story something like this: "What a heel Blank turned out to be. After all I've done for him, the first time I ask him to do something for me, he won't do it." The other may say: "What does he want from me? I've done plenty for him, but he wants you to do everything." In other words, the actions which were performed explicitly for the sake of friendship are now revealed as being part of a system of mutual obligations.

THE SOCIAL ROLE OF LEADER

Not all the corner boys live up to their obligations equally well, and this factor partly accounts for the differentiation in status among the men. The man with a low status may violate his obligations without much change in his position. His fellows know that he has failed to discharge certain obligations in the past, and his position reflects his past performances. On the other hand, the leader is depended upon by all the members to meet his personal obligations. He cannot often fail to do so without causing confusion and losing his position. The relationship of status to the system of mutual obligations is most clearly revealed when we consider the use of money. While all the men are expected to be generous, the flow of money between members can be explained only in terms of the group structure.

The Millers provide an illustration of this point. During the time that I knew them, Sam, the leader, was out of work except for an occasional odd job; yet whenever he had a little money, he spent it on Joe and Chichi, his closest friends, who were next to him in the structure of the group. When Joe or Chichi had money, which was less frequent, they reciprocated. Sam frequently paid for two members who stood close to the bottom of the structure and occasionally for others. The two men who held positions immediately below Joe and Chichi in the subgroups were considered very well off according to Cornerville standards. Sam said that he occasionally borrowed money from them, but never more than fifty cents at a time. Such loans he tried to repay at the earliest possible moment. There were four other members, with positions ranging from intermediate to the bottom, who nearly always had more money than Sam. He did not recall ever having borrowed from them. He said that the only time he had obtained a substantial sum from anyone around his corner was when he borrowed eleven dollars from a friend who was the *leader* of another corner-boy group.

The system is substantially the same for all the groups on which I have information. The leader spends more money on his followers than they on him. The farther down in the structure one looks, the fewer are the financial relations which tend to obligate the leader to a follower. This does not mean that the leader has more money than others or even that he necessarily spends more—though he must always be a free spender. It means that the financial relations must be explained in social terms. Unconsciously, and in some cases consciously, the leader refrains from putting himself under obligations to those with low status in the group.

Relations of rivalry or outright hostility with other groups are an important factor in promoting in-group solidarity, as has been well recognized. . . . Present-day corner gangs grew up in an atmosphere of street fighting against gangs of Irish or of fellow-Italians. While actual fights are now infrequent, the spirit of gang loyalty is maintained in part through athletic contests and political rivalries.

As the structures indicate, members have higher rates of interaction with men close to their own positions in their subgroups than with men who rank much higher or much lower or belong to a different subgroup. That is a significant fact for the explanation of group cohesion.

In the case of the Millers, Sam's best friends were Joe and Chichi. As his remarks have indicated, Sam realized that the solidarity of the Millers depended in the first instance upon the existence of friendly and cooperative relations between himself, Joe, and Chichi. A Cornerville friend, who was aware of the nature of my observations, commented in this manner:

> On any corner, you would find not only a leader but probably a couple of lieutenants. They could be leaders themselves, but they let the man lead

> them. You would say, they let him lead because they like the way he does things. Sure, but he leans upon them for his authority. . . . Many times you find fellows on a corner that stay in the background until some situation comes up, and then they will take over and call the shots. Things like that can change fast sometimes.

Such changes are the result not of an uprising of the bottom men but of a shift in the relations between men at the top of the structure. When a gang breaks into two parts, the explanation is to be found in a conflict between the leader and one who ranked close to him in the structure of the original gang.

The distinctive functions of the top men in promoting social cohesion are readily observable in the field. Frequently, in the absence of their leader the members of a gang are divided into a number of small groups. There is no common activity or general conversation. When the leader appears, the situation changes strikingly. The small units form into one large group. The conversation becomes general, and unified action frequently follows. The leader becomes the focal point in discussion. One observes a follower start to say something, pause when he notices that the leader is not listening, and begin again when he has the leader's attention. When the leader leaves the group, unity gives way to the divisions that existed before his appearance. To a certain extent the lieutenants can perform this unifying function; but their scope is more limited because they are more closely identified with one particular subgroup than is the leader.

The same Cornerville friend summed up the point in this way:

> If we leave the followers, they'll go find some other leader. They won't know what they're doing, but that's what they'll do, because by themselves they won't know what to do. They gather around the leader, and it is the leader that keeps them together.

The leader is the man who knows what to do. He is more resourceful than his followers. Past events have shown that his ideas were right. In this sense "right" simply means satisfactory to the members. He is the most independent in judgment. While his followers are undecided as to a course of action or upon the character of a newcomer, the leader makes up his mind. When he gives his word to one of "his boys," he keeps it. The followers look to him for advice and encouragement, and he receives more of the confidences of the members than any other man. Consequently, he knows more about what is going on in the group than anyone else. Whenever there is a quarrel among the boys, he will hear of it almost as soon as it happens. Each party to the quarrel may appeal to him to work out a solution; and, even when the men do not want to compose their differences, each one will take his side of the story to the leader at the first opportunity. A man's standing depends partly upon the leader's belief that he has been conducting himself as he should.

The leader is respected for his fair-mindedness. Whereas there may be hard feelings among some of the followers, the leader cannot bear a grudge against any man in the group. He has close friends (men who stand next to him in position), and he is indifferent to some of the members; but if he is to retain his reputation for impartiality, he cannot allow personal animus to override his judgment.

The leader need not be the best baseball player, bowler, or fighter, but he must have some skill in whatever pursuits are of particular interest to the group. It is natural for him to promote activities in which he excels and to discourage those in which he is not skillful; and, insofar as he is thus able to influence the group, his competent performance is a natural consequence of his position. At the same time his performance supports his position.

It is significant to note that the leader is better known and more respected outside of his group than is any of his followers. His social mobility is greater. One of the most important functions he performs is that of relating his group to other groups in the district. His reputation outside the group tends to support his standing within the group, and his position in the group supports his reputation among outsiders.

It should not be assumed from this discussion that the corner boys compete with one another for the purpose of gaining leadership. Leadership is a product of social interaction. The men who reach the top in informal groups are those who can perform skillfully the actions required by the situation. Most such skills are performed without long premeditation.

What the leader is has been discussed in terms of what he does. I doubt whether an analysis in terms of personality traits will add anything to such an explanation of behavior. One can find a great variety of personality traits among corner-boy leaders, just as one can among business or political leaders. Some are aggressive in social contacts, and others appear almost retiring. Some are talkative, and others have little to say. Few uniformities of this nature are to be found. On the other hand, there are marked uniformities to be observed in the functions performed by men who hold similar positions in society, and the study of them promises to provide the best clues for the understanding of social behavior.

THE GANGS AND THE WIDER COMMUNITY

For a community study, data upon five corner gangs are hardly more than a beginning. Two problems were involved in extending the research. First, I had to discover whether I could safely generalize my conclusions to apply them to all corner gangs in Cornerville. Second, I had to fit the corner gangs into the fabric of Cornerville society.

To accomplish the first end I solicited the aid of a number of corner-boy leaders, who made for me more or less systematic observations of their own groups and of groups about them. The generalizations, presented earlier, upon the functions of leaders, indicate why I found them the best sources of information upon their groups. This procedure could not be relied upon as a substitute for observation, for it is only through observation that the student can discover what his informants are talking about and understand their remarks in terms of group structure. Observation suggests a framework of significant behavior patterns and indicates subjects that are relevant for discussion with informants.

The student should realize that this procedure changes the attitude of the corner boy toward himself and his group. The quotations from Cornerville men presented here all show the effects of prior discussion with me. However, the effort of informants to make explicit statements upon unreflective behavior does not distort the factual picture as long as they are required to tell their stories in terms of observed interactions.

The most thorough study of this kind was made for me by Sam of the Millers upon his own group. The structure of the Millers was worked out by Sam over a period of months on the basis of such material as I have quoted. My function was to discuss Sam's observations with him, to point out gaps in his data, and to check them with some independent observations.

All the generalizations presented here have been checked against the experience and observations of four such informants. In this way I have been able to expand my study far beyond what I should have been able to cover alone.

Accomplishment of the second purpose—fitting corner gangs into the fabric of society—required study of the relations which linked group to group and the group to persons who held superior positions in Cornerville—politicians and racketeers, for example.

The observation that the leader is the person to relate his group to other people provides the most important lead for such a study. We see that the social behavior of groups pivots around the actions of certain men who hold strategic positions in them. This does not mean that the leader can make his followers do anything he desires. It does mean that he customarily leads the group activity and that outsiders, in order to influence the members, must deal with the group through him. This is to be observed particularly at the time of a political campaign when politicians seek to mobilize group support. Similar observations may be made in order to explain the position and influence of the racketeer in relation to corner-boy groups.

Brief reference to the Cornerville S. and A. study will indicate the nature of the results that may be obtained. Tony, the top man in the chart, was a prominent policy racketeer. The chart indicates that certain members were agents who turned their policy slips in to him. While

Tony belonged to the club, his interests were so widespread that he had little time to spend with the members. It was recognized that he held a higher status, that he was not a corner boy.

At the time of the formation of the club, Tony knew Dom, his agent, and recognized Dom's position among the lunchroom boys. He knew Carlo only casually and was not aware of his position as leader of the barbershop clique. In the course of a political campaign (November 1939) a conflict arose over the endorsement of a candidate for alderman. By playing off one clique against the other, Tony was able to secure the adoption of his policy, but Carlo opposed him vigorously and lost out in a close vote. Carlo's position was strengthened when his candidate defeated the man supported by Tony. Following the election, there was a marked change in Tony's actions. He began to attend every meeting and to spend more time with the members. For his purposes Carlo was the most important man in the club, and he made every effort to cement his social relations with Carlo and to place Carlo under obligations to him. During this period a basis for co-operation between the two men was established. When Tony turned his attention to other activities, he was able to deal with the club through Carlo as well as through Dom.

This story illustrates a method of study, not a set of conclusions. Through observing the interactions between Tony and Dom, Tony and Carlo, Dom and the members of his clique, and Carlo and the members of his clique, one can establish the position and influence of the racketeer in relation to this particular organization of corner boys. Other observations establish Tony's position in the racket organization, which extends throughout the district and far beyond it. They also point out Tony's relations with certain politicians. Only in the study of such specific situations can one arrive at reliable generalizations upon the positions and influence of men in the community.

CONCLUSION

The methods I have used call for precise and detailed observation of spatial positions and of the origination of action in pair and set events between members of informal groups. Such observations provide data by means of which one may chart structures of social relations and determine the basis of the structures—a system of mutual obligations growing out of the interactions of the members over a long period of time. Observations also point out the distinctive functions of the leader, who serves as chief representative of his group and director and coordinator of group activity. A knowledge of the structure and of the social processes carried on through it serves to explain the behavior of individual members in a manner which could not be accomplished if one considered the men as an unstructured aggregation.

Such an understanding of clique behavior seems a necessary first step in the development of knowledge of the nature of the larger social organization into which the cliques fit. Instead of seeking to place each clique member in relation to the total social organization, the investigator may concentrate his attention upon the actions of the leader, who relates his corner boys to other groups and to persons holding superior positions. By discovering these strategic points for social integration and by extending the network of social relations through them, the investigator can place a large number of the inhabitants of his community in their social positions.

This is a painstaking and time-consuming method. While it does not produce statistics which count all the inhabitants in terms of certain characteristics, it does provide the investigator with a close-up view of the social organization in action.

NOTES

1. *Measuring Human Relations: An Introduction to the Study of the Interaction of Individuals* ("Genetic Psychology Monographs" [Provincetown, Mass.: Journal Press, 1940]).
2. *Op. cit.*, p. 54. To terminate an action is to follow the initiative of another person.

Review Questions

1. How are various aspects of the groups studied by Whyte *similar to* and *different from* formal organizations?
2. According to Whyte, how do clique structures arise? How did his methods of research allow him to discover the answer to this question?
3. Explain Whyte's statement, "Leadership is a product of social interaction." Give examples from the groups he discussed as well as from your own experience.
4. Explain how providing aid to friends built up a network of obligations among the corner boys. Were they aware that they expected reciprocity from the friends they aided?

THE COLLEGE CLASSROOM: SOME OBSERVATIONS ON THE MEANINGS OF STUDENT PARTICIPATION

David A. Karp and William C. Yoels

A RECENT REPORT ON THE EMPLOYMENT OF SOCIOLOGISTS AND ANTHROPOLogists indicated that 97 percent of the sociologists in the United States were teaching either full-time or part-time in an institution of higher education (NIMH: 1969). While sociologists earn their "daily bread" by teaching, they earn their scholarly reputations by engaging in research studies of almost every conceivable kind of social setting except, it seems, that of the college classroom. The failure to explore the "routine grounds" of our everyday lives as teachers is testimony to the existence of the college classroom as part of what Alfred Schutz (1962) referred to as "the world as taken-for-granted."

• • •

Rarely have researchers attempted to consider the processes through which students and teachers formulate definitions of the classroom as a social setting. The problem of how students and teachers assign "meaning" to the classroom situation has been largely neglected in the various studies mentioned. Although writing about primary and secondary school classrooms, we would suggest that the following statement from Jackson's (1968:vii) *Life in Classrooms* holds true for college classrooms as well. He writes that:

> Classroom life . . . is too complex an affair to be viewed or talked about from any single perspective. Accordingly, as we try to grasp the meaning of what school is like for students and teachers, we must not hesitate to use all the ways of knowing at our disposal. This means we must read and look and listen and count things, and talk to people, and even muse introspectively.

The present study focuses on the meanings of student participation in the college classroom. Our examination of this problem will center on the way in which definitions of classrooms held by students and teachers relate to their actual behavior in the classroom.

SOURCE: David Karp & William C. Yoels: "The College Classroom: Some Observations on the Meanings of Student Participation." *Sociology and Social Research*, Vol. 60, No. 4, pp. 421–439. Reprinted by permission.

METHODS OF STUDY

In an attempt to investigate the issues mentioned above we initiated an exploratory study of classroom behavior in several classes of a private university located in a large city in the northeastern United States. Our familiarity with the literature on the "words-deeds" problem (Deutcher, 1973; Phillips, 1971) led us to employ a two-fold process of data collection—namely, systematic observation of classroom behavior in selected classes, accompanied by questionnaires administered at the end of the semester in the classes under observation. None of the previously reviewed studies employed this type of research strategy, and it was hoped that such an approach would yield insights not attainable from reliance on a single data gathering procedure. In addition to the foregoing procedures we also drew upon our numerous years of experience as both students and teachers in college classrooms.

Ten classes were selected for observation. The observers were undergraduate and graduate sociology students who were doing the research as part of a Readings and Research arrangement. The classes were not randomly selected but were chosen in terms of observers' time schedules and the possibility of their observing behavior in the classrooms on a regular basis throughout the semester. The observed classes were located in the following departments: sociology, philosophy, English, psychology, economics, theology. While the classes are certainly not a representative sample of all classes taught in this university, questionnaire responses from an additional sample of students in classes selected at random at the end of the semester indicate a remarkable similarity to the questionnaire responses of the students in the ten classes under observation.[1]

At the end of the semester a questionnaire was distributed in class to the students in the ten classes which had been under prior observation. A shortened version of this questionnaire was also given to the teachers of these classes. Questionnaire items centered on factors deemed important in influencing students' decisions on whether to talk or not in class.[2]

FINDINGS

Table 1 presents a summary of selected observational items by class size. Classes with less than 40 students have a higher average number of interactions per session than those with more than 40 students. More important, however, is the fact that in both categories of class size the *average number* of students participating is almost identical. Moreover, a handful of students account for more than 50 percent of the total interactions in both under 40 and over 40 classes. In classes with less

Table 1. Summary Table by Class Size of Selected Observational Items(a)

CLASS SIZE	AVERAGE NUMBER OF INTERACTIONS PER CLASS	AVERAGE NUMBER OF STUDENTS PARTICIPATING	AVERAGE % OF STUDENTS PRESENT PARTICIPATING	AVERAGE NUMBER OF STUDENTS MAKING TWO OR MORE COMMENTS	% OF THOSE PRESENT MAKING TWO OR MORE COMMENTS	% OF TOTAL INTERACTIONS ACCOUNTED FOR BY THOSE MAKING TWO OR MORE COMMENTS
Under 40	25.96	9.83	47.84	4.64	25.06	75.61
40 +	19.40	9.88	23.98	2.70	5.74	51.00

(a) THE SMALLEST CLASS CONTAINED 12 STUDENTS; THE LARGEST CLASS CONTAINED 65 STUDENTS.

than 40 students, between 4 and 5 students account for 75 percent of the total interactions per session; in classes of more than 40 students, between 2 and 3 students account for 51 percent of the total interactions per session. From the limited data presented here it would appear that class size has relatively little effect on the average number of students participating in class. Such a finding is particularly interesting in view of the fact, as indicated in Table 5, that more than 65 percent of both male and female students indicated that the large size of the class was an important factor in why students would choose not to talk in class.

Data also indicate that students have a conception of classroom participation as being concentrated in the hands of a few students. Ninety-three percent of the males and 94 percent of the females strongly agreed or agreed with the item "In most of my classes there are a small number of students who do most of the talking." Such a conception is in congruence with the observations of actual classroom behavior noted in Table 1.

The students' conception that a handful of students do most of the talking is also coupled with annoyance on the part of many students at those who "talk too much." Responses to a questionnaire item indicated that 62 percent of the males and 61 percent of the females strongly agreed or agreed with the item "I sometimes find myself getting annoyed with students who talk too much in class."

Students also believe it possible to make a decision very early in the semester as to whether professors really want class discussion. Ninety-four percent of the males and 96 percent of the females strongly agreed or agreed with the item "students can tell pretty quickly whether a professor really wants discussion in his/her class."

Students were also asked whether the teacher's sex is likely to influence their participation in class. The overwhelming response of both male and female students to this question is that the professor's sex makes *no difference* in their likelihood of participating in class. Over 93 percent of the males and 91 percent of the female students answered "No Difference" to this question. In effect, then, both male and female students tend to define the classroom as a situation in which the sexual component of the professor's identity is completely irrelevant.

The contrast between what students say about the previous item and what they actually do in the classroom is highlighted in Table 2. The data indicate a very clearcut relationship between the sex of the teacher and the likelihood of male or female participation in class. In male taught classes men account for 75.4 percent of the interactions, three times the percentage for women—24.6 percent. In female taught classes, men still account for more of the interactions than women—57.8 percent to 42.2 percent—but the percentage of female participation increases almost 75 percent from 24.7 percent in male taught classes to 42.2 percent in female taught classes. Female student participation is maximized under the influence of female professors.

Since the participation of men and women may be a function of their proportion in class, the right-hand side of Table 2 presents data on the composition of the male and female taught classes. In both male and female taught classes the percentage of male and female students is almost equal, therefore eliminating the possibility that the rate of male-female participation is a function of male student overrepresentation in these classes.

Table 3 presents observational data regarding what the students were responding to when they participated in classroom interactions. There was very little student-to-student interaction occurring in the ten classes under observation. Ten percent of the total number of classroom interactions involved cases in which students responded to the questions or comments of other students. Table 3 indicates quite dramatically that the actions of the teacher are indeed most crucial in promoting class-

Table 2. Observed Classroom Interaction by Sex of Student and Sex of Teacher

SEX OF TEACHER	% OF OBSERVED INTERACTIONS				% OF STUDENTS IN CLASSES(a)			
	Male	*Female*	*Total*	*N*	*Male*	*Female*	*Total*	*N*
Male	75.4	24.6	100.0	565	52.0	48.0	100.0	152
Female	57.8	42.2	100.0	774	51.5	48.5	100.0	163
Total	65.3	34.7	100.0	1339	51.7	48.3	100.0	315

Note: $X^2 = 44.05$, df = 1, $p < .001$

(a) REFERS TO THE NUMBER OF STUDENTS ANSWERING THE QUESTIONNAIRE IN CLASS.

Table 3. Source of Interaction by Sex of Student

	SOURCE OF "STIMULUS"								
Sex of Student	Teacher Question: Direct	Teacher Question: Indirect	Teacher Comment	Student Question	Student Comment	Source Not Specified	Total	N
Male	10.0%	46.5%	31.9%	3.6%	6.3%	1.5%	99.8%	840
Female	9.8%	45.9%	31.3%	1.6%	8.9%	2.2%	99.7%	437
Total	9.9%	46.3%	31.7%	2.9%	7.2%	1.8%	99.8%	1,277(a)

(a) 62 CASES WERE EXCLUDED BECAUSE OF INSUFFICIENT INFORMATION.

room interaction. Questions posed by the teacher and teacher comments accounted for 88 percent of the classroom interactions. Especially significant is the fact that very few cases occur in which the teacher directly calls on a particular student to answer a question (category labelled "Direct" under TQ). The percentage for the Direct Question category is 9.9 percent, compared to 46.3 percent for the Indirect Question in which the teacher poses a question to the class in general. Indeed, it might be argued that the current norm in college classrooms is for both students and teachers to avoid any type of direct *personal confrontation* with one another. It might be that "amicability" in the classroom is part of the larger process, described by Riesman (1950) in *The Lonely Crowd*, in which the desire to "get ahead" is subordinated to the desire to "get along." In the college classroom "getting along" means students and teachers avoiding any situation that might be potentially embarrassing to one or the other.

Table 4 indicates that in male-taught classes male students are more likely than female students to be directly questioned by the instructor (7.1 percent to 3.1 percent). In addition, men are twice as likely as female students (30.3 percent to 15.0 percent) to respond to a comment made by a male teacher. In female-taught classes the percentage of male and female responses are almost identical in each category under observation. Of interest here is the fact that female teachers are equally likely to directly question male and female students (12.8 percent versus 12.5 percent).

Table 5 presents the student responses to a series of items concerning why students would choose not to talk in class. The items are ranked in terms of the percentage of students who indicated that the particular item was important in keeping them from talking. As the rankings indicate, male and female students are virtually identical in their conceptions of what factors inhibit or promote their classroom participation. The items accorded the most importance—not doing the assigned reading, ignorance of the subject matter, etc.—are in the highest ranks.

Table 4. Source of Interaction by Sex of Student, Controlling for Sex of Teacher

	SOURCE OF "STIMULUS"							
Sex of Student	*Teacher Question Direct*	*Teacher Question Indirect*	*Teacher Comment*	*Student Question*	*Student Comment*	*Source Not Specified*	*Total*	*N*
			Male-Taught Classes					
Male	7.1%	55.3%	30.3%	1.9%	2.6%	2.6%	99.8%	419
Female	3.1%	67.4%	15.0%	3.9%	3.9%	6.3%	99.6%	126
Total	6.2%	58.1%	26.7%	2.3%	2.9%	3.4%	99.6%	545
			Female-Taught Classes					
Male	12.8%	37.7%	33.4%	5.4%	9.9%	.4%	99.6%	421
Female	12.5%	37.2%	37.9%	.6%	10.9%	.6%	99.7%	311
Total	12.7%	37.5%	35.3%	3.4%	10.3%	.5%	99.7%	732

The lowest ranking items are those dealing with students and teachers not respecting the student's point of view, the grade being negatively affected by classroom participation, etc.

In comparing the teachers' rankings of these same items with that of the students, it appears that, with one important exception, the rankings are very similar. About 42 percent of both male and female students ranked as important the item concerning the possibility that other students would find them unintelligent. Eighty percent of the teachers, on the other hand, indicated that this was likely an important factor in keeping students from talking.

DISCUSSION

Although we did not begin this study with any explicit hypotheses to be tested, we did begin with some general guiding questions. Most comprehensive among these, and of necessary importance from a symbolic interactionist perspective, was the question, "What is a college classroom?" We wanted to know how both students and teachers were defining the social setting, and how these definitions manifested themselves in the activity that goes on in the college classrooms. More specifically, we wanted to understand what it was about the definition of the situation held by students and teachers that led to, in most instances, rather little classroom interaction.

What knowledge, we might now ask, do students have of college classrooms that makes the decision not to talk a "realistic" decision?

There would seem to be two factors of considerable importance as indicated by our data.

First, students believe that they can tell very early in the semester whether or not a professor really wants class discussion. Students are also well aware that there exists in college classrooms a rather distinctive "consolidation of responsibility." In any classroom there seems almost inevitably to be a small group of students who can be counted on to respond to questions asked by the professor or to generally have comments on virtually any issue raised in class. Our observational data (Table 1) indicated that on the average a very small number of students are responsible for the majority of all talk that occurs in class on any given day. The fact that this "consolidation of responsibility" looms large in students' consciousness is indicated by the fact, reported earlier, that more than 90 percent of the students strongly agreed or agreed with the statement "In most of my classes there are a small number of students who do most of the talking."

Once the group of "talkers" gets established and identified in a college classroom the remaining students develop a strong expectation that these "talkers" can be relied upon to answer questions and make comments. In fact, we have often noticed in our own classes that when a question is asked or an issue raised the "silent" students will even begin to orient their bodies towards and look at this coterie of talkers with the expectation, presumably, that they will shortly be speaking.

Our concept of the "consolidation of responsibility" is a modification of the idea put forth by Latane and Darley (1970) in *The Unresponsive Bystander*. In this volume Latane and Darley developed the concept of "the diffusion of responsibility" to explain why strangers are often reluctant to "get involved" in activities where they assist other strangers who may need help. They argue that the delegation of responsibility in such situations is quite unclear and, as a result, responsibility tends to get assigned to no one in particular—the end result being that no assistance at all is forthcoming. In the case of the classroom interaction, however, we are dealing with a situation in which the responsibility for talking gets assigned to a few who can be relied upon to carry the "verbal load"—thus the *consolidation of responsibility*. As a result, the majority of students play a relatively passive role in the classroom and see themselves as recorders of the teacher's information. This expectation is mutually supported by the professor's reluctance to directly call on *specific* students, as indicated in Table 3.

While students expect that only a few students will do most of the talking, and while these talkers are relied upon to respond in class, the situation is a bit more complicated than we have indicated to this point. It would appear that while these talkers are "doing their job" by carrying the discussion for the class as a whole, there is still a strong feeling on the part of many students that they ought not to talk *too much*.

Table 5. Percentage of Students Who Indicated that an Item Was an Important Factor in Why Students Would Choose Not to Talk in Class, by Sex of Student (in Rank Order)

MALE			FEMALE		
Rank	*Item*	*%*	*Rank*	*Item*	*%*
1.	I had not done the assigned reading	80.9	1.	The feeling that I don't know enough about the subject matter	84.8
2.	The feeling that I don't know enough about the subject matter	79.6	2.	I had not done the assigned reading	76.3
3.	The large size of the class	70.4	3.	The feeling that my ideas are not well enough formulated	71.1
4.	The feeling that my ideas are not well enough formulated	69.8	4.	The large size of the class	68.9
5.	The course simply isn't meaningful to me	67.3	5.	The course simply isn't meaningful to me	65.1
6.	The chance that I would appear unintelligent in the eyes of the teacher	43.2	6.	The chance that I would appear unintelligent in the eyes of other students	45.4
7.	The chance that I would appear unintelligent in the eyes of other students	42.9	7.	The chance that I would appear unintelligent in the eyes of the teacher	41.4
8.	The small size of the class	31.0	8.	The small size of the class	33.6
9.	The possibility that my comments might negatively affect my grade	29.6	9.	The possibility that my comments might negatively affect my grade	24.3
10.	The possibility that other students in the class would not respect my point of view	16.7	10.	The possibility that the teacher would not respect my point of view	21.1
11.	The possibility that the teacher would not respect my point of view	12.3	11.	The possibility that other students in the class would not respect my point of view	12.5

As noted earlier, more than 60 percent of the students responding to our questionnaire expressed annoyance with students who "talk too much in class." This is interesting to the extent that even those who talk very regularly in class still account for a very small percentage of total class time. While we have no systematic data on time spent talking in class, the comments of the observers indicate that generally a total of less than five minutes of class time (in a fifty-minute period) is accounted for by student talk in class.

A fine balance must be maintained in college classes. Some students are expected to do most of the talking, thus relieving the remainder of the students from the burdens of having to talk in class. At the same time, these talkers must not be "rate-busters." We are suggesting here that students see "intellectual work" in much the same way that factory workers define "piecework." Talking too much in class, or what might be called "linguistic rate-busting," upsets the normative arrangement of the classroom and, in the students' eyes, increases the probability of raising the professor's expectations vis-á-vis the participation of other students. It may be said, then, that a type of "restriction of verbal output" norm operates in college classrooms, in which those who engage in linguistic rate-busting or exhibit "overinvolvement" in the classroom get defined by other students as "brown-noses" and "apostates" from the student "team." Other students often indicate their annoyance with these "rate-busters" by smiling wryly at their efforts, audibly sighing, rattling their notebooks and, on occasion, openly snickering.

A second factor that insures in students' minds that it will be safe to refrain from talking is their knowledge that only in rare instances will they be directly called upon by teachers in a college classroom. Our data (Table 3) indicate that of all the interactions occurring in the classes under observation only about 10 percent were due to teachers calling directly upon a specific student. The unwillingness of teachers to call upon students would seem to stem from teachers' beliefs that the classroom situation is fraught with anxiety for students. It is important to note that teachers, unlike students themselves, viewed the possibility that "students might appear unintelligent in the eyes of other students" as a very important factor in keeping students from talking (Table 6). Unwilling to exacerbate the sense of risk which teachers believe is a part of student consciousness, they refrain from directly calling upon specific students.

The direct result of these two factors is that students feel no obligation or particular necessity for keeping up with reading assignments so as to be able to participate in class. Such a choice is made easier still by the fact that college students are generally tested infrequently. Unlike high school, where homework is the teacher's "daily insurance" that students are prepared for classroom participation, college is a situation in which the student feels quite safe in coming to class without having

Table 6. Percentage of Teachers Who Indicated that an Item Was an Important Factor in Why Students Would Choose Not to Talk in Class (in Rank Order)

RANK	ITEM	%
1.5	The large size of the class	80
1.5	The chance that I would appear unintelligent in the eyes of other students	80
4.0	The feeling that I don't know enough about the subject matter	70
4.0	The feeling that my ideas are not well enough formulated	70
4.0	The possibility that my comments might negatively affect my grade	70
6.0	The course simply isn't meaningful to me	50
7.5	I had not done the assigned reading	40
7.5	The chance that I would appear unintelligent in the eyes of the teacher	40
9.5	The possibility that the teacher would not respect my point of view	30
9.5	The possibility that other students in the class would not respect my point of view	30
11.5	The small size of the class	10

done the assigned reading and, not having done it, safe in the secure knowledge that one won't be called upon.[3] It is understandable, then, why such items as "not having done the assigned reading" and "the feeling that one does not know enough about the subject matter" would rank so high (Table 5) in students' minds as factors keeping them from talking in class.

In sum, we have isolated two factors relative to the way that classrooms actually operate that make it "practically" possible for students not to talk in class. These factors make it possible for the student to pragmatically abide by an early decision to be silent in class. We must now broach the somewhat more complicated question: what are the elements of students' definitions of the college classroom situation that prompt them to be silent in class? To answer this question we must examine how students perceive the teacher as well as their conceptions of what constitutes "intellectual work."

By the time that students have finished high school they have been imbued with the enormously strong belief that teachers are "experts" who possess the "truth." They have adopted, as Freire (1970) has noted, a "banking" model of education. The teacher represents the bank, the huge "fund" of "true" knowledge. As a student it is one's job to make weekly "withdrawals" from the fund, never any "deposits." His teachers, one is led to believe, and often led to believe it by the teachers themselves, are possessors of the truth. Teachers are in the classroom to *teach*, not to *learn*.

If the above contains anything like a reasonable description of the way that students are socialized in secondary school, we should not find it strange or shocking that our students find our requests for criticism of ideas a bit alien. College students still cling to the idea that they are knowledge seekers and that faculty members are knowledge dispensers. Their view of intellectual work leaves little room for the notion that ideas themselves are open to negotiation. It is simply not part of their view of the classroom that ideas are generated out of dialogue, out of persons questioning and taking issue with one another, out of persons being *critical* of each other.

It comes as something of a shock to many of our students when we are willing to give them, at best, a "B" on a paper or exam that is "technically" proficient. When they inquire about their grade (and they do this rarely, believing strongly that our judgment is unquestionable), they want to know what they did "wrong." Intellectual work is for them dichotomous. It is either good or bad, correct or incorrect. They are genuinely surprised when we tell them that nothing is wrong, that they simply have not been critical enough and have not shown enough reflection on the ideas. Some even see such an evaluation as unfair. They claim a kind of incompetence at criticism. They often claim that it would be illegitimate for them to disagree with an author.

Students in class respond as uncritically to the thoughts of their professors as they do to the thoughts of those whom they read. Given this general attitude toward intellectual work, based in large part on students' socialization, and hence their definition of what should go on in classrooms, the notion of using the classroom as a place for generating ideas is a foreign one.

Part of students' conceptions of what they can and ought to do in classrooms is, then, a function of their understanding of how ideas are to be communicated. Students have expressed the idea that if they are to speak in class they ought to be able to articulate their point logically, systematically, and above all completely. The importance of this factor in keeping students from talking is borne out by the very high ranking given to the item (Table 5) "the feeling that my ideas are not well enough formulated."

In their view, if their ideas have not been fully formulated in advance, then the idea is not worth relating. They are simply unwilling to talk "off the top of their heads." They feel, particularly in an academic setting such as the college classroom, that there is a high premium placed on being articulate. This feeling is to a large degree prompted by the relative articulateness of the teacher. Students do not, it seems, take into account the fact that the teacher's coherent presentation is typically a function of the time spent preparing his/her ideas. The relative preparedness of the teacher leads to something of paradox vis-á-vis classroom discussion.

We have had students tell us that one of the reasons they find it difficult to respond in class involves the professor's preparedness; that is, students have told us that because the professor's ideas as presented in lectures are (in their view) so well formulated they could not add anything to those ideas. Herein lies something of a paradox. One might suggest that, to some degree at least, the better prepared a professor is for his/her class, the less likely are students to respond to the elements of his/her lecture.

We have both found that some of our liveliest classes have centered around those occasions when we have talked about research presently in progress. When it is clear to the student that we are ourselves struggling with a particular problem, that we cannot fully make sense of a phenomenon, the greater is the class participation. In most classroom instances, students read the teacher as the "expert,"[4] and once having cast the professor into that role it becomes extremely difficult for students to take issue with or amend his/her ideas.

It must also be noted that students' perceptions about their incapacity to be critical of their own and others' ideas leads to an important source of misunderstanding between college students and their teachers. In an open-ended question we asked students what characteristics they thought made for an "ideal" teacher. An impressionistic reading of these responses indicated that students were overwhelmingly uniform in their answers. They consensually found it important that a teacher "not put them down" and that a teacher "not flaunt his/her superior knowledge." In this regard the college classroom is a setting pregnant with possibilities for mutual misunderstanding. Teachers are working under one set of assumptions about "intellectual work" while students proceed under another. Our experiences as college teachers lead us to believe that teachers tend to value *critical* responses by students and tend to respond critically themselves to the comments and questions of college students. Students tend to perceive these critical comments as in some way an assault on their "selves" and find it difficult to separate a critique of their thoughts from a critique of themselves. Teachers are for the most part unaware of the way in which students interpret their comments.

The result is that when college teachers begin to critically question a student's statement, trying to get the student to be more critical and analytical about his/her assertions, this gets interpreted by students as a "put-down." The overall result is the beginning of a "vicious circle" of sorts. The more that teachers try to instill in students a critical attitude toward one's own ideas, the more students come to see faculty members as condescending, and the greater still becomes their reluctance to make known their "ill formulated" ideas in class. Like any other social situation where persons are defining the situation differently, there is bound to develop a host of interactional misunderstandings.

Before concluding this section, let us turn to a discussion of the differences in classroom participation rates of male versus female students. Given the fact that men and women students responded quite similarly to the *questionnaire items* reported here, much of our previous discussion holds for both male and female students. There are some important differences, however, in their *actual behavior* in the college classroom (as revealed by our observational data) that ought to be considered. Foremost among these differences is the fact that the sex of the teacher affects the likelihood of whether male or female teachers in these classes are "giving off expressions" that are being interpreted very differently by male and female students. Male students play a more active role in all observed classes regardless of the teacher's sex, but with female instructors the percentage of female participation sharply increases. Also of interest, as indicated in Table 4, is the fact that the male instructors are more likely to directly call on male students than on female students (7.1 percent to 3.1 percent), whereas female instructors are just as likely to call on female students as on male students (12.5 percent to 12.8 percent). Possibly female students in female-taught classes interpret the instructor's responses as being more egalitarian than those of male professors and thus more sympathetic to the views of female students. With the growing [awareness] of women faculty and students [of women's issues] it may not be unreasonable to assume that female instructors are more sensitive to the problems of female students both inside and outside the college classroom.

With the small percentage of women faculty currently teaching in American universities it may well be that the college classroom is still defined by both male and female students as a setting "naturally" dominated by men. The presence of female professors, however, as our limited data suggest, may bring about some changes in these definitions of "natural" classroom behavior.

IMPLICATIONS

For the reasons suggested in the last few pages, it may be argued that most students opt for noninvolvement in their college classroom. This being the case, and because organizational features of the college classroom allow for noninvolvement (the consolidation of responsibility, the unwillingness of professors to directly call on specific students, the infrequency of testing), the situation allows for a low commitment on the part of students. The college classroom, then, rather than being a situation where persons must be deeply involved, more closely approximates a situation of "anonymity" where persons' obligations are few.

We can now perceive more clearly the source of the dilemma for college instructors who wish to have extensive classroom dialogues with students. To use the terminology generated by Goffman (1963) in *Behavior in Public Places,* we can suggest that instructors are treating the classroom as an instance of "focused" interaction while students define the classroom more as an "unfocused" gathering. Focused gatherings are those where persons come into one another's audial and visual presence and see it as their obligation to interact. These are to be distinguished from unfocused gatherings where persons are also in a face-to-face situation but either feel that they are not privileged to interact or have no obligation to do so.[5]

It may very well be that students more correctly "read" how professors interpret the situation than vice versa.[6] Knowing that the teacher expects involvement, and having made the decision not to be deeply involved, students reach a compromise. Aware that it would be an impropriety to be on a total "away" from the social situation, students engage in what might be called "civil *attention.*" They must *appear* committed enough to not alienate the teacher without at the same time showing so much involvement that the situation becomes risky for them. Students must carefully create a show of interest while maintaining noninvolvement. A show of too great interest might find them more deeply committed to the encounter than they wish to be.

So, students are willing to attend class regularly, and they do not hold private conversations while the teacher is talking; they nod their heads intermittently, and maintain enough attention to laugh at the appropriate junctures during a lecture, and so on. Students have become very adept at maintaining the social situation without becoming too involved in it. Teachers interpret these "shows" of attention as indicative of a real involvement (the students' performances have proved highly successful) and are, therefore, at a loss to explain why their involvement is not even greater—why they don't talk very much in class.

NOTES

1. Some relevant demographic characteristics of the students in the ten classes under observation are as follows: sex: males—52 percent, females—48 percent; year in college: freshmen and sophomores—60 percent, juniors and seniors—40 percent; father's occupation: proprietor—7 percent, management or executive—21 percent, professional—34 percent, clerical and sales—15 percent, skilled worker—16 percent, unskilled worker—7 percent; religious affiliation: Catholic—79 percent, Protestant—7 percent, Other—14 percent. In comparing the students in the observed classes to those students in unobserved classes which were selected at random at the end of the semester, the following differences should be noted: the observed classes contain more women (48 percent)

than the unobserved classes (33 percent); there were twice as many freshmen in the observed classes (31 percent) than in the unobserved classes (14 percent); there were twice as many students whose fathers were in clerical and sales occupations in the observed classes (15 percent) than in the unobserved classes (8 percent).

The questionnaire responses of the students in the unobserved classes are not reported here since these were selected only to check on the representativeness of the students in the original ten classes under observation.

2. Spatial limitations preclude a full treatment of the methodology and findings. More complete details are available from the authors.

3. We have no "hard" data concerning student failure to do the assigned reading other than our own observations of countless instances where we posed questions that went unanswered, when the slightest familiarity with the material would have been sufficient to answer them. We have also employed "pop" quizzes and the student performance on these tests indicated a woefully inadequate acquaintance with the readings assigned for that session. The reader may evaluate our claim by reflecting upon his/her own experience in the college classroom.

4. This attribution of power and authority to the teacher may be particularly exaggerated in the present study due to its setting in a Catholic university with a large number of students entering from Catholic high schools. Whether college students with different religious and socioeconomic characteristics attribute similar degrees of power and authority to professors is a subject worthy of future comparative empirical investigation.

5. If we think of communication patterns in college classrooms as ranging along a continuum from open-discussion formats to lecture arrangements, the classes studied here all fall toward the traditional lecture end of the continuum. Thus, generalizations to other formats, such as the open discussion ones, may not be warranted by the present data.

6. Of interest here is the recent study by Thomas *et al.* (1972) in which support was found for the "theoretical proposition that role-taking ability varies inversely with the degree of power ascribed to social positions" (1972:612).

REFERENCES

Deutscher, I.
1973 *What We Say/What We Do.* Glenview, Ill: Scott, Foresman and Company.

Freire, P.
1970 *Pedagogy of the Oppressed.* New York: Seabury Press.

Goffman, E.
1963 *Behavior in Public Places.* New York: Free Press.

Jackson, P.
1968 *Life in Classrooms.* New York: Holt, Rinehart and Winston.

Latane, B. and J. Darley
1970 *The Unresponsive Bystander: Why Doesn't He Help?* New York: Appleton-Century-Crofts.

National Institute of Mental Health
1969 *Sociologists and Anthropologists: Supply and Demand in Educational Institutions and Other Settings.* Chevy Chase, Md: U.S. Government Printing Office.

Phillips, D.
1971 *Knowledge From What?* Chicago: Rand McNally and Co.

Riesman, D.
1950 *The Lonely Crowd.* New Haven: Yale University Press.

Schutz, A.
1962 *Collected Papers: I. The Problem of Social Reality.* Edited by Maurice Natanson, The Hague: Martinus Nijhoff.

Thomas, D. L., D. D. Franks, and J.M. Calonico
1972 "Role-Taking and Power in Social Psychology," *American Sociological Review* 37:605–614.

Review Questions

1. What is Karp and Yoels's "banking" model of education? What factors cause students to adopt this model? What are some sociological consequences of the model?
2. Summarize Karp and Yoels's findings regarding the number of students who participate in class and the frequency of participation. What factors affected the rate of participation and what factors didn't?
3. What differences exist in the expectations of students and teachers for their own role and for the reciprocal role?
4. What were students' attitudes toward those who participated in class? Why is it ironic that these attitudes were held? Incorporate the concept of "consolidation of responsibility" in your answer.
5. How did teachers and students differ in terms of why they thought students didn't participate in class?

GROWING OLD BETWEEN WALLS

Andrea Fontana

I HAD TAKEN A SUMMER JOB AT THE [SUNNY HILL] CONVALESCENT CENTER AS a janitor (actually, housekeeper was the definition given to my job) with the intention of studying the setting, and coming back later as a researcher, which I did the following summer. This [article] is based on the data gathered in these periods.

Having worked at the center proved very helpful to my research in three ways. First, I was part of the staff, thus being able to partake in "backstage" interaction.[1] By this I mean that I took part in "gripe sessions"; I listened to the aides' accounts, not in an official form or through formal work relations, but relaxedly over a cup of coffee, from one "low-rank" employee to another. In this fashion I learned how Joe did not have a bowel movement in two days, why Bill was so confused after the new medication, or why that "old bitch" down the hall wouldn't eat unless you pinched her nose closed; things one would not find in records or would not be told to an "outsider." This gave me an understanding of how the aides felt and allowed me to sit right in with them during breaks or to walk around with them while they worked in the center.

Second, I was able to spend time with the patients while cleaning their rooms, and I came to know some of them well. While this does not matter with some patients, who would talk to anybody willing to listen, it is important with others, who become suspicious and taciturn.

Third, I viewed the patients as a staff member, thus coming to see the patients in terms of my job. That summer I had a lot of patients classified:

> This one spits on the floor all the time; I'll have to give him a butt can. That one throws his food all over the floor; it'll be hard to mop. Old Anne always had a puddle of urine under her wheelchair. Sarah will walk away with the mop and the bucket if I don't watch her; Dan will talk my leg off so I'll skip his room today.[2]

I came to see the patients as "work objects" rather than as human beings. But I also slowly became aware of other important concerns which

SOURCE: Andrea Fontana: Excerpted from "The Last Frontier," *Sage Library of Social Research*, Vol. 4, (Sage Publications, 1977), pp. 143–145, 147–167. Reprinted with permission of Sage Publications.

made me realize the meaning of growing old between the walls of the convalescent center for the patients. This [article] is not an ethnography of the operations of a convalescent center;[3] it is not a collection of survey data on convalescent centers;[4] it is not a critical indictment of convalescent centers;[5] this [article] intends to explore what happens to the meaning of the "golden years," to the "consummatory period of life" for that handful of elderly[6] who come to "convalesce" in the waning years of their lives.

• • •

THE STAGE

The proscenium upon which this drama of life is played serves an important function as the setting for the interaction between the staff and the patients. Thus, before being introduced to the actors, as the curtain pulls back, the reader will be presented with a vision of the center itself. The brochure advertising the center reads:

> At the Sunny Hill Convalescent Center the guest wants for nothing... screened sunbathing and patio areas, television, telephone facilities, planned recreational activities and beautiful six-acre site are at the disposal of the guests... especially noted for the delicious food prepared in the spotless, modern kitchen.

However, as one looks closely around the center, the picture which emerges is quite different. The convalescent center is located in the middle of the small town of Verde, which is about twenty miles away from the nearest city. Although centrally located, the center is isolated from the town because it is situated atop a steep hill, which is accessible only by a road leading to the center; no other building is located on the hill.

The center comprises two wards, situated one below the other on the slope of the hill. The lower ward is a long one-story construction, while the upper one is a two-story building; both appear fairly new from the outside. The "six-acre" site is indeed there, but the "sunbathing and patio areas" are small and enclosed by a high chain-linked fence.

The inside is almost identical in both wards. It consists of a long corridor running the length of the slightly V-shaped buildings. Rooms with two beds in each are located at both sides of the corridor, with adjoining toilets between two rooms; the same toilet is at times shared by two men in one room and by two women in the next. Both wards have a large recreational lounge, with a view overlooking the town through a large, dark blue-tinted picture window. The recreation lounge is furnished with sofas, armchairs, chairs, and a television set.

Both wards have a kitchen right across from the recreation room. The upstairs kitchen is used only for warming up food, since all the cooking is done in the downstairs kitchen. Small dining rooms are adjacent to the kitchens. The kitchens contain some old, greasy-looking gas stoves, a large sink, a hot-water sterilizing unit (for dishes), refrigerators, and other assorted equipment. Both wards have a nursing station, which is a smallish place located behind a long counter. At the end of each corridor is a large bathroom containing a tub and a shower in which the aides wash the patients (four bathrooms in all). The lower ward has a small waiting hall for incoming visitors. This room can be separated from the rest of the ward by a heavily blue-tinted glass sliding door.

The only telephones available are in the offices and nursing station and are to be used only by the staff on official business. I only witnessed a couple of "emergency" personal calls by employees and none whatsoever by patients. All doors are locked at all times, and the staff are forever unlocking and locking doors and closets in their daily rounds. A couple of times the outside door was accidentally left unlocked, and a patient managed to "escape" but was soon found wandering in downtown Verde. One time I saw Wilma, a sixty-year-old ex-ballerina (she had a tracheotomy operation so she cannot speak and has a small hole at the base of her neck), gingerly vault over the high chain fence, and I had to unlock the gate and guide her back inside. One final point: One of my duties was to wash breakfast dishes in the "spotless kitchen," and the only spotless thing about the kitchen were my hands after I had summarily rinsed off a pile of muck-covered plates.

THE ACTORS

Having described the setting, it is time to introduce the cast. The staff consists of an administrator, who manages the facility, a bookkeeper, two janitors, a laundry person, the kitchen staff (a cook, two second-cooks, and part-time helpers), and the nursing staff.

The director of nurses is a registered nurse who is in charge of another nurse and the aides. The other nurse is a licensed vocational nurse managing the lower ward when the registered nurse is in the upper one, which is most of the time. The remainder of the staff is composed of nurse's aides.

The aides are either white women from nearby towns or Indian women from the reservation three miles away. The turnover is great due to the harshness of the job, the extremely low pay, and the nature of the place. I witnessed quite a few cases of aides who left aghast after their first day and never came back. Actually, that almost happened to me, as I was not yet trained in the arts of doing field research while cleaning toilets. There are two kinds of aides: the old "battle axes" who have seen it all, have been there forever, and are not shaken by anything that happens; the others are much younger women, usually fresh out of high school, often on their first job, who live in the town of Verde, where no other jobs are available, or are just filling a gap while waiting for a better job to materialize.

The other people on the payroll as staff members do not work in the center but make periodic visits. There are three doctors, each caring for a certain number of patients, who come by to visit the patients every other week. . . . There are others: a hairdresser, who comes over from the reservation once a week; a social worker, who comes every other week; a handyman, who is on call; and a dietician, who is consulted by telephone.

The rest of the cast is made up of the patients. The patients are not identified in any visible way and are not divided in the wards in any fashion. The only rule is to have two individuals of the same sex in a room, but if one is senile and incontinent and the other is not, it is of no concern to the staff; contingencies such as availability of rooms are much more pressing. Usually the center is filled to capacity; even the room supposed to be used as an emergency room has a patient in it, an old blind wrestler, who must at one time have been a giant, but now has stumps where legs used to be and has lost most of his cognitive ability on various rings across the country years ago.

Not being able to identify the patients at sight[7] was a problem for me, but it was not a problem for the staff, who classified the patients in terms of physical attributes related to their daily work routine. There are the "up and about," those patients who can walk and get in and out of bed by themselves, walk to the dining room for meals, go to the toilet, etc. The others are called "in chair," meaning that they are confined to a wheelchair and that they must be helped in and out of bed; they need containers to urinate in while sitting in their chair, etc. Another classification is that of "feeders" and "nonfeeders." "Nonfeeders" are those patients (whether "in chair" or "up and about") who are capable of eating in the dining room by themselves, whereas "feeders" need to be hand-fed by an aide. With this system of classification, the nurses and aides can categorize patients in terms of "work time." An "up-and-about nonfeeder" will require little of their time, while an "in-chair feeder" will take a lot more time: he will have to be fed, have his diapers changed, and his bed sores medicated. Most "in-chair" patients spend a lot of time in bed, hence developing bed sores. At one time I wondered out loud why they bothered getting them out of bed at all, and the licensed vocational nurse said that it was required by [the state] that all patients be up and out of bed for at least two hours daily. The classification system is an effective tool in planning one's daily work schedule. This is no different from my classification of patients while I was a janitor (spitter, wet-the-floor type, mess-up-the-toilet type, and so on).

• • •

The behavior of the patients was markedly different outside of the categories of "work time" invoked by the staff. By this it is meant that categorizing patients in classes based upon the care they require does not account for those periods which place no (or minimal) demands upon the staff. These periods comprise a large part of the day of the patients, and are spent in different ways by them.

Many elderly patients no longer have to worry about the problem of how to occupy their time in meaningful ways because their selves have escaped long ago, leaving behind babbling biological husks which are carted about by unkind hands and spend their time strapped to beds or wheelchairs. But there are others. And it is to these and to their attempts to keep their selves from escaping their weakened frames that attention shall now be paid.

THE INTERACTION

• • •

There are three kinds of interaction which are relevant to the understanding that shapes the everyday lives of the patients: staff-to-patient interaction, patient-to-staff interaction, and patient-to-patient interaction. It must be mentioned that Sunny Hill has a mental health license, hence mental patients can be found mixing freely with those whose only fault is to be old.[8]

STAFF TO PATIENT

Staff-to-patient interaction is characterized by what Strauss and Glaser call "work-time."[9] The same problem noticed by the two sociologists in their study of a hospital ward is found at the Sunny Hill center: The patients' and the staff's conceptions of time are very often at variance. There are not enough nurse's aides, and they consequently have a very busy work schedule and minimal time to give the patients any attention as human beings; the patients are work objects, as is exemplified by their categorization in terms of work (feeders, etc.).

Given that the staff-to-patient interaction takes place in terms of work, a typical daily work routine will be described. The aides begin getting the patients out of bed and into their wheelchairs at about 6:30 a.m. At 7:00 the day-shift aides come in and finish preparing the patients for breakfast. The aides distribute trays to the patients who sit in their rooms in their wheelchairs, while the ambulatory cases walk to the dining room. Next, the aides feed the "feeders":

> I was going around with Mary and Glenda feeding the patients. Mary was literally stuffing food in a woman's mouth, and the semi-liquid yellowish substance was dribbling down the woman's chin onto her nightgown, which had been washed so many times that it was now an amorphous gray sack.
>
> Louise was feeding lunch to an old patient, and she explained to me that he always refused his water and that was bad for his kidneys. After having finished feeding him, she held a glass of water to his mouth, which he shut tightly. So Louise turned to me and said, "See, I told you so" and left, making no further effort to give the man a drink.[10]

During breakfast the licensed vocational nurse goes around with a medicine cart slipping pills in bowls of cornflakes or oatmeal, while the janitor mops up the floor between the chairs, cleaning spilled oatmeal, wheelchair scuffs, and small puddles of urine underneath some of the chairs because the patients' requests to go to the toilet are being ignored by the aides. The aides are still feeding "feeders" down the wing somewhere (some patients do not ask for help to go to the toilet anymore, they just urinate in their wheelchairs).

After the chaos of breakfast, with things and people running around, everything calms down. The patients are dressed (or they dress themselves, or are put back in bed) and either sit in their rooms or are wheeled into the lounge room where the television is broadcasting its usual variety of morning quiz shows. The patients look at the television, but most of them are just staring at a box with light and colors. . . .

The 9:00 aide is here now[11] and she begins to make beds on her assigned wing. Some days I go around with her:

> Today the 9:00 aide is Louise and I join her. She is making beds in and around patients. As I talk to her, she is going right on making beds and talking to me. Some of the patients are up and in the wheelchairs, but others are in bed. Louise picks them up and sits them in a chair, then proceeds to make the beds. After having changed the linen and the plastic sheet, Louise puts the patients back to bed, either saying nothing to them or things like—here you go—that's good—while carrying on a conversation with me or with another aide if there is one nearby.

After the morning activities, the mealtime bedlam of rushing food trays, cleaning up floors, and pushing around patients begins all over. After lunch it is quiet again as some patients are wheeled into the lounge room to watch some soap operas while others are put to bed to take a nap.

At 3:00 P.M. the evening shift comes in while the day shift retires to the dining room to fill in their daily reports on the patients. These reports summarize the activities of the patients in terms of physical and mental functions. Emphasis is given by the aides to things such as b.m.'s (bowel movements) and unusual behavior; since each aide fills only some charts, there is a continuous negotiation on whether Billy had a bowel movement today or whether Elma had a quiet day or was restless. The reports are jotted down in about twenty minutes and the charts returned to the nursing station.

These reports are very important for the patients since the nurse in charge compiles her monthly reports by summarizing the aides' reports. The social worker also uses the aides' reports to give her account of the patients, and the various reports are used by the doctors to determine the status of the patients. A doctor comes in, sits behind the nurses' station, and inquires about his breakfast, which is promptly served. Having thumbed through the charts for a while, he walks quickly up and down the corridors, asking from time to time, "How are you today, Mr. Smith, and you, Mrs. Jones?" Without waiting for an answer, he keeps on walking. At times he visits one or two patients who may be experiencing serious problems, and then he is gone, not to be seen for another two weeks.

The following is an example of how the information in the reports is acquired in many cases. Mr. Anderson's medical records stated that he had been committed to the convalescent center as a manic-depressive case. The records made mention of the fact that he had been a former patient and had left to go to a boarding house. However, Dr. Bell (his doctor throughout this whole period) brought him back to the center, since Mr. Anderson was in a severe state of depression (listed as spitting and cursing at doctors and nurses).

I thumbed through the reports of the aides and found that Mr. Anderson was often reported as "depressed" (aides have five choices in their chart: satisfactory, confused, depressed, irritable, noisy). On the back of the report, under "nurses' progress notes," it was often generally stated that Mr. Anderson had shown signs of depression, and occasionally he was reported as having said things such as, "If I had a gun I would shoot myself."

I happened to be present during one of Mr. Anderson's "depressive" conditions.

> Mr. Anderson said that he could not understand why they locked the windows, that all it would take to get out would be a kitchen knife used as a screwdriver. The aide wrote down in her report that he was very agitated and talked about escaping from the center.

My impression of the "incident" was entirely different. I had heard Mr. Anderson make the comment about the windows to an aide.[12] The incident assumed new meaning in the aide's account of it. Dramatic overtones kept piling on until what had seemed to me a frustrated remark about the futility of certain security measures became a dramatic plan to escape from the center. The incident shows that the interpretation of Mr. Anderson's behavior as deviant was taken by an aide who had a preconceived notion of his depression and was in a hurry to finish her report. Her account became of extreme importance since the other members of the staff rely solely upon such reports to pass judgment on the patients.

After this example of "form filling," it is time to return to the daily scheduled events. The daily work routine is now in the hands of the evening shift. The circle starts all over again—getting patients up from their naps, making beds, getting patients ready for dinner. It is 5:00 p.m., the last meal of the day, the last moment of a kaleidoscope of colors, odors, noises. Food is served, forced into mouths, spat out, cleaned up, dropped on the floor, aides yell at patients, and patients scream in the hall, in their rooms, in their chairs, and then, silence again. Some patients, a few, walk back to the lounge room, the others are put to bed, the day at the center is over.

The rush imposed by a heavy work load leads the aides to treat the patients in the same fashion. It becomes legitimate to stuff food down their throats because the goal has become serving the meal, not nourishing the patient; or to lift them in and out of bed as if they were inanimate dummies because the goal is bed making not making the patient comfortable. The patients thus end up suffering from "organization contingencies" similar to those found by many sociologists in other settings.[13] But what is suffering here from problems stemming from work-flow contingencies is not a car malfunctioning from shoddy workmanship, but human beings who by being treated as inanimate objects end up becoming inanimate objects.

PATIENT TO STAFF

Patients find themselves competing for the staff's attention. The patients are not rushed by a busy work schedule, on the contrary they have nothing but time on their hands. Apart from the scheduled rounds of activities such as meals, baths, haircuts, etc., there are scarcely any other goings-on available to the patients. The patients who still have the physical and mental capabilities to do so return to their rooms after the scheduled activities are over; others never leave their rooms; the rest, who fall somewhere in between, are carted to the recreation room to watch television.

Confined to a restricted setting beyond their control, the patients attempt to break the monotony of the empty periods of waiting for the next scheduled activity. The patients employ various strategies to attract the attention of the aides. . . . "Bob waves his hand at the aide who is passing by and mumbles—toilet—she looks at him and says—oh you don't have to go—and goes on." When they attract someone's attention, usually a new aide or me, they smile and ask for a glass of water (or milk) or for a dime to buy a Coke. Five minutes later, up goes the same hand, and the same person asks for another glass of water. Doing beds or cleaning rooms is also a good time to attempt to engage the aide in conversation because she cannot just turn around and leave. These attempts to create diversions in the period between meals, or between a meal and a bath, are treated by the staff unanimously in the same fashion—they are ignored unless they become a problem which will disrupt the daily schedule: things such as a patient defecating in the hallway or pulling another patient's hair can no longer be ignored as they would soon attract the attention of the licensed vocational nurse or the administrator.

PATIENT TO PATIENT

• • •

The interaction among patients is mainly characterized by its absence. Patients do not have anything to do with each other. To fraternize with other patients would mean to place oneself at their level, to admit that one indeed belongs here.

Thus the others are ignored. Once I asked Al, who was a great sports fan, why he did not watch the ball games on television. He replied that he would not go into the recreation room during the day because he did not like to see and smell the result of other incontinent patients, and the aides would not let him watch the night games.

• • •

At Christmas I had sent Mr. Adams a set of checkers, and when I returned to the center the next summer, he invited me to play with him. The checker set had not been opened yet, and Mr. Adams said that there was nobody to play with at the center. Later I discovered that this was not true since I played with other patients. When I mentioned this to Mr. Adams, he claimed that they were not good enough players to play with him. But neither was I, because after an initial doubt as to whether I should let "poor old Mr. Adams" beat me at checkers, I realized that I had as much of a chance of beating him at checkers as I would have had of spotting Bobby Fischer a rook and then beating him at chess.

When interaction between patients does take place, it is not of a desirable kind. The following examples illustrate this point. The administrator decided to put Mr. Adams and Mr. Ritter, two of the "better" patients, in the same room. This arrangement did not last long. Both fellows liked their privacy and the freedom of doing what they liked in their rooms.... They tolerated each other for a while but began complaining about each other's quirks privately (often to me).... This eventually led to open confrontation, which occurred when they were both listening to their favorite program on their transistor radios and tried to outdo each other by a battle of volumes. The nurse rushed in to see what was going on, and as a result Mr. Adams went back upstairs to a new room.

• • •

At times, the interaction between patients became violent as when somebody grabbed hold of a hank of hair and pulled as hard as he or she could. A couple of times punches were thrown by some patients, but these flare-ups were rare. What caused most of the problems was the mixing of mental cases with normal patients. . . .

• • •

The patients respond in different ways to their confinement in the center. Those who manage to survive the heavy odds against them and retain a lucid mind are few indeed. They may or may not have reconciled themselves with spending the remainder of their days at the center, but they all agree that their stay is against their will, that they are for all practical purposes being kept prisoners in the center.

Mr. Anderson is a tall, thin man in his early eighties; his vivid, alert eyes peer at you from his hollow cheeks, and his long, bony hands are tightly held in his lap. He walks slowly, slightly hunched, but he walks.

Mr. Anderson used to live in a boarding house. One day the people who managed the house told him that he had to go to the doctor for a check-up. He was taken to the center and has been there ever since. He feels that this is illegal, and that the doctor signed his release to the center because he is a good patient, ambulatory and quiet, and they wanted his money. He has written to his daughter about it but has received no reply.

Mr. Anderson told me his story in a calm, resigned manner. He feels as if he were in a prison. He spends his days voraciously reading old novels and magazines. Mr. Anderson said that when he reads he loses track of time, and before he knows it, it is time for lunch or dinner. At times, however, he feels very depressed about being in the convalescent center; then he closes the door and stares out of the window since he doesn't feel like reading.

Mr. Ritter, a tall, heavy-set fellow in his late fifties, is another case. He used to be a minor-league pitcher, and he went on to become a professional heavy-weight fighter . . . . He was placed in custody in 1971 as decreed by court order after psychiatric examination . . . . He had trouble subtracting numbers from 100 in descending order, seven at a time (he became confused at 93). He also forgot to mention Kennedy when listing our presidents backward . . . . He has to be reexamined every year to determine whether his mental state warrants commitment. While no cure or therapy is prescribed for Mr. Ritter, he is being administered quite a few phenobarbital drugs as sedatives on an "as-needed" basis. . . . Mr. Ritter feels that he is being kept at the center as a captive, but he is resigned and he will not attempt to escape. He spends his days mending old trousers or sewing buttons on shirts and listens to the radio from time to time.

• • •

The regularity with which the "better" patients view themselves as prisoners seems to indicate that believing that they are being held by some conspiracy in a place in which they do not belong allows these individuals to reconcile themselves with their being at the center. . . . But as long as the "better" patients view themselves as prisoners, they can survive in the center: The other people here are not their equals, and the staff's treatment is a part of the conspiracy to keep them here.

• • •

THE OTHERS

There are other patients at the center who hang on to a remainder of self. It is often impossible to know how much lucidity they retain because it is hard to crack the solid wall that these patients have erected between themselves and the institution. At times, only at times, a crack appears, and one can catch a glimpse of life beneath the dull outside.

. . . Mrs. Leister had come to the center willingly because she had a heart condition and felt that she would want medical care nearby all the time. When she came in, she was an active and talkative lady. She walked up and down the corridors, talked to people, smiled a lot, and chirpily moved about. One day she was very excited because her daughter was coming to visit her from back East. She showed me a picture of her daughter and told me all about her daughter's husband and children. That very day I witnessed the kind of interaction that was to force Mrs. Leister behind her wall.

The aide came into the room without knocking and left the door opened behind her. Mrs. Leister was fully dressed, but she was lying on the bed awaiting her doctor's visit. The aide, taking no notice of either of us, began making the bed around Mrs. Leister. The doctor walked in and nodded good morning to the aide. He had no way of knowing who I was since he had never met me before, thus I was a stranger of the opposite sex of the patient he was examining; nevertheless, he casually unbuttoned Mrs. Leister's blouse while asking her about her health and began listening with a stethoscope to her heart. He left after a few minutes, and the nurse resumed making the bed while telling me what a terrible doctor that was.

That day Mrs. Leister had her first taste of what it is like to be treated as an object. When she attempted to be a human being, she was met by the unyielding iron hand of regulations. No, she could not go outside the center and take walks, that was against regulations; no, she could not watch television in the evenings, that would disturb the other patients, and it was not allowed; no, there was no portion of the six acres around the center that was set aside for gardening by the patients. Other patients spoke curtly to Mrs. Leister or returned her conversation with an idiotic grin. Old Maria, in her ramblings, once more reverted to the language of her youth when she was a prostitute in the streets of New York, and invested Mrs. Leister with a barrage of profanities, which brought laughter and a thorazine shot from the "battle axe" on duty.

Four months later, Mrs. Leister was spending all of her time on her bed. She no longer walked up and down the corridors. "I can look at the sky from here," she told me, perhaps in her last attempt to have something of her own.

Others who have been at the center longer have finished their wall and devised small ways to show that the center is an abhorrent entity outside of themselves. This enables them to keep a distance between themselves and the center.

And the rest of the patients? They are shadows who no longer possess a cognitive self. They wander aimlessly through the corridors or sit whimpering in a wheelchair, or groan as their bed sores grow redder. When one displays a spark and begins to rage against a ghost from the past which torments him, another pill is popped in his mouth. Slowly, the eyes turn glassy again and, as order and discipline are restored, the patient, a babbling idiot once more, slowly shuffles away.

• • •

In attempting to understand why patients present such a hostile front to others rather than unite and share the burden of their destiny, an analogy must be drawn. Seymour Margin Lipset and his associates, [14] in studying the typesetters union, discovered that typesetters fraternized with other typesetters in their off-duty activities. Lipset and the others attributed this to a problem of perceived status versus accorded status.

A group feels that it belongs to a certain status category and, therefore, believes that it should be its right to interact with groups in the same status bracket. However, the rest of society accords the group a status inferior to that which it itself perceives. The group is, in other words, rejected by others who feel superior to it and, in turn, rejects groups which it perceives as inferior.

In the center, a single patient can be considered the equivalent of the whole group of typesetters. The patient feels that he belongs to a certain status—being sane—and attempts to interact with individuals whom he considers sane: doctors, nurses, aides, janitors, etc. But they perceive the patient as belonging to an inferior status—work-object, insane, senile, etc.—and refuse to interact with him. On the other hand, the patient perceives the other patients as inferior because he assumes them to be bona fide patients deserving of being in the center and thus refuses to interact with them. The patient has only one group left with which to interact: himself.

NOTES

1. Erving Goffman, *The Presentation of the Self in Everyday Life* (Garden City, N.Y.: Anchor, 1959).

2. For a detailed account of patients in hospitals in terms of time and work, see Barney Glaser and Anselm Strauss, *Awareness of Dying*. Chicago: Aldine, 1965; *Time for Dying*, Chicago: Aldine, 1968; and *Anguish*. Mill Valley, Ca.: Sociology Press, 1970.

3. For a detailed ethnography of a convalescent center, see Jaber F. Gubrium, *Living and Dying at Murray Manor*. New York: St. Martin's Press, 1975.

4. Matilda W. Riley and Anne Foner, *Aging and Society*, (New York: Russell Sage, 1968) Vol. 1, Chapter 25.

5. Claire Townsend, *Old Age: The Last Segregation* (New York: Grossman, 1971); Mary Adelaide Mendelson, *Tender Loving Greed*. New York: Alfred A. Knopf, 1974.

6. Less than 5 percent of the people over sixty-five years of age in the United States are institutionalized. See *Social and Economic Characteristics of the Older Populations 1974*, U.S. Department of Commerce, Bureau of the Census. Washington, D.C.: U.S. Government Printing Office, 1975.

7. However, I had access to all the medical records of the patients.

8. In the latter part of my research an increasing number of young mental patients began replacing the old ones in the upper ward. At times I was mistaken by a new aide or a delivery man for a patient because I did not wear a white coat and wandered around the facilities.

9. Barney Glaser and Anselm Strauss, *Anguish*, op. cit.

10. This quote and the remainder . . . , unless otherwise noted, are from my field notes taken in the summer of 1974.

11. There are four aides on day shift (7:00 to 3:30), two per wing on each ward, plus two 9:00 aides (9:00 to 5:00).

12. The aide is an older lady in her sixties; she has been at the center for many years and somehow feels responsible for all that goes on in there. This leads her to become easily excitable, as I had the opportunity to witness many times.

13. See, for instance, Abraham Blumberg, *Criminal Justice*, Chicago: Quadrangle, 1967.

14. S. M. Lipset, Martin Trow, and James Coleman, *Union Democracy* (Garden City, N.Y.: Anchor, 1956).

Review Questions

1. Of all the types of actors on the "stage" at Sunny Hill, which ones had the most prestige and income? Which ones had the most contact with the patients?
2. What factors determined how the aides interacted with the patients? Are these the same factors that determine how teachers interact with students, how friends interact with each other, how guards interact with prisoners? Explain.
3. How did the "better" patients and those confined to beds and chairs develop responses to their treatment?
4. To what degree were there true groups among the patients? Why?
5. Overall, how much was the patient's life at Sunny Hill shaped by the staff and how much by the patients themselves?

Suggested Readings: Social Organization: Life in Groups

Adler, Patricia A. *Wheeling and Dealing: An Ethnography of an Upper-Level Drug Dealing and Smuggling Community*. New York: Columbia University Press, 1985.

Denzin, Norman K. "Notes on the Criminogenic Hypothesis: A Case Study of the American Liquor Industry," *American Sociological Review* 42, 6 (December 1977): 905–920.

Ellis, Carolyn S. *Fisherfolk: Two Communities on Chesapeake Bay*. Louisville, Ky.: University Press of Kentucky, 1988.

Farberman, Harvey A. "A Criminogenic Market Structure: The Automobile Industry," *Sociological Quarterly* 16 (Autumn 1975): 438–457.

Goffman, Erving. *Asylums: Essays on the Social Situation of Mental Patients and Other Inmates*. Chicago: Aldine, 1961.

Hummon, David M. *Commonplaces: Community Ideology and Identity in American Culture*. Stony Brook, N.Y.: State University of New York Press, 1990.

Roy, Donald F. "Quota Restriction and Goldbricking in a Machine Shop," *American Journal of Sociology* 57 (March 1952): 427–442.

Schwartz, Barry. "Notes on the Sociology of Sleep," *Sociological Quarterly* 11 (Fall 1970): 485–499.

Sudnow, David. *Passing On: The Social Organization of Dying*. Englewood Cliffs, N.J.: Prentice-Hall, 1967.

Tonnies, Ferdinand. *Community and Society.* East Lansing, Mich.: Michigan State University Press, 1957.

Whyte, William Foote. *Street Corner Society: The Social Structure of an Italian Slum.* Chicago: University of Chicago Press, 1943.

Zimbardo, Phillip. "Pathology of Imprisonment," *Society,* 9, 6, 1976.

Zurcher, Louis A. *Social Roles: Conformity, Conflict, and Creativity.* Beverly Hills, Calif.: Sage, 1983.

Part VI. Inequalities: Class, Race, and Gender

In nearly every known society, limited social and material rewards are distributed unevenly. Prestige, esteem, honor, and social power as well as wealth are granted to societal members unequally. Social groupings develop ranking, or *stratification,* systems in which various "ascribed" (determined at birth) and "achieved" (acquired) attributes—which may include gender, age, race or ethnicity, family name, occupation, and even sometimes physique—are weighted. One's attributes, once ranked in the stratification system, determine those societal rewards that one can claim and that others are willing to bestow.

The rewards and resources one is able to claim determine to a large extent one's *life chances.* By life chances we do not mean merely the opportunities to make a million dollars or to become president of the United States, but rather the chances of surviving infancy, avoiding malnutrition, obtaining education, securing a decent-paying and satisfying job, and living in good health to an advanced age. These life chances are *not* distributed equally in the United States or in any other modern nation.

Large categories of people who receive similar societal resources—and who have similar life chances—are termed *social classes.* Social-class ranking is usually applied to families, so that children inherit their parents' positions in the stratification hierarchy. They may remain in their inherited positions long after they have become independent from their parents, since *social mobility,* even in relatively "open" modern industrial societies, is not as common as we like to think. That is, individuals' rankings in the stratification system tend to be perpetuated.

The coherence and stability of stratification systems is maintained in part through social interaction. Interaction with people from other classes often involves "reminders" of one's own class position and actual barriers to upward movement. Interaction with those at one's own class level is, first of all, much more frequent, since many aspects of our lives, from residence to religious services, are somewhat segregated on the basis of social class and even sex, age, race, and the like. It is also more comfortable, because class members share similar life experiences and develop similar interpretations of those experiences. Those of you who have grown up in middle-class families may recall uncomfortable instances when you have crossed class boundaries. Have you ever been invited to a formal affair at an exclusive restaurant and wondered which of the three spoons to use first or what to do with the four forks? Have you come in contact with a prestigious personage who interrupted your conversation in order to talk to someone "more important"? Have you felt, or been made to feel, "out of place" because of your clothing, income, manners, or ignorance of upper-class customs? Have you been passed over for a job or promotion for these reasons? Have you judged people from a lower social class than your own on similar grounds?

The purpose of this section of our reader is to help you to become aware of the interactional bases of stratification and of the inequalities that result. Our selections place the dynamics of social inequality in an everyday context and illustrate how stratification can be viewed as a *social process* which begins in social interaction and which affects individuals' opportunities, self-conceptions, and even their survival. The "system" of distributing social power, prestige, and wealth is not some far-removed, nonhuman force. It consists of the everyday behavior of us all, as we socialize each other to accept both the cultural rationales for stratification and our own particular positions in the ranking system.

Judgments about people's class affiliations can have a profound effect on their life chances. In "The Saints and the Roughnecks," William Chambliss traces the interaction between authoritative agents of the community and two white, adolescent youth gangs—the upper-middle-class Saints and the lower-class Roughnecks. His study reveals a pattern of discrimination based on class.

The Saints and the Roughnecks differed little from each other aside from the crucial factors of class background; the visibility of their activities to others; and the biased perceptions of their activities on the part of schoolteachers and officials, the police, and the townspeople. Coming from wealthy families and having the mobility that wealth can buy, the Saints were able to carry out what the community, in ignorance, regarded as "pranks" in places beyond the townspeople's visibility. The Saints' low visibility, their polite demeanor before school and police authorities, and the community's bias in their favor combined to keep the gang free of any taint of delinquency. The way remained clear for the Saints to pursue the adult careers to which, in the community's eyes, their class status, school grades, and behavior entitled them.

The Roughnecks, by contrast, had no barriers to the visibility of their behavior to protect them. Both their defiant demeanor and the bias against them assured that their activities would be stamped with a criminal label. (For a discussion of labeling, see the section entitled *Deviance, Conformity, and Social Control*.) The attitudes of the community that produced the label affected the Roughnecks' expectations of their own futures. Thus, when the Roughnecks turned to adult criminal careers the community's prophecy was fulfilled. Chambliss's study shows us how class labels, imposed in the course of interaction between groups, have an enormous effect on life chances.

Many observers of American society have seen the great differences in the distribution of wealth as resulting from the values and attitudes that prevail within the different social classes. According to this view, middle-class values are different from lower-class values, the latter forming a pattern that has come to be called the "culture of poverty." The culture-of-poverty theory holds that lower-class values and attitudes form a way of life that keeps poor people from attaining job security and upward mobility. Whereas middle-class people are seen as future-oriented, lower-class people are seen as present-oriented. The middle class is said to defer its gratifications (they wait to have their desires fulfilled), an attitude favorable to saving; the lower class is said to seek immediate gratification of its needs, an attitude favorable to immediate consumption. The middle class is described as optimistic, and the lower class as fatalistic. These supposed differences between the cultures of the lower class and the middle class are assumed to explain poverty among the lower classes.

Elliot Liebow *challenges* the culture-of-poverty theory in the selection "Men and Jobs on Tally's Corner." He provides us with a detailed account of his observations of the attitudes and values that lower-class, black, streetcorner men hold toward their jobs, the attitudes that middle-class employers have with respect to those same jobs, and the objective conditions that surround the jobs available to men on the streetcorner.

From a superficial point of view, the men on Tally's Corner might seem to embody every value imputed to them by the culture-of-poverty theory. They appear to be irresponsible and indolent. But, as Liebow points out, most of the men on the corner have jobs—the least prestigious, lowest-paying jobs our society has to offer. Both the middle-class employer and the lower-class employee consider the jobs contemptible. Indeed, they are boring, dirty, and monotonous. The wages are insufficient to support a family, and the jobs provide no chance for advancement. Better-paying jobs are usually either physically debilitating, out of reach of the corner men, seasonal, weather-bound, machine-paced, or beyond the training of the corner men.

The system of paying extremely low wages for the retail and service jobs available to the streetcorner men provides an excellent illustration of how middle-class employers express their contempt for jobs that lower-class men perform. We see how the power of the employer can be used not only to demean the job but also to threaten whatever marginal security the job might provide.

The men on Tally's corner hold jobs that are "not much to talk about." They are convinced of their own incompetence. They cannot save, and they are reluctant to assume responsibility when responsible jobs are offered. Furthermore, these attitudes and experiences are likely to have been those of their fathers and their fathers' fathers. What is important, indeed critical, to note is that the attitudes expressed by the streetcorner men are not produced by a culture of poverty but, rather, are the results of objective, valid experience. The culture-of-poverty theory fails to explain why poverty and inequality exist, because it locates the faults in the victims instead of in the system. Liebow's essay demonstrates that the attitudes and values that support inequality are formed not in an isolated subculture but by a process of "self-fulfilling prophecy" in which the beliefs of the more powerful are translated into reality in the course of interaction between groups.

Lenore Weitzman sensitizes us to another way in which the social structure produces inequality in contemporary society. One of the most alarming trends in income stratification in recent years has been the increasing number of women and children in poverty. The U.S. Bureau of the Census estimates that, for the first time in history, *almost all* of the more than 30 million Americans who will live in poverty are *women and children*. Several factors are responsible for this phenomenal social transformation. One of them is the introduction of "no-fault" divorce laws. Weitzman's research and analysis of California's divorce laws are presented in "The Divorce Revolution and the Feminization of Poverty." She shows how and why these laws, in conjunction with more favorable treatment of men in the workplace, have had such dire, unanticipated consequences. Her findings send a warning to today's woman: your past social statuses, ascribed or achieved, are no guarantee of a comfortable future.

We turn our attention next to the ways in which *status reminders* are manifested in everyday interactions involving waiting. Time is, as we know, an important, scarce resource, and the use or waste of it can gain or deny us access to other valued resources. Since time can be socially used or abused, it entails social costs. And the ability to affect how other people use their time is an indicator of power. In his essay, "Waiting, Exchange, and Power," Barry Schwartz examines the social costs, uses, and abuses of time as a medium of exchange in the interactional relationship of waiting. Waiting, as Schwartz points out, affects the value of the goods, services, and persons one waits for. The social costs that whole categories of people bear in order to obtain some valued thing may be very high.

Waiting is closely related to power, because those who have power can impose waiting upon those who don't. The phrase, "being forced to wait," expresses the coercive power of waiting used as a policy. The power to make others wait is often held by those who have a monopoly on valued things. Our decision to wait expresses "status deference," the willingness to defer to others higher on the pecking order than we are. Yet it is not always the powerful for whom we wait. People low in power may impose waiting upon us because of their access to the powerful.

Schwartz examines the dynamics of waiting in terms of the value we give the objects for which we wait and the distribution of power between servers and their clients. Waiting is thus demonstrated to be not merely an annoyance, as it is often seen, but an indication and a reminder of inequality.

Most of the articles in this section focus on the social forces that determine our "places" in society's stratification system and the daily patterns of interaction that remind us to "stay in our places." The final article considers one type of reaction group members may have when they are relegated to low-prestige, low-power places in society. According to Charlotte Wolf, minority-group members compare themselves to other groups and often construct a definition of their own group as in some way superior.

In "Relative Advantage: Antidote to Low Status," Wolf examines historical records including diaries, letters, and tape-recorded interviews to gain insight into the reactions of three low-power groups: slaves and ex-slaves in the South, nineteenth-century American women, and Japanese-Americans whom the United States government forced to move from their homes to "relocation centers," or concentration camps, during World War II. In all of these groups, some members came to see their group as relatively advantaged, that is, as more worthy or privileged than at some other time or more worthy or privileged than some other groups. Wolf points out that it is not individuals but a group that creates and sustains a world view in which the group as a whole is superior.

What were the consequences of holding such world views for the groups Wolf studied? First individuals felt a sense of satisfaction that made coping with daily discrimination easier. At the macrosocial level, however, the sense of relative advantage seems to have a conservative effect. That is, the more satisfied people are with their situations in life, the less likely they may be to rebel against the existing stratification system. Only in the case of women did Wolf find that a sense of relative advantage led to a social movement to wrest power from the elite. In this case, the minority group (women) did not feel more privileged than the comparison group (men), but morally superior to them. Some branches of the nineteenth century feminist movement mobilized around this theme of women's moral worth, calling on "brutish" and "immoral" men to give up their leadership positions. More typically, however, a group's sense of relative advantage restrains its members from challenging "the system," effectively keeping them in their places and making them happy to be there.

THE SAINTS AND THE ROUGHNECKS

William J. Chambliss

EIGHT PROMISING YOUNG MEN—CHILDREN OF GOOD, STABLE, WHITE UPPER-middle-class families, active in school affairs, good pre-college students—were some of the most delinquent boys at Hanibal High School. While community residents knew that these boys occasionally sowed a few wild oats, they were totally unaware that sowing wild oats completely occupied the daily routine of these young men. The Saints were constantly occupied with truancy, drinking, wild driving, petty theft, and vandalism. Yet no one was officially arrested for any misdeed during the two years I observed them.

This record was particularly surprising in light of my observations during the same two years of another gang of Hanibal High School students, six lower-class white boys known as the Roughnecks. The Roughnecks were constantly in trouble with police and community even though their rate of delinquency was about equal with that of the Saints. What was the cause of this disparity? the result? The following consideration of the activities, social class, and community perceptions of both gangs may provide some answers.

THE SAINTS FROM MONDAY TO FRIDAY

The Saints' principal daily concern was with getting out of school as early as possible. The boys managed to get out of school with minimum danger that they would be accused of playing hookey through an elaborate procedure for obtaining "legitimate" release from class. The most common procedure was for one boy to obtain the release of another by fabricating a meeting of some committee, program or recognized club. Charles might raise his hand in his 9:00 chemistry class and ask to be excused—a euphemism for going to the bathroom. Charles would go to Ed's math class and inform the teacher that Ed was needed for a 9:30 rehearsal of the drama club play. The math teacher would recognize Ed and Charles as "good students" involved in numerous school activ-

SOURCE: William J. Chambliss, "The Saints and the Roughnecks." *Society* 11 Nov/Dec 1973, pp. 24–31.

ities and would permit Ed to leave at 9:30. Charles would return to his class, and Ed would go to Tom's English class to obtain his release. Tom would engineer Charles's escape. The strategy would continue until as many of the Saints as possible were freed. After a stealthy trip to the car (which had been parked in a strategic spot), the boys were off for a day of fun.

Over the two years I observed the Saints, this pattern was repeated nearly every day. There were variations on the theme, but in one form or another, the boys used this procedure for getting out of class and then off the school grounds. Rarely did all eight of the Saints manage to leave school at the same time. The average number avoiding school on the days I observed them was five.

Having escaped from the concrete corridors, the boys usually went either to a pool hall on the other (lower-class) side of town or to a cafe in the suburbs. Both places were out of the way of people the boys were likely to know (family or school officials), and both provided a source of entertainment. The pool hall entertainment was the generally rough atmosphere, the occasional hustler, the sometimes drunk proprietor and, of course, the game of pool. The cafe's entertainment was provided by the owner. The boys would "accidentally" knock a glass on the floor or spill cola on the counter—not all the time, but enough to be sporting. They would also bend spoons, put salt in sugar bowls and generally tease whoever was working in the cafe. The owner had opened the cafe recently and was dependent on the boys' business which was, in fact, substantial since between the horsing around and the teasing they bought food and drinks.

THE SAINTS ON WEEKENDS

On weekends the automobile was even more critical than during the week, for on weekends the Saints went to Big Town—a large city with a population of over a million 25 miles from Hanibal. Every Friday and Saturday night most of the Saints would meet between 8:00 and 8:30 and would go into Big Town. Big Town activities included drinking heavily in taverns or nightclubs, driving drunkenly through the streets, and committing acts of vandalism and playing pranks.

By midnight on Fridays and Saturdays the Saints were usually thoroughly high, and one or two of them were often so drunk they had to be carried to the cars. Then the boys drove around town, calling obscenities to women and girls; occasionally trying (unsuccessfully so far as I could tell) to pick girls up; and driving recklessly through red lights and at high speeds with their lights out. Occasionally they played "chicken." One boy would climb out the back window of the car and across the roof to the driver's side of the car while the car was moving at high speed (between 40 and 50 miles an hour); then the driver would move over and the boy who had just crawled across the car roof would take the driver's seat.

Searching for "fair game" for a prank was the boys' principal activity after they left the tavern. The boys would drive alongside a foot patrolman and ask directions to some street. If the policeman leaned on the car in the course of answering the question, the driver would speed away, causing him to lose balance. The Saints were careful to play this prank only in an area where they were not going to spend much time and where they could quickly disappear around the corner to avoid having their license plate number taken.

Construction sites and road repair areas were the special province of the Saints' mischief. A soon-to-be-repaired hole in the road inevitably invited the Saints to remove lanterns and wooden barricades and put them in the car, leaving the hole unprotected. The boys would find a safe vantage point and wait for an unsuspecting motorist to drive into the hole. Often, though not always, the boys would go up to the motorist and commiserate with him about the dreadful way the city protected its citizenry.

Leaving the scene of the open hole and the motorist, the boys would then go searching for an appropriate place to erect the stolen barricade. An "appropriate place" was often a spot on a highway near a curve in the road where the barricade would not be seen by an on-coming motorist. The boys would wait to watch an unsuspecting motorist attempt to stop and (usually) crash into the wooden barricade. With saintly bearing the boys might offer help and understanding.

A stolen lantern might well find its way onto the back of a police car or hang from a street lamp. Once a lantern served as a prop for a reenactment of the "midnight ride of Paul Revere" until the "play," which was taking place at 2:00A.M. in the center of a main street of Big Town, was interrupted by a police car several blocks away. The boys ran, leaving the lanterns on the street, and managed to avoid being apprehended.

Abandoned houses, especially if they were located in out-of-the-way places, were fair game for destruction and spontaneous vandalism. The boys would break windows, remove furniture to the yard and tear it apart, urinate on the walls and scrawl obscenities inside.

Through all the pranks, drinking, and reckless driving the boys managed miraculously to avoid being stopped by police. Only twice in two years was I aware that they had been stopped by a Big City policeman. Once was for speeding (which they did every time they drove whether they were drunk or sober), and the driver managed to convince the policeman that it was simply an error. The second time they were stopped they had just left a nightclub and were walking through an alley. Aaron stopped to urinate and the boys began making obscene remarks. A foot patrolman came into the alley, lectured the boys and sent them home. Before the boys got to the car one began talking in a loud voice again. The policeman, who had followed them down the alley, arrested this boy for disturbing the peace and took him to the police station where the other Saints gathered. After paying a $5 fine, and with the assurance that there would be no permanent record of the arrest, the boy was released.

The boys had a spirit of frivolity and fun about their escapades. They did not view what they were engaged in as "delinquency," though it surely was by any reasonable definition of that word. They simply viewed themselves as having a little fun and who, they would ask, was really hurt by it? The answer had to be no one, although this fact remains one of the most difficult things to explain about the gang's behavior. Unlikely though it seems, in two years of drinking, driving, carousing and vandalism no one was seriously injured as a result of the Saints' activities.

THE SAINTS IN SCHOOL

The Saints were highly successful in school. The average grade for the group was "B" with two of the boys having close to a straight "A" average. Almost all of the boys were popular and many of them held offices in the school. One of the boys was vice president of the student body one year. Six of the boys played on athletic teams.

At the end of their senior year, the student body selected ten seniors for special recognition as the "school wheels"; four of the ten were Saints. Teachers and school officials saw no problem with any of these boys and anticipated that they would all "make something of themselves."

How the boys managed to maintain this impression is surprising in view of their actual behavior while in school. Their technique for covering truancy was so successful that teachers did not even realize that the boys were absent from school much of the time. Occasionally, of course, the system would backfire and then the boy was on his own. A boy who was caught would be most contrite, would plead guilty and ask for mercy. He inevitably got the mercy he sought.

Cheating on examinations was rampant, even to the point of orally communicating answers to exams as well as looking at one another's papers. Since none of the group studied, and since they were primarily dependent on one another for help, it is surprising that grades were so high. Teachers contributed to the deception in their admitted inclination to give these boys (and presumably others like them) the benefit of the doubt. When asked how the boys did in school, and when pressed on specific examinations, teachers might admit that they were disappointed in John's performance, but would quickly add that they "knew that he was capable of doing better," so John was given a higher grade than he had actually earned. How often this happened is impossible to know. During the time that I observed the group, I never saw any of the boys take homework home. Teachers may have been "understanding" very regularly.

One exception to the gang's generally good performance was Jerry, who had a "C" average in his junior year, experienced disaster the next year, and failed to graduate. Jerry had always been a little more nonchalant than the others about the liberties he took in school. Rather than wait for someone to come get him from class, he would offer his own excuse and leave. Although he probably did not miss any more class than most of the others in the group, he did not take the requisite pains to cover his absences. Jerry was the only Saint whom I ever heard talk back to a teacher. Although teachers often called him a "cut up" or a "smart kid," they never referred to him as a troublemaker or as a kid headed for trouble. It seems likely, then, that Jerry's failure his senior year and his mediocre performance his junior year were consequences of his not playing the game the proper way (possibly because he was disturbed by his parents' divorce). His teachers regarded him as "immature" and not quite ready to get out of high school.

THE POLICE AND THE SAINTS

The local police saw the Saints as good boys who were among the leaders of the youth in the community. Rarely, the boys might be stopped in town for speeding or for running a stop sign. When this happened the boys were always polite, contrite, and pled for mercy. As in school, they received the mercy they asked for. None ever received a ticket or was taken into the precinct by the local police.

The situation in Big City, where the boys engaged in most of their delinquency, was only slightly different. The police there did not know the boys at all, although occasionally the boys were stopped by a patrolman. Once they were caught taking a lantern from a construction site. Another time they were stopped for running a stop sign, and on several occasions they were stopped for speeding. Their behavior was as before: contrite, polite, and penitent. The urban police, like the local police, accepted their demeanor as sincere. More important, the urban police were convinced that these were good boys just out for a lark.

THE ROUGHNECKS

Hanibal townspeople never perceived the Saints' high level of delinquency. The Saints were good boys who just went in for an occasional prank. After all, they were well dressed, well mannered, and had nice cars. The Roughnecks were a different story. Although the two gangs of boys were the same age, and both groups engaged in an equal amount of wild-oat sowing, everyone agreed that the not-so-well-dressed, not-so-well-mannered, not-so-rich boys were heading for trouble. Townspeople would say, "You can see the gang members at the drugstore, night after night, leaning against the storefront (sometimes drunk) or slouching around inside buying Cokes, reading magazines, and probably stealing old Mr. Wall blind. When they are outside and girls walk by, even respectable girls, these boys make suggestive remarks. Sometimes their remarks are downright lewd."

From the community's viewpoint, the real indication that these kids were in trouble was that they were constantly involved with the police. Some of them had been picked up for stealing, mostly small stuff, of course, "but still it's stealing small stuff that leads to big time crimes." "Too bad," people said. "Too bad that these boys couldn't behave like the other kids in town; stay out of trouble, be polite to adults, and look to their future."

The community's impression of the degrees to which this group of six boys (ranging in age from 16 to 19) engaged in delinquency was somewhat distorted. In some ways the gang was more delinquent than the community thought; in other ways they were less.

The fighting activities of the group were fairly readily and accurately perceived by almost everyone. At least once a month, the boys would get into some sort of fight, although most fights were scraps between members of the group or involved only one member of the group and some peripheral hanger-on. Only three times in the period of observation did the group fight together: once against a gang from across town, once against two blacks, and once against a group of boys from another school. For the first two fights the group went out "looking for trouble"—and they found it both times. The third fight followed a football game and began spontaneously with an argument on the football field between one of the Roughnecks and a member of the opposition's football team.

Jack had a particular propensity for fighting and was involved in most of the brawls. He was a prime mover of the escalation of arguments into fights.

More serious than fighting, had the community been aware of it, was theft. Although almost everyone was aware that the boys occasionally stole things, they did not realize the extent of the activity. Petty stealing was a frequent event for the Roughnecks. Sometimes they stole as a group and coordinated their efforts; other times they stole in pairs. Rarely did they steal alone.

The thefts ranged from very small things like paperback books, comics, and ballpoint pens to expensive items like watches. The nature of the thefts varied from time to time. The gang would go through a period of systematically shoplifting items from automobiles or school lockers. Types of thievery varied with the whim of the gang. Some forms of thievery were more profitable than others, but all thefts were for profit, not just thrills.

Roughnecks siphoned gasoline from cars as often as they had access to an automobile, which was not very often. Unlike the Saints, who owned their own cars, the Roughnecks would have to borrow their parents' cars, an event which occurred only eight or nine times a year. The boys claimed to have stolen cars for joy rides from time to time.

Ron committed the most serious of the group's offenses. With an unidentified associate the boy attempted to burglarize a gasoline station. Although this station had been robbed twice previously in the same month, Ron denied any involvement in either of the other thefts. When Ron and his accomplice approached the station, the owner was hiding in the bushes beside the station. He fired both barrels of a double-barreled shotgun at the boys. Ron was severely injured; the other boy ran away and was never caught. Though he remained in critical condition for several months, Ron finally recovered and served six months of the following year in reform school. Upon release from reform school, Ron was put back a grade in school, and began running around with a different gang of boys. The Roughnecks considered the new gang less delinquent than themselves, and during the following year Ron had no more trouble with the police.

The Roughnecks, then, engaged mainly in three types of delinquency: theft, drinking, and fighting. Although community members perceived that this gang of kids was delinquent, they mistakenly believed that their illegal activities were primarily drinking, fighting, and being a nuisance to passersby. Drinking was limited among the gang members, although it did occur, and theft was much more prevalent than anyone realized.

Drinking would doubtless have been more prevalent had the boys had ready access to liquor. Since they rarely had automobiles at their disposal, they could not travel very far, and the bars in town would not serve them. Most of the boys had little money, and this, too, inhibited their purchase of alcohol. Their major source of liquor was a local drunk who would buy them a fifth if they would give him enough to buy himself a pint of whiskey or a bottle of wine.

The community's perception of drinking as prevalent stemmed from the fact that it was the most obvious delinquency the boys engaged in. When one of the boys had been drinking, even a casual observer seeing him on the corner would suspect that he was high.

There was a high level of mutual distrust and dislike between the Roughnecks and the police. The boys felt very strongly that the police were unfair and corrupt. Some evidence existed that the boys were correct in their perception.

The main source of the boys' dislike for the police undoubtedly stemmed from the fact that the police would sporadically harass the group. From the standpoint of the boys, these acts of occasional enforcement of the law were whimsical and uncalled for. It made no sense to them, for example, that the police would come to the corner occasionally and threaten them with arrest for loitering when the night before the boys had been out siphoning gasoline from cars and the police had been nowhere in sight. To the boys, the police were stupid on the one hand, for not being where they should have been and catching the boys in a serious offense, and unfair on the other hand, for trumping up "loitering" charges against them.

From the viewpoint of the police, the situation was quite different. They knew, with all the confidence necessary to be a policeman, that these boys were engaged in criminal activities. They knew this partly from occasionally catching them, mostly from circumstantial evidence ("the boys were around when those tires were slashed"), and partly because the police shared the view of the community in general that this was a bad bunch of boys. The best the police could hope to do was to be sensitive to the fact that these boys were engaged in illegal acts and arrest them whenever there was some evidence that they had been involved. Whether or not the boys had in fact committed a particular act in a particular way was not especially important. The police had a broader view; their job was to stamp out these kids' crimes; the tactics were not as important as the end result.

Over the period that the group was under observation, each member was arrested at least once. Several of the boys were arrested a number of times and spent at least one night in jail. While most were never taken to court, two of the boys were sentenced to six months' incarceration in boys' schools.

THE ROUGHNECKS IN SCHOOL

The Roughnecks' behavior in school was not particularly disruptive. During school hours they did not all hang around together, but tended instead to spend most of their time with one or two other members of the gang who were their special buddies. Although every member of the gang attempted to avoid school as much as possible, they were not particularly successful and most of them attended school with surprising regularity. They considered school a burden—something to be gotten through with a minimum of conflict. If they were "bugged" by a particular teacher, it could lead to trouble. One of the boys, Al, once threatened to beat up a teacher and, according to the other boys, the teacher hid under a desk to escape him.

Teachers saw the boys the way the general community did, as heading for trouble, as being uninterested in making something of themselves. Some were also seen as being incapable of meeting the academic standards of the school. Most of the teachers expressed concern for this group of boys and were willing to pass them despite poor performance, in the belief that failing them would only aggravate the problem.

The group of boys had a grade point average just slightly above "C." No one in the group failed either grade, and no one had better than a "C" average. They were very consistent in their perception of the boys' achievement.

Two of the boys were good football players. Herb was acknowledged to be the best player in the school and Jack was almost as good. Both boys were criticized for their failure to abide by training rules, for refusing to come to practice as often as they should, and for not playing their best during practice. What they lacked in sportsmanship they made up for in skill, apparently, and played every game no matter how poorly they had performed in practice or how many practice sessions they had missed.

TWO QUESTIONS

Why did the community, the school, and the police react to the Saints as though they were good, upstanding, nondelinquent youths with bright futures but to the Roughnecks as though they were tough, young criminals who were headed for trouble? Why did the Roughnecks and the Saints in fact have quite different careers after high school—careers which, by and large, lived up to the expectations of the community?

The most obvious explanation for the differences in the community's and law enforcement agencies' reactions to the two gangs is that one group of boys was "more delinquent" than the other. Which group *was* more delinquent? The answer to this question will determine in part how we explain the differential responses to these groups by the members of the community and, particularly, by law enforcement and school officials.

In sheer number of illegal acts, the Saints were the more delinquent. They were truant from school for at least part of the day almost every day of the week. In addition, their drinking and vandalism occurred with surprising regularity. The Roughnecks, in contrast, engaged sporadically in delinquent episodes. While these episodes were frequent, they certainly did not occur on a daily or even a weekly basis.

The difference in frequency of offenses was probably caused by the Roughnecks' inability to obtain liquor and to manipulate legitimate excuses from school. Since the Roughnecks had less money than the Saints, and teachers carefully supervised their school activities, the Roughnecks' hearts may have been as black as the Saints', but their misdeeds were not nearly as frequent.

There are really no clear-cut criteria by which to measure qualitative differences in antisocial behavior. The most important dimension is generally referred to as the "seriousness" of the offenses.

If seriousness encompasses the relative economic costs of delinquent acts, then some assessment can be made. The Roughnecks probably stole an average of about $5 worth of goods a week. Some weeks the figure was considerably higher, but these times must be balanced against long periods when almost nothing was stolen.

The Saints were more continuously engaged in delinquency but their acts were not for the most part costly to property. Only their vandalism and occasional theft of gasoline would so qualify. Perhaps once or twice a month they would siphon a tankful of gas. The other costly items were street signs, construction lanterns and the like. All of these acts combined probably did not quite average $5 a week, partly because much of the stolen equipment was abandoned and presumably could be recovered. The difference in cost of stolen property between the two groups was trivial, but the Roughnecks probably had a slightly more expensive set of activities than did the Saints.

Another meaning of seriousness is the potential threat of physical harm to members of the community and to the boys themselves. The Roughnecks were more prone to physical violence; they not only welcomed an opportunity to fight, they went seeking it. In addition, they fought among themselves frequently. Although the fighting never included deadly weapons, it was still a menace, however minor, to the physical safety of those involved.

The Saints never fought. They avoided physical conflict both inside and outside the group. At the same time, though, the Saints frequently endangered their own and other people's lives. They did so almost every time they drove a car, especially if they had been drinking. Sober, their driving was risky; under the influence of alcohol it was horrendous. In addition, the Saints endangered the lives of others with their pranks. Street excavations left unmarked were a very serious hazard.

Evaluating the relative seriousness of the two gangs' activities is difficult. The community reacted as though the behavior of the Roughnecks was a problem, and they reacted as though the behavior of the Saints was not. But the members of the community were ignorant of the array of delinquent acts that characterized the Saints' behavior. Although concerned citizens were unaware of much of the Roughnecks' behavior as well, they were much better informed about the Roughnecks' involvement in delinquency than they were about the Saints'.

VISIBILITY

Differential treatment of the two gangs resulted in part because one gang was infinitely more visible than the other. This differential visibility was a direct function of the economic standing of the families. The Saints had access to automobiles and were able to remove themselves from the sight of the community. In as routine a decision as to where to go to have a milkshake after school, the Saints stayed away from the mainstream of community life. Lacking transportation, the Roughnecks could not make it to the edge of town. The center of town was the only practical place for them to meet since their homes were scattered throughout the town and any noncentral meeting place put an undue hardship on some members. Through necessity the Roughnecks congregated in a crowded area where everyone in the community passed frequently, including teachers and law enforcement officers. They could easily see the Roughnecks hanging around the drugstore.

The Roughnecks, of course, made themselves even more visible by making remarks to passersby and by occasionally getting into fights on the corner. Meanwhile, just as regularly, the Saints were either at the cafe on one edge of town or in the pool hall at the other edge of town. Without any particular realization that they were making themselves inconspicuous, the Saints were able to hide their time-wasting. Not only were they removed from the mainstream of traffic, but they were almost always inside a building.

On their escapades the Saints were also relatively invisible, since they left Hanibal and traveled to Big City. Here, too, they were mobile, roaming the city, rarely going to the same area twice.

DEMEANOR

To the notion of visibility must be added the difference in the responses of group members to outside intervention with their activities. If one of the Saints was confronted with an accusing policeman, even if he felt he was truly innocent of a wrongdoing, his demeanor was apologetic and penitent. A Roughnecks' attitude was almost the polar opposite. When confronted with a threatening adult authority, even one who tried to be pleasant, the Roughneck's hostility and disdain were clearly observable. Sometimes he might attempt to put up a veneer of respect, but it was thin and was not accepted as sincere by the authority.

School was no different from the community at large. The Saints could manipulate the system by feigning compliance with the school norms. The availability of cars at school meant that once free from the immediate sight of the teacher, the boys could disappear rapidly. And this escape was well enough planned that no administrator or teacher was nearby when the boys left. A Roughneck who wished to escape for a few hours was in a bind. If it were possible to get free from class, downtown was still a mile away, and even if he arrived there, he was still very visible. Truancy for the Roughnecks meant almost certain detection, while the Saints enjoyed almost complete immunity from sanctions.

BIAS

Community members were not aware of the transgressions of the Saints. Even if the Saints had been less discreet, their favorite delinquencies would have been perceived as less serious than those of the Roughnecks.

In the eyes of the police and school officials, a boy who drinks in an alley and stands intoxicated on the street corner is committing a more serious offense than is a boy who drinks to inebriation in a nightclub or a tavern and drives around afterwards in a car. Similarly, a boy who steals a wallet from a store will be viewed as having committed a more serious offense than a boy who steals a lantern from a construction site.

Perceptual bias also operates with respect to the demeanor of the boys in the two groups when they are confronted by adults. It is not simply that adults dislike the posture affected by boys of the Roughneck ilk; more important is the conviction that the posture adopted by the Roughnecks is an indication of their devotion and commitment to deviance as a way of life. The posture becomes a cue, just as the type of the offense is a cue, to the degree to which the known transgressions are indicators of the youths' potential for other problems.

Visibility, demeanor, and bias are surface variables which explain the day-to-day operations of the police. Why do these surface variables operate as they do? Why did the police choose to disregard the Saints' delinquencies while breathing down the backs of the Roughnecks?

The answer lies in the class structure of American society and the control of legal institutions by those at the top of the class structure. Obviously, no representative of the upper class drew up the operational chart for the police which led them to look in the ghettos and on street corners—which led them to see the demeanor of lower-class youth as troublesome and that of upper-middle-class youth as tolerable. Rather, the procedures simply developed from experience—experience with irate and influential upper-middle-class parents insisting that their son's vandalism was simply a prank and his drunkenness only a momentary "sowing of wild oats"—experience with cooperative or indifferent, powerless, lower-class parents who acquiesced to the laws' definition of their son's behavior.

ADULT CAREERS OF THE SAINTS AND THE ROUGHNECKS

The community's confidence in the potential of the Saints and the Roughnecks apparently was justified. If anything, the community members underestimated the degree to which these youngsters would turn out "good" or "bad."

Seven of the eight members of the Saints went on to college immediately after high school. Five of the boys graduated from college in four years. The sixth one finished college after two years in the army, and the seventh spent four years in the air force before returning to college and receiving a B.A. degree. Of these seven college graduates, three went on for advanced degrees. One finished law school and is now active in state politics, one finished medical school and is practicing near Hanibal, and one boy is now working for a Ph.D. The other four college graduates entered submanagerial, managerial or executive training positions with large firms.

The only Saint who did not complete college was Jerry. Jerry had failed to graduate from high school with the other Saints. During his second senior year, after the other Saints had gone on to college, Jerry began to hang around with what several teachers described as a "rough crowd"—the gang that was heir apparent to the Roughnecks. At the end of his second senior year, when he did graduate from high school, Jerry took a job as a used-car salesman, got married and quickly had a child. Although he made several abortive attempts to go to college by attending night school, when I last saw him (ten years after high school) Jerry was unemployed and had been living on unemployment for almost a year. His wife worked as a waitress.

Some of the Roughnecks have lived up to community expectations. A number of them were headed for trouble. A few were not.

Jack and Herb were the athletes among the Roughnecks and their athletic prowess paid off handsomely. Both boys received unsolicited athletic scholarships to college. After Herb received his scholarship (near the end of his senior year), he apparently did an about-face. His demeanor became very similar to that of the Saints. Although he remained a member in good standing of the Roughnecks, he stopped participating in most activities and did not hang around on the corner as often.

Jack did not change. If anything, he became more prone to fighting. He even made excuses for accepting the scholarship. He told the other gang members that the school had guaranteed him a "C" average if he would come to play football—an idea that seems far-fetched, even in this day of highly competitive recruiting.

During the summer after graduation from high school, Jack attempted suicide by jumping from a tall building. The jump would certainly have killed most people trying it, but Jack survived. He entered college in the fall and played four years of football. He and Herb graduated in four years, and both are teaching and coaching in high schools. They are married and have stable families. If anything, Jack appears to have a more prestigious position in the community than does Herb, though both are well respected and secure in their positions.

Two of the boys never finished high school. Tommy left at the end of his junior year and went to another state. That summer he was arrested and placed on probation on a manslaughter charge. Three years later he was arrested for murder; he pleaded guilty to second degree murder and is serving a 30-year sentence in the state penitentiary.

Al, the other boy who did not finish high school, also left the state in his senior year. He is serving a life sentence in a state penitentiary for first degree murder.

Wes is a small-time gambler. He finished high school and "bummed around." After several years he made contact with a bookmaker who employed him as a runner. Later he acquired his own area and has been working it ever since. His position among the bookmakers is almost identical to the position he had in the gang; he is always around but no one is really aware of him. He makes no trouble and he does not get into any. Steady, reliable, capable of keeping his mouth closed, he plays the game by the rules, even though the game is an illegal one.

That leaves only Ron. Some of his former friends reported that they had heard he was "driving a truck up north," but no one could provide any concrete information.

REINFORCEMENT

The community responded to the Roughnecks as boys in trouble, and the boys agreed with that perception. Their pattern of deviancy was reinforced, and breaking away from it became increasingly unlikely. Once the boys acquired an image of themselves as deviants, they selected new friends who affirmed that self-image. As that self-conception became more firmly entrenched, they also became willing to try new and more extreme deviances. With their growing alienation came freer expression of disrespect and hostility for representatives of the legitimate society. This disrespect increased the community's negativism, perpetuating the entire process of commitment to deviance. Lack of a commitment to deviance works the same way. In either case, the process will perpetuate itself unless some event (like a scholarship to college or a sudden failure) external to the established relationship intervenes. For two of the Roughnecks (Herb and Jack), receiving college athletic scholarships created new relations and culminated in a break with the established pattern of deviance. In the case of one of the Saints (Jerry), his parents' divorce and his failing to graduate from high school changed some of his other relations. Being held back in school for a year and losing his place among the Saints had sufficient impact on Jerry to alter his self-image and virtually to assure that he would not go on to college as his peers did. Although the experiments of life can rarely be reversed, it seems likely in view of the behavior of the other boys who did not enjoy this special treatment by the school that Jerry, too, would have "become something" had he graduated as anticipated. For Herb and Jack outside intervention worked to their advantage, for Jerry it was his undoing.

Selective perception and labeling—finding, processing, and punishing some kinds of criminality and not others—means that visible, poor, nonmobile, outspoken, undiplomatic "tough" kids will be noticed, whether their actions are seriously delinquent or not. Other kids, who have established a reputation for being bright (even though underachieving), disciplined, and involved in respectable activities, who are mobile and monied, will be invisible when they deviate from sanctioned activities. They'll sow their wild oats—perhaps even wider and thicker than their lower-class cohorts—but they won't be noticed. When it's time to leave adolescence most will follow the expected path, settling into the ways of the middle class, remembering fondly the delinquent but unnoticed fling of their youth. The Roughnecks and others like them may turn around, too. It is more likely that their noticeable deviance will have been so reinforced by police and community that their lives will be effectively channeled into careers consistent with their adolescent background.

Review Questions

1. What were the typical activities of the Saints? The Roughnecks? Which group committed more illegal acts?
2. Were the community's perceptions of the Saints accurate? Were the community's perceptions of the Roughnecks accurate? What role did the *visibility* of the two groups play in the community's perceptions of them?
3. How did the social-class backgrounds of the Saints and the Roughnecks affect their visibility to adult members of the community?
4. Why is it important to understand "surface variables"—visibility, demeanor, and bias—to explain the actions of the police?
5. How does Chambliss's research demonstrate the usefulness of looking beyond commonly accepted explanations of social life?

MEN AND JOBS ON TALLY'S CORNER

Elliot Liebow

IN SUMMARY OF OBJECTIVE JOB CONSIDERATIONS [OF STREETCORNER MEN], the most important fact is that a man who is able and willing to work cannot earn enough money to support himself, his wife, and one or more children. A man's chances for working regularly are good only if he is willing to work for less than he can live on, and sometimes not even then. On some jobs, the wage rate is deceptively higher than on others, but the higher the wage rate, the more difficult it is to get the job, and the less the job security. Higher-paying construction work tends to be seasonal and, during the season, the amount of work available is highly sensitive to business and weather conditions and to the changing requirements of individual projects.[1] Moreover, high-paying construction jobs are frequently beyond the physical capacity of some of the men, and some of the low-paying jobs are scaled down even lower in accordance with the self-fulfilling assumption that the man will steal part of his wages on the job.[2]

Bernard assesses the objective job situation dispassionately over a cup of coffee, sometimes poking at the coffee with his spoon, sometimes staring at it as if, like a crystal ball, it holds tomorrow's secrets. He is twenty-seven years old. He and the woman with whom he lives have a baby son, and she has another child by another man. Bernard does odd jobs—mostly painting—but here it is the end of January, and his last job was with the Post Office during the Christmas mail rush. It pays well (about $2 an hour) but he has twice failed the Post Office examination (he graduated from a Washington high school) and has given up the idea as an impractical one. He is supposed to see a man tonight about a job as a parking attendant for a large apartment house. The man told him to bring his birth certificate and driver's license, but his license was suspended because of a backlog of unpaid traffic fines. A friend promised to lend him some money this evening. If he gets it, he will pay the fines tomorrow morning and have his license reinstated. He hopes the man with the job will wait till tomorrow night.

A "security job" is what he really wants, he said. He would like to save up money for a taxicab. (But having twice failed the postal examination and having a bad driving record as well, it is highly doubtful that he could meet the qualifications or pass the written test.) That would be "a good life." He can always get a job in a restaurant or as a clerk in a drugstore but they don't pay enough, he said. He needs to take home at least $50 to $55 a week. He thinks he can get that much driving a truck somewhere. . . . Sometimes he wishes he had stayed in the army. . . . A security job, that's what he wants most of all, a real security job. . . .

When we look at what the men bring to the job rather than at what the job offers the men, it is essential to keep in mind that we are not looking at men who come to the job fresh, just out of school perhaps, and newly prepared to undertake the task of making a living, or from another job where they earned a living and are prepared to do the same on this job. Each man comes to the job with a long job history characterized by his not being able to support himself and his family. Each man carries this knowledge, born of his experience, with him. He comes to the job flat and stale, wearied by the sameness of it all, convinced of his own incompetence, terrified of responsibility—of being tested still again and found wanting. Possible exceptions are the younger men not yet, or just, married. They suspect all this but have yet to have it confirmed by repeated personal experience over time. But those who are or have been married know it well. It is the experience of the individual and the group; of their fathers and probably their sons. Convinced of their inadequacies, not only do they not seek out those few better-paying jobs which test their resources, but they actively avoid them, gravitating in a mass to the menial, routine jobs which offer no challenge—and therefore pose no threat—to the already diminished images they have of themselves.

Thus Richard does not follow through on [a] real estate agent's offer. He is afraid to do on his own—minor plastering, replacing broken windows, other minor repairs and painting—exactly what he had been doing for months on a piece-work basis under someone else (and which provided him with a solid base from which to derive a cost estimate).

Richard once offered an important clue to what may have gone on in his mind when the job offer was made. We were in the Carry-out, at a time when he was looking for work. He was talking about the kind of jobs available to him.

> I graduated from high school [Baltimore] but I don't know anything. I'm dumb. Most of the time I don't even say I graduated, 'cause then somebody asks me a question and I can't answer it, and they think I was lying about graduating. . . . They graduated me but I didn't know anything. I had lousy grades but I guess they wanted to get rid of me.
>
> I was at Margaret's house the other night and her little sister asked me to help her with her homework. She showed me some fractions and I knew

> right away I couldn't do them. I was ashamed so I told her I had to go to the bathroom.

And so it must have been, surely, with the real estate agent's offer. Convinced that "I'm dumb . . . I don't know anything," he "knew right away" he couldn't do it, despite the fact that he had been doing just this sort of work all along.

Thus, the man's low self-esteem generates a fear of being tested and prevents him from accepting a job with responsibilities or, once on a job, from staying with it if responsibilities are thrust on him, even if the wages are commensurately higher. Richard refuses such a job, Leroy leaves one, and another man, given more responsibility and more pay, knows he will fail and proceeds to do so, proving he was right about himself all along. The self-fulfilling prophecy is everywhere at work. In a hallway, Stanton, Tonk, and Boley are passing a bottle around. Stanton recalls the time he was in the service. Everything was fine until he attained the rank of corporal. He worried about everything he did then. Was he doing the right thing? Was he doing it well? When would they discover their mistake and take his stripes (and extra pay) away? When he finally lost his stripes, everything was all right again.

Lethargy, disinterest, and general apathy on the job, so often reported by employers, has its streetcorner counterpart. The men do not ordinarily talk about their jobs or ask one another about them.[3] Although most of the men know who is or is not working at any given time, they may or may not know what particular job an individual man has. There is no overt interest in job specifics as they relate to this or that person, in large part perhaps because the specifics are not especially relevant. To know that a man is working is to know approximately how much he makes and to know as much as one needs or wants to know about how he makes it. After all, how much difference does it make to know whether a man is pushing a mop and pulling trash in an apartment house, a restaurant, or an office building, or delivering groceries, drugs, or liquor, or, if he's a laborer, whether he's pushing a wheelbarrow, mixing mortar, or digging a hole. So much does one job look like every other that there is little to choose between them. In large part, the job market consists of a narrow range of nondescript chores calling for nondistinctive, undifferentiated, unskilled labor. "A job is a job."

A crucial factor in the streetcorner man's lack of job commitment is the overall value he places on the job. *For his part, the streetcorner man puts no lower value on the job than does the larger society around him.* He knows the social value of the job by the amount of money the employer is willing to pay him for doing it. In a real sense, every pay day, he counts in dollars and cents the value placed on the job by society at large. He is no more (and frequently less) ready to quit and look for another job than his employer is ready to fire him and look for another man. Neither the streetcorner man who performs these jobs nor the society which requires him to perform them assesses the job as one "worth doing and worth doing well." Both employee and employer are contemptuous of the job. The employee shows his contempt by his reluctance to accept it or keep it, the employer by paying less than is required to support a family.[4] Nor does the low-wage job offer prestige, respect, interesting work, opportunity for learning or advancement, or any other compensation. With few exceptions, jobs filled by the streetcorner men are at the bottom of the employment ladder in every respect, from wage level to prestige. Typically, they are hard, dirty, uninteresting, and underpaid. The rest of society (whatever its ideal values regarding the dignity of labor) holds the job of the dishwasher or janitor or unskilled laborer in low esteem if not outright contempt.[5] So does the streetcorner man. He cannot do otherwise. He cannot draw from a job those social values which other people do not put into it.[6]

Only occasionally does spontaneous conversation touch on these matters directly. Talk about jobs is usually limited to isolated statements of intention, such as "I think I'll get me another gig [job]," "I'm going to look for a construction job when the weather breaks," or "I'm going to quit. I can't take no more of this shit." Job assessments typically consist of nothing more than a noncomittal shrug and "It's O.K." or "It's a job."

One reason for the relative absence of talk about one's job is, as suggested earlier, that the sameness of job experiences does not bear reiteration. Another and more important reason is the emptiness of the job experience itself. The man sees middle-class occupations as a primary source of prestige, pride, and self-respect; his own job affords him none of these. To think about his job is to see himself as others see him, to remind him of just where he stands in this society.[7] And because society's criteria for placement are generally the same as his own, to talk about his job can trigger a flush of shame and a deep, almost physical ache to change places with someone, almost anyone, else.[8] The desire to be a person in his own right, to be noticed by the world he lives in, is shared by each of the men on the streetcorner. Whether they articulate this desire (as Tally does below) or not, one can see them position themselves to catch the attention of their fellows in much the same way as plants bend or stretch to catch the sunlight.[9]

Tally and I were in the Carry-out. It was summer, Tally's peak earning season as a cement finisher, a semiskilled job a cut or so above that of the unskilled laborer. His take-home pay during these weeks was well over a hundred dollars—"a lot of bread." But for Tally, who no longer had a family to support, bread was not enough.

> "You know that boy came in last night? That Black Moozlem? That's what I ought to be doing. I ought to be in his place."
>
> "What do you mean?"
>
> "Dressed nice, going to [night] school, got a good job."
>
> "He's no better than you, Tally. You make more than he does."

"It's not the money. [Pause] It's position, I guess. He's got position. When he finish school he gonna be a supervisor. People respect him. . . . Thinking about people with position and education gives me a feeling right here [pressing his fingers into the pit of his stomach]."

"You're educated, too. You have a skill, a trade. You're a cement finisher. You can make a building, pour a sidewalk."

"That's different. Look, can anybody do what you're doing? Can anybody just come up and do your job? Well, in one week I can teach you cement finishing. You won't be as good as me 'cause you won't have the experience but you'll be a cement finisher. That's what I mean. Anybody can do what I'm doing and that's what gives me this feeling. [Long pause] Suppose I like this girl. I go over to her house and I meet her father. He starts talking about what he done today. He talks about operating on somebody and sewing them up and about surgery. I knows he's a doctor 'cause of the way he talks. Then she starts talking about what she did. Maybe she's a boss or a supervisor. Maybe she's a lawyer and her father says to me, 'And what do you do, Mr. Jackson?" [Pause] You remember at the courthouse, Lonny's trial? You and the lawyer was talking in the hall? You remember? I just stood there listening. I didn't say a word. You know why? 'Cause I didn't even know what you was talking about. That's happened to me a lot."

"Hell, you're nothing special. That happens to everybody. Nobody knows everything. One man is a doctor, so he talks about surgery. Another man is a teacher, so he talks about books. But doctors and teachers don't know anything about concrete. You're a cement finisher and that's your specialty."

"Maybe so, but when was the last time you saw anybody standing around talking about concrete?"

The streetcorner man wants to be a person in his own right, to be noticed, to be taken account of, but in this respect, as well as in meeting his money needs, his job fails him. The job and the man are even. The job fails the man and the man fails the job.

Furthermore, the man does not have any reasonable expectation that, however bad it is, his job will lead to better things. Menial jobs are not, by and large, the starting point of a track system which leads to even better jobs for those who are able and willing to do them. The busboy or dishwasher in a restaurant is not on a job track which, if negotiated skillfully, leads to chef or manager of the restaurant. The busboy or dishwasher who works hard becomes, simply, a hard-working busboy or dishwasher. Neither hard work nor perseverance can conceivably carry the janitor to a sit-down job in the office building he cleans up. And it is the apprentice who becomes the journeyman electrician, plumber, steam fitter or bricklayer, not the common unskilled Negro laborer.

Thus, the job is not a stepping-stone to something better. It is a dead end. It promises to deliver no more tomorrow, next month, or next year than it does today.

Delivering little, and promising no more, the job is "no big thing." The man appears to treat the job in a cavalier fashion, working and not working as the spirit moves him, as if all that matters is the immediate satisfaction of his present appetites, the surrender to present moods, and the indulgence of whims with no thought for the cost, the consequences, the future. To the middle-class observer, this behavior reflects a "present-time orientation"—an "inability to defer gratification." It is this "present-time orientation"—as against the "future orientation" of the middle-class person—that "explains" to the outsider why Leroy chooses to spend the day at the Carry-out rather than report to work; why Richard, who was paid Friday, was drunk Saturday and Sunday and penniless Monday; why Sweets quit his job today because the boss looked at him "funny" yesterday.

But from the inside looking out, what appears as a "present-time" orientation to the outside observer is, to the man experiencing it, as much a future orientation as that of his middle-class counterpart.[10] The difference between the two men lies not so much in their different orientations to time as in their different orientations to future time or, more specifically, to their different futures.[11]

The future orientation of the middle-class person presumes, among other things, a surplus of resources to be invested in the future and a belief that the future will be sufficiently stable both to justify his investment (money in a bank, time and effort in a job, investment of himself in marriage and family, etc.) and to permit the consumption of his investment at a time, place, and manner of his own choosing and to his greater satisfaction. But the streetcorner man lives in a sea of want. He does not, as a rule, have a surplus of resources, either economic or psychological. Gratification of hunger and the desire for simple creature comforts cannot be long deferred. Neither can support for one's flagging self-esteem. Living on the edge of both economic and psychological subsistence, the streetcorner man is obliged to expend all his resources on maintaining himself from moment to moment.[12]

As for the future, the young streetcorner man has a fairly good picture of it. In Richard or Sea Cat or Arthur he can see himself in his middle twenties; he can look at Tally to see himself at thirty, at Wee Tom to see himself in his middle thirties, and at Budder and Stanton to see himself in his forties. It is a future in which everything is uncertain except the ultimate destruction of his hopes and the eventual realization of his fears. The most he can reasonably look forward to is that these things do not come too soon. Thus, when Richard squanders a week's pay in two days it is not because, like an animal or a child, he is "present-time oriented," unaware of or unconcerned with his future. He does so precisely because he is aware of the future and the hopelessness of it all.

Sometimes this kind of response appears as a conscious, explicit choice. Richard had had a violent argument with his wife. He said he was going to leave her and the children, that he had had enough of everything and could not take any more, and he chased her out of the house. His chest still heaving, he leaned back against the wall in the hallway of his basement apartment.

> "I've been scuffling for five years," he said. "I've been scuffling for five years from morning till night. And my kids still don't have anything; my wife don't have anything, and I don't have anything.
>
> "There," he said, gesturing down the hall to a bed, a sofa, a couple of chairs and a television set, all shabby, some broken. "There's everything I have and I'm having trouble holding onto that."
>
> Leroy came in, presumably to petition Richard on behalf of Richard's wife, who was sitting outside on the steps, afraid to come in. Leroy started to say something but Richard cut him short.
>
> "Look, Leroy, don't give me any of that action. You and me are entirely different people. Maybe I look like a boy and maybe I act like a boy sometimes but I got a man's mind. You and me don't want the same things out of life. Maybe some of the same, but you don't care how long you have to wait for yours and *I—want—mine—right—now.*"[13]

Thus, apparent present-time concerns with consumption and indulgences—material and emotional—reflect a future-time orientation. "I want mine right now" is ultimately a cry of despair, a direct response to the future as he sees it.[14]

In many instances, it is precisely the streetcorner man's orientation to the future—but to a future loaded with "trouble"—which not only leads to a greater emphasis on present concerns ("I want mine right now") but also contributes importantly to the instability of employment, family and friend relationships, and to the general transient quality of daily life.

Let me give some concrete examples. One day, after Tally had gotten paid, he gave me four twenty-dollar bills and asked me to keep them for him. Three days later he asked me for the money. I returned it and asked why he did not put his money in a bank. He said that the banks close at two o'clock. I argued that there were four or more banks within a two-block radius of where he was working at the time and that he could easily get to any one of them on his lunch hour. "No, man," he said, "you don't understand. They close at two o'clock and they closed Saturday and Sunday. Suppose I get into trouble and I got to make it [leave]. Me get out of town, and everything I got in the world layin' up in that bank? No good! No good!"

In another instance, Leroy and his girl friend were discussing "trouble." Leroy was trying to decide how best to go about getting his hands on some "long green" (a lot of money), and his girl friend cautioned him about "trouble." Leroy sneered at this, saying he had had "trouble" all his life and wasn't afraid of a little more. "Anyway," he said, "I'm famous for leaving town."[15]

Thus, the constant awareness of a future loaded with "trouble" results in a constant readiness to leave, to "make it," to "get out of town," and discourages the man from sinking roots into the world he lives in.[16] Just as it discourages him from putting money in the bank, so it discourages him from committing himself to a job, especially one whose payoff lies in the promise of future rewards rather than in the present. In the same way, it discourages him from deep and lasting commitments to family and friends or to any other persons, places or things, since such commitments could hold him hostage, limiting his freedom of movement and thereby compromising his security which lies in that freedom.

. . . The streetcorner man is under continuous assault by his job experiences and job fears. His experiences and fears feed on one another. The kind of job he can get—and frequently only after fighting for it, if then—steadily confirms his fears, depresses his self-confidence and self-esteem until finally, terrified of an opportunity even if one presents itself, he stands defeated by his experiences, his belief in his own self-worth destroyed and his fears a confirmed reality.

NOTES

1. The overall result is that, in the long run, a Negro laborer's earnings are not substantially greater—and may be less—than those of the busboy, janitor, or stock clerk. Herman P. Miller, for example, reports that in 1960, 40 percent of all jobs held by Negro men were as laborers or in the service trades. The average annual wage for nonwhite nonfarm laborers was $2,400. The average earning of nonwhite service workers was $2,500 (*Rich Man, Poor Man,* p. 90). Francis Greenfield estimates that in the Washington vicinity, the 1965 earnings of the union laborer who works whenever work is available will be about $3,200. Even this figure is high for the man on the streetcorner. Union men in heavy construction are the aristocrats of the laborers. Casual day labor and jobs with small firms in the building and construction trades, or with firms in other industries, pay considerably less.

2. For an excellent discussion of the self-fulfilling assumption (or prophecy) as a social force, see "The Self-Fulfilling Prophecy," Ch. XI, in Robert K. Merton's *Social Theory and Social Structure* (Glencoe, Ill.: Free Press, 1957).

3. This stands in dramatic contrast to the leisure-time conversation of stable, working-class men. For the coal miners (of Ashton, England), for example, "the topic [of conversation] which surpasses all others in frequency is work—the difficulties which have been encountered in the day's shift, the way in which a particular task was accomplished, and so on." Josephine Klein, *Samples from English Cultures,* Vol. 1(London: Routledge and Kegan Paul, 1956), p. 88.

4. It is important to remember that the employer is not entirely a free agent. Subject to the constraints of the larger society, he acts for the larger society as well as for himself. Child labor laws, safety and sanitation regulations, minimum wage scales in some employment areas, and other constraints, are already on the books; other control mechanisms, such as a guaranteed annual wage, are to be had for the voting.

5. See, for example, the U.S. Bureau of the Census, *Methodology and Scores of Socioeconomic Status.* The assignment of the lowest SES ratings to men who hold such jobs is not peculiar to our own society. A low SES rating for "the

shoeshine boy or garbage man . . . seems to be true for all [industrial] countries." Alex Inkeles, "Industrial Man," *American Journal of Sociology* 66 (July 1960), p. 8.

6. That the streetcorner man downgrades manual labor should occasion no surprise. Merton points out that "the American stigmatization of manual labor . . . *has been found to hold rather uniformly in all social classes*" (emphasis in original; *Social Theory and Social Structure,* p. 145). That he finds no satisfaction in such work should also occasion no surprise: "[There is] a clear positive correlation between the overall status of occupations and the experience of satisfaction in them." Inkeles, "Industrial Man," *American Journal of Sociology* 66 (July 1960), p. 12.

7. "[In our society] a man's work is one of the things by which he is judged, and certainly one of the more significant things by which he judges himself. . . . A man's work is one of the more important parts of his social identity, of his self; indeed, of his fate in the one life he has to live." Everett C. Hughes, *Men and Their Work* (Glencoe, Ill.: Free Press, 1958), pp. 42–43.

8. Noting that lower-class persons "are constantly exposed to evidence of their own irrelevance," Lee Rainwater spells out still another way in which the poor are poor: "The identity problems of lower-class persons make the soul-searching of middle-class adolescents and adults seem rather like a kind of conspicuous consumption of psychic riches," "Work and Identity in the Lower Class," in Sam Bass Warner, Jr., *Planning for a Nation of Cities* (Cambridge: Cambridge Univ. Press, 1966), p. 3.

9. Sea Cat cuts his pants legs off at the calf and puts a fringe on the raggedy edges. Tonk breaks his "shades" and continues to wear the horn-rimmed frames minus the lenses. Richard cultivates a distinctive manner of speech. Lonny gives himself a birthday party. And so on.

10. Taking a somewhat different point of view, S. M. Miller and Frank Riessman suggest that "the entire concept of deferred gratification may be inappropriate to understanding the essence of workers' lives." "The Working Class Subculture: A New View," *Social Problems* 9 (1961), p. 87.

11. This sentence is a paraphrase of a statement made by Marvin Cline at a 1965 colloquium at the Mental Health Study Center, National Institute of Mental Health.

12. And if, for the moment, he does sometimes have more money than he chooses to spend or more food than he wants to eat, he is pressed to spend the money and eat the food anyway since his friends, neighbors, kinsmen, or acquaintances will beg or borrow whatever surplus he has or, failing this, they may steal it. In one extreme case, one of the men admitted taking the last of a woman's surplus food allotment after she had explained that, with four children, she could not spare any food. The prospect that consumer soft goods not consumed by oneself will be consumed by someone else may be related to the way in which portable consumer durable goods, such as watches, radios, television sets or phonographs, are sometimes looked at as a form of savings. When Shirley was on welfare, she regularly took her television set out of pawn when she got her monthly check. Not so much to watch it, she explained, as to have something to fall back on when her money runs out toward the end of the month. For her and others, the television set or phonograph is her savings, the pawnshop is where she banks her savings, and the pawn ticket is her bankbook.

13. This was no simple rationalization for irresponsibility. Richard had indeed "been scuffling for five years" trying to keep his family going. Until shortly after

this episode, Richard was known and respected as one of the hardest-working men on the street. Richard had said, only a couple of months earlier, "I figure you got to get out there and try. You got to try before you can get anything." His wife Shirley confirmed that he had always tried. "If things get tough, with me I'll get all worried. But Richard get worried, he don't want to see me worried. . . . He *will* get out there. He's shoveled snow, picked beans, and he's done some of everything. . . . He's not ashamed to get out there and get us something to eat." At the time of the episode reported above, Leroy was just starting marriage and raising a family. He and Richard were not, as Richard thought, "entirely different people." Leroy had just not learned, by personal experience over time, what Richard had learned. But within two years Leroy's marriage had broken up and he was talking and acting like Richard. "He just let go completely," said one of the men on the street.

14. There is no mystically intrinsic connection between "present-time" orientation and lower-class persons. Whenever people of whatever class have been uncertain, skeptical or downright pessimistic about the future, "I want mine right now" has been one of the characteristic responses, although it is usually couched in more delicate terms: e.g., Omar Khayyam's "Take the cash and let the credit go," or Horace's "*Carpe diem.*" In wartime, especially, all classes tend to slough off conventional restraints on sexual and other behavior (i.e., become less able or less willing to defer gratification). And when inflation threatens, darkening the fiscal future, persons who formerly husbanded their resources with commendable restraint almost stampede one another rushing to spend their money. Similarly, it seems that future-time orientation tends to collapse toward the present when persons are in pain or under stress. The point here is that, the label notwithstanding, (what passes for) present-time orientation appears to be a situation-specific phenomenon rather than a part of the standard psychic equipment of Cognitive Lower Class Man.

15. And proceeded to do just that the following year when "trouble"—in this case, a grand jury indictment, a pile of debts, and a violent separation from his wife and children—appeared again.

16. For a discussion of "trouble" as a focal concern of lower-class culture, see Walter Miller, "Lower Class Culture as a Generating Milieu of Gang Delinquency," *Journal of Social Issues* 14 (1958), pp. 7, 8.

Review Questions

1. According to Liebow, for the streetcorner man, the job fails the man, and the man fails the job. Discuss this statement and give specific examples that support or refute it.
2. Describe Liebow's assessment of the present-time and future-time orientations of streetcorner men. Are there any indications that middle-class people are not always future-time oriented?
3. How do our society's sex roles contribute to the streetcorner men's feelings of failure?
4. Describe the sociological concept of self-fulfilling prophecy and give examples from Liebow's study of streetcorner men.

THE DIVORCE REVOLUTION AND THE FEMINIZATION OF POVERTY

Lenore J. Weitzman

INTRODUCTION

[STATES HAVE VARIED GREATLY THROUGH OUR COUNTRY'S HISTORY IN BOTH THE types of divorce laws they have and how the laws are interpreted by judges. California pioneered the introduction of a "no-fault" divorce law in 1970. The law is based on the modern idea that spouses can agree to divorce rather than fighting an adversarial battle in a court. In interpreting the new law, judges are not so quick to protect women as they once were. They award women alimony even more rarely than in the past. At the same time, the courts continue to give mothers primary responsibility for rearing children. Thus, the new law and its interpretation have contributed to a widening gender gap in income.]

Divorce has radically different economic consequences for men and women. While most divorced men find that their standard of living improves after divorce, most divorced women and the minor children in their households find that their standard of living plummets. This [article] shows that when income is compared to needs, divorced men experience an average 42 percent rise in their standard of living in the first year after the divorce, while divorced women (and their children) experience a 73 percent decline.

These apparently simple statistics have far-reaching social and economic consequences. For most women and children, divorce means precipitous downward mobility—both economically and socially. The reduction in income brings residential moves and inferior housing, drastically diminished or nonexistent funds for recreation and leisure, and intense pressures due to inadequate time and money. Financial hardships in turn cause social dislocation and a loss of familiar networks for emotional support and social services, and intensify the psycholog-

SOURCE: Lenore J. Weitzman, excerpted with permission from chapter 10 of: *The Divorce Revolution: The Unexpected Consequences for Women and Children in America.* by Dr. Lenore J. Weitzman. Copyright ©1985 by Dr. Lenore J. Weitzman. Published by The Free Press, a Division of Maxwell-Macmillan, Inc.

ical stress for women and children alike. On a societal level, divorce increases female and child poverty and creates an ever-widening gap between the economic well-being of divorced men, on the one hand, and their children and former wives on the other.

The data reviewed in this [article] indict the present legal system of divorce: it provides neither economic justice nor economic equality.

The economic consequences of the current system of divorce emerge from two different types of analysis. In the first analysis we focus on income. Here we compare men's and women's *incomes* before and after divorce. The second analysis focuses on *standards of living*. Here we ask how the husbands' postdivorce standards of living compare with that of their former wives. Since it is reasonable to expect postdivorce incomes and standards of living to vary with the length of marriage and the family income level before divorce, these two factors are controlled in the following analyses. . . .

LONG-MARRIED COUPLES AND DISPLACED HOMEMAKERS

Economically, older and longer-married women suffer the most after divorce. Their situation is much more drastic—and tragic—than that of their younger counterparts because the discrepancy between men's and women's standards of living after divorce is much greater than for younger couples, and few of these women can ever hope to recapture their loss.

Once again, among this group the discrepancy between former husbands and wives is evident at all income levels, and most pronounced—and severe—for those with predivorce family incomes of $40,000 or more a year.

When the courts project the postdivorce prospects for women after shorter marriages, they assume that most of these women will be able to build new lives for themselves.[1] They reason that a woman in her twenties or early thirties is young enough to acquire education or training and thus has the potential to find a satisfying and well-paid job. To be sure, such women will probably have a hard time catching up with their former husbands, but most of them will be able to enter or re-enter the labor force. In setting support for these younger women, the underlying assumption is that they will become self-sufficient. (I am not questioning that assumption. What has been questioned is the court's optimism about the ease and speed of the transition. Younger divorced women need more generous support awards for training and education to maximize their long-run job prospects.[2] But their potential for some level of "self-sufficiency" is not questioned.)

But what about the woman in her forties or fifties—or even sixties at the point of divorce? What are her prospects? Is it reasonable for judges to expect her to become self-sufficient? This woman's problems of job placement, retraining, and self-esteem are likely to be much more severe.[3] Her divorce award is likely to establish her standard of living for the rest of her life.

The hardest case is that of the long-married woman who has devoted her life to raising children who are now grown. Consider, for example, the hypothetical Ann Thompson, age fifty-three, who was formerly married to a wealthy corporate executive. She is much better off after divorce than the vast majority of divorced women her age because her former husband earns $6,000 a month net. The average Los Angeles judge would award Ann Thompson $2,000 a month in spousal support, giving her a total income of $24,000 a year in contrast to her former husband's $48,000 a year (after alimony payments are deducted from his income). Her former husband will be able to maintain his comfortable standard of living on his $48,000 income (which is likely to rise) and the tax benefits he gets from paying alimony. But Ann, with her house sold, no employment prospects, and the loss of her social status and social networks, will not be able to sustain anything near her former standard of living.

Since Ann Thompson's three children are over eighteen, she is not legally entitled to any child support for them.[4] She is likely, however, to be contributing to their college expenses. In addition, one or more of them is likely to still be living with her, and all probably return from time to time for extended visits. Thus she may well be providing as much if not more for their support than their well-to-do father.*

The combined effects of a less than equal income and a greater than equal share of the children's expenses invariably result in extreme downward mobility for long-married divorced women in California. They are both absolutely and relatively worse off than their former husbands. Although the courts are supposed to aim at balancing the resources of the two postdivorce households, the data reveal that they do not come near this goal. . . .

The data indicate that men married more than eighteen years have a much higher *per capita* income—that is, they have much more money to spend on themselves—than their former wives at every level of (predivorce family) income. Even where the discrepancy is smallest, in lower-income families, the husband and every member of this postdivorce family have *twice* as much money as his former wife and his children. In higher-income families, the discrepancy is enormous. The husband and each person in his postdivorce household—his new wife, cohab-

* When Stanford University students from divorced families were interviewed for a class research project most reported that they first asked their mother for money, even though they knew she had less than their father, because they found her more sympathetic and willing to support to them.

itor, or child—have three times as much disposable income as his former wife and the members of her postdivorce household. When we realize that the "other members" of the wife's postdivorce household are almost always the husband's children, the discrepancy between the two standards of living seems especially unjust. . . .

POSTDIVORCE STANDARDS OF LIVING: IMPOVERISHMENT OF WOMEN AND CHILDREN

The income disparity between men and women after divorce profoundly affects their relative standards of living.

To examine this effect we rely on an index of economic well-being developed by the U.S. government. The model for our analysis was constructed by Michigan researchers who followed a sample of 5,000 American families, weighted to be representative of the U.S. population. Economists Saul Hoffman and John Holmes compared the incomes of divorced men and divorced women over a seven-year period.*

A comparison of the married and divorced couples yielded two major findings. First, as might be expected, the dollar income of both divorced men and divorced women declined, while the income of married couples rose. Divorced men lost 19 percent in income while divorced women lost 29 percent.[5] In contrast, married men and women experienced a 22 percent rise in income.[6] These data confirm our commonsense belief that both parties suffer after a divorce. They also confirm that women experience a greater loss than their former husbands.

The second finding of the Michigan research is surprising. To see what the income loss meant in terms of family purchasing power, Hoffman and Holmes constructed an index of family income in relation to family needs.[7] Since this income/need comparison is adjusted for family size, as well as for each member's age and sex, it provides an individually tailored measure of a family's economic well-being in the context of marital status changes.

The Michigan researchers found that the experiences of divorced men and women were strikingly different when this measure was used. Over the seven-year period, the economic position of divorced men actually improved by 17 percent.[8] In contrast, over the same period divorced women experienced a 29 percent decline in terms of what their income could provide in relation to their needs.[9]

* Detailed information from the interviews provided the researchers with precise income data, including income from employment, intra-family transfers, welfare, and other government programs. Alimony and/or child support paid by the husband was subtracted from his income and added to the wife's postdivorce income. Finally, to facilitate direct comparisons, all income was calculated in constant 1968 dollars so that changes in real income could be examined without the compounding effect of inflation.

To compare the experiences of divorced men and women in California to those in Michigan, we devised a similar procedure to calculate the basic needs of each of the families in our interview sample. This procedure used the living standards for urban families constructed by the Bureau of Labor Statistics of the U.S. Department of Labor.[10] First, the standard budget level for each family in the interview sample was calculated in three different ways: once for the predivorce family, once for the wife's postdivorce family, and once for the husband's postdivorce family. Then the income in relation to needs was computed for each family. (Membership in postdivorce families of husbands and wives included any new spouse or cohabitor and any children whose custody was assigned to that spouse.) These data are presented in Figure 1.

Figure 1 reveals the radical change in the standards of living to which we alluded earlier. Just one year after legal divorce, *men experience a 42 percent improvement in their postdivorce standard of living, while women experience a 73 percent decline.*

Figure 1. Change in Standards of Living* of Divorced Men and Women (Approximately one year after divorce)

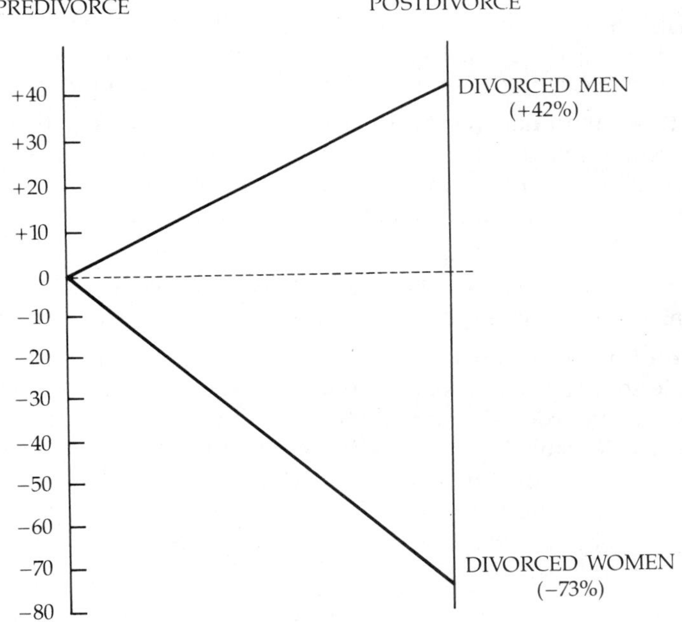

*Income in relation to needs with needs based on U.S. Department of Agriculture's low standard budget.

Based on weighted sample of interviews with divorced persons, Los Angeles County, California, 1978.

These data indicate that *divorce is a financial catastrophe for most women:* in just one year they experience a dramatic decline in income and a calamitous drop in their standard of living. It is hard to imagine how they deal with such severe deprivation: every single expenditure that one takes for granted—clothing, food, housing, heat—must be cut to one-half or one-third of what one is accustomed to.

It is difficult to absorb the full implications of these statistics. What does it mean to have a 73 percent decline in one's standard of living? When asked how they coped with this drastic decline in income, many of the divorced women said that they themselves were not sure. It meant "living on the edge" and "living without." As some of them described it:

> We ate macaroni and cheese five nights a week. There was a Safeway special for 39 cents a box. We could eat seven dinners for $3.00 a week. . . . I think that's all we ate for months.

> I applied for welfare. . . . It was the worst experience of my life. . . . I never dreamed that I, a middle class housewife, would ever be in a position like that. It was humiliating . . . they make you feel it. . . . But we were desperate, and I *had* to feed my kids.

> You name it, I tried it—food stamps, soup kitchens, shelters. It just about killed me to have the kids live like that. . . . I finally called my parents and said we were coming . . . we couldn't have survived without them.

Even those who had relatively affluent life-styles before the divorce experienced a sharp reduction in their standard of living and faced hardships they had not anticipated. For example, the wife of a dentist sold her car "because I had no cash at all, and we lived on that money—barely—for close to a year." And an engineer's wife:

> I didn't buy my daughter any clothes for a year—even when she graduated from high school we sewed together two old dresses to make an outfit.

The wife of a policeman told an especially poignant story about "not being able to buy my twelve-year-old son Adidas sneakers." The boy's father had been ordered to pay $100 a month child support but had not been paying. To make up that gap in her already bare-bone budget, she had been using credit cards to buy food and other household necessities. She had exceeded all her credit limits and felt the family just could not afford to pay $25 for a new pair of Adidas sneakers. But, as she said a year later,

> Sometimes when you are so tense about money you go crazy . . . and you forget what it's like to be twelve years old and to think you can't live without Adidas sneakers . . . and to feel the whole world has deserted you along with your father.

Others spoke of cutting out all the nonessentials. For one woman it meant "no movies, no ice cream cones for the kids." For another it meant not replacing tires on her son's bike "because there just wasn't the money." For another woman it meant not using her car—a real handicap in Los Angeles—and waiting for two buses in order to save the money she would have had to spend for gas. In addition to scaled-down budgets for food ("We learned to love chicken backs") and clothing ("At Christmas I splurged at the Salvation Army—the only 'new' clothes they got all year"), many spoke of cutting down on their children's school lunches ("I used to plan a nourishing lunch with fruit and juice; now she's lucky if we have a slice of ham for a sandwich") and school supplies and after-school activities ("he had to quit the Little League and get a job as a delivery boy").

Still, some of the women were not able to "make it." Fourteen percent of them moved onto the welfare rolls during the first year after the divorce, and a number of others moved back into their parents' homes when they had "no money left and nowhere to go and three children to feed."

EXPLAINING THE DISPARITY BETWEEN HUSBANDS' AND WIVES' STANDARDS OF LIVING

How can we explain the strikingly different economic consequences of divorce for men and women? How could a law that aimed at fairness create such disparities between divorced men and their former wives and children?

The explanation lies first in the inadequacy of the court's awards, second in the expanded demands on the wife's resources after divorce, and third in the husband's greater earning capacity and ability to supplement his income.

Consider first the court awards for child support (and in rarer cases, alimony). Since judges do not require men to support either their children or their former wives as they did during marriage, they allow the husband to keep most of his income for himself. Since only a few wives are awarded alimony, the only supplementary income they are awarded is child support and the average child support award covers less than half of the cost of raising a child. Thus, the average support award is simply inadequate: even if the husband pays it, it often leaves the wife and children in relative poverty. The custodial mother is expected to somehow make up the deficit alone even though she typically earns much less than her former husband.

In this regard, it is also important to note the role that property awards play in contributing to—rather than alleviating—the financial disparities between divorced women and men. Under the old law, when the wife with minor children was typically awarded the family home, she started her postdivorce life on a more equal footing because the home provided some stability and security and reduced the impact of the income loss suffered at divorce. Today, when the family home is more commonly sold to allow an "equal" division of property, there is no cushion to soften the financial devastations that low support awards create for women and children. Rather, the disruptive costs of moving and establishing a new household further strain their limited income—often to the breaking point.

The second explanation for the disparity between former husbands and wives lies in the greater demands on the wife's household after divorce, and the diminished demands on the husband's. Since the wife typically assumes the responsibility for raising the couple's children, her need for help and services increases as a direct result of her becoming a single parent. Yet at the very time that her need for more income and more financial support is greatest, the courts have drastically reduced her income. Thus the gap between her income and her needs is wider after divorce.

In contrast, the gap between the husband's income and needs narrows. Although he now has fewer absolute dollars, the demands on his income have diminished: he often lives alone and he is no longer financially responsible for the needs of his ex-wife and children. While he loses the benefits of economies of scale, and while he may have to purchase some services (such as laundry and cooking) that he did not have to buy during marriage, he is nevertheless much better off because he has so much more money to spend on himself. Since he has been allowed to retain most of his income for himself, he can afford these extra expenses and still have more surplus income than he enjoyed during marriage.

The final explanation for the large income discrepancy between former husbands and wives lies in the different earning capacities and starting points of the two adults at the time of the divorce. Not only do men in our society command higher salaries to begin with, they also benefit from the common marital pattern that gives priority to their careers. Marriage gives men the opportunity, support, and time to invest in their own careers. Thus marriage itself builds and enhances the husband's earning capacity. For women, in contrast, marriage is more likely to act as a career liability. Even though family roles are changing, and even though married women are increasingly working for pay during marriage, most of them nevertheless subordinate their careers to their husbands' and to their family responsibilities. This is especially true if they have children. Thus women are often doubly disadvantaged at the point of divorce. Not only do they face the "normal" 60 percent male/female income gap that affects all working women, they also suffer from the toll the marital years have taken on their earning capacity.

Thus marriage—and then divorce—impose a differential disadvantage on women's employment prospects, and this is especially severe for women who have custody of minor children. The responsibility for children inevitably restricts the mother's job opportunities by limiting her work schedule and location, her availability for overtime, and her freedom to take advantage of special training, travel assignments, and other opportunities for career advancement.

Although the combined income of the former spouses typically increases after divorce, most of the rise is a result of the husband's increased income. Even though women who have not been employed during marriage seek jobs after divorce, and part-time workers take full-time jobs, neither of these factors accounts for as much as the rise in male wages in the first year after divorce.

It is, in fact, surprising to see how many divorced men receive salary increases (and bonuses) immediately after divorce. While some of these are probably routine raises, and others may be the result of more intense work efforts or overtime work, it is also evident that some men manage to delay a bonus or commission or raise until after the divorce is final. This allows them to minimize the income they have to report to the court when child support (or alimony) awards are being made. . . .

During the same period, the obligations that these men have for alimony and child support typically remain fixed or diminish: some support obligations have been reduced or terminated by terms of the divorce settlement (and others have been reduced or stopped without the courts' permission). The result, once again, is that divorced men have more "surplus income" for themselves.

The discrepancy between divorced men and women has been corroborated by other research. Sociologist Robert Weiss and economist Thomas Espenshade . . . and Census Bureau data also document the disparities in both income and standards of living of men and women after divorce. In 1979, the median per capita income of divorced women who had not remarried was $4,152, just over half of the $7,886 income of divorced men who had not remarried.[11]

The situation of divorced women with young children is even more grim. The median income in families headed by women with children under six years of age was only 30 percent of the median income for all families whose children were under six.[12] Thus, for the United States as a whole, the "income of families headed by women is at best half that of other families; the income of families headed by women with young children is even less, one-third of that of other families."[13] . . .

SOCIETAL CONSEQUENCES

The rise in divorce has been the major cause of the increase in female-headed families,[14] and that increase has been the major cause of the feminization of poverty. Sociologist Diana Pearce, who coined the phrase "feminization of poverty," was one of the first to point to the critical link between poverty and divorce for women.[15] It was, she said, the mother's burden for the economic and emotional responsibility for child-rearing that often impoverished her family.

Contrary to popular perception, most female-headed single parent families in the United States are *not* the result of unwed parenthood: they are the result of marital dissolution.[16] Only 18 percent of the nearly ten million female-headed families in the United States are headed by an unwed mother: over 50 percent are headed by divorced mothers and the remaining 31 percent by separated mothers.[17]

When a couple with children divorces, it is probable that the man will become single but the woman will become a single parent. And poverty, for many women, begins with single parenthood. More than half of the poor families in the United States are headed by a single mother.[18]

The National Advisory Council on Economic Opportunity estimates that if current trends continue, the poverty population of the United States will be composed solely of women and children by the year 2000.[19] The Council declares that the "feminization of poverty has become one of the most compelling social facts of the decade."[20]

THE RISE IN FEMALE POVERTY

The well-known growth in the number of single-parent, female-headed households has been amply documented elsewhere. (The 8 percent of all children who lived in mother-child families in 1960, rose to 12 percent by 1970,[21] and to 20 percent by 1981.[22]) Also well-documented is the fact that these mother-headed families are the fastest growing segment of the American poor.[23]

What has not been well documented, and what appears to be relatively unknown—or unacknowledged—is the direct link between divorce, the economic consequences of divorce, and the rise in female poverty. The high divorce rate has vastly multiplied the numbers of women who are left alone to support themselves and their minor children. When the courts deny divorced women the support and property they need to maintain their families, they are relying, they say, on the woman's ability to get a job and support herself. But with women's current disadvantages in the labor market, getting a job cannot be the only answer—because it does not guarantee a woman a way out of poverty.[24] Even with full-time employment, one-third of the women cannot earn enough to enable them and their children to live above the poverty level.[25] The structure of the job market is such that *only half* of all full-time female workers are able to support two children without supplemental income from either the children's fathers or the government.[26]

In recent years there have been many suggestions for combating the feminization of poverty. Most of these have focused on changes in the labor market[27] (such as altering the sex segregation in jobs and professions, eliminating the dual labor market and the disparity between jobs in the primary and secondary sectors, eradicating the discriminatory structure of wages, and providing additional services, such as child care,[28] for working mothers) and on expanding social welfare programs (such as increasing AFDC benefits to levels above the poverty line, augmenting Medicaid, food stamp, and school lunch programs, and making housewives eligible for Social Security and unemployment compensation).[29]

A third possibility, which has not received widespread attention, is to change the way that courts allocate property and income at divorce. If, for example, custodial mothers and their children were allowed to remain in the family home, and if the financial responsibility for children were apportioned according to the means of the two parents, and if court orders for support were enforced, a significant segment of the population of divorced women and their children would not be impoverished by divorce.

THE RISE IN CHILD POVERTY AND ECONOMIC HARDSHIPS FOR MIDDLE-CLASS CHILDREN OF DIVORCE

Beyond question, the present system of divorce is increasing child poverty in America. From 1970 to 1982, the percentage of American children living in poverty rose from 14.9 percent to 21.3 percent.[30] According to demographer Samuel Preston, most of the growth in the number of children in poverty occurred in the category of female-headed families.[31]

While the vast majority (82 percent) of all children born in the United States today are born into two-parent families, more than half of these children are likely to experience the disruption of their parents' marriage before they reach age eighteen. As noted above, U.S. Census Bureau data show that close to 60 percent of the children born in 1983 *would not* spend their entire childhood living with both natural parents,[32] while Sandra Hofferth of the National Institute of Child Health and Human Development, projected that two-thirds of the children born in wedlock in 1980 would experience a parental divorce before they reach age seventeen.[33]

Whichever figures we use, the statistics suggest that we are sentencing a significant proportion of the current generation of American children to lives of financial impoverishment.

Clearly, living in a single-parent family does not have to mean financial hardship. The economic well-being of many of these children is in jeopardy only because their mothers bear the whole responsibility for their support. That jeopardy would end if courts awarded more alimony, higher amounts of child support, and a division of property that considered the interests of minor children. It would also be greatly reduced if the child support awards that the courts have already made were systematically enforced. Under the present legal system, however, the financial arrangements of divorce foster the financial deprivation of millions of children.

Although the deprivation is most severe below the poverty level, it affects children at every income level. In fact, middle-class children, like their mothers, experience the greatest relative deprivation. The economic dislocations of divorce bring about many changes which are particularly difficult for children: moving to new and less secure neighborhoods, changing schools, losing friends, being excluded from activities that have become too expensive for the family's budget, and having to work after school or help care for younger siblings.

Not surprisingly, the children of divorce often express anger and resentment when their standard of living is significantly less than that in their father's household.[34] They realize that their lives have been profoundly altered by the loss of "their home" and school and neighborhood and friends, and by the new expectations their mother's reduced income creates for them. . . .

The middle-class children of divorce may also feel betrayed by their disenfranchisement in their parents' property settlement. Since the law divides family property between the husband and wife and makes no provision for a child's share of the marital assets, many children feel they have been unfairly deprived of "their" home, "their" piano, "their" stereo set, and their college education. . . . The U.S. Census Bureau data on child support . . . indicated that even though child support awards are quite modest, less than half of all fathers comply fully with court orders for child support. Another quarter make some payment, and close to 30 percent do not pay anything at all.[35]

Inasmuch as about 1.2 million children's parents divorce each year, the 30 percent who receive no support from their fathers adds up to 360,000 new children each year. Over a ten-year period, this amounts to 4 million children. If we add to these the approximately 3 million over the years who receive only part of their child support (or receive it only some of the time), we find a ten-year total of 7 million children deprived of the support to which they are entitled. Remembering that fewer than 4 million children are born each year helps to put all these figures in perspective.[36]

The failure of absent parents to provide child support has taken an especially severe toll in recent years because of sharp cutbacks in public programs benefiting children since 1979. The Children's Defense Fund shows that children's share of Medicaid payments dropped from 14.9 percent in 1979, to 11.9 percent in 1982, despite a rise in the child proportion among the eligible.[37] The Aid to Families with Dependent Children (AFDC) program has also been sharply cut back. In 1979, there were 72 children in AFDC for every 100 children in poverty, but only 52 per 100 in 1982.[38]

It is not surprising to find a strong relationship between the economic and psychological effects of divorce on children. Economic deprivation following divorce has been linked to increased anxiety and stress among American children.[39] Mounting evidence also shows that children of divorce who experience the most psychological stress are those whose postdivorce lives have been impaired by inadequate income. For example, Hodges, Tierney, and Bushbaum find "income inadequacy" the most important factor in accounting for anxiety and depression among preschool children in divorced families.[40] When family income is adequate, there are no differences in anxiety-depression levels between children in divorced families and those in intact families. However, "children of divorced families with inadequate income had substantially higher levels of anxiety-depression."[41] Hodges, Wechsler, and Ballantine also find significant correlations between income and adjustment for preschool children of divorce (but not, interestingly, for preschool children of intact families).[42]

In summary, the accumulating evidence shows that children in divorced families are likely to suffer a variety of adjustment problems if they experience greater geographic mobility, lower income, and poorer adequacy of income. Unfortunately, these experiences are common to most children of divorce.

CONCLUSION: THE TWO-TIER SOCIETY

The economic consequences of the present system of divorce reverberate throughout our society. Divorce awards not only contribute heavily to the well-documented income disparity between men and women, they also lead to the widespread impoverishment of children and enlarge the ever-widening gap between the economic well-being of men and women in the larger society. Indeed, if current conditions continue unabated we may well arrive at a two-tier society with an underclass of women and children.

Thrust into a spiral of downward mobility by the present system of divorce, a multitude of middle-class women and the children in their charge are increasingly cut off from sharing the income and wealth of former husbands and fathers. Hampered by restricted employment opportunities and sharply diminished income, these divorced women are increasingly expected to shoulder alone the burden of providing for both themselves and their children.

Most of the children of divorce share their mother's financial hardships. Their presence in her household increases the strains on her meager income at the same time that they add to her expenses and restrict her opportunities for economic betterment.

Meanwhile, divorced men increasingly are freed of the major financial responsibility for supporting their children and former wives. Moreover, these men retain more than higher incomes. They experience less day-to-day stress than their ex-wives, they enjoy relatively greater mental, physical, and emotional well-being, and have greater freedom to build new lives and new families after divorce.

The economic disparities between men and women after divorce illuminate the long-standing economic disparities between the incomes of men and women during marriage. In theory, those differences did not matter in marriage, since they were partners in the enterprise and shared the husband's income. As Christopher Jencks observes, "As long as most American men and women married and pooled their economic resources, as they traditionally did, the fact the men received 70 percent of the nation's income had little effect on women's material well being."[43] But with today's high divorce rate, the ranks of unmarried women are vastly increased, and the relative numbers of women who share a man's income are greatly diminished.

The result is that the economic gulf between the sexes in the larger society is increasing. Some of this would have occurred even if the traditional divorce law remained everywhere in force. But the new divorce laws—and the way these laws are being applied—have exacerbated the effects of the high divorce rate by assuring that even greater numbers of women and children are being shunted out of the economic mainstream.

The data on the increase in female poverty, child poverty, and the comparative deprivation of middle-class women and children suggest that we are moving toward a two-tier society in which the upper economic tier is dominated by men (and the women and children who live with them). The former wives of many of these men, the mothers of their children, and the children themselves are increasingly found in the lower economic tier. Those in the first tier enjoy a comfortable standard of living; those in the lower tier are confined to lives of economic deprivation and hardship.

Obviously the two tiers are not totally segregated by sex: professional women for example, whether married or divorced, are more likely to be found in the first tier, and members of many minority groups, both men and women, are more likely to fall into the second. Yet among these groups, and among all families at the lower income levels, divorce brings a better economic future for men than for their former wives. . . .

Obviously, membership in the second tier is not necessarily permanent. Some women will find jobs or return to school or obtain training that will enable them to improve their status. Many of those who are under thirty and some of those who are under forty will accomplish the same result by remarrying. But even those women who manage eventually to improve their financial situation will typically spend their early postdivorce years in acute economic hardship. The fact that they are poor only temporarily does not mean that they and their children suffer any the less[44] or that they can ever recapture the losses of those wasted years.

NOTES

1. These assumptions are discussed in Chapters 6 and 7 of *The Divorce Revolution*, on alimony awards, pp. 157–158, 165–166, 176–177 in Chapter 6, and pp. 184–187, 197, 204–206, in Chapter 7.

2. See Chapter 7 of *The Divorce Revolution*, pp. 206, 209, and Chapter 6, 165–169.

3. The special problems that older women face at divorce are discussed in Chapter 7 of *The Divorce Revolution*, pp. 187–194, 198–201, 209–212.

4. The issue of support for dependent children over eighteen is discussed in Chapter 9 of *The Divorce Revolution*, pp. 278–281.

5. Ibid., p. 27 (Table 2.1), p. 31 (Table 2.2). Hoffman and Holmes are frequently cited as showing that divorced men have only a 10 percent decline in real money income. While this figure is shown in Table 2.1, it is based on the husband's total postdivorce income before alimony and/or child support is paid. Once these support payments are deducted from the husband's income, husbands experience a 19 percent decline in real income.

6. Ibid., p. 27 (Table 2.1).

7. This index, which is based on the Department of Agriculture's "Low-Cost Food Budget," adjusted for the size, age, and sex composition of the family, is described in note 10, below.

8. Saul Hoffman and John Holmes, "Husbands, Wives, and Divorce," in *Five Thousand Families—Patterns of Economic Progress* [Ann Arbor, MI.: Institute for Social Research, 1976], p. 27 (Table 2.1). This is closer to the rate of improvement of married couples who improved their standard of living by 21 percent. (Note that their income rose 22 percent, but their income in relation to needs rose 21 percent.)

9. Ibid., p. 31 (Table 2.2).

10. We assumed that the basic needs level for each family was the Lower Standard Budget devised by the Bureau of Labor Statistics, U.S. Department of Labor, *Three Standards of Living for an Urban Family of Four Persons* (1967). This budget is computed for a four-person urban family (husband and wife and two children) and kept current by frequent adjustments. See, e.g., McCraw, "Medical Care Costs Lead Rise in 1976-77 Family Budgets," *Monthly Labor Review*, Nov. 1978, p. 33. A Labor Department report devised a method for adjusting this standard budget to other types of families, depending on family size, age

of oldest child, and age of head of household. Bureau of Labor Statistics, U.S. Department of Labor, *Revised Equivalence Scale for Estimating Equivalent Incomes or Budget Costs by Family Type*, Bulletin No. 1570-2(1968). For example, the needs of a family of two persons (husband and wife) with the head of household of age thirty-five was calculated at 60 percent of the base figure for a Lower Standard Budget.

A Lower Standard Budget was calculated for each family in our interview sample three different ways: once for the predivorce family, once for the wife's postdivorce family, and once for the the husband's postdivorce family. The income over needs for each family was then computed. Membership in postdivorce families of husbands and wives included a new spouse or cohabitor (where applicable), and any children whose custody was assigned to that spouse. I am indebted to my research assistant, David Lineweber, for programming this analysis.

11. Bureau of the Census, U.S. Dept. of Commerce, "Money Income of Families and Persons in the United States: 1979," *Current Population Reports* Series P-60, No. 129, 1981, p. 23.

12. Bureau of the Census, U.S. Dept. of Commerce, "Families Maintained by Female Householders 1970-79," *Current Population Reports* Series P-23, No. 107, 1980, p. 36.

13. National Center on Women and Family Law, "Sex and Economic Discrimination in Child Custody Awards," *Clearinghouse Review* Vol. 16, no. 11, April 1983, p. 1132.

14. Jane R. Chapman and Gordon Chapman, "Poverty Viewed as a Woman's Problem—the U.S. Case," in *Women and the World of Work*, Anne Hoiberg, ed. (New York: Plenum, 1982).

15. Diana Pearce, "The Feminization of Poverty: Women, Work and Welfare," *Urban and Social Change Review*, Feb. 1978; and Diana Pearce and Harriette McAdoo, "Women and Children: Alone and in Poverty" (Washington, D.C.: National Advisory Council on Economic Opportunity, September 1981), p. 1 (hereafter cited as Pearce and McAdoo, "Women and Children in Poverty").

16. House Hearings on Child Support Enforcement legislation before the subcommittee on Public Assistance and Unemployment Compensation of the Committee on Ways and Means of the U.S. House of Representatives on July 14, 1983, p. 13 (Washington, D.C.: U.S. Government Printing Office, 1984) (hereafter cited as House Hearings 1983).

17. Ibid.

18. Barbara Ehrenreich and Francis Fox Piven, "The Feminization of Poverty: When the Family Wage System Breaks Down," *Dissent*, 1984, p. 162 (hereafter cited as Ehrenreich and Piven, "Feminization of Poverty").

19. National Advisory Council on Economic Opportunity, *Critical Choices for the '80s*, August 1980, p. 1 (Washington, D.C.: National Advisory Council, 1980).

20. Ibid.

21. Christopher Jencks, "Divorced Mothers, Unite," *Psychology Today*, November 1982, pp. 73-75 (hereafter cited as Jencks, "Divorced Mothers").

22. Ehrenreich and Piven, "Feminization of Poverty," p. 163.

23. Ibid., p. 162; Pearce and McAdoo, "Women and Children in Poverty"; Heather L. Ross and Isabel V. Sawhill, *Time of Transition: The Growth of Families Headed by Women* (Washington, D.C.: The Urban Institute Press, 1975).

24. Pearce and McAdoo, "Women and Children in Poverty," pp. 6, 18.

25. Briefing paper prepared for California Assemblyman Thomas H. Bates for hearings on "The Feminization of Poverty," San Francisco, Calif., April 8, 1983, mimeo, p. 6 (hereafter cited as Bates brief).

26. Ibid. Pearce and McAdoo, "Women and Children in Poverty."

27. See generally, Pearce and McAdoo, "Women and Children in Poverty," and Ehrenreich and Piven, "Feminization of Poverty."

28. Child care is clearly one of the most fundamental needs of single mothers, and yet, in 1983, fully 84 percent of the working mothers were *not* able to obtain government-licensed child care for their children. California Commission on the Status of Women, Briefing Paper for hearings on the Feminization of Poverty conducted by California Assemblyman Thomas H. Bates, April 8, 1983.

29. Ehrenreich and Piven, "Feminization of Poverty."

30. Samuel H. Preston, "Children and the Elderly: Divergent Paths for Americans' Dependents," Presidential address to the Population Association to be published in *Demography* Vol. 21, no. 4, forthcoming, citing Bureau of the Census, U.S. Dept. of Commerce, "Money Income and Poverty Status 1982," *Current Population Reports* Series P-60, No. 140, 1983. Citations that follow are to pages in the Preston manuscript.

31. Ibid., p. 15.

32. Interview with Dr. Arthur Norton, March, 1984.

33. Sandra Hofferth, "Updating Children's Life Course," Center for Population Research, National Institute for Child Health and Development, 1983.

34. Judith Wallerstein and Joan Kelly, *Surviving The Breakup: How Parents and Children Cope with Divorce* [New York: Basic Books, 1980], p. 231.

35. See Chapter 9, pp. 283-284, citing Bureau of the Census, "Child Support and Alimony, 1981," *Current Population Reports*, Series P-23, No. 124.

36. House Hearings 1983, p. 27.

37. Children's Defense Fund, *American Children in Poverty* (Washington, D.C.: Children's Defense Fund, 1984).

38. Ibid.

39. Ann Goetting, "Divorce Outcome Research: Issues and Perspectives," in *The Family in Transition*, Fourth Edition, Arlene S. Stolnick, eds. [Boston: Little Brown & Co., 1983]; and Nicholas Zil and James Peterson, "Trends in the Behavior and Emotional Well-Being of U.S. Children," Paper given at the 1982 Annual Meeting of the Association for the Advancement of Science, Washington, D.C., 1982.

40. William F. Hodges, Carol W. Tierney, and Helen K. Bushbaum, "The Cumulative Effect of Stress on Preschool Children of Divorced and Intact Families," *Journal of Marriage and the Family* Vol. 46, no. 3, August 1984, pp. 611-629, 614.

41. Ibid.

42. Ibid., citing their earlier work.

43. Jencks, "Divorced Mothers."

44. Ibid.

Review Questions

1. Based on the research findings cited by Weitzman, does the financial situation after a divorce improve or decline, on the average, for children? for women? for men? Explain why.

2. What are the three reasons that Weitzman gives for the differences in per capita income between divorced men's families and divorced women's families?

3. What does the phrase *feminization of poverty* mean? Why has poverty become feminized?

4. By the twenty-first century, what percentage of people living in poverty in the United States are women and children expected to make up? How does this fact relate to the "two-tier society" that social scientists predict?

5. What part does "no-fault" divorce legislation play in creating the two-tiered society?

WAITING, EXCHANGE, AND POWER: THE DISTRIBUTION OF TIME IN SOCIAL SYSTEMS[1]

Barry Schwartz

SO FAR AS IT LIMITS PRODUCTIVE USES OF TIME, WAITING GENERATES distinct social and personal costs. The purpose of this paper is to explore the way these costs are distributed throughout a social structure and to identify the principles to which this allocation gives expression. The main proposition of our analysis is that the distribution of waiting time coincides with the distribution of power. . . . The broader implications of this correlation allow us to characterize stratification systems in terms of the apportionment of time as well as the distribution of other kinds of resources.

Delay and congestion are relevant to the analysis of social systems because they undermine the efficiency with which these systems conduct their business. Indeed, one Russian economist (Liberman 1968–69) recently observed that because of its enormous cost in terms of more productive activities foregone, delay in waiting rooms and queues merit the status of a social problem (pp. 12–16). A gross estimate of the dimensions of this problem is furnished by Orlov, who reports that the Soviet population wastes about 30 billion hours a year waiting during their shopping tours alone. This is the equivalent of a year's work for no less than 15 million men (*New York Times,* May 13, 1969, p. 17). Another study shows that monthly queuing for the payment of rent and utilities wastes as least 20 million man-hours a year in Moscow alone (*New York Times,* June 25, 1972, p. 23). If figures like these were aggregated for the entire service sector of the labor force, social inefficiency occasioned by clients waiting would stand out even more dramatically.

The problem of delay may be more acute in some societies than in others; however, no modern society can claim immunity in this respect. Every social system must "decide" not only how much different members are to be given from a collective supply of goods and services; there must also be a decision as to the priority in which their needs are to be

SOURCE: Barry Schwartz, "Waiting, Exchange, and Power," *American Journal of Sociology,* Vol. 79, No. 4 (January, 1974), pp. 841–870 (with deletions).

satisfied. Queuing for resources is in this sense a fundamental process of social organization, regardless of the specific level of its affluence. Indeed, though the amount of waiting time per unit consumption may be minimal in the richer, consumer-oriented societies, a higher volume of consumption leaves open the possibility that more time is lost in waiting under conditions of affluence than under conditions of scarcity.

On the other hand, it may be said that the social costs of waiting, no matter where they are incurred or what their absolute level may be, merely derive from the summation over an entire population of rather negligible individual losses. But this does not seem to be the case. As one American commentator (Bradford 1971) puts it: "None of us would think of throwing away the nickels and quarters and dimes that accumulate in our pockets. But almost all of us do throw away the small-change time—five minutes here, a quarter hour there—that accumulates in any ordinary day. I figure I probably threw away a full working day in the dentist's office this past year, flicking sightlessly through old magazines" (p. 82). Even in the more opulent of modern societies, then, waiting time creates significant deficits for the individual as well as the system. At issue, however, is (1) the way such cost is distributed throughout a social structure and (2) the principles which govern this distribution. These questions are the subject of the present inquiry.

We begin with the assumption that delay is immediately caused by the relations of supply and demand: when the number of arrivals in some time unit is less than the number an organization can accommodate, waiting time will be relatively brief; but if the arrival rate exceeds the service rate, a "bottleneck" is created and a longer waiting period results. Delay is in this sense occasioned by limitations of access to goods and services. However, this model does not explain socially patterned variations in waiting time. We must therefore explore the institutional constraints which sustain observable levels of scarcity and which organize the priorities granted to different groups of clients. These constraints are shown to be the expressions of existing power relations.

• • •

WAITING, SCARCITY, AND POWER

• • •

Stratification of Waiting

Typical relationships obtain between the individual's position within a social system and the extent to which he waits for and is waited for by other member of the system. In general, the more powerful and important a person is, the more others' access to him must be regulated.

Thus, the least powerful may almost always be approached at will; the most powerful are seen only "by appointment." Moreover, because of heavy demands on their time, important people are most likely to violate the terms of appointments and keep their clients waiting. It is also true that the powerful tend not to ask for appointments with their own subordinates; rather, the lowly are summoned—which is grounds for them to cancel their own arrangements so as not to "keep the boss waiting."

The lowly must not only wait for their appointments with superiors; they may also be called upon to wait during the appointment itself. This may be confirmed in innumerable ways. For one, consider everyday life in bureaucracies. When, in their offices, superordinates find themselves in the company of a subordinate, they may interrupt the business at hand to, say, take a phone call, causing the inferior to wait until the conversation is finished. Such interruption may be extremely discomforting for the latter, who may wish not to be privy to the content of the conversation but, having no materials with which to express alternative involvement, must wait in this exposed state until his superior is ready to reengage him. The event becomes doubly disturbing when the superior is unable to recover from distraction, loses his train of thought, and is unable to properly devote himself to the moment's business. Of course, the subordinate is demeaned not only by the objective features of this scene but also by his realization that for more important clients the superior would have placed an embargo on all incoming calls or visitors. He would have made others wait. The assumption that the client correctly makes is that his own worth is not sufficient to permit the superior to renounce other engagements; being unworthy of full engagement, he is seen, so to speak, between the superior's other appointments. In this way, the client is compelled to bear witness to the mortification of his own worthiness for proper social interaction.

While the derogatory implications for self are clear when the person must repeatedly step aside and wait until the superordinate decides that the granting of his time will not be excessively costly, debasement of self may be attenuated by the client's own consideration that his superior is, after all, in a position of responsibility and assailed by demands over which he may not exercise as much control as he would like. But even this comforting account may be unavailable when the server himself initiates the interruption. It is possible for him to make a call, for example, or to continue his work after the client enters, perhaps with the announcement that he will "be through in a minute."

It is especially mortifying when the superior initiates a wait when an engagement is in progress. Thus, a subordinate, while strolling along a corridor in conversation with his superior may find himself utterly alone when the latter encounters a colleague and breaks off the ongoing relationship in his favor. The subordinate (who may not do the same when encountering one of his peers) is compelled to defer by standing aside and waiting until the unanticipated conversation is finished. Nothing less is expected by his superior, who, finding himself gaining less from the engagement than his inferior, assumes the right to delay or interrupt it at will if more profitable opportunities should arise.

THE IMMUNITY OF THE PRIVILEGED: The relationship between rank and accessibility implies that waiting is a process which mediates interchanges between those who stand on different sides of a social boundary. These divisions and the rules of access which correspond to them are found in organizations which are themselves bounded with respect to the outside world. This fact raises the problem of access when outsiders or clients (as well as insiders, that is, employees or co-workers) seek contact with persons situated at different points in a service hierarchy:

> Low down on the scale are the men you can walk right up to. They are usually behind a counter waiting to serve you on the main floor, or at least on the lower floors. As you go up the bureaucracy you find people on the higher floors and in offices: first bull pens, then private offices, then private offices with secretaries—increasing with each step in inaccessibility and therefore the necessity for appointments and the opportunity to keep people waiting. Recently, for example, I had an experience with a credit card company. First, I went to the first floor where I gave my complaint to the girl at the desk. She couldn't help me and sent me to the eighth floor to talk to someone in a bullpen. He came out, after a suitable waiting time, to discuss my problem in the reception room. I thought that if I were to straighten this matter out I was going to have to find a vice-president in charge of something, who would keep me waiting the rest of the day. I didn't have time to wait so I took my chances with said clerk, who, of course, didn't come through. I'm still waiting for the time when I have an afternoon to waste to go back and find that vice-president to get my account straightened out.[2]

The above statement suggests that delaying a typical client may be a prerogative of important servers. However, we must also recognize that powerful clients are relatively immune from waiting. This remark accords with Tawney's (1931) emphasis on the asymmetry of power relations. "Power," he writes, "may be defined as the capacity of an individual, or group of individuals, to modify the conduct of other individuals or groups in the manner which he desires, *and to prevent his own conduct being modified in the manner in which he does not*" (p. 229; emphasis added).

The relative immunity from waiting which the powerful enjoy is guaranteed because they have the resources to refuse to wait; that is, because they can often afford to go elsewhere for faster service or cause others, such as servants or employees, to wait in their places. Thus, while the relationship between privilege and the necessity of waiting cannot be generalized in any deterministic way, there appears nevertheless to be a relationship between the two, with the least-privileged clients compelled to do the most waiting. This general statement is consistent with Mann's (1969) more specific observations regarding the stratification of waiting in lined queues:

> The relationship between cultural equality and public orderliness is attenuated in the area of queuing because waiting in line is not a habit of all social classes in Western society. It is reasonable to suppose that if Mrs. Gottrocks joined a theater or a football line in the United States, Australia, or England, she would not be treated differently than anyone else, but it would be a rare event for someone of Mrs. Gottrock's status to use a line. Ordinarily, in both class-conscious and relatively class-free societies, the privileged class circumvent the line altogether and get their tickets through agents or other contacts.[3] Our point, then, is that queuing is confined largely to the less-privileged groups in society. [p. 353]

The privileged also wait less because they are least likely to tolerate its costs; they are more inclined to renege* from as well as balk† at entering congested waiting channels. On the other hand, the less advantaged may wait longer not only because of their lack of resources but also because their willingness to wait exceeds the readiness of those in higher strata. While they might have something else to do besides sitting and waiting, they might not have anything better to do. As a result, the least advantaged may pay less in profitable alternatives foregone and therefore suffer less than even those whose objective wait is shorter.

This relationship may be informed by another consideration, for which health-care delivery systems provide an example. Because of their scarcity, those who are able to pay for medical services are often forced to wait well beyond the time a server agreed to provide them. Yet there is some limit to the server's inconsiderateness, for, in principle at least, the client may decide that he has waited long enough and go elsewhere. On the other hand, those who are unable to pay for medical care may spend the better part of the day in outpatient waiting rooms, for consideration of the value of clients' time is far less imperative when these clients cannot take their business to someone else. In Britain's government-run maternity hospitals, for example, "a major complaint was that women dependent on the health service are treated offhandedly in hospitals and frequently have to wait more than an hour for checkups at antenatal clinics. Women who paid up to $700 for private treatment were dealt with speedily and efficiently" (*Chicago Tribune,* June 12, 1971, p. 10). Thus, while long, agonizing waiting pe-

* "Reneging" refers to giving up waiting after initially committing oneself to a line or waiting room.

† "Balking" means refusal to wait at all.

riods may be avoided only if one is willing to settle for more expensive service, the poor may avoid waiting only if they are willing to settle for no service at all. (The frequency with which they do select this option, is of course, unknown—as is the consequence of the selection.)

The above principle may be further illustrated in other, altogether different connections. It is noticeable, for one example, that in the "best" of urban department stores a customer is met by a salesperson as soon as he enters; the customer makes a selection under his guidance and makes payment to him. In establishments which are a grade below the best, customers may have difficulty finding someone to serve them during busy periods but, when they do, are accompanied by him, that is, "waited on," until the transaction is consummated by payment. The lowest-grade stores, however, provide few servers; as a result, customers must for the most part wait on themselves, then line up behind others at a cashier counter in order to make payment.

The above patterns are to be observed within as well as among organizations. In the typical department store, customers surveying high-priced goods like furniture and appliances will typically be approached immediately by a salesperson. Those in the process of selecting a handkerchief or pair of socks will not be so quickly attended and, when they finally are, will be dealt with more quickly. Likewise, clients who show interest in very expensive jewelry will be served at once and at length; those who are fascinated with costume jewelry will wait.

In general, it may be said that establishments which cater to a relatively wealthy clientele must serve them quickly (if the clients desire) not only because of the objective or assumed value of clients' time but also because they have the means to take their business elsewhere if it is not respected. Commercial places which service the less wealthy are less constrained in this respect because they tend to deal with a larger and/or less independent clientele. Within organizations, clients who promise to bring the most profit to a server enjoy a competitive advantage; they wait the least, to the disadvantage of their lesser endowed brethren who can find no one to honor the value of their time.[4]

Waiting and the Monopolization of Services

The above rule, however, rests on the assumption that faster alternative services are available to those who want and can pay for them. In fact, the availability of such alternatives is itself variable. Waiting is therefore affected not only by clients' resources and consequent ability to go elsewhere for service but also by the opportunity to do so.

It follows that establishments with many competitors are most likely to be concerned about the amount of time they keep clients waiting. Chicago Loop banks are among such organizations. In the words of one banking consultant, "The industry is too competitive to allow a dozen people waiting in line when they could just as easily take their business across the street where there is a teller at every window, a customer at every teller and waiting time is less than one minute" (*Chicago Tribune,* September 28, 1971, p. 7). However, organizations with few or no competitors are less obliged to reduce the waiting time of clients. (This condition makes waiting a national pastime in the Soviet Union, where most services are rendered by government-run establishments that are not subject to market forces.)

The enormous amounts of waiting time expended in dealings with public people-serving bureaucracies is directly related to monopolization of the various services which they offer or impose. Monopolization accords governmental units the power to maximize their efficiency of operation by minimizing service costs and, in so doing, maximizing client waiting. This "optimum solution" is exemplified by bureaus which distribute welfare benefits to long lines of disadvantaged people:

> The number of Medicaid and public assistance applicants and recipients has become so great that [New York's] Department of Social Services is literally shutting its doors in their faces.
>
> Many of the 45 social service centers close their doors early—12, 1 or 2 o'clock—rather than admit persons the workers realistically know cannot be seen that particular day.
>
> The Medicaid office advises applicants to line up outside the doors before dawn. "You'd better get down here around 6:30 or 7 o'clock," said a person answering the telephone at the Medicaid office. . . . "We can only see 200 persons a day. If you want to be in the first 200 you better get here then—with your application filled out." The Medicaid office does not open until 8:30 A.M. . . .
>
> Last week the department announced it had saved $39 million by employing fewer case workers. [*New York Times,* November 21, 1971, p. 58]

However, the relatively wealthy as well as the poor are put to inconvenience by having to wait in person for licenses, permits, visas, tickets, information and the like. Dealings with government-sponsored transportation facilities can also be cited as an example:

> Before Amtrak took over, I would have had to call the Illinois Central to go to Miami. If I wanted to go to New York, I'd call the Penn Central. To go west, the Santa Fe. But now, under the streamlined, tax-supported Amtrak, one number, one central office, makes the reservations. They have computers and other modern devices the old system didn't have.
>
> At 10 minutes after noon, I dialed the new Amtrak reservation number. The line was busy, so I hung up and waited a few minutes and dialed again. It was still busy. Five minutes later, I tried again. It was busy. By 1 o'clock I had tried 10 times, and had heard only busy signals.
>
> Enough was enough. I phoned the Amtrak executive office, to ask what was wrong with their reservation number. A woman there put me on hold. I

> was on hold for seven minutes. Then when she finally took me off hold, she switched me to somebody's office, and a secretary laughed and said: "Oh, yes, our lines are very busy."
>
> At 2 P.M. it finally happened. Instead of getting a busy signal, it rang. It actually rang. . . . It rang. And it rang. And it rang. For eight minutes it rang. . . . So I hung up, got another cup of coffee and tried again. That was a mistake, because I heard another busy signal.
>
> Then at 2:47 it happened. It rang. And somebody answered. I listened closely to make sure it wasn't a recorded message. No, it was really somebody alive. After that it was easy. In about eight or nine minutes the reservations were made.
>
> The clock said 3 P.M. So I have to congratulate Amtrak. It took me only two hours and 50 minutes to complete a telephone call and make reservations. It would have probably taken me at least 10 minutes more than that to take a cab to O'Hare, board a plane, fly to Miami, and get off the plane. [*Chicago Daily News*, June 9, 1972, p. 3]

This instance is an especially informative one, for it demonstrates that the amount of time clients of an organization are called upon to wait is in large measure determined by the broader competitive structure in which the organization is situated. Longitudinal and cross-sectional means are brought to bear in this assessment. By reference to the temporal barrier to access to rail service after centralization and monopolization, relative ease of access before the transformation is implicitly affirmed. And after documenting the lengthy waiting time required in a noncompetitive service market, we find explicit reference to the ready availability of service offered in highly competitive ones (airlines, in this case). In this double sense, the institutional grounding of waiting time is a conclusion warranted by the facts.

We now turn to public services which by their very nature admit of no alternatives and which at the same time are so organized as to constitute the most radical instance of the principle we are now discussing.

A DAY IN COURT: Discrepancy between demand for and supply of "authoritative judgment" is perhaps the most notorious source of waiting for both rich and poor. In fact, those who look forward to their "day in court," whether civil, criminal, or juvenile, very often find themselves spending their day in the courthouse corridor (many courts do not provide waiting rooms). In some courts, in fact, all parties whose cases are scheduled to be heard on a particular day are instructed to be present at its beginning when the judge arrives.[5] This is a most pronounced manifestation of what we earlier referred to as "overscheduling," which in this case ensures that the judge (whose bench is separated from his office or working area) will not be left with idle time that cannot be put to productive use—a consideration which may help us understand the seemingly irrational practice of assembling together at the beginning of the day those who are to be served during its course. While this tactic guarantees that the judge's valuable time will not be wasted, it also ensures that most parties will be kept waiting for a substantial period of time; some, all day long. Indeed, because they have no means to retaliate against the judge's own tardiness or excessive lunch breaks, some individuals may not be served at all and must return on the next day to wait further. Clients' attorneys, incidentally, keep them company during much of this time—a service for which the former pay dearly.

All of this is not to say that the organization of justice profits. It must, on the contrary, pay a very high price for support of its prima donnas. As one juvenile-court officer puts it: "[W]aiting to be called into court . . . is the most serious problem. Just from an internal point of view this means that a probation counselor usually accomplishes nothing in the hour or more he often has to wait to get his case into court. Usually during this waiting period he sees no people, does no counselling, can't do dictation or other 'desk-work'—his wait is complete, unproductive waste. These same problems apply to other professional people: caseworkers from the Department of Social Services, school principals, lawyers, etc." (Fairfax County [Virginia] Juvenile and Domestic Relations Court, Memorandum, 1971, p. 1). While attorneys[6] and other professionals are fortunate enough to claim a fee for doing nothing in a professional way, others are often denied this luxury. Authorities who are mindful of civil security, for example, wisely find it more expedient to dismiss cases (particularly such misdemeanants as traffic violators) for lack of witnesses and evidence than to tie up a large sector of the police force for the better part of a day in a crowded corridor. In this particular sense, the police are too important—their time too valuable—to be kept waiting. On the other hand, it may be claimed that by tying up defendants all day long in these same corridors justice may be served—provided, of course, that the defendants are in fact guilty as charged. However, the situation is quite different in felony cases, where casual dismissals are less probable. Under these circumstances police wait as long as defendants. In the Chicago Gun Court, for example, "40 or 45 police are waiting to testify at 9:30 A.M., when court begins. Cases are not scheduled for specific times, so most of them wait and wait. One recent day 31 were still waiting around at 1 P.M. The next day 20 were there at 1 P.M. and 23 the following day." The same conditions prevail at the Narcotics Court where police waiting time "translates on an annual basis to 13,000 police days lost and $700,000 in expenses" (*Chicago Daily News*, August 21, 1973, p. 14).

Two observations emerge from and transcend the particular content of what has just been said. First, the assertion that clients may pay a high price, in terms of time, in their dealings with public bureaucracies means that a societal cost, expressed in terms of aggregate client time diverted from more productive activities, must be written into the usually implicit but sometimes explicit "optimum solution formulae" by which particular "public service" organizations maximize their own efficiency. Because of this factor, the real cost of governmental services is not to be obviated by budgetary considerations alone.

Second, minimization of a powerful server's idle time may subtract from the productivity of the organization as well as its clients. This observation, which is merely grotesquely evident in court settings, reflects the general principle that increments in efficiency in one part of a social organization often entail malfunction in other sectors. Accordingly, just as high concentration of power in an organization may lend itself to societal inefficiency, indexed by more productive client-time foregone, so concentration of power and honor in an elevated server may render organizations ineffective by maximizing idle time of subordinated servers. The more general import of this statement is that it amends the overly simplistic scarcity theory of waiting, which fixates our attention upon server shortage as a condition of client delay. The present statement shows that the organization of services, as well as their volume, provides occasion for waiting.

An additional point is that some persons and groups are relatively exempt from waiting. If we turn our attention once more to the courtroom, we find that the powerful are most likely to enjoy such advantage. In making up the docket, for example, resources are taken into account. Defendants who are represented by an attorney are very often scheduled before those who are not (in Chicago traffic courts, at least). And cases involving important and powerful contestants, witnesses, and/or lawyers may be scheduled at their convenience and not be delayed for long periods of time. Similarly, attorneys who enjoy favor with the court clerk are also able to avoid long waits because they are allowed to schedule their case early.[7] Thus, while waiting time may be maximized by persons or in organizations which enjoy full or near monopoly on the services they offer, the relationship between the power and waiting time of their clients is probably attenuated rather than negated. For, while the powerful may lack the opportunity to take their business elsewhere, they nevertheless possess the resources to ensure that their needs will be accommodated before the needs of those with fewer means.

• • •

SOCIAL PSYCHOLOGICAL ASPECTS OF DELAY

Making Others Wait

• • •

Because the worth of a person is not independent of the amount of time others must wait for him, that person can maintain and dramatize his worth by purposely causing another to wait.

Of course, the imposition of a waiting period does not in itself make a person or his services valuable; it can only magnify existing positive evaluations or transform neutral feelings into positive ones. If these initial feelings are not favorable, or at least neutral, the waiting caused by a server may lower clients' estimations of his worth. Instead of a sought-after and important man, the server becomes an incompetent who cannot perform his job properly; thus is his initial inferiority confirmed. (This is why subordinates who know where they stand do not like to keep their superiors waiting.) Generally, the dramatization of ascendency by keeping another waiting will do a server the most good when his social rank exceeds that of his client or when the difference between their ranks is ambiguous. In the latter case, ascendency accrues to him who can best dramatize it; in the former, ascendency may be dramatized by him to whom it already accrues.

Thus, just as authority is affirmed by the placement of social distance between super and subordinate, so temporal distance subserves the ascendency of the person who imposes it. More precisely, the restriction of access to oneself by forcing another to "cool his heels" is instrumental to the cultivation of social distance.

• • •

The Imposition of Waiting as an Aggressive Act

If the temporal aspect of relationships between those occupying different social positions may be stated in terms of who waits for whom, then we would expect to find a reversal of the waiting-delaying pattern when persons "switch" positions. Furthermore, this reversal may be accentuated through retaliation by the one who suffered under the initial arrangement. A former president furnishes us with an example:

> Ken Hechler, who was director of research at the White House from 1948 to 1952, recalled the day Mr. Truman kept Winthrop Aldrich, president of the Chase Manhattan Bank, waiting outside the White House office for 30 minutes. Hechler quoted Mr. Truman as saying:
>
> "When I was a United States senator and headed the war investigation committee, I had to go to New York to see this fella Aldrich. Even though I had an appointment he had me cool my heels for an hour and a half. So just relax. He's got a little while to go yet." [*Chicago Daily News,* December 27, 1972, p. 4]

Punitive sanctioning through the imposition of waiting is met in its most extreme forms when a person is not only kept waiting but is also kept ignorant as to how long he must wait, or even of what he is waiting for. One manifestation of the latter form is depicted by Solzhenitsyn (1968*a*):

> Having met the man (or telephoned him or even especially summoned him), he might say: "Please step into my office tomorrow morning at ten." "Can't I

drop in now?" the individual would be sure to ask, since he would be eager to know what he was being summoned for and get it over with. "No, not now," Rusanov would gently, but strictly admonish. He would not say that he was busy at the moment or had to go to a conference. He would on no account offer a clear, simple reason, something that could reassure the man being summoned (for that was the crux of this device). He would pronounce the words "not now" in a tone allowing many interpretations—not all of them favorable. "About what?" the employee might ask, out of boldness or inexperience. "You'll find out tomorrow," Pavel Nikolaevich would answer in a velvet voice, bypassing the tactless question. But what a long time it is until tomorrow. [p. 222]

The underlying technique for the aggressive use of delay involves the withdrawal or withholding of one's presence with a view to forcing another into an interactionally precarious state wherein he might confront, recognize, and flounder in his own vulnerability or unworthiness.[8] By such means, the superordinate not only affirms his ascendency but does so at the direct expense of his inferior's dignity. Russian bureaucrats are masters at invoking this routine in their dealings with waiting clients:

Casting a disapproving eye at the janitor's wet overshoes, and looking at him severely, Shikin let him stand there while he sat down in an armchair and silently looked over various papers. From time to time, as if he was astonished by what he was reading . . . , he looked up at him in amazement, as one might look at a maneating beast that has finally been caged. All this was done according to the system and was meant to have an annihilating effect on the prisoner's psyche. A half-hour passed in the locked office in inviolate silence. The lunch bell rang out clearly. Spiridon hoped to receive his letter from home, but Shikin did not even hear the bell; he rifled silently through thick files, he took something out of a box and put it in another box, he leafed, frowning, through various papers and again glanced up briefly in surprise at the dispirited, guilty Spiridon.

All the water from Spiridon's overshoes had dripped on the rubber runner, and they had dried when Shikin finally spoke: "All right, move closer!" [Solzhenitsyn 1968*b*, pp. 482–83]

This kind of strategy can only be employed by superordinates who have power over a client in the first place. The effect on the client is to further subordinate him, regardless of a server's initial attractiveness or a client's realization that the delay has been deliberately imposed. Furthermore, this practice leaves the client in a psychologically as well as a ritually unsatisfactory state. The two presumably act back on each other in a mutually subversive way, for by causing his client to become tense or nervous the server undermines the self-confidence necessary for him to maintain proper composure. This tendency, incidentally, is routinely applied by skillful police interrogators who deliberately ignore a suspect waiting to be questioned, assuming that a long, uncertain wait will "rattle him" sufficiently to disorganize the kinds of defenses he could use to protect himself (Arthur and Caputo 1959, p. 31).

Ritual Waiting and Autonomy

We have tried to show that while servers may cause others to wait in order to devote their attention to other necessary matters, they may also make people wait for the pure joy of dramatizing their capacity to do so. Such elation, we saw, is understandable, for by effecting a wait the server demonstrates that his presence is not subject to the disposition or whim of another and that access to him is a privilege not to be taken lightly. And, if access is a privilege, then one may sanction another by deliberately holding oneself apart from him. But we must now make explicit a point that was only implied in our previous discussions: that the imposition of waiting expresses and sustains the autonomy as well as the superiority of the self.

While the imposition of delay allows a superordinate to give expression to his authority, waiting may also be imposed in protest against that authority. The latter achievement is valued, naturally, among those of despised status and low rank. Because they lack the wherewithal to do so in most of their other relations, the powerless, in their capacity as servers, delight in keeping their superiors waiting. The deliberately sluggish movements of many store clerks, telephone operators, cashiers, toll collectors, and the like, testify to the ability of the lowly as well as the lofty to dramatize their autonomy. This accords with Meerloo's (1966) assertion that "the strategy of delay is an ambivalent attack on those who command us" (p. 249). This kind of aggression is perhaps most pronounced under sociologically ambivalent conditions: as the legitimacy of the existing distribution of status honor ceases to be taken for granted, prescribed deference patterns give way to institutionalized rudeness, which may be expressed by appearing late for appointments with a superordinate as well as by dillydallying while he waits for his needs to be serviced.

• • •

SUMMARY

[V]alue foregone through idleness is an extrinsic disadvantage. On the other hand, the degradational implications of being kept idle are intrinsic to waiting and can arise in no way other than through involuntary delay. The purpose of this paper was to explore the way these costs are distributed throughout the social structure and to identify the principles to which this allocation gives expression.

We have introduced the category of power . . . as the ultimate determinant of delay, the main assertion being that the distribution of waiting time coincides with the distribution of power . . . [R]esourceful persons wait less within both competitive and monopolistic markets, while delay will be more pronounced in the latter regardless of personal power.

If waiting is related to a person's position in a power network, then a server may confirm or enhance his status by deliberately making another wait for him. In a more general sense, this is to say that the management of availability itself, regardless of the purpose for which an individual makes himself available, carries with it distinct psychological implications. Because a person's access to others indexes his scarcity as a social object, that person's social worth may only be realized by demonstrated inaccessibility. Openness to social relations may therefore be restricted not only to regulate interactional demands but also to enhance the self that one brings to an interaction. . . . The initial relationship between waiting and power thus gives rise to processes which strengthen it. . . .

The broader implication of this essay is that it finds . . . time itself a generalized resource whose distribution affects life chances with regard to the attainment of other, more specific kinds of rewards. This is true in a number of respects. Time, like money, is valuable because it is necessary for the achievement of productive purposes; ends cannot be reached unless an appropriate amount of it is "spent" or "invested" on their behalf. On the other hand, the power that a time surplus makes possible may be protected and/or expanded by depriving others of their time. By creating queues to reduce idle periods, for example, a server exploits clients by converting their time to his own use. A server does the same by "overcharging" in the sense of deliberately causing a particular client to wait longer than necessary.

The monetary analogies we have used are not without some justification. Just as money possesses no substantive value independent of its use as a means of exchange, time can only be of value if put to substantive use in an exchange relationship. Both time and money may be regarded as generalized means because of the infinity of possibilities for their utilization: both are possessed in finite quantities; both may be counted, saved, spent, lost, wasted, or invested . . . . Accordingly, while the powerful can allocate monetary means to their own desired ends by controlling the *budget*, they also regulate the distribution of time—rewarding themselves, depriving others—through their control of the *schedule*. What is at stake in the first instance is the *amount* of resources to which different parts of a system are entitled; in the second, it is the *priority* of their entitlements. Far from being a coincidental by-product of power, then, control of time comes into view as one of its essential properties.

NOTES

1. This paper was supported by grant 1-5690-00-4335 from the Ford Foundation and by the Center for Health Administration Studies, University of Chicago. The writer wishes to acknowledge the very useful comments made on this paper by Peter Blau and Morris Janowitz.

2. Personal communication from Florence Levinsohn.

3. Other "contacts" include the radio, over which Saturday and Sunday morning waiting times at many metropolitan golf courses are broadcast. This service, which saves many players many long delays, is performed almost exclusively for the middle and upper-middle classes.

4. Even when circumstances make it necessary for the resourceful to wait, they suffer less than their inferiors. As a general rule, the wealthier the clientele, the more adequate the waiting accommodations. Thus, persons who can afford bail can await their trial (or, far more frequently, the attorneys' bargaining on their behalf) in the free community. The poor must wait in jail. The same is true of facilities. In airports, for example, those who can afford it may simultaneously avoid contamination by the masses and engross themselves in a variety of activities, including fabulous eating and drinking, in "VIP lounges." The term "lounge" instead of the vulgar "waiting area" or "gate" is also applied to facilities set aside for those who travel a specified number of miles with (and pay a substantial sum of money to) a particular airline. In this as in many other settings, waiting locales for the poor and less rich lack the elaborate involvement supplies, pleasant decor, and other physical and psychological comforts that diminish the pain of waiting among those who are better off.

5. A functional equivalent is found in the Soviet Union. "Aleksandr Y. Kabalkin and Vadim M. Khinchuk . . . describe what they termed 'classic cases' in everyday life in the Soviet Union, in which customers wait for the television repairman or for a messenger delivering a train or plane ticket that had been ordered by phone. To the question 'About what time can I expect you?' the stereotyped reply is, 'It can be any time during the day.' And people have to excuse themselves from work and wait—there is no other way out" (*New York Times*, November 7, 1971, p. 5).

6. It may not be assumed that all lawyers earn while they wait. For example, the *New York Times* (August 25, 1971, p. 24) recently reported: "A lawyer who specializes in prosecuting landlords' claims against tenants asked permission in Bronx Supreme Court yesterday to bring his cases there rather than in Civil Court because . . . he spent much time 'just sitting and waiting.' And consequently, he said, he was suffering 'financial loss' and felt he could not continue working in Civil Court."

7. This is to say that, as a scarce commodity, time or priority of service routinely becomes the object of struggle. Recognizing this, a court intake officer writes in a memo to his supervisor: "Intake counselors should assume more control over the setting of cases on the docket, with a proportionate decrease in the control now exercised by clerks" (Fairfax County [Virginia] Juvenile and Domestic Relations Court, Memorandum, 1971, p. 1).

8. Of course, the impulse of stationary servers to make others wait for reasons that are independent of the scarcity of time is paralleled by the tactic used by mobile servers, of keeping them waiting for these same reasons. Thus, a person may simultaneously exhibit contempt for a gathering and underscore his own presence (Parkinson 1962, pp. 73–74) by purposely arriving late. This measure is particularly effective when the proceedings require his presence.

REFERENCES

Arthur, R., and R. Caputo
1959 *Interrogation for Investigators.* New York: Copp.

Bradford, Jean
1971 "Getting the Most out of Odd Moments." *Reader's Digest* (June), pp. 82–84.

Liberman, E. G.
1968–69 "The Queue: Anamnesis, Diagnosis, Therapy." *Soviet Review* 9 (Winter): 12–16.

Mann, Leon
1969 "Queue Culture: The Waiting Line as a Social System." *American Journal of Sociology* 75 (November): 340–54.

Meerloo, Joost
1966 "The Time Sense in Psychiatry." In *The Voices of Time,* edited by J. T. Fraser. New York: Braziller.

Parkinson, C., Northcote
1962 *Parkinson's Law.* Boston: Houghton-Mifflin.

Solzhenitsyn, Aleksandr
1968*a* *The Cancer Ward.* New York: Dial.
1968*b* *The First Circle.* New York: Harper & Row.

Tawney, R. H.
1931 *Equality.* London: Allen & Unwin.

Review Questions

1. Compare and contrast the positions in the hierarchy of a formal organization such as a factory or school in terms of control over one's own and others' time.

2. Explain how waiting may differ in monopolistic as opposed to competitive types of organizations. In which type of organization will the most waiting on the part of the clients occur? Will powerful clients have an advantage over the lowly in both types of organizations? Explain.

3. Discuss the practice of consciously *forcing* others to wait as it is engaged in by (1) the powerful, and (2) the lowly.

4. When are "reneging" and "balking" likely to occur? Are powerful people or subordinates more likely to renege and balk? Explain your answer.

5. Schwartz contends that waiting is structured (that is, occupants of some positions will usually spend more time waiting than occupants of other positions). Furthermore, waiting entails costs which are both material and psychological. Discuss these contentions, giving evidence from your own experience.

RELATIVE ADVANTAGE: ANTIDOTE TO LOW STATUS

Charlotte Wolf

RELATIVE ADVANTAGE

. . . RELATIVE ADVANTAGE IS A COLLECTIVE PROCESS BY WHICH A GROUP OF people come to define their situation, values, or character in reference to that of another group's or to that of their own group at a different time in a manner which gives them a sense of satisfaction. It is a group phenomenon, emerging from its experience and meaning context. The constructed definition eventually might take on a certain stability, an objectification of feeling and hope, becoming a part of the way in which a group's social world is organized, and possibly serving as a bulwark of this organized reality. It is likely to have multiple effects on group members, such as: the reinforcement of membership and the sharpening of the lines of group identification; the possible enhancement of group solidarity; and some awareness of how relative satisfaction or superiority reflects on who he or she is, with consequent effects on self-esteem. By defining others as less advantaged, this, by reference, turns one's group or self or circumstances into that which is *more* advantaged. Thus, there occurs the social construction of possible dissimilarity or inferiority of the other, with the resultant sense of superiority of self or group, and thus of relative advantage.

How does the social construction of relative advantage take place? What is the process? Although with historical data it is difficult, often impossible, to demonstrate the initiation of this idea, the competing definitions that possibly arise, and the negotiation that likely occurs, still, some conjecture is probably in order.

Social interpretations emerging out of the conditions and desires and ideas of subordinate groups are always in the process of being reconstructed. As part of this, people compare: people are "apparently and irretrievably" comparers (M. Gordon 1978, pp. 81–82), not only heeding their own needs but making judgments on the basis of what other

SOURCE: Charlotte Wolf, "How Minority Groups React." *Symbolic Interaction* 13 (1990): 37–61.

people have. What oppressed people see that they and others have, then, become ingredients of a "recipe" for interpreting the social world (Schutz 1971, II, p. 73). What is important or what is the focus or what are comparables will vary, depending upon the historical conditions of the group, the extent and duration of their oppression, and the range of perceived alternatives to their own circumstances. The extent of their accommodation to oppression and of their conservatism might tend to define their "need" for this type of comparison. Comparative others or objects would ordinarily be selected from within the purview of the politically safe, serving a social distancing function from dominant others.

At times the currency of comparability might be meager, and status borrowing (Wolf 1986, p. 222; 1978) might be brought into play. To borrow status implies that position or that which is associated with the status of superior groups is assumed to belong also to one's own subordinate group. For example, black slaves "borrowed" some of the arrogance and imperiousness of their white masters to feel superior to "poor white trash." Status borrowing, then, can become a weapon of the weak to justify feelings of relative advantage over another group.

Although the variability of oppressed responses will be apparent in the subsequent examples, still there are some conditions that generally appear to be met by those groups claiming to be advantaged. Oppressed groups who make these comparisons must recognize to some extent that they have definable characteristics or values or conditions that distinguish them from others or from themselves, if comparing their situation at the present with that of either their possible future situation or of their past situations. Some of these characteristics might well have been impressed on the subordinate group by their rulers, and certainly their status had been.[1] Second, given their own distinctiveness, it is expected that there be some agreement among group members that the comparison has merit. And, third, it is further suggested that the construction reflexively makes a difference in how the group sees itself. And, as a consequence, it is possible that this difference sharpens the lines of group identification and enhances group solidarity.

A typology of possible group comparisons, then, might be as follows:

(1) comparison with others of:
   (a) a similar status;
   (b) a lower status;
   (c) a superior status.[2]

(2) comparison with one's own group, differentiating:
   (a) present circumstances from those of its past;
   (b) present circumstances from those of its future;
   (c) some combination of comparative time frameworks.

Perspectives on Subordinate Position or "Place"

Each group studied—black slaves of the Antebellum period, Japanese-Americans of the 1940s, and Nineteenth Century American women—was treated by the dominant group as if its members were the same, inferior, and as part of a homogenous entity who belonged together in a specific "place." In this regard, Blumer said (1958: p. 4):

> The dominant group is not concerned with the subordinate group as such, but it is deeply concerned with its position vis-á-vis the subordinate group. This is epitomized in the key and universal expression that a given race is all right 'in its place.'

In this same article, he emphasized the importance of "a sense of group position," as constructed by the dominant group. Yet for subordinate groups, as well, their place, their sense of group position has overwhelming import. Charles Ball's remarks in his slave narrative are illustrative of this:

> My master gave me better clothes than the little slaves of my age generally received in Calbert, and often told me that he intended to make me his waiter, and that if I behaved well I should become his overseer in time. These stations of waiter and overseer appeared to me to be the highest points of honor and greatness in the whole world . . . (1859, p. 16).

Woman as "guardian of the home fires, nestled by the hearth" (Ryan 1975, p. 113) was a mark of the Nineteenth Century American woman's station (Jeffrey 1979, p. 72; Welter 1978, p. 313; Degler 1980, p. 150). As Susan Mansfield Huntington succinctly wrote in her diary on June 14, 1819:

> To render *home* happy is women's peculiar province; home is *her* world (Cott 1977, p. 73).

Thus, the image and sense of being members of a group, regardless of how disparate the members were, could become forged as chains of belief in a long, complicated historical process. For the black slaves in the South, few by the 1800s had any memory of freedom. Women's oppression had had a long history, although in the Nineteenth Century the shades of domination commenced to lighten. Japanese-Americans had been discriminated against since immigration into the United States, culminating with the advent of World War II in their forced evacuation from the West Coast to the relocation camps. The meaning of these peoples' "places," then, issued from that knot of relationship they shared with the dominant group, a relationship of power. It was subordination to which these groups had had to come to terms. To claim relative advantage was one way that this was done.

Comparisons with Others of Similar Status

It was not unusual for black slaves to comment that their circumstances or conditions were better than those of other black groups whom they knew. They knew the conditions well. This informational grapevine, as Feldstein tells us (1971, p. 186):

> reached into the quarters and great houses of other plantations. Even if the master did not permit any association with the slaves of another plantation, his people knew of the conditions of others. Many plantations used mills which were not located on their grounds, and slaves of several planters would meet, and, while conducting business exchange information which enabled the slave to make comparisons and interpretations of his life, the lives and conditions of other slaves, and, generally, of the institution.

The narratives indicate that this was not extraordinary.[3] Mrs. Marriah Hines, who had been born in 1835, for example, made this comparison:

> When we would look and see how the 'jining farm was faring, 'twould almost shed tears. It made us feel like we was gittin' 'long most fine. Dat's why we loved, 'spected master, 'course he was so good to us (Perdue et al 1976, p. 140).

And from the Fisk University files came this comment:

> Our white folks was good to us, yes'm, awful good to us. They didn't allow the overseer to whip the darkies. . . . You know, the man next to our field, he was the meanest white man you most ever saw. No'm, nobody never did run away from my white folks; you see they was so good to us; but they sho did run away from that other plantation (Fisk University 1945, p. 201).

Relative advantage was strongly felt by black slaves over those who had been sold away and had been taken west to the very large plantations in such states as Alabama, Mississippi, and Louisiana. Comments regarding this surfaced again and again (Smedes 1900, p. 78; Johnson 1969, p. 125; Yetman 1970, pp. 98, 166, 174; Perdue et al 1976, pp. 72, 99, 139, 140, 166; Raboteau 1978, p. 220), bearing witness to the sense of advantage, as well as sadness with their loss of kin and friends, of those who remained behind.

Frederick Douglass sums up the fine points of intragroup comparison, when he writes:

> I always measured the kindness of my master by the standard of kindness set up by slaveholders around us. However, slaves are like other people, and imbibe similar prejudices. They are apt to think *their condition* better than that of others. Many, under the influence of this prejudice, think their own masters are better than the masters of other slaves; and this, too, in some cases, when the very reverse is true. Indeed, it is not uncommon for slaves even to fall out and quarrel among themselves about the relative kindness of their masters, contending for the superior goodness of his own over that of others (1970, p. 91).

He continued this with a comment that underlines the importance of status borrowing for counters of superiority in such arguments:

> They seemed to think that the greatness of their masters are transferable to themselves (1970, p. 92).

Japanese-Americans frequently commented that *their* relocation center, in which *they* were incarcerated, had advantages not shared by others. Bogardus commented with surprise (1943, p. 389):

> In the Relocation Centers conflicts have arisen between those who came from different Assembly Centers because of loyalties developed in a short time in the latter.

Women, of course, distinguished between the group to which they belonged and others to which they felt they did not belong. However, most acerbic were the distinctions made between *different kinds* of women, as, for that matter, were also made by black slaves and Japanese-Americans about different kinds of people within their own oppressed entities.

As Nineteenth Century women saw it, there were "good women" and "bad women," and there were "ladies" and just women. These were differentiations that were no longer made on the basis of circumstances, but were made on the bases of character and values. Hymowitz and Weissman explain: "Nineteenth Century Americans referred to women who observed the proprieties demanded by women's sphere as 'ladies.' In the 1800s this term applied to middle-class women whose husbands 'supported them.'" (1978, p. 67). It was apparent that to be a "lady" was considered to be much better than not to be, the term becoming one of approval for some and used as a verbal whip for conformity to those who stepped out of line. Ann Scott elucidates the social control of such appelations when she says: ". . . in the South the image of the lady took deep root and had far-reaching consequences. The social role of women was unusually confining there, and the sanctions used to enforce obedience peculiarly effective" (1970, p. x–xi). When it came to "good" women and "bad" women, indeed, the line was drawn with severity.[4] But, of course, it was not possible to be a "good" woman, unless there were "bad" women with which to compare them, or as Barbara Berg tells us, "the prostitute was crucial to the continued existence of the woman-belle ideal" (1978, p. 179).

Japanese-Americans made crucial distinctions of character on the basis of generational and cultural differences. Adverse comparisons were made by both Issei, or first generation Japanese-Americans, and Nisei, or second generation Japanese-Americans, about each other. Charles Kikuchi in his diary of the relocation years mentions the superiority felt by the Nisei with their Americanized ways toward the "Old Country" Issei, and tells of his sister who smugly believed herself better than those Japanese in the camp who could not speak English well (Kikuchi 1973, p. 124; also Leighton 1945, p. 74; and Smith 1948, p. 245). Morimitsu sums this up when he talks of the Niseis' "callow" attitude toward their Issei parents:

> Reared in an American environment, their speech, dress, customs, ideals, all American, they had acquired with years a certain disdain for things Japanese. And their aged parents represented all that was Japanese (1943, p. 588).

On the other hand, the Isseis were not innocent of this sense of advantage over the Niseis:

> The Isseis on their part, feeling something like the hen who has hatched a duckling, gave the Niseis equally severe criticism. They said that the Niseis were soft, selfish, ignorant, and only interested in movies, dances, and a good time. They lack the spiritual qualities, character, and stamina of a real Japanese (Leighton 1945, p. 74).

There was a further cleavage between the Kibeis (second-generation Japanese-Americans who had been sent back to Japan for some of their education, and upon their return to the United States appeared to be much closer culturally to the Isseis than to the Niseis) and other groups. Bogardus points to the painful marginality of the Kibeis:

> They [the Kibei] are not wholly at home with the Issei, and they are made fun of and taunted by many of the Nisei (Bogardus 1943, p. 389; Ten Broek further explicates this in a later reference, 1968, p. 281).

One Japanese-American Nisei, writing in his diary in 1942, noted with a touch of gleeful arrogance:

> At the engineers' party last night all the fellows were supposed to bring with them a girl. One Kibei fellow didn't know exactly what they meant and brought his mother along (Japanese-American Relocation Records 9/12/1942).

Black slaves distinguished between field workers and house workers and between those who had been raised by "quality" folk or rich owners versus not-quality people or poor owners who had few slaves, suggesting that a complex hierarchical structure of plantation, farm, and city life existed at the lower levels (Feldstein 1971, p. 284). Daisy Anderson Leonard has repeated what her father, a former slave, told her:

> There was a social distinction with the slaves. The house and personal servants were on a higher social plane than the field slaves (Leonard 1967, p. 28).

One black man, in recalling how superior he had felt as a house slave vis-á-vis a field slave, also gives insight into the effectiveness of dominant group cooptation:

> Yes, I was a house slave; I slept under the stairway in the closet. I was sorta mistress' pet, you know. . . . We house slaves thought we was better 'n the others what worked in the fields. We really was raised a little different, you know. . . . Yes'm, we was raised; they, that is the field hands, wasn't (Fisk University 1945, p. 221).

John Thompson, who became a private body servant for his master's son, graphically illustrates this point in his narrative:

> Then my business was to wait upon him, attend to his horse, and go with him to and from school; for neglect of which, as he fancied, I often got severe floggings from him. Still, I did not wish my situation changed, for I considered my station a very high one; preferring an occasional licking, to being thrown out of office. Being a gentleman's body servant, I had nothing more to do with plantation affairs, and, consequently, thought myself much superior to those children who had to sweep the yard (Thompson 1968, pp. 24–25).

The distinctions made between those slaves who belonged to rich or "quality" masters and those who did not were made again and again in the slave literature. Kate Billingsley, an old black woman in Kentucky, emphasized during the course of an interview her superiority to other black slaves who had not been raised as she had been:

> No, I'se don' belief in no ghosts hants or anything of that kind, my white folks being quality. I'se been raised by quality! Why I'se a quality nigger! (Federal Writers Project 16, 1972, p. 60).

Daisy Anderson Leonard's father, a man with a clearly analytical mind, told her:

> The slaves belonging to the lower class of white folks were not considered on the same level as those belonging to the 'quality folks', and the slaves of these families were always proud of, and bragged of their connection with the better families. Thus we had our social distinctions, which were based largely on the social standing of the masters, and within the inner circle, on the position occupied in the plantation or home affairs (Leonard 1967, p. 28).

Once again, Frederick Douglass sums up in a tersely elegant manner:

> To be a SLAVE was thought to be bad enough, but to be a *poor man's* slave was deemed a disgrace, indeed (Douglass 1970, p. 91).

Japanese-Americans and American women, of course, also had strongly developed ideas of socio-economic hierarchy; and they, too, built walls of advantage and turned chilly shoulders on others of their kind. For example, one Japanese-American woman writing in her diary at Tanforan Relocation Center in 1942:

> We again discussed the unconventional behavior and mannerisms of the country people here. They are really crude in our eyes, though we may seem snobbish to them (Japanese-American Relocation Records, June 28, 1942).

In all of these cases, then, separateness and social distance were reinforced by beliefs of superiority and tended to fragment and weaken any incipient organization of protest and to make less likely the emergence of rebellious ideas.

Comparison with Others of Dominant or Inferior Status

Usually the sense of superiority over ruling groups by oppressed people took either the form of the oppressed having better character or the form of upholding a higher morality and having superior values. With black slaves this was the case among those who were "openly scornful of white religion" (Escott 1979, p. 113); but in some instances, the social peculiarities of the slave system were also looked on, at least by young slaves, as being quite remarkable and surely better than what the dominant group might have. Genovese relates:

> And then, there was the game of playing auction. One child would play the auctioneer and pretend to sell others to prospective buyers. They learned early in life that they had a price tag, and as children are wont to do, took pride in their prospective value. They could in fact turn it to some advantage with their white playmates. Two boys were boasting to each other about how much they were worth, when a white boy asked about himself. The scornful reply: "Lord, Marse Frank, you'se white. You ain't worth nothing!" (1976, p. 506).

The slave literature is replete with statements of superiority over "pore white trash" (Blassingame 1972, p. 202; Steward 1957, p. 101). They perceived poor white people as their inferiors, taking the currency of arrogance or status borrowing from their white masters. The concept they felt was deep and harsh and angry, as the statement of one old black man illustrates:

> When I was a boy we used to sing, "Rather be a nigger than a poor white man" (Botkin 1945, p. 242).

Daisy Anderson Leonard's father said bleakly:

> The most contemptible term we could think of to apply to any one was to call them "po no-count white trash" (Leonard 1967, p. 29).

Andy Marion from South Carolina at the age of 92 recalled:

> Marster had a overseer twice. They was pore white trash, not as de niggers (Yetman 1970, p. 222).

And Reuben Rosborough from South Carolina still proudly related:

> Us knowed dat our gran'pappy was a white man back in Verginny. . . . Us come on one side from de F.F.V.'s. I's proud of dat, and you can put down dere dat deres no poor white trash in dese old veins, too (Federal Writer's Project III, 1972, p. 45).

Of Japanese-Americans, perhaps only the Issei and Kibei expressed a belief in the superiority of Japanese culture over that of American culture; and as the mass evacuation exacerbated these feelings, it pushed, as Leighton says, "many of the Isseis toward more active support of Japan" (Leighton 1945, p. 71).

Nineteenth Century American women, perhaps more than either of the other groups, increasingly came to express over the period a defiant sense of moral superiority.[5] Eliza Southgate Bowne, who had been writing to her cousin Moses Porter, responded in May of 1801 to his earlier letter with a show of spirit:

> But she is a *female*, say you, with a *manly contempt*. Oh you Lords of the world, what are you that your unhallowed lips should dare to profane the fairest part of creation! (Bowne 1887, p. 52).

However, in a later letter Bowne moderated this, retrieving the glove of provocation by acknowledging that men had the superior qualities of "profundity" and "discernment" (Bowne 1887, p. 62).

These ideas of moral superiority became more frequently voiced by women as the century progressed. Lantz, Keyes, and Schultz (1975), in their review of the popular literature published between 1825 and 1850, mention that the theme of women's moral superiority was pervasive. And, for example, Lucy Breckinridge, a young, well-brought-up, well-to-do Southern woman in Virginia, writing during the Civil War, exclaimed in her journal:

> I rather incline to the opinion that women are purer and better than men. . . . [Men] have not the moral courage that women have (Breckinridge 1979, p. 22).

Even as time went by, she continued to say much the same thing:

> Women are so lovely, so angelic, what a pity they have to unite their fates with such coarse, brutal creatures as men (Breckinridge 1979, p. 134).

By mid-century and on to the 1900s a number of women's organizations were formed, both for social and feminist purposes. Through these to a great extent and the flowering of the Women's Movement were released impassioned and indignant declarations, first, of equality with men and, later, of superiority to them. At the Seneca Falls meeting on Women's Rights, held on July 19, 1848, Eliza Farnham declared that women's "position in the scale of life is the most exalted—the Sovereign one" (Stanton et al, 1881–1922, 3, p. 448). Elizabeth Cady Stanton and Susan B. Anthony, two of the great feminist leaders, who had commenced pressing the argument for equality with men, came to state in an 1848 speech read at the Waterloo Convention that: "Man is infinitely woman's inferior in every moral virtue" (Stoper and Johnson 1977, p. 199).

Toward the end of the Nineteenth Century, American native-born, white women both in the eastern and western parts of the country, were less tentative in their acceptance that not only were they moral guardians of the home, but, indeed, they were more pure and of higher moral character than men. This led to feelings that men should perhaps imitate the behavior of their unworldly but gentle and sweet and virtuous "womenfolk" (Hymowitz and Weissman 1978, pp. 174, 176, 218; Cott 1977; Sinclair 1966, p. 236). These beliefs had mixed effects. On the one hand, they operated to keep women out of the public life, still in their domestic place in order to protect them from the harshness of the world, and thus they helped to assure that the old system of male dominance remained intact. On the other hand, as wielded by some of the more outspoken and radical feminist leaders, these ideas served to question the legitimacy of a system that elevated "morally impure" and "brutal" males to higher authority over these upright and virtuous women. The feminist newspaper of that period REVOLUTION bluntly stated:

> If women used their influence they would eliminate lying, cheating, fraud, and other male characteristics: by applying feminine intuition women would replace bad male attitudes with such feminine traits as peace, understanding, sympathy, benevolence, piety and higher morality. "Should not women, who manage their households so well, assist in saving the nation? . . . Man needs refining. Let woman fulfill her God-like mission" (As quoted in Riegel 1970, p. 236).

Comparison between Present and Future Situations

In comparing the group history over time, it is often believed that group life will be better in the future: that is, tomorrow is compared with today as promising better things or "pie in the sky." It is obvious that if things are bad today, it would be helpful to people to feel that good days are coming. Thus, in this reconstructed time frame, many of those women who believed themselves oppressed felt that the shades of oppression were lifting, and that in the future they would be treated as the equals of men. Many blacks looked ahead to heaven as the ultimate solution to their problems on earth. Blacks were given a sense of hope by their religion, believing that the "promised land" would someday be theirs, and they would be free at last. At first, when they were being evacuated, Japanese-Americans believed that the relocation period could not last, and that they would be able to return soon to their West Coast homes. Later, many of them, particularly the older members, resisted leaving the relocation camps.

Comparison between the Present and the Past

Sometimes the present is seen as superior to that of the past for the group. Sam Boulware, an old black man from South Carolina, believed that being enslaved to white people had produced distinct advantages for blacks in comparison with what they had had or had been like earlier in Africa.

> If white folks had drapped us long ago, us would now be next to de rovin' beasts of de woods. Slavery was hard I knows, but it had to be, it seem lak. They tells me they eats each other in Africa. Us don't do dat and you knows dat is a heap to us (Federal Writers' Project, South Carolina II, 1972, p. 67).

Surely many women felt that the present was better than in a past in which they had had few legal rights and were highly restricted as a group.

Interestingly enough, a number of Japanese-Americans saw themselves as more advantaged in the relocation centers than when they had been free in a very discriminatory West Coast setting. A Nisei man told his interviewer:

> The second day in camp I went to the employment office to see if I could get some work that I was interested in. I was in the second contingent to arrive at Poston and the camp was entirely new. When I went to the employment interviewer I was elated at all of the job opportunities offered to us. This raised my hopes a little. Before the evacuation, the only jobs the Nisei ever got were in produce stands, farm work, and menial domestic tasks. At Poston I thought there was more of a chance for Nisei in the way of jobs (Thomas 1952, p. 172).

Eighth grade children in relocation camps made comparisons, as well. One young boy in an essay on life in Topaz, written for a composition class, said that it was "not quite as good as in Santa Anita," which had been an earlier assembly point for the evacuees. He went on to list the good points of Santa Anita:

> We had much bushes, grass, and tall palm trees. We had a large Grandstand. . . . we had our school right on the grandstand seats. There is a statue of Seabiscuit in front of the grandstand.

And he waxed on proudly about having two race tracks right there in his home, "one in front of the grandstand and the other was Anita Chiquita." A Japanese-American girl, in the same composition class, wrote in her essay how much she had liked Tanforan Race Track as a place to live, and how much better it had been than Topaz Relocation Center:

> The talent shows, carnivals, stables, lakes, and the grandstand. All of these things are lacking here. One thing I miss here is the grandstand. I'll never forget the address 49–1 where I lived (Japanese-American Relocation Records, February 3, 1943).

In short, these young people were seeing a place representative of the past as better than what they now had.

One well-educated man welcomed the new life in the camps because it provided an escape from the restrictions of the old life:

> The war came with terrible suddenness, even more violently broke the shell in which we lived. In my heart I secretly welcomed the evacuation because it was a total escape from the world I knew. Even when the bus took me away to the tar-papered barracks I felt for the first time in my life a complete sense of relief. The struggle against a life which seemed so futile and desperate was ended. Never again would I have to live it, never again see it, never again be haunted by its specters (Smith 1948, p. 243).

Some Japanese-Americans viewed the evacuation as a kind of vacation from economic pressures and were delighted to have the time to enjoy one another. A restaurant keeper summed this up:

> My general impression was that the assembly center, in spite of the restrictions, gossiping, and other handicaps, was more or less a holiday for everyone. The people as a whole did not have to work their heads off any more in order to make a living since the food and shelter was provided by the government. All in all, the evacuees felt that they were a part of a community more than ever before because of the fact that they were all in the same boat facing an unknown future (Thomas 1952, pp. 334–335).

Charles Kikuchi confided in his journal that his mother and father "actually like it here," mostly because they no longer had any economic problems. His mother, moreover, took particular joy in the new experiences because for the first time she was not restricted to her home "raising children and doing housework," and it also gave her "a great deal of pleasure to make all of these new social contacts" (Kikuchi 1973, pp. 122, 252). Teenagers and women, in particular, welcomed the freedom of the camps, so different from living in the tightly organized, patriarchally dominated Japanese-American community.

Comparison between Past and Present Situations

Lastly, there is the perceived advantage of the past over the present: this might be called a relative advantage by nostalgia. For those members of oppressed groups who could recall a different kind of past, some looked back at it as a period of greater contentment and happiness. Not surprisingly, there were many Japanese-Americans who looked back at the years before the evacuation as those of freedom and growing economic security; and some young university students thought wistfully of their school years and angrily that they had not been permitted to complete them.

There were more conservative American women, of course, who longed for the past, thinking it had been better in earlier times when women as a group minded their manners and their homes, kept silence, and stayed in their "place." People like Catherine Beecher in her lectures and particularly in her book *A Treatise on Domestic Economy* worked at making a science of these past virtues.

During the slavery period, certainly, there seemed to be very little general nostalgia for the past, a past that by the Nineteenth Century was likely to have been one of slavery, also. Of course, there were individual cases where a past situation or master was thought to have been much better than that which was the case at present.

Although it is beyond the purview of this paper, it could be mentioned that many black ex-slaves during their federally-supported interviews of the 1930s thought back on slavery days as the "good old days" (for example, Federal Writers' Project II, pp. 59, 67; Federal Writers' Project XII, p. 134; Federal Writers' Project IV, p. 26; Yetman 1970, pp. 12, 79, 140; Botkin 1945, pp. 65, 144, 152; Berry 1935, pp. 68–69; Bruce 1979, p. 148, etc.). It is apparent that either the slave days for these particular ex-slaves had not been as harsh as for others, or possible that the post-slave days were very difficult, or even that the past became mellow in memory as time went on, or perhaps for all of these reasons.

DISCUSSION AND CONCLUSION

To briefly reiterate: in the crucible of inferior power relations with a dominant group, relative advantage is a group-perceived discrepancy between what it has versus what another group has or between what it has, or had, or will have versus its situation at a different time. For the oppressed groups studied, it was found that more than one type of relative advantage construction was made by each of them, and these group interpretations of their comparative situation or relationships became part of their overall sense of reality. The criteria of what the perceived advantages were varied in accord with the group's position and history, reflecting the perspectives and world view of the oppressed group. Once again it should be emphasized that, undoubtedly, the response of relative advantage was not universal to the group and that not all the members responded in the same way at the same time. Probably, some never did; but many did upon occasion.

All three groups made comparisons that favored them as against other like-status groups.[6] However, the levels of comparison also included those of upper and lower statuses. The bases of these comparisons were those of circumstances, character, and value. Such comparisons tended to support not only a sense of advantage, but often a sense of group smugness[7] or contentment with their lot, as well, even becoming sufficiently stable over time as to be a part of the normative structure. If a comparison was made with a like-status group on the basis of discrepant circumstances, it did not cause division necessarily, the response of the advantaged often being one of sympathy. If the comparison was related to either character or morality or cultural superiority, it was divisive. Making pejorative contrasts in these regards emphasized, of course, the negative aspects of another like-situated group, delineating barriers between them and detracting from possible feelings of community and sympathy. Major problems which worked against group cohesiveness of the Japanese-Americans in the relocation centers had to do with the contentiousness aroused by perceived intergenerational and cultural differences between the Nisei, Issei, and Kibei. And thus, in general, by fragmenting the possibilities for enlarged group cohesiveness or coalitions, group attention can tend to focus on intragroup divisions and to be deflected from hostility toward the oppressor.[8]

The sense of advantage over dominant groups held by subordinate peoples has further complexities. Years ago Max Scheler (1961) defined *ressentiment* as feelings of sour grapes issuing from people in inferior positions against those perceived as more privileged. In using his idea of the value delusion of ressentiment, it can be seen that marginal or oppressed groups could construct a sense of group superiority: women more moral and virtuous than men; blacks more elevated in regard to their religion over whites and generally superior to poor whites. The resentment at being subordinate is apparent, perhaps, in these cases. Some of the implications within a religious framework, as with black slaves, was that sooner or later there would be divine retributive justice visited upon the white masters.

The sense of advantage over dominant others by oppressed people, if handled by them with care and not with dangerous disregard in the face of superior power, can effect two results: the first is that it gives one's own group a sense of dignity and honor, of being worthy, even though one's group is the target of negative evaluations by dominant people; and second, when an oppressed group's image and perspective and purposes can to some extent be independently shaped away from dominant control, a certain amount of resistance to oppression is already mounted. For example, black slaves, feeling that they had a relative advantage of deep religious beliefs as against what they perceived as the more superficial religiosity of many whites, chose a weapon at hand to defend their sense of dignity. This battle was never entirely secured. Still, in regard to their beliefs of superiority over poor whites, their sense of group honor blossomed. Though dependent on degrading poor whites, still it tended to chip away at the mystique of white skin and white superiority in general.

By the first half of the Nineteenth Century, there were a number of American women who felt they should receive expanded legal rights. With murmurings of protest also emerged a "cult of true womanhood." Though the locating of women as having a "place" in the home, and in the sentimentalizing of this place where they were expected to be domestic, pure, sweet, and good continued to place restrictions on the ambits of their lives, it also permitted them a certain amount of localized power and a sense of relative advantage. However, it did not take long before the early feminists picked up that torch of relative advantage over men, limited as it was, and marched it out of the kitchen and into the public arena.

If better times are believed to be coming in the future, or to have existed in the past, or are seen as existing in the present, and these are perceived in such a way that resistance to the oppressive system is irrelevant and there is nothing that can be done to rectify the group's position, relative advantage as measured to these dimensions tends to be apathy-inducing and to support accommodation to the system. Specifically in regard to the three groups studied, it appeared that the belief that things would be better in the future or that rewards would be forthcoming in heaven, a "pie in the sky" syndrome, spoke most directly to black slaves. It is possible that this kind of belief in relative advantage provides a dissociation from the cruelties of everyday life for the most highly oppressed peoples.[9] And, as mentioned earlier, there was the further advantage constructed by black slaves, brought out most clearly in the slave literature, that not only would their own group be going to heaven but their superiors might very well not be going that direction.

Thus, I have suggested various types of reality construction that can occur as an oppressed group phenomenon. Emerging from the conditions of dependency and forced subjection, the construction of relative advantage can be seen as permitting a group to achieve some control over the circumstances of their lives. In doing so, it has some positive effects for the group, such as creating a consciousness of group belonging and emphasizing its superiority in some regard; and the group is not only seen as better than or as having some advantage over another group, but also that it is a group that has a difference, that has some extraordinary characteristic. The building and preservation of a beneficial sense of group identity reflects upon the individual member as well, enhancing the sense of self by reference to the group's advantage. For both group and individual, then, relative advantage gives a feeling of importance, self-esteem, of control within the oppressed boundaries, limiting the feelings of deprivation and oppression, contributing to feelings of contentment.

At this juncture, it is perhaps appropriate to at least pose the questions that were noted earlier as having been neglected in the sociological literature: how were the "comparison others" chosen by individuals or groups; and what were the reasons or needs or motives for making these comparisons. First, the historical data studied in this paper appear to demonstrate that comparison others or frameworks were chosen for the reasons of structural or geographical or temporal proximity, and also that such others were politically safe objects for comparison.

Second, these data, fragmented and limited as the historical resources are, do not lend themselves easily to conjecture on what these comparisons *meant* to the group members, that is, what these members' *underlying* motives or needs or reasons initiated the comparative process. However, they do illustrate that, given the choice of comparison others, if the enhancement of a sense of self or group worth or if felicitous appraisals of group life were the underlying motives, then such comparisons appeared to be effective.

In conclusion, then, it is suggested that in varying circumstances, relative advantage might make the oppressed situation more bearable, more dignified, and in this way it has a conservative influence. No matter what the situation, judgments of relative advantage make it more likely that the group will try to hang on to or conserve what they have. This, of course, tends to protect the group from harsh retaliation, but it also constrains it into the traces of accommodation.

Ultimately, relative advantage could be a strategic factor in the tamping down of discontent, in muffling protest, and in modifying alienation. Although, as it was seen, relative advantage can be pressed into the service of the disaffected to be worn as a banner for resistance, its strength in this regard could be questioned. It is more likely that while it might help the group to survive as a dignified entity, relative advantage works to support the status quo and to encourage the tendency toward the "legitimation of oppression" (Wolf 1986).

NOTES

1. In some of Blumer's early work on racial prejudice (1958), he presents the idea of group position as the way in which a racial group collectively defines another group.

2. Eugene D. Genovese (1976, p. 533) states that inferiors do not compare themselves with acknowledged superiors. The data in this study demonstrate quite the opposite in some instances.

3. The article "Rethinking Subculture: An Interactionist Analysis" by Gary Alan Fine and Sherryl Kleinman serves to give theoretical credence to the importance of such community linkages as illustrated in this text and to explicate an understanding of "a subsociety as a grounded network" (1979, p. 17).

4. It should be emphasized here, if it needs to be, that those who held the reins of social control over women most firmly and uncompromisingly were members of the dominant group, men. However, women also cooperated in this system.

5. Space precludes a discussion of the kind of out-group hostility expressed by both Japanese-Americans and native-born, white American women toward blacks and other minority groups. It has been noted many times, and most persuasively years ago by Gordon Allport (1954).

6. Where there is little hope for change, relative advantage appears to operate among like-status groups as a kind of vehicle of upward mobility by imagination.

7. It is apparent, of course, that the idea of relative advantage in some instances bears similarity to that of ethnocentrism. However, relative advantage is far more unidimensional and limited, rather than the generalized group belief in the inherent superiority of one's group and culture, as referred to by ethnocentrism.

8. The extent to which dominant groups actively encourage these comparative processes of relative advantage by subordinate groups is beyond the scope of this paper, although it would surely make for an interesting study.

9. Vittorio Lanternari in his excellent book RELIGIONS OF THE OPPRESSED (1963) lends insight into the meaning and hope that religion, promising relief in the future, holds out for oppressed people.

REFERENCES

Ball, C.
1859 *Fifty Years in Chains: Or the Life of an American Slave.* New York: H. Dayton.

Berg, B.
1978 *The Remembered Gate: Origins of American Feminism: The Woman and the City.* New York: Oxford University Press.

Berry, J. Brewton
1935 "Silver Spoon: The Autobiography of Daddy June." *Story* (August): 65–79.

Blair, Karen J.
1980 *The Clubwoman as Feminist: True Womanhood Redefined, 1868–1914.* New York: Holmes & Meier Publishers.

Blassingame, J. W.
1972 *The Slave Community: Plantation Life in the Antebellum South.* Oxford; Oxford University Press.
1958 "Race Prejudice as a Sense of Group Position." *Pacific Sociological Review* I (Spring): 3–7.

Bogardus, E. S.
1943 "Culture Conflicts in Relocation Centers." *Sociology and Social Research* 27: 381–390.

Botkin, B. A., ed.
1945 *Lay My Burden Down: A Folk History of Slavery.* Chicago: University of Chicago Press.

Bowne, E. S.
1887 *A Girl's Life Eighty Years Ago: Selections from the Letters of Eliza Southgate Bowne.* New York: Charles Scribner's Sons.

Breckinridge, L.
1979 *Lucy Breckinridge of Grove Hill: The Journal of a Virginia Girl, 1862–1864,* edited by Mary D. Robertson. Kent, Ohio: Kent State University Press.

Bruce, Jr., D. D.
1979 *Violence and Culture in the Antebellum South.* Austin: University of Texas Press.

Clarke, L. and M. Clarke
1969 *Sufferings of Lewis and Milton Clarke, Sons of a Soldier of the Revolution, During a Captivity of More than Twenty Years among Slave-Holders of Kentucky, One of the So-Called Christian States of North America.* New York: Arno Press.

Cott, N. F.
1972 *Root of Bitterness: Documents of the Social History of American Women.* New York: E. P. Dutton.
1977 *The Bonds of Womanhood: 'Woman's Sphere' in New England, 1780–1835.* New Haven: Yale University Press.

Degler, C. N.
1980 *At Odds: Women and Family in America from the Revolution to the Present.* New York: Oxford University Press.

Douglass, F.
1970 *My Bondage and My Freedom.* Chicago: Johnson Publishing Company.

Drew, B.
1968 *The Refugee: Or the Narratives of Fugitive Slaves in Canada, Related by Themselves.* New York: Negro Universities Press.

Escott, P. D.
1979 *Slavery Remembered: A Record of Twentieth-Century Slave Narratives.* Chapel Hill: University of North Carolina Press.

Farragher, J. M.
1979 *Women and Men on the Overland Trail.* New Haven: Yale University Press.

Federal Writers' Project
1972 *The American Slave: A Composite Autobiography.* 17 vols. Edited by George P. Rawick. Westport, CT: Greenwood Press.

Feldstein, S.
1971 *Once a Slave: The Slave's View of Slavery.* New York: William Morrow and Company.

Fine, G. A. and S. Kleinman
1979 "Rethinking Sub-Culture: An Interactionist Analysis." *American Journal of Sociology* 85: 1–20.

Fisk University. Social Sciences Institute
1945 *Social Science Source Documents, No. 1: Unwritten History of Slavery, Autobiographical Account of Negro Ex-Slaves.* Nashville, TN: Fisk University.

Freire, P.
1974 *Pedagogy of the Oppressed.* New York: Seabury Press.

Genovese, E. D.
1976 *Roll, Jordan, Roll: The World the Slaves Made.* New York: Vintage Book.

Glick, I., R. S. Weiss, and C. M. Parkes
1974 *The First Year of Bereavement.* New York: Wiley-Science.

Gordon, M. M.
1978 *Human Nature, Class, and Ethnicity.* New York: Oxford University Press.

Holmes, Sarah Katherine (Stone)
1955 *Brokenburn: The Journal of Kate Stone, 1861–1868.* Baton Rouge: Louisiana State University Press.

Huggins, N. I.
1979 *Black Odyssey: The Afro-American Ordeal in Slavery.* New York: Vintage Books.

Hymowitz, C. and M. Weissman
1978 *A History of Women in America.* New York: Bantam Books.

Japanese American Relocation Records
1941–1950 Unpublished. Bancroft Library Collection. Berkeley: University of California.

Jeffrey, J. R.
1979 *Frontier Women: The Trans-Mississippi West, 1840–1880.* New York: Hill and Wang.

Johnson, G. G.
1969 *A Social History of the Sea Islands.* New York: Negro Universities Press.

Kashima, T.
1980 "Japanese-American Internees Return, 1945–1955: Readjustment and Social Amnesia." *Python* 41: 102–115.

Kikuchi, C.
1973 *The Kikuchi Diary: Chronicle from an American Concentration Camp. The Tanforan Journals of Charles Kikuchi.* Champaign-Urbana: University of Illinois Press.

Lanternari, V.
1963 *Religions of the Oppressed.* New York: Alfred A. Knopf, Inc.

Lantz, H., J. Keyes, and M. Schultz
1975 "The American Family in the Preindustrial Period: From Baselines in History to Change." *American Sociological Review* 40: 21–36.

Lebsock, S.
1984 *The Free Women in Petersburg: Status and Culture in a Southern Town, 1784–1860.* New York: W. W. Norton.

Leighton, A.
1945 *The Governing of Men: General Principles and Recommendations Based on Experience at a Japanese Relocation Camp.* Princeton, N.J.: Princeton University Press.

Leonard, D. A.
1967 *From Slavery to Affluence: Memoirs of Robert Anderson, Ex-Slave.* Steamboat Springs, Colorado: The Steamboat Pilot.

Litwack, L. F.
1980 *Been in the Storm So Long: The Aftermath of Slavery.* New York: Vintage Press.

Mead, G. H.
1967 *Mind, Self, and Society.* Chicago: University of Chicago Press.

Moore, Jr., B.
1978 *Injustice: The Social Bases of Obedience and Revolt.* White Plains, N.Y.: M. E. Sharpe, Inc.

Morimitsu, G.
1943 "These Are Our Parents." *Asia and the Americas* 43: 586–589.

Parker, Gail
1972 *The Oven Birds: American Women on Womanhood, 1820–1920.* New York: Anchor Books.

Perdue, Jr., C. L., T. E. Barden, and R. K. Phillips
1976 *Weevils in the Wheat: Interviews with Virginia Ex-Slaves.* Charlottesville: University Press of Virginia.

Popkin, S. L.
1979 *The Rational Peasant; The Political Economy of the Rural Society in Vietnam.* Berkeley: University of California Press.

Raboteau, A. J.
1978 *Slave Religion: The "Invisible Institution" in the Antebellum South.* New York: Oxford University Press.

Riegal, R. E.
1970 *American Women: A Story of Social Change.* Lehigh, PA: Dickinson University Press.
1973 "Patterns of Nineteenth Century Feminism." Pp. 183–201 in *The Women Question in American History,* edited by Barbara Welter. Hinsdale, IL: Dryden Press.

Ropes, H.
1980 *Civil War Nurse: The Diary and Letters of Hannah Ropes.* Knoxville, TN: University of Tennessee Press.

Rossi, A. S., ed.
1973 *The Feminist Papers: From Adams to De Beauvoir.* New York: Columbia University Press.

Ryan, M. P.
1975 *Womanhood in America: From Colonial Times to the Present.* New York: New Viewpoints.

Scott, A. F.
1970 *The Southern Lady: From Pedestal to Politics, 1830–1930.* Chicago: University of Chicago Press.

Scott, J. C.
1976 *The Moral Economy of the Peasant: Rebellion and Subsistence in Southeast Asia.* New Haven: Yale University Press.

Seeman, M.
1981 "Intergroup Relations." Pp. 378–410 in *Social Psychology,* edited by Morris Rosenberg and Ralph Turner. New York: Basic Books.

Shibutani, T. and K. M. Kwan
1968 *Ethnic Stratification: A Comparative Approach.* New York: Macmillan.

Sinclair, A.
1966 *The Emancipation of the American Woman.* New York: Harper Brothers, Publishers.

Smedes, S.
1900 *A Southern Planter: Social Life in the Old South.* New York: James Pott & Company.

Smith, B.
1948 *Americans from Japan.* Philadelphia: J. B. Lippincott Company.

Smith, D. S.
1979 "Family Limitation, Sexual Control, and Domestic Feminism in Victorian America." Pp. 222–245 in *A Heritage of Her Own,* edited by Nancy F. Cott and Elizabeth H. Pleck. New York: Simon & Schuster.

Spicer, E., K. Luomala, A. T. Hanson, and M. K. Opler
1946 *Impounded People: Japanese Americans in Relocation Centers.* Washington, D.C.: War Relocation Authority, United States Department of Interior.

Stampp, K.
1971 "Rebels and Sambos: The Search for the Negro's Personality in Slavery." *Journal of Southern History* 37: 367–392.

Stanton, E. C., S. B. Anthony, M. J. Gage, I. H. Harper, eds.
1881–1922 *History of Women Suffrage.* 6 vols. New York: Fowler and Wells.

Steward, A.
1957 *Twenty-Two Years a Slave and Forty Years a Freeman.* Rochester, N.Y.: William Alling.

Stoper, E. and R. A. Johnson
1977 "The Weaker Sex and the Better Half: The Idea of Women's Moral Superiority in the American Feminist Movement." *Polity* X: 192–217.

Tateishi, J.
1984 *And Justice for All: An Oral History of the Japanese American Detention Camps.* New York: Random House.

Ten Broek, J., E. Barnhard, and F. W. Matson
1968 *Prejudice, War and the Constitution.* Berkeley: University of California Press.

Thomas, D. (with the assistance of Charles Kikuchi and James Sakoda)
1952 *The Salvage: Japanese American Evacuation and Resettlement.* Berkeley: University of California Press.

Thompson, J.
1968 *The Life of John Thompson, A Fugitive Slave: Containing His History of 25 Years in Bondage and His Providential Escape* (written by himself). New York: Negro Universities Press.

Van Deburg, W. L.
1979 *The Slave Drivers: Black Agricultural Labor Supervisors in the Antebellum South.* Westport, CT: Greenwood Press.

Welter, B.
1978 "The Cult of True Womanhood: 1820–1860." Pp. 313–333 in *The American Family in Social-Historical Perspective,* edited by M. Gordon. New York: St. Martin's Press.

Wolf, C.
1969 *Garrison Community: A Study of an Overseas Military Colony.* Westport, CT: Greenwood Press.
1986 "Legitimation of Oppression: Response and Reflexivity." *Symbolic Interaction* 9: 217–234.

Yetman, N. R.
1970 *Voices from Slavery.* New York: Holt, Rinehart & Winston.

Review Questions

1. What does Wolf mean by "relative advantage"?
2. What types of comparisons did the following minority groups make to improve their collective self-images?
   (a) Slaves and ex-slaves
   (b) Nineteenth-century American women
   (c) Japanese-Americans
3. Cite examples of the use of relative advantage by groups other than those Wolf studied.
4. What are the consequences of a minority group's creation of a sense of relative advantage? How does a minority group's sense of relative advantage help to maintain the existing power structure?

Suggested Readings: Inequalities: Class, Race, and Gender

Anderson, Elijah. *A Place on the Corner: Identity and Rank among Black Streetcorner Men.* Chicago: University of Chicago Press, 1981.

Blau, Peter. *Exchange and Power in Social Life.* New York: Wiley, 1964.

Coser, Lewis A., and Rose Laub Coser. "The Housewife and Her 'Greedy Family,' " pp. 89–100 in Coser and Coser, *Greedy Institutions: Patterns of Undivided Commitment.* New York: Free Press, 1974.

Gold, Ray. "Janitors Versus Tenants: A Status Income Dilemma," *American Journal of Sociology* 57 (1962): 486–493.

Henley, Nancy M. *Body Politics: Power, Sex and Nonverbal Communication.* Englewood Cliffs, N.J.: Prentice-Hall, 1977.

Hughes, Langston. "That Powerful Drop," p. 93, in Gregory P. Stone and Harvey A. Farberman, eds., *Social Psychology Through Symbolic Interaction.* Waltham, Mass.: Ginn-Blaisdell, 1970.

Jencks, Christopher. *Who Gets Ahead?* New York: Basic Books, 1979.

Liebow, Elliot. *Tally's Corner: A Study of Negro Streetcorner Men.* Boston: Little, Brown, 1967.

MacLeod, Jay. *Ain't No Makin' It: Leveled Aspirations in a Low-Income Neighborhood.* New York: Westview, 1988.

Mills, C. Wright. *The Power Elite.* New York: Oxford University Press, 1956.

Pearce, Diana. "The Feminization of Poverty: Women, Work and Welfare," *Urban and Social Change Review* (Feb. 1978).

Ross, Catherine E., and John Mirowsky. "Worst Place and Best Face," *Social Forces* 62 (Dec. 1983): 529–536.

Rubin, Lillian. *Worlds of Pain.* New York. Basic Books, 1976.

Schwartz, Barry. *Queuing and Waiting: Studies in the Social Organization of Access and Delay.* Chicago: University of Chicago Press, 1975.

Sennett, Richard, and Jonathan Cobb. *The Hidden Injuries of Class.* New York: Vintage, 1973.

Stone, Gregory P. "The Circumstance and Situation of Social Status," in Gregory P. Stone and Harvey A. Farberman, eds., *Social Psychology Through Symbolic Interaction.* Waltham, Mass.: Ginn-Blaisdell, 1970.

Zetterberg, Hans. "The Secret Ranking," *Journal of Marriage and the Family* (1966): 134–142.

Part VII. Deviance, Conformity, and Social Control

FOR MANY YEARS, MOST SOCIOLOGISTS VIEWED DEVIANCE AND CONFORMITY as states that could be easily distinguished on the basis of whether a norm had been violated or not. A deviant was defined as a person who violated a custom, rule, or law; conformists were those who did not violate norms. In reality, there is often no way to determine validly who has or has not actually violated a norm, and researchers using this approach usually had to rely on the definitions of the courts, the schools, and other authorities to classify criminals and juvenile delinquents. (Such a procedure is of questionable usefulness, of course, since not everyone who violates rules gets caught, and not everyone who is "caught" has violated rules.) What these sociologists then attempted to do was to understand *why some individuals broke the rules and others did not*. They searched for social forces such as poverty, social disruption of neighborhoods, broken homes, or improper socialization which might be associated with rule violation.

More recently, the limitations of the early approach have been widely recognized. It was, in a word, too simple to reflect the complexities of deviance and conformity. By asking a limited set of questions, it paid too little attention to the social forces that *produce deviant labels* and *attach them* to some people and not others. A newer approach, called labeling theory or societal-reaction theory, focuses our attention on *social-control agents*—lawmakers, prison guards, parents, the local gossip, and the like—who have various amounts of power to decide what conditions and behaviors will be considered deviant and/or to decide who should receive negative societal sanctions for alleged deviance. As Edwin Schur explained, in every society labeling processes occur on the levels of (1) *collective rule making*, as when legislatures enact a law or members of a peer group informally arrive at a norm to guide the members' behavior; (2) *interpersonal reactions* such as stares, gossip, "dirty looks," and rule-enforcement techniques including whistle-blowing by sports officials; and (3) *organizational processing*, from detention after school to incarceration in a prison or mental hospital. These are the rule-enforcement processes that students of deviance and conformity are now examining.

One of the most important assumptions of labeling theory is that almost no behaviors are automatically considered deviant across all societies. What is "right" and what is "wrong" are decided upon by societal members within their own cultural, or even subcultural, frameworks. The cannibalism of certain native American groups would be considered deviant in our own society, and the relatively free interaction between girls and boys in American society today would be viewed as sinful in many Latin American societies and even by our own ancestors. Walking about a college campus with a brick tied to one's ankle may appear foolish to many, but the individual who engages in this act may be conforming to the norms of the fraternity. What is to be deemed deviant, then, is *relative* to a given culture's or subculture's normative framework. If we accept that behavior is not automatically deviant, it follows that the *creation of rules* for behavior *creates deviants*. Society, not individuals, makes deviance.

Furthermore, as we noted above, not everyone who engages in a culturally disapproved behavior is reacted to as a deviant. And, equally important, not all people who conform to the norms are seen as conformists. Almost anyone who has grown up with brothers and sisters can remember cases in which two children engaged in exactly the same behavior, yet one was punished and the other was not. Not uncommon also are cases in which a child who is conforming is blamed for deviant acts which she or he did not commit. In the larger society as well, labeling "mistakes" such as these are commonplace. Referring to the table below, we can find many instances which could be classified into cells b and c. What's more, *it may be more important in the long run if a person has been labeled than if a person has actually deviated from a norm*. That is, the consequences of labels for the individual's life chances and future interactions may be of greater weight than the individual's own conforming or deviating behavior. In fact, many sociologists argue that one is not deviant unless defined as deviant by other members of society. Deviance is, thus, a social label.

Finally, any given act is usually sufficiently *ambiguous* that it (and its perpetrator) could be interpreted in a number of ways. Norms are often situationally tied, which means that the context of one's behavior must also be evaluated. Killing someone in an officially declared war is not considered murder, for instance, while killing an adulterous spouse may or may not be so viewed. Contracting arthritis may be considered

		ENGAGED IN A DEVIANT ACT?	
		Yes	No
RECEIVED A DEVIANT LABEL?	Yes	a	b
	No	c	d

deviant among the young, but not among the elderly. Just how a condition or act comes to receive meaning within a society of interacting individuals is an important issue for labeling theory.

What factors determine if someone will be labeled as a conformist or a deviant? We know that some types of individuals are more likely to be labeled than others, regardless of their actions. The wealthy person who has several martinis and a bottle of wine with dinner each night is called a "social drinker," while the poor person imbibing an equal amount of (less expensive) liquor is deemed a "drunk" or an "alcoholic." It may be easier for a middle-class person who has political influence or access to lawyers than for a poor person with no "contacts" to escape labeling from police officers, judges, and other agents of the criminal-justice system. Minority-group members may commit no more serious offenses than the WASP, yet because of stereotyping be more readily perceived as deviants (or less readily perceived as conformists). In our society, the poor are often considered less "worthy" in general than are those of greater means.

Moreover, once an individual has been successfully labeled by public opinion, by the courts, by parents, or by teachers, other labels may be attached more easily—as with the child who was once caught breaking a family heirloom and who continues to get blamed for all manner of breakage that occurs thereafter, or with the teenager who has a police record and elicits a greater negative reaction from the police officer than the "nice kid." We have seen examples of the latter in Chambliss's article, "The Saints and the Roughnecks," in Part VI.

Another important question is whose interests are served by the laws and rules of society and on whose behalf the agents of social control act when they administer sanctions. The issue of power comes into play here, and there is much evidence to suggest that, in most societies, the rules and rule enforcers function to maintain existing power relations. In the U.S., for instance, the legal system provides more serious punishments for offenses such as burglary and theft committed by individuals than for corporate crimes, from price fixing to the marketing of dangerous products. Deaths resulting from unnecessary surgery are rarely punished as severely as deaths resulting from a barroom brawl. In other words, those with prestige and power may engage in behavior with consequences as serious as those ensuing from the actions of the less powerful and prestigious, but the societal reactions to the former are less severe than reactions to the latter.

Thus, the labeling perspective on deviance and conformity directs our attention *away from* those who have been labeled *toward* those who do the labeling. The questions that researchers are led to ask include: What are the characteristics of the social-control agents who are empowered to make and enforce rules? What systems are developed to define deviance and label deviants? What are the consequences of the labeling process for the individual and for society? Who benefits from the labels and designations of deviance that gain acceptance in a society? How do societal members cope with or attempt to avoid labels?

The articles gathered in this section address a number of these questions. First, Spencer Cahill examines the question, What happens when children (newcomers to society) violate rules that reflect deeply held societal values? Are they automatically labeled as deviant? Or, does their rule violation actually contribute to their later conformity—and contribute to the social order as well?

Cahill's study rests on Erving Goffman's ideas about the rules of civility in contemporary societies. Goffman saw civility as a "secular religion," a creed or faith that does not rest on conceptions of God. Instead, the new religion of civility embraces as "sacred" the individual self and individual rights. By contrast, many traditional societies (including some Native American, Asian, and feudal European groups) do not hold individuality or individual rights to be important at all.

In the present-day West, Goffman argued, many ceremonies of civility have arisen to elevate the individual. These ceremonies prescribe what one can and cannot expose other people to, how to open and close interaction with others, how to protect others' self-concepts and self-presentations, how close one can come to others without invading their "personal space," and how to remedy breaches of the rules. All these ceremonies are rituals that attest to the importance of the individual.

Cahill describes what happens when American children come into contact with others in the civil arena of everyday life. Not knowing the ceremonies of civility, children often stare, point, screech loudly, invade others' privacy, and engage in other norm violations. Parents and other adults attempt to control, punish, and make children atone for these offenses. But because children do not yet receive much respect for their own individual rights, they may deliberately refuse to obey the rules, inviting even greater social control efforts from adults.

Cahill believes that for most children, "ceremonial deviance" is a temporary phase in which they explore and learn more about the society's moral boundaries and the kinds of sanctions that deviants might incur. In addition, by attempting to exercise control over children, adults reinforce for themselves the rules of the civil religion. Thus Cahill's analysis echoes Emile Durkheim, who held that deviance is a necessary element in the process of creating social order.

In the next selection, psychologist D. L. Rosenhan asks how people come to be labeled as mentally ill, how they are controlled in mental hospitals, and what the consequences of psychiatric labels might be for those who receive them. By having a number of normal, "sane" people approach mental hospitals for help with a (false) complaint, he discovered that the psychiatric branch of medicine was quick to attribute mental illness to his pseudo-patients. Furthermore, once an individual received a psychiatric label, the hospital staff reinforced the label by interpreting much of the "normal" behavior that occurred as evidence of insanity. Rosenhan's study shows us how ambiguous conditions and behavior can easily come to be viewed from a deviance perspective. It also shows the constraints of the institutional environment, and especially, of drug treatment, on the behavior of the inmates. We see many ways in which social control creates deviance.

Next, in Marcia Millman's article, "Kids at Fat Camp," we find a poignant example of how social control can have lasting effects on people's self-concepts, thereby creating a self-fulfilling prophecy. It is common knowledge that definitions of fatness and attitudes toward weight vary dramatically from one society to another and from one time period to another. In some societies, thin people are the deviants. In our own society today, however, thinness is the ideal. As one consequence, obese and even plump adolescents are candidates for weight-loss camps.

Parents and camp personnel are the agents of social control who restrict, cajole, and humiliate in order to produce thin children. Whether these agents of social control are successful or not depends on the time frame we adopt: in the short run, pounds come off; in the long run, they return. Millman gives us first-hand data that show that the social-control processes themselves serve to perpetuate the problem, in part by creating "fat" self-concepts. The children internalize the society's labeling scheme and become their own agents of humiliation.

The final article in this section illustrates the point that people do not always label norm violators as deviant, even when they suffer as a result of the violation. It concerns woman battering and, specifically, how victims react to it. From observations and interviews at battered women's shelters, Kathleen Ferraro and John Johnson discovered that women commonly were reluctant to label their abusers as deviant. Instead they often rationalized their partners' violence, at least until something happened to change their perceptions of the relationship.

The researchers were able to identify a variety of rationalizations that battered women use to explain or excuse their partners' violence. Some of these rationalizations provide alternative, sympathetic ways to view the abusers, while some involve the women blaming themselves. Finally, the researchers found that a number of catalysts could cause women in battering relationships to redefine their partners, themselves, or their relationships. Coming to view their partners as deviant allows them to seek help to leave the abusive situation. Seeking help involves "outsiders" in the couple's lives, and formal and informal agents of social control may then respond to the violent partner.

Ferraro and Johnson's study shows that the labeling process is neither automatic nor unambiguous. Complicated patterns of meaning, social structural arrangements, and personal hopes, dreams, and fears all play their parts in it.

CHILDREN AND CIVILITY: CEREMONIAL DEVIANCE AND THE ACQUISITION OF RITUAL COMPETENCE

Spencer E. Cahill

When Erving Goffman (1955, p. 95) described our secular world as "not so irreligious as we might like to think," he may have been metaphorically stretching Durkheim's (1915, p. 63) classic sociological definition of religion, but not by much.... As Goffman (1971, p. 63) observed, in our contemporary civil society rituals performed to stand-in for supernatural entities may be everywhere in decay, yet there remain

> brief rituals one individual performs for and to another, attesting to civility and good will on the performer's part and the recipient's possession of a small patrimony of sacredness.

In an important sense, our routine performance of such interpersonal rituals, and the belief in the sacredness of the human personality which those rituals implicitly express, unite members of our contemporary civil society into a single, albeit fragile, moral community, a defining characteristic of religion according to Durkheim.... This article is concerned with the processes through which initiates into contemporary American society are converted to and, consequently, shaped by that religion.

CONVERSION TO CIVILITY

If our contemporary civil society is to retain its distinctive moral shape, then successive generations of initiates into that society must be mobilized as *self*-regulating performers of the... rituals of our "religion of civility." That requires that they do somewhat more than simply learn the code of ceremonial conduct which we commonly call etiquette. In a sense, they must have certain elements of behavior "built into them." ... The process through which initiates into our contemporary civil society acquire such ritual competence is the most fundamental socialization of

Source: "Children and Civility: Ceremonial Deviance and the Acquisition of Ritual Competence." Spencer E. Cahill. *Social Psychology Quarterly 50*: 312–321 (1987).

all, since they thereby learn about the nature they are to have as actors (Goffman, 1971, p. 157).

This most fundamental socialization of all shapes not only the behavior but also the inner emotional life of initiates into our contemporary civil society. They are taught to have feelings attached to a self which is expressed through "face" or effective claims to positive social value. They are also taught that such claims are both made and validated through performances of the constituent interpersonal rituals of our religion of civility. In learning these lessons, they acquire an emotional commitment to the code of ceremonial conduct which characterizes that religion. . . .

One of the first and, perhaps, most fundamentally important components of the process through which ceremonially relevant elements of behavior are built into the individual is toilet training. . . . Children are taught in a variety of ways, including temporary imprisonment in bathrooms, that failure to avoid befouling themselves or exposing others to bodily excreta results in social condemnation and isolation. They thereby learn that bodily excreta have profaning power and pose a danger to both their own and others' sacred human personalities. For the most part, children incorporate this lesson into their own inner conversation and come to evaluate their self-worth in terms of their ability to uphold the associated code of excretory conduct. . . .

Of course, toilet training as well as various other component processes of children's socialization to civility occur primarily or at least begin in the context of interaction with members or friends of the child's own family. However, many of the lessons which the child learns in such relatively benign interactional contexts eventually must be generalized to other social situations. . . .

The remainder of this article is concerned with young children's socialization to civility in public settings. Over a two-year period, several research assistants and I spent a total of nearly 300 hours observing young children in such public settings as city streets, shopping malls, parks, restaurants and laundromats at various locations. . . . The following analysis of the process through which children acquire ritual competence in public settings is [based on those observations.]

• • •

YOUNG CHILDREN'S PARTICIPATION IN PUBLIC LIFE

Young children are implicitly required to be under the presumed protection of an accompanying adult whenever they are in a public setting. . . . When it is not immediately obvious that an adult is accompanying a young child in public, adults who are present typically scan the setting in an apparent attempt to identify one of their kind as the child's immediate caretaker. If this visual search for an adult caretaker is unsuccessful, more elaborate measures are sometimes taken . . .

[However,] for the most part, young children not only are accompanied by an adult caretaker when in public, but their relationship to that adult is also clearly displayed to the audience-at-large. For example, young children in public settings are sometimes perched upon an adult's shoulders and are often confined to strollers and shopping carts which are propelled by an adult. Even when young children in public are under their own locomotive power, an adult commonly has a firm grasp of one of their hands, or the child is within easy reach of an adult whose eyes seldom wander from the child for more than a few seconds. Of course, young children in public settings sometimes attempt to venture beyond the physical and visual reach of their adult caretakers, but those attempts are usually frustrated. . . . In brief, young children are not allowed to participate in public life as individuals. Rather, they are either explicitly or implicitly required to be part of a "with" or multi-person participation unit (Goffman 1971, p. 19) which includes at least one adult.

No doubt this requirement is in part for young children's own protection, but it also serves to protect the ceremonial order which adults strive to maintain in public settings . . . as long as young children are within the reach of an adult caretaker, their disruptive or otherwise offensive acts do not pose a serious threat to the ceremonial order of public life. If necessary, young children's adult caretakers draw upon their superior size or strength in order to contain their charges' ceremonial deviance.

Indeed . . . young children's caretakers . . . can be counted upon to not only contain but to also ritually repair their charges' disruptions of the ceremonial order of public life. For example, I observed the following in a discount department store.

> While a young woman is inspecting a rack of clothing, an approximately five-year-old boy who had been standing next to the young woman runs between the surrounding racks of clothing and collides with an elderly woman. The elderly woman (E) loudly exclaims; "Oh, MY LORD!" The young woman (Y) quickly comes to the scene of the accident and apologizes to the elderly woman.
>
> Y: Oh, I'm sorry about that. B–, come over here right now.
> E: That's okay. He just frightened me.
> Y: Sorry again.
> E: Oh really, no problem.

Note that . . . it is "I" not "he" who is "sorry about that." In other words, the young woman does not apologize on the boy's behalf but apparently for her own failure to prevent his disruptive behavior. That is, she assumes moral responsibility for the collision. . . . In an important sense, this transference of moral responsibility from the child offender to his or her adult caretaker propels the process through which young children are socialized to civility in public places.

SOCIALIZATION TO CIVILITY IN PUBLIC SETTINGS

The fact that young children typically are accompanied by an adult caretaker in public settings virtually ensures that children will routinely witness competent performances of interpersonal rituals. . . . [Yet] young children will not learn much from their caretakers' example unless they attend to [its] ceremonially relevant aspects . . . [and] caretakers seldom interrupt their own or others' public activities in order to direct their charges' attention to ceremonially relevant aspects of those activities. For the most part, they only do so in response to their charges' disruptive or otherwise offensive acts.

In their attempts to contain and repair their charges' disruptions and threatened disruptions of the ceremonial order of public life, young children's public caretakers often explicitly or implicitly instruct their charges regarding ritually important aspects of behavior in public places. For example . . . young children often intrusively stare at those with whom they are unacquainted, as illustrated by the following incident which was observed at a fast-food restaurant.

> A woman is sitting across a table from an approximately five-year-old girl. The girl is looking intently at a man who is sitting at the table directly behind the woman and facing the girl. The woman looks up from the sandwich she is eating, glances over her shoulder, and tells the girl: "C–, it's not polite to stare."

. . . Similar to this woman, young children's public caretakers commonly respond to their charges' ceremonially inappropriate conduct with such "rule statements". . . .

The code of ceremonial conduct which adults commonly sustain in public places is typically unspoken, however. Thus, even though young children's public caretakers may readily recognize and decisively respond to their charges' violations of that code of conduct, they often have difficulty articulating and explaining its constituent rules, as the following incident illustrates.

> While a woman is inspecting cans on a supermarket shelf, an approximately four-year-old boy leaves her side, walks over to a shelf on the opposite side of the aisle, picks up a piece of previously used chewing gum, and starts to put in his mouth. The woman glances over her shoulder and loudly commands the boy to 'STOP.' Still holding the gum in his hand, the boy points to the shelf from which he removed the gum and objects that "it was there." The

woman responds: "I don't care where you found it. It's been in someone else's mouth."

This incident suggests that while children may learn to avoid befouling themselves with or exposing others to certain forms of bodily excreta in the course of their toilet training, they must subsequently be taught to generalize that ceremonial proscription to other forms of bodily excreta such as saliva and to objects contaminated by such substances. Yet, the response of the boy's caretaker in the preceding example to his attempted recycling of previously chewed gum does not clearly convey that lesson. . . . Indeed, adults' instructions to children concerning rules of ceremonial conduct are typically incomplete and often seem more confusing than enlightening. . . .

The following conversation between an approximately five-year-old girl (J) and her mother (M) was overheard in a busy laundromat and illustrates adults' difficulties in instructing children regarding civility.

J: Mommy, do you see that baby?
(M does not respond to the question).
J: His face is so fat and . . .
M: DON'T talk so loudly about other people.
M: They might hear you.
J: heh heh but the baby won't understand.
M: That's not the point. It's not polite.

. . . In this conversation, the girl's mother interrupts her daughter's unflattering description of the "baby" and instructs her to take care so as not to be overheard by the subjects of such tactless remarks. However, the girl objects that in this case the subject of the remark would not be offended. . . . Clearly, this girl had not yet acquired the "protective orientation" toward saving the face of others that characterizes competent members of contemporary civil society (Goffman 1955). Without such a taken-for-granted sense of considerateness and tact, the mother's instructions to the girl seem unreasonable and arbitrary. By implication, this example seems to suggest that the process through which children acquire ritual competence necessarily involves something more than observational learning and instruction.

• • •

[I]n order to truly become members of contemporary civil society, children must learn to provide corrective readings for a variety of potentially offensive acts. . . . [Although] young children witness their caretakers' provision of corrective readings, . . . it is doubtful that [they] recognize the ceremonial importance of such remedial work . . . or even that they are expected to provide similar corrective readings for their own acts, as suggested by the following incident which occurred in a large toy store.

> A clerk has just stacked a number of boxes containing toy trucks at the end of an aisle and steps back to admire her work. An approximately five-year-old boy comes running around the corner, collides with the stack of boxes, and knocks a number of them to the floor. A man immediately follows the boy around the corner and instructs him to "tell the lady you're sorry." The boy objects that "you're supposed to say that." The man and store clerk laugh. The boy furrows his brow and looks at the floor.

This boy apparently assumed on the basis of past experience that it was not he but his caretaker who should apologize for his disruptive act. In other words, he had not yet learned to assume ceremonial responsibility for his own behavior and, therefore, to provide corrective readings for his own potentially offensive acts.

Despite this boy's failure to apologize to the victim of his negligence, his caretaker's attempt to prompt him to perform such a remedial act is exemplary of a common response to young children's failures to voluntarily provide corrective readings for their ceremonially offensive acts. For the most part, these prompts or "elicitation routines" have a standard form. The child's public caretaker uses the word "tell" or "say" to signal the child to "repeat the following words in virtually unchanged form" (Greif and Gleason 1980, p. 163). As in the preceding example, often the child is also explicitly instructed as to whom the repeated words should be addressed. Moreover, in addition to using such prompts in an attempt to elicit performances of remedial acts from their charges, young children's public caretakers also prompt their charges to preface requests with "please" and to "say thank you" when an expression of gratitude is ceremonially due. They also employ such prompts as "say hi to the nice man" and "say bye now" in their attempts to encourage their charges to ceremonially open and close interpersonal encounters. . . .

Children's public caretakers not only explicitly prompt performances of ceremonial routines when their charges fail to voluntarily fulfill ceremonial expectations, but also employ what Goffman (1971) appropriately termed "priming moves." For example, the following incident concretely illustrates Goffman's (1971, p. 157) more general observation that a child's failure to provide a corrective reading for ceremonially inappropriate conduct often leads to a halt in the proceedings, this accomplished by an adult's use of the common priming move "what do you say?"

> A man, a woman and two boys are sitting around a table in a fast-food restaurant. One of the boys belches so loudly that the diners who are sitting at nearby tables glance at the boy. The woman immediately asks the boy: "What do you say?" He smiles and answers: "Excuse me."

Clearly, unlike explicit prompting, the use of such a priming move by a child's public caretaker does not simply encourage the child to perform some ceremonial routine. It also requires the child to determine which such routine to perform.

By implication, the use of priming moves by children's public caretakers implicitly tests their charges' understanding of ceremonially appropriate responses to different kinds of interpersonal events. For example, the following occurred in a fast-food restaurant.

> An approximately four-year-old girl who is sitting at a table across from a man loudly announces that she "wants ketchup." The man informs her that "daddy will get it," walks to the service counter and quickly returns with two small packets. While still standing, he holds the packets in front of the girl but slightly out of her reach and asks: "What do you say?" She quickly responds "thank you," and the man gives her the packets.

Like this man, children's public caretakers often withhold or encourage others to withhold some indulgence from their charges until they pass the implicit tests posed by the caretakers' priming moves. Such dramatizations of the potential consequences of failing to perform ritual acts when situationally appropriate may well encourage children to voluntarily do so in the future.

In summary, children's ceremonially deviant acts are essential elements of the process through which they are socialized to civility.... [C]hildren's ceremonial deviance occasions remedial work by their caretakers which children observe, instructions to children regarding conventionalized expressions of interpersonal respect and regard, and the use of prompts and priming moves to encourage children to actively transform their ceremonially deviant acts into expected forms of ritual conduct.

Notably, however, young children often are not the recipients of the expressions of respect and regard that they are instructed and encouraged to give others. As previously illustrated, for example, young children are commonly instructed that "it's not polite to stare" or otherwise violate adults' implicit right to be let alone. Yet, under a variety of circumstances, such as when waiting in supermarket check-out queues or riding on public transport vehicles, adults often steadily gaze at young children with whom they are not acquainted, smile, wink or in some other way attempt to seduce such children into . . . interaction. . . . Thus, children are not expected to do unto others what is done unto them, but what others instruct and encourage them to do. . . .

Although children are often emancipated relatively early from the direct control of adult caretakers when in public settings, they remain subject to adult direction for some time. If children who are unaccompanied by an adult caretaker step out of ceremonial line, any adult may quickly bring them back into line. For example, I observed the following in a fast-food restaurant.

> An approximately nine-year-old and eight-year-old boy are looking at the overhead menu and discussing the offerings. The younger of the two suddenly exclaims "wait," turns, and starts to run toward an exit only to collide

with a woman. The woman grabs the boy's shoulders and informs him that "you shouldn't run."

In contrast to adults, as this example illustrates, children may be subjected to explicit reprimands from total strangers even before they have an opportunity to provide corrective readings for offensive acts. In a sense, they are on a kind of ceremonial probation when in public settings.

Moreover, children do not ceremonially fare much better in public settings when they are in the presence of adults with whom they are acquainted.... [I]t often seems as if adults assume that the young do not experience anger, shame, and embarrassment when ceremonial expectations are unfulfilled, as the following suggests.

> An approximately eight-year-old boy runs through an entrance to a fast-food restaurant while a woman holds open the door. He slips on the recently mopped floor, stumbles, and falls to the ground. Those who are waiting in the queue in front of the counter turn and look. The woman who was holding the door loudly exclaims: "God, get up!" She turns to the onlookers, smiles and shakes her head from side to side. A number of the onlookers audibly giggle as the boy gets back on his feet.

Notably, instead of exercising tactful blindness or offering assistance as they no doubt would have if an adult had been the victim of such a mishap, witnesses to the boy's misfortune readily accepted the woman's invitation to enjoy a laugh at the boy's expense....

Of course ... [s]chool-age children, adolescents and even some young adults sometimes do engage in what Gary Alan Fine (1986) aptly describes as "playful terrorism" against the ceremonial order which adults strive to maintain in public places. However, such ceremonial deviance may not be the unmistakable symptoms of unenlightened barbarism that many adults apparently assume that it is. Rather, such strategically disruptive acts may be "meaningful nonadherences" (Goffman 1971, p. 61) through which the young express their alienation from the social circle of well-demeaned adults....

Yet ... the young's playful terrorism against the ceremonial order which adults strive to maintain in public places may simply be a temporary detour along a path that eventually leads to civility. Through such exploration of the moral frontiers of our contemporary civil society, the young may acquire detailed knowledge of that society's moral boundary and an intimate understanding of the potential consequences of behaviorally crossing it. Moreover, like proverbial thieves, they may also learn that the only protection against betrayal is the honor of one's partners in crime. No doubt such training will serve them well if and when they become well-demeaned adults' partners in reproducing the moral boundary of our contemporary civil society.

• • •

CONCLUSION

[O]thers . . . have previously argued that deviance cannot be dismissed simply as pathological or disruptive, because in controlled quantities it actually promotes social stability. That is, deviance provides occasions for societal members to reaffirm the moral boundary which both binds them together and separates them from those who are not part of their moral community. No doubt children's ceremonial deviance performs a similar function. Their disruptive and offensive acts serve to remind adults of what they must not do nor allow others to do if the ceremonial order of contemporary civil society is to be maintained. Moreover, the preceding analysis demonstrates that children's ceremonial deviance contributes to the stability of our contemporary civil society in yet another way. That is, it occasions responses from adults that serve to intergenerationally transmit the code of ceremonial conduct around which the distinctive moral shape of our contemporary civil society is fashioned.

Of course, simply transmitting the code of ceremonial conduct which characterizes our religion of civility to children does not ensure that they will abide by it. . . . After all, adults in public places often treat children as if they are of meager sacred value regardless of how they act. Thus, the young have little to lose and possibly even something to gain by sometimes strategically disrupting the ceremonial order which adults strive to maintain in public places. In a sense, they have paid in advance for the very sins that might earn them the admiration of their ceremonially profane kind.

Yet, even the young's playful terrorism against the ceremonial order of our contemporary civil society may indirectly contribute to the historical continuity of that society's moral shape . . . . They may thereby acquire a deeper appreciation and understanding of the unwritten catechism about which they initially learned from others' responses to their earlier and less sophisticated forms of ceremonial deviance. Thus, the ceremonial deviance of initiates into our contemporary civil society apparently fuels the very process whereby they are converted to civility and consequently come to reproduce that society's moral boundary.

REFERENCES

Durkheim, Emile (1915)
1965 *The Elementary Forms of Religious Life*, translated by J. W. Swain. New York: Free Press.

Fine, Gary Alan
1986 "The Dirty Play of Little Boys." *Society* 24: 63–67.

Goffman, Erving
1982 (1955) *Interaction Ritual.* New York: Pantheon.
1971 *Relations in Public.* New York: Basic Books.

Greif, Esther Blank and Jean Berko Gleason
1980 "Hi, Thanks, and Goodbye: More Routine Information." *Language and Society* 9: 159–166.

Review Questions

1. What are the elements of contemporary society's "civil religion"? Why do we call it a religion? What does the civil religion hold sacred?
2. How are children likely to deviate from the prescribed ceremonies of the civil religion?
3. Why are adults' efforts at social control likely to fail to regulate children's behavior? That is, what contradictions between how children are expected to treat others and how they are treated themselves lead them to persist in their deviance?
4. What are the long-term consequences of children's repeated, calculated ceremonial deviance for the children, for adults, and for the society as a whole?

ON BEING SANE IN INSANE PLACES

D. L. Rosenhan

IF SANITY AND INSANITY EXIST, HOW SHALL WE KNOW THEM?

The question is neither capricious nor itself insane. However much we may be personally convinced that we can tell the normal from the abnormal, the evidence is simply not compelling. It is commonplace, for example, to read about murder trials wherein eminent psychiatrists for the defense are contradicted by equally eminent psychiatrists for the prosecution on the matter of the defendant's sanity. More generally, there are a great deal of conflicting data on the reliability, utility, and meaning of such terms as "sanity," "insanity," "mental illness," and "schizophrenia."[1] Finally, as early as 1934, Benedict suggested that normality and abnormality are not universal.[2] What is viewed as normal in one culture may be seen as quite aberrant in another. Thus, notions of normality and abnormality may not be quite as accurate as people believe they are.

To raise questions regarding normality and abnormality is in no way to question the fact that some behaviors are deviant or odd. Murder is deviant. So, too, are hallucinations. Nor does raising such questions deny the existence of the personal anguish that is often associated with "mental illness." Anxiety and depression exist. Psychological suffering exists. But normality and abnormality, sanity and insanity, and the diagnoses that flow from them may be less substantive than many believe them to be.

At its heart, the question of whether the sane can be distinguished from the insane (and whether degrees of insanity can be distinguished from each other) is a simple matter: do the salient characteristics that lead to diagnoses reside in the patients themselves or in the environments and contexts in which observers find them? From Bleuler, through Kretchmer, through the formulators of the recently revised *Diagnostic and Statistical Manual* of the American Psychiatric Association, the belief has been strong that patients present symptoms, that those

SOURCE: D. L. Rosenhan, "On Being Sane in Insane Places" published in *Science*, 1/19/73. Volume 179, beginning on pg. 250.

symptoms can be categorized, and, implicitly, that the sane are distinguishable from the insane. More recently, however, this belief has been questioned. Based in part on theoretical and anthropological considerations, but also on philosophical, legal, and therapeutic ones, the view has grown that psychological categorization of mental illness is useless at best and downright harmful, misleading, and pejorative at worst. Psychiatric diagnoses, in this view, are in the minds of the observers and are not valid summaries of characteristics displayed by the observed.[3–5]

Gains can be made in deciding which of these is more nearly accurate by getting normal people (that is, people who do not have, and have never suffered, symptoms of serious psychiatric disorders) admitted to psychiatric hospitals and then determining whether they were discovered to be sane and, if so, how. If the sanity of such pseudopatients were always detected, there would be prima facie evidence that a sane individual can be distinguished from the insane context in which he is found. Normality (and presumably abnormality) is distinct enough that it can be recognized wherever it occurs, for it is carried within the person. If, on the other hand, the sanity of the pseudopatients were never discovered, serious difficulties would arise for those who support traditional modes of psychiatric diagnosis. Given that the hospital staff was not incompetent, that the pseudopatient had been behaving as sanely as he had been outside of the hospital, and that it had never been previously suggested that he belonged in a psychiatric hospital, such an outcome would support the view that psychiatric diagnosis betrays little about the patient but much about the environment in which an observer finds him.

This article describes such an experiment. Eight sane people gained secret admission to 12 different hospitals.[6] Their diagnostic experiences constitute the data of the first part of this article; the remainder is devoted to a description of their experiences in psychiatric institutions. Too few psychiatrists and psychologists, even those who have worked in such hospitals, know what the experience is like. They rarely talk about it with former patients, perhaps because they distrust information coming from the previously insane. Those who have worked in psychiatric hospitals are likely to have adapted so thoroughly to the settings that they are insensitive to the impact of that experience. And while there have been occasional reports of researchers who submitted themselves to psychiatric hospitalization,[7] these researchers have commonly remained in the hospitals for short periods of time, often with the knowledge of the hospital staff. It is difficult to know the extent to which they were treated like patients or like research colleagues. Nevertheless, their reports about the inside of the psychiatric hospital have been valuable. This article extends those efforts.

PSEUDOPATIENTS AND THEIR SETTINGS

The eight pseudopatients were a varied group. One was a psychology graduate student in his 20's. The remaining seven were older and "established." Among them were three psychologists, a pediatrician, a psychiatrist, a painter, and a housewife. Three pseudopatients were women, five were men. All of them employed pseudonyms, lest their alleged diagnoses embarrass them later. Those who were in mental health professions alleged another occupation in order to avoid the special attentions that might be accorded by staff, as a matter of courtesy or caution, to ailing colleagues.[8] With the exception of myself (I was the first pseudopatient and my presence was known to the hospital administrator and chief psychologist and, so far as I can tell, to them alone), the presence of pseudopatients and the nature of the research program w[ere] not known to the hospital staffs.[9]

The settings were similarly varied. In order to generalize the findings, admission into a variety of hospitals was sought. The 12 hospitals in the sample were located in five different states on the East and West coasts. Some were old and shabby, some were quite new. Some were research-oriented, others not. Some had good staff-patient ratios, others were quite understaffed. Only one was a strictly private hospital. All of the others were supported by state or federal funds or, in one instance, by university funds.

After calling the hospital for an appointment, the pseudopatient arrived at the admissions office complaining that he had been hearing voices. Asked what the voices said, he replied that they were often unclear, but as far as he could tell they said "empty," "hollow," and "thud." The voices were unfamiliar and were of the same sex as the pseudopatient. The choice of these symptoms was occasioned by their apparent similarity to existential symptoms. Such symptoms are alleged to arise from painful concerns about the perceived meaninglessness of one's life. It is as if the hallucinating person were saying, "My life is empty and hollow." The choice of these symptoms was also determined by the *absence* of a single report of existential psychoses in the literature.

Beyond alleging the symptoms and falsifying name, vocation, and employment, no further alterations of person, history, or circumstances were made. The significant events of the pseudopatient's life history were presented as they had actually occurred. Relationships with parents and siblings, with spouse and children, with people at work and in school, consistent with the aforementioned exceptions, were described as they were or had been. Frustrations and upsets were described along with joys and satisfactions. These facts are important to remember. If anything, they strongly biased the subsequent results in favor of detecting sanity, since none of their histories or current behaviors were seriously pathological in any way.

Immediately upon admission to the psychiatric ward, the pseudopatient ceased simulating *any* symptoms of abnormality. In some cases, there was a brief period of mild nervousness and anxiety, since none of the pseudopatients really believed that they would be admitted so easily. Indeed, their shared fear was that they would be immediately exposed as frauds and greatly embarrassed. Moreover, many of them had never visited a psychiatric ward; even those who had, nevertheless had some genuine fears about what might happen to them. Their nervousness, then, was quite appropriate to the novelty of the hospital setting, and it abated rapidly.

Apart from that short-lived nervousness, the pseudopatient behaved on the ward as he "normally" behaved. The pseudopatient spoke to patients and staff as he might ordinarily. Because there is uncommonly little to do on a psychiatric ward, he attempted to engage others in conversation. When asked by staff how he was feeling, he indicated that he was fine, that he no longer experienced symptoms. He responded to instructions from attendants, to calls for medication (which was not swallowed), and to dining-hall instructions. Beyond such activities as were available to him on the admissions ward, he spent his time writing down his observations about the ward, its patients, and the staff. Initially these notes were written "secretly," but as it soon became clear that no one much cared, they were subsequently written on standard tablets of paper in such public places as the dayroom. No secret was made of these activities.

The pseudopatient, very much as a true psychiatric patient, entered a hospital with no foreknowledge of when he would be discharged. Each was told that he would have to get out by his own devices, essentially by convincing the staff that he was sane. The psychological stresses associated with hospitalization were considerable, and all but one of the pseudopatients desired to be discharged almost immediately after being admitted. They were, therefore, motivated not only to behave sanely, but to be paragons of cooperation. That their behavior was in no way disruptive is confirmed by nursing reports, which have been obtained on most of the patients. These reports uniformly indicate that the patients were "friendly," "cooperative," and "exhibited no abnormal indications."

THE NORMAL ARE NOT DETECTABLY SANE

Despite their public "show" of sanity, the pseudopatients were never detected. Admitted, except in one case, with a diagnosis of schizophrenia,[10] each was discharged with a diagnosis of schizophrenia "in remission." The label "in remission" should in no way be dismissed as a formality, for at no time during any hospitalization had any question been raised about any pseudopatient's simulation. Nor are there any indications in the hospital records that the pseudopatient's status was suspect. Rather, the evidence is strong that, once labeled schizophrenic, the pseudopatient was stuck with that label. If the pseudopatient was to be discharged, he must naturally be "in remission"; but he was not sane, nor, in the institution's view, had he ever been sane.

The uniform failure to recognize sanity cannot be attributed to the quality of the hospitals, for, although there were considerable variations among them, several are considered excellent. Nor can it be alleged that there was simply not enough time to observe the pseudopatients. Length of hospitalization ranged from 7 to 52 days, with an average of 19 days. The pseudopatients were not, in fact, carefully observed, but this failure clearly speaks more to traditions within psychiatric hospitals than to lack of opportunity.

Finally, it cannot be said that the failure to recognize the pseudopatients' sanity was due to the fact that they were not behaving sanely. While there was clearly some tension present in all of them, their daily visitors could detect no serious behavioral consequences—nor, indeed, could other patients. It was quite common for the patients to "detect" the pseudopatients' sanity. During the first three hospitalizations, when accurate counts were kept, 35 of a total of 118 patients on the admissions ward voiced their suspicions, some vigorously. "You're not crazy. You're a journalist, or a professor [referring to the continual note-taking]. You're checking up on the hospital." While most of the patients were reassured by the pseudopatient's insistence that he had been sick before he came in but was fine now, some continued to believe that the pseudopatient was sane throughout his hospitalization.[11] The fact that the patients often recognized normality when staff did not raises important questions.

Failure to detect sanity during the course of hospitalization may be due to the fact that physicians operate with a strong bias toward what statisticians call the type 2 error. This is to say that physicians are more inclined to call a healthy person sick (a false positive, type 2) than a sick person healthy (a false negative, type 1). The reasons for this are not hard to find: it is clearly more dangerous to misdiagnose illness than health. Better to err on the side of caution, to suspect illness even among the healthy.

But what holds for medicine does not hold equally well for psychiatry. Medical illnesses, while unfortunate, are not commonly pejorative. Psychiatric diagnoses, on the contrary, carry with them personal, legal, and social stigmas.[12] It was therefore important to see whether the tendency toward diagnosing the sane insane could be reversed. The following experiment was arranged at a research and teaching hospital whose staff had heard these findings but doubted that such an error could occur in their hospital. The staff was informed that at some time during the following 3 months, one or more pseudopatients would attempt to be admitted into the psychiatric hospital. Each staff member was asked to rate each patient who presented himself at admissions or on the ward according to the likelihood that the patient was a pseudopatient. A 10-point scale was used, with a 1 and 2 reflecting high confidence that the patient was a pseudopatient.

Judgments were obtained on 193 patients who were admitted for psychiatric treatment. All staff who had had sustained contact with or primary responsibility for the patient—attendants, nurses, psychiatrists, physicians, and psychologists—were asked to make judgments. Forty-one patients were alleged, with high confidence, to be pseudopatients by at least one member of the staff. Twenty-three were considered suspect by at least one psychiatrist. Nineteen were suspected by one psychiatrist *and* one other staff member. Actually, no genuine pseudopatient (at least from my group) presented himself during this period.

The experiment is instructive. It indicates that the tendency to designate sane people as insane can be reversed when the stakes (in this case, prestige and diagnostic acumen) are high. But what can be said of the 19 people who were suspected of being "sane" by one psychiatrist and another staff member? Were these people truly "sane," or was it rather the case that in the course of avoiding the type 2 error the staff tended to make more errors of the first sort—calling the crazy "sane"? There is no way of knowing. But one thing is certain: any diagnostic process that lends itself so readily to massive errors of this sort cannot be a very reliable one.

THE STICKINESS OF PSYCHODIAGNOSTIC LABELS

Beyond the tendency to call the healthy sick—a tendency that accounts better for diagnostic behavior on admission than it does for such behavior after a lengthy period of exposure—the data speak to the massive role of labeling in psychiatric assessment. Having once been labeled schizophrenic, there is nothing the pseudopatient can do to overcome the tag. The tag profoundly colors others' perceptions of him and his behavior.

From one viewpoint, these data are hardly surprising, for it has long been known that elements are given meaning by the context in which they occur. Gestalt psychology made this point vigorously, and Asch[13] demonstrated that there are "central" personality traits (such as "warm" versus "cold") which are so powerful that they markedly color the meaning of other information in forming an impression of a given personality.[14] "Insane," "schizophrenic," "manic-depressive," and "crazy" are probably among the most powerful of such central traits. Once a person is designated abnormal, all of his other behaviors and characteristics are colored by that label. Indeed, that label is so powerful that many of the pseudopatients' normal behaviors were overlooked entirely or profoundly misinterpreted. Some examples may clarify this issue.

Earlier I indicated that there were no changes in the pseudopatient's personal history and current status beyond those of name, employment, and where necessary, vocation. Otherwise, a[n accurate] description of personal history and circumstances was offered. Those circumstances were not psychotic. How were they made consonant with the diagnosis of psychosis? Or were those diagnoses modified in such a way as to bring them into accord with the circumstances of the pseudopatient's life, as described by him?

As far as I can determine, diagnoses were in no way affected by the relative health of the circumstances of a pseudopatient's life. Rather, the reverse occurred: the perception of his circumstances was shaped entirely by the diagnosis. A clear example of such translation is found in the case of a pseudopatient who had had a close relationship with his mother but was rather remote from his father during his early childhood. During adolescence and beyond, however, his father became a close friend, while his relationship with his mother cooled. His present relationship with his wife was characteristically close and warm. Apart from occasional angry exchanges, friction was minimal. The children had rarely been spanked. Surely there is nothing especially pathological about such a history. Indeed, many readers may see a similar pattern in their own experiences, with no markedly deleterious consequences. Observe, however, how such a history was translated in the psychopathological context, this from the case summary prepared after the patient was discharged.

> This white 39-year-old male . . . manifests a long history of considerable ambivalence in close relationships, which begins in early childhood. A warm relationship with his mother cools during his adolescence. A distant relationship to his father is described as becoming very intense. Affective stability is absent. His attempts to control emotionality with his wife and children are punctuated by angry outbursts and, in the case of the children, spankings. And while he says that he has several good friends, one senses considerable ambivalence embedded in those relationships also. . . .

The facts of the case were unintentionally distorted by the staff to achieve consistency with a popular theory of the dynamics of a schizophrenic reaction.[15] Nothing of an ambivalent nature had been described in relations with parents, spouse, or friends. To the extent that ambivalence could be inferred, it was probably not greater than is found in all human relationships. It is true the pseudopatient's relationships with his parents changed over time, but in the ordinary context that would hardly be remarkable—indeed, it might very well be expected. Clearly, the meaning ascribed to his verbalizations (that is, ambivalence, affective instability) was determined by the diagnosis: schizophrenia. An entirely different meaning would have been ascribed if it were known that the man was "normal."

All pseudopatients took extensive notes publicly. Under ordinary circumstances, such behavior would have raised questions in the minds of observers, as, in fact, it did among patients. Indeed, it seemed so certain that the notes would elicit suspicion that elaborate precautions were taken to remove them from the ward each day. But the precautions proved needless. The closest any staff member came to questioning these notes occurred when one pseudopatient asked his physician what kind of medication he was receiving and began to write down the response. "You needn't write it," he was told gently. "If you have trouble remembering, just ask me again."

If no questions were asked of the pseudopatients, how was their writing interpreted? Nursing records for three patients indicate that the writing was seen as an aspect of their pathological behavior. "Patient engages in writing behavior" was the daily nursing comment on one of the pseudopatients who was never questioned about his writing. Given that the patient is in the hospital, he must be psychologically disturbed. And given that he is disturbed, continuous writing must be a behavioral manifestation of that disturbance, perhaps a subset of the compulsive behaviors that are sometimes correlated with schizophrenia.

One tacit characteristic of psychiatric diagnosis is that it locates the sources of aberration within the individual and only rarely within the complex of stimuli that surrounds him. Consequently, behaviors that are stimulated by the environment are commonly misattributed to the patient's disorder. For example, one kindly nurse found a pseudopatient pacing the long hospital corridors. "Nervous, Mr. X?" she asked. "No, bored," he said.

The notes kept by pseudopatients are full of patient behaviors that were misinterpreted by well-intentioned staff. Often enough, a patient would go "berserk" because he had, wittingly or unwittingly, been mistreated by, say, an attendant. A nurse coming upon the scene would rarely inquire even cursorily into the environmental stimuli of the patient's behavior. Rather, she assumed that his upset derived from his pathology, not from his present interactions with other staff members. Occasionally, the staff might assume that the patient's family (especially when they had recently visited) or other patients had stimulated the outburst. But never were the staff found to assume that one of themselves or the structure of the hospital had anything to do with a patient's behavior. One psychiatrist pointed to a group of patients who were sitting outside the cafeteria entrance half an hour before lunchtime. To a group of young residents he indicated that such behavior was characteristic of the oral-acquisitive nature of the syndrome. It seemed not to occur to him that there were very few things to anticipate in a psychiatric hospital besides eating.

A psychiatric label has a life and an influence of its own. Once the impression has been formed that the patient is schizophrenic, the expectation is that he will continue to be schizophrenic. When a sufficient amount of time has passed, during which the patient has done nothing bizarre, he is considered to be in remission and available for discharge. But the label endures beyond discharge, with the unconfirmed expectation that he will behave as a schizophrenic again. Such labels, conferred by mental health professionals, are as influential on the patient as they are on his relatives and friends, and it should not surprise anyone that the diagnosis acts on all of them as a self-fulfilling prophecy. Eventually, the patient himself accepts the diagnosis, with all of its surplus meanings and expectations, and behaves accordingly.

The inferences to be made from these matters are quite simple. Much as Zigler and Phillips have demonstrated that there is enormous overlap in the symptoms presented by patients who have been variously diagnosed,[16] so there is enormous overlap in the behaviors of the sane and the insane. The sane are not "sane" all of the time. We lose our tempers "for no good reason." We are occasionally depressed or anxious, again for no good reason. And we may find it difficult to get along with one or another person—again for no reason that we can specify. Similarly, the insane are not always insane. Indeed, it was the impression of the pseudopatients while living with them that they were sane for long periods of time—that the bizarre behaviors upon which their diagnoses were allegedly predicated constituted only a small fraction of their total behavior. If it makes no sense to label ourselves permanently depressed on the basis of an occasional depression, then it takes better evidence than is presently available to label all patients insane or schizophrenic on the basis of bizarre behaviors or cognitions.

• • •

THE EXPERIENCE OF PSYCHIATRIC HOSPITALIZATION

The term "mental illness" is of recent origin. It was coined by people who were humane in their inclinations and who wanted very much to raise the station of (and the public's sympathies toward) the psychologically disturbed from that of witches and "crazies" to one that was akin to the physically ill. And they were at least partially successful, for the treatment of the mentally ill *has* improved considerably over the years. But while treatment has improved, it is doubtful that people really regard the mentally ill in the same way that they view the physically ill. A broken leg is something one recovers from, but mental illness allegedly endures forever.[17] A broken leg does not threaten the observer, but a crazy schizophrenic? There is by now a host of evidence that attitudes toward the mentally ill are characterized by fear, hostility, aloofness, suspicion, and dread.[18] The mentally ill are society's lepers.

That such attitudes infect the general population is perhaps not surprising, only upsetting. But that they affect the professionals—attendants, nurses, physicians, psychologists, and social workers—who treat and deal with the mentally ill is more disconcerting, both because such attitudes are self-evidently pernicious and because they are unwitting. Most mental health professionals would insist that they are sympathetic toward the mentally ill, that they are neither avoidant nor hostile. But it is more likely that an exquisite ambivalence characterizes their relations with psychiatric patients, such that their avowed impulses are only part of their entire attitude. Negative attitudes are there too and can easily be detected. Such attitudes should not surprise us. They are the natural offspring of the labels patients wear and the places in which they are found.

Consider the structure of the typical psychiatric hospital. Staff and patients are strictly segregated. Staff have their own living space, including their dining facilities, bathrooms, and assembly places. The glassed quarters that contain the professional staff, which the pseudopatients came to call "the cage," sit out on every dayroom. The staff emerge primarily for caretaking purposes—to give medication, to conduct a therapy or group meeting, to instruct or reprimand a patient. Otherwise, staff keep to themselves, almost as if the disorder that afflicts their charges is somehow catching.

So much is patient-staff segregation the rule that, for four public hospitals in which an attempt was made to measure the degree to which staff and patients mingle, it was necessary to use "time out of the staff cage" as the operational measure. While it was not the case that all time spent out of the cage was spent mingling with patients (attendants, for example, would occasionally emerge to watch television in the dayroom), it was the only way in which one could gather reliable data on time for measuring.

The average amount of time spent by attendants outside of the cage was 11.3 percent (range, 3 to 52 percent). This figure does not represent only time spent mingling with patients, but also includes time spent on such chores as folding laundry, supervising patients while they shave, directing ward clean-up, and sending patients to off-ward activities. It was the relatively rare attendant who spent time talking with patients or playing games with them. It proved impossible to obtain a "percent mingling time" for nurses, since the amount of time they spent out of the cage was too brief. Rather, we counted instances of emergence from the cage. On the average, daytime nurses emerged from the cage 11.5 times per shift, including instances when they left the ward entirely (range, 4 to 39 times). Late afternoon and night nurses were even less available, emerging on the average 9.4 times per shift (range, 4 to 41 times). Data on early morning nurses, who arrived usually after midnight and departed at 8 A.M., are not available because patients were asleep during most of this period.

Physicians, especially psychiatrists, were even less available. They were rarely seen on the wards. Quite commonly, they would be seen only when they arrived and departed, with the remaining time being spent in their offices or in the cage. On the average, physicians emerged on the ward 6.7 times per day (range, 1 to 17 times). It proved difficult to make an accurate estimate in this regard, since physicians often maintained hours that allowed them to come and go at different times.

The hierarchical organization of the psychiatric hospital has been commented on before,[19] but the latent meaning of that kind of organization is worth noting again. Those with the most power have least to do with patients, and those with the least power are most involved with them. Recall, however, that the acquisition of role-appropriate behaviors occurs mainly through the observation of others, with the most powerful having the most influence. Consequently, it is understandable that attendants not only spend more time with patients than do any other members of the staff—that is required by their station in the hierarchy—but also, insofar as they learn from their superiors' behavior, spend as little time with patients as they can. Attendants are seen mainly in the cage, which is where the models, the action, and the power are.

I turn now to a different set of studies, these dealing with staff response to patient-initiated contact. It has long been known that the amount of time a person spends with you can be an index of your significance to him. If he initiates and maintains eye contact, there is reason to believe that he is considering your requests and needs. If he pauses to chat or actually stops and talks, there is added reason to infer that he is individuating you. In four hospitals, the pseudopatient approached the staff member with a request which took the following form: "Pardon me, Mr. [or Dr. or Mrs.] X, could you tell me when I will be eligible for grounds privileges?" (or " . . . when I will be presented at the staff meeting?" or " . . . when I am likely to be discharged?"). While the content of the question varied according to the appropriateness of the target and the pseudopatient's (apparent) current needs the form was always a courteous and relevant request for information. Care was taken never to approach a particular member of the staff more than once a day, lest the staff member become suspicious or irritated. In examining these data, remember that the behavior of the pseudopatients was neither bizarre nor disruptive. One could indeed engage in good conversation with them.

The data for these experiments are shown in Table 1, separately for physicians (column 1) and for nurses and attendants (column 2). Minor

Table 1. Self-initiated Contact by Psuedopatients with Psychiatrists and Nurses and Attendants, Compared to Contact with Other Groups

	PSYCHIATRIC HOSPITALS		UNIVERSITY CAMPUS (NONMEDICAL)	UNIVERSITY MEDICAL CENTER PHYSICIANS		
	(1)	(2)	(3)	(4)	(5)	(6)
CONTACT	*Psychiatrists*	*Nurses and attendants*	*Faculty*	*"Looking for a psychiatrist"*	*"Looking for an internist"*	*No additional comment*
Responses						
Moves on, head averted (%)	71	88	0	0	0	0
Makes eye contact (%)	23	10	0	11	0	0
Pauses and chats (%)	2	2	0	11	0	10
Stops and talks (%)	4	0.5	100	78	100	90
Mean number of questions answered (out of 6)	*	*	6	3.8	4.8	4.5
Respondents (No.)	13	47	14	18	15	10
Attempts (No.)	185	1283	14	18	15	10

* NOT APPLICABLE.

differences between these four institutions were overwhelmed by the degree to which staff avoided continuing contacts that patients had initiated. By far, their most common response consisted of either a brief response to the question, offered while they were "on the move" and with head averted, or no response at all.

The encounter frequently took the following bizarre form: (pseudopatient) "Pardon me, Dr. X. Could you tell me when I am eligible for grounds privileges?" (physician) "Good morning, Dave. How are you today?" (Moves off without waiting for a response.)

It is instructive to compare these data with data recently obtained at Stanford University. It has been alleged that large and eminent universities are characterized by faculty who are so busy that they have no time for students. For this comparison, a young lady approached individual faculty members who seemed to be walking purposefully to some meeting or teaching engagement and asked them the following six questions.

1. "Pardon me, could you direct me to Encina Hall?" (at the medical school: ". . . to the Clinical Research Center?").
2. "Do you know where Fish Annex is?" (there is no Fish Annex at Stanford).
3. "Do you teach here?"
4. "How does one apply for admission to the college?" (at the medical school: ". . . to the medical school?").
5. "Is it difficult to get in?"
6. "Is there financial aid?"

Without exception, as can be seen in Table 1 (column 3), all of the questions were answered. No matter how rushed they were, all respondents not only maintained eye contact, but stopped to talk. Indeed, many of the respondents went out of their way to direct or take the questioner to the office she was seeking, to try to locate "Fish Annex," or to discuss with her the possibilities of being admitted to the university.

Similar data, also shown in Table 1 (columns 4, 5, and 6), were obtained in the hospital. Here too, the young lady came prepared with six questions. After the first question, however, she remarked to 18 of her respondents (column 4), "I'm looking for a psychiatrist," and to 15 others (column 5), "I'm looking for an internist." Ten other respondents received no inserted comment (column 6). The general degree of cooperative responses is considerably higher for these university groups than it was for pseudopatients in psychiatric hospitals. Even so, differences are apparent within the medical school setting. Once having indicated that she was looking for a psychiatrist, the degree of cooperation elicited was less than when she sought an internist.

POWERLESSNESS AND DEPERSONALIZATION

Eye contact and verbal contact reflect concern and individuation; their absence, avoidance and depersonalization. The data I have presented do not do justice to the rich daily encounters that grew up around matters of depersonalization and avoidance. I have records of patients who were beaten by staff for the sin of having initiated verbal contact. During my own experience, for example, one patient was beaten in the presence of other patients for having approached an attendant and told him, "I like you." Occasionally, punishment meted out to patients for misdemeanors seemed so excessive that it could not be justified by the most radical interpretations of psychiatric canon. Nevertheless, they appeared to go unquestioned. Tempers were often short. A patient who had not heard a call for medication would be roundly excoriated, and the morning attendants would often wake patients with, "Come on, you m— —f— —s, out of bed!"

Neither anecdotal nor "hard" data can convey the overwhelming sense of powerlessness which invades the individual as he is continually exposed to the depersonalization of the psychiatric hospital. It hardly matters *which* psychiatric hospital—the excellent public ones and the very plush private hospital were better than the rural and shabby ones in this regard, but, again, the features that psychiatric hospitals had in common overwhelmed by far their apparent differences.

Powerlessness was evident everywhere. The patient is deprived of many of his legal rights by dint of his psychiatric commitment.[20] He is shorn of credibility by virtue of his psychiatric label. His freedom of movement is restricted. He cannot initiate contact with the staff, but may only respond to such overtures as they make. Personal privacy is minimal. Patient quarters and possessions can be entered and examined by any staff member, for whatever reason. His personal history and anguish is available to any staff member (often including the "grey lady" and "candy striper" volunteer) who chooses to read his folder, regardless of their therapeutic relationship to him. His personal hygiene and waste evacuation are often monitored. The water closets may have no doors.

At times, depersonalization reached such proportions that pseudopatients had the sense that they were invisible, or at least unworthy of account. Upon being admitted, I and other pseudopatients took the initial physical examinations in a semipublic room, where staff members went about their own business as if we were not there.

On the ward, attendants delivered verbal and occasionally serious physical abuse to patients in the presence of other observing patients, some of whom (the pseudopatients) were writing it all down. Abusive behavior, on the other hand, terminated quite abruptly when other staff members were known to be coming. Staff are credible witnesses. Patients are not.

A nurse unbuttoned her uniform to adjust her brassiere in the presence of an entire ward of viewing men. One did not have the sense that she was being seductive. Rather, she didn't notice us. A group of staff persons might point to a patient in the dayroom and discuss him animatedly, as if he were not there.

One illuminating instance of depersonalization and invisibility occurred with regard to medications. All told, the pseudopatients were administered nearly 2100 pills, including Elavil, Stelazine, Compazine, and Thorazine, to name but a few. (That such a variety of medications should have been administered to patients presenting identical symptoms is itself worthy of note.) Only two were swallowed. The rest were either pocketed or deposited in the toilet. The pseudopatients were not alone in this. Although I have no precise records on how many patients rejected their medications, the pseudopatients frequently found the medications of other patients in the toilet before they deposited their own. As long as they were cooperative, their behavior and the pseudopatients' own in this matter, as in other important matters, went unnoticed throughout.

Reactions to such depersonalization among pseudopatients were intense. Although they had come to the hospital as participant observers and were fully aware that they did not "belong," they nevertheless found themselves caught up in and fighting the process of depersonalization. Some examples: a graduate student in psychology asked his wife to bring his textbooks to the hospital so he could "catch up on his homework"—this despite the elaborate precautions taken to conceal his professional association. The same student, who had trained for quite some time to get into the hospital, and who had looked forward to the experience, "remembered" some drag races that he had wanted to see on the weekend and insisted that he be discharged by that time. Another pseudopatient attempted a romance with a nurse. Subsequently, he informed the staff that he was applying for admission to graduate school in psychology and was very likely to be admitted, since a graduate professor was one of his regular hospital visitors. The same person began to engage in psychotherapy with other patients—all of this as a way of becoming a person in an impersonal environment.

THE SOURCES OF DEPERSONALIZATION

What are the origins of depersonalization? I have already mentioned two. First are attitudes held by all of us toward the mentally ill—including those who treat them—attitudes characterized by fear, distrust, and horrible expectations on the one hand, and benevolent intentions on the other. Our ambivalence leads, in this instance as in others, to avoidance.

Second, and not entirely separate, the hierarchical structure of the psychiatric hospital facilitates depersonalization. Those who are at the top have least to do with patients, and their behavior inspires the rest of the staff. Average daily contact with psychiatrists, psychologists, residents, and physicians combined ranged from 3.9 to 25.1 minutes, with an overall mean of 6.8 (six pseudopatients over a total of 129 days of hospitalization). Included in this average are time spent in the admissions interview, ward meetings in the presence of a senior staff member, group and individual psychotherapy contacts, case presentation conferences, and discharge meetings. Clearly, patients do not spend much time in interpersonal contact with doctoral staff. And doctoral staff serve as models for nurses and attendants.

There are probably other sources. Psychiatric installations are presently in serious financial straits. Staff shortages are pervasive, staff time at a premium. Something has to give, and that something is patient contact. Yet, while financial stresses are realities, too much can be made of them. I have the impression that the psychological forces that result in depersonalization are much stronger than the fiscal ones and that the addition of more staff would not correspondingly improve patient care in this regard. The incidence of staff meetings and the enormous amount of recordkeeping on patients, for example, have not been as substantially reduced as has patient contact. Priorities exist, even during hard times. Patient contact is not a significant priority in the traditional psychiatric hospital, and fiscal pressures do not account for this. Avoidance and depersonalization may.

Heavy reliance upon psychotropic medication tacitly contributes to depersonalization by convincing staff that treatment is indeed being conducted and that further patient contact may not be necessary. Even here, however, caution needs to be exercised in understanding the role of psychotropic drugs. If patients were powerful rather than powerless, if they were viewed as interesting individuals rather than diagnostic entities, if they were socially significant rather than social lepers, if their anguish truly and wholly compelled our sympathies and concerns, would we not *seek* contact with them, despite the availability of medications? Perhaps for the pleasure of it all?

THE CONSEQUENCES OF LABELING AND DEPERSONALIZATION

Whenever the ratio of what is known to what needs to be known approaches zero, we tend to invent "knowledge" and assume that we understand more than we actually do. We seem unable to acknowledge that we simply don't know. The needs for diagnosis and remediation of behavioral and emotional problems are enormous. But rather than acknowledge that we are just embarking on understanding, we continue to label patients "schizophrenic," "manic-depressive," and "insane," as if in those words we had captured the essence of understanding. The facts of the matter are that we have known for a long time that diagnoses are often not useful or reliable, but we have nevertheless continued to use them. We now know that we cannot distinguish insanity from sanity. It is depressing to consider how that information will be used.

Not merely depressing, but frightening. How many people, one wonders, are sane but not recognized as such in our psychiatric institutions? How many have been needlessly stripped of their privileges of citizenship, from the right to vote and drive to that of handling their own accounts? How many have feigned insanity in order to avoid the criminal consequences of their behavior, and, conversely, how many would rather stand trial than live interminably in a psychiatric hospital—but are wrongly thought to be mentally ill? How many have been stigmatized by well-intentioned, but nevertheless erroneous, diagnoses? On the last point, recall again that a "type 2 error" in psychiatric diagnosis does not have the same consequences it does in medical diagnosis. A diagnosis of cancer that has been found to be in error is cause for celebration. But psychiatric diagnoses are rarely found to be in error. The label sticks, a mark of inadequacy forever.

Finally, how many patients might be "sane" outside the psychiatric hospital but seem insane in it—not because craziness resides in them, as it were, but because they are responding to a bizarre setting, one that may be unique to institutions which harbor nether people? Goffman calls the process of socialization to such institutions "mortification"—an apt metaphor that includes the processes of depersonalization that have been described here. And while it is impossible to know whether the pseudopatients' responses to these processes are characteristic of all inmates—they were, after all, not real patients—it is difficult to believe that these processes of socialization to a psychiatric hospital provide useful attitudes or habits of response for living in the "real world." . . .[21]

REFERENCES AND NOTES

1. P. Ash, *J. Abnorm. Soc. Psychol.* 44, 272 (1949); A. T. Beck, *Amer. J. Psychiat.* 119, 210 (1962); A. T. Boisen, *Psychiatry* 2, 233 (1938); N. Kreitman, *J. Ment. Sci.* 107, 876 (1961); N. Kreitman, P. Sainsbury, J. Morrisey, J. Towers, J. Scrivener, *ibid.*, p. 887; H. O. Schmitt and C. P. Fonda, *J. Abnorm. Soc. Psychol.* 52, 262 (1956); W. Seeman, *J. Nerv. Ment. Dis.* 118, 541 (1953). For an analysis of these artifacts and summaries of the disputes, see J. Zubin, *Annu. Rev. Psychol.* 18, 373 (1967); L. Phillips and J. G. Draguns, *ibid.* 22, 447 (1971).

2. R. Benedict, *J. Gen. Psychol.* 10, 59 (1934).
3. See in this regard H. Becker, *Outsiders: Studies in the Sociology of Deviance* (Free Press, New York, 1963); B. M. Braginsky, D. D. Braginsky, K. Ring, *Methods of Madness: The Mental Hospital as a Last Resort* (Holt, Rinehart & Winston, New York, 1969); G. M. Crocetti and P. V. Lemkau, *Amer. Sociol. Rev.* 30, 577 (1965); E. Goffman, *Behavior in Public Places* (Free Press, New York, 1964); R. D. Laing, *The Divided Self: A Study of Sanity and Madness* (Quadrangle, Chicago, 1960); D. L. Phillips, *Amer. Sociol. Rev.* 28, 963 (1963); T. R. Sarbin, *Psychol. Today* 6, 18 (1972); E. Schur, *Amer. J. Sociol.* 75, 309 (1969); T. Szasz, *Law, Liberty and Psychiatry* (Macmillan, New York, 1963); *The Myth of Mental Illness: Foundations of a Theory of Mental Illness* (Hoeber-Harper, New York, 1963). For a critique of some of these views, see W. R. Gove, *Amer. Sociol. Rev.* 35, 873 (1970).
4. E. Goffman, *Asylums* (Doubleday, Garden City, N. Y., 1961).
5. T. J. Scheff, *Being Mentally Ill: A Sociological Theory* (Aldine, Chicago, 1966).
6. Data from a ninth pseudopatient are not incorporated in this report because, although his sanity went undetected, he falsified aspects of his personal history, including his marital status and parental relationships. His experimental behaviors therefore were not identical to those of the other pseudopatients.
7. A. Barry, *Bellevue Is a State of Mind* (Harcourt Brace Jovanovich, New York, 1971); I. Belknap, *Human Problems of a State Mental Hospital* (McGraw-Hill, New York, 1956); W. Caudill, F. C. Redlich, H. R. Gilmore, E. B. Brody, *Amer. J. Orthopsychiat.* 22, 314 (1952); A. R. Goldman, R. H. Bohr, T. A. Steinberg, *Prof. Psychol.* 1, 427 (1970); unauthored, *Roche Report* 1 (No. 13), 8 (1971).
8. Beyond the personal difficulties that the pseudopatient is likely to experience in the hospital, there are legal and social ones that, combined, require considerable attention before entry. For example, once admitted to a psychiatric institution, it is difficult, if not impossible, to be discharged on short notice, state law to the contrary notwithstanding. I was not sensitive to these difficulties at the outset of the project, nor to the personal and situational emergencies that can arise, but later a writ of habeas corpus was prepared for each of the entering pseudopatients and an attorney was kept "on call" during every hospitalization. I am grateful to John Kaplan and Robert Bartels for legal advice and assistance in these matters.
9. However distasteful such concealment is, it was a necessary first step to examining these questions. Without concealment, there would have been no way to know how valid these experiences were; nor was there any way of knowing whether whatever detections occurred were a tribute to the diagnostic acumen of the staff or to the hospital's rumor network. Obviously, since my concerns are general ones that cut across individual hospitals and staffs, I have respected their anonymity and have eliminated clues that might lead to their identification.
10. Interestingly, of the 12 admissions, 11 were diagnosed as schizophrenic and one, with the identical symptomatology, as manic-depressive psychosis. This diagnosis has a more favorable prognosis, and it was given by the only private hospital in our sample. On the relations between social class and psychiatric diagnosis, see A. deB. Hollingshead and F. C. Redlich, *Social Class and Mental Illness: A Community Study* (Wiley, New York, 1958).
11. It is possible, of course, that patients have quite broad latitudes in diagnosis and therefore are inclined to call many people sane, even those whose

behavior is patently aberrant. However, although we have no hard data on this matter, it was our distinct impression that this was not the case. In many instances, patients not only singled us out for attention, but came to imitate our behaviors and styles.

12. J. Cumming and E. Cumming, *Community Ment. Health* 1, 135 (1965); A. Farina and K. Ring, *J. Abnorm. Psychol.* 70, 47 (1965); H. E. Freeman and O. G. Simmons, *The Mental Patient Comes Home* (Wiley, New York, 1963); W. J. Johannsen, *Ment. Hygiene* 53, 218 (1969); A. S. Linsky, *Soc. Psychiat.* 5, 166 (1970).

13. S. E. Asch, *J. Abnorm. Soc. Psychol.* 41, 258 (1946); *Social Psychology* (Prentice-Hall, New York, 1952).

14. See also I. N. Mensh and J. Wishner, *J. Personality* 16, 188 (1947); J. Wishner, *Psychol. Rev.* 67, 96 (1960); J. S. Bruner and R. Tagiuri, in *Handbook of Social Psychology*, G. Lindzey, Ed. (Addison-Wesley, Cambridge, Mass., 1954), vol. 2, pp. 634–654; J. S. Bruner, D. Shapiro, R. Tagiuri, in *Person Perception and Interpersonal Behavior*, R. Tagiuri and L. Petrullo, Eds. (Stanford Univ. Press, Stanford, Calif., 1958), pp. 277–288.

15. For an example of a similar self-fulfilling prophecy in this instance dealing with the "central" trait of intelligence, see R. Rosenthal and L. Jacobson, *Pygmalion in the Classroom* (Holt, Rinehart & Winston, New York, 1968).

16. E. Zigler and L. Phillips, *J. Abnorm. Soc. Psychol.* 63, 69 (1961). See also R. K. Freudenberg and J. P. Robertson, *A.M.A. Arch. Neurol. Psychiatr.* 76, 14 (1956).

17. The most recent and unfortunate instance of this tenet is that of Senator Thomas Eagleton.

18. T. R. Sarbin and J. C. Mancuso, *J. Clin. Consult. Psychol.* 35, 159 (1970); T. R. Sarbin, *ibid.* 31, 447 (1967); J. C. Nunnally, Jr., *Popular Conceptions of Mental Health* (Holt, Rinehart & Winston, New York, 1961).

19. A. H. Stanton and M. S. Schwartz, *The Mental Hospital: A Study of Institutional Participation in Psychiatric Illness and Treatment* (Basic, New York, 1954).

20. D. B Wexler and S. E. Scoville, *Ariz. Law Rev.* 13, 1 (1971).

21. I thank W. Mischel, E. Orne, and M. S. Rosenhan for comments on an earlier draft of this manuscript.

Review Questions

1. According to Rosenhan, how easy is it for mental-health workers to determine who is "really" sane and who is "really" insane?
2. How did the staff members of mental hospitals act to legitimate the labels that psychiatrists gave to the "mental patients"?
3. How does psychiatric labeling in general serve social-control functions for society? What particular social-control techniques were used in the hospitals studied here to make the everyday routine run smoothly?
4. Why were none of the "patients" in Rosenhan's study turned away from the mental hospitals?

KIDS AT FAT CAMP

Marcia Millman

Girl Camper: Adele, is toothpaste fattening? Because some kids are eating it.

Adele (Camp Owner and Director): Very nice. Now what does that tell you?

Second Girl Camper: (Shouts out, laughing) It tells you that we're hungry.

Adele: No, it doesn't tell me you're hungry. It tells me that you are obsessed with eating and that's all you think about.

CAMP LAUREL, WHICH USED TO BE A MOTEL, CONSISTS OF TWO DOZEN BUNGALOWS arranged in a circle around a concrete driveway. In the middle of the circle is a dirt playground with swings, seesaws, and a turning platform.

For the hundreds of fat children who have been sent here for the summer to lose weight, the camp represents many contradictory things: a prison, a refuge, a place to be transformed.

Camp Laurel is attended by children and teenagers, both male and female, from ages seven to eighteen, and by older counselors who have also come to lose weight. Although some of the children are very heavy (100 pounds or more overweight) others are barely plump, and certainly not more than five or ten pounds overweight. Most are from Jewish middle-class families. The cost for each camper will come close to $1,800. Throughout the summer each will be restricted to a daily diet of under twelve hundred calories and forced to exercise as much as possible.

We can already see among these campers the early stages of life themes [that are recounted by adults as well]. It is well known that the great majority (80 to 90 percent) of fat children become fat adults. But as early as childhood we can also see the beginnings of experiences and world views that will probably follow the overweight person all through life: being excluded and separated from normal society because of their weight, believing that losing weight will solve all their problems, and experiencing dieting as unjust punishment imposed from the outside.

"Girls Bunks one through four, and Boys three through nine, get to the dining hall, *now!* Judy Cohen come to the office for a phone call. David Goodman report to your bunk."

It is noontime, and the camp owner's voice booms over the loudspeaker, reaching every corner of the grounds. The voice comes often. There is rarely more than five minutes of respite from the loudspeaker.

The announcement that it is time to eat is hardly necessary, for as usual, lunch has been eagerly anticipated all morning, and speculations about what will be served have dominated talk around the camp for the past two hours. But as the children file through the food line, collect their portions, and take places with their bunk-mates at the long tables and benches, their fantasies dissolve before the paltry meal. Lunch today is a slice of bologna and a slice of American cheese on a single thin piece of white bread, a small portion of canned mandarin oranges, washed of their syrup, and served in a little accordion paper cup (the size used at lunch counters to serve mayonnaise), four ounces of reconstituted instant nonfat milk mixed with artificial sweetener, and a small serving of iceberg lettuce topped with a ring of green pepper. The meal is served on paper plates and eaten with plastic utensils.

While they silently eat, more information comes over the loudspeaker, and one girl is sent out of dining hall for talking to her neighbor before the announcements are completed. Although they have been instructed to eat slowly, lunch is finished in ten minutes and soon the campers congregate in small groups in the playground outside. Reminiscing about the foods they used to eat, their faces and voices becoming animated once again.

"My mother makes them with *both* chocolate chips and butterscotch bits," boasts one camper. "Does your mother make them with nuts?" counters another. Across the playground a camper recalls the "s'mores" they used to serve at the camp she went to the previous summer and still another proudly announces that the very block she lives on in Manhattan's Upper West Side has a Baskin-Robbins ice cream parlor and both a Barton's and Barricini's candy store.

What makes diet camp seem so much like a prison is that, by being sent there, the child is implicitly told that he or she is not fit to be with normal children. And although some eventually come to believe (or partly believe) that they are being sent for their own good, few are happy about it at first. Not only does the experience segregate fat children from the world of normals, but it also takes a happy time—summer—and turns it into a season of deprivation and labor. It denies these children what they most enjoy doing—eating—and substitutes what they hate most: strenuous exercise. Several campers lie to their winter friends about where they are going for the summer, because they are ashamed and feel that being sent to a special camp will further mark them as fat and different in the eyes of their peers.

Some of the younger children are first-timers to the camp and are especially upset at the news of being sent there. Several are hardly overweight but have parents who are fat and want to make sure their children won't be. Indeed, one slightly overweight ten-year-old recalls that her mother forced her to come. The girl had no part in the decision, even though when the camp brochures arrived in the mail, she ripped them up and ran to her room, threatening to leave home.

Not only do the children feel constantly starved for food (and indeed, one might well ask whether young children should be on such a restricted diet) but to some extent they also regard the staff as jailers. The presumption is made by the staff that without constant surveillance many of the children will be importing forbidden food into the camp, cheating on their diets, and avoiding exercise. The enforcement of diets and exercise is both a cause and outcome of the children's noncompliance.

Feeling pushed around, the children do rebel wherever they can. Complaining of how the camp is "killing them," many approach exercises and sports that children usually enjoy with a lethargy and disdain that is remarkable. And excuses for sitting out activities are made so frequently that the counselors quite rightly argue, "Girls, you can't be having your period for a month at a time." The counselors also calculate that if all the complained-of ailments were legitimate, roughly a quarter of the camp children might be considered badly injured at any given time. This is difficult to believe, considering the care with which the children move themselves.

But most rebellious of all are the food smugglers. Dreaming up ways to cheat on the diet is a continuous project among campers, pursued with far more interest and enthusiasm than the exercises. The camp has a fairly tight food control system. For example, all packages arriving in the mail must be opened in a counselor's presence, and even money is forbidden to campers since it might be used to commission the purchase of candy when someone gets permission to go into town. The camp expects this mutiny from the diet. The older children know that all campers are sent to the movies the afternoons after parents' visiting days so their bunks and mattresses can be thoroughly searched by counselors for hidden food.

Finally, many campers are cynical about whose interests are served by camp policies. While they do not believe that they are really the victims of staff cruelty (most of the campers think the counselors, being fat themselves, are sympathetic), they do suspect that the profit motive rather than concern for their welfare is behind most of the policies. For example, when some campers petitioned for a higher ration of protein in their diet they were skeptical of the camp owner's explanations: that she served such foods as cereal for breakfast because the children would always be exposed to foods like these, and needed to learn how to eat them in modified portions.

The children's skepticism is logical. Many have attended the camp during previous summers and always regained the lost weight by New Year's. And many admit that even though they want to lose weight, if left free of external control, they would be eating fattening foods.

What ultimately undermines their faith in the camp and makes it seem even more like a prison is the hypocrisy of the staff. The counselors are supposed to be role models for the campers in diet and exercise, but they frequently show the smallest weight losses. It is obvious why: they are allowed into town so they have more opportunities to cheat. Despite their presumed greater maturity the counselors illustrate the principle that once external control is removed, many will abandon the diet.

Furthermore, the camp owner herself is overweight, and though her lectures are wise and she is the object of some affection from the campers, she, too, is considered a hypocrite. Because she allowed some of the "homesick" campers to come to her house (on the camp grounds) and do chores like make her bed, they have had opportunities to observe her own eating habits. Word got around and now campers complain that "Adele doesn't practice what she preaches. She eats half a cherry pie and washes it down with nonfat milk." Other children gossip about how she has not one, but *two* refrigerators in her kitchen and how one is always filled with ice cream and cake.

If the children are cynical about the ultimate benefits of the diet camp, so are the staff and management. Asked whether the camp could be the subject of a story in the media, the top administrators considered among themselves whether they had anything to lose by this kind of coverage. One administrator speculated, "Well, they could say that 95 percent of diets fail and people gain the weight back, but even if they do say it, that can't hurt us. All the parents who send their children here think their kids will be one of the 5 percent."

One of the most significant dangers of sending children to a diet camp is that they learn to associate dieting with punishment or at least arbitrary external rule rather than as something voluntarily pursued as a way of being good to themselves. The source of control for what can or can't be eaten rests outside the child, and the child's sense of control can then come only from cheating or resisting. Thus begins a long career of associating dieting with oppressive restrictions imposed from the outside and to be resisted or abandoned. Thus the camp may be experienced as a prison in a fundamental way; put someone in prison and all they will think about is how to get out. Put people on a diet with external monitors and enforcement and all they will think about is how to cheat. What campers may be learning, like first-time offenders in jail, may be why they should resent the authorities and how to circumvent them rather than why and how they should "rehabilitate" themselves.

Of course, the children at Camp Laurel complain in the same ways that children always complain about camp: that the management is repressive, that there aren't enough good activities, that the food is terrible. Slender children at regular camps, too, often feel that camp is like a prison and fight with the staff about unfair rules. The difference between Camp Laurel and the others is that for the fat children struggles with authority are centered around food and dieting, just as fat adults often focus exclusively on weight as the cause of their troubles.

It would be very mistaken, however, to think that Camp Laurel represents merely a prison for its residents. It is also a refuge from a hostile world. Although children new to the camp may at first resent being sent, many come to like it. Some of the older children even come of their own choice. For them, Camp Laurel is a last resort, all other diets having failed. Some already feel excluded from the world of normal teenagers, so the camp represents a friendly, comfortable home rather than bitter exile.

Having acknowledged that they are indeed fat, many children find pleasure in being with others of their own kind. It is often said at Camp Laurel that the kids there are "nicer" than children at regular camps. Indeed, given the teasing and exclusion these children would probably experience among slim children, this is probably true. Many children also remark that only among other fat children could they feel comfortable enough to wear bathing suits, shorts, and halters and participate in sports and physical activities.

Many are relieved to learn that others use the very same lies and deceits they have used to obtain and eat forbidden foods. Others are comforted in discovering that others have suffered through the same fights with parents and humiliations in gym class or embarrassment from being unable to keep up with other children in physical activities. In the special world of the camp, their sensitivity about weight is even reduced enough for some to willingly adapt to fat-associated nicknames such as Blimp or Stubby—names they would never tolerate in the outside world.

Learning to be comfortable around other fat children is just one of the many identity experiences children have at camp. In some ways, being with other fat children minimizes the salience of their weight for their social identities. Since all the children are fat, they can see and relate to each other and themselves in terms of other characteristics. But in other ways being segregated from the normal world also underscores and enlarges the importance of their weight. In an ironic way the camp actually schools them in the ways of surviving as a fat person in a hostile, unsympathetic world and, indeed, teaches them to view the world from the perspective of a member of an oppressed minority group. Whether the camp is considered a refuge or a prison, one thing is certain: the outside world is a place to be dealt with guardedly. A much-talked-about camp episode . . . illustrates this point.

During an athletic meet between Camp Laurel and a neighboring (regular) boy's camp, the Laurel boys were successfully baited by their adversaries. While the counselors weren't around, the "normal" boys taunted the fat children with Oreo cookies. Dangling the cookies before them, the thinner boys teased, "Here, doggie. Have a cookie, doggie." Starved for long-missed sweets and not knowing when they would have such an opportunity again, the Laurel boys gratefully grabbed the cookies and ate them.

In a camp meeting that followed this event, the camp owner lectured about the disgrace the campers had brought on themselves by eating the cookies. This was placed in the context of reminding the children that they must always remember their disadvantaged position in the world:

Adele: They weren't being friendly when they offered you the cookies. They don't look at you the way we see ourselves. Thin people look at us differently. They don't understand us. When they offered you food it was like offering food to the animals at the zoo. They are offering you food as a big joke and they are laughing *at* you, not with you.

Despite the lethargy and occasional cheating, and the doubtfulness of the camp's programs as a long-term solution, most of the children do lose a substantial amount of weight (over 20 pounds) during the summer. For the smaller ones, this amount of weight loss can transform a fat child into a slim one. Moreover, since the children are separated from their families and friends all summer, the change in appearance takes on the dramatic character of a life transformation.

If food is one of the main topics of conversation among campers, losing weight is the other. Over the weeks as they lose weight they constantly ask one another, "If you saw me on the street and you didn't know me, would you think I was fat?" Undaunted by their previous experiences of gaining back lost weight, they frequently vow that this will be their last year at the camp and that they are confident of the future: "When I lose weight, I'll be *perfect.*" Their exhilaration goes beyond the certainty that they will be slim, for after all, they have been raised to believe that their weight is the cause of all their unhappiness. All kinds of major benefits are expected to follow: "When I lose weight, I'll do better in school and I'll be more extroverted." Faith in the millennium even carries them through trying experiences. Said one camper, "When the kids from the other camp tease me and call me a fat pig I say, 'I may be fat, but I'm doing something about it. You're stupid; what can you do about that?' If you're ugly or stupid, you're stuck with it, but fat you can always lose."

"Half of you is missing when you go home," one camper explains. It is an interesting way to describe the transformation, for it suggests the feeling that part of their identities will be left behind with the weight that is shed. When one considers what it must feel like to come from a family where slimness is associated with upward social mobility and fatness with one's ethnic origins (as it is among many Jewish and Italian Americans), this statement has special poignancy.

The contradictory meanings and nature of the camp are nowhere better expressed than in the weekly nutrition classes held for each division. It is the time, once a week, when the campers are weighed and thus rewarded for their week's labors.

The owner of the camp starts each class by reading the "ideal" weights for every height represented in the group, and the children listen, transfixed, asking her to repeat the weights over and over again. A few argue with the "ideal" and point out that individual build should be taken into account, and to this point Adele always agrees. One boy can be heard complaining, "According to that chart I should lose 15 more pounds. If I lost another 15 pounds I'd be *dead*."

One nutrition class for twelve-year-old girls got under way when Adele invited them to raise problems or questions:

Adele: While we're waiting for the counselors to set up the scales, let me take some questions.

Girl: Adele, will I ever be able to eat cake?

Adele: I wouldn't say you can never eat cake, but you have to remember we're different from other people. Thin people only eat when they're hungry. Do you ever turn down food? After dinner, when you have company and your mother serves cake do you ever say no? Skinny people only eat when they're hungry.

There were no other questions, so Adele decided to grill them. "Let me ask *you* a question. Who can tell us all a good reason for losing weight? Raise you hand."

One small girl raised her hand and answered, "I don't *like* being fat." Another volunteered, "You're fat and people laugh at you." A third added, "You can't go places."

By now the scales were set up on the auditorium stage and the children lined up. One came running down the steps screaming and crying. "Five pounds—I lost five pounds." Tears of joy rolled down her face. Others repeated the gesture, hugging their friends and wildly jumping up and down. They seemed to mimic contestants on a television game show. One girl called to her friends, "I can't believe it—I'm in my *teens*" (meaning she weighed under 120). More quietly, another told a friend that she weighed under 200 pounds for the first time since she was ten years old.

But there were also disappointments. Some had lost only a pound or two in the last week, or perhaps only 10 pounds since camp had started four weeks earlier, and they complained that the small losses didn't justify the costs and sacrifice. Adele had an answer ready.

Adele: This is a small town and I hear everything that goes on. If you belch at the other end of town, I can hear it here. Of those of you who lost less than two pounds, how many of you went horseback riding in town on Tuesday?
[Several raise hands]

Adele: Of you girls, is there anyone who has something to tell the group?
[Silence]

Adele: Doesn't anyone have anything they would like to share?

Girl [near tears]: I cheated.

Adele: You what? Say it louder.

Girl: I cheated.

Adele: O.K. I knew this happened. [To the girl] Would you tell me where you got the money to buy food?

Girl: I'm not telling.

Adele: You know it's against the rules for you to have money, so I'm asking you where you got it.

Girl: I'm not saying.

Adele: You don't have to tell me any names—just tell me whether it was a friend who gave you the money, or did you steal the candy?

Girl: No, it was a friend.

Adele: That was no friend. A friend wouldn't give you money to do something self-destructive. You might think she's a friend, but she's not. Girls, you're just going to have to ask yourselves what's more important to you—eating or your self-respect.
[Silence, then another girl raises her hand]

2nd Girl: Adele, what's for lunch?

Adele: I'm not going to answer that question.

The conversation now turned to the controversial question of chewing gum. All the campers had been asked to turn in their gum, but a few had hoarded their supply and gotten caught when they threw the wrappers on the lawn. Because of this, Adele had prohibited gum for another few weeks:

Adele: Because of Dana, no one in camp will be getting gum. Come up here, Dana. Where did you get that gum?

Dana: Somebody gave it to me.

Adele: Who?

Dana: Somebody.

Adele: I want you to learn how to live with one another. You were told that until everyone stops chewing, no one will. Now, Dana, you are personally responsible for stopping everyone from chewing. How do you feel about it?

Dana: [Shrugs her shoulders].

Adele: You don't care.

Because parents' visiting day was coming up soon, and the campers would be going out for the day, Adele handed out copies of sample menus from restaurants in order to drill them on what they could order.

"Okay, girls. What would be better, french fried potatoes or baked potatoes?"

In chorus, they answered back, "Baked potatoes," but a few giggled, "French fries!"

"What would be better, steak or fish?"

"Fish!"

Time was running out, but Adele had a moment for one more question. A slim girl raised her hand: "Adele, if you're on maintenance, are you allowed to eat french fries?" "Girls, I've answered that question a million times. I hate to cut this short, but the next class is waiting." As they started to file out of the room she called some final advice after them, "Girls, are you chewing your food well and eating slowly?"

Comparisons between the campers in nutrition class are inevitable. The fact that some have reached their goal and become slim and that for most this would have been impossible in one summer points out the wide range of sizes among the campers. And sadly, there are strains between the groups. For if the camp generally has the aura of a sanctuary, it is also true that some of the painful experiences the children encounter in the outside world are reproduced within the camp as well. As one of the larger fourteen-year-old girls explained, a small group of the thinnest girls in the camp formed an elite clique and made mean remarks to the fatter girls, gossiping behind their backs about what size pants the larger girls wore. According to this camper, these thin "beauties" of the camp would frequently admire themselves in the mirror while complaining. "Oh, I'm so fat," in front of the larger girls in a deliberate attempt to make them feel uncomfortable. In the view of the fatter campers, several girls of essentially normal weight had come to camp so they could feel "superior" to the others and have all the boys chasing after them.

There is some evidence to support these observations and interpretations. There are many fewer boys than girls attending Camp Laurel, and most of the boys are indeed interested in dating the slimmer girls. For example, one seventeen-year-old male counselor who was quite a bit overweight himself admitted that he preferred the thinner girls and would certainly never date a fat girl at home, because his parents had told him that he should have "the best." Fat girls, in his estimation, had no self-respect because they had to settle for what they could get. He also expressed concern about how fat girlfriends would reflect on him: "If I dated a fat girl and walked down the street, someone would say, 'Oh look at that fat couple. Aren't they cute.' But if I was with a thin girl, I wouldn't mind if someone said, 'How did that fat guy get that beautiful girl—he must be pretty good.' " Asked if he thought it was worse to be a fat woman than a fat man he replied, "A guy can be big, but a girl should be petite. Girl goes with petite like pie goes with coffee or bagels go with cream cheese."

The relationship between the slimmer and fatter girls is complicated. To the larger girls, the thin ones represent both their persecutors and also what they might become. For even though there is a division, all are on a continuum of suffering and triumph, symbolized by their ritual of trading clothes up the weight line as the campers get slimmer. As their clothes become too big, each passes the discarded items along to others who can just now fit into them. So, even if all cannot become thin over the summer, they all can experience some taste of transformation. If all do not go home transformed into "normal" children, each has had an opportunity to see herself in a different way. When their parents collect them at the end of the summer, most go home looking forward to a new life.

For many, this taste of transformation will not be enough to sustain their weight loss. Even on visiting day, it is already obvious that the transformation is only skin deep, and once free of external control they will revert to their old habits. Despite what they learned in nutrition class and even in the presence of their parents, many go on a binge, jamming so much eating into their day-long furlough that they actually make themselves sick with indigestion after weeks of dieting. And like paroled prisoners who go back to the old neighborhood, once on the loose at the end of summer many of the campers will reacquaint themselves with all their old friends: pizza, ice cream, candy, and french fries. Many will be back at Camp Laurel the next summer.

Review Questions

1. Why do sociologists view the fat children at Camp Laurel as deviant?
2. What other types of deviants could the fat children be compared to? Contrasted with? Why?
3. How did the treatment of the campers by the camp owner, the counselors, and the other children differ from how they were treated outside the camp?
4. What evidence does Millman present to demonstrate that the self-concepts of the fat children were affected by their treatment in the camp?
5. How did this treatment guarantee that any changes in the campers would be temporary? That is, what aspects of the treatment actually taught the children how to enact the "fat role" and remain fat?

HOW WOMEN EXPERIENCE BATTERING

Kathleen Ferraro and John Johnson

ALTHOUGH THE EXISTENCE OF VIOLENCE AGAINST WOMEN IS NOW PUBLICLY ACknowledged, the experience of being battered is poorly understood. . . . Interviews with battered women make it apparent that the experience of violence inflicted by a husband or lover is shocking and confusing. Battering is rarely perceived as an unambiguous assault demanding immediate action to ensure future safety. In fact, battered women often remain in violent relationships for years (Pagelow, 1981).

Why do battered women stay in abusive relationships? Some observers answer facilely that they must like it. The masochism thesis was the predominant response of psychiatrists writing about battering in the 1960s (Saul, 1972; Snell *et al.*, 1964). More sympathetic studies of the problem have revealed the difficulties of disentangling oneself from a violent relationship (Hilberman, 1980; Martin, 1976; Walker, 1979). These studies point to the social and cultural expectations of women and their status within the nuclear family as reasons for the reluctance of battered women to flee the relationship. The socialization of women emphasizes the primary value of being a good wife and mother, at the expense of personal achievement in other spheres of life. The patriarchal ordering of society assigns a secondary status to women, and provides men with ultimate authority, both within and outside the family unit. Economic conditions contribute to the dependency of women on men; in 1978 U.S. women earned, on the average, 58 percent of what men earned (U.S. Department of Labor, 1980). In sum, the position of women in U.S. society makes it extremely difficult for them to reject the authority of men and develop independent lives free of marital violence (Dobash and Dobash, 1979; Pagelow, 1981).

Material and cultural conditions are the background in which personal interpretations of events are developed. Women who depend on their husbands for practical support also depend on them as sources of self-esteem, emotional support, and continuity. This paper looks at how women make sense of their victimization within the context of these de-

SOURCE: Kathleen J. Ferraro and John M. Johnson, "How Women Experience Battering: The Process of Victimization," © 1976 by the Society for the Study of Social Problems. Reprinted from *Social Problems*, Vol 30, no. 3, pp. 325–339 by permission.

pendencies. Without dismissing the importance of the macro forces of gender politics, we focus on inter and intrapersonal responses to violence. We first describe six techniques of rationalization used by women who are in relationships where battering has occurred. We then turn to catalysts which may serve as forces to reevaluate rationalizations and to initiate serious attempts at escape. Various physical and emotional responses to battering are described, and finally, we outline the consequences of leaving or attempting to leave a violent relationship.

THE DATA

The data for this study were drawn from diverse sources. From July, 1978 to September, 1979 we were participant observers at a shelter for battered women located in the southwestern United States. The shelter was located in a suburban city of a major urban center. The shelter served [a] population of 170,000. It was funded primarily by the state through an umbrella agency concerned with drug, mental health, and alcoholism problems. It was initially staffed by paraprofessionals and volunteers, but since this research it has become professionalized and is run by several professional social workers.

During the time of the research, 120 women passed through the shelters; they brought with them 165 children. The women ranged in age from 17 to 68, generally had family incomes [close to or below the poverty level], and did not work outside the home. The characteristics of shelter residents are summarized in Table 1.

We established personal relationships with each of these women, and kept records of their experiences and verbal accounts. We also tape-recorded informal conversations, staff meetings, and crisis phone conversations with battered women. This daily interaction with shelter residents and staff permitted first-hand observation of feelings and thoughts about the battering experience. Finally, we taped interviews with 10 residents and five battered women who had left their abusers without entering the shelter. All quotes in this paper are taken from our notes and tapes.

In addition to this participant study, both authors have been involved with the problem of domestic violence for more than 10 years. In 1976–77, Ferraro worked as a volunteer at Rainbow Retreat, the oldest shelter still functioning in the United States. In 1977–78, we both helped to found a shelter for battered women in our community. This involvement has led to direct contact with hundreds of women who have experienced battering, and many informal talks with people involved in the shelter movement in the United States and Europe.

The term battered woman is used in this paper to describe women who are battered repeatedly by men with whom they live as lovers.

Table 1. Demographic Characteristics of Shelter Residents during First Year of Operation (N = 120)

Age		*Education*	
–17	2%	Elementary School	2%
18–24	33%	Junior High	8%
25–34	43%	Some High School	28%
35–44	14%	High School Graduate	43%
45–54	6%	Some college	14%
55+	1%	College graduate	2%
		Graduate School	1%
Ethnicity		*Number of Children*	
White	78%	0	19%
Black	3%	1	42%
Mexican-American	10%	2	21%
American Indian	8%	3	15%
Other	1%	4	2%
		5+	1%
		Pregnant	7%
Family Income		*Employment Status*	
–$5,000	27%	Full time	23%
$ 6,000–10,000	36%	Part time	8%
$11,000–15,000	10%	Housewife	54%
$16,000+	10%	Student	5%
No Response*	17%	Not employed	8%
		Receiving welfare	2%

NOTE: *MANY WOMEN HAD NO KNOWLEDGE OF THEIR HUSBANDS' INCOME.

Marriage is not a prerequisite for being a battered woman. Many of the women who entered the shelter we studied were living with, but were not legally married to, the men who abused them.

RATIONALIZING VIOLENCE

Marriages and their unofficial counterparts develop through the efforts of each partner to maintain feelings of love and intimacy. In modern, Western cultures, the value placed on marriage is high; individuals invest a great amount of emotion in their spouses, and expect a return on that investment. The majority of women who marry still adopt the roles of wives and mothers as primary identities, even when they work outside the home, and thus have a strong motivation to succeed in their domestic roles. Married women remain economically dependent on their husbands. . . . Given these high expectations and dependencies, the costs of recognizing failures and dissolving marriages are significant. Divorce is an increasingly common phenomenon in the United States, but it is still labeled a social problem and is seldom undertaken without serious deliberations and emotional upheavals (Bohannan, 1971). Levels of commitment vary widely, but some degree of commitment is implicit in the marriage contract.

When marital conflicts emerge there is usually some effort to negotiate an agreement or bargain, to ensure the continuity of the relationship (Scanzoni, 1972). Couples employ a variety of strategies, depending on the nature and extent of resources available to them, to resolve conflicts without dissolving relationships. It is thus possible for marriages to continue for years, surviving the inevitable conflicts that occur (Sprey, 1971).

In describing conflict-management, Spiegel (1968) distinguishes between "role induction" and "role modification." Role induction refers to conflict in which "one or the other parties to the conflict agrees, submits, goes along with, becomes convinced, or is persuaded in some way" (1968:402). Role modification, on the other hand, involves adaptations by both partners. Role induction seems particularly applicable to battered women who accommodate their husbands' abuse. Rather than seeking help or escaping, as people typically do when attacked by strangers, battered women often rationalize violence from their husbands, at least initially. Although remaining with a violent man does not indicate that a woman views violence as an acceptable aspect of the relationship, the length of time that a woman stays in the marriage after abuse begins is a rough index of her efforts to accommodate the situation. In a U.S. study of 350 battered women, Pagelow (1981) found the median length of stay after violence began was four years; some left in less than one year, others stayed as long as 42 years.

Battered women have good reasons to rationalize violence. There are few institutional, legal, or cultural supports for women fleeing violent marriages. In Roy's (1977:32) survey of 150 battered women, 90 percent said they "thought of leaving and would have done so had the resources been available to them." Eighty percent of Pagelow's (1981) sample indicated previous, failed attempts to leave their husbands. Despite the development of the international shelter movement, changes in police practices, and legislation to protect battered women since 1975, it remains extraordinarily difficult for a battered women to escape a violent husband determined to maintain his control. At least one woman, Mary Parziale, has been murdered by an abusive husband while residing in a shelter (Beverly, 1978) others have been murdered after leaving shelters to establish new, independent homes (Garcia, 1978). When these practical and social constraints are combined with love for and commitment to an abuser, it is obvious that there is a strong incentive—often a practical necessity—to rationalize violence.

Previous research on the rationalizations of deviant offenders has revealed a typology of "techniques of neutralization," which allow *offenders* to view their actions as normal, acceptable, or at least justifiable (Sykes and Matza, 1957). A similar typology can be constructed for *victims*. Extending the concepts developed by Sykes and Matza, we assigned the responses of battered women we interviewed to one of six categories of rationalization: (1) the appeal to the salvation ethic; (2) the denial of the victimizer; (3) the denial of injury; (4) the denial of victimization; (5) the denial of options; and (6) the appeal to higher loyalties. The women usually employed at least one of these techniques to make sense of their situations; often they employed two or more, simultaneously or over time.

1) *The appeal to the salvation ethic:* This rationalization is grounded in a woman's desire to be of service to others. Abusing husbands are viewed as deeply troubled, perhaps "sick," individuals, dependent on their wives' nurturance for survival. Battered women place their own safety and happiness below their commitment to "saving my man" from whatever malady they perceive as the source of their husbands' problems (Ferraro, 1979a). The appeal to the salvation ethic is a common response to an alcoholic or drug-dependent abuser. The battered partners of substance-abusers frequently describe the charming, charismatic personality of their sober mates, viewing this appealing personality as the "real man" being destroyed by disease. They then assume responsibility for helping their partners to overcome their problems, viewing the batterings they receive as an index of their partners' pathology. Abuse must be endured while helping the man return to his "normal" self. One woman said:

> I thought I was going to be Florence Nightingale. He had so much potential; I could see how good he really was, and I was going to "save" him. I thought I was the only thing keeping him going, and that if I left he'd lose his job and wind up in jail. I'd make excuses to everybody for him. I'd call work and lie when he was drunk, saying he was sick. I never criticized him, because he needed my approval.

2) *The denial of the victimizer:* This technique is similar to the salvation ethic, except that victims do not assume responsibility for solving their abusers' problems. Women perceive battering as an event beyond the control of both spouses, and blame it on some external force. The violence is judged situational and temporary, because it is linked to unusual circumstances or a sickness which can be cured. Pressures at work, the loss of a job, or legal problems are all situations which battered women assume as the causes of their partners' violence. Mental illness, alcoholism, and drug addiction are also viewed as external, uncontrollable afflictions by many battered women who accept the medical perspective on such problems. . . .

> He's sick. He didn't used to be this way, but he can't handle alcohol. It's really like a disease, being an alcoholic. . . . I think too that this is what he saw at home, his father is a very violent man, and alcoholic too, so it's really not his fault, because this is all he has ever known.

3) *The denial of injury:* For some women, the experience of being battered by a spouse is so discordant with their expectations that they simply refuse to acknowledge it. When hospitalization is not required—and it seldom is for most cases of battering[1]—routines quickly return to normal. Meals are served, jobs and schools are attended, and daily chores completed. Even with lingering pain, bruises, and cuts, the normality of everyday life overrides the strange, confusing memory of the attack. When husbands refuse to discuss or acknowledge the event, in some cases even accusing their wives of insanity, women sometimes come to believe the violence never occurred. The denial of injury does not mean that women feel no pain. They know they are hurt, but define the hurt as tolerable or normal. Just as individuals tolerate a wide range of physical discomfort before seeking medical help, battered women tolerate a wide range of physical abuse before defining it as an injurious assault. One woman explained her disbelief at her first battering:

> . . . I could not believe it had happened, and I didn't want to believe it. We had only been married a year, and I was pregnant and excited about starting a family. Then all of a sudden, this! The next morning he told me he was sorry and it wouldn't happen again, and I gladly kissed and made up. I wanted to forget the whole thing, and wouldn't let myself worry about what it meant for us.

4) *The denial of victimization:* Victims often blame themselves for the violence, thereby neutralizing the responsibility of the spouse. Pagelow (1981) found that 99.4 percent of battered women felt they did *not* deserve to be beaten, and 51 percent said they had done nothing to provoke an attack. The battered women in our sample did not believe violence against them was justified, but some felt it could have been avoided if they had been more passive and conciliatory. Both Pagelow's and our samples are biased in this area, because they were made up almost entirely of women who had already left their abusers, and thus would have been unlikely to feel major responsibility for the abuse they received. Retrospective accounts of victimization in our sample, however, did reveal evidence that some women believed their right to leave violent men was restricted by their participation in the conflicts. One subject said:

[1] National crime survey data for 1973–76 show that 17 percent of persons who sought medical attention for injuries inflicted by an intimate were hospitalized. Eighty-seven percent of injuries inflicted by a spouse or ex-spouse were bruises, black eyes, cuts, scratches, or swelling (National Crime Survey Report, 1980).

> Well, I couldn't really do anything about it, because I did ask for it. I knew how to get at him, and I'd keep after it and keep after it until he got fed up and knocked me right out. I can't say I like it, but I shouldn't have nagged him like I did.

As Pagelow (1981) noted, there is a difference between provocation and justification. A battered woman's belief that her actions angered her spouse to the point of violence is not synonymous with the belief that violence was therefore *justified.* But belief in provocation may diminish a woman's capacity for retaliation or self-defense, because it blurs her concept of responsibility. A woman's acceptance of responsibility for the violent incident is encouraged by an abuser who continually denigrates her and makes unrealistic demands. Depending on the social supports available, and the personality of the battered woman, the man's accusations of inadequacy may assume the status of truth. Such beliefs of inferiority inhibit the development of a notion of victimization.

5) *The denial of options:* This technique is composed of two elements: practical options and emotional options. Practical options, including alternative housing, source of income, and protection from an abuser, are clearly limited by the patriarchal structure of Western society. However, there are differences in the ways battered women respond to these obstacles, ranging from determined struggle to acquiescence. For a variety of reasons, some battered women do not take full advantage of the practical opportunities which are available to escape, and some return to abusers voluntarily even after establishing an independent lifestyle. Others ignore the most severe constraints in their efforts to escape their relationships. For example, one resident of the shelter we observed walked 30 miles in her bedroom slippers to get to the shelter, [while] a woman who had a full-time job, had rented an apartment, and had been given by the shelter all the clothes, furniture, and basics necessary to set up housekeeping, returned to her husband two weeks after leaving the shelter. . . . (Ferraro, 1981b). . . . The belief of battered women that they will not be able to make it on their own—a belief often fueled by years of abuse and oppression—is a major impediment to acknowledging that one is a victim and taking action.

The denial of *emotional* options imposes still further restrictions. Battered women may feel that no one else can provide intimacy and companionship. . . . It is not uncommon for battered women to express the belief that their abuser is the only man they could love. . . . One woman said:

> He's all I've got. My dad's gone, and my mother disowned me when I married him. And he's really special. He understands me, and I understand him. Nobody could take his place.

6) *The appeal to higher loyalties:* This appeal involves enduring battering for the sake of some higher commitment, either religious or traditional.

The Christian belief that women should serve their husbands as men serve God is invoked as a rationalization to endure a husband's violence for later rewards in the afterlife. Clergy may support this view by advising women to pray and try harder to please their husbands (Davidson, 1978; McGlinchey, 1981). Other women have a strong commitment to the nuclear family, and find divorce repugnant. They may believe that for their children's sake, any marriage is better than no marriage. One woman we interviewed divorced her husband of 35 years after her last child left home. More commonly women who have survived violent relationships for that long do not have the desire or strength to divorce and begin a new life. When the appeal to higher loyalties is employed as a strategy to cope with battering, commitment to and involvement with an ideal overshadows the mundane reality of violence.

CATALYSTS FOR CHANGE

Rationalization is a way of coping with a situation in which, for either practical or emotional reasons, or both, a battered woman is stuck. For some women, the situation and the beliefs that rationalize it may continue for a lifetime. For others, changes may occur within the relationship, within individuals, or in available resources which serve as catalysts for redefining the violence. When battered women reject prior rationalizations and begin to view themselves as true victims of abuse, the victimization process begins.[2]

There are a variety of catalysts for redefining abuse; we discuss six: (1) a change in the level of violence; (2) a change in resources; (3) a change in the relationship; (4) despair; (5) a change in the visibility of violence; and (6) external definitions of the relationship.

1) *A change in the level of violence:* . . . [One factor that seems] to serve as a catalyst is a sudden change in the relative level of violence. Women who suddenly realize that battering may be fatal may reject rationalizations in order to save their lives. One woman who had been severely beaten by an alcoholic husband for many years explained her decision to leave on the basis of a direct threat to her life:

> It was like a pendulum. He'd swing to the extremes both ways. He'd get drunk and beat me up, then he'd get sober and treat me like a queen. One day he put a gun to my head and pulled the trigger. It wasn't loaded. But that's when I decided I'd had it. I sued for separation of property. I knew what was coming again, so I got out. I didn't want to. I still loved the guy, but I knew I had to for my own sanity.

• • •

[2] Explanation of why and how some women arrive at these feelings is beyond the scope of this paper. Our goal is to describe feelings at various stages of the victimization process.

2) *A change in resources:* Although some women rationalize cohabiting with an abuser by claiming they have no options, others begin reinterpreting violence when the resources necessary for escape become available. The emergence of safe homes or shelters since 1970 has produced a new resource for battered women. While not completely adequate or satisfactory, the mere existence of a place to go alters the situation in which battering is experienced (Johnson, 1981). Public support of shelters is a statement to battered women that abuse need not be tolerated. Conversely, political trends which limit resources available to women, such as cutbacks in government funding to social programs, increase fears that life outside a violent marriage is economically impossible.

• • •

3) *A change in the relationship:* Walker (1979), in discussing the stages of a battering relationship, notes that violent incidents are usually followed by periods of remorse and solicitude. Such phases deepen the emotional bonds, and make rejection of an abuser more difficult. But as battering progresses, periods of remorse may shorten, or disappear, eliminating the basis for maintaining a positive outlook on the marriage. After a number of episodes of violence, a man may realize that this victim will not retaliate or escape, and thus feel no need to express remorse. . . . One woman recalled:

> At first, you know, we used to have so much fun together. He has kind've, you know, a magnetic personality; he can be really charming. But it isn't fun anymore. Since the baby came, it's changed completely. He just wants me to stay at home, while he goes out with his friends. He doesn't even talk to me, most of the time. . . . No, I don't really love him anymore, not like I did.

4) *Despair:* Changes in the relationship may result in a loss of hope that "things will get better." When hope is destroyed and replaced by despair, rationalizations of violence may give way to the recognition of victimization. Feelings of hopelessness or despair are the basis for some efforts to assist battered women, such as Al-Anon.[3] The director of an Al-Anon organized shelter explained the concept of "hitting bottom":

> Before the Al-Anon program can really be of benefit, a woman has to hit bottom. When you hit bottom, you realize that all of your own efforts to control the situation have failed; you feel helpless and lost and worthless and completely disenchanted with the world. Women can't really be helped unless they're ready for it and want it. Some women come here when things get bad, but they aren't really ready to be committed to Al-Anon. Things haven't gotten bad enough for them, and they go right back. We see this all the time.

[3]Al-Anon is the spouse's counterpart to Alcoholics Anonymous. It is based on the same self-help, 12-step program that A. A. is founded on.

5) *A change in the visibility of violence:* Creating a web of rationalizations to overlook violence is accomplished more easily if no intruders are present to question their validity. Since most violence between couples occurs in private, there are seldom conflicting interpretations of the event from outsiders. Only 7 percent of the respondents in Gelles's (1976) study who discussed spatial location of violence indicated events which took place outside the home, but all reported incidents within the home. Others report similar findings (Pittman and Handy, 1964; Pokorny, 1965; Wolfgang, 1958). If violence does occur in the presence of others, it may trigger a reinterpretation process. Battering in private is degrading, but battering in public is humiliating, for it is a statement of subordination and powerlessness. . . .

> He never hit me in public before—it was always at home. But the Saturday I got back [returned to husband from shelter], we went Christmas shopping and he slapped me in the store because of some stupid joke I made. People saw it, I know, I felt so stupid, like, they must all think what a jerk I am, what a sick couple, and I thought, "God, I must be crazy to let him do this."

6) *External definitions of the relationship:* A change in visibility is usually accomplished by the interjection of external definitions of abuse. External definitions vary depending on their source and the situation; they either reinforce or undermine rationalizations. Battered women who request help frequently find others—and especially officials—don't believe their story or are unsympathetic (Pagelow, 1981; Pizzey, 1974). Experimental research by Shotland and Straw (1976) supports these reports. Observers usually fail to respond when a woman is attacked by a man, and justify nonintervention on the grounds that they assumed the victim and offender were married. One young woman discussed how lack of support from her family left her without hope:

> It wouldn't be so bad if my own family gave a damn about me. . . . Yeah, they know I'm here, and they don't care. They didn't care about me when I was a kid, so why should they care now? I got raped and beat as a kid, and now I get beat as an adult. Life is a big joke.

Clearly, such responses from family members contribute to the belief among battered women that there are no alternatives and that they must tolerate the abuse. However, when outsiders respond with unqualified support of the victim and condemnation of violent men, their definitions can be a potent catalyst toward victimization. . . .

> My mother-in-law knew what was going on, but she wouldn't admit it. . . . I said, "Mom, what do you think these bruises are?" and she said "Well, some people just bruise easy." . . . And he just denied it, pretended like nothing happened, and if I'd said I wanted to talk about it, he'd say, "life goes on, you can't just dwell on things". . . . But this time, my neighbor *knew* what happened, she saw it, and when he denied it, she said, "I can't believe it!

> You know that's not true!" . . . and I was so happy that finally, somebody else saw what was goin' on, and I just told him then that this time I wasn't gonna' come home!

Shelters for battered women serve not only as material resources, but as sources of external definitions which contribute to the victimization process. . . . Within a shelter, women meet counselors and other battered women who are familiar with rationalizations of violence and the reluctance to give up commitment to a spouse. . . . (Ferraro, 1981a). The goal of many shelters is to overcome feelings of guilt and inadequacy so that women can make choices in their best interests. In this atmosphere, violent incidents are reexamined and redefined as assaults in which the woman was victimized.

How others respond to a battered woman's situation is critical. The closer the relationship of others, the more significant their response is to a woman's perception of the situation. Thus, children can either help or hinder the victim. Pizzey (1974) found adolescent boys at a shelter in Chiswick, England, often assumed the role of the abusing father and themselves abused their mothers, both verbally and physically. On the other hand, children at the shelter we observed often became extremely protective and nurturing toward their mothers. . . . Children who have been abused by fathers who also beat their mothers experience high levels of anxiety, and rarely want to be reunited with their fathers. A 13-year-old, abused daughter of a shelter resident wrote the following message to her stepfather:

> I am going to be honest and not lie. No, I don't want you to come back. It's not that I am jealous because mom loves you. It is [I] am afraid I won't live to see 18. I did care about you a long time ago, but now I can't care, for the simple reason you['re] always calling us names, even my friends. And another reason is, I am tired of seeing mom hurt. She has been hurt enough in her life, and I don't want her to be hurt any more.

• • •

The relevance of these catalysts to a woman's interpretation of violence vary with her own situation and personality. The process of rejecting rationalizations and becoming a victim is ambiguous, confusing, and emotional. We now turn to the feelings involved in victimization.

THE EMOTIONAL CAREER OF VICTIMIZATION

As rationalizations give way to perceptions of victimization, a woman's feelings about herself, her spouse, and her situation change. These feelings are imbedded in a cultural, political, and interactional structure. Initially, abuse is contrary to a woman's cultural expectations of behavior between intimates, and therefore engenders feelings of betrayal. The husband has violated his wife's expectations of love and protection, and thus betrayed her confidence in him. The feeling of betrayal, however, is balanced by the husband's efforts to explain his behavior, and by the woman's reluctance to abandon faith. Additionally, the political dominance of men within and outside the family mediate women's ability to question the validity of their husband's actions.

At the interpersonal level, psychological abuse accompanying violence often invokes feelings of guilt and shame in the battered victim. Men define violence as a response to their wives' inadequacies or provocations, which leads battered women to feel that they have failed. Such character assaults are devastating, and create long-lasting feelings of inferiority (Ferraro, 1979b):

> I've been verbally abused as well. It takes you a long time to . . . you may say you feel good and you may . . . but inside, you know what's been said to you and it hurts for a long time. You need to build up your self-image and make yourself feel like you're a useful person, that you're valuable, and that you're a good parent. You might think these things, and you may say them. . . . I'm gonna prove it to myself.

Psychologists working with battered women consistently report that self-confidence wanes over years of ridicule and criticism (Hilberman and Munson, 1978; Walker, 1979).

Feelings of guilt and shame are also mixed with a hope that things will get better, at least in the early stages of battering. Even the most violent man is nonviolent much of the time, so there is always a basis for believing that violence is exceptional and the "real man" is not a threat. The vascillation between violence and fear on the one hand, and nonviolence and affection on the other was described by a shelter resident:

> First of all, the first beatings—you can't believe it yourself. I'd go to bed, and I'd cry, and I just couldn't believe this was happening. And I'd wake up the next morning thinking that couldn't of happened, or maybe it was my fault. It's so unbelievable that this person that you're married to and you love would do that to you, but yet you can't leave either because, ya'know, for the other 29 days of the month that person loves you and is with you.

Hope wanes as periods of love and remorse dwindle. Feelings of love and intimacy are gradually replaced with loneliness and pessimism. Battered women who no longer feel love for their husbands but remain in their marriages enter a period of emotional dormancy. They survive each day, performing necessary tasks, with a dull depression and lack of enthusiasm. While some battered women live out their lives in this emotional desert, others are spurred by catalysts to feel either the total despair or mortal fear which leads them to seek help.

Battered women who perceive their husbands' actions as life-threatening experience a penetrating fear that consumes all their thoughts and energies. The awareness of murderous intent by a presumed ally who is a central figure in all aspects of her life destroys all bases for safety. There is a feeling that death is imminent, and that there is nowhere to hide. Prior rationalizations and beliefs about a "good marriage" are exploded, leaving the woman in a crisis of ambiguity (Ridington, 1978).

Feelings of fear are experienced physiologically as well as emotionally. Battered women experience aches and fatigue, stomach pains, diarrhea or constipation, tension headaches, shakes, chills, loss of appetite, and insomnia. Sometimes, fear is expressed as a numbed shock, similar to rape trauma syndrome (Burgess and Holmstrom, 1974), in which little is felt or communicated.

If attempts to seek help succeed, overwhelming feelings of fear subside, and a rush of new emotions are felt: the original sense of betrayal re-emerges, creating strong feelings of anger. For women socialized to reject angry feelings as unfeminine, coping with anger is difficult. Unless the expression of anger is encouraged in a supportive environment, such women may suppress anger and feel only depression (Ball and Wyman, 1978). When anger is expressed, it often leads to feelings of strength and exhilaration. Freedom from threats of violence, the possibility of a new life, and the unburdening of anger create feelings of joy. The simple pleasures of going shopping, taking children to the park, or talking with other women without fear of criticism or punishment from a husband, constitute amazing freedoms. One middle-aged woman expressed her joy over her newly acquired freedom this way:

> Boy, tomorrow I'm goin' downtown, and I've got my whole day planned out, and I'm gonna' do what *I* wanna' do, and if somebody doesn't like it, to *hell* with them! You know, I'm having so much fun, I should've done this years ago!

Probably the most typical feeling expressed by women in shelters is confusion. They feel both sad and happy, excited and apprehensive, independent, yet in need of love. Most continue to feel attachment to their husbands, and feel ambivalent about divorce. There is grief over the loss of an intimate, which must be acknowledged and mourned. Although shelters usually discourage women from contacting their abusers while staying at the shelter, most women do communicate with their husbands—and most receive desperate pleas for forgiveness and reconciliation. If there is not strong emotional support and potential material support, such encouragement by husbands often rekindles hope for the relationship. Some marriages can be revitalized through counseling, but most experts agree that long-term batterers are unlikely to change (Pagelow, 1981; Walker, 1979). Whether they seek refuge in shelters or with friends, battered women must decide relatively quickly what actions to take. Usually, a tentative commitment is made, either to independence or working on the relationship, but such commitments are usually ambivalent. As one woman wrote to her counselor:

> My feelings are so mixed up sometimes. Right now I feel my husband is really trying to change. But I now that takes time. I still feel for him some. I don't know how much. My mind still doesn't know what it wants. I would really like when I leave here to see him once in a while, get my apartment, and sort of like start over with our relationship for me and my baby and him, to try and make it work. It might. It kind of scares me. I guess I am afraid it won't. . . . I can only hope this works out. There's no telling what could happen. No one knows.

The emotional career of battered women consists of movement from guilt, shame, and depression to fear and despair, to anger, exhilaration, and confusion. Women who escape violent relationships must deal with strong, sometimes conflicting, feelings in attempting to build new lives for themselves free of violence. The kind of response women receive when they seek help largely determines the effects these feelings have on subsequent decisions . . . . Some battered women, however, develop a feeling of repugnance to romantic involvements. They may feel that "men are no good," or simply enjoy their freedom too much to consider entering a relationship.

• • •

CONCLUSION

The process of victimization is not synonymous with experiencing violent attacks from a spouse. Rationalizing the violence inhibits a sense of outrage and efforts to escape abuse. Only after rationalizations are rejected, through the impact of one or more catalysts, does the victimization process begin. When previously rationalized violence is reinterpreted as dangerous, unjustified assault, battered women actively seek alternatives. The success of their efforts to seek help depends on available resources, external supports, reactions of husbands and children, and their own adaptation to the situation. Victimization includes not only cognitive interpretations, but feelings and physiological responses. Creating a satisfying, peaceful environment after being battered involves emotional confusion and ambiguity, as well as enormous practical and economic obstacles. It may take years of struggle and aborted attempts before a battered woman is able to establish a safe and stable lifestyle; for some, this goal is never achieved.

REFERENCES

Ball, Patricia G., and Elizabeth Wyman
1978 "Battered wives and powerlessness: What can counselors do?" *Victimology* 2(3–4):545–552.

Beverly
1978 "Shelter resident murdered by husband." *Aegis*, September/October: 13.

Bohannan, Paul (ed.)
1971 *Divorce and After.* Garden City, New York: Anchor.

Burgess, Ann W., and Lynda Lytle Holmstrom
1974 *Rape: Victims of Crisis.* Bowie, Maryland: Brady.

Davidson, Terry
1978 *Conjugal Crime.* New York: Hawthorn.

Dobash, R. Emerson, and Russell P. Dobash
1979 *Violence Against Wives.* New York: Free Press.

Ferraro, Kathleen, J.
1979a "Hard love: Letting go of an abusive husband." *Frontiers* 4(2):16-18.
1979b "Physical and emotional battering: Aspects of managing hurt." *California Sociologist* 2(2): 134–149.
1981a *Battered women and the shelter movement.* Unpublished Ph.D. dissertation, Arizona State University.
1981b "Processing battered women." *Journal of Family Issues* 2(4):415–438.

Garcia, Dick
1978 "Slain women 'lived in fear.'" *The Times* (Erie, Pa.). 6 14:B1.

Gelles, Richard J.
1976 "Abused wives: Why do they stay?" *Journal of Marriage and the Family* 38(4):659–668.

Hilberman, Elaine
1980 "Overview: The 'wife-beater's wife' reconsidered." *American Journal of Psychiatry* 137(11):1336–1347.

Hilberman, Elaine, and Kit Munson
1978 "Sixty battered women." *Victimology* 2(3–4):460–470.

Johnson, John M.
1981 "Program enterprise and official cooptation of the battered women's shelter movement." *American Behavioral Scientist* 24(6):827–842.

McGlinchey, Anne
1981 "Woman battering and the church's response." Pp. 133–140 in Albert R. Roberts (ed.), *Sheltering Battered Women.* New York: Springer.

Martin, Del
1976 *Battered Wives.* San Francisco: Glide.

National Crime Survey Report
1980 *Intimate Victims.* Washington, D.C.: U.S. Department of Justice.

Pagelow, Mildred Daley
1981 *Woman-Battering*. Beverly Hills: Sage.

Pittman, D. J. and W. Handy
1964 "Patterns in criminal aggravated assault." *Journal of Criminal Law, Criminology, and Police Science* 55(4):462–470.

Pizzey, Erin
1974 *Scream Quietly or the Neighbors Will Hear.* Baltimore: Penguin.

Pokorny, Alex. D.
1965 "Human violence: A comparison of homicide, aggravated assault, suicide, and attempted suicide." *Journal of Criminal Law, Criminology, and Police Science* 56(12): 488–497.

Ridington, Jillian
1978 "The transition process: A feminist environment as reconstitutive milieu." *Victimology* 2(3–4):563-576.

Roy, Maria (ed.)
1977 *Battered Women.* New York: Van Nostrand.

Saul, Leon J.
1972 "Personal and social psychopathology and the primary prevention of violence." *American Journal of Psychiatry* 128(12):1578–1581.

Scanzoni, John
1972 *Sexual Bargaining.* Englewood Cliffs, N.J.: Prentice-Hall.

Shotland, R. Lance, and Margret K. Straw
1976 "Bystander response to an assault: When a man attacks a woman." *Journal of Personality and Social Psychology* 34(5):990–999.

Snell, John E., Richard Rosenwald, and Ames Robey
1964 "The wifebeater's wife: A study of family interaction." *Archives of General Psychiatry* 11(8):107–112.

Spiegel, John P.
1968 "The resolution of role conflict within the family." Pp. 391–411 in N. W. Bell and E. F. Vogel (eds.), *A Modern Introduction to the Family.* New York: Free Press.

Sprey, Jetse
1971 "On the management of conflict in families." *Journal of Marriage and the Family* 33(4):699–706.

Sykes, Gresham M., and David Matza
1957 "Techniques of neutralization: A theory of delinquency." *American Sociological Review* 22(6):667–670.

U.S. Department of Labor
1980 *Handbook of Labor Statistics.* Washington, D.C.: U.S. Government Printing Office.

Walker, Lenore E.
1979 *The Battered Woman.* New York: Harper and Row.

Wolfgang, Marvin E.
1958 *Patterns in Criminal Homicide.* New York: John Wiley.

Review Questions

1. What does this study show us about the process of labeling norm violators?
2. What are six rationalizations that battered women use to excuse or justify their partners' violent behavior? Which ones focus on the partner and which ones on the woman?
3. What are six catalysts that can propel battered women to leave their relationships?
4. What part do social-control agents outside the couple normally play in labeling the batterer? In influencing the battered woman to stay in the relationship?

Suggested Readings: Deviance, Conformity, and Social Control

Becker, Howard S. *Outsiders.* New York: Free Press, 1963.
Campbell, Anne. *Girls in the Gang.* Oxford, England: Basil Blackwell Ltd., 1984.
Chambliss, William J. *On the Take.* Bloomington, Ind.: Indiana University Press, 1978.
Conrad, Peter. "The Myth of Cut-Throats among Premedical Students: On the Role of Stereotypes in Justifying Failure and Success," *Journal of Health and Social Behavior* 27 (June, 1986), 150–160).
———, and Joseph W. Schneider. *Deviance and Medicalization: From Badness to Sickness.* St. Louis: C. V. Mosby, 1980.
Erikson, Kai T. *Wayward Puritans.* New York: Wiley, 1966.
Goffman, Erving. *Stigma: Notes on the Management of Spoiled Identity.* Englewood Cliffs, N. J.: Prentice-Hall, 1963.
Katz, Jack. *Seductions of Crime: The Moral and Sensual Attractions of Doing Evil.* New York: Basic, 1988.
McIntyre, Lisa J. *The Public Defender: The Practice of Law in the Shadows of Repute.* Chicago: University of Chicago Press, 1987.
Molstad, Clark. "Choosing and Coping with Boring Work," *Urban Life* 15 (July 1986): 215–236.
Scheff, Thomas J. *Being Mentally Ill,* 2nd ed. New York: Aldine, 1984.

Schur, Edwin M. *Crimes Without Victims—Deviant Behavior and Public Policy.* Englewood Cliffs, N. J.: Prentice-Hall, 1965.

———. *Labeling Women Deviant: Gender, Stigma, and Social Control.* New York: Random House, 1984.

Szasz, Thomas. *The Manufacture of Madness.* New York: Harper & Row, 1970.

Wiseman, Jacqueline P. *Stations of the Lost: The Treatment of Skid Row Alcoholics.* Chicago: University of Chicago Press, 1979.

Part VIII. Interaction in Institutional Contexts

Individuals face a host of problems as they attempt to survive in their environments. Societies, too, must develop strategies, plans, or systems to deal with problems that occur *at the collective level*. That is, in order for the *group* to survive—regardless of what happens to any given individual—solutions to group problems must be worked out and agreed upon, formally or informally, by societal members. A complex system of attitudes, norms, beliefs, and roles outlining what *should* occur to solve a societal problem is called an *institution*.

Suppose your sociology class were stranded on a Caribbean island, with no prospect of contact with or aid from any other human society. A number of threats to the survival of your group will sooner or later arise, requiring the interdependent action of societal members. For instance, the society will no longer exist if all of its members die of starvation or exposure, so some coordinated system of producing and distributing food and shelter will have to be worked out. That system—a plan, or set of norms, governing the behavior of your societal members with regard to who engages in what productive functions and what will have to be done to acquire goods once they are produced—is called the *economic institution* of your society. Literally thousands of interrelated norms may be involved in the institution: One should begin work promptly at 7 A.M. and work for ten hours. One should take all goods produced to a central storehouse. All members who need or want any of the goods merely collect them from the storehouse. No private property will be permitted. People who work too hard or not hard enough will receive negative sanctions. Women should do one kind of work, while men do another. People must begin their work activities when they are eight years old. And so on. The specific rules will vary from one culture to another—your sociology class might not develop the same economic institution as ours—but some economic system is sure to emerge.

Your society will face other problems and develop other institutional solutions. Questions of how to create new members to replace those who eventually die will probably be answered with a *family institution* specifying who is allowed to marry whom (marriage seems to be a cultural universal), how the spouses will interact, who will be allowed to have how many children and at what times in their lives, how children are to be cared for and socialized, and so on. To keep your societal members from killing each other off or being killed by outsiders before they can reproduce enough people to take their places, you will develop a system to control and protect your members, or a *political institution*. Problems of *health and illness* will be met by an *institution* which includes rules for defining what should be seen as health and what as illness and how the latter should be treated. Transmitting your culture to new members may require the creation of an *institution* or system of rules and roles to provide *education*. Questions about aspects of your world which defy other culturally available explanations may be answered by a *religious institution*, a set of beliefs, rules for religious expression, and roles for religious leaders and followers.

There are several important points regarding social institutions which the articles in this section address. First, a *society's institutions are taught and learned in the process of socialization*, once they have been created. Although the general problems societies confront are similar, the emergent institutions which attempt to cope with these problems vary from one society to another and from one historical period to another. They are not fixed or immutable, nor are they automatically understood by the society's children. Institutions must be transmitted from one generation to the next, and of course they may be changed somewhat in the process.

Second, once these arrangements or systems are incorporated into the culture, *they constrain the behavior of individuals in many ways*. Institutions are not usually so rigid that people are allowed *no* choice in type of work, marriage partners, religious beliefs, and the like. At the same time, the individual does not have total freedom to work, marry, or believe as he or she chooses without running the risk of receiving negative sanctions from other societal members.

Moreover, institutions tend to structure one's time and activities. For instance, beliefs about how best to prepare children for adult life have resulted in the school—a social organization of rules and roles which requires some people to spend long periods of time sitting in small rooms at desks facing toward an older person who stands or sits in front of the room. The young people may be separated by age into classes. One result of this arrangement is that the population becomes "age-segregated." Old people have fewer and fewer structured opportunities to interact with children, and children themselves are not always allowed free interaction with other children of different ages. As one consequence, children (and all students) are much better able to distinguish small differences in age than are adults. The structural constraints produced by age-segregation and age-grading in schools may entail benefits *and/or* costs for individuals and for societies; the point here is that the educational institution channels and limits human activity and interaction.

As another example of the constraining effects of social institutions, consider the norms of the economic institution of the United States. They specify that one must use money in order to obtain goods and services and, further, that this money may be gained by inheritance, by work, or by providing capital (factories, equipment, and the like) for the production process. Permitting money and other valuable assets to be passed from one generation to the next automatically ensures that the children of poor parents will have fewer chances to acquire wealth than the children of affluent parents. In other words, the structural arrangement that allows for inheritance of money, wealth, and capital creates inequality as a feature of social life. Thus, while our society's myths tell us that poverty and wealth are the results of individual efforts, the sociological perspective allows us to see that the way a society is organized, including its institutional systems, actually produces its own effects on the individual's behavior and life chances.

A third important point regarding institutions is that *they tend to be interrelated* so that a change in one area—say a declaration of war to protect a society's interests—will have effects in other institutional areas—the rules about marriage and childbearing may change as young people are removed from their normal activities to perform military duties. Many sociologists contend that the one institution which is most likely to affect all the others is the economic system. The society's economic norms may have a powerful impact on the system of courtship and marriage; the system of educating the young for adult roles; the system of laws, law making, and law enforcement; and so on. The change from an agricultural economy to one based on industry, for example, upsets prior beliefs and norms concerning work itself as well as beliefs and norms about religious observance, family size, and what constitutes a proper education. Furthermore, the *structural changes* in the way society is organized that accompany industrialization have a limiting effect on other institutions, and on individuals as well. Consider the consequences of the change from working on one's own homesite to working in a factory or office.

As we move to a discussion of the nature and consequences of several specific institutions in the United States, try to keep in mind these general characteristics of institutions: they are learned sets of norms which represent collective responses to collective problems, they constrain human activity and interaction, and they are interrelated.

Part A. Family

THE FIRST INSTITUTIONAL CONTEXT FOR HUMAN INTERACTION THAT WE WILL examine here is the one that first affects our lives—the family system. Everyone knows a great deal about families. After all, most of us grew up in one and were probably socialized to want to form new families as adults. Our own personal family involvements, however, form a very *poor* base of knowledge about family norms and patterns of the larger society. We must step outside our own lives to gain a sociological perspective on the family.

Sociologically, a society's family institution serves several important functions. It provides societal members with ascribed statuses—a position in the social-class structure and racial, ethnic, and sexual identities. The family system also affects sexual behavior and reproduction. It further provides a plan for socializing infants and children and for providing emotional support and stability to family members. It is in interaction with family members that our self-concepts are initially developed.

Within the family circle—whatever members the society defines this as including—intensive interaction takes place. This interaction is not unstructured, however, since a division of labor is usually present, with parents and children, and perhaps men and women, performing different tasks to meet the needs of the group as a whole. Thus learned social roles generally guide our family relationships and interaction.

But social roles are not fixed. A given society may always have some sort of family system, but the content of that system—the rules for constituting families and carrying out the daily activities within the family—can and does change. A host of social trends have assailed the American family in recent decades: postponement of marriage, decreased fertility rates, postponement of childbearing, increased labor-force participation for women, longer life expectancies, and increasing divorce rates. And the family system has been modified as a result.

It is interesting to note, though, that changes in our family system usually have not represented radical departures from previous values and norms, but have instead represented adaptations that preserve a great deal from the past. Adaptations are the subject of the three articles in this section.

The first sociological question addressed is, "What is a family?" To most Americans, the image conjured up by this question is a *nuclear* family with a mother, father, and their nonadult children. But this is not the only type of family possible. Nor is it even the most common form, since divorce, death, and children leaving the "nest" can truncate families, more than two generations may live together in what we call *extended* families, and (as we saw in the article by Horowitz) non-kin can be drawn into *expanded* families.

Sociologically speaking, a family is any group of people who interact with one another on the basis of familial roles—who act toward one another *as if* they were a family. Carol Stack's research shows clearly that the role obligations being fulfilled by a set of people are more important than the biological or legal ties among them. In "Sex Roles and Survival Strategies in an Urban Black Community," Stack reports on the flexible families formed by people living in The Flats, an extremely poor area of a midwestern city that she calls "Jackson Harbor." In doing so, she also explains why these families have to be flexible: their economic situations are so tenuous and so variable that mutual support networks are essential to survival. The data she gathered from living in The Flats and becoming part of these families herself contradict many common American stereotypes about the families of poor people.

Families contain within them several types of relationships—such as those between parents and children, husbands and wives, in-laws, and others. One of the most important elements of a family is the relationship between husband and wife: marriage. The second selection in this section addresses the social processes produced by the dissolution of marriage.

The norms of our culture specify that a newly married couple should live in a private household, interacting frequently and intensely with each other. These norms create an isolated setting in which each couple is likely to develop a unique world view. In essence, the partners alter their definitions of themselves, of their daily lives, of their past experiences, and of their futures. All of these come to be seen from a perspective different from the one either partner had before marriage. Marriage, then, is much more than an agreement to live with another person. Marriage has consequences for the individual in all spheres of public and private life—even to the extent of determining how one views the world.

We can see the far-reaching changes that marriage produces when we examine those who are *leaving* a marriage, and a coupled world view, because of the death of a spouse or divorce. The formerly married must adjust in a number of obvious ways to their change in marital status. One *less* obvious problem of adaptation involves creating a new "single" world view. Consider the husband who was uninterested in the theater before his marriage to a theater "buff." Over the years, he has heard his wife discussing the theater a great deal and has himself come to see himself as a "theatergoer," to pay attention to new performers, openings on Broadway, and such. After his divorce, he hears on the radio an announcement of a new play and automatically thinks, "We should get tickets to that." Then he realizes that "we" no longer exist, and he's really not very interested in sitting in some stuffy theater straining to understand the play's existential message anyway. In this hypothetical incident, we see in a small way that the former husband is caught between a coupled identity created in his marriage and a new single identity that reflects his own views (or the views of his new associates) more closely.

Diane Vaughan explores the theme of shifting identities corresponding to shifting marital statuses in "Uncoupling: The Social Construction of Divorce." Previously, "uncoupling" was thought to be a chaotic period in the lives of those involved, characterized by pain, guilt, and anxiety about their uncertain futures. Through intensive interviews with people who have undergone this experience, Vaughan uncovers the order that lies behind the apparent chaos. She finds that the individual usually goes through identifiable stages, gradually shedding his or her marital identity and gaining a new world view and a new self-concept as a single adult, possibly available for future "re-coupling."

The final selection concerns adaptations within the family system that result from a new economic fact: the increasing number of two-job families. Arlie Russell Hochschild, aided by Anne Machung, observed the home lives of working spouses with young children and conducted intensive interviews with the family members. Hochschild concludes that the current historical period represents a "stalled revolution" in the American family system.

On the one hand, wives have increasingly taken on economic responsibilities, joining their husbands in the paid labor force. On the other hand, most men have not joined their wives by taking on an equal share of the family's housework and childcare duties. The result is that, on the average, working women end up doing thirty 24-hour days more of housework every year than their husbands do. That adds up to about twenty extra work weeks per year—overall, women are spending forty per cent more time than men on the combination of paid and household labor. Thus, women's roles have been partly revolutionized, but men's roles remain much the same as they were half a century ago. A "new man" who takes equal responsibility for housework is emerging, but so far his numbers are small.

Our excerpt from Hochschild's book on the "second shift" focuses on both the average woman's extra household labor and on the relatively rare man who does his share. We have included Part One of the excerpt, "When Working Wives Get Home," in this section; Part Two, "The New Man," can be found in the section on Social and Cultural Change.

In "When Working Wives Get Home," Hochschild details the kinds of work that most wives do on their second shift. She also describes men's and women's gender ideologies and gender strategies that underpin the unequal division of household labor. Finally, she reports on the tensions that this new arrangement engenders, tensions that tend to erode gratitude and love between spouses. Some marriages Hochschild observed were held together only by "family fictions" that the husbands were doing their share.

Hochschild believes that more adaptation is necessary. The stalled family revolution will have to pick up steam and move ahead to a fairer division of labor, and perhaps the society will have to create new institutions and permit more flexibility in work schedules to allow families time to handle their household chores and rear their children. Until then, wives, husbands, and especially children—all of whom are caught in this in-between historical phase—will continue to suffer.

SEX ROLES AND SURVIVAL STRATEGIES IN AN URBAN BLACK COMMUNITY

Carol B. Stack

THE POWER AND AUTHORITY ASCRIBED TO WOMEN IN THE BLACK GHETTOS OF America, women whose families are locked into lifelong conditions of poverty and welfare, have their roots in the inexorable unemployment of Black males and the ensuing control of economic resources by females. These social-economic conditions have given rise to special features in the organization of family and kin networks in Black communities, features not unlike the patterns of domestic authority that emerge in matrilineal societies, or in cultures where men are away from home in wage labor (Gonzalez, 1969, 1970). The poor in Black urban communities have evolved, as the basic unit of their society, a core of kinsmen and non-kin who cooperate on a daily basis and who live near one another or co-reside. This core, or nucleus, has been characterized as the basis of the consanguineal household (Gonzalez, 1965) and of matrifocality (Tanner, 1975; Abrahams, 1963; Moynihan, 1965; Rainwater, 1966).

The concept of "matrifocality," however, has been criticized as inaccurate and inadequate. Recent studies (Ladner, 1971; Smith, 1970; Stack, 1970; Valentine, 1970) show convincingly that many of the negative features attributed to matrifocal families—that they are fatherless, unstable, and produce offspring that are "illegitimate" in the eyes of the folk culture—are not general characteristics of low-income Black families in urban America. Rather than imposing widely accepted definitions of the family, the nuclear family, or the matrifocal family on the ways in which the urban poor describe and order their world, we must seek a more appropriate theoretical framework. Elsewhere I have proposed an analysis based on the notion of a domestic network (Stack, 1974). In this view, the basis of familial structure and cooperation is not the nuclear family of the middle class, but an extended cluster of kinsmen related chiefly through children but also through marriage and friendship, who align to provide domestic functions. This cluster, or domestic network,

SOURCE: Carol B. Stack, "Sex Roles and Survival Strategies in an Urban Black Community," in Michelle Z. Rosaldo and Louise Lamphere, eds., *Women, Culture and Society*, Stanford, Calif: Stanford University Press, 1975. Reprinted by permission of Carol B. Stack.

is diffused over several kin-based households, and fluctuations in individual household composition do not significantly affect cooperative arrangements.

In this paper I shall analyze the domestic network and the relationships within it from a woman's perspective—from the perspective that the women in this study provided and from my own interpretations of the domestic and social scene. Many previous studies of the Black family (e.g. Liebow, 1967 and Hannerz, 1969) have taken a male perspective, emphasizing the streetcorner life of Black men and viewing men as peripheral to familial concerns. Though correctly stressing the economic difficulties that Black males face in a racist society, these and other studies (Moynihan, 1965; Bernard, 1966) have fostered a stereotype of Black families as fatherless and subject to a domineering woman's matriarchal rule. From such simplistic accounts it is all too easy to come to blame juvenile delinquency, divorce, illegitimacy, and other social ills on the Black family, while ignoring the oppressive reality of our political and economic system and the adaptive resiliency and strength that Black families have shown.

My analysis will draw on life-history material as well as on personal comments from women in The Flats, the poorest section of a Black community in the Midwestern city of Jackson Harbor.[1] I shall view women as strategists—active agents who use resources to achieve goals and cope with the problems of everyday life. This framework has several advantages. First, because the focus is on women rather than men, women's views of family relations, often ignored or slighted, are given prominence. Second, since households form around women because of their role in child care, ties between women (including paternal aunts, cousins, etc.) often constitute the core of a network; data from women's lives, then, crucially illuminate the continuity in these networks. Finally, the life-history material, taken chiefly from women, also demonstrates the positive role that a man plays in Black family life, both as the father of a woman's children and as a contributor of valuable resources to her network and to the network of his own kin.

I shall begin by analyzing the history of residential arrangements during one woman's life, and the residential arrangements of this woman's kin network at two points in time, demonstrating that although household composition changes, members are selected or self-selected largely from a single network that has continuity over time. Women and men, in response to joblessness, the possibility of welfare payments, the breakup of relationships, or the whims of a landlord, may move often. But the very calamities and crises that contribute to the constant shifts in residence tend to bring men, women, and children back into the households of close kin. Newly formed households are successive recombinations of the same domestic network of adults and children, quite often in the same dwellings. Residence histories, then, are an important reflection of the strategy of relying on and strengthening the domestic kin network, and also reveal the adaptiveness of households with "elastic boundaries." (It may be worth noting that middle-class whites are beginning to perceive certain values, for their own lives, in such households.)

In the remainder of the paper, the importance of maximizing network strength will be reemphasized and additional strategies will be isolated by examining two sets of relationships within kin networks—those between mothers and fathers and those between fathers and children. Women's own accounts of their situations show how they have developed a strong sense of independence from men, evolved social controls against the formation of conjugal relationships, and limited the role of the husband-father within the mother's domestic group. All of these strategies serve to strengthen the domestic network, often at the expense of any particular male-female tie. Kin regard any marriage as a risk to the woman and her children, and the loss of either male or female kin as a threat to the durability of the kin network. These two factors continually augment each other and dictate, as well, the range of socially accepted relationships between fathers and children.

RESIDENCE AND THE DOMESTIC NETWORK

In The Flats, the material and cultural support needed to sustain and socialize community members is provided by cooperating kinsmen. The individual can draw upon a broad domestic web of kin and friends—some who reside together, others who do not. Residents in The Flats characterize household composition according to where people sleep, eat, and spend their time. Those who eat together may be considered part of a domestic unit. But an individual may eat in one household, sleep in another, contribute resources and services to yet another, and consider himself or herself a member of all three households. Children may fall asleep and remain through the night wherever the late-evening visiting patterns of the adult females take them, and they may remain in these households and share meals perhaps a week at a time. As R. T. Smith suggests in an article on Afro-American kinship (1970), it is sometimes difficult "to determine just which household a given individual belongs to at any particular moment." These facts of ghetto life are, of course, often disguised in the statistical reports of census takers, who record simply sleeping arrangements.

Households in The Flats, then, have shifting memberships, but they maintain for the most part a steady state of three generations of kin: males and females beyond child bearing age; a middle generation of mothers raising their own children or children of close kin; and the children. This observation is supported in a recent study by Ladner (1971: 60), who writes, "Many children normally grow up in a three-generation household and they absorb the influences of a grandmother and grandfather as well as a mother and father." A survey of eighty-three residence changes among welfare families, whereby adult females who are heads of their own households merged households with other kin, shows that the majority of moves created three-generation households. Consequently, it is difficult to pinpoint structural beginning or end to household cycles in poor Black urban communities (Buchler and Selby, 1968; Fortes, 1958; Otterbein, 1970). But it is clear that authority patterns within a kin network change with birth and death; with the death of the oldest member in a household, the next generation assumes authority.

Residence changes themselves are brought on by many factors, most related to the economic conditions in which poor families live. Women who have children have access to welfare, and thus more economic security than women who do not, and more than all men. Welfare regulations encourage mothers to set up separate households, and women actively seek independence, privacy, and improvement in their lives. But these ventures do not last long. Life histories of adults show that the attempts by women to set up separate households with their children are short-lived: houses are condemned; landlords evict tenants; and needs for services among kin arise. Household composition also expands or contracts with the loss of a job, the death of a relative, the beginning or end of a sexual partnership, or the end of a friendship. But fluctuations in household composition rarely affect the exchanges and daily dependencies of participants. The chronology of residence changes made by Ruby Banks graphically illuminates these points (see Table 1).

Ruby's residential changes, and the residences of her own children and kin, reveal that the same factors contributing to the high frequency of moving also bring men, women, and children back into the household of close kin. That one can repeatedly do so is a great source of security and dependence for those living in poverty.

A look in detail at the domestic network of Ruby's parents, Magnolia and Calvin Waters, illustrates the complexity of the typical network and also shows kin constructs at work both in the recruitment of individuals to the network and in the changing composition of households within the network, over less than three months (see Table 2).

These examples do indeed indicate the important role of the Black woman in the domestic structure. But the cooperation between male and female siblings who share the same household or live near one another has been underestimated by those who have isolated the female-headed household as the most significant domestic unit among the urban Black poor. The close cooperation of adult siblings arises from

Table 1.

AGE	HOUSEHOLD COMPOSITION AND CONTEXT OF HOUSEHOLD FORMATION
Birth	Ruby lived with her mother, Magnolia, and her maternal grandparents.
4	To be eligible for welfare, Ruby and Magnolia were required to move out of Ruby's grandparents' house. They moved into a separate residence two houses away, but ate all meals at the grandparents' house.
5	Ruby and Magnolia returned to the grandparents' house and Magnolia gave birth to a son. Magnolia worked and the grandmother cared for her children.
6	Ruby's maternal grandparents separated. Magnolia remained living with her father and her (now) two sons. Ruby and her grandmother moved up the street and lived with her maternal aunt Augusta and maternal uncle. Ruby's grandmother took care of Ruby and her brothers, and Magnolia worked and cooked and cleaned for her father.
7–16	The household was now composed of Ruby, her grandmother's new husband, Augusta and her boyfriend, and Ruby's maternal uncle. At age sixteen Ruby gave birth to a daughter.
17	Ruby's grandmother died and Ruby had a second child, by Otis, the younger brother of Ruby's best friend, Willa Mae. Ruby remained living with Augusta, Augusta's boyfriend, Ruby's maternal uncle and her daughters.
18	Ruby fought with Augusta and she and Otis moved into an apartment with her two daughters. Ruby's first daughter's father died. Otis stayed with Ruby and her daughters in the apartment.
19	Ruby broke up with Otis. Ruby and her two daughters joined Magnolia, Magnolia's "husband," and her ten half-siblings. Ruby had a miscarriage.
19½	Ruby left town and moved out of state with her new boyfriend, Earl. She left her daughters with Magnolia and remained out of state for a year. Magnolia then insisted she return home and take care of her children.
20½	Ruby and her daughters moved into a large house rented by Augusta and her mother's brother. It was located next door to Magnolia's house, where Ruby and her children ate. Ruby cleaned for her aunt and uncle, and gave birth to another child, by Otis, who had returned to the household.
21	Ruby and Otis broke up once again. She found a house and moved there with her daughters, Augusta, and Augusta's boyfriend. Ruby did the cleaning, and Augusta cooked. Ruby and Magnolia, who now lived across town, shared child care, and Ruby's cousin's daughter stayed with Ruby.
21½	Augusta and her boyfriend have moved out because they were all fighting, and the two of them wanted to get away from the noise of the children. Ruby has a new boyfriend.

Table 2.

HOUSEHOLD	DOMESTIC ARRANGEMENTS, APRIL 1969	DOMESTIC ARRANGEMENTS, JUNE 1969
1	Magnolia, her husband Calvin, their eight children (4–18.)	Unchanged.
2	Magnolia's sister Augusta, Augusta's boyfriend, Ruby, Ruby's children, Ruby's boyfriend Otis.	Augusta and boyfriend have moved to #3 after a quarrel with Ruby. Ruby and Otis remain in #2.
3	Billy (Augusta's closest friend), Billy's children, Lazar (Magnolia's sister Carrie's husband, living in the basement), Carrie (from time to time—she is an alcoholic).	Augusta and boyfriend have moved to a small, one-room apartment upstairs from Billy.
4	Magnolia's sister Lydia, Lydia's daughters Georgia and Lottie, Lydia's boyfriend, Lottie's daughter.	Lottie and her daughter have moved to an apartment down the street, joining Lottie's girl friend and child. Georgia has moved in with her boyfriend. Lydia's son has moved back into Lydia's home #4.
5	Ruby's friend Willa Mae, her husband and son, her sister, and her brother James (father of Ruby's daughter).	James has moved in with his girl friend, who lives with her sister; James keeps most of his clothes in household #5. James's brother has returned from the army and moved into #5.
6	Eloise (Magnolia's first son's father's sister), her husband, their four young children, their daughter and her son, Eloise's friend Jessie's brother's daughter and her child.	Unchanged.
7	Violet (wife of Calvin's closest friend Cecil, now dead several years), her two sons, her daughter Odessa, and Odessa's four children.	Odessa's son Raymond has fathered Clover's baby. Clover and baby have joined household #7.

the residential patterns typical of young adults (Stack, 1970). Owing to poverty, young women with or without children do not perceive any choice but to remain living at home with their mothers or other adult female relatives. Even when young women are collecting welfare for their children, they say that their resources go further when they share food and exchange goods and services daily. Likewise, the jobless man, or the man working at a part-time or seasonal job, often remains living at home with his mother—or, if she is dead, with his sisters and brothers. This pattern continues long after such a man becomes a father and establishes a series of sexual partnerships with women, who are in turn living with their own kin or friends or are alone with their children. A result of this pattern is the striking fact that households almost always have men around: male relatives, affines, and boyfriends. These men are often intermittent members of the households, boarders, or friends who come and go—men who usually eat, and sometimes sleep, in these households. Children have constant and close contact with these men, and especially in the case of male relatives, these relationships last over the years. The most predictable residential pattern in The Flats is that individuals reside in the households of their natal kin, or the households of those who raised them, long into their adult years.

Welfare workers, researchers, and landlords in Black ghetto communities have long known that the residence patterns of the poor change frequently and that females play a dominant domestic role. What is much less understood is the relationship between household composition and domestic organization in these communities. Household boundaries are elastic, and no one model of a household, such as the nuclear family, extended family, or matrifocal family, is the norm. What is crucial and enduring is the strength of ties within a kin network; the maintenance of a strong network in turn has consequences for the relationships between the members themselves, as demonstrated in the following discussion of relationships between mothers and fathers and between fathers and their children.

MOTHERS AND FATHERS

Notwithstanding the emptiness and hopelessness of the job experience in the Black community, men and women fall in love and wager buoyant new relationships against the inexorable forces of poverty and racism. At the same time, in dealing with everyday life, Black women and men have developed a number of attitudes and strategies that appear to mitigate against the formation of long-term relationships. Even when a man and woman set up temporary housekeeping arrangements, they both maintain primary social ties with their kin. If other members of a kin network view a particular relationship as a drain on the network's resources, they will act in various and subtle ways to break up the relationship. This is what happened in the life of Julia Ambrose, another resident of The Flats.

When I first met Julia, she was living with her baby, her cousin Teresa, and Teresa's "old man." After several fierce battles with Teresa over the bills, and because of Teresa's hostility toward Julia's boyfriends, Julia decided to move out. She told me she was head over heels in love with Elliot, her child's father, and they had decided to live together.

For several months Julia and Elliot shared a small apartment, and their relationship was strong. Elliot was very proud of his baby. On weekends he would spend an entire day carrying the baby around to his sister's home, where he would show it to his friends on the street. Julia, exhilarated by her independence in having her own place, took great care of the house and her baby. She told me, "Before Elliot came home from work I would have his dinner fixed and the house and kid clean. When he came home he would take his shower and then I'd bring his food to the bed. I'd put the kid to sleep and then get into bed with him. It was fine. We would get in a little piece and then go to sleep. In the morning we'd do the same thing."

After five months, Elliot was laid off from his job at a factory that hires seasonal help. He couldn't find another job, except part-time work for a cab company. Elliot began spending more time away from the house with his friends at the local tavern, and less time with Julia and the baby. Julia finally had to get back "on aid" and Elliot put more of his things back in his sister's home so the social worker wouldn't know he was staying with Julia. Julia noticed changes in Elliot. "If you start necking and doing the same thing that you've been doing with your man, and he don't want it, you know for sure that he is messing with someone else, or don't want you anymore. Maybe Elliot didn't want me in the first place, but maybe he did 'cause he chased me a lot. He wanted me and he didn't want me. I really loved him, but I'm not in love with him now. My feelings just changed. I'm not in love with no man, really. Just out for what I can get from them."

Julia and Elliot stayed together, but she began to hear rumors about him. Her cousin, a woman who had often expressed jealousy toward Julia, followed Elliot in a car and told her that Elliot parked late at night outside the apartment house of his previous girl friend. Julia told me that her cousin was "nothing but a gossip, a newspaper who carried news back and forth," and that her cousin was envious of her having an "old man." Nevertheless, Julia believed the gossip.

After hearing other rumors and gossip about Elliot, Julia said, "I still really liked him, but I wasn't going to let him get the upper hand on me. After I found out that he was messing with someone else, I said to myself, I was doing it too, so what's the help in making a fuss. But after that, I made him pay for being with me!

"I was getting a check every month for rent from welfare and I would take the money and buy me clothes. I bought my own wardrobe and I gave my mother money for keeping the baby while I was working. I worked here and there while I was on aid and they were paying my rent. I didn't really need Elliot, but that was extra money for me. When he asked me what happened to my check I told him I got off and couldn't get back on. My mother knew. She didn't care what I did so long as I didn't let Elliot make an ass out of me. The point is a woman has to have her own pride. She can't let a man rule her. You can't let a man kick you in the tail and tell you what to do. Anytime I can make an ass out of a man, I'm going to do it. If he's doing the same to me, then I'll quit him and leave him alone."

After Elliot lost his job, and kin continued to bring gossip to Julia about how he was playing around with other women, Julia became embittered toward Elliot and was anxious to hurt him. There had been a young Black man making deliveries for a local store who would pass her house every day, and flirt with her. Charles would slow down his truck and honk for Julia when he passed the house. Soon she started running out to talk to him in his truck and decided to "go" with him. Charles liked Julia and brought nice things for her child.

"I put Elliot in a trick," Julia told me soon after she stopped going with Charles. "I knew that Elliot didn't care nothing for me, so I made him jealous. He was nice to the kids, both of them, but he didn't do nothing to show me he was still in love with me. Me and Elliot fought a lot. One night Charles and me went to a motel room and stayed there all night. Mama had the babies. She got mad. But I was trying to hurt Elliot. When I got home, me and Elliot got into it. He called me all kinds of names. I said he might as well leave. But Elliot said he wasn't going nowhere. So he stayed and we'd sleep together, but we didn't do nothing. Then one night something happened. I got pregnant again by Elliot. After I got pregnant, me and Charles quit, and I moved in with a girl friend for a while. Elliot chased after me and we started going back together, but we stayed separate. In my sixth month I moved back in my mother's home with her husband and the kids."

Many young women like Julia feel strongly that they cannot let a man make a fool out of them, and they react quickly and boldly to rumor, gossip, and talk that hurts them. The power that gossip and information have in constraining the duration of sexual relationships is an important cultural phenomenon. But the most important single factor affecting interpersonal relationships between men and women in The Flats is unemployment. The futility of the job experience for street-corner men in a Black community is sensitively portrayed by Elliot Liebow in *Tally's Corner*. As Liebow (1967: 63) writes, "The job fails the man and the man fails the job." Liebow's discussion (p. 142) of men and jobs leads directly to his analysis of the streetcorner male's exploitive relationships with women: "Men not only present themselves as economic exploiters of women but they expect other men to do the same." Ghetto-specific male roles that men try to live up to at home and on the street, and their alleged round-the-clock involvement in peer groups, are interpreted in *Soulside* (Hannerz, 1969) as a threat to marital stability.

Losing a job, then, or being unemployed month after month debilitates one's self-importance and independence and, for men, necessitates sacrificing a role in the economic support of their families. Faced with these familiar patterns in the behavior and status of men, women call upon life experiences in The Flats to guide them. When a man loses his job, that is the time he is most likely to begin "messing around."

And so that no man appears to have made a fool of them, women respond with vengeance, out of pride and self-defense. Another young woman in The Flats, Ivy Rodgers, told me about the time she left her two children in The Flats with her mother and took off for Indiana with Jimmy River, a young man she had fallen in love with "the first sight I seen." Jimmy asked Ivy to go to Gary, Indiana, where his family lived. "I just left the kids with my mama. I didn't even tell her I was going. My checks kept coming so she had food for the kids, but I didn't know he let his people tell him what to do. While he was in Gary, Jimmy started messing with another woman. He said he wasn't, but I caught him. I quit him, but when he told me he wasn't messing, I loved him so much I took him back. Then I got to thinking about it. I had slipped somewhere. I had let myself go. Seems like I forgot that I wasn't going to let Jimmy or any man make an ass out of me. But he sure was doing it. I told Jimmy that if he loved me, he would go and see my people, take them things, and tell them we were getting married. Jimmy didn't want to go back to The Flats, but I tricked him and told him I really wanted to visit. I picked out my ring and Jimmy paid thirty dollars on it and I had him buy my outfit that we was getting married in. He went along with it. What's so funny was when we come here and he said to me, 'You ready to go back?' and I told him, 'No, I'm not going back. I never will marry you.' "

Forms of social control in the larger society also work against successful marriages in The Flats. In fact, couples rarely chance marriage unless a man has a job; often the job is temporary, low-paying, and insecure, and the worker is arbitrarily laid off whenever he is not needed. Women come to realize that welfare benefits and ties within kin networks provide greater security for them and their children. In addition, caretaker agencies such as public welfare are insensitive to individual attempts for social mobility. A woman may be immediately cut off the welfare rolls when a husband returns home from prison or the army, or if she gets married. Unless there is either a significant change in employment opportunities for the urban poor or a livable guaranteed minimum income, it is unlikely that urban low-income Blacks will form lasting conjugal units.

Marriage and its accompanying expectations of a home, a job, and a family built around the husband and wife have come to stand for an individual's desire to break out of poverty. It implies the willingness of an individual to remove himself from the daily obligations of his kin network. People in The Flats recognize that one cannot simultaneously meet kin expectations and the expectations of a spouse. Cooperating kinsmen continually attempt to draw new people into their personal network; but at the same time they fear the loss of a central, resourceful member in the network. The following passages are taken from the detailed residence life history of Ruby Banks. Details of her story were substantiated by discussions with her mother, her aunt, her daughter's father, and her sister.

"Me and Otis could be married, but they all ruined that. Aunt Augusta told Magnolia that he was no good. Magnolia was the fault of it, too. They don't want to see me married! Magnolia knows that it be money getting away from her. I couldn't spend the time with her and the kids and be giving her the money that I do now. I'd have my husband to look after. I couldn't go where she want me to go. I couldn't come every time she call me, like if Calvin took sick or the kids took sick, or if she took sick. That's all the running I do now. I couldn't do that. You think a man would put up with as many times as I go over her house in a cab, giving half my money to her all the time? That's the reason they don't want me married. You think a man would let Aunt Augusta come into the house and take food out of the icebox from his kids? They thought that way ever since I came up.

"They broke me and Otis up. They kept telling me that he didn't want me, and that he didn't want the responsibility. I put him out and I cried all night long. And I really did love him. But Aunt Augusta and others kept fussing and arguing so I went and quit him. I would have got married a long time ago to my first baby's daddy, but Aunt Augusta was the cause of that, telling Magnolia that he was too old for me. She's been jealous of me since the day I was born.

"Three years after Otis I met Earl. Earl said he was going to help pay for the utilities. He was going to get me some curtains and pay on my couch. While Earl was working he was so good to me and my children that Magnolia and them started worrying all over again. They sure don't want me married. The same thing that happened to Otis happened to many of my boyfriends. And I ain't had that many men. I'm tired of them bothering me with their problems when I'm trying to solve my own problems. They tell me that Earl's doing this and that, seeing some girl.

"They look for trouble to tell me every single day. If I ever marry, I ain't listening to what nobody say. I just listen to what he say. You have to get along the best way you know how, and forget about your people. If I got married they would talk, like they are doing now, saying, 'He ain't no good, he's been creeping on you. I told you once not to marry him. You'll end up right back on aid.' If I ever get married, I'm leaving town!"

Ruby's account reveals the strong conflict between kin-based domestic units and lasting ties between husbands and wives. When a mother in The Flats has a relationship with an economically nonproductive man, the relationship saps the resources of others in her domestic network. Participants in the network act to break up such relationships, to maintain kin-based household groupings over the life cycle, in order to maximize potential resources and the services they hope to exchange. Similarly, a man's participation is expected in his kin network, and it is understood that he should not dissipate his services and finances to a sexual or marital relationship. These forms of social control made Ruby afraid to take the risks necessary to break out of the cycle of poverty. Instead, she chose the security and stability of her kin group. Ruby, recognizing that to make a marriage last she would have to move far away from her kin, exclaimed, "If I ever get married, I'm leaving town!" While this study was in progress, Ruby did get married, and she left the state with her husband and her youngest child that very evening.

FATHERS AND CHILDREN

People in The Flats show pride in all their kin, and particularly new babies born into their kinship networks. Mothers encourage sons to have babies, and even more important, men coax their "old ladies" to have their babies. The value placed on children, the love, attention, and affection children receive from women and men, and the web of social relationships spun from the birth of a child are all basic to the high birthrate among the poor.

The pride that kinsmen take in the children of their sons and brothers is seen best in the pleasure that the mothers and sisters of these men express. Such pride was apparent during a visit I made to Alberta Cox's home. She introduced me to her nineteen-year-old son Nate and added immediately, "He's a daddy and his baby is four months old." Then she pointed to her twenty-two-year-old son Mac and said, "He's a daddy three times over," Mac smiled and said, "I'm no daddy," and his friend in the kitchen said, "Maybe going on four times, Mac." Alberta said, "Yes you are. Admit it, boy!" At that point Mac's grandmother rolled back in her rocker and said, "I'm a grandmother many times over, and it make me proud." A friend of Alberta's told me later that Alberta wants her sons to have babies because she thinks it will make them more responsible. Although she usually dislikes the women her sons go with, claiming they are "no-good trash," Alberta accepts the babies and asks to care for them whenever she has a chance.

Although Blacks, like most Americans, acquire kin through their mothers and fathers, the economic insecurity of the Black male and the availability of welfare to the mother-child unit make it very difficult for an unemployed Black husband-father to compete with a woman's kin for authority and control over her children. As we have seen, women seek to be independent, but also, in order to meet everyday needs, they act to strengthen their ties with their kin and within their domestic network. Though these two strategies, especially in the context of male joblessness, may lead to the breakup of a young couple, a father will maintain his ties with his children. The husband-father role may be limited, but contrary to the stereotype of Black family life, it is not only viable but culturally significant.

Very few young couples enter into a legal marriage in The Flats, but a father and his kin can sustain a continuing relationship with the father's children if the father has acknowledged paternity, if his kin have activated their claims on the child, and if the mother has drawn these people into her personal network. Widely popularized and highly misleading statistics on female-headed households have contributed to the assumption that Black children derive nothing of sociological importance from their fathers. To the contrary, in my recent study of domestic life among the poor in a Black community in the Midwest (Stack, 1972), I found that 70 percent of the fathers of 1,000 children on welfare recognized their children and provided them with kinship affiliations. But because many of these men have little or no access to steady and productive employment, out of the 699 who acknowledged paternity, only 84 (12 percent) gave any substantial financial support to their children. People in The Flats believe a father should help his child, but they know that the mother cannot count on his help. Community expectations of fathers do not generally include the father's *duties* in relation to a child; they do, however, assume the responsibilities of the father's kin. Kinship through males in The Flats is reckoned through a chain of acknowledged genitors, but social fatherhood is shared by the genitor with his kin, and with the mother's husband or with her boyfriends.

Although the authority of a father over his genealogical children or his wife's other children is limited, neither the father's interest in his child nor the desire of his kin to help raise the child strains the stability of the domestic network. Otis's kin were drawn into Ruby's personal network through his claims on her children, and through the long, close friendship between Ruby and Otis's sister, Willa Mae. Like many fathers in The Flats, Otis maintained close contact with his children, and provided goods and care for them even when he and Ruby were not on speaking terms. One time when Otis and Ruby separated, Otis stayed in a room in Ruby's uncle's house next door to Ruby's mother's house. At that time Ruby's children were being kept by Magnolia each day while Ruby went to school to finish working toward her high school diploma. Otis was out of work, and he stayed with Ruby's uncle over six months helping Magnolia care for his children. Otis's kin were proud of the daddy he was, and at times suggested they should take over the raising of Otis and Ruby's children. Ruby and other mothers know well that those people you count on to share in the care and nurturing of your children are also those who are rightfully in a position to judge and check upon how you carry out the duties of a mother. Shared responsibilities of motherhood in The Flats imply both a help and a check on how one assumes the parental role.

Fathers like Otis, dedicated to maintaining ties with their children, learn that the relationship they create with their child's mother largely determines the role they may assume in their child's life. Jealousy between men makes it extremely difficult for fathers to spend time with their children if the mother has a boyfriend, but as Otis said to me, "When Ruby doesn't have any old man then she starts calling on me, asking for help, and telling me to do something for my kids." Between such times, when a man or a woman does not have an ongoing sexual relationship, some mothers call upon the fathers of their children and temporarily "choke" these men with their personal needs and the needs of the children. At these times, men and women reinforce their fragile but continuing relationship, and find themselves empathetic friends who can be helpful to one another.

A mother generally regards her children's father as a friend of the family whom she can recruit for help, rather than as a father failing his parental duties. Although fathers voluntarily help out with their children, many fathers cannot be depended upon as a steady source of help. Claudia Williams talked to me about Harold, the father of her two children. "Some days he be coming over at night saying, 'I'll see to the babies and you can lay down and rest, honey,' treating me real nice. Then maybe I don't even see him for two or three months. There's no sense nagging Harold. I just treat him as some kind of friend even if he is the father of my babies." Since Claudia gave birth to Harold's children, both of them have been involved in other relationships. When either of them is involved with someone else, this effectively cuts Harold off from his children. Claudia says, "My kids don't need their daddy's help, but if he helps out then I help him out, too. My kids are well behaved, and I know they make Harold's kinfolk proud."

CONCLUSIONS

The view of Black women as represented in their own words and life histories coincides with that presented by Joyce Ladner: "One of the chief characteristics defining the Black woman is her [realistic approach] to her [own] resources. Instead of becoming resigned to her fate, she has always sought creative solutions to her problems. The ability to utilize her existing resources and yet maintain a forthright determination to struggle against the racist society in whatever overt and subtle ways necessary is one of her major attributes" (Ladner, 1971: 276–77).

I have particularly emphasized those strategies that women can employ to maximize their independence, acquire and maintain domestic authority, limit (but positively evaluate) the role of husband and father, and strengthen ties with kin. The last of these—maximizing relationships in the domestic network—helps to account for patterns of Black family life among the urban poor more adequately than the concepts of nuclear or matrifocal family. When economic resources are greatly limited, people need help from as many others as possible. This requires expanding their kin networks—increasing the number of people they hope to be able to count on. On the one hand, female members of a network may act to break up a relationship that has become a drain on their resources. On the other, a man is expected to contribute to his own kin network, and it is assumed that he should not dissipate his services and finances to a marital relationship. At the same time, a woman will continue to seek aid from the man who has fathered her children, thus building up her own network's resources. She also expects something of his kin, especially his mother and sisters. Women continually activate these lines to bring kin and friends into the network of exchange and obligation. Most often, the biological father's female relatives are poor and also try to expand their network and increase the number of people they can depend on.

Clearly, economic pressures among cooperating kinsmen in the Black community work against the loss of either males or females—through marriage or other long-term relationships—from the kin network. The kin-based cooperative network represents the collective adaptations to poverty of the men, women, and children within the Black community. Loyalties and dependencies toward kinsmen offset the ordeal of unemployment and racism. To cope with the everyday demands of ghetto life, these networks have evolved patterns of co-residence: elastic household boundaries; lifelong, if intermittent, bonds to three-generation households; social constraints on the role of the husband-father within the mother's domestic group; and the domestic authority of women.

NOTES

1. This work is based on a recent urban anthropological study of poverty and domestic life of urban-born Black Americans who were raised on public welfare and whose parents had migrated from the South to a single community in the Urban North (Stack, 1972). Now adults in their twenties to forties, they are raising their own children on welfare in The Flats. All personal and place names in this paper are fictitious.

Review Questions

1. While place of residence and family may coincide for many people in our society, for the poor community described by Stack they do not. What can we say about the meaning of the term "family" in light of this fact?

2. What is the importance of economic factors in shaping both the residence patterns and family interactions of residents of The Flats?

3. What are the roles played by men in the family system of this poor neighborhood? What features of our society affect which family roles men occupy and how they are performed?

4. Despite the fact that the poor families described here have developed flexible household boundaries and extensive networks of kin support and obligations not characteristic of the nuclear family, family life in The Flats can be seen as embodying and responding to many of the central values and norms of the family institution of the larger culture. Give examples of conformity to cultural norms and values.

UNCOUPLING: THE SOCIAL CONSTRUCTION OF DIVORCE

Diane Vaughan

BERGER AND KELLNER (1964) DESCRIBE MARRIAGE AS A DEFINITIONAL PROCESS. Two autonomous individuals come together with separate and distinct biographies and begin to construct for themselves a subworld in which they will live as a couple. A redefinition of self occurs as the autonomous identity of the two individuals involved is reconstructed as a mutual identity. This redefinition is externally anticipated and socially legitimated before it actually occurs in the individual's biography.

Previously, significant conversation for each partner came from nonoverlapping circles, and self-realization came from other sources. Together, they begin to construct a private sphere where all significant conversation centers in their relationship with each other. The coupled identity becomes the main source of their self-realization. Their definitions of reality become correlated, for each partner's actions must be projected in conjunction with the other. As their worlds come to be defined around a relationship with a significant other who becomes *the* significant other, all other significant relationships have to be reperceived, regrouped. The result is the construction of a joint biography and a mutually coordinated common memory.

Were this construction of a coupled identity left only to the two participants, the coupling would be precarious indeed. However, the new reality is reinforced through objectivation, that is, "a process by which subjectively experienced meanings become objective to the individual, and, in interaction with others, become common property, and thereby massively objective" (Berger and Kellner, 1964:6). Hence, through the use of language in conversation with significant others, the reality of the coupling is constantly validated.

Of perhaps greater significance is that this definition of coupledness becomes taken for granted and is validated again and again, not by explicit articulation, but by conversing around the agreed [upon] definition of reality that has been created. In this way a consistent reality is maintained, ordering the individual's world in such a way that it validates his identity. Marriage, according to Berger and Kellner, is a

SOURCE: Diane Vaughan: "Uncoupling: The Social Construction of Divorce" was written for the first edition of *Social Interaction*.

constructed reality which is "nomos-building" (1964:1). That is, it is a social arrangement that contributes order to individual lives, and therefore should be considered as a significant validating relationship for adults in our society.

Social relationships, however, are seldom static. Not only do we move in and out of relationships, but the nature of a particular relationship, though enduring, varies over time. Given that the definitions we create become socially validated and hence constraining, *how do individuals move from a mutual identity, as in marriage, to assume separate, autonomous identities again?* What is the process by which new definitions are created and become validated?

The Berger and Kellner analysis describes a number of interrelated yet distinguishable stages that are involved in the social construction of a mutual identity; for example, the regrouping of all other significant relationships. In much the same way, the *demise* of a relationship should involve distinguishable social processes. Since redefinition of self is basic to both movement into and out of relationships, the social construction of a singular identity also should follow the patterns suggested by Berger and Kellner. This paper is a qualitative examination of this process. Hence, the description that follows bears an implicit test of Berger and Kellner's ideas.

The dimensions of sorrow, anger, personal disorganization, fear, loneliness, and ambiguity that intermingle every separation are well known.[1] Their familiarity does not diminish their importance. Though in real life these cannot be ignored, the researcher has the luxury of selectivity. Here, it is not the pain and disorganization that are to be explored, but the existence of an underlying orderliness.

Though the focus is on divorce, the process examined appears to apply to *any* heterosexual relationship in which the participants have come to define themselves and be defined by others as a couple. The work is exploratory and, as such, not concerned with generalizability. However, the process may apply to homosexual couples as well. Therefore, the term "uncoupling" will be used because it is a more general concept than divorce. Uncoupling applies to the redefinition of self that occurs as mutual identity unravels into singularity, regardless of marital status or sex of the participants.

The formal basis from which this paper developed was in-depth, exploratory interviews. The interviews, ranging from two to six hours, were taped and later analyzed. All of the interviewees were at different stages in the uncoupling process. Most were divorced, though some were still in stages of consideration of divorce. Two of the interviews were based on long-term relationships that never resulted in marriage. All of the relationships were heterosexual. The quality of these interviews has added much depth to the understanding of the separation process. The interviewees were of high intellectual and social level, and their sensitivity and insight have led to much valuable material, otherwise unavailable.

A more informal contribution to the paper comes from personal experiences and the experiences of close friends. Further corroboration has come from autobiographical accounts, newspapers, periodicals, and conversations, which have resulted in a large number of cases illustrating certain points. Additional support has come from individuals who have read or heard the paper with the intent of proving or disproving its contentions by reference to their own cases.

Since the declared purpose here is to abstract the essential features of the process of uncoupling, some simplification is necessary. The separation of a relationship can take several forms. To trace all of them is beyond the scope of this study. Therefore, to narrow the focus, we must first consider the possible variations.

Perhaps the coupled identity was not a major mechanism for self-validation from the outset of the union. Or the relationship may have at one time filled that function, but, as time passed, this coupled identity was insufficient to meet individual needs. Occasionally this fact has implications for both partners simultaneously, and the uncoupling process is initiated by both. More frequently, however, one partner still finds the marriage a major source of stability and identity, while the other finds it inadequate. In this form, one participant takes the role of initiator of the uncoupling process. However, this role may not consistently be held by one partner, but instead may alternate between them, due to the difficulty of uncoupling in the face of external constraints, social pressure not to be the one responsible for the demise of the marriage, and the variability in the self-validating function of the union over time. For the purpose of this study, the form of uncoupling under consideration is that which results when one partner, no longer finding the coupled identity self-validating, takes the role of initiator in the uncoupling process. The other partner, the significant other, still finds the marriage a major source of stability and identity.

UNCOUPLING: THE INITIATION OF THE PROCESS

> I was never psychologically married. I always felt strained by attempts that coupled me into a marital unit. I was just never comfortable as "Mrs." I never got used to my last name. I never wanted it. The day after my marriage was probably the most depressed day of my life, because I had lost my singularity. The difference between marriage and a deep relationship, living together, is that you have this ritual, and you achieve a very definite status, and it was *that* that produced my reactions—because I became in the eyes of the world a man's wife. And I was never comfortable and happy with it. It didn't make any difference who the man was.

An early phase in the uncoupling process occurs as one or the other of the partners begins to question the coupled identity. At first internal, the challenging of the created world remains for a time as a doubt within one of the partners in the coupling. Though there is a definition of coupledness, subjectively the coupledness may be experienced differently by each partner. Frequently, these subjective meanings remain internal and unarticulated. Thus, similarly, the initial recognition of the coupling as problematic may be internal and unarticulated, held as a secret. The subworld that has been constructed, for some reason, doesn't "fit."

A process of definition negotiation is begun, initiated by the one who finds the mutual identity an inadequate definition of self. Attempts to negotiate the definition of the coupledness are likely to result in the subjective meaning becoming articulated for the first time, thus moving the redefinition process toward objectivation. The secret, held by the initiator, is shared with the significant other. When this occurs, it allows both participants to engage in the definitional process.

Though the issue is made "public" in that private sphere shared by the two, the initiator frequently finds that a lack of shared definitions of the coupled identity stalemates the negotiations. While the initiator defines the marriage as a problem, the other does not. The renegotiation of the coupled identity cannot proceed unless both agree that the subworld they have constructed needs to be redefined. Perhaps for the significant other, the marriage as it is still provides important self-validation. If so, the initiator must bring the other to the point of sharing a common definition of the marriage as "troubled."

ACCOMPANYING RECONSTRUCTIONS

Though this shared definition is being sought, the fact remains that, for the initiator, the coupled identity fails to provide self-validation. In order to meet this need, the initiator engages in other attempts at redefining the nature of the relationship. Called "accompanying reconstructions," these *may* or *may not* be shared with the significant other. They may begin long before the "secret" of the troubled marriage is shared with the other, in an effort to make an uncomfortable situation more comfortable without disrupting the relationship. Or they may occur subsequent to sharing the secret with the significant other, as a reaction to the failure to redefine the coupledness satisfactorily. Time order for their occurrence is not easily imposed—thus, "accompanying reconstructions."

The initiator's accompanying reconstructions may be directed toward the redefinition of (1) the coupledness itself, (2) the identity of the significant other, or (3) the identity of the initiator. A change in definition of either of the three implies a change in at least one of the others. Though they are presented here separately, they are interactive rather than mutually exclusive and are not easily separable in real life.

The first form of accompanying reconstruction to be considered is the initiator's redefinition of the coupledness itself. One way of redefining the coupledness is by an unarticulated conversion of the agreed-upon norms of the relationship.

> I had reconceptualized what marriage was. I decided sexual fidelity was not essential for marriage. I never told her that. And I didn't even have anyone I was interested in having that intimate a relationship with—I just did a philosophical thing. I just decided it was O.K. for me to have whatever of what quality of other relationship I needed to have. Something like that—of that caliber—was something I could never talk to her about. So I did it all by myself. I read things and decided it. I was at peace with me. I knew that we could stay married, whatever that meant. O.K., I can stay legally tied to you, and I can probably live in this house with you, and I can keep working the way I have been. I decided I can have my life and still be in this situation with you, but you need some resources, because I realize now I'm not going to be all for you. I don't want to be all for you, and I did tell her that. But I couldn't tell her this total head trip I'd been through because she wouldn't understand.

Or, the coupledness may be redefined by acceptance of the relationship with certain limitations. Boundaries can be imposed on the impact that the relationship will have on the total life space of the initiator.

> I finally came to the point where I realized I was never going to have the kind of marriage I had hoped for, the kind of relationship I had hoped for. I didn't want to end it, because of the children, but I wasn't going to let it hurt me any more. I wasn't going to depend on him any more. The children and I were going to be the main unit, and, if he occasionally wanted to participate, fine—and if not, we would go ahead without him. I was no longer willing to let being with him be the determining factor as to whether I was happy or not. I ceased planning our lives around his presence or absence and began looking out for myself.

A second form of accompanying reconstruction occurs when the initiator attempts to redefine the significant other in a way that is more compatible with his own self-validation needs. The initiator may direct efforts toward specific behaviors, such as drinking habits, temper, sexual incompatibilities, or finance management. Or, the redefinition attempt may be of a broader scope.

> I was aware of his dependence on the marriage to provide all his happiness, and it wasn't providing it. I wanted him to go to graduate school, but he postponed it, against my wishes. I wanted him to pursue his own life. I didn't want him to sacrifice for me. I wanted him to become more exciting

> to me in the process. I was aware that I was trying to persuade him to be a different person.

Redefinition of the significant other may either be directed toward maintaining the coupledness, as above, or moving away from it, as in the case following.

> The way I defined being a good wife and the way John defined being a good wife were two different quantities. He wanted the house to look like a hotel and I didn't see it that way. He couldn't see why I couldn't meet his needs. . . . When he first asked for a divorce and I refused, he suggested I go back to school. I remembered a man who worked with John who had sent his wife back to school so she could support herself, so he could divorce her. I asked John if he was trying to get rid of me. He didn't answer that. He insisted I go, and I finally went.

A third form of accompanying reconstruction may be directed toward the redefinition of the initiator. Intermingled with attempts at redefinition of the significant other and redefinition of the coupledness itself is the seeking of self-validation outside the marriage by the initiator. A whole set of other behaviors may evolve that have the ultimate effect of moving the relationship away from the coupledness toward a separation of the joint biography.

What was at first internally experienced and recognized as self-minimizing takes a more concrete form and becomes externally expressed in a search for self-maximization. Through investment of self in career, in a cause requiring commitment, in a relationship with a new significant other, in family, in education, or in activities and hobbies, the initiator develops new sources of self-realization. These alternative sources of self-realization confirm not the coupled identity but the singularity of the initiator.

Furthermore, in the move toward a distinct biography, the initiator finds ideological support that reinforces the uncoupling process. Berger and Kellner (1964:3) note the existence of a supporting ideology which lends credence to marriage as a significant validating relationship in our society. That is, the nuclear family is seen as the site of love, sexual fulfillment, and self-realization. In the move toward uncoupling, the initiator finds confirmation for a belief in *self* as a first priority.

> I now see my break with religion as a part of my developing individuality. At the time I was close friends with priests and nuns, most of whom have since left the church. I felt a bitterness toward the church for its definition of marriage. I felt constrained toward a type of marriage that was not best for me.

Whether this ideology first begins within the individual, who then actively *seeks* sources of self-realization that are ideologically congruent, or whether the initiator's own needs come to be met by a serendipitous "elective affinity" of ideas (Weber: 1930), is difficult to say. The interconnections are subtle. The supporting ideology may come from the family of orientation, the women's movement, the peer group, or a new significant other. It may grow directly, as through interaction, or indirectly, as through literature. No matter what the source, the point is that, in turning away from the marriage for self-validation, a separate distinct biography is constructed in interaction with others, and this beginning autonomy is strengthened by a supporting belief system.

The initiator moves toward construction of a separate subworld wherein significant conversation comes from circles which no longer overlap with those of the significant other. And, the significant other is excluded from that separate subworld.

> I shared important things with the children that I didn't share with him. It's almost as if I purposefully punished him by not telling him. Some good thing would happen and I'd come home and tell them and wouldn't tell him.

The initiator's autonomy is further reinforced as the secret of the troubled marriage is shared with others in the separate subworld the initiator is constructing. It may be directly expressed as a confidence exchanged with a close friend, family member, or children, or it may be that the sharing is indirect. Rather than being expressed in significant conversation, the definition of the marriage as troubled is created for others by a variety of mechanisms that relay the message that the initiator is not happily married. The definition of the marriage as problematic becomes further objectivated as the secret, once held only by the initiator, then shared with the significant other, moves to a sphere beyond the couple themselves.

Other moves away occur that deeply threaten the coupled identity for the significant other and at the same time validate the autonomy of the initiator.

> I remember going to a party by myself and feeling comfortable. She never forgot that. I never realized the gravity of that to her.

> Graduate school became a symbolic issue. I was going to be a separate entity. That's probably the one thing I wanted to do that got the biggest negative emotional response from him.

> All that time I was developing more of a sense of being away from her. I didn't depend on her for any emotional feedback, companionship. I went to plays and movies with friends.

The friendship group, rather than focusing on the coupledness, relies on splintered sources that support separate identities. Though this situation can exist in relationships in which the coupled identity is validating for both participants, the distinction is that, in the process of uncoupling, there may not be shared conversation to link the separate subworld of the initiator with that of the significant other.

These movements away by the initiator heighten a sense of exclusion for the significant other. Deep commitment to other than the coupled identity—to a career, to a cause, to education, to a hobby, to another person—reflects a lessened commitment to the marriage. The initiator's search for self-validation outside the marriage even may be demonstrated symbolically to the significant other by the removal of the wedding ring or by the desire, if the initiator is a woman, to revert to her maiden name. If the initiator's lessened commitment to the coupled identity is reflected in a lessened desire for sexual intimacy, the challenge to the identity of the significant other and the coupledness becomes undeniable. As the significant other recognizes the growing autonomy of the initiator, he, too, comes to accept the definition of the marriage as "troubled."

The roles assumed by each participant have implications for the impact of the uncoupling on each. Whereas the initiator has found other sources of self-realization outside the marriage, usually the significant other has not. The marriage still performs the major self-validating function. The significant other is committed to an ideology that supports the coupled identity. The secret of the "troubled" marriage has not been shared with others as it has by the initiator, meaning for the significant other the relationship in its changed construction remains unobjectivated. The challenge to the identity of the significant other and to the coupledness posed by the initiator may result in increased commitment to the coupled identity for the significant other. With the joint biography already separated in these ways, the couple enters into a period of "trying."

TRYING

Trying is a stage of intense definition negotiation by the partners. Now both share a definition of the marriage as troubled. However, each partner may seek to construct a new reality that is in opposition to that of the other. The significant other tries to negotiate a shared definition of the marriage as savable, whereas the initiator negotiates toward a shared definition that marks the marriage as unsavable.[2]

For the initiator, the uncoupling process is well underway. At some point the partner who originally perceived the coupled identity to be problematic and sought self-validation outside the coupled identity has experienced "psychological divorce." Sociologically, this can be defined as the point at which the individual's newly constructed separate subworld becomes a major nomos-building mechanism in his life space, replacing the nomos-building function of the coupled identity.

The initiator tries subtly to prepare the significant other to live alone. By encouraging the other to make new friends, find a job, get involved in outside activities, or seek additional education, the initiator hopes to decrease the other's commitment to and dependence upon the coupled identity for self-validation and move the other toward autonomy. This stage of preparation is not simply one of cold expediency for the benefit of the initiator, but is based on concern for the significant other and serves to mitigate the pain of the uncoupling process for both the initiator and the other.

For both, there is a hesitancy to sever the ties. In many cases, neither party is fully certain about the termination of the marriage. Mutual uncertainty may be more characteristic of the process. The relationship may weave back and forth between cycles of active trying and passive acceptance of the status quo due to the failure of each to pull the other to a common definition and the inability of either to make the break.

> I didn't want to hurt him. I didn't want to be responsible for the demise of a marriage I no longer wanted. I could have forced him into being the one to achieve the breach, for I realized it was never going to happen by itself.

> I didn't want to be the villain—the one to push her out into the big, bad world. I wanted to make sure she was at the same point I was.

> I kept hoping some alternative would occur so that he would be willing to break. I kept wishing it would happen.

Frequently, in the trying stage, the partners turn to outside help for formal negotiation of the coupled identity. Counseling, though entered into with apparent common purpose, becomes another arena in which the partners attempt to negotiate a shared definition from their separately held definitions of the marriage as savable or unsavable. For the initiator, the counseling may serve as a step in the preparation of the significant other to live alone. Not only does it serve to bring the other to the definition of the marriage as unsavable, but also the counseling provides a resource for the significant other, in the person of the counselor. Often it happens that the other has turned to no one for comfort about the problem marriage. The initiator, sensitive to this need and unable to fill it himself, hopes the counselor will fill this role. The counseling has yet another function. It further objectivates the notion of the coupled identity as problematic.

At some point during this period of trying, the initiator may suggest separation. Yet, separation is not suggested as a formal leave-taking but as a *temporary* separation meant to clarify the relationship for both partners. Again, the concern on the part of the initiator for the significant other appears. Not wanting to hurt, yet recognizing the coupled identity as no longer valid, the temporary separation is encouraged as a further means of bringing the other to accept a definition of the marriage as unsavable, to increase reliance of the other on outside resources of self-realization, and to initiate the physical breach gently.

> Even at that point, at initial separation, I wasn't being honest. I knew fairly certainly that when we separated, it was for good. I let her believe that it was a means for us first finding out what was happening and then eventually possibly getting back together.

Should the initiator be hesitant to suggest a separation, the significant other may finally tire of the ambiguity of the relationship. No longer finding the coupling as it exists self-validating, the significant other may be the one to suggest a separation. The decision to separate may be the result of discussion and planning, or it may occur spontaneously, in a moment of anger. It may be mutually agreed upon, but more often it is not. However it emerges, the decision to separate is a difficult one for both partners.

OBJECTIVATION: RESTRUCTURING OF THE PRIVATE SPHERE

The separation is a transitional state in which everything needs definition, yet very little is capable of being defined. Economic status, friendship networks, personal habits, and sex life are all patterns of the past which need simultaneous reorganization. However, reorganization is hindered by the ambiguity of the relationship. The off-again, on-again wearing of the wedding rings is symbolic of the indecision in this stage. Each of the partners searches for new roles, without yet being free of the old.

For the initiator who has developed outside resources, the impact of this uncertainty is partially mitigated. For the significant other, who has not spent time in preparation for individual existence, the major self-validating function of the marriage is gone and nothing has emerged as a substitute.

> I had lost my identity somewhere along the way. And I kept losing my identity. I kept letting him make all the decisions. I couldn't work. I wasn't able to be myself. I was letting someone else take over. I didn't have any control over it. I didn't know how to stop it. I was unsure that if anything really happened I could actually make it on my own or not.

The separation precipitates a redefinition of self for the significant other. Without other resources for self-validation, and with the coupled identity now publicly challenged, the significant other begins a restructuring of the private sphere.

This restructuring occurs not only in the social realm but also entails a form of restructuring that is physical, tangible, and symbolic of the break in the coupled identity. For instance, if the initiator has been the one to leave, at some point the significant other begins reordering the residence they shared to suit the needs of one adult rather than two. Furniture is rearranged or thrown out. Closets and drawers are reorganized. A thorough house-cleaning may be undertaken. As the initiator has moved to a new location that reinforces his singularity, the significant other transforms the home that validated the coupling into one that likewise objectivates the new definition. Changes in the physical appearance of either or both partners may be a part of the symbolic restructuring of the private sphere. Weight losses, changes of hair style, or changes in clothing preferences further symbolize the yielding of the mutual identity and the move toward autonomy.

Should the significant other be the one to leave, the move into a new location aids in the redefinition of self as an autonomous individual. For example, the necessity of surviving in a new environment, the eventual emergence of a new set of friends that define and relate to the significant other as a separate being instead of as half of a couple, and the creation of a new residence without the other person are all mechanisms which reinforce autonomy and a definition of singularity.

Though the initiator has long been involved in objectivating a separate reality, frequently for the significant other this stage is just beginning. Seldom does the secret of the troubled marriage become shared with others by this partner until it can no longer be deferred. Although the initiator actively has sought objectivation, the significant other has avoided it. Confronted with actual separation, however, the significant other responds by taking the subjectively experienced meanings and moving them to the objective level—by confiding in others, perhaps in writing, in letters or in diaries—any means that helps the other deal with the new reality.

There are some who must be told of the separation—children, parents, best friends. Not only are the two partners reconstructing their own reality, but they now must reconstruct the reality for others. Conversation provides the mechanism for reconstruction, simultaneously creating common definitions and working as a major objectivating apparatus. The longer the conversation goes on, the more massively real do the objectivations become to the partners. The result is a stabilization of the objectivated reality, as the new definition of uncoupledness continues to move outward.

Uncoupling precipitates a reordering of all other significant relationships. As in coupling, where all other relationships are reperceived and regrouped to account for and support the emergence of *the* significant other, in uncoupling the reordering supports the singularity of each partner. Significant relationships are lost, as former friends of the couple now align with one or the other or refuse to choose between the two. Ties with families of orientation, formerly somewhat attenuated because of the coupling, are frequently renewed. For each of the partners, pressure exists to stabilize characterizations of others and of self so that the world and self are brought toward consistency. Each partner approaches groups that strengthen the new definition each has created, and avoids those that weaken it. The groups with which each partner associates help co-define the new reality.

OBJECTIVATION: THE PUBLIC SPHERE

The uncoupling is further objectivated for the participants as the new definition is legitimized in the public sphere. Two separate households demand public identification as separate identities. New telephone listings, changes of mailing address, separate checking accounts, and charge accounts, for example, all are mechanisms by which the new reality becomes publicly reconstructed.

The decision to initiate legal proceedings confirms the uncoupling by the formal negotiation of a heretofore informally negotiated definition. The adversary process supporting separate identities, custody proceedings, the formal separation of the material base, the final removal of the rings all act as means of moving the new definition from the private to the public sphere. The uncoupling now becomes objectivated not only for the participants and their close intimates, but for casual acquaintances and strangers.

Objectivation acts as a constraint upon whatever social identity has been constructed. It can bind a couple together, or hinder their recoupling, once the uncoupling process has begun. Perhaps this can better be understood by considering the tenuous character of the extramarital affair. The very nature of the relationship is private. The coupling remains a secret shared by the two and seldom becomes objectivated in the public realm. Thus, the responsibility for the maintenance of that coupling usually rests solely with the two participants. When the relationship is no longer self-validating for one of the participants, the uncoupling does not involve a reconstruction of reality for others. The constraints imposed by the objectivation of a marital relationship which function to keep a couple in a marriage do not exist to the same extent in an affair. The fragility of the coupling is enhanced by its limited objectivation.

Berger and Kellner (1964:6) note that the "degree of objectivation will depend on the number and intensity of the social relationships that are its carriers." As the uncoupling process has moved from a nonshared secret held within the initiator to the realm of public knowledge, the degree of objectivation has increased. The result is a continuing decline in the precariousness of the newly constructed reality over time.

DIVORCE: A STAGE IN THE PROCESS

Yet a decrease in precariousness is not synonymous with a completion of the uncoupling process. As marriage, or coupling, is a dramatic act of redefinition of self by two strangers as they move from autonomous identities to the construction of a joint biography, so uncoupling involves yet another redefinition of self as the participants move from mutual identity toward autonomy. It is this redefinition of self, for each participant, that completes the uncoupling. Divorce, then, may not be the final stage. In fact, divorce could be viewed as a nonstatus that is at some point on a continuum ranging from marriage (coupling) as an achieved status, to autonomy (uncoupling), likewise an achieved status. In other words, the uncoupling process might be viewed as a status transformation which is complete when the individual defines his salient status as "single" rather than "divorced." When the individual's newly constructed separate subworld becomes nomos-building—when it creates for the individual a sort of order in which he can experience his life as making sense—the uncoupling process is completed.

The completion of uncoupling does not occur at the same moment for each participant. For either or both of the participants, it may not occur until after the other has created a coupled identity with another person. With that step, the tentativeness is gone.

> When I learned of his intention to remarry, I did not realize how devastated I would be. It was just awful. I remember crying and crying. It was really a very bad thing that I did not know or expect. You really aren't divorced while that other person is still free. You still have a lot of your psychological marriage going—in fact, I'm still in that a little bit because I'm still single.

For some, the uncoupling may never be completed. One or both of the participants may never be able to construct a new and separate subworld that becomes self-validating. Witness, for example, the widow who continues to call herself "Mrs. John Doe," who associates with the same circle of friends, who continues to wear her wedding ring and observes wedding anniversaries. For her, the coupled identity is still a major mechanism for self-validation, even though the partner is gone.

In fact, death as a form of uncoupling may be easier for the significant other to handle than divorce. There exist ritual techniques for dealing with it, and there is no ambiguity. The relationship is gone. There will be no further interaction between the partners. With divorce, or any uncoupling that occurs through the volition of one or both of the partners, the interaction may continue long after the relationship has been formally terminated. For the significant other—the one left behind, without resources for self-validation—the continuing interaction between the partners presents obstacles to autonomy.

There's a point at which it's over. If your wife dies, you're a lot luckier, I think, because it's over. You either live with it, you kill yourself, or you make your own bed of misery. Unlike losing a wife through death, in divorce, she doesn't die. She keeps resurrecting it. I can't get over it, she won't die. I mean, she won't go away.

CONTINUITIES

Continuities are linkages between the partners that exist despite the formal termination of the coupled identity. Most important of these is the existence of shared loved ones—children, in-laws, and so on. Though in-laws may of necessity be excluded from the separately constructed subworlds, children can rarely be and, in their very existence, present continued substantiation of the coupled identity.

In many cases continuities are actively constructed by one or both of the participants after the formal termination of the relationship. These manufactured linkages speak to the difficulty of totally separating that common biography, by providing a continued mechanism for interaction. They may be constructed as a temporary bridge between the separated subworlds, or they may come to be a permanent interaction pattern. Symbolically, they seem to indicate caring on the part of either or both of the participants.

The wife moves out. The husband spends his weekend helping her get settled—hanging pictures, moving furniture.

The husband moves out, leaving his set of tools behind. Several years later, even after his remarriage, the tools are still there, and he comes to borrow them one at a time. The former wife is planning to move within the same city. The tools are boxed up, ready to be taken with her.

The wife has moved out, but is slow to change her mailing address. Rather than marking her forwarding address on the envelopes and returning them by mail, the husband either delivers them once a week or the wife picks them up.

The wife moves out. The husband resists dividing property with her that is obviously hers. The conflict necessitates many phone calls and visits.

The husband moves out. Once a week he comes to the house to visit with the children on an evening when the wife is away. When she gets home, the two of them occasionally go out to dinner.

A nice part of the marriage was shared shopping trips on Sunday afternoons. After the divorce, they still occasionally go shopping together.

The holidays during the first year of separation were celebrated as they always had been—with the whole family together.

During a particularly difficult divorce, the husband noted that he had finally succeeded in finding his wife a decent lawyer.

Continuities present unmeasurable variables in the uncoupling process. In this paper, uncoupling is defined as a reality socially constructed by the participants. The stages that mark the movement from a coupled identity to separate autonomous identities are characterized, using divorce for an ideal-type analysis. Yet, there is no intent to portray uncoupling as a compelling linear process from which there is no turning back. Such conceptualization would deny the human factor inherent in reality construction. Granted, as the original secret is moved from private to public, becoming increasingly objectivated, reconstructing the coupled identity becomes more and more difficult.

Each stage of objectivation acts as a closing of a door. Yet at any stage the process may be interrupted. The initiator may not find mechanisms of self-validation outside the coupling that reinforce his autonomy. Or the self-validation found outside the coupling may be the very stuff that allows the initiator to stay *in* the relationship. Or continuities may intervene and reconstruction of the coupled identity may occur, despite the degree of objectivation, as in the following case.

> Ellen met Jack in college. They fell in love and married. Jack had been blind since birth. He had pursued a college career in education and was also a musician. Both admired the independence of the other. In the marriage, she subordinated her career to his and helped him pursue a masters degree, as well as his musical interests. Her time was consumed by his needs—for transportation and the taping and transcribing of music for the musicians in his group. He was teaching at a school for the blind by day and performing as a musician at night. They had a son, and her life, instead of turning outward, as his, revolved around family responsibilities. She gained weight. Jack, after twelve years of marriage, left Ellen for his high school sweetheart. Ellen grieved for a while, then began patching up her life. She got a job, established her own credit, went back to college, and lost weight. She saw a lawyer, filed for divorce, joined Parents Without Partners, and began searching out singles groups. She dated. Throughout, Jack and Ellen saw each other occasionally and maintained a sexual relationship. The night before the divorce was final, they reconciled.

The uncoupling never was completed, though all stages of the process occurred, including the public objectivation that results from the initiation of the legal process. Ellen, in constructing an autonomous identity, became again the independent person Jack had first loved.[3] This, together with the continuities that existed between the two, created the basis for a common definition of the coupling as savable.

DISCUSSION

Berger and Kellner describe the process by which two individuals create a coupled identity for themselves. Here, we have started from the point of the coupled identity and examined the process by which people move out of such relationships. Using interview data, we have found that, although the renegotiation of separate realities is a complex web of subtle modifications, clear stages emerge which mark the uncoupling process. The emergent stages are like benchmarks which indicate the increasing objectivation of the changing definitions of reality, as these definitions move from the realm of the private to the public.

Beginning within the intimacy of the dyad, the initial objectivation occurs as the secret of the troubled marriage that the initiator has held is shared with the significant other. With this, the meaning has begun to move from the subjective to the objective. Definition negotiation begins. While attempting to negotiate a common definition, the initiator acts to increase the validation of his identity and place in the world by use of accompanying reconstructions of reality. The autonomy of the initiator increases as he finds self-validation outside the marriage and an ideology that supports the uncoupling. The increased autonomy of the initiator brings the significant other to accept a definition of the marriage as troubled, and they enter into the stage of "trying." The process continues, as counseling and separation further move the new definition into the public sphere.

The telling of others, the symbolic physical signs of the uncoupling, and the initiation of formal legal proceedings validate the increasing separation of the partners as they negotiate a new reality which is different from that constructed private sphere which validated their identity as a couple. Eventually, a redefinition of the mutual identity occurs in such a way that the joint biography is separated into two separate autonomous identities. As Berger and Kellner state that marriage is a dramatic act of redefinition of self by two individuals, so uncoupling is characterized by the same phenomenon. Self-realization, rather than coming from the coupledness, again comes from outside sources. Significant conversation again finds its source in nonoverlapping circles. The new definition of the relationship constructed by the participants has, in interaction with others, become common property.

Language is crucial to this process. Socially constructed worlds need validation. As conversation constantly reconfirms a coupled identity, so also does it act as the major validating mechanism for the move to singularity, not by specific articulation, but by the way in which it comes to revolve around the uncoupled identity as taken for granted.

The notion that the stages uncovered do broadly apply needs to be further confirmed. We need to know whether the process is invariant regardless of the heterosexuality, homosexuality, or social class of couples. Does it also apply for close friends? In what ways does the sex of the interviewer bias the data? Additionally, the stages in the process should be confirmed by interviews with both partners in a coupling. Due to the delicacy of the subject matter, this is difficult. In only one instance were both partners available to be interviewed for this study.

Notwithstanding these limitations, the findings which emerge deserve consideration.

Most significant of these is the existence of an underlying order in a phenomenon generally regarded as a chaotic and disorderly process. Undoubtedly the discovery of order was encouraged by the methodology of the study. The information was gained by retrospective analysis on the part of the interviewees. Certainly the passage of time allowed events to be reconstructed in an orderly way that made sense. Nonetheless, as was previously noted, the interviewees were all at various stages in the uncoupling process—some at the "secret" stage and some five years hence. Yet, the stages which are discussed here appeared without fail in every case and have been confirmed repeatedly by the other means described earlier.

In addition to this orderliness, the examination of the process of uncoupling discloses two other little-considered aspects of the process that need to be brought forth and questioned.

One is the caring. Generally, uncoupling is thought of as a conflict-ridden experience that ends as a bitter battle between two adversaries intent on doing each other in. Frequently, this is the case. Yet, the interviews for this study showed that in all cases, even the most emotion generating, again and again the concern of each of the participants for the other revealed itself. Apparently, the patterns of caring and responsibility that emerge between the partners in a coupling are not easily dispelled and in many cases persist throughout the uncoupling process and after, as suggested by the concept of continuities.

A second question that emerges from this examination of uncoupling is related to Berger and Kellner's thesis. They state that, for adults in our society, marriage is a significant validating relationship, one that is nomos-building. Marriage is, in fact, described as "a crucial nomic instrumentality" (1964:4). Though Berger and Kellner at the outset do delimit the focus of their analysis to marriage as an ideal type, the question to be answered is, To what degree is this characterization of marriage appropriate today?

Recall, for example, the quote from one interviewee: "I was never psychologically married. I always felt strained by attempts that coupled me into a marital unit. I was just never comfortable as 'Mrs.'" The interviews for this study suggest that the nomos-building quality assumed to derive from marriage to the individual should be taken as problematic rather than as given. Gouldner (1959) suggests that the parts of a unit vary in the degree to which they are interdependent. His concept of functional autonomy may be extended to illuminate the variable forms that marriage, or coupling, may take and the accompanying degree of nomos. A relationship may exist in which the partners are highly interdependent, and the coupled identity does provide the major mechanism for self-validation, as Berger and Kellner suggest. Yet it is equally as likely that the participants are highly independent, or "loosely coupled" (Weick, 1976; Corwin, 1977), wherein mechanisms for self-validation originate *outside* the coupling rather than from the coupling itself. The connection between the form of the coupling, the degree to which it is or is not nomos-building, and the subsequent implications for uncoupling should be examined in future research.

NOTES

1. For a sensitive and thought-provoking examination of these as integral components of divorce, see Willard Waller's beautiful qualitative study, *The Old Love and the New.*

2. This statement must be qualified. There are instances when the partners enter a stage of trying with shared definitions of the marriage as savable. The conditions under which the coupling can be preserved have to be negotiated. If they can arrive at a common definition of the coupling that is agreeable to both, the uncoupling process is terminated. But this analysis is of uncoupling, and there are two alternatives: (1) that they enter with common definitions of the marriage as savable but are not able to negotiate the conditions of the coupling so that the self-validation function is preserved or (2) that they enter the period of trying with opposing definitions, as stated here.

3. Waller interprets this phenomenon by using Jung's conceptualization of the container and the contained, analogous to the roles of initiator and significant other, respectively, in the present discussion. Notes Waller, "Or the contained, complicated by the process of divorcing, may develop those qualities whose lack the container previously deplored" (Waller: 163–168).

REFERENCES

Berger, Peter L. and Hansfried Kellner
1964 "Marriage and the Construction of Reality," *Diogenes,* 46: 1–23.

Berger, Peter L. and Thomas Luckmann
1966 *The Social Construction of Reality.* New York: Doubleday.

Bohanon, Paul
1971 *Divorce and After.* Garden City, N.Y.: Anchor.

Corwin, Ronald G.
1976 "Organizations as Loosely Coupled Systems: Evolution of a Perspective," Paper presented, Seminar on Educational Organizations as Loosely Coupled Systems. Palo Alto, Calif.

Davis, Murray S.
1973 *Intimate Relations,* New York: Free Press.

Epstein, Joseph E.
1975 *Divorce: The American Experience.* London: Jonathan Cape.

Goode, William J.
1956 *Women in Divorce.* New York: Free Press.

Gouldner, Alvin W.
1959 "Organizational Analysis," in R. K. Merton, L. Bloom, and L. S. Cottrell, Jr., eds. *Sociology Today.* New York: Basic Books, pp. 400–428.

Krantzler, Mel
1973 *Creative Divorce.* New York: New American Library.

Nichols, Jack
1975 *Men's Liberation: A New Definition of Masculinity.* New York: Penquin.

Sullivan, Judy
1974 *Mama Doesn't Live Here Anymore.* New York: Pyramid.

Waller, Willard
1930 *The Old Love and the New.* Carbondale: Southern Illinois University Press.

Walum, Laurel Richardson
1977 *The Dynamics of Sex and Gender: A Sociological Perspective.* Chicago: Rand McNally.

Weber, Max
1930 *The Protestant Ethic and the Spirit of Capitalism,* translated by Talcott Parsons. New York: Charles Scribner's Sons.

Weick, Karl E.
1976 "Educational Organizations as Loosely Coupled Systems," *Administrative Science Quarterly,* 21: 1–19.

Weiss, Robert
1975 *Marital Separation.* New York: Basic Books.

Review Questions

1. Briefly describe the following stages of "uncoupling": (1) initiation, (2) accompanying reconstructions and redefinitions, (3) self-validation outside marriage, (4) trying, (5) objectivation in the private sphere, (6) objectivation in the public sphere, (7) divorce, and (8) continuities.
2. Once a couple moves through several or all of these stages, is uncoupling inevitable? Why, or why not?
3. How do the "initiator" and the "significant other" each work to define the marital situation differently?
4. Vaughan's research shows that divorce is neither the beginning nor the end of the uncoupling process. Why? What part does the coupled world view play in the various stages of the process?

THE SECOND SHIFT, PART ONE: WHEN WORKING WIVES GET HOME

Arlie Russell Hochschild with Anne Machung

INTRODUCTION

She is not the same woman in each magazine advertisement, but she is the same idea. She has that working-mother look as she strides forward, briefcase in one hand, smiling child in the other. Literally and figuratively, she is moving ahead. Her hair, if long, tosses behind her; if it is short, it sweeps back at the sides, suggesting mobility and progress. There is nothing shy or passive about her. She is confident, active, "liberated." She wears a dark tailored suit, but with a silk bow or colorful frill that says, "I'm really feminine underneath." She has made it in a man's world without sacrificing her femininity. And she has done this on her own. By some personal miracle, this image suggests, she has managed to combine what 150 years of industrialization have split wide apart—child and job, frill and suit, female culture and male.

When I showed a photograph of a supermom like this to the working mothers I talked to in the course of [my] research, many responded with an outright laugh. One daycare worker and mother of two, ages three and five, threw back her head: "Ha! They've got to be *kidding* about her. Look at me, hair a mess, nails jagged, twenty pounds overweight. Mornings, I'm getting my kids dressed, the dog fed, the lunches made, the shopping list done. That lady's got a maid." Even working mothers who did have maids couldn't imagine combining work and family in such a carefree way. "Do you know what a baby *does* to your life, the two o'clock feedings, the four o'clock feedings?" Another mother of two said: "They don't show it, but she's whistling"—she imitated a whistling woman, eyes to the sky—"so she can't hear the din." They envied the apparent ease of the woman with the flying hair, but she didn't remind them of anyone they knew.

The women I interviewed—lawyers, corporate executives, word processors, garment pattern cutters, daycare workers—and most of their

SOURCE: From *The Second Shift: Working Parents and the Revolution at Home,* by Arlie Hochschild with Anne Machung.

husbands, too—felt differently about some issues: how right it is for a mother of young children to work a full-time job, or how much a husband should be responsible for the home. But they all agreed that it was hard to work two full-time jobs and raise young children.

How well do couples do it? The more women work outside the home, the more central this question. The number of women in paid work has risen steadily since before the turn of the century, but since 1950 the rise has been staggering. In 1950, 30 percent of American women were in the labor force; in 1986, it was 55 percent. In 1950, 28 percent of married women with children between six and seventeen worked outside the home; in 1986, it had risen to 68 percent. In 1950, 23 percent of married women with children under six worked. By 1986, it had grown to 54 percent. We don't know how many women with children under the age of one worked outside the home in 1950; it was so rare that the Bureau of Labor kept no statistics on it. Today half of such women do. Two-thirds of all mothers are now in the labor force; in fact, more mothers have paid jobs (or are actively looking for one) than nonmothers. Because of this change in women, two-job families now make up 58 percent of all married couples with children.

Since an increasing number of working women have small children, we might expect an increase in part-time work. But actually, 67 percent of the mothers who work have full-time jobs—that is, thirty-five hours or more weekly. That proportion is what it was in 1959.

If more mothers of young children are stepping into full-time jobs outside the home, and if most couples can't afford household help, how much more are fathers doing at home? As I began exploring this question I found many studies on the hours working men and women devote to housework and childcare. One national random sample of 1,243 working parents in forty-four American cities, conducted in 1965–66 by Alexander Szalai and his coworkers, for example, found that working women averaged three hours a day on housework while men averaged seventeen minutes; women spent fifty minutes a day of time exclusively with their children; men spent twelve minutes. On the other side of the coin, working fathers watched television an hour longer than their working wives, and slept a half hour longer each night. A comparison of this American sample with eleven other industrial countries in Eastern and Western Europe revealed the same difference between working women and working men in those countries as well. In a 1983 study of white middle-class families in greater Boston, Grace Baruch and R. C. Barnett found that working men married to working women spent only three-quarters of an hour longer each week with their kindergarten-aged children than did men married to housewives.

Szalai's landmark study documented the now familiar but still alarming story of the working woman's "double day," but it left me wondering how men and women actually felt about all this. He and his coworkers studied how people used time, but not, say, how a father felt about his twelve minutes with his child, or how his wife felt about it. Szalai's study revealed the visible surface of what I discovered to be a set of deeply emotional issues: What should a man and woman contribute to the family? How appreciated does each feel? How does each respond to subtle changes in the balance of marital power? How does each develop an unconscious "gender strategy" for coping with the work at home, with marriage, and, indeed, with life itself? These were the underlying issues.

But I began with the measurable issue of time. Adding together the time it takes to do a paid job and to do housework and childcare, I averaged estimates from the major studies on time use done in the 1960s and 1970s, and discovered that women worked roughly fifteen hours longer each week than men. Over a year, they worked an *extra month of twenty-four-hour days a year.* Over a dozen years, it was an extra year of twenty-four-hour days. Most women without children spend much more time than men on housework; with children, they devote more time to both housework and childcare. Just as there is a wage gap between men and women in the workplace, there is a "leisure gap" between them at home. Most women work one shift at the office or factory and a "second shift" at home.

Studies show that working mothers have higher self-esteem and get less depressed than housewives, but compared to their husbands, they're more tired and get sick more often. In Peggy Thoits's 1985 analysis of two large-scale surveys, each of about a thousand men and women, people were asked how often in the preceding week they'd experienced each of twenty-three symptoms of anxiety (such as dizziness or hallucinations). According to the researchers' criteria, working mothers were more likely than any other group to be "anxious."

In light of these studies, the image of the woman with the flying hair seems like an upbeat "cover" for a grim reality, like those pictures of Soviet tractor drivers smiling radiantly into the distance as they think about the ten-year plan. The Szalai study was conducted in 1965–66. I wanted to know whether the leisure gap he found in 1965 persists, or whether it has disappeared. Since most married couples work two jobs, since more will in the future, since most wives in these couples work the extra month a year, I wanted to understand what the wife's extra month a year meant for each person, and what it does for love and marriage in an age of high divorce.

With my research associates Anne Machung and Elaine Kaplan, I interviewed fifty couples very intensively, and I observed in a dozen homes. We first began interviewing artisans, students, and professionals in Berkeley, California, in the late 1970s. This was at the height of the women's movement, and many of these couples were earnestly and self-consciously struggling to modernize the ground rules of their marriages. Enjoying flexible job schedules and intense cultural support to do so, many succeeded. Since their circumstances were unusual they became our "comparison group" as we sought other couples more typical of mainstream America. In 1980 we located more typical couples by sending a questionnaire on work and family life to every thirteenth name—from top to bottom—of the personnel roster of a large, urban manufacturing company. At the end of the questionnaire, we asked members of working couples raising children under six and working full time jobs if they would be willing to talk to us in greater depth. Interviewed from 1980 through 1988, these couples, their neighbors and friends, their children's teachers, daycare workers and baby-sitters, form the heart of this [research].

When we called them, a number of baby-sitters replied as one woman did, "You're interviewing us? Good. We're human too." Or another, "I'm glad you consider what we do work. A lot of people don't." As it turned out, many daycare workers were themselves juggling two jobs and small children, and so we talked to them about that, too.

We also talked with other men and women who were not part of two-job couples; divorced parents who were war-weary veterans of two-job marriages, and traditional couples, to see how much of the strain we were seeing was unique to two-job couples.

I also watched daily life in a dozen homes during a weekday evening, during the week-end, and during the months that followed, when I was invited on outings, to dinner, or just to talk. I found myself waiting on the front doorstep as weary parents and hungry children tumbled out of the family car. I shopped with them, visited friends, watched television, ate with them, walked through parks, and came along when they dropped their children at daycare, often staying on at the baby-sitter's house after parents waved good-bye. In their homes, I sat on the living-room floor and drew pictures and played house with the children. I watched as parents gave them baths, read bedtime stories, and said good night. Most couples tried to bring me into the family scene, inviting me to eat with them and talk. I responded if they spoke to me, from time to time asked questions, but I rarely initiated conversations. I tried to become as unobtrusive as a family dog. Often I would base myself in the living room, quietly taking notes. Sometimes I would follow a wife upstairs or down, accompany a child on her way out to "help Dad" fix the car, or watch television with the other watchers. Sometimes I would break out of my peculiar role to join in the jokes they often made about acting like the "model" two-job couple. Or perhaps the joking was a subtle part of my role, to put them at ease so they could act more naturally. For a period of two to five years, I phoned or visited these couples to keep in touch even as I moved on to study the daily lives of other working couples—black, Chicano, white, from every social class and walk of life.

I asked who did how much of a wide variety of household tasks. I asked who cooks? Vacuums? Makes the beds? Sews? Cares for plants? Sends Christmas or Hanukkah cards? I also asked: Who washes the car? Repairs household appliances? Does the taxes? Tends the yard? I asked who did most household planning, who noticed such things as when a child's fingernails need clipping, cared more how the house looked or about the change in a child's mood.

Inside the Extra Month a Year

The women I interviewed seemed to be far more deeply torn between the demands of work and family than were their husbands. They talked with more animation and at greater length than their husbands about the abiding conflict between them. Busy as they were, women more often brightened at the idea of yet another interviewing session. They felt the second shift was *their* issue and most of their husbands agreed. When I telephoned one husband to arrange an interview with him, explaining that I wanted to ask him about how he managed work and family life, he replied genially, "Oh, this will *really* interest my *wife*."

It was a woman who first proposed to me the metaphor, borrowed from industrial life, of the "second shift." She strongly resisted the *idea* that homemaking was a "shift." Her family was her life and she didn't want it reduced to a job. But as she put it, "You're on duty at work. You come home, and you're on duty. Then you go back to work and you're on duty." After eight hours of adjusting insurance claims, she came home to put on the rice for dinner, care for her children, and wash laundry. Despite herself her home life *felt* like a second shift. That was the real story and that was the real problem.

Men who shared the load at home seemed just as pressed for time as their wives, and as torn between the demands of career and small children. . . . But the majority of men did not share the load at home. Some refused outright. Others refused more passively, often offering a loving shoulder to lean on, an understanding ear as their working wife faced the conflict they both saw as hers. At first it seemed to me that the problem of the second shift was hers. But I came to realize that those husbands who helped very little at home were often indirectly just as deeply affected as their wives by the need to do that work, through the resentment their wives feel toward them, and through their need to steel themselves against that resentment. Evan Holt, a warehouse furniture salesman, did very little housework and played with his four-year-old son, Joey, at his convenience. Juggling the demands of work with family at first seemed a problem for his wife. But Evan himself suffered enormously from the side effects of "her" problem. His wife did the second shift, but she resented it keenly, and half-consciously expressed her frustration and rage by losing interest in sex and becoming overly absorbed with Joey. One way or another, most men I talked with do suffer the severe repercussions of what I think is a transitional phase in American family life.

One reason women take a deeper interest than men in the problems of juggling work with family life is that even when husbands happily shared the hours of work, their wives felt more *responsible* for home and children. More women kept track of doctors' appointments and arranged for playmates to come over. More mothers than fathers worried about the tail on a child's Halloween costume or a birthday present for a school friend. They were more likely to think about their children while at work and to check in by phone with the baby-sitter.

Partly because of this, more women felt torn between one sense of urgency and another, between the need to soothe a child's fear of being left at daycare, and the need to show the boss she's "serious" at work. More women than men questioned how good they were as parents, or if they did not, they questioned why they weren't questioning it. More often than men, women alternated between living in their ambition and standing apart from it.

As masses of women have moved into the economy, families have been hit by a "speed-up" in work and family life. There is no more time in the day than there was when wives stayed home, but there is twice as much to get done. It is mainly women who absorb this "speed-up." Twenty percent of the men in my study shared housework equally. Seventy percent of men did a substantial amount (less than half but more than a third), and 10 percent did less than a third. Even when couples share more equitably in the work at home, women do two-thirds of the *daily* jobs at home, like cooking and cleaning up—jobs that fix them into a rigid routine. Most women cook dinner and most men change the oil in the family car. But, as one mother pointed out, dinner needs to be prepared every evening around six o'clock, whereas the car oil needs to be changed every six months, any day around that time, any time that day. Women do more childcare than men, and men repair more household appliances. A child needs to be tended daily while the repair of household appliances can often wait "until I have time." Men thus have more control over *when* they make their contributions than women do. They may be very busy with family chores but, like the executive who tells his secretary to "hold my calls," the man has more control over his time. The job of the working mother, like that of the secretary, is usually to "take the calls."

Another reason women may feel more strained than men is that women more often do two things at once—for example, write checks and return phone calls, vacuum and keep an eye on a three-year-old, fold laundry and think out the shopping list. Men more often cook dinner *or* take a child to the park. Indeed, women more often juggle three spheres—job, children, and housework—while most men juggle two—job and children. For women, two activities compete with their time with children, not just one.

Beyond doing more at home, women also devote *proportionately more* of their time at home to housework and proportionately less of it to childcare. Of all the time men spend working at home, more of it goes to childcare. . . . Since most parents prefer to tend to their children than clean house, men do more of what they'd rather do. More men than women take their children on "fun" outings to the park, the zoo, the movies. Women spend more time on maintenance, feeding and bathing children, enjoyable activities to be sure, but often less leisurely or "special" than going to the zoo. Men also do fewer of the "undesirable" household chores: fewer men than women wash toilets and scrub the bathroom.

As a result, women tend to talk more intently about being overtired, sick, and "emotionally drained." Many women I could not tear away from the topic of sleep. They talked about how much they could "get by on" . . . six and a half, seven, seven and a half, less, more. They talked about who they knew who needed more or less. Some apologized for how much sleep they needed—"I'm afraid I need eight hours of sleep"—as if eight were "too much." They talked about the effect of a change in baby-sitter, the birth of a second child, or a business trip on their child's pattern of sleep. They talked about how to avoid fully waking up when a child called them at night, and how to get back to sleep. These women talked about sleep the way a hungry person talks about food.

All in all, if in this period of American history, the two-job family is suffering from a speed up of work and family life, working mothers are its primary victims. It is ironic, then, that often it falls to women to be the "time and motion expert" of family life. Watching inside homes, I noticed it was often the mother who rushed children, saying, "Hurry up! It's time to go," "Finish your cereal now," "You can do that later," "Let's go!" When a bath is crammed into a slot between 7:45 and 8:00 it was often the mother who called out, "Let's see who can take their bath the quickest!" Often a younger child will rush out, scurrying to be first in bed, while the older and wiser one stalls, resistant, sometimes resentful: "Mother is always rushing us." Sadly enough, women are more often the lightning rods for family aggressions aroused by the speed-up of work and family life. They are the "villains" in a process of which they are also the primary victims. More than the longer hours, the sleeplessness, and feeling torn, this is the saddest cost to women of the extra month a year.

MARRIAGE IN THE STALLED REVOLUTION

Each marriage bears the footprints of economic and cultural trends which originate far outside marriage. A rise in inflation which erodes the earning power of the male wage, an expanding service sector which opens up jobs for women, new cultural images—like the woman with the flying hair—that make the working mother seem exciting, all these changes do not simply go on *around* marriage. They occur *within* marriage, and transform it. Problems between husbands and wives, problems which seem "individual" and "marital," are often individual experiences of powerful economic and cultural shock waves that are not caused by one person or two. Quarrels that erupt . . . result mainly from a friction between faster-changing women and slower-changing men, rates of change which themselves result from the different rates at which the industrial economy has drawn men and women into itself.

There is a "his" and "hers" to the economic development of the United States. In the latter part of the nineteenth century, it was mainly men who were drawn off the farm into paid, industrial work and who changed their way of life and their identity. At that point in history, men became more different from their fathers than women became from their mothers. Today the economic arrow points at women; it is women who are being drawn into wage work, and women who are undergoing changes in their way of life and identity. Women are departing more from their mothers' and grandmothers' way of life, men are doing so less.[1]

Both the earlier entrance of men into the industrial economy and the later entrance of women have influenced the relations *between* men and women, especially their relations within marriage. The former increase in the number of men in industrial work tended to increase the power of men, and the present growth in the number of women in such work has somewhat increased the power of women. On the whole, the entrance of men into industrial work did not destabilize the family whereas *in the absence of other changes,* the rise in female employment has gone with the rise in divorce. . . . Beneath the image of the woman with the flying hair, there has been a real change in women without much change in anything else.

The exodus of women into the economy has not been accompanied by a cultural understanding of marriage and work that would make this transition smooth. The workforce has changed. Women have changed. But most workplaces have remained inflexible in the face of the family demands of their workers, and at home, most men have yet to really adapt to the changes in women. This strain between the change in women and the absence of change in much else leads me to speak of a "stalled revolution."

A society which did not suffer from this stall would be a society *humanely* adapted to the fact that most women work outside the home. The workplace would allow parents to work part time, to share jobs, to work flexible hours, to take parental leaves to give birth, tend a sick child, or care for a well one. As Delores Hayden has envisioned in *Re-*

designing the American Dream, it would include affordable housing closer to places of work, and perhaps community-based meal and laundry services. It would include men whose notion of manhood encouraged them to be active parents and share at home. In contrast, a stalled revolution lacks social arrangements that ease life for working parents, and lacks men who share the second shift.

If women begin to do less at home because they have less time, if men do little more, if the work of raising children and tending a home requires roughly the same effort, then the questions of who does what at home and of what "needs doing" become key. Indeed they may become a source of deep tension in the marriage, tensions I explore here one by one.

• • •

My first question about who does what gave way to a series of deeper questions: What leads some working mothers to do all the work at home themselves—to pursue what I call a supermom strategy—and what leads others to press their husbands to share the responsibility and work of the home? Why do some men genuinely want to share housework and childcare, others fatalistically acquiesce, and still others actively resist?

How does each husband's ideas about manhood lead him to think he "should feel" about what he's doing at home and at work? What does he really feel? Do his real feelings conflict with what he thinks he should feel? How does he resolve the conflict? The same questions apply to wives. What influence does each person's consequent "strategy" for handling his or her feelings and actions with regard to the second shift affect his or her children, job, and marriage? Through this line of questioning, I was led to the complex web of ties between a family's needs, the sometime quest for equality, and happiness in modern marriage. . . .

We can describe a couple as rich or poor and that will tell us a great deal about their two-job marriage. We can describe them as Catholic, Protestant, Jewish, black, Chicano, Asian, or white and that will tell us something more. We can describe their marriage as a combination of two personalities, one "obsessive compulsive," say, and the other "narcissistic," and again that will tell us something. But knowledge about social class, ethnicity, and personality takes us only so far in understanding who does and doesn't share the second shift, and whether or not sharing the work at home makes marriages happier.

When I sat down to compare one couple that shared the second shift with another three that didn't, many of the answers that would seem obvious—a man's greater income, his longer hours of work, the fact that his mother was a housewife or his father did little at home, his ideas about men and women—all these factors didn't really explain why some women work the extra month a year and others don't. They didn't explain why some women seemed content to work the extra month, while others were deeply unhappy about it. When I compared a couple who was sharing and happy with another couple who was sharing but miserable, it was clear that purely economic or psychological answers were not enough. Gradually, I felt the need to explore how *deep* within each man and woman gender ideology goes. I felt the need to understand the ways in which some men and women seemed to be egalitarian "on top" but traditional "underneath," or the other way around. I tried to sensitize myself to the difference between shallow ideologies (ideologies which were contradicted by deeper feelings) and deep ideologies (which were reinforced by such feelings). I explored how each person reconciled ideology with his or her own behavior, that of a partner, and with the other realities of life. I felt the need to explore what I call loosely "gender strategies."

The Top and Bottom of Gender Ideology

A gender strategy is a plan of action through which a person tries to solve problems at hand, given the cultural notions of gender at play. To pursue a gender strategy, a man draws on beliefs about manhood and womanhood, beliefs that are forged in early childhood and thus anchored to deep emotions. He makes a connection between how he thinks about his manhood, what he feels about it, and what he does. It works in the same way for a woman.

A woman's gender ideology determines what sphere she *wants* to identify with (home or work) and how much power in the marriage she wants to have (less, more, or the same amount). I found three types of ideology of marital roles:—traditional, transitional, and egalitarian. Even though she works, the "pure" traditional wants to identify with her activities at home (as a wife, a mother, a neighborhood mom), wants her husband to base his at work and wants less power than he. The traditional man wants the same. The "pure" egalitarian, as the type emerges here, wants to identify with the same spheres her husband does, and to have an equal amount of power in the marriage. Some want the couple to be jointly oriented to the home, others to their careers, or both of them to jointly hold some balance between the two. Between the traditional and the egalitarian is the transitional, any one of a variety of types or blending of the two. But, in contrast to the traditional, a transitional woman wants to identify with her role at work as well as at home. Unlike the egalitarian, she believes her husband should base his identity more on work than she does. A typical transitional wants to identify *both* with the caring for the home, and with helping her husband earn money, but wants her husband to focus on earning a living. A typical transitional man is all for his wife working, but expects her to take the main responsibility at home too. Most men and women I talked with were "transitional." At least, transitional ideas came out when I asked people directly what they believed.

In actuality, I found there were contradictions between what people said they believed about their marital roles and how they seemed to *feel* about those roles. Some men seemed to me egalitarian "on top" but traditional "underneath." Others seemed traditional on top and egalitarian underneath.[2] Often a person attached deep feelings to his or her gender ideology in response to what I call early "cautionary tales" from childhood, as well as in response to his or her present situation. Sometimes these feelings *reinforced* the surface of a person's gender ideology. For example, the fear Nancy Holt was to feel of becoming a submissive mother, a "doormat," as she felt her mother had been, infused emotional steam into her belief that her husband Evan should do half the second shift.

On the other hand, the dissociation Ann Myerson was to feel from her successful career undermined her ostensible commitment both to that career and to sharing the second shift. Ann Myerson's surface ideology was egalitarian; she *wanted* to feel as engaged with her career as her husband was with his. This was her view of the "proper experience" of her career. She thought she *should* love her work. She *should* think it mattered. In fact, as she confessed in a troubled tone, she didn't love her work and didn't think it mattered. She felt a conflict between what she thought she ought to feel (according to her surface ideology)—emotionally involved in her career—and what she did feel—uninvolved with it. Among other things, her gender strategy was a way of trying to resolve that conflict.

The men and women I [interviewed], seem to have developed their gender ideology by unconsciously synthesizing certain cultural ideas with feelings about their past. But they also developed their ideology by taking opportunity into account. Sometime in adolescence they matched their personal assets against the opportunities available to men or women of their type; they saw which gender ideology best fit their circumstances, and—often regardless of their upbringing—they identified with a certain version of manhood or womanhood. It "made sense" to them. It felt like "who they were." For example, a woman sizes up her education, intelligence, age, charm, sexual attractiveness, her dependency needs, her aspirations, and she matches these against her perception of how women like her are doing in the job market and the "marriage market." What jobs could she get? What men? What are her chances for an equal marriage, a traditional marriage, a happy marriage, any marriage? Half-consciously, she assesses her chances—chances of an interesting, well-paid job are poor? her courtship pool has very traditional men? She takes these into account. *Then* a certain gender ideology, let's say a traditional one, will "make sense" to her.

She will embrace the ideology that suits her perception of her chances. She holds to a certain version of womanhood (the "wilting violet," say). She identifies with its customs (men opening doors), and symbols (lacy dress, long hair, soft handshakes, and lowered eyes). She tries to develop its "ideal personality" (deferential, dependent), not because this is what her parents taught her, not because this corresponds to how she naturally "is," but because these particular customs now *make sense* of her resources and of her overall situation in a stalled revolution. The same principle applies to men. However wholehearted or ambivalent, a person's gender ideology tends to fit their situation.

Gender Strategies

When a man tries to apply his gender ideology to the situations that face him in real life, unconsciously or not he pursues a gender strategy.[3] He outlines a course of action. He might become a "superdad"—working long hours and keeping his child up late at night to spend time with him or her. Or he might cut back his hours at work. Or he might scale back housework and spend less time with his children. Or he might actively try to share the second shift.

The term "strategy" refers both to his plan of action and to his emotional preparations for pursuing it. For example, he may require himself to suppress his career ambitions to devote himself more to his children, or suppress his responsiveness to his children's appeals in the course of steeling himself for the struggle at work. He might harden himself to his wife's appeals, or he might be the one in the family who "lets" himself see when a child is calling out for help.

In the families I [interviewed], then, I have tried to be sensitive to the fractures in gender ideology, the conflicts between what a person thinks he or she ought to feel and what he or she does feel, and to the emotional work it takes to fit a gender ideal when inner needs or outer conditions make it hard.

As this social revolution proceeds, the problems of the two-job family will not diminish. If anything, as more couples work two jobs these problems will increase. If we can't return to traditional marriage, and if we are not to despair of marriage altogether, it becomes vitally important to understand marriage as a magnet for the strains of the stalled revolution, and to understand gender strategies as the basic dynamic of marriage.

The Economy of Gratitude

The interplay between a man's gender ideology and a woman's implies a deeper interplay between his gratitude toward her, and hers toward him. For how a person wants to identify himself or herself influences what, in the back and forth of a marriage, will seem like a gift and what will not. If a man doesn't think it fits the kind of "man" he wants to be to have his wife earn more than he, it may become his "gift" to her to "bear it" anyway. But a man may also feel like the husband I interviewed, who said, "When my wife began earning more than me I thought I'd struck gold!" In this case his wife's salary is the gift, not his capacity to accept it "anyway." When couples struggle, it is seldom simply over who does what. Far more often, it is over the giving and receiving of gratitude.

FAMILY MYTHS

As I watched couples in their own homes, I began to realize that couples sometimes develop "family myths"—versions of reality that obscure a core truth in order to manage a family tension.[4] Evan and Nancy Holt managed an irresolvable conflict over the distribution of work at home through the myth that they now "shared it equally." Another couple unable to admit to the conflict came to believe "we aren't competing over who will take responsibility at home; we're just dreadfully busy with our careers." Yet another couple jointly believed that the husband was bound hand and foot to his career "because his work demanded it," while in fact his careerism covered the fact that they were avoiding each other. Not all couples need or have family myths. But when they do arise, I believe they often manage key tensions which are linked, by degrees, to the long hand of the stalled revolution.

• • •

[Toward the end of my twelve years of interviewing, I found that] more couples *wanted* to share and imagined that they did. Dorothy Sims, a personnel director, summed up this new blend of idea and reality. She eagerly explained to me that she and her husband Dan "shared all the housework," and that they were "equally involved in raising their nine-month-old son Timothy." Her husband, a refrigerator salesman, applauded her career and "was more pleased than threatened by her high salary"; he urged her to develop such competencies as reading ocean maps, and calculating interest rates (which she'd so far "resisted learning") because these days "a woman should." But one evening at dinner, a telling episode occurred. Dorothy had handed Timothy to her husband while she served us a chicken dinner. Gradually, the baby began to doze on his father's lap. "When do you want me to put Timmy to bed?" Dan asked. A long silence followed during which it occurred to Dorothy—then, I think, to her husband—that this seemingly insignificant question hinted to me that it was *she*, not he, or "they," who usually decided such matters. Dorothy slipped me a glance, put her elbows on the table, and said to her husband in a slow, deliberate voice, "So, what do *we* think?"

When Dorothy and Dan described their "typical days," their picture of sharing grew even less convincing. Dorothy worked the same nine-hour day at the office as her husband. But she came home to fix dinner and to tend Timmy while Dan fit in a squash game three nights a week from six to seven (a good time for his squash partner). Dan read the newspaper more often and slept longer.

Compared to the early interviews, women in the later interviews seemed to speak more often in passing of relationships or marriages that had ended for some other reason but of which it "was also true" that he "didn't lift a finger at home." Or the extra month alone did it. . . . But women like Dorothy Sims, who simply add to their extra month a year a new illusion that they aren't doing it, represent a sad alternative to the woman with the flying hair—the woman who doesn't think that's who she is.

NOTES

1. This is more true of white and middle-class women than it is of black or poor women, whose mothers often worked outside the home. But the trend I am talking about—an increase from 20 percent of women in paid jobs in 1900 to 55 percent in 1986—has affected a large number of women.

2. In a 1978 national survey, Joan Huber and Glenna Spitze found that 78 percent of husbands think that if husband and wife both work full time, they should share housework equally (*Sex Stratification: Children, Housework and Jobs.* New York: Academic Press, 1983). In fact, the husbands of working wives at most average a third of the work at home.

3. The concept of "gender strategy" is an adaptation of Ann Swidler's notion of "strategies of action." In "Culture in Action—Symbols and Strategies," *American Sociological Review* 51 (1986): 273–86, Swidler focuses on how the individual uses aspects of culture (symbols, rituals, stories) as "tools" for constructing a line of action. Here, I focus on aspects of culture that bear on our ideas of manhood and womanhood, and I focus on our emotional preparation for and the emotional consequences of our strategies.

4. For the term *family myth* I am indebted to Antonio J. Ferreira, "Psychosis and Family Myth," *American Journal of Psychotherapy* 21 (1967): 186–225.

REFERENCES

Baruch, Grace K., and Rosalind Barnett
1983 "Correlates of Fathers' Participation in Family Work: A Technical Report." Working paper no. 106. Wellesley College, Center for Research on Women, Wellesley, Mass.

Szalai, Alexander (ed.).
1972 *The Use of Time: Daily Activities of Urban and Suburban Populations in Twelve Countries.* The Hague: Mouton.

Thoits, Peggy.
1986 "Multiple Identities: Examining Gender and Marital Status Differences in Distress." *American Sociological Review* 51 : 259–72.

Review Questions

1. Why does Hochschild call the unequal division of labor in households of working parents a "stalled revolution"?
2. In Hochschild's study, which spouse usually did more of the daily (as opposed to occasional) chores, did two things at once, and spent more time on housework than on child care?
3. What differences did Hochschild find among the traditional, transitional, and egalitarian couples? How did husbands' and wives' espoused gender ideologies match what they actually felt and did?
4. What is the result of the stalled revolution for the marital economy of gratitude?

Suggested Readings: Interaction in Institutional Contexts: Family

Goode, William. *After Divorce.* New York: Free Press, 1956.
——. "The Theoretical Importance of Love," *American Sociological Review,* 24 (February 1959): 38–47.
Gutman, Herbert G. *The Black Family in Slavery and Freedom, 1750–1925.* New York: Pantheon, 1976.
Lopata, Helena Z. *Occupation Housewife.* New York: Oxford University Press, 1971.
Motz, Annabelle B. "The Family as a Company of Players," *Transaction,* 2 (March–April 1965): 27–30.
Riessman, Catherine Kohler. *Divorce Talk: Women and Men Make Sense of Personal Relationships.* New Brunswick, N.J.: Rutgers University Press, 1990.
Rothman, Barbara Katz. *Recreating Motherhood.* New York: Norton, 1989.
Rubin, Lillian Breslow. *Worlds of Pain: Life in the Working-Class Family.* New York: Basic Books, 1976.

——. *Intimate Strangers.* New York: Harper & Row, 1983.

——. *Erotic Wars: What Happened to the Sexual Revolution?* New York: Farrar, Straus, and Giroux, 1990.

Stack, Carol B. *All Our Kin: Strategies for Survival in a Black Community.* New York: Harper & Row, 1974.

Stein, Peter, ed. *Single Life: Unmarried Adults in Social Context.* New York: St. Martin's Press, 1981.

Vaughan, Diane. *Uncoupling: Turning Points in Intimate Relationships.* New York: Oxford University Press, 1988.

Waller, Willard, "The Rating and Dating Complex," *The American Sociological Review,* 2 (1937): 727–734.

Weitzman, Lenore J. *The Marriage Contract: Spouses, Lovers and the Law.* New York: Free Press, 1983.

B. Education

THE CONCEPT OF EDUCATION AS A SET OF ACTIVITIES SEPARATE FROM WHAT transpires in the course of everyday interactions is relatively new. Although all societies throughout human history have developed family systems, it is only in the past two or three centuries that the roles of teacher and student have occupied more than a tiny fraction of the population. Schooling has become so widespread and highly valued today that we can scarcely imagine that it was not always so. We begin dividing our time and attention between the family and the school at about the same age that generation after generation of people living in pre-industrial societies were beginning to move directly into work and apprenticeship roles.

How did we come from the point where schooling was a luxury for those (of any age) who had sufficient money and leisure time to the point where schooling is compulsory for many years of one's life and intimately tied to other institutions of our culture? The most obvious answer is that the skills required of individuals by an industrial, technological society are more *diverse* and more *specialized* than the skills needed to survive in an agricultural age. Parents today simply cannot give their children enough information to carry them through their adult lives, while earlier generations of parents usually could. Furthermore, factories and corporations benefit from having skills taught in schools, rather than having to train and educate workers themselves. Thus, one explanation for the rise of a separate educational institution is that it is functional in economic terms, both for soon-to-be workers and for employers.

Other less obvious factors have also contributed to the growth and spread of schooling in the United States. Legislation removing children from factory work in the late 1800s, often seen as a humanitarian movement to protect children from dreadful working conditions, was actually passed in order to keep children from competing with adults for employment opportunities in the urban centers. Once large numbers of children were "freed" from employment by this legislation, the question became what to do with them. The answer was often schooling, and in time education came to be seen as a duty of the young.

But schooling was not made *compulsory* until the early 1900s, when vast waves of Southern- and Eastern-European immigrants arrived in our country. These groups were less likely to speak English or to have economically valued skills than previous immigrants, and "Americanizing" their children was attempted by enacting compulsory-education laws. Schooling thus came to be seen as a vehicle for socialization, and education as a prime factor in upward social mobility.

As a result of the growing number of students, more and more jobs were created in the educational field and in allied industries—from teacher to administrator, from text-book publisher to cap-and-gown manufacturer. It is, you will agree, unlikely that individuals who earn a living from these activities would favor decreasing the role of schooling in society. In fact, these categories of people have worked consistently throughout this century to protect their own employment by expanding the educational sector.

As for post-secondary education, many of the same forces (except for compulsory legislation) have been operating to increase its importance. In addition, the G.I. Bill (providing tuition and living expenses for former military personnel) and the availability of federally financed college loans led to a virtual explosion of college enrollments in the post-World War II period. That explosion continues to the present day in terms of the *proportion* of "college-age" people who are enrolled (rather than the actual number, which is declining because of lower birth rates after the post-war baby boom). Currently, over half of those graduating from high school are attending college. Only about half of these will complete a four-year course, but the trend is sufficient to lead many observers to speak of the United States as a mass-educated society, especially when we consider that many adults are entering or returning to college and that graduate education is also being pursued at unprecedented rates. The "pull" of the learning environment is only part of the story; a "push" is also provided by employers who rely on the college or graduate degree as a criterion for employment. The meaning and value of these degrees has changed substantially in recent decades, because of the increasing number of college graduates. A college diploma may be the required ticket to board the economic train, but it no longer guarantees one a seat.

The institutionalization of schooling has had a number of important consequences for the ways in which we form our self-concepts and interact with others. The reader will recall our earlier discussion of the effects of age-segregation and age-grading on social interaction among the old and the young. We can further note that the age-segregation associated with mass schooling has, in conjunction with other societal trends, shaped new social roles—childhood, adolescence, and youth. Childhood was little different from adulthood until industrialization, urbanization, schooling, and a new religious view of the very young as needing moral molding were underway. Adolescence was not seen as a stage of life until around 1900, when educators began arguing that teenagers (the age of high-school students) had special needs. Of course, teenagers probably did *not* have special needs before this time, since their lives were essentially indistinguishable from the lives of their elders. Since the Second World War, another stage of movement toward adulthood has been created—youth—corresponding to the ages of college (and perhaps graduate-school) attendance. Each of these stages now has a special role specifying rights and obligations of those occupying the age-status. In sum, as entry into work roles is postponed for longer and longer periods, and as new stages of schooling emerge to occupy the time and energy of the postponers, our conceptions of what it means to be a certain age have changed and new social roles have been added.

These processes have also meant that the young person today interacts with new types of significant others within new organizational arrangements. The *teacher* and the *peer group* of age-mates have become sources of socialization to be reckoned with. Both may have a significant impact on the values, self-concept, aspirations, and behavior of the young in their roles as student, child, adolescent, and youth, as well as in their future roles as adults. The *bureaucratic* style of organizing the activities of large numbers of students and educators is a rather rigid system for keeping order and processing people. Some of the key features of educational bureaucracies, such as the grading system of evaluating student performance, have often been cited as producing competition and frustration among students. The informal systems emerging to cope with bureaucratic rules and regulations—often termed the *student culture*—are also modern developments that could not have arisen without schools.

The articles in this section cannot, of course, detail all the consequences of the rise of schooling or of educational systems for social interaction. In the first selection, entitled "Skimming and Dumping at Penrose High: Career Mobility and the Perpetuation of Inequality," Demie Kurz takes a close look at the teachers, students, administrators, and parents associated with "Penrose High School." She approaches the school as an example of a bureaucratic organization with formal and informal rules and processes. What she documents is a fairly common practice of teachers trying to enhance their own prestige by attempting to select classes with prestigious students. The students they considered to be ideal were the high achievers. Low achievers were often "dumped" into the classes of teachers with less power and seniority in the system. How does this practice come about? What do parents and administrators contribute to the dumping process? What are the consequences of dumping for public-school students? These are some of the important questions Kurz addresses.

The college campus was the focus of research by Howard Becker, Blanche Geer, and Everett C. Hughes. Over twenty years ago, they examined in detail the workings of a midwestern state university. What struck them most forcibly was the degree to which students' and professors' academic roles were structured around grades, as we see in "Making the Grade." Faculty members often deplored the students' emphasis on grades, and students themselves often felt that grades interfered with learning. Both groups, however, found that their actions and interactions centered on the giving and receiving of grades.

Dissension, upheaval, and even revolution have shaken college and university campuses in the decades since this piece of research was undertaken. As we noted previously, economic and social changes have also affected the importance and value of a college education. One enduring structural feature of most colleges, however, is the grading system. Although college students now face a different set of contingencies after college than the students whom Becker, Geer, and Hughes observed, we submit that much still hinges on grades and that, therefore, this research can tell us much about the formal and informal structuring of the school experience today, as it did in that earlier generation.

Both of the articles in this section present pictures that are at odds with the official version of what is, and what is supposed to be, taking place in the educational process. By looking behind the scenes at the lives of the actors involved in the school, and by listening to those who are actually "processing" or being "processed" by the bureaucracies, the authors are able to document some of the ways in which the educational institution can shape the lives of the young.

SKIMMING AND DUMPING AT PENROSE HIGH: CAREER MOBILITY AND THE PERPETUATION OF INEQUALITY

Demie Kurz

INTRODUCTION

SOCIOLOGISTS AND EDUCATIONAL RESEARCHERS HAVE LONG BEEN CONcerned with what causes and perpetuates inequality in schools (Coleman et al., 1961, 1966; Coleman and Hoffer, 1986; Ryan, 1976; Jencks et al., 1972, 1979; Lightfoot, 1978, 1983; Bowles and Gintis, 1976). We still find today that many students labeled "low-achieving"—those most in need of positive educational experiences—are precisely the ones whom some, maybe most, teachers consider undesirable. Teachers who have the most power and seniority often manage to "skim" for their own classes the students who "achieve" in conventional terms and to "dump" undesirable students into the classes of the newest and least powerful teachers.

Why does this situation persist? Why do teachers skim and dump? What social processes foster an educational system that often labels as undesirable and fails to serve a segment of the school's clientele?

In this article, I look in depth at one school—and especially at its teachers—to suggest answers to these questions. We should keep in mind as we study teachers that this occupational group is not totally unique. It shares features with other occupations, especially those with clients to serve. Julius Roth (1973) has noted that many professionals (like physicians) and semiprofessionals (like nurses) attempt to control who their clients are. Everett Hughes (1956) was first to point out that as workers advance in their jobs, they try to delegate "dirty work," or unrewarding, low-prestige work, to others. For workers who are client-servers, dirty work consists of work with undesirable clients (Walsh and Elling, 1968). As a consequence, undesirable clients are often delegated by the most senior and powerful to be served by workers who are less powerful and are said to be less qualified (Becker, 1955).

Psychiatrists, for example, tend to prefer young, intelligent clients of at least middle-class background. Such clients have a higher probability of achieving success as adults than working-class clients. Psychiatry, like teaching, is a field in which practitioners have little means of assessing the quality of their work. Therefore, when well-established psychiatrists in private practice choose clients who are likely to succeed in life, they can employ these successes as testaments to their professional effectiveness. In the same vein, by avoiding lower-status and/or severely ill clients, these psychiatrists can minimize doubting their own abilities. Undesirable patients, in turn, get dumped on younger, less established psychiatrists, clinical psychologists, psychiatric social workers, and paraprofessionals who are employed by public mental-health facilities (Lorber and Satow, 1977).

Like other client-serving professionals, teachers want "clean" clients to enhance their work experiences, their sense of accomplishment, and their status. Teachers, however, have special problems actually controlling their clientele. First, the fact that schooling is compulsory guarantees that *some* teachers will have to do dirty work. Second, teaching is a "horizontal" career (Becker, 1952). There is no formal career ladder for teachers, no set of distinctive ranks like, say, "junior teacher," "regular teacher," "super teacher." If teachers advance, they become administrators and no longer teach. Because of the lack of ranks, there are no formal mechanisms for passing *down* dirty clients. Finally, teachers have less power to resist dumping by administrators than do other professional groups (Bidwell, 1965; Corwin, 1965; Lortie, 1969).

Given these constraints, how do teachers manage to skim and dump particular clients? We turn now to the staff and students of Henry Penrose High School to see how one school—typical, I believe, of many suburban high schools—has systematized the processes of skimming and dumping.

THE RESEARCH SITE AND METHOD

A decade ago, I undertook a year of fieldwork at Henry Penrose High School, a recently constructed, large, two-story brick building located in a middle-class suburb of 80,000 inhabitants. Penrose High enrolls some 5,000 students, of whom 80 percent are white, 19 percent are black, and 1 percent are other ethnic and foreign students. The teaching staff consists of slightly more than 200 faculty members, most of whom are well educated and hold at least a masters degree. Over 90 percent of the faculty are white. School officials claim that Penrose High has an outstanding academic record and even a national reputation for excellence.

In my year at Henry Penrose High School, I conducted interviews and conversations with representative samples of the school's staff: teachers, department heads, counselors, assistant principals, all four principals, and department supervisors. I observed classes and faculty meetings. I analyzed school documents and literature.

CAREER ENHANCEMENT AND THE PERPETUATION OF INEQUALITY

In the following section I examine the origins and nature of "skimming" and "dumping." First I consider why the students who are below average in academic performance are shunned as undesirables by those who are hired to teach them. I then examine how teachers negotiate with their supervisors to skim and dump. Last, I discuss how these practices are tolerated in a community that is well aware of them.

Like many or most teachers, those at Penrose High prefer to teach students who perform well. They are rewarded by administrators and the school board for evidence of achievement—producing students who score high on standardized tests, win competitions and awards, and gain admission to prestigious colleges. Obviously, it is more difficult to produce the desired product if one begins with lower-achieving students. Furthermore, the self-images of many Penrose teachers militate against an interest in teaching such students. These teachers feel they were trained to teach their disciplines at higher levels than the abilities of their students permit. They report feeling bored by the elementary level of the material. Finally, teachers expect lower-track classes to present discipline problems that they are eager to avoid.

As a result, most teachers at Penrose High are in the business of negotiating with department heads and administrators to win as many high- or at least middle-track classes as possible and avoid low-track classes. Competition also exists for the senior students (thought to be most capable), while freshmen (thought to be least capable) are avoided. A few teachers are repeatedly more successful than others in these negotiations (in which seniority is important but not, by itself, sufficient). A small number of those most junior and least adept at negotiation habitually find themselves with large numbers of low-track students. The most and least desirable students having been accounted for, most of the faculty teach the majority of students in between. Teachers in each of these groups frequently negotiate to better or maintain their positions.

In their attempts to select their clientele, Penrose teachers face certain obstacles, as well as gaining a certain amount of support, from the community and from school administrators. For instance, upper-middle-class parents—whose children tend to do well in school—are active in promoting classes and programs for high-achieving students.

Several nearby communities that are predominantly upper-middle class provide a point of reference for Penrose parents, who are able to say with conviction and credibility, "The moment they let the standards go down around here, that's the moment I move to— —." Because the prospect of mass migration of the socioeconomic cream of the community into a more attractive school district is a serious issue in any prosperous town, these parents exert considerable influence on policy and curriculum.

The option of moving into a more desirable school district is not open, by and large, to parents of lower-tracked students, who come disproportionately (but not solely) from less wealthy households and from minority backgrounds. These parents, who cannot use economic pressure or presume on social acquaintance to promote their wishes, must rely principally on verbal protest in public meetings and on the desire of district officials to avoid embarrassment and confrontation.

The parents of low-tracked students do succeed in extracting some concessions and improved services for their children; but Penrose's reputation for "academic excellence"—that is, for the production of nationally high-achieving students—remains the dominant concern and rule for action among administrators. So the influence of pressure groups poses only a *potential* threat to Penrose teachers' freedom to select their clientele. In practice the overall effect has been to promote, rather than constrain, the tendency of senior, more competent, and more favored teachers to dump unattractive clients on their less well-protected colleagues.

Administrators have the power and authority to pose more of a problem. In general, though, top-level administrators feel that their own careers are best served by protecting and nurturing Penrose's outstanding performance on such traditional indicators of academic success as test scores, college acceptance rates, and state and national student prizes. This usually means giving priority to educating those students most likely to pull off winning performances—those already performing at average or above average levels. Rarely did any school board members or superintendents suggest changing the indicators of success by, for example, trying to dramatically raise the showing of students beginning from a lower point on the ladder.

Lower-level administrators with different sorts of concerns can also constrain teachers' autonomy in selecting students. Department heads must somehow staff all classes. They are constantly in the business of negotiating with individual teachers to try to assign lower-track classes without creating morale problems among the faculty. Principals and assistant principals, whose job is to maintain a satisfactory level of order in halls and classrooms, negotiate with teachers over the placement of notorious student troublemakers. These pressures militate against teacher control of clientele.

As I observed the array of actors vying in the complex system of negotiation at Penrose High, I noted that teachers tend to remain in, and become identified with, one of the three categories mentioned above: the small number who manage to get most of the "top" students; the small number who habitually teach the "bottom" students; and the majority, who spend their years teaching middle-level students. In the following section I examine each of the three groups and the processes by which they gain, maintain, and lose the ability to select their clienteles.

TEACHERS AND SELECTIVITY

Elite Teachers: The Academic "Specialists"

Among senior teachers, a handful are recognized as having special expertise in their subjects. (A prestigious graduate degree or a publication often confers this status.) Because of their perceived expertise, members of this small elite teach mostly Advanced Placement (college-level) and Honors classes with upper-level students. To secure and maintain this position of privilege, the "specialist" must first pursue a good working relationship with the department head, generally by supporting his or her aims and policies. Second, the teacher must produce high enrollments and exceptional student performance. Finally, the teacher should, if possible, court and utilize the support of parents of superior students.

Competition from other departments as well as successful attacks from parents lobbying for the interests of average and below-average students are ever-present threats to the autonomy of these teachers and to their resulting privileged access to superior students. When, in a particular case, administrators forced a selective social studies-English program to open its doors to a random selection of students, teacher job satisfaction among the elite declined noticeable. ("Regular" teachers, who had lobbied for the change, reported increased satisfaction.)

Changes in the tracking system also pose a major threat to the quality-control strategies of elite teachers. Parents of average and below-average students persuaded the administration to reduce the number of tracks (ability levels) so that their children would have more contact with brighter students and better teachers. The morale of the "elite" teachers dropped. They complained they could not teach at the high level to which they were accustomed.

Teachers at the Middle Level

The majority of teachers who have been at Penrose High more than three years learn and put into practice strategies for avoiding the dirtiest work (i.e., assignment to the lowest-performing classes). They cannot rise to the level of their academic-specialist colleagues and have little contact with outstanding students. There is, however, a range of "middle" students; teachers use several means to get to teach students at its upper end.

First, teachers at the same level of seniority frequently strike bargains to "take turns" with colleagues, teaching "better" classes in alternate years. Teachers feel some assurance that they will have the opportunity to teach a variety of middle-range students during their tenure at the school. Still, most teachers also want the rewarding experience of teaching some of the higher-achieving students. Those with close ties to their department heads may ask for more prestigious assignments, but mobility through this route is limited because department heads are wary of charges of favoritism.

Realizing the importance of gaining a reputation as something of a specialist fairly early in one's career, a teacher may develop a new class or a new approach to a subject. For example, one social studies teacher created a non-Western cultures class that he found very satisfying to teach. While it was not a "top-level" (or most selective) class, prerequisites eliminated the least-desirable students, and self-selection took care of a good many more in the below-average group. Developing this course gave a significant boost to the teacher's status; he is someone with a "special" class and "special" abilities to teach it. He strengthens this identity by producing "results," "good" students, and then uses this identity to try to bargain for greater selectivity next time around.

But a successful result is not automatic. Another teacher, younger and newer, developed a course in Afro-American studies. Not wanting to exclude anyone from what she thought was an important subject, she placed no restrictions on enrollment. Her class drew some top performers, but counselors also sent students who did not fit in anywhere else and needed an elective. Shortly, she began to feel that the program had become a "dumping ground," a place for unwanted students. She found in addition that, because of the disparate levels of student interest and ability, it was a difficult class to teach.

In the Penrose High system, the teacher who does not complain about teaching a few less desirable students will soon be teaching many more of them. Praise from superiors—encouragement to keep teaching "open" classes—comes quickly. Younger teachers may initially welcome such flattery, but its appeal is short-lived:

> When you teach low-ability students they give you this line: "You're so good with these kids." It's just a line to make you believe you should keep teaching them.

> If you get low-ability students they tell you you should be a specialist because you're good at teaching low-ability students. They try to flatter your ego that way, but it's really a con.

Too much interest in low-achieving students may block or delay upward career mobility. The teacher is effectively "typecast."

> *Teacher:* I don't want to be considered the specialist who just takes these classes. I think that's happening and that people will come to say that I'm good at low-ability but not at academic teaching.
>
> *Interviewer:* You think that's happened already?
>
> *Teacher:* Yes, I definitely do. I think it's happened already. As a matter of fact, someone who was pretty high up in this school, almost to the top, told me that in terms of my future career, I should stop teaching so many of these students.

Teachers' concerns to advance on the career ladder thus may conflict with the interests of department heads who are eager to identify and label "low-achiever specialists" so that they will have uncomplaining staff on whom to foist dirty work. As one department chair said:

> We really need the specialists. Otherwise it would affect the morale of the department. Things would be very difficult if we had to force people to take these jobs.

In addition to developing special classes, teachers at the middle level sometimes create specialized programs. Again the goal may have more to do with skimming and dumping than education, and allies in the school administration and the public are helpful.

One program director illustrated the successful use of skimming. He developed materials and techniques for bringing students working just below par up to their grade level. He convinced the principal to give him exactly the population that he needed for his program, and the students' scores improved. Since the production of "results" looked good for the school, the principal was also able to claim credit for these achievements. Not surprisingly then, the principal continued to grant this teacher the privilege of choosing his students.

In a similar case, however, a department head actively intervened to reduce selectivity. He feared that if the program skimmed close-to-average students, other teachers would resent getting those even further below average.

A third program, an evening program for dropouts, demonstrates the substitution of dumping strategies for skimming. Despite the high status of the program director, a former principal, he could not secure the right to select students. Through persistent negotiating—in which he made use of his seniority and the success of his students in college admissions—he did gain the right to expel students who had three unexcused absences. The director was confident he could use this power to dump those with little interest or ability. Still, principals have pressured him to take in troublesome students. He feels that when he retires and is replaced by someone with less power, the program will lose all control over its clientele.

At Penrose High, all programs for middle-level students faced pressure to accept discipline problems and low achievers. An assistant principal said:

> I do not try to put acting-out kids in the programs, because they'll destroy them. But sometimes I must.

For their part, program directors and teachers fear the results. One teacher put it:

> Trying to avoid being a dumping ground is trying to avoid other people putting their problems in your classes.

The middle-level teacher who cannot maintain selectivity gets not only "problems" but also a loss of prestige.

Teachers of the Lowest-Achieving Students

Two groups consistently are assigned primarily low-achieving students. The first is the small number of teachers who choose lower-track assignments, who believe that the teaching profession should focus on helping students who most need help. These ideological "deviants" feel they must find kindred spirits and role models among like-minded teachers at other schools, because their own colleagues at Penrose High denigrate them and their efforts. As one said:

> I tried to explain to other teachers what I was attempting to accomplish with my classes, but they still asked me how I could stand it.

According to another:

> Teachers look down on those of us who teach low-ability students as less professional. They have a snotty attitude. They don't understand it, and they think it's less professional to teach these students.

These teachers may be shunned because they remind the careerists of a more idealistic, self-sacrificing philosophy.

The other group consistently assigned low-performance students is new teachers. The stated rationale for this policy is that new teachers are not yet prepared for academically higher-level students—that it takes a teacher longer to develop the expertise for higher-level students than for lower-achieving ones. What is more likely is that schools, like many other organizations, start newcomers off with the dirty work that no one else wants. Factory workers, for example, must often spend years working on the night shift before they have earned the seniority necessary to transfer to the preferred day shift (Robboy, 1979). In many organizations, starting at the bottom is justified as a means for newcomers to "learn the ropes" and to prove their loyalty.

Some new teachers believe the school's "official" rationale; the organization can, therefore, play on their insecurities. The majority, however, readily state that the main reason new teachers are given these students is that "no one else wants them." The presence of new teachers to staff unwanted classes keeps senior teachers from having to take more of them. New teachers tolerate this situation because they expect to be tenured after three years, at which time they, too, will be able to dump undesirables on their younger colleagues.

SUMMARY AND CONCLUSIONS

I have analyzed how teachers in one high school attempt to improve their work conditions and gain prestige and status in their school and community. The primary mechanism they use is skimming and dumping students, that is, avoiding dirty clients and dirty work. Like other professionals, teachers want to develop their own expertise based on their own image of what constitutes an ideal client, free from outside interference (Becker, 1955). Teachers accomplish skimming and dumping by foisting low-achieving students onto willing teachers or newcomers, winning political favors from department heads, developing specialized and advanced classes, and shrewdly using parental pressure.

One unintended consequence of teachers' pursuit of career advancement and job satisfaction is a low level of concern and effort for all but the highest-achieving students. Because low-achieving students are defined as dirty clients, they systematically are denied the best teachers and a proportionate share of the school's resources. This system actively creates failure: once a program or a class is labeled a dumping ground, a further denial of resources and a lowering of expectations result (Rosenthal and Jacobsen, 1966). Its teacher may be incapable of producing successes.

The practices of skimming and dumping at Penrose, or at any other high school, do not operate in isolation. They result from the norms and values of both the community and the larger society. Like most schools, Penrose High functions to socialize students to accept and perpetuate the status quo. For the most part, the high achievers are unaware of the social factors that make their successes possible. Students who are skimmed believe they are superior and more meritorious than the others. Likewise, students who are dumped in large part internalize their failures, rather than seeing sociological factors such as classism and racism as sources of their woes.

Teachers, then, pursuing what they see as their legitimate professional goals, are part of a system that insures unequal treatment for students. Aside from the schoolroom itself, does this result have other ramifications? Inasmuch as schools' sorting affects later placement in the larger society (Cicourel and Kitsuse, 1963), teachers' actions contribute to social inequality.

There is little if any evidence that the skimming and dumping procedures described at Penrose High differ from the status-attainment mechanisms employed by teachers at similar high schools throughout the United States. Approaching the issues from the students' point of view, William Chambliss's now classic study of "The Saints and the Roughnecks" (included in Part V of this book) illustrates similar institutional structures and processes in a high school in Seattle. Nationally, systems of ability tracking, specialized programs for the gifted and for the impaired, as well as narrowly focused curricula emphasizing vocational and career preparation all contribute to the reproduction of the present class structure—constraining the social actors who occupy its ranks.

From a societal point of view, Penrose High is a "rational" institution: the individuals thought to be of greatest value in perpetuating the present society benefit most. It also successfully coopts most of the teachers, administrators, and students into acting in their own self-interest at the expense of equality. Like many other institutions in contemporary society, Penrose High offers least to those who need the most.

REFERENCES

Becker, Howard S.

1952 "The Career of the Chicago School Teacher," *American Journal of Sociology* 57: 470–77.

1955 "Schools and Systems of Social Status," *Phylon* 16: 159–170.

Berg, Ivan E.

1970 *Education and Jobs; The Great Training Robbery.* New York: Praeger.

Bidwell, Charles

1965 "The School as a Formal Organization." Pp. 972–1022 in J. G. March, ed., *Handbook of Organizations.* Chicago: Rand McNally.

Bluestone, Barry, William Murphy, and Mary Stephenson

1975 "Education and Industry." Pp. 161–173 in Martin Cornoy, ed., *Schooling in a Corporate Society*, 2nd ed. New York: David McKay and Co.

Bowles, Samuel, and Herbert Gintis

1976 *Schooling in Capitalist America.* New York: Basic Books.

Boudon, Raymond

1973 *Education, Opportunity and Social Inequality.* New York: Wiley.

Callahan, Raymond
1962 *Education and the Cult of Efficiency.* Chicago: University of Chicago Press.

Cicourel, Aaron V., and Kitsuse, John I.
1963 *The Educational Decision-Makers.* Indianapolis: Bobbs Merrill.

Coleman, James S. et al.
1961 *The Adolescent Society.* Glencoe, Ill.: Free Press of Glencoe.
1966 *Equality of Educational Opportunity.* Washington, D.C.: United States Government Printing Office.

——., and Thomas Hoffer
1986 *Public and Private High Schools: The Impact of Communities.* New York: Basic Books.

Corwin, Ronald G.
1965 *A Sociology of Education.* New York: Appleton-Century-Crofts.

Cremin, Lawrence
1961 *The Transformation of the American School: Progressivism in American Education,* 1876–1957. New York: Vintage.

Gintis, Herbert
1971 "Education, Technology and the Characteristics of Worker Productivity," *American Economic Review* 61: 266–279.

Hughes, Everett C.
1956 "Social Role and the Division of Labor." Pp. 304–310 in Everett C. Hughes, *The Sociological Eye.* Chicago: Aldine.

Jencks, Christopher, et al.
1972 *Inequality: A Reassessment of the Effects of Family and Schooling in America.* New York: Basic Books.
1979 *Who Gets Ahead? The Determinants of Economic Success in America.* New York: Basic Books.

Karabel, Jerome
1972 "Community Colleges and Social Stratification: Submerged Class Conflict in American Higher Education," *Harvard Educational Review* 42: 521–562.

Katz, Michael
1975 *Class, Bureaucracy and Schools.* New York: Praeger.

Lightfoot, Sarah Lawrence
1978 *Worlds Apart: Relationships Between Families and Schools.* New York: Basic Books.
1983 *The Good High School: Portraits of Character and Culture.* New York: Basic Books.

Lorber, Judith, and Roberta Satow
1977 "Creating a Company of Unequals: Sources of Occupational Stratification in a Ghetto Community Mental Health Center," *Sociology of Work and Occupations* 4: 281–301.

Lortie, Dan C.
1969 "The Balance of Control and Autonomy in Elementary School Teaching." Pp. 1–53 in Amitai Etzioni, ed., *The Semi Professions and Their Organizations.* New York: Free Press.

Persell, Caroline
1973 *The Urban School: Factory for Failure.* Cambridge, Mass.: M.I.T. Press.
1977 *Education and Inequality.* New York: Free Press.

Robboy, Howard
1979 "At Work with the Night Worker." Pp. 365–77 in Howard Robboy, Sidney Greenblatt, and Candace Clark, eds., *Social Interaction.* New York: St. Martin's Press. [pp. 471–85 in this edition]

Rosenthal, Robert, and Lenore Jackson
1968 *Pygmalion in the Classroom: Teacher Expectation and Pupils' Intellectual Development.* New York: Holt, Rinehart and Winston.

Roth, Julius
1973 "The Right to Quit," *Sociological Review* 21: 250–58.

Ryan, William
1976 *Blaming the Victim,* rev. ed. New York: Vintage.

Walsh, James L., and Ray H. Elling
1968 "Professionalism and the Poor—Structural Effects and Professional Behavior," *Journal of Health and Social Behavior* 9: 16–28.

Review Questions

1. How did the school board rate the Penrose High School teachers' performance? On what bases did the teachers gain prestige and promotions?
2. How are teachers similar to and different from other occupational groups in their control of their clientele?
3. What techniques did the Penrose High teachers use to "skim" and "dump"?
4. What roles did administrators and parents play in promoting or preventing skimming and dumping?
5. How do the processes of skimming and dumping perpetuate society's stratification system?

MAKING THE GRADE

Howard S. Becker, Blanche Geer, and Everett C. Hughes

IN OUR STUDY, THREE OBSERVERS ([INCLUDING] BECKER [AND] GEER...) spent more than two years working with students at the University of Kansas. We went to classes with them, spent time with them in their residential units, attended formal and informal meetings of all kinds of campus organizations, and participated in many aspects of informal campus social life. We did not pretend to be students, nor did we assume any of the formal obligations of students; though we went to class with them, we did not do homework or take examinations. The nature of our fieldwork will become clear in the quotations from our field notes that appear throughout the [article].

A fourth observer (Hughes) spent two semesters at the University as a visiting professor and in that capacity gathered data on the perspectives of faculty and administration. The other observers occasionally gathered similar material and, in addition, made extensive use of documents prepared by the administration and by other organizations, largely to characterize the environment in which students act.

• • •

GENERALIZED GOALS

[P]erspectives are modes of collective action groups develop under the conditions set by the situations in which they have to act. The thrust of our analysis is largely situational, emphasizing the constraints and opportunities of the [college] situation and minimizing the influence of ideas and perspectives that students bring with them to college. Yet students do bring with them some notions about college and what they are going to do there, and these have bearing on what actually happens, even though they are transformed in the student's later experience.

Students have, in a rudimentary way when they enter college and in more elaborated form afterward, a *generalized goal,*[1] a point of view about why they have come to college and what they may reasonably expect

SOURCE: Howard S. Becker, Blanche Geer, and Everett C. Hughes: *Making the Grade: The Academic Side of College Life*. New York: Wiley, 1968. Reprinted by permisson of the authors.

to get out of their stay there. Generalized goals are, when the student first enters, a mixture of vague generalities and fragmentary specific desires, between which the student dimly apprehends some kind of connection. As he goes through school, he will probably (though not necessarily) come to a more precise definition of the general goal and will discern more complicated and precise relations between it and the specific goals he develops in particular areas of college life.

• • •

The chief characteristic of students' generalized goal, in its fully developed form, is an emphasis on college as a place in which one grows up and achieves the status of a mature adult. To manage one's college life properly (whatever meaning is attributed to that vague statement) shows that one has what it takes to be a mature adult, for the problems of college life are seen as much more like those of the adult world than anything that has come before. To do well in college, one must have the qualities students attribute to adults: the ability to manage time and effort efficiently and wisely, to meet responsibilities to other people and to the organizations one belongs to, and to cope successfully with the work one is assigned.

• • •

The generalized goal students have on entering [college] may be no more than an idea that they are going to take their academic work seriously, work hard, and do well. That goal, broadened and its connections to other areas of college life made specific, exerts an influence on the perspective students develop on their academic work. It does not tell the student how to act while he is in college; it only points the direction in which an answer must be sought and specifies a criterion against which any solution to the problems of college life will have to be measured. The generalized goal does not tell students the precise perspective they should adopt toward their academic work; many perspectives might satisfy its requirements. But the generalized goal does stand ready to tell students when a potential perspective is not in keeping with their long-range aims.

THE GRADE POINT AVERAGE PERSPECTIVE

The student's generalized goal enjoins him to be serious about college: to recognize it as a serious place where important things happen and to try to do well in all areas of college life as a sign of having achieved maturity. His perspective on academic work develops as he interacts with other students in an environment in which, as we shall see, grades are the chief form of institutionalized value and the institutional basis of punishment and reward in academic pursuits.

The perspective students develop on their academic work—we can call it the *grade point average perspective*[2]—reflects the environmental emphasis on grades. It describes the situation in which students see themselves working, the rewards they should expect from their academic work, the appropriate actions to take in various circumstances, the criteria by which people should be judged, and relevant conflicts in goals. In general, the perspective specifies the grade point average as the criterion of academic success and directs students to undertake those actions that will earn "good" or adequate grades.[3]

The main elements of the grade point average perspective are these:

Definition of the situation

1. The college is so organized that one can neither remain as a student nor graduate without receiving adequate grades. Furthermore, a number of other rewards that students desire cannot be achieved without sufficiently high grades.

2. A successful student, one who is achieving maturity in college, will "do well" in his academic work, however "doing well" is measured, thus demonstrating that he is capable of meeting the demands of the environment and also opening the way to success in other areas of campus life.

3. Doing well in academic work can be measured by the formal institutional rewards one wins. Since the major academic rewards are grades, success consists of getting a "good" grade point average.

4. Intellectual or other interests may suggest other rewards than grades to be sought in academic experience. Where the actions necessitated by the pursuit of grades conflict with other interests, the latter must be sacrificed.

Actions

5. To be successful a student should do whatever is necessary to get "good" grades, not expending effort on any other goal in the academic area until that has been achieved.

Criteria of judgment

6. Since any student who wants to can achieve adequate grades, failure to do so is a sign of immaturity. Grades can, therefore, be used as a basis of judging the personal worth of other students and of oneself.

7. Faculty members may be judged, among other ways, according to how difficult they make it to achieve adequate or "good" grades.

To say that student perspectives emphasize grades does not mean that there is a unitary standard for all students. What is considered "good" may vary considerably among various groups on the campus.

An average of B may be considered adequate in one fraternity house but substandard in another. The grade point average that will satisfy an engineering student may not satisfy a business student or vice versa. The definition of "good" grades depends, as well, on the student's aspirations in other spheres of campus life. Failing grades are satisfactory to no one, but any other set of grades may be acceptable to some student. Although the acceptable level of grades varies from group to group and person to person, the perspective directs students to orient their activities toward getting "good" grades.

• • •

An analogy with a money economy . . . is instructive. Anyone participating in such an economy will want to make what might variously be described as "enough money," "good money," or "a decent living." But the conception of "enough" or "decent" will vary widely among social classes, occupations, regions—and between individuals as well. Some will be satisfied only if they are millionaires; some will settle for a bare subsistence; most are in between. Almost everyone recognizes that "money isn't everything," that one must balance the need for money against other needs which are equally important.

Similarly, students vary in the degree to which they personally accept and live according to the rules suggested by the perspective. To some it seems completely normal: "How else could things be?" Others recognize that things might, in some other institutional setting, be quite different, but find the perspective acceptable. And some are irked by it, find it constraining and uncongenial. But it has two features that cause most students to accept it, however they feel about it, as a reasonable way to view the campus world and act in it. First, it is a *realistic way to orient oneself toward the academic aspects of campus life.* To be sure, it may not be the only realistic orientation; but it takes account of what are objectively discernible features of the campus environment. For this reason, it works; a student who adopts it as a standard of action will probably not have academic troubles. Thus, even though other perspectives might produce equally acceptable results, students will probably use this one, because it has worked in the past.

Second, the grade point average perspective is *widely accepted and thus has the force of being "what everyone knows."* Most people the students come in contact with talk and act in ways congruent with it; it embodies the accepted commonsense of his world. To question it or act in ways that deny it requires the student to violate the commonsense assumptions his fellows share; it is easier and more natural to accept them.

• • •

Whatever the student's private reservations—and, indeed, no matter how many students may have such private reservations—the terms and assumptions of conventional discourse are those contained in the perspective. To recur to the analogy with money, an adult may feel that money is not very important and privately decide that he will ignore it; but as long as he lives in a money economy, surrounded by people and institutions that assume the importance of money, he will be constrained to accept that assumption in his dealings with them. Just so with students and grades; however the student feels privately, campus life is organized around the terms and assumptions of the grade point average perspective.

• • •

THE FACULTY VIEWPOINT: AN ALTERNATIVE DEFINITION

We have described the university social structure, as students define its effects in the area of academic work, as one that emphasizes grades, grades being the chief and most important valuable. Because this is a matter on which students and faculty have widely differing viewpoints, and because we tend to give more weight to the student viewpoint than academicians commonly do, we want here to indicate what seems to us the typical faculty viewpoint and to criticize it for failing to give sufficient weight to the structural imperatives we have described.

• • •

Some faculty members, no doubt, believe that the grades they give accurately reflect the amount of knowledge the student has acquired and are perfectly content that students should work for grades; in doing so they will learn what they are supposed to know. Other faculty members despise grades and would like to do away with them and all the associated paraphernalia of grade point averages, cumulative averages, and the like. Still others feel great ambivalence. They find it necessary, whether out of inner conviction or because of bureaucratic rules, to give grades and try to do it in a serious and responsible way. But they do not believe that the grades they give adequately reflect student ability; there are always some students who do well on tests although their classroom performance casts doubt on their grasp of the material presented, and others who know the material but get poor grades, perhaps because of poor test-taking skill. The faculty want to reward true achievement rather than the cunning of the accomplished grade-getter.

Faculty in the last two categories probably feel that students should be concerned about grades, but not *that* concerned. In particular, they object to what they see as the student tendency to reduce everything to grades, to raise interminable questions about "what we are responsible for," about the grading system and the criteria that will be used in assigning grades, about the number of questions on the exam—all the common questions that seem to them at best extraneous to the true business of learning and at the worst a deliberate mockery of it.[4]

Faculty are usually at a loss to explain student interest in grades and see no rational basis for it. They may attribute it to misguided competitiveness or to other kinds of irrationality. They do not see its basis in the structure of campus life, do not understand that the student definition of the situation is largely based on the realities of college life.

Faculty members, in complaining about student concern with grades instead of scholarship, complain, we may argue, because they feel that student concern with "beating" the system of tests and assignments designed to test achievement interferes with the true assessment of student ability. Students have a different view. They take tests and grades at face value and see a connection between doing their academic work properly—in such a fashion as to get adequate grades—and the emphasis on maturity contained in their generalized goal. They believe that when they achieve a satisfactory GPA they have demonstrated their ability to do their work and meet their obligations to themselves . . . and their college—in short, their ability to act as responsible adults.

THE CONFLICT BETWEEN GRADES AND LEARNING

Despite what we have just said, some students share the faculty viewpoint in part. They incorporate it into their definition of the situation as one horn of a dilemma they see the college as posing for them. They feel that the workaday world of academic requirements, which forms the basis of the GPA perspective, causes them to miss something they might otherwise get from their courses, that they must meet the requirements before they can attempt to "learn for themselves." Insofar as the dilemma reflects a persisting definition of grades as important, it does not indicate the existence of a different and alternative perspective.

We do not mean to imply that students feel the conflict most of the time or that most students do at one time or another; the implication is not necessary to our argument, which is only that where the conflict is felt it reflects the belief that grades are important. For the most part, indeed, students believe that their courses are "good"; what they are required to do to pass the course is just what they ought to do anyhow to learn the substance of that course. Even when they fail to become excited by the content they are learning, they reason that the teacher knows the subject and that what he is teaching them must be what is important to know. If one gets a good grade, one has therefore necessarily learned something worth knowing. Where students do not accept the rationale, and feel a conflict between grades and learning, we have counted the incident as evidence of the existence of the GPA perspective.

Here is an extended statement of the problem by a successful student leader who himself had very high grades:

> There's an awful lot of work being done up here for the wrong reason. I don't exactly know how to put it, but people are going through here and not learning anything at all. Of course, there are a lot of your classes where you can't really learn anything at all. . . . There's a terrific pressure on everybody here to get good grades. It's very important. They tell you that when you come in, we tell our own pledges that. We have to, because it's true. And yet there are a lot of courses where you can learn what's necessary to get the grade and when you come out of the class you don't know anything at all. You haven't learned a damn thing, really.
>
> In fact, if you try to really learn something, it would handicap you as far as getting a grade goes. And grades are important. . . .
>
> And, you see, it says in the catalog, if you read it, that C is a satisfactory grade. Well, do they mean that or don't they? Actually it's the minimum grade here. But it's supposed to be a satisfactory grade. OK. Supposing you wanted to work on something in your own way and didn't mind if you got a C. Well, if C was really a satisfactory grade it wouldn't hurt you any. But that's not the truth. C is just barely passing. The most satisfactory thing is an A, and next is a B.
>
> The grading systems are so cockeyed around here you can't tell what's going on. One guy does it this way and another guy does it that way and, as I say, in a lot of these courses the only thing you can do is get in there and memorize a lot of facts. I've done that myself. I've gone into classes where that's all you could do is memorize . . . memorize and memorize. And then you go in to take the final and you put it all down on the paper, everything you've memorized, and then you forget it. You walk out of the class and your mind is purged. Perfectly clean. There's nothing in it. Someone asks you the next week what you learned in the class and you couldn't tell them anything because you didn't learn anything.
>
> There are a lot of guys around here who are very expert at doing that. They can take any course and learn what has to be learned and get through the course with an A. And yet, I don't think those guys are really that smart, not to me anyway. In my opinion there are plenty of people around here who have much greater potential and they just haven't found the classes where you can use it . . . We've got these kids coming in and I don't know what it is, they're not interested themselves in accumulating knowledge for its own sake or because it will be of any use to them. All they want to do is get a grade. Now, of course, grades are important. We tell them [pledges] to go out and get that grade. What else can you tell them? It's very important for the house and it's important for them to get the grade. They want to be offered those good jobs when they graduate. I don't blame them. I would myself. I've always tried to get high grades and I've done pretty well. —*fraternity senior*

This articulate student has presented most of the major themes of this aspect of the perspective, themes that recur more briefly in statements by others: Grades are important, for many reasons; one can get good grades without learning; indeed, trying to learn may interfere with grade-getting; the point of view is passed on in his fraternity.

• • •

INDIVIDUAL ACTIONS

Having sized up their situation by discovering what needs to be done in each of their classes and projecting their semester GPA, students take action based on their definition of the importance of grades. Specifically, they express the GPA perspective when they take actions that have as their object getting a "good" grade, a grade sufficient for them in the light of their other grades, the total GPA they desire, and their other responsibilities and desires; in short, when they set their level and direction of effort with an eye to its effect on their GPA.

Student actions designed to get desired grades can take two forms. First, students may attempt to meet the requirements presented to them: they study and try to master the materials and skills they are supposed to acquire. But they may fail in that attempt or decide that they will fail if that is all they do. Then they undertake other actions which, rather than being designed to meet the requirements, try to achieve the reward of grades through other, less legitimate means such as arguing with the instructor, "getting next to" him, or cheating. If they can do the job, they do it, putting their major efforts into academic work; if they cannot, they try to influence their grade in some other way.

Under some circumstances, students making use of the GPA perspective will, instead of raising their effort to meet requirements or looking for alternative forms of action, actually lower their level of effort substantially, leading (as we shall see) to the paradoxical result that an emphasis on grades leads to decreased effort to achieve them.

DOING THE JOB: Students study; they are supposed to. But they study harder at some times than at others, and the variation in effort is not a function of anything in the material they study itself, but rather of whether or not a term paper is due or an examination looms ahead. They study harder, too, when their GPA is lower than they would like it to be.

This may seem overly obvious and not necessarily connected with the perspective we are describing. After all, what do students come to college for if not to study? Why do we think it necessary to explain that they do so? Even if we were to grant this (ignoring the possibility that students might come to college for other reasons and have no intention of studying at all), it is still not obvious why a student should study in any particular rhythm, with peaks of effort at one time and periods of relaxation at another.

Consider the following example. A student says that his work is "piling up" on him, that he is "getting behind." Does he say this because he has come to college to study and learn and feels that he is not learning fast enough? On the contrary, he feels his work is "piling up" because he has a given amount of work to do in a specified amount of time; if he does not keep to a daily schedule, getting so much done every day, he will fall behind and have more to do on the following days.[5] He did not choose those amounts of work and time; because of the relationship of subjection in the academic area, they are set for him by the faculty. He must meet faculty demands because his grades will be based on how well he does just that.

We frequently found students who were not doing well working extremely hard. The poorer student probably studies longest; he has so much difficulty that he must devote all his time to his work. Here is an example, from a conversation with a freshman . . . on the verge of flunking out:

> Well, I start studying after dinner and I study all night until midnight and sometimes until one o'clock. And sometimes I start at six o'clock and just keep going right through. And I've been getting awfully tired, I think that's why I got that cold. Last weekend I went home and I slept thirteen hours until three o'clock in the afternoon. —*freshman woman*

Most instances are less dramatic. The student indicates that he has a great deal of work to do because of previous low grades and that he is doing what he thinks will be needed to improve them:

> I said to Harry, "How are things going with you?" He immediately replied, "Oh, I got a down slip [a midterm notice that one is likely to fail a course] in one of my courses and that's what I'm studying for now. I have a test in it tomorrow. . . ." I said, "How are your other courses going?" Harry replied, "They're OK, C's and B's. I'm doing all right in those and I think if I can work a little harder on this I can get it up to at least a C by the final. . . . Of course, I have no social life this semester and about all I'm doing is studying." —*freshman independent man*

Students need not be failing to behave this way; they may simply find it necessary to devote all their time to finishing required work in time to meet a deadline. Thus a student who had previously been quite prepared to engage in long conversations with the observer said: "Gee, you've caught me at a kind of bad time. I'm just trying to finish up a paper for Soc." (*senior man, scholarship hall*). (Most of the few occasions when students were unwilling to talk to us involved similar situations; the student had too much work to do to allow him to take the time off.)

When devoting more time and effort to study does not work, students who want higher grades seek help. They may, for instance, take advantage of services organized by the faculty, such as tutorial instruction, the Reading Clinic or the University Counseling Center.

More commonly, however, students get help from other students or from files, maintained by their living group, of old examinations, term papers, and the like. During dinner at a fraternity house, an observer overheard the following:

> You know how to study for Professor Jones, now, do you? Did you follow the file? Well, if you follow that file the way the course is outlined, then you can't go wrong, because he's been giving that course in the same way for the past ten years. Just be sure that you memorize all of those definitions, just the way that they are set up in the files, and you can't go wrong, you'll be sure of an A if you do.—*junior fraternity man*

Files of old examinations and papers are a tradition on many campuses. But students rely on fellow members of their living group for more than access to already accumulated files. They also ask for help in completing current assignments:

> The observer was lounging around in a student's room in the dormitory.... Long said, "[Bracket is] really busy in there. He's got a theme to turn in tomorrow and I don't think he's done anything on it yet." A little later Bracket arrived saying, "Does anybody know anything about Karl Marx? I've just run out of ideas. That's all there is to it. Where is Tucker? ...He promised to give me an old term paper of his on Karl Marx that I could use." I said, "Johnny Bracket! Don't tell me that you would turn in somebody else's term paper?" He looked around quite seriously and said, "Oh, no. I didn't mean that. I just wanted to get some ideas out of it for the last two pages of my paper. I need about two more pages." Albright said, "I see. You would just copy the last two pages, is that it?" Bracket said, "Well, I wouldn't exactly copy them."—*sophomore independent man*

The pressure of assignments and the need to get grades thus push students to do the academic work assigned them. But, if pressure supplies a motive for work, its absence makes work less necessary. If the material need not be mastered now, but can be put off until later, the student may decide to work only as much as is required and no more. If he were sincerely interested in learning for its own sake, he would presumably continue to work on a topic until he lost interest in it or felt that he had learned enough to suit his purpose. But many students do only what is required of them:

> A student described having led a very extensive social life during the last semester. I said, "Did you get pretty good grades with all that?" He said, "I can't complain, I did just about as well as I expected." I said, "What was your grade point average?" He said, "2.6" [B plus]. I said, "Wow, that's pretty good, isn't it?" He said, "Yes, it is pretty good, it really could have been higher if I had applied myself more in English, but I didn't. I think 2.6

is plenty high enough. There's no harm in that. But I didn't have to apply myself to get it. And I didn't have any intention of applying myself. . . .

"I don't mean to say that it was all a breeze. I had to put myself out occasionally. I had to get all those English themes in and so on. But frankly, with the exception of English, I didn't do any work at all the whole last month of school. I was caught up on all my other courses. I had done all the work for the rest of the semester. And the only reason that I hadn't done it in English is that you couldn't tell ahead of time what kind of themes he would assign. Otherwise I would have done all of that too. I really had all the whole last month perfectly free to do whatever I wanted."

I said, "You might have gone out and read some things that weren't assigned. Did you do that?" He smiled very broadly and said, "No, sir, you don't catch me doing that. I'll do just as much as I have to to get the grades and that's all." —*sophomore fraternity man*

Students who take this point of view make it their business to discover just what is required so that they can do the minimum necessary for the GPA they want. As soon as they discover that some action that seems necessary for a grade in fact is not, they dispense with it, even giving up going to class when that can be managed without running afoul of rules about "cuts":

I don't know about these classes. I've got one class where the fellow lectured about one set of things and then gave us an exam on a completely different set of things out of the book. I really don't think I'm going to go to that class any more. I mean, what's the sense of sitting there and taking notes if he's going to ask questions straight out of the book? I might as well just read the book and let it go at that. —*independent man, year in school unknown*

The emphasis on what is required is reflected even in the interior decoration of student rooms. We repeatedly noticed that many students' bookshelves contained nothing but textbooks. Many other students, of course, had sizable collections of books that were only distantly related, if at all, to their course work. But a substantial number of students apparently had no use for books that would not be helpful in attempting to meet requirements.[6]

ILLEGITIMATE ACTIONS: Some of the actions that students take in pursuit of grades would be regarded as illegitimate by most faculty members. Faculty believe that students should work as well as they are able, and that they will do so if the faculty member can find a way to interest them. If called on to do so, faculty tend to justify the use of grades by defining them as some kind of combined measure of ability and interest. But some student actions make a mockery of that definition, being designed to produce the end product—grades—without an appropriate input of ability, interest, and effort.

Actions designed to circumvent the ability-effort equation, then, may be regarded as illegitimate. We have already noted that students attempt to get information on instructors' prejudices and idiosyncrasies. They act on that information, and even act when they have no information and must rely on guesswork. They want to affect the instructor's judgment of their work and thus raise their grade, either by catering to his prejudices or by getting to know him personally and taking advantage of the personal acquaintance in some way.

The conception underlying such actions is embodied in the commonly used phrase "brownie points." The vulgar origins of the expression are quite lost on campus; innocent young girls and boys use it freely. One gains brownie points, of course, by "brown-nosing," by doing things that will gain the instructor's favor other than simply doing the assigned classwork. The phrase is commonly used in a half-joking way, but its import is perfectly serious. One student explained the technique in detail (though he used a more refined term):

> What I do is apple-polishing, but it's not so obvious as that. It all depends on the teacher. Mainly, I just get to know them. I go up to their offices and talk with them. [What do you talk about?] Anything, anything they feel like talking about. I might figure out a good question to ask them. That'll show them that I'm really thinking about the course. And sometimes I just go up and say hello and we sit down and start talking about things. Maybe we'll talk about new cars. I'll say I don't like the new Ford this year, what do you think of it? And he'll tell me what he thinks of it.
>
> Just different problems like that. You know, these teachers don't like to talk about their subject all the time, they get tired of it, day in, day out, the same thing. I just size them up and see what I think they will go for. Now my English teacher last year, he was a tough one to figure out the second semester. It took me almost a whole semester to figure out what to do about him. Finally, I figured it out. I praised him, that's what he liked. It paid off, too. I got my mark raised a whole grade.—*sophomore fraternity man*

One can get negative brownie points as well—lose points by doing something formally extraneous to the course work which irritates or annoys the instructor; he is thought to retaliate by lowering one's grade:

> Prentice said, "Boy, I've got minus brownie points in my speech class. I'm about 200 in the hole to her." His friend said, "What do you mean?" Prentice said, "Well, she just doesn't like me. She's got some reasons too. I mean, they're pretty good reasons." The observer said, "For instance?" Prentice said, "Well, for one thing, I didn't show up for an appointment with her, you know, it was supposed to be for my benefit. She was going to help me out. I just didn't show up, so that doesn't go over too good. And I haven't been to class in a long time."—*freshman independent man.*

Students fear particularly that disagreeing with the instructor, in class or in a paper, will have bad results:

> You can write a very good theme on some subject—I mean, the grammar can be perfect and the spelling and the punctuation and everything—and

> they'll flunk you, if you write something they don't agree with. I've seen it happen. They don't like for you to have a different interpretation than the one they think is right. You take a piece of poetry, for instance. They'll pretty much tell you what you should get out of it, how it should impress you. They'll ask you to write a theme about it. Well, you'd better get the same impressions from it that they told you you should have, or you're going to be in trouble.... It just doesn't pay to disagree with them, there's no point in it. The thing to do is find out what they want you to say and tell them that.—*junior fraternity man*

• • •

Students also act illegitimately when they attempt to improve their grade by disputing the instructor's interpretation of a term paper or an examination question. As every faculty member knows, returning papers or exams often provokes spirited debate designed to demonstrate that the answer the teacher thought incorrect was really correct, that the paper he thought inadequate actually measured up to the requirements he had set. And, as every teacher also knows, a student can often raise his grade by such tactics; students are ingenious in discovering hidden ambiguities in examination questions and term paper assignments. Here is an example:

> I had to wring a C out of the psychology man [the instructor]. I had to argue with him, you should have seen me. The thing was, on that essay question he took off because I didn't give a name [a heading] for each point. There were eight points and I got each one in the discussion but I thought I would be different and just describe it and not give the name, so he counted off two points for each one, but I made him put some back and that gives me a C.—*junior independent woman*

Arguments over the interpretation of an answer or assignment seem illegitimate to faculty because, again, they are ways of circumventing the equation of ability and effort with grades. They turn the grade into something that can be achieved by using the academically extraneous skills of a "Philadelphia lawyer."

Some students engage in the ultimate illegitimate act—cheating. A national survey of academic dishonesty among college students suggests, however, that students and faculty differ with respect to the definition of cheating.[7] Students seldom consider that they have cheated when they consult one another about an assignment. But faculty members, who see the teacher-student relationship as a one-to-one relationship between themselves and each individual student (a dyadic model of learning), sometimes feel that if the student consults anyone else he has acted dishonestly. By doing so, he has made his grade depend in some part on the ability and effort of others. (In view of the common scholarly practice of circulating work before publication for collegial comment and criticism, this faculty notion seems unduly rigorous.)

Some acts are on the borderline. A good many students might agree with faculty members that the following chemistry "shortcut" is illegitimate:

> They give you a sample of something and you're supposed to figure out what's in it. They only give you so much of it. The idea is if you use it all up making the wrong tests then you're just out of luck, you fail on that experiment. But guys are getting another sample out of them. You know, they say that their partner knocked the jar over or that they tripped while they are carrying it and spilled it or something like that. I've seen two fellows get away with it. So I don't think it'll be all that tough, if you can get around things like that.—*sophomore fraternity man*

• • •

The same national survey reveals that grosser forms of cheating are quite widespread. Fifty percent of the students questioned admitted that they had, at least once during their college careers, copied during an examination, used crib notes, plagiarized published materials for a term paper, or turned in someone else's paper. We saw very little obvious cheating, although we saw many borderline actions. One case of copying on an examination came to our attention, and one theft of an examination from a departmental office occurred during the time we were in the field. Nevertheless, some cheating must have occurred that we did not see; the nature of the act and students' shame at engaging in it (also documented in the survey referred to) make it hard to detect.

The most important point about illegitimate actions is that *they are a consequence of the existence of a system of examinations, grades, and grade point averages.* If the faculty uses examinations and other assignments to evaluate the student's abilities or progress, some students will attempt to influence the outcome of the evaluation "illegally," by "brown-nosing," arguing, or cheating. Illegitimate actions would be foolish if nothing important could be gained from them. It is because they may be rewarded by a raised grade that students engage in them.

THE GPA AND LOWERED STUDENT EFFORT: The grade point average perspective does not always intensify student academic effort. In fact, it can depress the level of effort a student puts forth, if he feels that he is already in such serious trouble that no conceivable amount of effort will get him out; when he sees his situation this way, he may stop working altogether. If we compare students to the industrial workers studied by Donald Roy, the analogy to a monetary system is again revealing. The workers Roy studied felt that they were "entitled" to a certain hourly average when they worked on piecework. If piecework rates were set so tightly that workers could not achieve the specified amount, they then worked at well below their capacity.[8] Since they could not "make out," they might as well simply collect their hourly wage and be done with it. They saw no sense in expending effort when nothing could be gained.

College students act much the same way. When they know they cannot possibly win, they resign themselves to losing and do not throw good money after bad. Failing students refuse even to calculate their grade point average; they know that they are going to fail and are not interested in the exact degree of failure:

> Brown said, "I sure am going to have to work and pull my grade average up if I want to stay here." The observer said, "What is it now?" He laughed and said, "I haven't even figured it out. It's too awful to think about." Carlson said, "I haven't either. I don't know what I'm going to get in some of these courses, but I know it's going to be pretty bad and I don't really want to bother figuring what my average is. What good would it do? I know I've got to bring everything up."—*two independent men, freshman and sophomore*

Likewise, students who are so far behind that it seems impossible to catch up do not bother to do assigned work anymore and sometimes stop doing all schoolwork completely; they report (to the observers and to each other) that they are unable to muster the energy or spirit to do the work:

> Tucker said, "Well, you're a damn fool. You just don't even try." Long said, "Buddy, I just can't get my spirit up. I don't know what's the matter with me." Tucker said, "I know how you feel. I feel the same way. There just doesn't seem to be any point to studying. I mean, I don't feel that I can learn anything and if I did it wouldn't be worth it so the hell with it."—*two independent men, a freshman, and a junior*

The importance students attach to grades is thus exhibited in reverse. If one has already done so poorly that nothing can be salvaged, there is no point in studying or working.

• • •

CONCLUSION

Grades are universally defined as important because they are institutionalized; scholarship need not be recognized as important by everyone because its status as a valuable is not ratified by a set of rules and embodied in the organization and daily routine of the college. In the same way, participants in our society may consider beauty or truth more important than money. But one can ignore beauty and truth in one's life because they are not institutionalized; no one can ignore money, no matter how unimportant he thinks it. Not to have money has consequences one must reckon with. To have grades of the wrong kind likewise has consequences one cannot ignore.

Nevertheless, just as economic achievement is not the only important thing in a man's life, so academic achievement is not the only important thing in a student's life. A certain minimum is essential in each case, because of the way the valuable is institutionalized, with other kinds of rewards contingent on reaching that minimum. But beyond the minimum, which represents the level necessary in order to have the privilege of choosing where to put one's remaining time and effort, choice becomes possible, and the person finds that he must balance the various rewards available against one another in making that choice. One may decide to sacrifice the higher grade that would come with more work in a course, choosing to devote that time instead to a political career or a girl friend.

It is at this point that both economic man and the grade-getting student achieve some measure of autonomy. To be sure, they are both captives of a system of performance and reward imposed on them by others; the student is still in a relation of subjection to faculty and administration. But, having achieved the minimum without which participation is impossible, they can then choose to go no farther, to pursue instead other valuables in other areas of life. They become, thus, men in a community, fully alive to all the possibilities available to them in that communal life. . . . [S]tudents make use of that autonomy, though not in the ways that faculty members often hope they will.

NOTES

1. The concept of generalized goal is related to, but not the same as, the concept of long-range perspective used in Howard S. Becker, Blanche Geer, Everett C. Hughes, and Anselm L. Strauss, *Boys in White: Student Culture in Medical School* (Chicago: University of Chicago Press, 1961), pp. 35–36, 68–79. They are alike in pointing to very general definitions of the meaning of one's participation in an organization. They differ in that long-range perspective refers the meaning to some state of affairs that lies beyond the end of the period of participation, while generalized goal refers the meaning to changes that take place during participation.

For further discussion of the relation between the understanding people bring with them to a situation and those they acquire in it, see Howard S. Becker and Blanche Geer, "Latent Culture: A Note on the Theory of Latent Social Roles," *Administrative Science Quarterly*, 5 (September 1960), pp. 304–313. The question has been pursued in studies of prison culture; see, especially, John Irwin and Donald R. Cressey, "Thieves, Convicts and the Inmate Culture," *Social Problems*, 10 (Fall 1962), pp. 142–155, and David A. Ward and Gene G. Kassebaum, *Women's Prison: Sex and Social Structure* (Chicago: Aldine, 1965), pp. 56–79.

2. We occasionally shorten this, in what follows, and refer to the GPA perspective.

3. We will use the expression "good grades" to refer to the level of grades that a student finds satisfactory, given the standards that he, his living group, and his other associates have developed. Those standards will take into account the various other obligations and opportunities relevant to the achievement of a mature balancing of effort and activity. "Good grades" will thus vary among students, living groups, and possibly along other dimensions as well. In contrast, we will use the expression "adequate grades" when we wish to refer to grades that are sufficient to meet some formal requirement; unless otherwise specified, "adequate grades" will refer to the GPA necessary to remain in school. Adequate grades, of course, do not vary, except as the requirement to which they refer varies.

4. See the discussion of medical faculty views in Howard S. Becker, Blanche Geer, Everett C. Hughes, and Anselm L. Strauss, *Boys in White, op. cit.*, pp. 110 and 132–134. Several essays in Nevitt Sanford, ed., *The American College* (New York: John Wiley and Sons, 1962), give evidence of the viewpoint of college faculty members.

5. *Ibid.*, pp. 92–106.

6. We made a practice of describing in detail the student rooms we visited and were thus able to check this point in our field notes.

7. William Bowers, *Student Dishonesty and Its Control in College* (New York: Bureau of Applied Social Research, Columbia University, 1964).

8. Donald Roy, "Quota Restriction and Goldbricking in a Machine Shop," *American Journal of Sociology*, 57 (March 1952), pp. 427–442.

Review Questions

1. Becker, Geer, and Hughes draw a parallel between "making the grade" in college and being financially successful in the larger society. What is this parallel?

2. Students come to college with generalized goals of working hard and doing well. Faculty come to class to impart knowledge and to promote critical thinking. Why and how are these two definitions of the situation subverted?

3. What techniques do students employ to "make the grade"?

4. How does the grading system of evaluating student performance sometimes boomerang, leading to a lack of motivation?

5. The students observed and interviewed by Becker, Geer, and Hughes attended college twenty-five years ago. Are the processes and systems which affected those students still affecting orientations for success in college in your generation? Could you devise another system for motivating and evaluating students which would promote learning rather than "making the grade"?

Suggested Readings: Interaction in Institutional Contexts: Education

Adler, Patricia, and Peter Adler. *Backboards and Blackboards: College Athletics and Role Engulfment*. New York: Columbia University Press, 1990.

Collins, Randall. *The Credential Society: An Historical Sociology of Education and Stratification*. New York: Academic Press, 1979.

Illich, Ivan. *Deschooling Society*. New York: Harper & Row, 1971.

Larkin, Ralph. *Suburban Youth in Cultural Crisis*. New York: Oxford University Press, 1979.

Rosenthal, Robert, and Lenore Jacobson. *Pygmalion in the Classroom*. New York: Holt, Rinehart and Winston, 1968.

Waller, Willard. *The Sociology of Teaching*. New York: John Wiley, 1967.

C. Work and Economics

We have noted repeatedly that the economic institution of a society—that cluster of norms and values that guides the production and distribution of food, shelter, clothing, and the host of other services and material goods we require and want—has major consequences for all other institutions. The rules we must follow in order to survive have changed drastically over the past century, as agriculture gave way to industry. For one thing, we have become in large part a nation of employees, dependent not on the seasons and the climate but on the corporation, the company, the agency, or the factory. A greater *variety* of skills are required in an industrial society, and the systems for interrelating workers with different job descriptions are much more complicated. In a great many instances, the organizations that hire us have adopted bureaucratic methods to coordinate work and workers.

Sociologists take a great interest in work, because it has symbolic meaning both on a social and a personal level. Not all jobs are viewed with equal esteem, and occupational prestige affects both one's position in the class structure and one's self-esteem. The kind of work we do defines us to other members of society by indicating, in many cases, our sex, the income we are likely to earn, the amount of education we are likely to have, and the lifestyles we are likely to pursue. Being an attorney, for example, conveys a social meaning different from being a factory worker or a housewife, meanings that are likely to affect how people interact with us in a variety of situations and how we see ourselves. The importance of the work identity is driven home at an early age to most children, who are repeatedly asked, "And what are you going to be when you grow up?"

The workplace itself has also received much attention from sociologists. How do various types of formal organization affect the workers? What informal norms and patterns of behavior emerge among workers in the factory, the university, the corporation? What, in short, are the social processes that surround a job?

Our first selection in this section looks at a group of factory workers, but the processes occurring here can be recognized in other work environments, such as hospitals, prisons, and the like. Howard Robboy, in "At Work with the Night Worker," discusses that small but significant portion of the labor force who think of the night as a time for work rather than sleep. It would be easy to view night workers merely as deviants, but to do so would give us no clues as to why they have broken from the usual workaday pattern. Robboy shows that the incentives that motivate the night worker are both economic and social. Night workers receive a pay differential (a slightly higher hourly wage) and are free to operate businesses of their own during the day. There is, moreover, a strong sense of solidarity that is not found in the factory at other times. And because night workers do not have the multitude of bosses hovering over them that day workers do, they can claim both greater personal freedom and more control over their duties.

The issue of playing the role of a fantasy character is the core of the second article in this section, "Becoming the Easter Bunny." In this selection the authors report on their field research in a Midwestern shopping center where the Easter Bunny made appearances for the public's amusement and entertainment. The photographers who hired the Easter Bunny had another purpose—getting the public to buy what the Easter Bunny is selling.

Through their participant observation, the researchers became aware of meanings attributed to this fantasy character, meanings that derive from the media, mythology, and history. They discovered that various age groups held different perceptions of the character and reacted differently to him under certain circumstances—for example, whether or not an adult was accompanied by a child.

Most important, the researchers learned that the process of becoming socialized to the Easter Bunny role was more complicated and more consequential for the role player's self-concept than they had believed. The professor who played the Bunny responded to the photographer, the public, and to his own feelings. For the person inside the bunny suit, donning the costume literally meant putting on a new identity. If a temporary fantasy role has such an impact, what does this say about the power of more typical work roles to mold and shape us?

This section of the book can by no means be said to detail even a fraction of the norms, systems, and behavior patterns pertaining to work in our society. It is our hope that the reader will begin to see how work activities can be viewed sociologically and will apply this vantage point in looking at other occupations and settings. We try to show here that work is not motivated *solely* by the promise of economic reward and that, in fact, people will often work very hard for little return or even forego income. The informal social nature of the workplace *combines* with formal structures, rules, and economic incentives to set its tone and character. We also try to indicate the variety of meanings that can be attached to economic activities and to those who perform them.

AT WORK WITH THE NIGHT WORKER

Howard Robboy

AT 11 P.M. OR MIDNIGHT EACH NIGHT, AS MOST AMERICANS ARE EITHER ASLEEP or thinking about going to sleep, a small but significant number of people are just beginning their night's work.

Working nights means that one's entire daily schedule is thrown out of line from the temporal flow of society. Eating, sleeping, having sexual intercourse, socializing, visiting family members, and seeing one's children must be carefully scheduled by those who work the night shift. In a sense, these people become loners. The entire family must endure the strain of living in and between two time worlds.

In this study, the focus is on married male factory workers who reside and work in central and northern New Jersey and who work at night. The question explored in this article is why these workers agree to work the night shift despite the limitations on their social, family, and personal lives.

The period defined as night—perhaps from 11 P.M. to the breaking of the dawn—exists as a unique time zone in the course of social life (Melbin, 1978). It is here that we find fewer rules governing behavior than at any other time during the twenty-four hour cycle. For example, at this time we find blinking traffic lights and no time-specific norms pertaining to dress or food preferences.

The freer atmosphere of the night is not restrained by the walls of a factory and thus permeates the work experience of those employed on the night shift. Generally, night workers speak of less pressure, less tension, and a more congenial atmosphere than exist for their counterparts on the day shift in the same organization. The more amiable atmosphere manifests itself in many subtle ways during the night workers' time on the job.

SOURCE: Howard Robboy: "At Work With the Night Worker," is taken from "They Work by Night: Temporal Adaptations in an Industrial Society," the author's doctoral dissertation and was published in the first edition of *Social Interaction*.

THE FREER WORKING ATMOSPHERE ON THE NIGHT SHIFT

When a worker begins to work nights, his work experience is different from that of his counterpart on the day shift. For one thing, he finds that many of the regulations enforced on the day shift are ignored by supervision at night. In most cases, the workers have to report only to their foremen.[1]

The foremen are usually the only ones in charge at night and thus are themselves freed from the scrutiny of superiors. As long as the required amount of work is accomplished, they allow certain things to slide by. After all, they are working nights too.

> *Case 10*
> There are fewer supervisors around. The foremen are likely to overlook shop rules like going for extra coffee or goofing off. On this shift you can read or do crossword puzzles to keep your mind from getting tired. You can't do this on days.

> *Case 34*
> You don't have to wear safety plugs in your ears. On this job it is dangerous to wear earplugs. There is less pressure on third shift. There are no bigwigs from New York walking around. Also the supervisors don't bug you as much. There are no big shots putting pressure on them

aving fewer supervisors gives the night worker greater control over his work. This is important for several reasons.[2] First, it means that the worker can move at his own pace while running the machines, controlling the speed at which he works, rather than following the dictum of management. It can be argued, in fact, that reports of alienated workers are less likely to come out of the night shift. It is not that night workers do less work but, rather, that they have some say about how much work will be done, and when, during their eight hours on the job.

> *Case 24*
> No one ever bothers me. My boss hardly ever comes to see me. As long as I do my work, things are OK.

A further consequence of working at one's own pace is that on third shift the workers don't have to "dog their job"—go through the motions of working when in fact they are not—as night-shift workers claim day shift workers do to avoid the omnipresent eye of supervision. Not having to "look busy" also lessens the night worker's role distance—there is greater correspondence between what is expected of him and what he accomplishes than is true of day workers.

> *Case 12*
> On third shift you don't have to dog your job because you have someone standing over you. You might do in six hours what someone else on day

shift drags out to eight. If you have decent supervision they won't mind if you lie down. This is where the other shifts complain.

Third-shift workers often have the opportunity to use their own methods of operation rather than depend on procedures set by management. In my own experience as a bull-block operator in a copper-tubing factory, I was taught that when the machines were "running good" and the copper we were using was of high quality, we were allowed to run the machines faster than permitted by management—and so achieve production bonuses. Rarely did our foreman check up on us, as we were told was done on the first shift.[3]

Case 26
I have to carry seventy pounds of material between these two machines. It was really hard on my wrists, so I devised a little cart so I could wheel the material between the two machines. On first shift they have to carry the stuff back and forth like horses. . . . We used to have two guys who worked out a system where one of them would run two machines for an hour while the other guy took a break. They showed this to others and soon it was done on the second and third shifts. Meanwhile, on first shift they have two guys doing the job dragging their feet.

Another feature of the third shift is that workers are frequently permitted to stretch their breaks. This adds to their feeling of having greater control over their lives while on the job.

Case 14
We get a little more wash-up time. The shifts overlap in our favor. So if we finish early we can disappear. We don't have all the snoopers around, the white shirts who are always watching over you. . . . They are more lenient about breaks. They are also this lenient on second shift, but not on first.[4]

Case 18
We can stretch our breaks where you can't on days. We can take a walk through the locker room and talk to the guys on breaks. On first shift, if you are not at your machine, you will get caught and get yelled at.

From the literature in industrial sociology, the data reported here, and my own experiences at the copper-tubing factory, it is the bargaining-conflict model of social relationships that most clearly depicts labor-management relationships (see Shelling, 1960; Handelman, 1976). The opportunities for rule breaking by a third-shift worker, seen through this perspective, are important for several reasons. On one level, they provide outlets for worker resentment against management. By breaking the rules, the worker feels that he is getting away with something or getting back at management. When the worker is supervised closely, as he is on the day shift, few opportunities exist for the channeling of resentments. My hunch is that, if the problem of industrial sabotage were to be thoroughly investigated, one would find that it occurs more frequently on the day shift (with adjustment made, of course, for the number of the workers on each of the shifts). For if there are few outlets for a worker's resentments, one of the options remaining when conditions become intolerable is to stop the machines.

On another level, the opportunity to break the rules can be viewed as a way to humanize the workplace. The authoritarian rule of management generates the expectation that the worker is supposed to work during his eight hours on the job (except for his coffee and lunch breaks) and do nothing else. The question then raised is, how often can people realistically do only one thing for such a prolonged period of time? Night workers, because they are able to manage their own time, can, to some extent, create a more humane atmosphere in which to work.

Working nights also provides the worker with the chance to "goof off" occasionally. A colleague, Noel Byrne, relates his experiences while working nights in a mill in Northern California:

> During the night, production would stop as the workers began waging bets on forklift truck races. The forklift trucks, normally used to transport the materials used in production, would be raced against one another. One night the brakes failed on one of the trucks as it went out the door, over a ten-foot embankment and finally stopped as it went head on into a creek which ran alongside the factory. It got so bad that the vice president of the company had to come into the plant one night to stop this practice. The foremen, who normally were the only ones in charge at this time, were the ones who drove the trucks during the races.[5]

In my own experience at the copper-tubing factory, workers were constantly throwing things at the drivers of cranes that rode on monorails attached to the roof of the building. The noise level in the plant was very high, and most of the workers wore their required earplugs. Unless one looked up from his work and saw the crane approaching, it would pass unnoticed. The crane operator, however, seeing the workers below busy at their work, would throw various articles at them. This folly would continue throughout the night.

The opportunity to smoke or drink coffee while working, to control both the pace of work and the production routines, to stretch their breaks, and occasionally to "goof off' on the job becomes an important feature of work on the night shift. Such advantages, along with a quantitative and qualitative difference in supervision, greatly affect the working atmosphere.

The working conditions often give rise to a greater sense of solidarity among third shift workers than among those on other shifts. Solidarity develops not only from the looser atmosphere, which makes greater interaction among the workers possible, but from the stigma of being labeled night workers by the workers on the first and second shifts.

Although working at night doesn't lead to the formation of a deviant identity off the job, there is evidence that a deviant identity does emerge during the hours of work. Such an identity is temporally situated at the workplace and reinforced as the night workers are compared with those on the other shifts.[6] In the nonwork world night workers identify themselves, and are identified by others, as being just working men, but at work they pick up the stigmatized identity of being night workers.[7] And, as the deviance literature suggests, a deviant or stigmatized identity acts as a strong bonding mechanism.

Case 21
People on the third shift are much closer. They confide in each other. They help one another. There is a much closer relationship on this shift.[8]

Case 30
When I go on vacation, I leave the key to my toolbox in case anyone needs anything. At work we share our tools. This is not done on day shift. We share information about the different machines. On days, everyone keeps to themselves and they don't help one another. There is a rivalry between them. . . . The workers are friendlier on night shift. There is more camaraderie. If you are on days the men bitch more. On third, if you are in trouble, someone will come over. There are only eight guys on this shift and they will give you a hand. We are a close-knit group. There are more soreheads on days. On nights the guys are easygoing.

In addition to the issues already discussed, other advantages of working at night emerged during the course of the interviews.

In the summer the night worker is spared from working under the heat of the day, which, along with the heat generated from the work itself, can be oppressive. In my own work experience, bull-block operators on the day shift were issued salt tablets by the plant nurse. These were a necessity to make it through the hot, humid days of New Jersey; on the night shift, these tablets were required only occasionally.

In some cases a night worker has a greater chance of working overtime than he would if he worked days. Usually the third shift is smaller in size than the other shifts, and so the probability is increased that any one worker will get overtime work when it is available.

Case 29
There are fewer people on our shift, so there is a greater probability of getting overtime. I get $2,000 to $3,000 a year in overtime. There is less supervision and we can work at our own speed. We are more united, closer together than they are on the day shift.

Having a smaller number of men working at night can also result in a reduction of the overall noise level in the factory. This is cited as an advantage of the night shift.

Case 15
It is also quieter on nights. The noise is incredible on days if I have to stay over. At my age, more things anger you. There is less aggravation on this shift.

Case 25
There is no hubbub like on second or days. There are fewer bosses and fewer employees. You are closer toward your fellow employees. You don't have the cutthroat attitude like on days and second.

SHIFT DIFFERENTIAL

All the workers interviewed in this study receive a nightshift differential in pay for working the third shift. The shift differential ranges from 12 to 71 cents an hour. Most of the workers view this as a compensation for having to work nights. A minority of the workers, those who like working nights, see the shift differential as a bonus. In any event, the shift differential allows the worker to earn an additional $5 to $28 a week and enables him to feel that he is doing better than his day-shift neighbors. Certainly such an awareness can add to his feelings of competence as a breadwinner of the family. Thus the shift differential provides a second major explanation of why workers agree to work the night shift—it can mean the difference between staying afloat financially or sinking. It can also be the difference between their being forced to work a second or third job and/or their wives being forced to seek employment.

Case 27
I was on day shift for two years until a few months ago. I went back on third because we needed the ten percent. The doctor told me not to work a parttime job any more. Whenever I work two jobs I wind up in the hospital. I have bronchitis, asthma, and emphysema. I got off third shift last time because my wife wanted me to. The kids were getting older and she wanted me to spend more time with them. When I was on days, she worked part-time. Then she stopped working and we needed the ten percent so I went back on third.

MOONLIGHTING

Having the daytime hours to himself gives the night worker the opportunity to obtain a part-time job or start his own business. In his study of moonlighters, Wilensky (1964) found that 6 percent of the male labor force moonlighted.[9] In this sample of night workers, sixteen men, or 40 percent of the forty workers interviewed, either had second jobs or owned small businesses to supplement the earnings from their night-shift positions. Of the sixteen night workers reporting second sources of income, ten operated their own businesses.

> *Case 16*
> I work third by choice. The kids were young then and we needed the money. I always worked two jobs. I am a carpenter and a fencer. Working third gave me my days free for a second job. You only work this shift for the money.

> *Case 28*
> I chose to work this shift as it gives me time to do other things. I have a part-time job as a handyman as well as a catering business.

Chinoy (1955), in his study of automobile workers, reports that some of the workers considered leaving the assembly line to start their own businesses. Although they are part of the American Dream and the Horatio Alger mystique, small businesses—the kind typically started by blue-collar workers—have a high failure rate. The night shift provides a safety valve for workers who want to set up a business of their own. They can work their night jobs and still run the business. If the business fails or doesn't produce sufficient income to support a family, they still have their jobs. Thus the night shift provides them with a trial period to get their businesses going. This is an option open to few day shift workers.

For workers with businesses of their own, the night shift can be important in other ways. Consider the following night worker who is self-employed during the day as a fence builder.

> *Case 16*
> I have a fence business. When someone wants a fence put around their house they want it done right away. Maybe their dog almost got run over, their kid ran out into the street, or they just had a big fight with one of their neighbors. In any case, they want you there the next day. If I was on the day shift I would have to do it on weekends or after five o'clock during the week if it is summer. If you do this, they figure they are getting a half-assed job because you are trying to moonlight. It means that you are not a regular contractor. They are paying a good buck for the work, and they want to get workman's quality. They figure that you can't do quality work at five o'clock. And on weekends they don't want to be bothered by you being there. By working nights I can be there by 9 A.M. They feel that they are getting a real contractor. This way I can charge full price and do a first-rate job. If you come in the afternoon or on a weekend, they want to pay you less because you are not a real fencer.

THE NIGHT-WORK TRAP

A night worker can become a blue-collar entrepreneur. He can work in a factory yet be free of many of the disagreeable features of the workplace that day shift workers encounter. He can earn the shift differential and have the opportunity to hold down a second job or manage a business of his own. But it is not for these reasons that most night workers choose the third shift. More often, little choice is available when they begin employment.

One of the initial reasons why workers agree to work on the night shift is that they have little or no seniority to qualify for the preferred position on the day shift. If a young worker, newly married, wants a job at a factory, he may have to choose between the second and third shifts. He may make the selection with the idea that, once he gains sufficient seniority, he will be able to go onto the day shift. In some cases the wait can be from five to ten years.

The second shift (beginning between 3P.M. and 4P.M. and ending between 11P.M. and midnight) seems to be almost as disagreeable as the night shift. A second-shift worker with a working wife may see his wife and children only on weekends. He can sleep with his wife at night, but "night" often begins at two or three in the morning—because many workers find that they need a few hours to unwind before they are tired enough to go to bed. Many of the workers in this study had had some work experience on the second shift and, because of the scheduling difficulties, chose to transfer to the third shift.[10]

> *Case 30*
> I hate second shift. All you do is eat, sleep, and work. You come home at 12:45 A.M. wide awake. When you work nine to five, you have at least four hours free before you go to bed. What do you do at 12:45A.M.? There is no one to talk to. You watch television until six in the morning, sleep until one-thirty, and then go to work. I call second shift the get-rich shift. All you can do is work and save.

> *Case 41*
> I would prefer nights to the afternoon shift. You start work at 2:30 before the kids come home from school. You come home after they are in bed and wake up after they've left for school. I would like to work days. But I prefer nights to the afternoons.

Choosing to work nights with the hope of eventually accumulating enough seniority to go on the day shift is a common strategy among night-shift workers. Consider the plight of a young worker, with a wife and family, who agrees to work nights. When he gains enough seniority to bid successfully for a job on the day shift, he may be faced with a financial dilemma. To go on days would require him to forfeit not only his shift differential but his second job or small business as well. To get off the night shift would entail, then, a substantial loss in income and a corresponding drop in his family's standard of living. For the blue-collar family, whose life style is already far from extravagant, this might prove quite difficult. Thus the night-shift differential and the opportunities for moonlighting, although they are economically seductive at the outset, can prove to be a trap that makes it difficult for a worker to leave the shift.

Case 47
I would much prefer working days. It would be the ultimate to have a straight nine-to-five job. I could work days, but my other involvements stop it. Eventually I will go over to days. This will be when the kids are older and can take care of themselves.

ADDITIONAL REASONS FOR WORKING THE NIGHT SHIFT

For some workers, going on nights means an advancement to a higher-paying position.

Case 1
I want to qualify for a foreman's job. The foreman's job includes a salary increase and job on the day shift. That is why I took this job as a mechanic. I know that if I wanted to advance, I couldn't just be an operator. A mechanic is a step to a foreman. If I knew that I would have to remain a mechanic, I would have stayed an operator and worked days.

Case 18
I have another five years on third in my department before I can go on days. If I switched to another department I could go on days tomorrow. Another job would mean a lower paying job, 13 cents an hour less plus the 10 percent shift differential.

During the course of the interviews, incidents were related of factories suddenly closing and workers finding themselves unemployed. With a family to support, working nights becomes attractive if it means a steady job with a secure future.

Case 12(Wife)
Bud used to work at G.E. All of a sudden they moved to Texas and left us with nothing.

Case 21
I worked at Studebaker for two years until they closed up. So I went looking for work and I got a job in construction—building homes. This lasted for about a year, but then I got laid off when the weather got bad. I wound up in ——— on the second shift shift. I worked there for two years but wanted a job on days, so I went to the Mack in Plainfield to work the day shift. I was at the Mack exactly five years, because I got a five-year pin. Then Mack moved out in '61, and I went to ——— again on the third shift. *(Wife)* When Mack moved out it was really hard to get a job. All those men were thrown out of work. In fact, we used up most of our savings and it was rough. We were just glad that he had a job. *(Husband)* I needed a job and I was glad to work there.

> When you look for a job, you try to get the most for the least. Some of the places I went to paid so little that it wouldn't cover my mortgage payments. I am very grateful for the job I do have. No one around here pays the money ——— does. We also get great benefits. The hospitalization and the other benefits can't be matched. At first I didn't like the third shift. I couldn't get used to it. But I made up my mind, and I got used to it.

If a night worker doesn't have a second job or a business on the side, having the day free provides time to pursue hobbies, care for preschool children, and clean the house.

> *Case 14*
> I work nights for the money and to be able to babysit during the day while she is working. I am on third shift now primarily because of our youngest child. . . . I would like to go on days in a few years when my youngest child is older and can take care of herself after school. Right now our lives are set up for me on the third shift. Everything is going so well. I don't know whether I would want to go on days now. Things are going well.

> *Case 41*
> I have more time with my family, especially in the winter. I get up when the kids get home from school, and I am with them until they go to bed at night and I go to work.

The third shift is also advantageous for activities like shopping. The worker can leisurely shop away from the evening and weekend crowds.

> *Case 4*
> The biggest advantage of the shift is that you can shop with no crowds. If you need a doctor's appointment, shopping, and things done around the house, it is good. You don't have to fight crowds on weekends.

Another advantage of the shift is that if the worker is not tied down by a second job, he can use some of his nonwork time for recreaction and avoid the crowded periods which day shift workers utilize for leisure.

> *Case 37*
> I love to fish and hunt. On this shift I can come home, change my clothes, and be hunting and fishing in fifteen minutes.

> *Case 10*
> It is a perfect shift for camping. I work the Sunday to Thursday schedule and can come home Friday morning and sleep for a few hours. Then I can leave and not return until Sunday night. If I was on the regular third shift, I would have to leave Saturday morning and be back Sunday night for my wife to get to work on Monday morning.

> *Case 19*
> During the summer, I can go to the beach during the day and not fight traffic. I can sleep on the beach, and I don't have to fight the weekend crowds.

The night shift can also provide the worker with ample time to pursue his hobbies.

Case 17
If I could take you downstairs and show you my hobby, you would understand why I like this shift so much. I raise show parakeets, and working nights allows me time to take care of them. We also go to bird shows in New York, Boston, and Washington. If we have to go into New York for the day, I don't have to take a day off from work. I also have a greenhouse outside where I raise azaleas. On day shift you can have your evening activities, but you don't have time for a hobby.

Another feature of the night shift is that the workers save time driving to and from work because they do not have to fight rush-hour traffic. This adds to their amount of daily nonwork time.

Case 30
I can go from here to the plant in seventeen minutes. On days it would take thirty-five to forty minutes. I save an hour this way.

One worker used his nonwork time to build a new house for himself and his family.

Case 16
I built this house three years ago. I saved the money from working the two jobs and from my wife working part-time. *(Wife)* We worked six hours a day on this house and in ten months we built it. He came home from work, had breakfast, and worked on the house for six hours. Then he went home and went to sleep. We now rent our old house, and that pays for the mortgage on this house. We pay the smaller mortgage on that house, and we own land in Florida. Now we don't need the money from the third shift. *(Husband)* If I had worked days, I wouldn't have been able to accomplish as much. No one helped us with this. We did it ourselves. We could not have built this house if I wasn't on third shift. I was home when the materials were delivered and could check to make sure there were no shortages or that the wrong materials weren't sent.

It should be noted that all of the "features" of the night shift cited by the workers bespeak a degree of social isolation. The nonwork activities act as "side bets" in embellishing their careers as loners. An element common to their remarks is that they are able to avoid crowds.

NEGATIVE ASPECTS OF WORKING THE NIGHT SHIFT

Although the advantages of the night shift are significantly greater than the limitations, still, in the course of the interviews, the workers speak of the negative features.

One of the slang terms used for the third shift is the "dead-man's shift." The phrase symbolizes the feelings on the part of workers that management doesn't care about them or even notice their existence. The feelings manifest themselves in several ways. First, decisions about production and product development are made by management officials who work the day shift. The night workers claim that decisions are made on the basis of day-shift operations, with no consideration given to night-shift needs.

> *Case 4*
> You are always left out of new information or new projects being developed. Management decisions are made on the basis of the first shift and not the third. You are never noticed by anyone, so it's hard to advance. You don't get the exposure.

> *Case 20*
> If you get a new machine, the person on day shift will know more about the machine. If there is a question about the machine, there is no one to go to.

Night workers are also unknown to management except on paper. This factor may be significant if the worker hopes to advance to a higher position.

> *Case 12*
> I know a lot of young guys who are strapped and need the 10 percent. They can't get into training programs or foremanships. No one knows them. You can apply, but when they get into the office, they say, "Who is that guy?"

The night workers complain that fewer plant facilities are open at night. I experienced these difficulties. One night we were working hard trying to make production bonuses, and a 270-pound coil of hot copper tubing began falling off the conveyor belt as it approached my section of the bull block. As I grabbed the coil with my insulated gloves, a section of the tubing hit my arm. The burn wasn't serious enough to require emergency treatment in a local hospital, but a Band-Aid proved to be insufficient. Since there was no nurse on duty on the night shift, I had to wait until 7A.M. to see the nurse, who came on duty with the day shift.

> *Case 26*
> On third shift you can't buy safety shoes or glasses when you want. The foreman has to do it for me. There is no nurse on duty either.

> *Case 30*
> On first shift they have a full cafeteria. On third they have a lunch wagon. If I have a problem, I have to see the personnel man on my own time. No one is there at 7A.M.

SUMMARY AND CONCLUSIONS

This research provides numerous explanations as to why married male factory workers agree to work the night shift despite serious limitations in their family, social, and private lives.

The desires for a good job, easier working conditions, control over one's work, less supervision, and a small bonus becomes immediately apparent as explanations for working this shift. As one looks at the night shift in terms of a career, however, one discovers social and economic factors that serve as traps and consequently make it difficult for a night worker to return to a normal day-shift routine if an opportunity arose.

NOTES

1. Of all the advantages of working nights cited by the workers interviewed, having less supervision was mentioned most often. Twenty-six of the forty workers interviewed raised this issue.

2. For a further discussion of the issue of worker's control, see Gerry Hunnius, G. David Garson, and John Case, eds., *Worker's Control: A Reader on Labor and Social Change*. New York: Vintage, 1973.

3. Donald Roy, in "Efficiency and the Fix: Informal Intergroup Relations in a Piecework Machine Shop," *American Journal of Sociology* 60, 255–266, reports a similar finding.

4. A colleague, Noel Byrne, reports the following account from his night-work job in a mill in northern California.

> One of the advantages of night work was that you didn't have to hide when you finished your work. One night it was almost time to quit when the owner of the plant who lived in Chicago made a tour. He was unknown to us as we had never seen him before. One guy was just standing around, killing time before he could punch out. The owner came up to him and said, "What are you doing?" The worker replied, "Just fucking the dog." The owner, startled, retorted with, "You're fired, because I'm the dog you are fucking."

5. Another colleague, Howard Finkelstein, verifies Byrne's experience in his account of a night shift job he held in a swimming pool factory in New Jersey.

> I worked at a place where they manufactured prefab swimming pools. We used to bust our asses getting our work done by lunch time (3:30 A.M.) so that we could goof off the rest of the night. We used to bring in gallon containers of pink lemonade and gin. Following their consumption, we used to have forklift truck races on the loading platforms. This practice ended one night when the brakes on one of the trucks failed, and the truck went off the loading platform into a pile of wood.

6. For a discussion of situated identities in relationship to the self, see Edward Gross and Gregory P. Stone, "Embarrassment and the Analysis of Role Requirements," *The American Journal of Sociology* 70 (July 1964): 1–15.

7. Although Pigors and Pigors (1944:3) and Sergean (1971:165) claim that there is a social stigma attached to night work, I found no evidence for this in the course of the interviews.

8. Sergean (1971), Davis (1973), and Kozak (1974) report similar findings in their studies of night workers.

9. According to Michelotti (1975:56–62), the latest statistics show that men between the ages of 25 and 54 have the highest percentage of moonlighting (between 6 and 7 percent). As expected, there is no available national data on the percentage of night workers who moonlight.

10. To complete the "picture" of the American labor force, ethnographies are needed on second and rotating shift workers. For example, the second shift has a reputation among night workers for being a haven for bad marriages. If the couple schedules it "correctly," they can see each other only on weekends, thus minimizing the friction periods when they are together. Meanwhile they can appear married to the outside world.

REFERENCES

Becker, Howard S.

1953–54 "Some Contingencies of the Professional Dance Musician's Career," *Human Organization,* 12 (Spring), 22–26.

1960 "Notes on the Concept of Commitment," *American Journal of Sociology,* 65 (July), 32–40.

Chinoy, Ely

1955 *The Automobile Worker and the American Dream.* Garden City, N.Y.: Doubleday.

Davis, Murray

1973 *Intimate Relations.* New York: Free Press.

Goffman, Erving

1961 *Encounters.* Indianapolis: Bobbs-Merrill.

Gross, Edward and Gregory P. Stone

1964 "Embarrassment and the Analysis of Role Relationships," *American Journal of Sociology,* 70 (July), 1–15.

Handleman, Don

1976 "Rethinking Banana Time," *Urban Life,* 4 (January), 433–448.

Hunnius, G., David Garson, and John Case, eds.

1973 *Workers Control.* New York: Vintage.

Kozak, Lola Jean

1974 "Night People: A Study of the Social Experiences of Night Workers," *Summation,* 4 (Spring/Fall), 40–61.

Melbin, Murry

1978 "Night as Frontier," *American Sociological Review,* 43 (February), 1–22.

Michelatti, Kopp

1975 "Multiple Jobholders in May, 1975," *Monthly Labor Review* (November), 56–62.

Pigors, Paul and Faith Pigors

1944 *Human Aspects of Multiple Shift Work.* Cambridge: Department of Economics and Social Science, Massachusetts Institute of Technology.

Roy, Donald F.
1952 "Quota Restriction and Goldbricking in a Machine Shop," *American Journal of Sociology,* 57 (March), 427–442.
1955 "Efficiency and 'The Fix': Informal Intergroup Relations in a Piecework Machine Shop," *American Journal of Sociology,* 60, 255–266.
1959–60 "Banana Time," *Human Organization,* 18 (Winter), 158–168.

Sergean, Robert
1971 *Managing Shiftwork.* London: Gower Press-Industrial Society.

Shelling, Thomas
1960 *The Strategy of Conflict.* Cambridge, Mass.: Harvard University Press.

Shostak, Arthur
1969 *Blue Collar Life.* New York: Random House.

Slater, Phillip
1969 *On the Pursuit of Loneliness: American Culture at the Breaking Point.* Boston: Beacon Press.

Stone, Gregory P.
1971 "American Sports: Play and Display," in Eric Dunning, ed., *The Sociology of Sport.* London: Frank Cass, pp. 46–65.
1974 "Remarks," at *The Minnesota Symposium on Symbolic Interaction.* Hudson, Wis., June.

Wilensky, Harold L.
1964 "The Moonlighter: A Product of Relative Deprivation," *Institute of Industrial Relations* (Reprint No. 219). Berkeley: University of California, pp. 105–124.

Review Questions

1. A young married worker in need of a job accepts a position on the night shift. He or she hopes to earn enough seniority to switch to the day shift eventually. According to Robboy's study of night-shift workers, what social and economic traps might prevent an eventual switch to the day shift?

2. Robboy's research indicates that there are numerous advantages and disadvantages to working the night shift. What are they, and why do they exist on the night shift rather than on other shifts?

3. How can we explain the fact that there is less worker alienation and industrial sabotage on the night shift than on the day shift?

BECOMING THE EASTER BUNNY: SOCIALIZATION INTO A FANTASY ROLE

Joseph V. Hickey, William E. Thompson, and Donald L. Foster

TO MOST AMERICANS BOTH THE EASTER BUNNY ROLE AND ITS FANTASY MEANings seem relatively clear-cut. The mall Easter Bunny is that funny looking, adorable, fantasy creature with the long ears, oversized incisors and prominent cottontail, who annually visits American shopping centers, and proffers candy and plastic rings to children and their parents. Like Santa Claus, the Easter Bunny holds infants in his lap so that they may have their photographs taken to be shown to family members during the holiday celebrations and placed in family photo albums and scrapbooks for posterity.

• • •

Popular notions suggest that playing a fantasy character, whether the Easter Bunny, Santa Claus, or a character at Disneyland, is a relatively simple act that requires little effort. However, our research indicates that it is a far more complex task than is generally assumed, for taking on a role such as that of the Easter Bunny is not an *act*, but a *process*. Moreover, as symbolic interactionists have effectively demonstrated, a concept of "self" is not generated from within, but emerges and develops through the course of interaction with others (e.g., Blumer, 1969; Cooley, 1902). As Gary Fine wrote in his book *Shared Fantasy* (1983: 241):

> The extent of "getting into" a role, and the subsequent sense of "getting out," constitute a dimension along which secondary roles vary—whether of golfer, . . . blind date, or nude model. What is necessary for . . . identification is the self conscious realization that the role to be assumed is different from the "real self" but is nonetheless important to one's own self-image as a role taker.

Assuming the role of a fantasy character takes on special and perhaps unique dimensions as compared to other roles that people fulfill in

SOURCE: Excerpted from Joseph Hickey, William E. Thompson, and Donald L. Foster, "Becoming the Easter Bunny: Socialization into a Fantasy Role," *Journal of Contemporary Ethnography*, Vol. 17, no.1 (April 1988, p. 67–95). Reprinted by permission of Sage Publications, Inc.

the course of their daily lives. As a golfer, blind date, or nude model, the individual is still a human; consequently, his/her personal identity and concept of "self" are never totally submerged. In contrast, when an individual dons a costume that completely masks his/her human identity some unique accommodations must be made to playing the role.

On the one hand, there is a certain element of "safety" in being hidden in a costume. Persons playing a "human role" must adjust their actions to coincide with public expectations associated with the roles they play, and their personal identity is directly tied to those roles. Hence it is not merely a case that a golfer is having a bad day, but in fact that Joe or Lucy Smith the golfer is having a bad day. Likewise, it is not merely the nude model who is too fat, or does not hold poses well, but it is Bill or Mary Jones the nude model. This is not the case with the individual playing a fantasy character. If the Easter Bunny does not "act right" or Santa Claus is "grumpy," that is the final assessment by those who interact with them—the *Easter Bunny* did not act right and *Santa Claus* was grumpy. There is no apparent threat to one's self concept nor "loss of face" for the individual playing the part (although too many complaints of that nature and the person playing the part will lose his/her job, which would, of course, impact upon one's concept of self).

On the other hand, in some ways one's sense of personal identity is even more "on the line" when playing a well-known fantasy character, for most Americans have fairly clear-cut notions of how fantasy characters ought to behave. Moreover, to violate the social expectations associated with fantasy characters is not only to temporarily disrupt social interaction, but also to threaten traditional understandings about them that have become so institutionalized in our culture that they border on the "sacred." Further, because stereotypic notions about fantasy characters are defined so narrowly, the individual playing them does not enjoy the flexibility usually associated with ordinary roles. That is, when the public encounters the Easter Bunny it defines the bunny as exciting and fun, and no matter how the person in the bunny costume may behave, the public tends to associate his/her actions with its fantasy images. As Berger and Luckmann (1966) have suggested, the public tends to react to the *typification* of the Easter Bunny as well as to the bunny itself.

Each spring at shopping centers across America the Easter Bunny makes its annual holiday appearance. At first glance, the bunny's visit appears to be made solely for the purpose of amusing and entertaining the public. However, beneath the clever bunny disguise lies another objective—to sell rather expensive photographs to a willing public. The Easter Bunny must achieve this commercial objective in actual social interaction with humans, most of whom choose to define the role solely in fantasy terms. Consequently, in order to effectively fulfill this mission the individual must undergo a socialization process into the role.

The theoretical framework for this analysis is based upon the dramaturgical analysis of everyday life as utilized by Goffman (1959; 1961; 1963; 1967; 1969; 1971). It is our contention that during the course of social interaction, the photo company draws upon the mutual understanding of people who associate the Easter Bunny with its fantasy meanings, while using the role to promote its own commercial interests. By carefully constructing a scenario and effectively manipulating the course of social interaction, the photo company creates a situation in which mall visitors eventually become willing participants in their scheme. A critical element for the success of this commercial venture, however, is the ability of the individual "playing" the Easter Bunny to fulfill the role expectations associated with it. In the course of social interaction, he/she must go beyond the mere act of putting on a bunny suit, and in effect, "become" the Easter Bunny. This involves a socialization process unique to the assumption of a fantasy role. This process is the focal point for our study. . . .

METHODOLOGY

The method used in this study was eleven days of full-time participant observation without disclosure of research intentions by one of the authors, who played the role of the Easter Bunny. . . . The Easter Bunny job was discovered in the want ads. In order to enter the setting, one of the authors visited the job service employment office and went through a standard application process. During the interview, he was told that the mall was embarking upon a promotional photo campaign and that someone was needed to play the role of the Easter Bunny. Because of his background in amateur photography, and because the authors believed he could better observe the public interacting with the Easter Bunny, he indicated that he would prefer the job of photographer. He was informed that a photographer had already been hired, but that they still needed somebody to wear the Easter Bunny costume. As it turned out, by having one of the authors "be" the Easter Bunny, our study not only allowed us to observe the public in interaction with the Easter Bunny, but also to gain valuable insights into the complex process by which an individual is socialized into such a fantasy role.

After initial screening by a representative of the photo company, he was hired to work the noon-to-seven shift for eleven days in March. He kept a detailed journal of his experiences. [He] was visited by the other two authors [who observed] his interactions with the public. . . . As Douglas (1976: 218) has noted, this approach offered the necessary balance between "the cool detachment of the outsider and the committed view of the insider." It also reduced the "uncertainty effects" of individual research (Douglas, 1976: 218). Additionally, by meeting during the field study and discussing our observations, we gained special insights into the actor's understandings of the Easter Bunny role and how he perceived his interactions with the public. More importantly, as Douglas (1976: 219) noted, we were able to "cross-check each other" and "balance each other in the collective grasps, understandings and reports that emerge[d] from the work."

• • •

SETTING

The setting for our ethnographic fieldwork was a shopping mall in a midwestern college town of approximately 26,000 people. The mall appears to be typical of others in the region.[1] At the time of the study it contained about twenty businesses including such large chains as Wal-Mart and Montgomery Ward. It also included the usual mix of small regional shoe stores, clothing shops, and other small business ventures. . . .

Initially, the photo company set up its booth in the center of the mall to make it accessible to the public. However, this location did not afford sufficient control over the environment in which social interaction took place. Consequently, the photo booth was moved to an empty store in the mall that the company believed better suited its needs. Mall businesses would have preferred that the Easter Bunny move about the shopping center and visit their stores, and certainly the children would have liked a "mobile" Easter Bunny. However, from the photo company's perspective, the Easter Bunny was meant to be a stationary prop, for the company believed the bunny could achieve its best commercial results only in a carefully structured environment.[2] . . .

The photo company required few props. A large wooden platform where photos were taken was used to divide paying customers from the merely curious. A red imitation-velvet sofa, that could seat the Easter Bunny and several children, rested on the platform. Other than the camera, and a small table where Easter cards, photos, and the cash drawer rested, only two other props were needed. On either side of the platform two placards, each containing a 5×7 child's photo with the Easter Bunny, and a $4.99 price tag were displayed. With these few props strategically arranged, the appropriate fantasy environment was achieved and the Easter Bunny was ready to encounter the public.

THE MALL EASTER BUNNY

Mythology, Hollywood, television, and newspaper cartoon characters have all contributed to our understandings of the Easter Bunny role. In ancient and medieval times the rabbit was strongly associated with fertility and renewal; its public mating rituals may account for this association. Moreover, rabbits are quite prolific, producing several large litters each year. This may explain the curious association between rabbits and colored eggs in the folklore of many people. In ancient Egypt, and in western Europe and America today, "children are told not that a hen laid them [colored eggs], but rather that a rabbit brought them in a basket" (Lonsdale, 1981: 102). . . .

Like all social roles, the mall Easter Bunny has no fixed meanings. Rather, it is defined and redefined through the process of social interaction. From the symbolic interactionist perspective, meanings are viewed as "social products, as creations that are formed in and through the defining activities of people as they interact" (Blumer, 1969: 5). In addition to media contributions, the meanings attached to the mall Easter Bunny are primarily derived from the interaction of three main actors, each of which has its own needs and objectives. A central player in the role's definition is the photo company that uses the Easter Bunny for one reason—to make a profit. The photo company designs the Easter Bunny suits, arranges for a place to sell its products, and hires people to promote its commercial goals. The public also brings to the interaction its own special definitions of the Easter Bunny role, which usually are void of any commercial connotations. Finally, the individual hired to play the Easter Bunny contributes to our understanding of the role. . . . For an individual to fulfill the requirements of the Easter Bunny role successfully, he/she must go through a socialization process whereby he/she is no longer merely a person in a bunny suit, but instead, *is* the Easter Bunny. As Fine (1983: 241) has indicated;

> When one takes on a role that is distinct from one's primary role, one must decide how to embrace it. How should one manifest identification with that new self? Should one play the role or play oneself in the contours of the environment in which the role is set?

The meanings that the individual attributes to the role and communicates to others emerge "by virtue of this process of communicating with himself" (Blumer, 1969:5).

THE PHOTO COMPANY AND THE EASTER BUNNY

In late March, one of the authors was told to report to the janitor's office at the mall where he would be provided an Easter Bunny costume. The photographic company carried a variety of Easter Bunny suits to fit persons of average size. The bunny costume was snow white and contained thousands of cotton-polyester curls that were meant to represent rabbit fur. No part of the human anatomy was allowed to show. The bunny suit stretched from neck to ankle, with pull-over socks covering the feet. Hands were hidden within white mittens. A large cotton tail that is usually part of the outfit, had been removed from the suit for some unknown reason.[3]

Most elements of the Bunny attire directed one's attention to the rabbit's head and face—the central focus of interaction. A blue vest with two rows of false red and gold buttons embellished the rabbit's upper torso, along with a double gold tie around the neck. The eyes dominated the face. Two black ovals with triangular white discs in each, gave the rabbit a permanent gleeful expression (a twinkle in his eyes). A tiny pink button nose called attention to the rabbit's mouth, which displayed oversized incisors and a permanently fixed pleasant smile. The puffy cheeks gave the Easter Bunny an infantile look, while the two cocked ears reinforced the image of the bunny as a playful or comic figure.

It was no accident that the photo company chose these particular features to be crafted onto the Bunny costume. The rabbit's kindly and playful visage was meant to amuse and entertain, but more important, it was designed to serve as a kind of neon sign that beckoned to children in a nonthreatening way, saying "come over here, kids, and have fun; visit the Easter Bunny." . . .

Only one other element was needed to make the enterprise work—the commercial photographer. If the Easter Bunny embodied fantasy, the photographer was pure commerce. Children were generally delighted after seeing the Easter Bunny. They laughed and shouted for joy, ran to him and often hugged and kissed his furry face. While this fantasy was played out, the photographer, usually in a very businesslike manner, discussed with their parents the price and quality of photos. After the sale was made, he carried the child to the Easter Bunny's lap, took his/her picture, and collected the fee. To the public the rabbit seemed fun and exciting. The photographer was usually perceived in opposite terms. He was viewed as dull, menial, or even bad—"someone out to get your money" or worse still, a person who probably didn't like kids, a public understanding that even the bunny actor initially shared.

Despite his initial negative reaction, the author soon adopted a very different attitude about the photographer. After playing the role briefly, he discovered that he was almost totally dependent upon the photographer for most of his human needs. The photographer was his "seeing-eye dog," literally leading him from location to location. For example, at break time he had to be led to the bathroom, and there the photographer assisted in removing the costume. Most importantly, he provided the one human contact with which the author could exhibit "backstage behavior" and for a brief moment resume his human and personal identity (Goffman, 1959: 112).

While the public tended to perceive the photographer in negative terms, relatively few seemed to recognize that without this role there would be no mall Easter Bunny. By taking responsibility for all commercial transactions, and providing for the bunny's earthly needs, the photographer allowed the Easter Bunny to remain in the realm of fantasy. If the Easter Bunny needed more candy or plastic rings, it was the photographer's responsibility to see that he was resupplied. He also picked up small children and placed them on the bunny's lap for their photo, and then removed them when finished.

The photographer's role was vitally linked to the bunny fantasy in that it enabled both the photo company and the public to deny that the Easter Bunny had any association with that most earthly of human endeavors—the making of money. . . . [T]he public was shielded from the fact that the rabbit was, in fact, a *shill*, an agent hired to promote purely commercial objectives.[4] This area was so sensitive that even the slightest association between the Easter Bunny and commerce was met with strong public disapproval, as we discovered during our research. . . . Midway through the study, the photographer made the mistake of displaying two photos of the Easter Bunny alone, each with a $4.99 price tag, instead of the typical photos of bunny and child. After hearing several negative comments including "that Bunny costs too much," the photographer realized his error, and he replaced the bunny photos with those which included children. Upon doing so, public hostility immediately subsided.[5]

PUBLIC UNDERSTANDINGS OF THE EASTER BUNNY

The mall Easter Bunny is a uniquely American invention. . . . In such an environment, the irrational may fill an obvious void granting the individual a sense of worth and allowing for the public expression of emotion, in the dehumanizing and impersonal context of buyer and seller. Although they stand on ground where human worth is measured by money alone, people get misty-eyed as they watch their children hug and caress the Easter Bunny and the rabbit respond in kind.

• • •

Only infants and children to about the age of two seemed to have difficulty responding to the Easter Bunny as a fantasy creature; in fact, many initially responded to him with uncertainty and fear.[6] As recorded in the bunny's journal, "they loved me at a distance, but getting to touch them took work." In most cases, it was only after receiving treats, and with much encouragement from their parents that they came to accept the Easter Bunny as a "good bunny" and define it in positive terms. Older children, aged three to seven, having watched their parents' positive responses to the bunny for a number of years, and having been exposed to many comic and playful rabbits on television, almost always reacted to the bunny with affection and joy. As logged in his journal, "they ran to me, hugged me and even kissed my false face."

Children from the ages of two or three up to about five years old largely perceived the Easter Bunny as a purveyor of gifts or rewards. Upon seeing the Easter Bunny, many children instantly extended their arms, palms up for their reward. As noted in his journal, the author wrote: "They were only interested in what I could do for them." Several children told the Bunny that Easter was very near their birthdays, and thus they should receive two presents. The childhood association of the Easter Bunny with gifts was so strong that many children seemed to consider the Easter Bunny and Santa Claus as almost one and the same. On numerous occasions, children asked the Easter Bunny if he were Santa Claus in a disguise. One child asked the bunny if he and Santa Claus exchanged gifts, and many others attempted to give the Easter Bunny a list of desired gifts that were to be delivered on Easter day.

If the Easter Bunny is perceived as a giver of gifts, he may, like parents everywhere, also deny such things, or even withdraw favors as punishment for improper behavior. Having witnessed their parents using such sanctions on many occasions, children seemed to clearly recognize the possibility. One young girl asked the Easter Bunny for candy, noting that she had been good the previous week. But in the same breath she told the bunny not to give her brother a treat, for during the same period he had hit her. Parents occasionally used the Easter Bunny to sanction a child's behavior, even in the Bunny's presence. One mother confessed to the Easter Bunny that she had told her daughter that if she kept sucking her thumb the Easter Bunny "would steal it."

By the time children had reached school age there was obvious recognition that the mall Easter Bunny was, in fact, a "man or woman" inside a bunny suit. Children of this age investigated the bunny's human characteristics, making their discoveries known to the actor. Questions were often couched in expressions of a concern for the bunny's welfare. At other times, children told the actor that certain human traits they discovered during their investigations were, in fact, desirable. One child noticing a green band showing the actor's tube socks, expressed concern that the bunny's shoes were too big for his feet. Another child, peering under the bunny head noticed eyeglasses, and told the actor that "it was good the Easter Bunny wore glasses." These discoveries on the part of children rarely upset the interaction, for as Goffman (1959: 91) noted, "Insofar as children are defined as 'non-persons' they have some license to commit gauche acts without requiring the audience to take the expressive implications of these acts too seriously." However, as he also pointed out, these discoveries potentially threatened the interaction because "whether treated as non-persons or not, children are in a position to disclose crucial secrets" (Goffman, 1959: 91).

School-aged children were fully aware that a fantasy was being played out, and that they could potentially disrupt it. However, other than revealing this fact to the bunny actor, they, like their parents, were unwilling to expose the rabbit's deceit. . . . Children protected the bunny fantasy not only for their own benefit and that of their parents, but also for younger children who they knew believed in such fantasies. By six, children recognized that they, along with their parents and the Easter Bunny, were in fact co-conspirators in a fiction promoted for the benefit of others. In his journal the actor wrote, "they [school age children] go up to the bunny, tell him their names and grade in school, politely receive their candy and leave . . . it seems they only wish to make their parents happy." But more may be involved. By participating in a social reality tacitly created by their parents, the photo company and the bunny actor, children may also show that they are making satisfactory progress toward adulthood.

There was an exception to this observation, and that was the behavior of male teenagers in groups. While others took considerable pains to promote the bunny fantasy, teenagers (especially teenage boys in groups), went to great lengths to expose, challenge, and ridicule the bunny fantasy. When alone, teenagers behaved much like adults, generally promoting the Easter Bunny fantasy. In contrast, groups of teenage males often taunted and teased the Easter Bunny. On one occasion, three 13-year-olds discovered the rabbit had a blind spot, and they took turns walking behind him and poking him in the back. The author found this doubly offensive; not only did he perceive it as a challenge to the Easter Bunny fantasy, but more importantly, it overtly challenged his human persona. On other occasions, a cub scout (in front of his peers) asked the bunny if he wanted to buy "Scout-O-Rama" tickets, and another teenager, after smelling the actor's after shave, called the Easter Bunny "musk rabbit," in a loud voice so that everyone could hear.

Of all age groups, adult responses, especially when the individual was alone, were most varied. Some adults ignored the bunny and did not respond to his waves. Others, especially men, met the bunny's greetings with hostile glares. The elderly almost always responded in a very positive way. They returned the bunny's waves, and many shook his hand or even hugged him.[7] The behavior of adult women was the most surprising to the author, for many responded to him in sexual terms. In one case, a woman winked at the bunny and ran her tongue suggestively over her lips. Another time, a woman asked if there was a "boy bunny" inside the suit and another young woman declared that he was a "hot to trot" bunny. Although one woman told the author that he was a "gay bunny," another told the photographer that "she wanted to take the bunny into a back room and rape him."

The strongest predictor of an adult's response to the Easter Bunny was whether he or she was in the presence of a child. In the presence of children, adults not only promoted the bunny fantasy, they seemed to "overact." As noted in his journal, "they made funny sounds (baby talk) and strange faces, called to their children and even played games." Much of their behavior seemed to be an attempt to show young children how they "ought" to respond to such a creature. . . .

In the presence of small children, adults apparently believed that it was so important that the bunny fantasy be maintained that they reacted negatively to anything interpreted as a threat to the fantasy. . . .

The parental need to perpetuate the bunny fantasy was readily capitalized upon by the photographer. By encouraging parent-bunny interaction, the photographer subtly applied added pressure on parents to purchase a photo. In some cases, parental commitment actually seemed to be called into the public limelight. In other words, after "playing with the bunny," encouraging the child to sit on his lap, etc., the photographer subtly implied that any *caring* parent could not possibly pass up the opportunity for a photo of his/her child with the Easter Bunny. Amid onlookers, many parents seemingly recognized that their fulfillment of the role of "good parent" had been publicly questioned. As Goffman (1971: 163) has noted, individuals need to maintain a favorable impression during social interaction, and consequently, "when the scene around him ceases to provide this information . . . he is likely to feel compelled to act to control the undesired impression of himself he may have made." In private, most adults would be unwilling to pay $4.99 for a photo valued at approximately twenty-five cents. However, when publicly acting out the fantasy scenario and responding to a challenge to their parental commitment, the reinterpretation of the situation transformed the photo price into a seeming bargain. For *only* $4.99, parents received the photo of their child with the Easter Bunny, while at the same time, their role of "good parents" was publicly confirmed.

THE ACTOR'S CONTRIBUTIONS TO THE BUNNY ROLE

While the public and photo companies try to shape understandings of the Easter Bunny role, they are not the only contributors. Those who play the Easter Bunny, usually young men and women who are often college students, also help shape its definition. There is considerable room for subjective interpretations and experimentation, for bunny actors receive little formal training; they are given a small list of the do's and don'ts of bunny behavior, given a costume, and sent out to play the part.

The public assumes that the Easter Bunny role is so simple and stereotypic that anyone can play it well. Our research indicates otherwise, for not only is there little latitude in playing a fantasy role, but the individual must also decide how much of one's "self" should be submerged in that role. Moreover, as Berger and Luckmann (1966: 77) have indicated,

> To learn a role it is not enough to acquire the routines immediately necessary for its "outward" performance. One must also be initiated into the various cognitive and even affective layers of the body of knowledge that is directly and indirectly appropriate to this role.

On his first day on the job, the author donned the Easter Bunny costume and, accompanied by the photographer, entered the mall. His initial reaction was one of acute embarrassment. He felt like a "man trying to be a bunny." Before he had put on the bunny costume, he thought that it would be like Halloween costumes he had worn as a child, outfits that were moderately comfortable and which to his thinking allowed him to express some semblance of "self." In contrast, the bunny costume was awkward and uncomfortable, and his every movement seemed stiff and unnatural. Guided by the photographer, he felt totally helpless. Moreover, the bunny head was inordinately heavy, and his visibility was poor. Hot and sweaty, and barely five minutes on the job, his greatest desire was to beat a hasty retreat from the mall and remove the detested costume.

Then he noticed that a large number of people had detected him. Their reactions were shocking. Not only did they fail to recognize his deceit or judge his appearance as foolish, they responded to him in a most positive way. Children shrieked and waved with obvious joy. With a basket in one hand and the photographer holding the other arm, the author could not immediately respond to their waves. So he decided to nod his head up and down, a tactic that apparently worked, for the slightest nod increased the children's expressions of glee. Even some adults waved and smiled at him, but he felt no need to respond to their greetings. To the author, it seemed silly for adults to wave to "a man dressed in a bunny suit."

By the time he reached the photo platform he felt more relaxed. But he still was unable to separate his bunny and human personas. He sat on the velvet sofa and the photographer began to place one child after another on his lap to have their pictures taken. At first, he watched them laugh and happily pose for their pictures without emotional reaction; all he could do was stare inside the bunny mask noting its every stitch and seam. The author also remained preoccupied with the heat generated inside the bunny suit; sweat ran in his eyes and down his nose reinforcing the author's belief that he was a man "trapped" within a bunny suit.

Surprisingly, these initial feelings and sensations quickly dissipated. As more children arrived to have their pictures taken, he focused his attention less on himself and the costume, and more on the children, noticing more and more how extremely happy they were in the Easter Bunny's presence. Soon he began to smile and laugh and to respond to the children's needs rather than his own. By the end of the day, after posing with dozens of children, he felt transformed. His journal entry that day read: "They know I am good . . . I have let myself go . . . and am happy go-lucky . . . I walk the mall and mingle with humans enjoying their hugs and smiles . . . I gave them gifts and freely returned their embraces . . . I have even become accustomed to being called cute, darling, and adorable." In short, he had become the Easter Bunny.

Several days into the job he began to feel guilty about his association with the commercial aspects of the role, and as the author noted in his journal "being a part of the photo racket."[8] Yet, at the same time, he found it impossible to separate their interests from his. For example, some people tried to cheat the photo company by claiming dissatisfaction with their photo, which, according to company policy, entitled them to a free photo. The actor, knowing their intent, recorded in his diary, "It is really strange how people could steal from the Easter Bunny."

Despite this notable transformation from being a "man in a bunny suit" to being a fantasy character, the author did not lose his sense of personal identity. For as Fine (1983: 206) has noted, "despite the ability of some [fantasy] players to *become* their characters . . . these roles are too temporary and compartmentalized for us to speak meaningfully of a role-self merger." Adopting a fantasy role, then, could more accurately be described as "role embracement" rather than "role merger" (Goffman, 1961: 106). Consequently, the author learned to balance his various roles, alternately or simultaneously being a man in a bunny suit, a researcher observing public interaction with a fantasy character, and/or the Easter Bunny. More importantly, he developed the skills necessary to adopt any of those roles with relative ease.

Although he learned that he could effectively perform a variety of roles, he also discovered that the public was unwilling to recognize any but the fantasy role. Speaking was his most obvious means of expressing both his human and individual identities, and occasionally, although it was against company rules, he tried to speak. However, he soon discovered that the photo company had designed the bunny suit in such a way that his speech, which according to Goffman (1967: 37), might not only place the speaker in jeopardy but others present as well, had little or no significant impact on the nature of bunny-human interaction. The head was designed in such a way that the author's voice resonated within the rabbit head rather than without. Thus, to the author it seemed he was always shouting. In contrast, the public heard only hollow whispering sounds which they could not clearly understand. Again, the photographer filled a critical need, serving in this case as the Easter Bunny's interpreter. After briefly attempting to understand the bunny's garbled sounds, many mall visitors turned to the photographer with a quizzical look, and as might be expected, the photographer was more than willing to help. The photographer's interpretation of what the bunny had said was almost always some variation of: "The Easter Bunny said that he would like to have his picture made with you, wouldn't that be fun?" Having heard these words many people needed no further encouragement, but proceeded directly to the photographic platform to fulfill the rabbit's request.

Another example of how the design of the suit negated the human persona was made apparent when the author's wife and two nephews visited him a week into the job. They approached him cautiously until they heard him speak. His speech, however, did not ensure that the interaction would be smooth, for his voice was too garbled to be understood and more importantly they were unable to separate voice from bunny persona. For example, when his normally affectionate nephews sat on their uncle's lap, they could not fully respond to either the uncle or bunny. Even the author's wife who sat on her husband's lap for a photo felt uncomfortable; she could hear her husband's voice coming from the bunny's head, but she could not overcome the feeling that she was "talking to the Easter Bunny."

The author also found that he was "entrapped" in the bunny role as the result of a variety of other public expectations. For example, the bunny suit was extremely hot, and thus he was constantly thirsty and in need of a soft drink. At first he tried to drink soda in a back room, but the public reacted negatively to his absence. So he began to drink his soda discretely through a straw, but in their presence. It was under these circumstances that the actor realized why the photo company had no need to establish elaborate rules of bunny behavior. Whenever his behavior deviated too far from public notions of the role, there were strong negative reactions. As he recorded in his diary "everyone who saw me doing these things stopped and stared in disbelief." In effect, the actor learned, as Goffman had predicted, that

> if he is willing to find out from hints and glances and tactful cues what his place is, and keep it—then there will be no objection to his furnishing this place . . . with all the comfort, elegance, and nobility that his wit can muster for him [Goffman 1967: 43].

Accepting public definitions of the role had other unanticipated results. As the author learned that the public expected a cheerful and playful bunny, he in turn, began to expect a warm and loving public. He expected people to respond to him with affection and joy and when they did not, he became upset and angry. He began to measure his days in the number of waves and hugs received. It only took two or three people to ignore him for him to define them as "hateful" and the entire day as a "grump day." As Fine (1983: 217) wrote, "In playing a character for a long time, identification grows and the player begins to feel what the character feels."

As the Easter Bunny, the author also learned that he had to temper his anger. For example, when poked in the back by teenagers, he had to understand that they were not merely poking at the human inside the bunny suit but the Easter Bunny as well, and that the public would not tolerate any expressions of hostility from a fantasy character. He also had to learn to live with human failings, as fantasy characters must do. He was often appalled by adults' behavior toward their children—especially if it alienated them from the Easter Bunny. Parents often forcibly pushed their children onto the bunny's lap. In his journal the actor noted, "some parents shoved kids down my throat so that neither of us was happy." Parents also punished their children in the Easter Bunny's presence, often by denying the bunny or his rewards to their children. On one occasion, because his child had initially rejected the Easter Bunny, a father took and ate candy presented to the child, and would allow the child none of it. On another occasion, for some unknown reason, a father had his picture taken with the bunny, but over the protests of his wife and children, would not allow their pictures to be taken.

If the "Easter Bunny" could express displeasure with such behavior he found that he had to temper it in the extreme. Although his smiling face might say "come hither," his body and hands could be used to express the opposite message. Children who became pests or demanded too much candy, might be unable to detect the bunny's ire by studying his countenance, but few failed to recognize the negative meanings in his body language. If small children pestered him too much, the bunny only had to stand and turn away. If adults irritated him, he disappeared into a back room in the mall and returned when they had departed.

By the end of the study, the author had come full circle in his socialization into the Easter Bunny role. He had learned to ignore physical discomforts and overcome feelings of embarrassment associated with being inside the bunny suit, and he had learned to successfully fulfill the bunny role while maintaining his individual and human personas. He also had come to understand the public's expectations of the role and the demands of him as a fantasy character. Finally, he learned that despite the severe limitations placed on his behavior by the photo company and the public, he could express his personal feelings by couching them in a socially acceptable way—the end result of any effective socialization process.

• • •

CONCLUSION

Socialization into the Easter Bunny role involves all of the complex social learning processes that are involved in the assumption of any social role. As we have clearly demonstrated, assuming the Easter Bunny role requires the acquisition of a complex set of attitudes and behaviors in interaction with a variety of social audiences. However, there are some unique characteristics involved in the assumption of a fantasy role that lend special insights into the socialization process. By assuming the Easter Bunny role one is afforded the rare opportunity (because of the anonymity involved) of taking on a role with very little, if any, risk to one's sense of personal identity. Moreover, the public totally disassociates the role from the actor. Significantly, however, the actor does not. Due to the socialization process the actor feels a need and, as we have described, finds a variety of ways to express his/her multiple selves. In other words, social roles take on meaning to those who occupy them that go beyond the structured cultural meanings assigned to the role. Consequently, when an individual is socialized into a role, even one which involves a fantasy character to be portrayed only for a very brief period of time in a special setting, it becomes a significant part of his/her overall concept of self.

NOTES

1. Jacobs in *The Mall* noted that there are 23,000 shopping malls in the United States and that they account for about half of all annual retail sales in the categories of general merchandise and clothing (Jacobs, 1984: v, 1).

2. According to Real (1977:85), Disneyland involves all the senses of the visitor by controlling the entire environment. A visitor is removed from the normal environment, thereby suspending usual reality-testing mechanisms. Persuasive techniques disguised as value-free entertainment actively involve the visitor in the ongoing themes and symbols of the park, creating a group consensus around these central themes and symbols.

3. We discovered later that the tail had been pulled off by some teenaged boys the previous spring.

4. This disassociation from the collection of money by a person whose motive is commercial, but perceived as altruistic, is not at all uncommon in other social arenas. For example, doctors almost never directly collect fees for their services. The doctor is perceived only as interested in helping the patient, while the receptionist or cashier is the person who insists on being paid, or having proper insurance forms completed.

5. Commercial photographers seem to be particularly adept at using fantasy to sell photos. One studio we have encountered uses "Mother Goose" as its trademark and utilizes a person dressed as Mother Goose to promote and display photos and to assist the photographer in posing children.

6. Hagstrom (1966:25) in his article "What is the meaning of Santa Claus" remarked that Marxist authors have shown that "children are often distressed by Santa and anxious in his presence and that adults can recall only happiness in their childhood experiences with Santa."

7. This supports Jacobs' (1984: 93) notion that for teenagers, suburban housewives, and retirees, "malls are . . . not . . . one of many alternative settings in which to pursue social interaction, but . . . [are] the *only* setting for such an undertaking."

8. Interestingly, while playing the Easter Bunny, the actor strongly resented the photographer for using the bunny fantasy to make money, totally ignoring the fact that for most actors the primary motivation for taking on the bunny role was also money. This seemingly hypocritical position may be a classic example of Goffman's (1959) dramaturgical analysis of sincerity as merely being a person taken in by his own act.

BIBLIOGRAPHY

Berger, P. L. and T. Luckmann
1966 *The Social Construction of Reality: A Treatise in the Sociology of Knowledge.* New York: Anchor.

Blumer, H.
1969 *Symbolic Interactionism: Perspective and Method.* Englewood Cliffs, NJ: Prentice-Hall.

Cooley, C. H.
1902 *Human Nature and the Social Order.* New York: Charles Scribner's Sons.

Douglas, J. D.
1976 *Investigative Social Research.* Beverly Hills: Sage.

Fine, G. A.
1983 *Shared Fantasy: Role Playing Games As Social Worlds.* Chicago: Univ. of Chicago Press.

Goffman, E.
1959 *The Presentation of Self in Everyday Life.* New York: Anchor.
1961 *Encounters.* Indianapolis: Bobbs-Merrill.
1963 *Behavior in Public Places.* New York: Free Press.
1967 *Interaction Ritual.* New York: Anchor.
1969 *Strategic Interaction.* Philadelphia: Univ. of Pennsylvania Press.
1971 *Relations in Public.* New York: Basic Books.

Hagstrom, W.
1966 "What is the meaning of Santa Claus?" *Amer. Sociologist.* 1:248-252.

Jacobs, J.
1984 *The Mall.* Prospect Heights, IL.: Waveland.

Longdale, S.
1981 *Animals and the Origins of Dance.* New York: Thames & Hudson.

Real, M.
1977 *Mass Mediated-Culture.* Englewood Cliffs, NJ: Prentice-Hall.

REVIEW QUESTIONS

1. Describe the impact of the following on the Easter Bunny role. Give concrete examples from the article.
   (a) The public
   (b) The photography company and the photographer
   (c) The individual inside the costume
2. How did the "Easter Bunny's" self-concept change when he stepped into the costume and played the role?
3. What aspects of socialization to the role of Easter Bunny might also occur in socialization to non-costumed, non-fantasy work roles? What aspects would be different?

Suggested Readings: Interaction in Institutional Context: Work and Economics

Biggart, Nicole. *Charismatic Capitalism: Direct Selling in America*. Chicago: University of Chicago Press, 1988.

Lorber, Judith. *Women Physicians: Careers, Status and Power.* New York: Tavistock, 1984.

Miller, Gale. *It's a Living: Work in Modern Society.* New York: St. Martin's Press, 1981.

Reimer, Jeffery. *Hard Hats: The Work World of Construction Workers.* Beverly Hills, Calif.: Sage, 1979.

Ritzer, George, and David Walczak. *Working: Conflict and Change*, 3rd ed. Englewood Cliffs, N.J.: Prentice-Hall, 1986.

Roy, Donald F. "Quota Restriction and Goldbricking in a Machine Shop," *American Journal of Sociology* 57 (1952): 427–442.

Schrank, Robert. *Ten Thousand Working Days.* Cambridge, Mass.: The M.I.T. Press, 1979.

Sell, Ralph. "Transferred Jobs: A Neglected Aspect of Migration and Occupational Change," *Work and Occupations* 10 (1983): 179–206.

Spradley, James P., and Brenda J. Mann. *The Cocktail Waitress: Woman's Work in a Man's World.* New York: John Wiley, 1979.

Stenross, Barbara, and Sherryl Kleinman. "The Highs and Lows of Emotional Labor: Detectives Encounters with Criminals and Victims," *Journal of Contemporary Ethnography:* 17 (1989): 435–452.

Terkel, Studs. *Working.* New York: Random House, 1974.

Williams, Bruce B. *Black Workers in an Industrial Suburb: The Struggle against Discrimination.* New Brunswick, N.J.: Rutgers University Press, 1987.

D. Health and Illness

IN CONTEMPORARY WESTERN SOCIETIES A HOST OF SPECTACULAR MEDICAL procedures and technologies permits us to trade in our kidneys and hearts, to rejuvenate our eyes and ears, and to prolong life itself beyond the capacities of our organs. These spectacular developments overshadow many other aspects of health, illness, and treatment in our society: a large number of people have little or no access to medical treatment; a great deal of mundane, repetitive, ameliorative treatment is rendered; a wide variety of health problems is caused by medical treatment itself; and the price tag attached to staying healthy and getting treated now consumes well over 10 percent of our national economy. Sociologists looking at America's present system of defining and dealing with health and illness cannot overlook any of these issues. While some sociologists study the social consequences of kidney dialysis machinery and artificial heart implants, others inquire into the types and prevalence of medical mistakes, the implications of the medical insurance system (or "third-party payers"), and the economic benefits some people reap at the expense of the sick.

The first article in this section is an overview of many sociological insights about our health-and-illness system. Candace Clark's review essay, "Sickness and Social Control," summarizes a large body of research on our society's ways of defining illness and disease, the organization of medical treatment, and a process called the "medicalization of deviance." This process involves changing conceptions of what an illness is and what causes people to stray from normality, or health. Such changes have led to a shift in the locus of social control in our society. In all human groups, healers have been in charge of controlling those deviant conditions defined as illness. In the Western world, over the past century or so, more and more conditions and behaviors have come to be *interpreted* as illnesses rather than as sin, criminality, or other types of deviance. And as more deviant conditions have come to be viewed as illnesses, medical personnel have been given a larger and larger role in controlling deviance than ever before in history. Surgery, drugs, hospitalization, and other techniques of medical intervention have gained tremendously in recent years, often replacing the old techniques of social control employed by religious leaders, teachers, parents, and the courts.

The ideas in Clark's article challenge the taken-for-granted ways in which most of us think about illness and deviance, medical treatment, and social control. Since Americans have more faith and trust in the expertise and good intentions of physicians than of any other occupational group, it is often difficult for us to stand back and assess the societal functions of medical theories and treatments. Yet just because we are not used to thinking of the social-control aspects of medicine does not mean that they do not exist. If we are to understand life in the United States in the late twentieth century, we must come to grips with the expanded role of medicine in defining and enforcing our norms.

The second selection, "The Social Meaning of AIDS" by Peter Conrad, examines why people blame the victims of disease, particularly in areas of sex- and behavior-related conditions. Public fear of AIDS and overreaction to its perils have made life more difficult for those who suffer from the disease but have not brought about the medical and social changes that could keep people safe from it.

Conrad also explores strategies for making the image of AIDS less frightening to the public. To confront the stigma and to prevent unnecessary fears of the disease, Conrad argues, professionals must do no less than change the social meaning of the disease. Doing so would reduce both the social and physical suffering of AIDS victims.

SICKNESS AND SOCIAL CONTROL

Candace Clark

INTRODUCTION

JUST AS EVERY SOCIETY HAS DEVELOPED A FAMILY SYSTEM AND AN ECONOMIC system, every society known to social scientists has developed a normative system to define, locate, and control illness (Wellin, 1978; Fábrega, 1974). What is considered illness in one society may be a mark of health in another—that is, illness categories are devised or constructed differently from one culture to another—yet every human group recognizes something as constituting illness and mobilizes resources in response to illness. I hope to demonstrate in this review essay that *the control of illness and sick people is one form of the more general phenomenon of social control.* Social control, any behavior or social-structural arrangement which encourages people to conform to societal norms and values, is an essential feature of all societies. Medical forms of social control have increased tremendously in importance in American society over the past century, edging aside religious, legal, educational, and familial forms and techniques of social control. An accurate and comprehensive picture of life and interaction in modern Western societies cannot omit the expanded role of medical models offering explanations of human experience and of medical means of transforming human behavior.

A first step in presenting this sociological view of the role of medicine is the clarification of the key terms illness, sickness, and disease, all of which have distinct and specific meanings here. As the terms are understood by sociologists today (Twaddle and Hessler, 1977:97), "illness"[1] refers to the *individual's perception* or claim of a problematic physiological experience, state, or change that he or she is feeling which is presumed to have biological causes. By "sickness" we mean the state of being defined and reacted to by *other societal members,* including relatives, friends, and employers, as having a problem or condition with presumed biological causes.

SOURCE: Candace Clark: "Sickness and Social Control" was written for the second edition of *Social Interaction*.

While all societies recognize illness and sickness, the concept of disease is a relatively new product of Western culture. "Disease" is used here to refer to *whatever medical practitioners define* as a cause of illness (Freidson, 1970:206, passim). This explanation may seem overly general, but it is impossible to be more specific when the phenomena considered as disease in our society, let alone others, are as varied as bacterial infection, diabetes, alcohol "dependence," and *anorexia nervosa* (an inability or unwillingness to eat). It is commonly believed by the public that a condition seen as a disease has a known biophysiological cause and cure. There is widespread acceptance within Western biomedicine of the theory that certain bacteria produce toxic reactions in human hosts; but the causes and cures of the other conditions mentioned above are not well understood at all. With regard to alcohol dependence, there is at present no single accepted theory as to its cause, nor is there even an adequate definition of "dependence" (Conrad and Schneider, 1980:82–102). And even with the bacterium, it is not necessarily the case that a disease will be recognized.

As Dubos (1959), Freidson (1970), and Dingwall (1976) have argued, diseases do not exist "in nature," but rather are culturally created *meanings* attached to particular conditions by human beings. As Sedgwick put it, "the blight that strikes at corn or potatoes is a *human invention*, for if man wished to cultivate parasites (rather than corn or potatoes) there would be no 'blight.' " And, "the invasion of a human organism by cholera germs carries with it no more the stamp of 'illness' than the souring of milk by other forms of bacteria" (Sedgwick, 1972:211). In order for a condition to come to be seen or interpreted as a disease, *it must first be considered a problem* by many members of a society. In societies in which diarrhea is widespread, for instance, this condition may be seen as normal rather than problematic, although in our own culture it is viewed as a problem to be dealt with by medicine and, therefore, evidence of disease.

If a problematic condition is related in some way to biological functioning, and if no means of control by other than medical techniques (for instance, prayer or legal action) are considered acceptable, medical practitioners may attempt to deal with it. In some cases, a medical treatment is discovered *before* the problem comes to be seen in medical terms. For instance, the discovery that the stimulant Ritalin has a tranquilizing effect on children led to the interpretation of children's disruptive behavior, short attention span, and fidgeting as a disease called hyperkinesis. Previously, such children were simply defined as "bad" and dealt with by teachers and parents as such (Conrad, 1975). In other cases, the medical profession has come to view certain conditions as diseases even though there is little evidence as to biological causes and no medical cure or effective treatment. Such was the case with many of the conditions which have come to be seen as "mental illness" rather than as sinful or illegal behavior (Szasz, 1961, 1970; Conrad and Schneider, 1980).

The process by which a condition comes to be viewed as a disease is in some respects a political one. That is, some groups may lobby for or against a disease interpretation. In our own society, a major lobbying effort by various homosexual organizations led to the removal of homosexuality from the list of mental illnesses in 1974 (Conrad and Schneider, 1980:204–8). Pediatric radiologists lobbied to have Battered Child Syndrome seen as a mental illness of parents who use violent techniques of child-rearing (Conrad and Schneider, 1980:163–66). Such behavior was not even viewed as a "problem" two centuries ago, let alone a "disease."

The final decisions as to whether a condition will be interpreted as a disease are made by those physicians who are in charge of preparing the diagnostic manuals of the profession. The U.S. government's National Institutes of Health and the World Health Organization based in Geneva, Switzerland, are in large part responsible for the listing of diseases. There may be widespread agreement among medical practitioners as to the decisions reached by these groups, or there may be less of a consensus. In some cases, votes have been taken of medical practitioners throughout the country, with the majority view determining whether a condition is or is not a disease.

It is often difficult for us to accept the position that the diseases recognized by Western biomedicine are socially constructed, because medical models for interpreting conditions have become deeply embedded in our culture's common stock of knowledge and are now part of our taken-for-granted reality. In fact, social scientists have sometimes argued that some diseases are "real" while some (such as alcohol use, violence toward children, and *anorexia nervosa*) are "abnormal" *behaviors* which happen to have physiological consequences but which are *not* "real" diseases. In doing so, they are participating in part in our culture's taken-for-granted reality. Rather than arguing what should and should not properly be called a disease, I have adopted the view here that disease is what medical practitioners say it is. This view will allow us to focus on *how practitioners treat* those they define as diseased.

Following these three definitions, we can see that one may *define oneself* as "ill" or claim to have an illness; be *diagnosed* as having a "disease" by a medical practitioner; and/or come to be *seen as* "sick" by parents, teachers, and co-workers. A moment's reflection will illustrate that these three distinct statuses are not necessarily occupied simultaneously. For instance, one may perceive oneself to be healthy, yet be diagnosed as having a disease and come to be viewed by significant others as sick. Or, one may feel ill, but be regarded as healthy (disease free) by medical practitioners and as healthy (not sick) by one's spouse and boss. In societies such as ours where the legitimacy of medical practitioners as experts is great, definitions of disease have a strong influence on the individual's definition of him- or herself as ill and the significant others' determination of sickness.

SICKNESS AS DEVIANCE

To understand the conceptual link between the control of sickness and social control in general, it is helpful first to come to view sickness (or impairment) as a special case or form of *deviance,* as medical sociologist Eliot Freidson argued cogently over two decades ago (1970:205–23; see also Mechanic, 1968:44–48; Goffman, 1963; Zola, 1972; Twaddle, 1973).

Deviance as a Label

Deviance is *not* a quality of an act or state which exists outside the confines of culture, but is rather a meaning, designation, or label which is both created by societal members and attached to particular individuals and/or to their behavior in the course of social interaction (Becker, 1973; Lemert, 1962, 1972; Katz, 1975). A behavior itself has no meaning unless societal members assign it one within their cultural framework of norms and within their understanding of situational contexts. Two individuals may engage in precisely the same behavior, yet one will be viewed as normal and the other as a criminal. The labeling process involves locating the individual within a more or less elaborate classification system as, say, a sex pervert or a check forger. In short, as situations are defined (Thomas, 1923), so are individuals—some as deviant, some as normal.

Sickness as a Label

As implied in my introduction above, a similar labeling process occurs regarding illness, sickness, and disease. This labeling process involves the use of the culture's "common stock of knowledge" and its stock of "expert knowledge" to make sense of or interpret a societal member's problematic physiological states and experiences. It must first be determined if the individual is to be seen as healthy or unhealthy. Then the unhealthy individual is classified (by self or others) as suffering from a particular type of ill health. The problematic physiological conditions or states we experience ourselves or recognize in others are almost always *ambiguous;* that is, they could be interpreted in a number of different ways even within one culture. For example, if an individual notices some physiological change, that change may be attributed to illness or it may (1) be seen as a non-problem or (2) be seen as a consequence of tiredness, possession by the devil, laziness, or some other "cause" that is culturally acceptable. ("Is this pain 'normal,' or am I having a heart attack?," "I may be getting the flu, or I may just be working too hard," "I've never thought about it this way before, but maybe his behavior does indicate that he is mentally ill.")

Recent research by David Locker indicates that a general pattern often followed by lay individuals in Western societies is first to define a problematic experience tentatively as "normal" until later evidence or the input of others causes a change in interpretation (1981:87–92; see also Zola, 1973). Medical practitioners, on the other hand, tend to view even the most ambiguous symptoms as evidence of disease (Freidson, 1970:263; Scheff, 1966:105–27; Rosenhan, 1973). Whatever the general tendencies of the parties involved in interpreting states of health, it is clear that the process of definition is a negotiated one. Our own interpretations are "validated" by checking them with others (Berger and Luckmann, 1966; Locker, 1981:62, passim). ("What do you think, Doctor? Is this sore throat serious?" "Do you think these spots are measles, Mom?" A physician says, "It doesn't *look* serious to me, but how do you *feel*?") All stages of the process of interpretation, validation, reinterpretation, and so on are rooted in interaction. The label "unhealthy" is, therefore, a negotiated social product. And the process of defining always involves comparison against a similarly socially constructed definition of "health" or "normality" (Lewis, 1953).

Societal Reaction to Labels

The act of labeling someone as either deviant or unhealthy usually implies that some sorts of responses will be made by societal members which are different from their responses to those labeled as nondeviants or healthy. As Lennard et al. put it, labels are instructions or messages for treatment, not just descriptive categories (1971). The sick person is considered "not normal," as is the deviant; and the reactions of societal members to the mugger, to the drunk driver, to the genius, or to the sick are not the same as responses to "normal" people. Various attempts, legal or medical, are often made to return deviants and the sick to a relatively normal state of functioning and/or to protect other societal members from interaction with them. In fact, it is by viewing these societal reactions that sociologists determine whether or not deviance or sickness exists. That is, an individual can be said to be deviant or sick *when others respond as if* that person belonged in the category (Becker, 1973; Sudnow, 1967). Moreover, the sick are labeled and reacted to as deviants.

Blame and Discreditation

To be sure, the term deviance usually carries negative connotations (except in the case of the "positive" deviant, e.g., the genius or the hero), while the term sickness may not (Locker, 1981:4–5). It is a general norm in most cultures that people viewed as sick are not to be blamed for their conditions or states (a "right"), if they act in ways that indicate their desire to improve (a "duty") (Parsons, 1951). On the other hand, those recognized as deviants are commonly felt to be able to control their actions and are therefore blamed for them (Locker, 1981:4–5). While the sick are described as "victims of" or "suffering from" diseases which they "contract," deviants presumably choose to act or think in certain ways—and are viewed by some as having more in common with disease than with the sick.

This generalization breaks down, however, when we consider the cases of AIDS, venereal disease and obesity, all of which are conditions recognized as diseases that evoke blame from many members of society (Cahnman, 1979). Studies of physicians' attitudes toward those labeled as alcoholics show that the majority hold alcoholics personally responsible for drinking (Conrad and Schneider, 1980:98). It is also common for medical practitioners to complain that some of their clients "bring their illness on themselves" by their living habits or by their disregard of medically meaningful symptoms until they reach an advanced state (Millman, 1976; Locker, 1981: 138–39).[2] These practitioners are blaming the sick.

More important, there is a "moral" aspect to sickness; sickness may not evoke blame, but neither does it evoke credit. Many sicknesses call forth severe negative evaluations of the moral worth of the sick, resulting in revulsion or ostracism—as in the cases of Typhoid Mary, those with disfiguring birth defects, the mentally ill, epileptics, and lepers (Goffman, 1963). In fact, medical anthropologist Horacio Fábrega (1974) has concluded from extensive research that, in all known societies, designating an individual as sick *inevitably involves discreditation* of that person. Over and above the fact that the sick person may not be blamed for his or her condition, he or she is not viewed as being as worthy, as creditable, as reliable, or as adequate as the healthy. Thus, the amputee and the flu sufferer, the cancer patient and the mentally ill are seen (to a greater or lesser degree) as less desirable prospective interactants than the healthy—even though the sick can claim a certain amount of sympathy and attention from the healthy. Discreditation in many ways sets up barriers to routine interaction between the sick and the "normal" population in everyday life. It should come as no surprise to find that there is often some reluctance to accept the label of sickness. On the contrary, we should expect an imperfect fit between definitions of disease and sickness, on the one hand, and definitions of illness, on the other.

We now see that sickness, though unique because of its actual or presumed biological causes, has a great deal in common with what is more commonly considered deviance and can, indeed, be seen as one form of deviance. Since the mere fact of defining deviance implies social control, it follows that diagnosing and defining disease and sickness imply social control as well.

CONTROL OF SICKNESS

What do gossip, smiles, frowns, awards, imprisonment, stares, fines, and the prescribing of antibiotics have in common? They are all behaviors or structural arrangements which serve to encourage societal members to conform to social norms—to think, to act, and indeed to look in ways which are within the culture's acceptable limits—or to discourage thinking or acting or looking outside acceptable limits. As such they constitute *social control.* Negative sanctions addressed to the deviant may induce return to normality; positive sanctions reward normality. Furthermore, negative sanctions allow those people seen as normal to view the consequences of their potential deviance, and a better understanding of what the boundaries of normality are considered to be is fostered (Dentler and Erikson, 1959).

Cultural norms, values, and beliefs tend to become manifested in our social organization and social structure. "Specialist" social statuses emerge, and patterned ways of dealing with nonconformity develop. Social-control specialists are charged with more than the ordinary degree of responsibility for exercising control, and are commensurately empowered to punish, reward, and treat. These specialists, in general, are termed *agents of social control.* Examples include teacher, judge, prison guard, child-guidance professional, advice columnist, and medical practitioner.

Practitioners and Social Control

Assume for a moment that we are societal engineers attempting to create a system for organizing and controlling the behavior of societal members so that the group can maintain its existence into the future. One problem we would have to face would be how to insure a reasonable supply of productive members to carry out tasks which are important for societal survival. Our society could not long persist if most of its members were sick most of the time, since sickness is almost universally seen as a legitimate reason for not engaging in one's regular social functions, such as feeding and dressing oneself, going to school, going to work, and caring for others. That is, one of the norms of the sick role is that those recognized as legitimately sick should not be required to carry out their normal responsibilities (Parsons, 1951). One societal problem, then, is to guarantee that not everyone is sick—enters the sick role—at the same time.

Additionally, we may find that continual performance of social functions by our societal members, day in and day out, rain or shine, may prove difficult and stressful. An occasional release from the demands of work, family, and community roles may make it easier for our members to function—and the population easier to control—over the long run. Thus, another problem is to provide "safety valves," occasional releases from constant drudgery, for our societal members.

As societal engineers, we might devise any number of strategies to deal with these problems. One such strategy might be to rely on medical practitioners as our agents of social control. While the process is by no means as conscious and formal as this hypothetical case makes it seem, we submit that practitioners have come to function in just such a manner in all societies.

Treatment as Social Control

Let us take up these problems in order, beginning with supplying productive societal members. The reader will recall that the designation of sickness brings with it discreditation. It might be suggested that this discreditation, coupled with pain and suffering, could be sufficient to motivate people to return to normality or to feel inadequate enough to shun association with normal individuals. Rather than trusting solely to the motivation and abilities of the afflicted individuals to get better, however, all societies have evolved one or more "specialist" positions of medical practitioner (Hughes, 1968). Practitioners—shamans, mechanists, physicians, and the like—are relied upon by their societies to develop models or theories of what illness is, how it is caused, and how it can be eliminated or controlled, thereby contributing to the maintenance of a reasonable supply of productive societal members.

A rather small number of *techniques* of medical treatment have been devised in the course of human history. Drugs, poultices, surgery, bone setting, confinement and isolation, instrumental interventions (such as acupuncture, electric shock, or leeching), talking, ritual, magic, and appeal to the supernatural—all are techniques which have been used by medical practitioners in a wide variety of societies to control sickness and the sick. These techniques have been put to use in several *forms* or *modes* of social control: (1) returning the sick to normal functioning, (2) punishment, (3) isolation, and—occasionally—(4) altering society to prevent or alleviate sickness.

A few words are in order concerning the general implications of the disease concept of Western biomedicine for treatment in our society. Some belief systems, including Christian Science, see the causes of illness in the supernatural rather than in disease. Other systems have pointed to the social conditions of poverty and crowding as the causes of illness (Twaddle and Hessler, 1977:9–11). Our current belief system views illness as a result of foreign organisms attacking a person or an organ of a person or as a result of the malfunctioning of the body itself. In a word, we view disease as the cause of illness and as "person-centered" rather than societally, environmentally, or supernaturally centered. Our searches for cures and treatments for those conditions we interpret as disease-caused are, therefore, likely to focus on the individual level. The great success of germ theory in controlling illness related to microbial infection has probably been responsible for this thrust in Western biomedicine, although germ theory has come to be recognized as not very useful for understanding chronic, degenerative, or mental illnesses (Strauss, 1975; Twaddle and Hessler, 1977:13–15). *As a result of the person-centered disease concept, control and treatment of sickness often means control and treatment of the sick individuals, as we shall see below.*

RETURN TO NORMALITY: First, medical techniques may be used in an effort to return the sick to a level of functioning as close as possible to, or better than, that existing before the onset of sickness. (Of course, the societal expert, the medical practitioner, has a large voice in determining what is "normal.") Thus, the physician prescribes drugs in an attempt to rid the body of toxic microbes or to reduce the effects of stress, sets a broken bone, or removes abnormal tissues. The shaman or *curandero* (curer) administers herbs to try to reduce fever. Early physicians in the U.S. who viewed "Negritude" (the state of being Negro) as a disease used drugs, poultices, and the like to change blacks into whites (Szasz, 1970:153–59). All of these activities have as their goal, at least partially, the return of the sick person to "normality." This form of social control is the one which is most widely recognized as an appropriate goal of medical treatment, since it is usually assumed to be in line with the interests of the individual sufferer as well as the interests of the society.

PUNISHMENT: Second, both treatment itself and certain healers in specific may serve to punish the sick, whether the healers are conscious of this effect or not.[3] Punishment may encourage return to normality among the sick as well as signaling to the normal the consequences of their potential lapses from normality.

Confinement in a hospital is often deemed punishing by the hospital's clients (Roth, 1972:426–28). The restrictions and routines of the bureaucratically organized hospital demand that the client give up claims to privacy, mobility, and liberty in general. Diet and sleeping times are out of the control of the client. Even ambulatory clients are often refused permission to leave the hospital temporarily; those who do so may forfeit the benefits of medical insurance and the right to future care (Roth, 1973).

A more extreme case of this general rule applies in the case of incarceration in a mental hospital (especially involuntary incarceration). Not only are daily activities regimented, conformity to dress regulations enforced, and personal liberty circumscribed, but civil rights are forfeited (Szasz, 1970:65–66). All of these practices lead to a redefinition of self for the client (Goffman, 1961; Scheff, 1966). Additionally, non-ordinary measures are adopted in the mental hospital to ensure conformity to the bureaucratic regimen, such as routine administration of large quantities and dosages of tranquilizing drugs (Rosenhan, 1973), assignment to solitary confinement, and the use of the straitjacket. These techniques may be painful and/or dangerous, as is electroconvulsive shock, still a common form of "treatment" for the depressed which is quite often viewed explicitly as punishment by the clients. Psychiatrist Thomas Szasz has noted the punishing aspects of the treatment of mental patients, stating that "people often prefer a cure that kills to no cure at all" (1982).

Moreover, incarceration in a mental hospital produces *stigma* so great as to limit the ex-patient's ability to participate in society after his or her release (Goffman, 1961). Ex-convicts may be more readily accepted as neighbors, workers, and friends than ex-mental patients. Phillips (1963) reports that public views of the so-called mentally ill are more negative in cases where hospitalization has occurred than when less formalized treatment has been given or when no treatment at all was administered. Hospitalization, rather than the individual's behavior, elicited stigma.

Outside the realm of the hospital as well, examples of the use of medical techniques as punishment can be found. Barker-Benfield (1976) documents, for instance, the widespread practice during the late 1800s and early 1900s in the United States of performing hysterectomies and clitoroidectomies to eliminate "non-feminine" behavior in women. Sterilization operations performed on the poor and the mentally retarded (usually women) without their informed consent serve to remove the rewards of parenthood from people considered unworthy (Davis, 1974; Caress, 1975) as the family-planning movement of the 1960s may also have done (Kammeyer et al., 1975).

Additionally, programs to "help" handicapped or impaired populations are often punitive in their effects (Freidson, 1966; Sussman, 1966; Wiseman, 1979), a point of which many handicapped are painfully aware. Scott (1969) found that the blind, for example, very often attempted to avoid the label of blindness and the services of agencies to aid the blind. They recognized that, by accepting the label, they would be set apart from sighted society both symbolically—as when white canes and guide dogs signal a deviant condition—and physically—as a result of work and leisure activities organized for the blind only. These consequences of defining themselves as blind and accepting "help" were considered punishments by many.

In a less severe form, contacts with medical personnel in our society involve a host of other *degradations* and *inconveniences* related to the unequal distribution of power in the client-practitioner relationship. In most cases these days, the client (the sufferer) must leave his/her own surroundings and travel to receive services from the practitioner on the latter's home "turf." The cost in time and money is added to the *interactional* disadvantage to the client of trying to maintain poise in strange surroundings. As Barry Schwartz points out elsewhere in this book, the expenditure of time in waiting is a cost also borne disproportionately by the client. The use of mystifying terminology and jargon by medical personnel underscores the client's feelings of ignorance and the practitioner's status as an "insider." Outright condescension by the practitioner that challenges the client's competence may also occur (Locker, 1981: 155–65).

Although the client is the one who has the problematic condition, it is common in our society to treat the sick as though they cannot be trusted to be "in their right minds" when giving accounts of what they are experiencing. Clients' assessments of their own conditions are, therefore, often ignored or discounted, adding to their feelings of helplessness. The "good patient" is one who asks no questions, turning control over his or her fate to the practitioner (Glogow, 1973).

As if this were not enough, the client may be asked to disrobe. In most settings in our society, nudity or semi-nudity puts one at a severe interactional disadvantage. Members of what other occupational groups are allowed to remain clothed while interacting with clients who sit or lie *sans* apparel? The gynecological exam is an example of one situation fraught with embarrassment and uneasiness, in part for this reason (Emerson, 1970).

If medical treatment can be costly or punishing in terms of loss of liberty, pain, danger, stigmatization, and degradation, it is also costly in *monetary* terms in our society. The United States is one of the very few industrialized countries in the world today in which the sick person is expected to pay the costs of services as they are rendered—i.e., when he or she is ill (Waitzkin and Waterman, 1974; Navarro, 1976).[4] Other societies finance medical care with public funds, the practitioners receiving salaries or yearly "capitation" payments for each client under their care, rather than collecting a fee from the ill for each service performed (Anderson, 1972). Some segments of our population—the poor and the elderly—receive some aid with medical bills, and medical insurance (itself very costly) eases or diffuses the financial burden for many others. Still, ours is a nation in which high medical costs lead many to delay or forgo treatment and in which a catastrophic condition or accident may result in severe financial difficulty for the sick and their family members. Medical costs, then, may be seen as a type of disincentive to seek treatment, or as a punishment similar to a fine levied by a judge or jury.

Closely related to the financing issue is that of *"unnecessary"* medical procedures. In essence, the practitioner in the United States can create a portion of the "demand" for his or her services by recommending that clients be observed and/or treated. The fee-for-service method of paying physicians encourages high rates of service, since procedures ranging from laboratory tests to surgery are financially beneficial to the practitioner. Some examples of commonly overrecommended procedures are hysterectomies, tonsillectomies, routine blood work, and the annual physical checkup (Scully, 1980; Millman, 1976; Freidson, 1970:257–58). The costs to the client of unnecessary procedures can be measured in terms of pain and suffering (occasionally death), money, time, and inconvenience.

Many of us are not used to thinking of medical treatment as having such a wide variety of punishing aspects. Or, we calculate the benefits of medical care as outweighing the costs. Nevertheless, medical treatment does entail costs and punishments. To the extent that these punishments encourage those who are sick to return to "normal" and those who are not sick to remain healthy, society "benefits" from them and they function as social control.

ISOLATION: A third major form of medical social control over sickness involves *protecting the healthy by removal of the sick person* from his or her normal environment. A quarantine approach such as this is based on a *contagion model* of the cause of illness, in which the removal of the "bad apple" is deemed appropriate to prevent the spread of the condition to others. It has been most often applied when evidence exists that a microbe is causing an illness. Room (1975) argues, however, that the contagion-quarantine model is the logic increasingly applied in the case of drug use (a newly recognized disease). The drug user is seen as capable of "infecting" others and thus must be removed from normal society to a special location, for the protection of the larger group. Additionally, the public relies on the staff of the mental hospital to isolate those mental patients believed to be dangerous to others. Thus, we can see that some aspects of incarcerating people in mental hospitals and segregating the handicapped, in addition to punishing them, fit with this model of protection of the healthy.

In a similar vein, medical diagnosis and treatment may serve as a sorting process for other societal institutions. By certifying who is healthy, the physician aids employers, the military, sports teams, and the like to select healthy members and reject others (Daniels, 1969; Illich, 1976; 76–77).

ALTERING SOCIETY: Fourth, and more rarely, social organization itself may be altered in order to control sickness. Stressful working conditions may be eliminated, sanitation systems may be put into operation, pollution-producing industrial practices may be controlled, and so on. (See Reverby, 1972, for further discussion of health-promoting measures as distinct from illness-response measures.) Such practices are usually regarded in our society as in the province of public health, a branch of medicine which is distinctly lower in prestige and monetary rewards than those branches which take a more person-centered approach to control. The concern is often voiced that altering societal conditions is more expensive than treating persons; yet, with more than one of every ten dollars of the total Gross National Product of the United States being spent on medicine ($425 billion, or more than $1300 per person, in 1985; *World Almanac*, 1987), it is difficult to view costs alone as the reason for the limited use of societal alterations. For whatever reasons, we see again that control of sickness is often accomplished by controlling the sick.

Sickness As Social Control

We turn now to the issue of release from the lifelong burden of societal responsibilities. Vacations provide a degree of release (except for mothers who attend to child-care duties whether the family is at home or away). Sleep also, in addition to having physiological benefits, allows the individual to escape temporarily from the pressures of interaction (Schwartz, 1970). Another form of release occurs when one is defined as sick and enters the sick role, as Talcott Parsons noted over forty years ago (1951). Because most conditions are temporary and self-limiting, and because the sick person is expected (1) to want to improve and (2) to cooperate with the experts in order to do so, the release associated with sickness is usually temporary and controlled. Medical practitioners, as the primary legitimate definers of sickness, serve as *gatekeepers* channeling people into the sick role. They serve as societal agents controlling "release time." The uses of treatment discussed above are then brought into play to channel the sick out of the temporary role. Thus, sickness itself, defined and controlled by medical practitioners, may serve an important social-control function for society.

The importance of the sick role as a safety valve has long been recognized by prison officials who must maintain control over their "societies of inmates." Prisoners in most penal facilities are routinely cycled through sick bay, presenting their claims of illness to practitioners who confirm or deny them (Twaddle, 1976). When prison physicians adopt get-tough policies and refuse to legitimate claims to illness, control of the prisoners often becomes difficult or impossible to accomplish (Waitzkin and Waterman, 1974:46–52).[5] In the prison context—and in the military as well (Waitzkin and Waterman, 1974:56)—allowing people to enter the sick role on a temporary basis facilitates social control in the long run. The medical practitioner may be seen as providing an important social-control service here as in the larger society.

THE MEDICALIZATION OF SOCIAL CONTROL IN THE UNITED STATES

It should be clear by this point that medical practitioners have a great potential for wielding power to the end of social control. In our own society, that power has increased dramatically over the past half century or so, for several interrelated reasons. First, our own trust and faith in the medical profession has increased, legitimating and reinforcing the power of healers (Krause, 1977). Few question the expertise of the medical profession, the benefits of prescribed treatments, or the size of the medical bill. Medical models of defining problematic experiences and medical techniques of treating them have caught on in the lay public's consciousness and imagination. Whereas medical explanations of events—or definitions of situations—were once regarded with suspicion or hostility or amused tolerance, the medical approach has become not only accepted but also popularized and has entered the common stock of knowledge of our culture. That is, the lay public themselves increasingly invoke medical models to define situations, states, and events. Medical metaphors abound: "There is a cancer growing on the presidency." "We live in a sick world." "If you don't take that offer, you're crazy." "Surgery is required to rid ourselves of the tangle of laws governing this area." Medical diagnoses by lay persons are legion: "That's just a virus." "John has strep throat." "Of course, your headache is due to stress." Furthermore, many occupational groups such as social workers and parole officers are adopting medical and para-medical approaches to their clients, thereby borrowing a degree of prestige from medicine (Chalfant, 1977).

Second, the profession of medicine has achieved a state of professional autonomy of impressive magnitude (Freidson, 1970; Brown, 1979). Physicians, unlike most other occupational groups, control the production of new members by determining the content of medical education and the numbers and types of new recruits. Licensing of physicians also rests solely in the hands of the medical profession. Medical mistakes (deviance among the agents of social control) are dealt with mainly within the medical community, despite what the widespread publicity of some recent legal suits brought against physicians might lead us to believe (Millman, 1976). Fees for medical services are also subject to little outside regulation. The terms, hours, and content of physicians' jobs are dictated by no outside source, except perhaps the clients' willingness and ability to pay for certain types of services. Physicians enjoy a great deal of autonomy and freedom from outside intervention in their own profession, and they also exercise control and influence over other medical groups, such as nursing, pharmacy, and the like (Freidson, 1970:47–70). The trend toward group- and hospital-based practice, and especially the rise of medical "empires" connected with university research-and-teaching hospitals, have contributed to a heightening and consolidation of medical control over their own and other occupational groups (Ehrenreich and Ehrenreich, 1970).

Third, and perhaps most important, more and more conditions have come to be defined as diseases every year by the medical profession. Currently there are more than a thousand categories of disease. A large proportion of the new diseases recognized since World War II are behavioral rather than physiological in origin, and most fall into the general category of "functional" mental illness (Conrad and Schneider, 1980: 53). Hundreds of conditions have been added to the medical nosology in recent decades, including obesity, sociopathy, alcoholism, hyperactivity in children, *anorexia nervosa*, minimal brain dysfunction, and drug addiction. These conditions once were interpreted in terms of "sin" or "badness" or "illegality" but are now routinely conceived of as actual diseases. Another candidate for disease status is *hysteroid dysphoria*, a recently coined term to describe "love junkies" who feel a need to be in love. "Limerance" is another recently created term for this love obsession, although some prefer the less mystifying "lovesickness." Drug therapy is offered by some physicians for this condition (Sobel, 1980). Although *hysteroid dysphoria* may not ultimately come to be widely recognized as a disease, many other conditions undoubtedly will. Thus, the domain of medicine is expanding, and the proportion of the population subject to treatment with medical techniques is growing correspondingly. The increase in the number of disease categories explains in part the increased expenditures for medicine in our society, from about five percent of the Gross National Product in 1950 to ten percent today (Fenninger and Meeker, 1980:6).

In sum, social control can be said to be increasingly medicalized, because both the power and domain of medicine have expanded, with the blessing of the lay public.

SOCIOLOGICAL IMPLICATIONS

In concluding, I should note a few of the implications of the increased medicalization of social control for American society which are of particular sociological importance. First, social control is achieved over many types of problems without the imposition of extreme degrees of discreditation. Since blame is often not assigned to the sick, they may receive attention and support not available under other systems of social control. Furthermore, much medical treatment is more effective and efficient than previous methods of control. In these cases, employing medical models to define and treat conditions is actually useful to individuals and/or to society. This outcome, which may be more humane than the effects of legal social control, is balanced, however, with others not as sanguine.

Second, medical treatment is less readily recognized as social control than is legal intervention. While the court and the prison are seen as overtly "on society's side," medicine is presumed (as is religion) to act in the interests of the individual. This presumption is particularly dangerous given the great power, prestige, and influence of medical practitioners vis-à-vis their clients. If the social-control functions of medical treatments are not obvious, we are less likely to provide safeguards for individual rights in this arena (Kittrie, 1971; Mechanic, 1973). Social control is not recognized as such and, in a manner of speaking, goes underground. Currently, legal and ethical debates are surfacing over the rights of clients to refuse treatment, to be informed of medical diagnoses and procedures, and to ask questions of medical practitioners regarding their bills. These debates may signal a degree of public awareness of the problems of "hidden" social control.

A third consequence of the medicalization of social control is not unique to medicine, but it is nonetheless important. The person-centered nature of much medical treatment focuses attention away from societal problems and "privatizes" them. That is to say, what *could* be viewed as a failure of societal organization and structure comes to be interpreted as the "failure" of the individual. Conrad (1975) gives a telling example to illustrate this point in his analysis of hyperactivity in children. What could have been seen as a problem of rigidly organized schools has become a disease located in the child. Treatment involves drug therapy for the individual rather than a restructuring of the school environment.

Stress provides yet another example. Stress has increasingly come to be seen as related to any manner of other problematic conditions, from digestive-tract problems to suicide to the susceptibility to influenza. Medical models of stress have tended to focus on the individual and to find solutions in psychoanalysis or tranquilizers or physical exercise. By focusing thus, attention is shifted from societal conditions—time clocks, traffic jams, deadlines, competition, rapid social change, and unemployment—to the person. Taking the opposite, society-centered approach, Brenner has found evidence for increases in suicides and heart problems corresponding to increases in unemployment (1973). Evidence such as this calls into question the usefulness of person-centered approaches to disease. That is, from the standpoint of the individual or from the standpoint of the society, medical models for defining and treating some human problems may not be useful at all, *over the long run*. The society, by not paying attention to social-structural problems, may allow them to grow to the point that they are insoluble.

NOTES

1. Impairment and disability may also be considered as categories similar to illness (Freidson, 1966); but, for the sake of brevity, I will not make continued reference to impairment and disability.

2. Of course, clients may also be criticized for presenting themselves to their physicians with "unimportant" or "nonexistent" symptoms (Locker, 1981:62, passim)—a classic double-bind situation for the client.

3. I am ignoring in this discussion the issue of iatrogenic (treatment- or physician-produced) disease or impairment, since I assume that most cases of this type are accidental. Nonetheless, iatrogenic conditions are a common feature of treatment. It is estimated that about 20 per cent of hospital clients leave the hospital with a problem they did not have when they entered (Roth, 1972). Illich contends that the increased tendency of the population to seek care in modern times has meant that treatment has become a considerable public-health problem (Illich, 1976:26–34, passim). To the extent that clients and potential clients are aware of the dangers involved in medical treatment, that aspect of treatment may be seen as a deterrent or punishment.

4. For a more detailed discussion of the problems inherent in the U.S. system of medical-care financing, see Fuchs (1974) and Carlson (1976).

5. Note that I am not attempting to judge whose claims are more valid, the prisoner's or the physician's. In fact, in most cases it probably makes little difference, since the power to define rests so one-sidedly with the practitioner in the prison setting.

REFERENCES

Anderson, Odin W.
1972 *Health Care: Can There be Equity? The United States, Sweden and England.* New York: Wiley.

Barker-Benfield, G. J.
1976 *The Horrors of the Half-Known Life.* New York: Harper & Row.

Becker, Howard S.
1973 *Outsiders: Studies in the Sociology of Deviance* (2nd ed.). New York: Free Press.

Berger, Peter, and Thomas Luckmann
1966 *The Social Construction of Reality: A Treatise in the Sociology of Knowledge.* Garden City, N.Y.: Doubleday.

Brenner, M. Harvey
1973 *Mental Illness and the Economy.* Cambridge: Harvard University Press.

Brown, E. Richard
1979 *Rockefeller Medicine Men: Medicine and Capitalism in America.* Berkeley: University of California Press.

Cahnman, Werner
1979 "The Moral Treatment of Obesity." Pp. 439–54 in Howard Robboy, Sidney L. Greenblatt, and Candace Clark, eds., *Social Interaction* (1st ed.). New York: St. Martin's Press.

Caress, Barbara
1975 "Sterilization: Fit to Be Tied," *Health/PAC Bulletin* 62:1–6, 10–13.

Carlson, Rick J.
1976 *The End of Medicine.* New York: Wiley-Interscience.

Chalfant, Paul
1977 "Professionalization and the Medicalization of Deviance: The Case of Probation Officers," *Offender Rehabilitation* 2:77–85.

Conrad, Peter
1975 "The Discovery of Hyperkinesis: Notes on the Medicalization of Deviant Behavior," *Social Problems* 23:12–21.

Conrad, Peter and Joseph Schneider
1980 *Deviance and Medicalization: From Badness to Sickness.* St. Louis: Mosby.

Daniels, Arlene Kaplan
1969 "The Captive Professional: Bureaucratic Limitation in the Practice of Military Psychiatry," *Journal of Health and Social Behavior* 10:255–65.

Davis, Morris E.
1974 "Involuntary Sterilization: A History of Social Control," *Journal of Black Perspectives* 1:46.

Dentler, Robert A. and Kai T. Erikson
1959 "The Functions of Deviance in Groups," *Social Problems* 7:98–107.

Dingwall, Robert
1959 *Aspects of Illness.* New York: St. Martin's Press.

Dubos, Rene
1976 *Mirage of Health.* Garden City, N.Y.: Doubleday.

Ehrenreich, Barbara and John E. Ehrenreich
1970 *The American Health Empire.* New York: Random House.

Emerson, Joan P.
1970 "Behavior in Private Places: Sustaining Definitions of Reality in Gynecological Examinations." Pp. 74-97 in Hans P. Dreitzel, ed., *Recent Sociology* No. 2. New York: Macmillan.

Fábrega, Horacio, Jr.
1974 *Disease and Social Behavior.* Cambridge: M.I.T. Press.

Fenninger, Randolph B. and Edward F. Meeker
1980 "Decade of the 1970's: Window on the 1980's: A Review of Health Care Policy." Pp. 3–21 in Gerald L. Glandon and Roberta Shapiro, eds., *Profile of Medical Practice 1980.* Monroe, Wisc.: American Medical Association.

Freidson, Eliot
1966 "Disability as Social Deviance." Pp. 71–99 in Marvin Sussman, ed., *Sociology and Rehabilitation.* Washington, D.C.: American Sociological Association.
1970 *Profession of Medicine.* New York: Dodd, Mead.

Fuchs, Victor
1974 *Who Shall Live? Health, Economics, and Social Choice.* New York: Basic Books.

Glogow, Eli
1973 "The Bad Patient Gets Better Quicker," *Social Policy* 4:72–76.

Goffman, Erving
1961 *Asylums.* Garden City, N.Y.: Doubleday.
1963 *Stigma: Notes on the Management of a Spoiled Identity.* Englewood Cliffs, N.J.: Prentice-Hall.

Hughes, Charles C.
1968 "Medical Care: Ethnomedicine." Pp. 87–97 in David Sills, ed., *International Encyclopedia of the Social Sciences,* Vol. 10. New York: Crowell, Collier & Macmillan.

Illich, Ivan
1976 *Medical Nemesis: The Expropriation of Health.* New York: Pantheon.

Kammeyer, Kenneth C. W., Norman R. Yetman, and McKee J. McClendon
1975 "Race and Public Policy: Family Planning Services and the Distribution of Black Americans." Pp. 402–21 in Norman R. Yetman and C. Hoy Steele, *Majority and Minority: The Dynamics of Racial and Ethnic Relations,* 2nd ed. Boston: Allyn & Bacon.

Katz, Jack
1975 "Essences as Moral Identities," *American Journal of Sociology* 80:1369–90.

Kittrie, Nicholas
1971 *The Right to Be Different: Deviance and Enforced Therapy.* Baltimore: Johns Hopkins University Press.

Krause, Elliott A.
1977 *Power and Illness: The Political Sociology of Health and Medical Care.* New York: Elsevier.

Lemert, Edwin
1962 "Paranoia and the Dynamics of Exclusion," *Sociometry* 25:2–20.
1972 *Human Deviance, Social Problems, and Social Control* (2nd ed.). Englewood Cliffs, N.J.: Prentice-Hall.

Lennard, Henry, et al.
1971 *Mystification and Drug Misuse.* New York: Perennial Library.

Lewis, Aubrey
1953 "Health as a Social Concept," *British Journal of Sociology* 4:109–24.

Locker, David
1981 *Symptoms and Illness: The Cognitive Organization of Disorder.* London: Tavistock.

Mechanic, David
1968 *Medical Sociology: A Selective View.* New York: Free Press.
1973 "Health and Illness in Technological Societies," *Hastings Center Studies* 1:7–18.

Millman, Marcia
1976 *The Unkindest Cut: Life in the Backrooms of Medicine.* New York: Morrow.

Navarro, Vicente
1976 *Medicine under Capitalism.* New York: Prodist.

Parsons, Talcott
1951 *The Social System,* Chapter 10. Glencoe, Ill.: Free Press.

Phillips, Derek L.
1963 "Rejection: A Possible Consequence of Seeking Help for Mental Disorders," *American Sociological Review* 28:963–72.

Reverby, Susan
1972 "A Perspective on the Root Causes of Illness," *American Journal of Public Health* 62:1140–42.

Room, Robin
1975 "The Epidemic Model and Its Assumptions," *Quarterly Journal of Studies in Alcohol* 1:16–21.

Rosenhan, David L.
1973 "On Being Sane in Insane Places," *Science* 179:250–58.

Roth, Julius
1972 "The Necessity and Control of Hospitalization," *Social Science and Medicine* 6:425–46.
1973 "The Right to Quit," *Sociological Review* 21:381–96.

Scheff, Thomas
1966 *Being Mentally Ill.* Chicago: Aldine.

Schwartz, Barry
1970 "Notes on the Sociology of Sleep," *Sociological Quarterly* 11:485–99.

Scott, Robert A.
1969 *The Making of Blind Men.* New York: Russell Sage.

Scully, Diana.
1980 *Men Who Control Women's Health.* Boston: Houghton Mifflin.

Sedgwick, Peter
1972 "The Concept of Disease," *Salmagundi.*

Sobel, Dava
1980 "In Pursuit of Love: Three Current Studies," *New York Times,* Jan. 22, III, 1; 5.

Strauss, Anselm L.
1975 *Chronic Illness and the Quality of Life.* St. Louis: Mosby.

Sudnow, David
1967 *Passing On: The Social Organization of Dying.* Englewood Cliff, N.J.: Prentice-Hall.

Sussman, Marvin (ed.)
1966 *Sociology and Rehabilitation.* Washington, D.C.: American Sociological Association.

Szasz, Thomas
1961 *The Myth of Mental Illness.* New York: Hoeber-Harper.
1970 *The Manufacture of Madness.* New York: Harper-Colophon.
1982 "The Lady in the Box," editorial, *New York Times,* Feb. 16.

Thomas, W. I.
1923 *The Unadjusted Girl.* Boston: Little, Brown.

Twaddle, Andrew C.
1973 "Illness and Deviance," *Social Science and Medicine* 7:751–62.
1976 "Utilization of Medical Services by a Captive Population: Analysis of Sick Call in a State Prison," *Journal of Health and Social Behavior* 17:236–48.

Twaddle, Andrew C. and Richard M. Hessler
1977 *A Sociology of Health.* St. Louis: Mosby.

Vaughan, Denton and Gerald Sparer
1974 "Ethnic Group and Welfare Status of Women Sterilized in Federally Funded Family Planning Programs," *Family Planning Perspectives* 6:224–229.

Waitzkin, Howard B. and Barbara Waterman
1974 *The Exploitation of Illness in Capitalist Society.* Indianapolis: Bobbs Merrill.

Wellin, Edward
1978 "Theoretical Orientations in Medical Anthropology: Change and Continuity over the Past Half Century." Pp. 23–39 in Michael H. Logan and Edward E. Hunt, Jr., eds., *Health and the Human Condition: Perspectives on Medical Anthropology.* North Scituate, Mass.: Duxbury.

Wiseman, Jacqueline P.
1979 *Stations of the Lost: The Treatment of Skid Row Alcoholics.* Chicago: University of Chicago Press.

World Almanac.
1987 New York: Pharos Books.

Zola, Irving K.
1972 "Medicine as an Institution of Social Control," *Sociological Review* 20:487–504.
1973 "Pathways to the Doctor: From Person to Patient," *Social Science and Medicine* 7:677–88.

Review Questions

1. What are the distinctions among illness, sickness, and disease made by Clark?
2. How can sickness be seen as one form of deviance? Discuss situations from your own experience in which a person considered sick was treated, or reacted to, as "not normal."
3. How does the sick role contribute to social control?
4. How does medical treatment contribute to social control?
5. What are some of the consequences for society and for individuals of the medicalization of social control?

THE SOCIAL MEANING OF AIDS

Peter Conrad

Disease and illness can be examined on different levels. Disease is best understood as a biophysiological phenomenon, a process or state that affects the body. Illness, by contrast, has more to do with the social and psychological phenomena that surround the disease. The world of illness is the subjective world of meaning and interpretation, how a culture defines an illness and how individuals experience their disorder.

In this article I am going to examine the social and cultural meanings of Acquired Immunodeficiency Syndrome or AIDS as it is manifested in late-20th-century America and relate these meanings to the social reaction that it has engendered. When I talk about the social meaning of AIDS, I am including what Susan Sontag has termed the metaphorical aspects of illness: those meanings of diseases that are used to reflect back on some morally suspect element of society.[1] As Sontag suggests, metaphorical aspects of illness are especially prevalent with dread diseases that have great unknowns about them. We need to look at AIDS not only as a biomedical entity, but as an illness that has a socially constructed image and engages particular attitudes. The social meanings of AIDS are simultaneously alarmingly simple and bafflingly complex, but are key to understanding the social reaction to AIDS.

THE SOCIAL REACTION TO AIDS

[In 1981] virtually no one had heard of AIDS. [By 1985] AIDS had become a household term and a feared intruder in the society.

The medical reality of AIDS, as we know it, remains puzzling but is becoming clearer. AIDS is a disease caused by a virus that breaks down the immune system and leaves the body unprotected against "opportunistic infections" that nearly invariably lead to death. The number of AIDS cases is growing dramatically and AIDS is considered an epidemic in the society. . . .

Over 90 percent of AIDS victims come from two risk groups: homosexual or bisexual men and intravenous drug users. (Hemophiliacs and others requiring frequent blood transfusions and infants born to moth-

SOURCE: Peter Conrad, "The Social Meaning of AIDS," *Social Policy* (Summer 1986): 51–56. Published by Social Policy Corporation, New York, NY 10036.

ers with AIDS are also considered risk groups.) The evidence is clear that the AIDS virus is transmitted through the direct exchange of bodily fluids, semen and blood; the most common mode of transmission is anal intercourse among male homosexuals and unsterile needle-sharing among intravenous drug users. There is virtually *no* evidence that the virus can be transmitted by everyday "casual contact," including kissing or shaking hands, or exposure to food, air, water, or whatever.[2] With the exception of very specific modes of semen- or blood-related transmission, it does not appear that the AIDS virus is very easy to "catch."

Yet the public reaction to AIDS has bordered on hysteria. Below are a few examples of reactions to AIDS or AIDS victims.

> 11,000 children were kept out of school in Queens, New York, as parents protested the decision to allow a 7-year-old girl with AIDS to attend second grade (despite no evidence of transmission by school children).
>
> Hospital workers in San Francisco refused to enter the room of an AIDS patient. When ordered to attend the patient, they appeared wearing masks, gowns, and goggles.
>
> A Baltimore policeman refused to enter the office of a patient with AIDS to investigate a death threat and donned rubber gloves to handle the evidence.
>
> A local school district in New Jersey tried to exclude a healthy 9-year-old boy whose sister has ARC (despite no sign of sibling transmission).
>
> An Amarillo, Texas, hospital fired a cafeteria worker who participated in a blood drive. This worker showed no signs of being ill or unable to perform his duties, but his blood had registered seropositive.
>
> In early 1985, Delta Airlines proposed a rule (later dropped) forbidding the carrying of AIDS patients.
>
> In New York, undertakers refused to embalm AIDS victims, householders fired their Haitian help, and subway riders wore gloves, all from fear of contracting AIDS.
>
> One child, hospitalized with AIDS, had a "do not touch" sign on her bed and was isolated from all physical contact with her parents.
>
> *The New York Times* reported cases of dentists who refused to treat gay patients (not just confirmed AIDS cases).
>
> In Dallas, a small group of doctors and dentists formed Dallas Doctors Against AIDS and began a campaign to reinstate Texas' sodomy laws.
>
> In a Boston corporation, employees threatened to quit en masse if the company forced them to work with an AIDS patient.
>
> Dade County, Florida, voted to require the county's 80,000 food workers to carry cards certifying they are free of communicable diseases, including AIDS, despite no known cases of AIDS transmitted through food and even though public health officials opposed this policy.
>
> The U.S. military is beginning to screen all new recruits for AIDS antibodies, with the likely result of declaring those who test seropositive ineligible for service.
>
> Several major life insurance companies are requiring certain applicants (young, single, male, living in certain areas) to undergo an HIV antibody test.

> Public health officials in Texas passed a measure allowing quarantine of certain AIDS patients. A candidate with a platform calling for the quarantining of all people with AIDS won the Democratic party's nomination for lieutenant governor in Illinois.

The list could go on. There is clearly a great fear engendered by the spectre of AIDS, a fear that has led to an overreaction to the actual problem. This is in no way to say that AIDS is not a terrible and devastating disease—it is—or to infer that it is not a serious public health concern. What we are seeing is an overblown, often irrational, and pointless reaction to AIDS that makes the disease more difficult for those who have it and diverts attention from the real public health concerns.

THE SOCIAL AND CULTURAL MEANINGS OF AIDS

To better understand the reaction to AIDS, it is necessary to examine particular social features of the disease: 1) the effect of marginal and stigmatized "risk groups"; 2) sexually-related transmission; 3) the role of contagion; and 4) the deadly nature of the disease.

The Effect of Marginal and Stigmatized "Risk Groups"

There are some illnesses that carry with them a certain moral devaluation, a stigma. Leprosy, epilepsy, mental disorder, venereal disease, and by some accounts, cancer, all reflect moral shame on the individuals who had the ill luck to contract them. Stigmatized illnesses are usually diseases that in some fashion are connected to deviant behavior: either they are deemed to produce it as with epilepsy or they are produced by it, as in the case of VD.

The effect of the early connection of AIDS to homosexual conduct cannot be underestimated in examining its stigmatized image. The early designation of the disorder was Gay Related Immune Deficiency Syndrome (GRID) and was publicly proclaimed as a "gay plague." It was first thought to be caused by the use of "poppers" (amylnitrate) and later by promiscuity. Something those fast-track gays were doing was breaking down their immune system. However, AIDS is not and never was specifically related to homosexual conditions; viruses don't know homosexuals from heterosexuals.

Within a short time, other "risk" groups were identified for what was now called AIDS—intravenous drug users, Haitians, and hemophiliacs. With the exception of hemophiliacs (who made up less than two percent of the cases), AIDS' image in the public eye was intimately connected with marginal populations. It was a disease of "those deviants," considered by some as deserved punishment for their activities. In 1983

Patrick J. Buchanan, who later became a White House staffer, wrote: "Those poor homosexuals. They have declared war on nature, and nature is exacting an awful retribution."[4] It is certain that fear of AIDS was amplified by the widespread and deeply rooted "homophobia" in American society.

Sexually Related Transmission

The dominant vector of transmission of AIDS is through sexual activity, particularly anal intercourse of male homosexuals. Although scientifically AIDS is better seen as a "blood disease" (since contact with blood is necessary for transmission), this common form of transmission has contributed to its image as a sexually transmitted disease.

Venereal diseases are by nature also stigmatized. They are deemed to be the fault of the victims and would not occur had people behaved better. As Allen Brandt points out, venereal diseases have become a symbol of pollution and contamination: "Venereal disease, the palpable evidence of unrestrained sexuality became a symbol for social disorder and moral decay—a metaphor of evil."[5]

AIDS, with its connection to multiple sex encounters and once-forbidden "sodomy," touches deep Puritanical concerns and revives alarms of promiscuity and "sexual permissiveness" that have become more muted in recent decades. The connection of AIDS to "sexual irresponsibility" has been made repeatedly.

Now that it appears AIDS can be transmitted through heterosexual intercourse as well, although apparently not as efficiently and rapidly, there is increasing concern among sexually active people that they may be betrayed in their most intimate moments. This connection with intimacy and sexuality amplifies our anxieties and creates fears that one sexual act may bring a lifetime of pollution and ultimately death.

The Role of Contagion

We have almost come to believe that large-scale deadly epidemics were a thing of the past. The polio panics of the early 1950s have receded far into our collective memory, and the wrath of tuberculosis, cholera, or diphtheria have become, in American society at least, artifacts of the past. Everyday models of contagion are more limited to the likes of herpes, chicken pox, and hepatitis. When we encounter AIDS, which is contagious but apparently in a very specific way, our fear of contagion erupts almost without limits. When little is known about a disease's transmission, one could expect widespread apprehensions about contagion. But a great deal is known about AIDS' transmission—it appears only to be transmitted through the exchange of bodily fluids and in *no* cases through any type of casual contact. In fact, compared to other contagious diseases it has a relatively low infectivity. Yet the fear of contagion fuels the reaction to AIDS.

Given our extant medical knowledge, what are the sources of fear? We live in a society where medicine is expected to protect us from deadly contagious diseases, if not by vaccine, then by public health intervention. And when medicine does not do this, we feel we must rely on our own devices to protect ourselves and our loved ones. Contagion, even of minor disorders, can engender irrational responses. Several months ago my 5-year-old daughter was exposed to a playmate who came down with chicken pox. A good friend of mine, who happens to be a pediatrician, did not want his 4-year-old to ride in the car with my daughter to gymnastics class, even though he knew medically that she could not yet be infectious. He just did not want to take any chances. And so it is with us, our reactions to contagion are not always rational.

With AIDS, of course, the situation is much worse. When we read in the newspapers that the AIDS virus has been found in saliva or tears, though only occasionally, we imagine in our commonsense germ-theory models of contagion that we could "catch AIDS" in this manner. Reports that no transmission has ever occurred in this fashion become secondary. The public attitudes seem to be that exposure to the AIDS virus condemns one to the disease.

While AIDS is contagious, so is the fear and stigma. The fear of AIDS has outstripped the actual social impact of the disease. But, more importantly for families of people who suffer from AIDS, the stigma of AIDS becomes contagious. They develop what Erving Goffman has called a courtesy stigma, a taint that has spread from the stigmatized to his or her close connections.[6] Family members of people with AIDS are shunned and isolated by former friends and colleagues, for fear that they too might bring contagion.

A Deadly Disease

AIDS is a devastating and deadly disease. It is virtually 100 percent lethal: 75 percent of people with AIDS die within two years. There are few other diseases that, like AIDS, attack and kill people who are just reaching the prime of their lives. Currently, AIDS is incurable; since there are no treatments for it, to contract AIDS [now] is to be served with a death warrant. Many sufferers waste away from Kaposi's Sarcoma or some rare form of chronic pneumonia.

As various researchers have shown, caretakers and family alike tend to distance themselves from sufferers who are terminally ill with diseases that waste away their bodies.[7] The pain of suffering and the pollution of dying are difficult for many people to encounter directly in a society that has largely removed and isolated death from everyday life.

Taken together, these features form a cultural image of AIDS that is socially as well as medically devastating. It might even be said that AIDS is an illness with a triple stigma: it is connected to stigmatized groups (homosexuals and drug users); it is sexually transmitted; and, like cancer, it is a terminal, wasting disease. It would be difficult to imagine a scenario for a more stigmatizing disease, short of one that also makes those infected obviously visible.

THE EFFECTS OF AIDS

The social meaning affects the consequences of AIDS, especially for AIDS sufferers and their families and the gay community but also for medicine and the public as well.

The greatest consequences of AIDS are of course for AIDS sufferers. They must contend with a ravaging disease and the stigmatized social response that can only make coping with it more difficult. In a time when social support is most needed, it may become least available. And in the context of the paucity of available medical treatments, those with AIDS must face the prospect of early death with little hope of survival.

People with ARC or those who test antibody positive must live with the uncertainty of not knowing what the progression of their disorder will be. And living with this uncertainty, they must also live with the fear and stigma produced by the social meanings of AIDS. This may mean subtle disenfranchisement, overt discrimination, outright exclusion, or even total shunning. The talk of quarantine raises the anxiety of "why me?" Those symptomless sero-positive individuals, who experts suggest have a 5 to 20 percent chance of developing full-blown AIDS, must live with the inner conflict of who to tell or not to tell, of how to manage their sexual and work lives, and the question of whether and how they might infect others. The social meanings of AIDS make this burden more difficult.

Families and lovers of people with AIDS, ARC, or an antibody-positive test are placed in an uncomfortable limbo status. Many live in constant fear that they might contract the AIDS virus, and thus limit their contact with the infected individual. Others wonder whether they too might be or become infectious. As mentioned earlier, families often share the AIDS stigma, as others see them as tainted, cease visiting their home, or even sever all contact with them. In one recent study of screening for AIDS among blood donors, the researchers noted they "have interviewed people in the pilot phase of [their] identification program who have been left by their spouses or significant others after telling them about their blood test results."[8]

The gay community has been profoundly affected by AIDS. The late 1960s and 1970s were an exciting and positive period of the American gay community. Thousands of gay men and women came "out of the closet" and proclaimed in a variety of ways that "gay is good." Many laws forbidding gay sexual activity were removed from the books. Gay people developed their own community institutions and more openly experimented and practiced alternative lifestyles. Although the celebration of anonymous sex among some gay males resulted in high rates of sexually-transmitted diseases and hepatitis B, the social atmosphere in the gay community remained overwhelmingly positive. While the attitudes toward homosexuality never became totally accepting, public moral opprobrium toward gays was perceptibly reduced.[9]

And along came AIDS. With its image as a "gay disease" related to a fast-track gay male lifestyle, the fear of AIDS tapped into a reservoir of existing moral fear of homosexuals. It was a catalyst to the reemergence of a latent "homophobia" that had never really disappeared. Now there was a new reason to discriminate against gays. Thus AIDS has led to a restigmatization of homosexuality. Every avowed male homosexual is a suspected carrier of AIDS and deemed potentially dangerous. This, of course, has pushed many gay men back into the closet, living their lives with new fears and anxieties. It is clear that AIDS threatens two decades of social advances for the gay community.

Concern about AIDS has also become the overriding social and political concern of the gay community, consuming energy that previously went toward other types of social and political work. The gay community was the first to bring the AIDS problem into the public arena and to urge the media, medicine, and government to take action. Action groups in the gay community have engaged in extensive AIDS education campaigns. This was done out of concern, but not without a fear of government surveillance and invasion of privacy. There was also apprehension that the images of "bad blood" and depictions of gays as health risks might lead to new exclusions of gays.[10]

The scourge of AIDS in the gay community has led, on the one hand, to divisions among gays (e.g., should bath houses be closed) and, on the other, to unprecedented changes in sexual behavior (e.g., witness the dramatic drop in the number of sex partners and types of sexual encounters reported in several studies and indexed by the large decrease in new cases of rectal gonorrhea).[11]

There is also a great emotional toll from the AIDS epidemic in the gay community. Nearly everyone in the community has friends or acquaintances who have died from the disease. As one gay activist recently put it, many people in the gay community were suffering a "grief overload" as a result of the losses from AIDS.[12]

The social image of AIDS has affected medical care and scientific research as well. In general, the medical voice concerning AIDS, at least in terms of describing it to the public and outlining its perils, has on the whole been cautious and evenhanded. The tenor of information has been factual and not unduly emotional. The Center for Disease Control (CDC) has again and again declared that AIDS is not transmitted by casual contact and, although it is a major epidemic and a public health threat, it is one with specific risk groups.

However, some medical scientists have placed the dangers of AIDS in a highly negative light either to raise the public's concern or to elicit private or governmental research funds. For example, "Dr. Alvin Friedman-Kein, an AIDS researcher who saw the first cases, said that AIDS will probably be the plague of the century."[13] Dr. Mathlide Krim was quoted in *The New York Post*... as saying that "it is only a matter of time before it afflicts heterosexuals on a large scale" while presenting no evidence or data to support the claim.[14] The media, of course, picks up these assertions, often highlighting them in headlines, which reinforces the public fear.

The stigma of AIDS in a few cases has affected medical practice. There have been some reports of doctors, health workers, or hospitals who have refused to treat AIDS patients. But fortunately, these extreme examples are rare and, for the most part, AIDS sufferers seem to have received at least adequate care from most medical facilities. But a mistrust of the ramifications of the public attitudes toward AIDS may well keep some "high risk" individuals from seeking medical diagnosis or care. The fear of being found seropositive and becoming a social pariah might well keep carriers of the AIDS virus from medical attention.

Finally, stigmatized attitudes toward a disease can constrain medical progress. As Allen Brandt points out, the negative social meanings attached to VD actually obstructed medical efforts. He noted that research funding was somewhat limited because the issue was thought to be best dealt with behaviorally. Among many VD researchers the discovery of penicillin was treated with ambivalence, since they were afraid a cure of syphilis would promote promiscuity.[15]

While medical scientists have recently gained a great deal of knowledge about AIDS, including isolating the virus, describing the modes of transmission, and developing a test for screening HIV antibodies in blood (although it is imperfect for screening people[16]), the stigma AIDS presents has probably limited public funding for AIDS research and deterred some types of community research on AIDS' natural history. Several commentators have noted that federal funding for research and prevention of AIDS was slow in emerging because AIDS was seen as a "gay disease." It was only when it threatened blood transfusions and blood products that public consciousness was aroused and federal support was forthcoming. Unfortunately, this increased support for research and education was "misinterpreted as an indicator that AIDS was a universal threat destined to work its way inexorably through all segments of society."[17]

One of the most striking aspects about the social reaction to AIDS is how fear and stigma have led to resistance to information about AIDS. While at times the media has sensationalized AIDS, there has also been a great deal of information communicated concerning AIDS, its characteristics, and its modes of transmission. Yet study after study finds a small but substantial and consistent proportion of the population that exhibits profound misinformation about AIDS. An October, 1985, Harris Poll reported that 50 percent of those asked believed one could get AIDS from living in the same house with someone who had it or from "casual contact," and one-third of the respondents thought that one could catch it from "going to a party where someone with AIDS is."[18]

Another study of high school students in San Francisco found that 41.9 percent believed you could get AIDS if kissed by someone with the disease; 17.1 percent thought if you touched someone with the disease you could get AIDS; 15.3 percent believed just being around someone with AIDS can give you the disease; and 11.6 percent thought all gay men have AIDS.[19] In a study of adolescents in Ohio, fully 60 percent believed that touching or coming near a person with AIDS might transmit the disease.[20] These authors contend that low knowledge of AIDS is correlated with high perceived susceptibility.

In a survey in San Francisco, New York, and London, the researchers found that "more knowledge was significantly negatively correlated with general fear of AIDS and with anti-gay attitudes among risk groups."[21] It appears that rather than low knowledge creating fear, the social meaning of AIDS creates resistance and barriers to taking in accurate information about AIDS.

Such misinformation is also prevalent among health-care providers. In a Massachusetts study of the effect of AIDS educational programs on health-care providers, the researchers reported that before the program, "20.5 percent of providers thought AIDS could be transmitted by shaking hands and 17.2 percent thought it could be acquired simply by being in the same room with a patient."[22] Many of these beliefs seem resistant to change. In the Massachusetts study, "after the [educational] programs, 15 percent of the providers still thought AIDS could be transmitted by sneezing or coughing, and 11.3 percent thought it could be transmitted by shaking hands. [In addition] after the... programs, the majority (66.2 percent) still thought that gowns were always necessary and a substantial minority (46.3 percent) still considered quarantine necessary."[23] While the educational programs affected some change in knowledge about AIDS, the researchers found a strong resistance to changing knowledge and attitudes among a substantial minority of health-care providers. Such misinformation among health-care providers can only have negative effects on AIDS patients.

One of the social tragedies of the fear and stigma is that it has constrained compassion for AIDS sufferers. In our culture, we generally show caring and compassion for severely and terminally ill patients. The social meaning of AIDS mutes this compassion in families, among health-care providers, and with the public at large. It is a shame that a victim of any disease in our society must suffer the plight of Robert Doyle of Baltimore. After discovering he had pneumonia brought on by AIDS, no nursing home or hospice would take him. His family rejected him and his lover demanded that he move out of the apartment. With only months to live, he had no support, resources, or place to die. He finally rented a room in a run-down hotel, where the staff refused to enter the room and left food for him in the hallway. After a newspaper story, a stranger took him into her home, only to ask him to leave in a few days; next an elderly couple took him in, until threatening phone calls and vandalism forced him to move again. He finally found a home with three other adults, one also an AIDS victim. Soon he was returned to the hospital where he died.[24] The fear of AIDS turned this sick and dying man into a social outcast.

CONCLUSION

The social meaning of AIDS has added to the victim-blaming response common to sexually and behaviorally-related diseases a powerful victim-fearing component. This has engendered an overreaction to the perils of AIDS and fueled the public fears of the disease. Some dangers and threats are, of course, very real, but the triple stigma of AIDS presents a frightening picture to the public, which leads to misguided attempts at "protection" and to resistance to contrary information. This only makes managing life more difficult for the sufferers and does not make the world "safer" from AIDS.

Since a medical cure or prevention for AIDS in the near future is unlikely, it is important that efforts be made to reduce the "hysteria" and overreaction surrounding this disease. We need to redouble our efforts to diffuse the unwarranted aspects of the fear of AIDS and to reduce its stigma. There are several strategies for attempting to accomplish this.

AIDS appears to be "out of control." If some type of medical intervention emerged that could limit the spread and/or symptoms of the disease, this sense of lack of control might be decreased and the public expectations of medicine's protective function might be somewhat restored. But given the historical examples of epilepsy and syphilis, available and efficacious medical treatments do not in themselves alter the image of a disorder. The stigma of these diseases, while perhaps reduced, are still prevalent in our society.

Activists, policymakers, and medical personnel must directly attempt to change the image of the disease. Sometimes a disease's stigmatized image is reinforced by incorrect information. A classic example is the notion that leprosy was highly contagious and sufferers needed to be placed in isolated colonies. We know now that leprosy is not easily communicable. With epilepsy, myths developed that both emerged from and sustained the stigma, including notions like epilepsy is an inherited disease or it causes crime. These myths often gained professional policies such as forbidding marriage or immigration.[25] Such incorrect information and mythology must be unmasked and not be allowed to become the basis for social policies.

Another strategy to reduce stigma is to "normalize" the illness; that is, to demonstrate that not only "deviants" get the disease. It is important to show that conventional people can suffer the disease and, to the extent possible, lead normal lives. For example, Rock Hudson's belated public disclosure of his AIDS was an important symbol. He was identified as a solid, clean-cut American man, almost an ideal. He was also a movie hero with whom many people had made some kind of vicarious relationship. To a certain extent Rock Hudson helped bring AIDS out of the closet.* An important policy strategy should be to "normalize" AIDS as much as possible—to present exemplars of people who can still live relatively normal, if difficult, lives, with positive antibodies, ARC, or even AIDS. The media has done this to a degree with children—depicted as innocent victims of the disease—but we need to bring other AIDS sufferers back into our world and recreate our compassion for them.

We need to develop policies that focus on changing the image of AIDS and confront directly the stigma, resistance to information, and the unnecessary fears of the disease. Given the social meaning of AIDS, this won't be easy. While studies have shown us how difficult it is to change public attitudes toward illness,[26] images of diseases like leprosy (Hanson's disease) and, to a lesser degree, epilepsy have changed. We must develop the professional and public resolve to change the social meanings and response to AIDS and make this a high priority, along with the control, treatment, and eventual eradication of the disease. It is incumbent upon us to reduce the social as well as the physical suffering from AIDS.

NOTES

1. Susan Sontag, *Illness as Metaphor* (New York: Farrar, Straus and Giroux, 1978).

2. Merle A. Sande, "The Transmission of AIDS: The Case Against Casual Contagion," *New England Journal of Medicine*, vol. 314 (1986), pp. 380–82. See

*Sports figure Magic Johnson may be able to accomplish even more.

also, June E. Osborn, "The AIDS Epidemic: An Overview of the Science," *Issues in Science and Technology* (Winter, 1986), pp. 40–55.

3. Jacques Liebowitch, *A Strange Virus of Unknown Origin* (New York: Ballantine, 1985), pp. 3–4.

4. Cited in Matt Clark et al., "AIDS," *Newsweek* (October 12, 1984), pp. 20–24, 26–27.

5. Allen M. Brandt, *No Magic Bullet* (New York: Oxford University Press, 1985), p. 92.

6. Erving Goffman, *Stigma* (Englewood Cliffs, NJ: Prentice-Hall, 1963), pp. 30–31.

7. Sontag, 1978. See also, Anselm Strauss and Barney Glaser, *Awareness of Dying* (Chicago: Aldine, 1965).

8. Paul D. Cleary et al., "Theoretical Issues in Health Education about AIDS Risk." Unpublished paper, Department of Social Medicine and Health Policy, Harvard Medical School, 1986.

9. Peter Conrad and Joseph W. Schneider, *Deviance and Medicalization: From Badness to Sickness* (St. Louis: C. V. Mosby, 1980).

10. Ronald Bayer, "AIDS and the Gay Community: Between the Specter and the Promise of Medicine," *Social Research* (Autumn, 1985), pp. 581–606.

11. Donald E. Riesenberg, "AIDS-Prompted Behavior Changes Reported," *Journal of the American Medical Association* (January 10, 1986), pp. 171–72; Ronald Stall, "The Behavioral Epidemiology of AIDS: A Call for Anthropological Contributions," *Medical Anthropology Quarterly* (February, 1986), pp. 36–37; Jonathan Lieberson, "The Reality of AIDS," *New York Review of Books* (January 16, 1986), p. 47.

12. Christopher Collins, "Homosexuals and AIDS: An Inside View." Paper presented to the American Society of Law and Medicine conference on "AIDS: A Modern Plague?" Boston, April, 1986.

13. Lieberson, 1986, p. 45.

14. Ibid., p. 46.

15. Brandt, 1985, p. 137.

16. Carol Levine and Ronald Bayer, "Screening Blood: Public Health and Medical Uncertainty." *Hastings Center Report* (August, 1985), pp. 8–11.

17. George F. Grady, "A Practitioner's Guide to AIDS," *Massachusetts Medicine* (January/February, 1986), pp. 44–50. See also, Kenneth W. Payne and Stephen J. Risch, "The Politics of AIDS," *Science for the People* (September/October, 1984), pp. 17–24.

18. Cited in Lieberson, 1986, p. 44.

19. Ralph J. DiClemente, Jim Zorn, and Lydia Temoshok, "A Large-Scale Survey of Adolescents' Knowledge, Attitudes, and Beliefs About AIDS in San Francisco: A Needs Assessment." Paper presented at the meetings of the Society for Behavioral Medicine, March, 1986.

20. Cited in ibid., p. 4.

21. Lydia Temoshok, David M. Sweet, and Jane Zich, "A Cross-Cultural Analysis of Reactions to the AIDS Epidemic." Paper presented at the meeting of the Society for Behavioral Medicine, March, 1986.

22. Dorothy C. Wertz et al., "Research on the Educational Programs of the AIDS Action Committee of the Fenway Community Health Center: Final Re-

port." Submitted to the Massachusetts Department of Public Health, AIDS Research Program, 1985, p. 11.

23. Ibid., p. 12.

24. Jean Seligman and Nikki Fink Greenberg, "Only Months to Live and No Place to Die," *Newsweek* (August 12, 1985), p. 26.

25. Joseph W. Schneider and Peter Conrad, *Having Epilepsy; The Experience and Control of Illness* (Philadelphia: Temple University Press, 1983), pp. 22–46.

26. Elaine Cumming and John Cumming, *Closed Ranks* (Cambridge: Harvard University Press, 1957).

Review Questions

1. What are the American public's common misconceptions about AIDS?
2. How have the following factors contributed to the public's misconceptions and overreactions to AIDS?
   (a) Marginal and stigmatized "risk groups"
   (b) Sexually related transmission
   (c) Contagion
   (d) Deadliness
3. What effect have the AIDS epidemic and the public reaction had on the gay community? The medical community?
4. How does Conrad believe we can change the public's misconceptions and negative attitudes toward AIDS? What would be the benefits of doing so?

Suggested Readings: Interaction in Institutional Context: Health and Illness.

Freidson, Eliot. *Profession of Medicine.* New York: Dodd-Mead, 1970.

McGuire, Meredith, with Debra Kantor. *Ritual Healing in Suburban America.* New Brunswick, N.J.: Rutgers University Press, 1988.

Millman, Marcia. *The Unkindest Cut: Life in the Backrooms of Medicine.* New York: Williams Morrow, 1978.

Starr, Paul. *The Social Transformation of American Medicine.* New York: Basic Books, 1982.

Strauss, Anselm L. *Chronic Illness and the Quality of Life.* St. Louis: Mosby, 1975.

Weitz, Rose. *Life with AIDS.* New Brunswick, N.J.: Rutgers University Press, 1991.

E. Religion

THERE IS MUCH THAT IS SOCIAL ABOUT RELIGIONS. REGARDLESS OF THEIR particular beliefs and rituals, religions emerge and flourish within societies, and nonreligious aspects of those societies affect them. Religions generate social processes and serve social functions. They are characterized by social structures and roles. The early sociologist Emile Durkheim noted a century ago that religion serves societal functions by bringing its members together and providing a common element around which group solidarity may form. Religious rituals such as weddings, baptisms, and funerals give some structure to possible disruptive events and changes. In a country such as ours where religious diversity is a long-standing fact of life, different kinds of issues arise. How do various ethnic groups develop styles of religious practice that are uniquely their own? How does one's religious status affect opportunities for interacting with other people, for marrying, for making employment contacts, and for experiencing discrimination? What is the importance of competing religious world views? How does one decide to change one's religious affiliation, to enter a religious career, or even to become an atheist? How does social interaction shape the individual's religious affiliations and beliefs?

The two articles in this section focus on opposing trends in American religion: a movement away from traditional religion toward humanism, and a counter trend away from humanism in favor of a return to traditional values and religion. Although they are concerned with widely divergent groups, both studies examine "new recruits," and both show the interplay between the secular and sacred worlds.

Western societies today are, on the average, much more human-centered and less God-centered than was the case a few centuries ago. Even compared to the early part of this century, fewer people today adhere strictly to the literal tenets of religious writings than to more abstract codes of ethics and morality. And more people "segregate" religious matters from their weekday lives. This trend toward humanism and secularism has, of course, had major implications for religions and for the roles of religious leaders.

In "Equals before God: Humanistic Seminarians and New Religious Roles," Sherryl Kleinman takes us inside a Midwestern Protestant seminary. When ministerial students first arrived at the seminary, they were astonished by their professors' behavior, by the tenor of their courses, and by their co-seminarians. Their prior assumptions about the role of minister—the expected demeanor, language, piety, and purpose—were all called into question. Much to their surprise, the role they were taking up turned out to be closer to the role of counselor than to their image of a minister. Kleinman's study shows us how important the larger social context can be in framing even religious leaders' conceptions of religion. It also illuminates the particular processes that shaped the self-concepts, attitudes, and behavior of these future ministers, bringing them closer to secular humanism.

On the other hand, American Society (and indeed the world) has also recently witnessed the revitalization of a variety of fundamentalist, evangelical, and other conservative religions. Traditional religions (and branches of religions) gained membership, increased their coffers, and become more outspoken in the 1980s and early 1990s, even affecting the American political scene. Candidates have had to alter their appeals to reach a variety of conservative religious bodies who are calling for a return to familism and other religious values. There is little doubt that a backlash against the trend toward secularism is under way.

Debra Kaufman's article, "Patriarchal Women: A Case Study of Newly Orthodox Jewish Women," gives us a close-up view of women who had once participated in the secular society but renounced it in the 1970s and 1980s to join extremely traditional, ultra-Orthodox Jewish communities. In these communities, rules spelled out in the Old Testament and the ancient Talmud govern most aspects of everyday life. The rules prohibit women from studying religious writings and taking a role in the synagogue, call for the physical segregation of men and women and even husbands and wives during certain times, and require women to enact a host of Biblical rituals listed in Leviticus, including rituals of purification. From an outsider's perspective, it would appear that Orthodox Judaism relegates women to minority-group status.

Kaufman wanted to understand why modern women would voluntarily enter religious groups that kept them subordinate. She discovered that the women felt a sense of identity and specialness as women that they had lacked when they lived in the larger society. To use Charlotte Wolf's term (see Part VII of this book), the newly Orthodox women had constructed a world view in which they had a "relative advantage." First, they believed they were advantaged compared to non-Orthodox and non-Jewish women because of the power they wielded in their homes. Second, they believed that they were advantaged relative to men because God had given them a special role more important and powerful than men's roles. Kaufman concludes that Orthodox Jewish women do not, in fact, have more power and influence in their communities than men. Yet they perceive themselves as powerful. It was their previous immersion in modern secular society, with its emphasis on women's rights and empowerment, that prompted them to look for power once they converted—and to "find" it.

EQUALS BEFORE GOD: HUMANISTIC SEMINARIANS AND NEW RELIGIOUS ROLES

Sherryl Kleinman

[This article reports on six months of field research at Midwest Seminary, a liberal Protestant theological school. The author, herself an "agnostic Jew," lived on the campus with the approximately 200 ministry students, eating in the residence hall, attending classes, and conducting interviews with students, faculty, and administrators. The focus of this article is on the resocialization of the students. They came expecting to find restrictions, theology, and piety. They discovered, however, that the new human-centered trend in theology had created quite a different set of teachings and expectations.]

Humanistic religion is grounded in the human situation rather than in the transcendent [in the here-and-now rather than the spiritual]. In this view, the distinction between transcendent and mundane realities no longer exists, for everyday reality takes on a religious significance. Hence, humanistic religion has a this-worldly emphasis. Religion becomes a matter of human symbolism rather than a God-given truth (Gilkey 1967).

A conception of religion as symbolic, situated in time and place, and of this world suggests that religiosity is relative. Religion becomes subjective, individualized, and privatized (Lemert 1974a, 1974b; Luckmann 1967; Miller 1975). Consequently, ministers no longer set the standards for or enforce moral purity and orthodoxy (Bellah 1964). Rather, individuals become responsible, more than the Church, for their religiosity and even for determining what religious behavior is (Hiller 1969, 183). The Church simply provides an environment for the individual's spiritual growth and ministers become enablers rather than truth givers or standard setters. Consequently, the faculty at Midwest Seminary do not expect the students to be devoted to traditionally religious duties or to serve as traditional moral exemplars in the community. In addition, the subjectivizing of religion has led to a bias against intellectualizing and an emphasis on "feeling-talk."

SOURCE: Excerpt from Sherryl Kleinman *Equals before God: Seminarians as Humanistic Professionals* (Chicago: University of Chicago Press, 1984), pp. 49–62.

WORLD-OPENNESS

In the new theology, "liberation is obtained from rigid and closed world views, and the world is accepted as sanctioned ground for action" (Hiller 1969, 80). The less rigid and closed world view tends to be associated with less rigid standards for conventional ministerial behavior. As the world becomes an open place for religiosity, ministers can participate in many activities once considered off limits for them.

Instructional personnel at Midwest Seminary do not advocate partying, smoking, drinking, and swearing, but neither do they say that such behaviors are bad. Within the humanistic framework, these behaviors become matters students should deal with themselves and do not determine whether they will become good ministers. Students discover this view when they note that the organization does not interfere in their leisure activities. Student dorm life, including parties, are not monitored by the school. Further, faculty sometimes say that behavior people usually think of as routine deviance for most people, but "real" deviance for religious people, is not necessarily bad. For example, in a class called "The Changing Conception of the Church's Self-Image" (the course title itself indicates the new orientation), the following interchange occurred:

> The professor said, "When I was younger I saw someone smoking after a revival meeting. At that time I thought that anyone who smoked or drank was a sinner. When I saw this person smoking, I thought, 'Oh, the revival didn't work.' " A male, second-year student said, "Yeah, it didn't take." The class laughed. The professor said, "We are *all* born into the Body of Christ, yet we set up standards for who should be let in and let out." (Field notes)

The professor implies that he used to think smoking indicated the absence of religiosity but now he knows better.

Just as the faculty do not equate abstaining from deviant activities as good, they do not emphasize participating in traditionally pious activities as the way to self-betterment. The organization institutionalizes few conventionally religious activities. One of them, a half-hour chapel service, is held twice a week. But even participation in chapel is officially and informally defined as optional. My observations indicate that the high point of chapel service for students and others is the sociability of the reception following the service. Here, students, faculty, administrators, and staff chat, drink coffee, and eat doughnuts for about fifteen minutes.

Faculty sometimes show role distance from traditional expectations of piety and respect for conventional religion in their classes. They usually do this through their jokes:

> I went with Jean over to Assessment Services. Jean said to the secretary, "I signed up for assessment last year but I couldn't take it. So I'd like to sign

up again." One of the seminary faculty standing nearby said, smiling, "Isn't there some penalty for that? Hmm, well, say 5,000 Hail Mary's." The three of us laughed. After we left, Jean decided to fill the form out right away and hand it in. She told me later, "When I handed it in, Anderson was still there. I told him it would be a good idea to hand in the form right away. He said, 'That's intelligent. Take off some Hail Mary's.' " (Field notes)

In a class on pastoral psychotherapy the instructor was discussing a "case." He then said, "I asked the client who her heroes are, maybe I should ask *you* [the class]." He then suddenly did an imitation of Christ on the Cross. Some of the class laughed nervously, others just laughed. He said, "Some of you seemed shocked at that." The third-year, male student sitting next to me smiled and said, "Only the first-years." (Field notes)

In a time-management seminar, the class was divided into groups of three in which students discussed problems with their schedules. One group said their problem was having self-expectations that were too high. Someone in the class responded, "Yes, if it hurts it must be good." The instructor said, "Oh, the joy of suffering. Jesus did it, so can I." The class laughed. (Field notes)

Because faculty fail to emphasize the religious in the traditional sense but do emphasize that ministers should be egalitarian—ministers are, after all, only human—students get the idea that people who show their religiosity are using it to establish a sense of superiority and are therefore acting inappropriately. Since the conventional ministerial role is that of a superordinate, demystifying the role involves getting rid of the signs and displays of religious specialness, such as robes, the collar, talk about God, and pious behaviors. (Hence, the students had allowed me to wear traditional garb as a means to a humanistic end.) In a dorm room in which three female students were present, the following interchange took place:

One student said: "I ran into this guy I used to know, who's Fundamentalist. Anyway, he took some of us out to lunch, to McDonald's. And you know what he said? He said, 'Let's pray.'" The other student said, "Oh, gross!" I said, "What's so gross about it?" The first student said, "It's too public, it looks like he was trying to tell everyone that he's pious. It's as if he's saying, 'I'm pious, why can't you be?' It's like saying he's superior." The other students nodded in agreement. (Field notes)

Students might have challenged this man's behavior primarily on the basis of its inappropriateness for the setting—McDonald's. The fact that they challenged him on the basis of his lack of humanism is evidence for the strength of their humanistic beliefs.

The demystification of "religious people" was made explicit in the following interview with a member of the faculty.

It's in preaching that people see their prejudices, their hangups, it's a personal thing. Now some preachers don't see it that way. They gloss over what attitudes they're showing by saying, "It's the Word of God." I don't see it that

> way. I make the students hear and see what they're saying. That's why I use the videotape. . . . One student whose sermon I was commenting on yesterday started off the sermon by saying "There's a story about a boy who . . ." I told him it sounded like the boy was *him*—you know, the classic case of "I have a *friend* with a problem, and it's *you*." So I told him that either he should *say* the story's about him and be open about his problem; or if the person's problem is too intense or personal for the pulpit, then leave it out entirely. But why should he leave it open, why leave me with that curiosity? If it's a problem he can talk about then he *should*, because it's good for the congregation to see that even people into religion have problems.

In the lounge one evening, a former student of the seminary who had returned for a visit was speaking with one first-year female student and one second-year male student:

> The returning student said, "What would you say the students are like here, pious or what?" The first-year female student said, "We're not pious at all." The former student replied, "That's good. Three years ago, we had some of those holy people around, who really could not relate to the real world. They went around like, 'I'm Christian, I'm holy, I'm happy.' They were all clean-shaven, short hair, conservative dress. I'm glad there have been some changes." The second-year student said, "The problem is we're not concerned with being pious at all." The female student said in a sarcastic tone, "Well, listen to him—*pious*." The second-year student replied, "I know. To you pious has a negative connotation. You think it means holier-than-thou. . . . It's as if there's an understanding that you shouldn't talk about faith here. It's understood." (Field notes)

Given humanistic notions of religion, it is understandable that students did not treat me as an outsider. In their view, even a Jewish agnostic can become part of the minister's religious experience, for almost everything and everyone is defined as part of God's reality. For example, a student I had interviewed a few days earlier came to my room and said to me:

> Remember in my interview I said that I felt I had to be called to be a minister? And I've been called, I *know*, to be here *this year*, I've been called to consider the ministry. But I don't know if I've been called to be ordained. [Well, I don't think I'm qualified to . . . um] God's will is communicated through *people*, so by talking to *you*, for instance, it may help me to find God's guidance. (Field notes)

Indeed, with an understanding of religion and ministering as interpersonal and all-inclusive, some students who thought I was a good listener suggested I become a minister.

ANTI-INTELLECTUALISM

Most of the faculty emphasize the heart of ministry as interpersonal rather than intellectual. Intellectualizing did go on in class, but it was often treated as secondary or deprecated. For example, during the break period in a small theology seminar which had had an intellectual-personal mix, one of the students asked the instructor a question about something he had written on the blackboard. The instructor looked a little embarrassed and said in an apologetic tone, "Yes, I like to keep up my image, that I'm a theological thinker." The instructor expressed role distance from the image of the "cold thinker" presumably evidenced by his having written some theological terms on the blackboard! In another class, another professor said, smiling, "Since I guess most of you expect a course on theology to talk about God, the next two sessions will be it." He then went on to emphasize the "experiential" as the most important part of the theology. In still another class, a professor was making the point that students should refrain from using big words the congregation might not understand. He mentioned a cartoon in which the minister is speaking to a snoring congregation. He said the caption read, "Look, I know you're thinking Sabelleus, but . . . ," indicating that the minister was insensitive to the congregation's boredom at hearing an intellectual sermon.

Consequently, students believe that those few peers who engage in intellectual talk are arrogant (and therefore bad) or are defensive and need therapy. Students who tried to discuss theology in the cafeteria, for instance, made people noticeably uncomfortable and were often resented by their peers. One third-year student who attempted to intellectualize matters also recognized that by doing so he could bring out theological divisions among the students that would otherwise be left unstated:

> There's a lot of unspoken tension about faith issues . . . I mean some people should really be erupting at each other! If they knew how different they really are they should be asking, "How can we both be here and should we both be here?" And they should talk about these things, but they don't. (Interview)

This student was atypical. Most learn to refrain from intellectualizing or come to believe it is bad. For example, one student wrote the following in his ministry project:

> As I enlarge my world view, I also have found that I must look inward toward a better self-understanding. With the help of Assessment Services and new friendships, I have been made aware of the areas where I personally need to grow. I tend to intellectualize my way through emotional situations which I seem to set up for myself. . . . I use overpowerful language in order to get my point across and to break communication barriers which often should be handled more carefully. I let the debater in me come through.

In his ministry project, another student put it:

> In ministry we must give up the security of a system of verbal, intellectual formulations and enter into human relationships through love and trust.

After about three weeks in the field, I remarked to a few students that I had yet to hear a theological discussion. In response to that remark, students would now and then call me over if they were discussing anything remotely intellectual, saying things like "Quick, Sherryl, we're having a theological discussion," or "Let's have a theological discussion for Sherryl." They were making fun of my expectation that a seminary would be pervaded by religious talk. Also, they sometimes used jokes to stop others from intellectualizing. For example, at breakfast one morning, a first-year student was discussing Zimbardo's well-known prison experiment [in which he assigned students to play the roles of inmates and guards in a mock prison] relating it to questions of human nature. Two other students continued to eat their breakfast, but didn't participate in the conversation. After about ten minutes, one of them got up to leave. She said, mocking an upper-class British accent, "Well, thank you for this theological, spiritual, intellectual discussion." The other student chuckled.

Because of the new definition of religious people as "normal," or "like everyone else," students come to reject their earlier expectation that a seminary should be characterized by conventional religious behavior and theological talk:

> I thought that everyone else here who came to ministry would be concerned only with religion. This is absurd, as absurd as thinking that when I was in music I would think only about music, or that you, in sociology, would be concerned only with sociology. Why I didn't grasp that before I came, I don't know. I wouldn't expect people in journalism, say, to only talk about journalism. But people expect that with religion, *even* people who come here to study. (Interview, female, first-year student)

A third-year student who had just returned from an intern year said in an interview:

> I expected the dinner table talk to be theologically oriented, you know, "Well, did you study Martin Luther's 95 Theses today?" And to show you how much my mind has changed on these things, well, last week I was sitting, talking to Beth [another third-year woman] across the table [in the cafeteria]. There were two guys sitting next to us—first-year students—and they were into a deep theological discussion, kind of like what I imagined would go on long ago. We just kind of looked at them and said to each other later, "Gee, I wonder how long it's going to take them to get out of *that*?" [laughing]. (Field notes)

SOCIALIZATION PROBLEMS

Students initially have strong conventional expectations of religiosity, both ideologically and behaviorally. They enter the seminary expecting their peers and teachers to act in religious ways. In short, students expect an institution of religion to be a religious institution. Many of them talked about what they thought they would have to give up in seminary (partying, dancing, smoking, drinking, swearing) and what they thought they would have to do (daily devotions, talk about God, prayer groups).

> I went out for dessert with four female students. After about fifteen minutes of joking around, Donna said, "Gee, I wish we could have done this last year, before coming here, then I wouldn't have worried about coming." Belle said, "You mean going out with seminary students before we became seminary students?" Donna said, "Yes, I remember talking to Nancy about that last quarter. It turns out we were both worried, before we got here, that there wouldn't be any fun people at seminary." Belle said, laughing, "Oh, but you should have realized that *you're* fun, and you're going to seminary, so there must be others—I know what you mean; I wondered about that, too." (Field notes)

It is quite common in occupational socialization settings that students' initial expectations are incorrect. In the case of the ministry, however, the students' experience is one of reality shock, for the realities of seminary life are not just different but the opposite of what they expected. For example, what was previously defined as deviant behavior (drinking, smoking, swearing) isn't, now, and what was once defined as religious behavior (piety) is now defined as deviant.

The students are in fact ambivalent about their initial conventional expectations of religiosity; they want to become ministers, but fear the "monastic" life. Their ambivalence perhaps paralleled mine. As a field worker in a seminary, I expected and was willing to make certain sacrifices, such as suspending skepticism about religion, becoming more polite, going to chapel, being proselytized, and altering other acts or attitudes. Students and I also reacted similarly to the lack of religiosity—some relief at having our tasks made easier mixed with an uneasy feeling about the legitimacy of the organization. They wonder: "Can an unconventional seminary really be a seminary?"

STUDENTS' RESPONSES

Students largely accept the redefinition of religious deviance, acting "publicly" against traditional expectations and notions of religiosity, often through cynical remarks and jokes. Entering the seminary with traditional expectations, I, like many new recruits, was surprised at ministry students' lack of "pious" behavior. I was equally struck by the prevalence of jokes with religious content, such as making a pun on "saving a chair" for someone (and asking the chair to repent) or calling poor typing "typing in tongues." Students often point out discrepancies between their behavior and outsiders' expectations of them, saying things like, "You wouldn't know this is a seminary, right?" In light of the dominant humanistic expectations in the seminary, and the intensity of traditional expectations on the outside, this joking behavior is less surprising. Students are enacting collective role distance from traditional expectations. The behavior seems to say "We do not assume the traditional role which you outsiders are giving us." The students, like the faculty, made jokes and cynical remarks about religion among themselves.

> In the evening, one male student, three female students, and I were in one of the women's rooms. There was a lull in the conversation. One of the women was leaning on the towel rack that was nailed to the closet. Suddenly the rack fell, which startled us a bit. The woman who had been leaning on it said, "Oh, it's the Holy Spirit! Wait, the Devil made me do it." We laughed. (Field notes)

After having arrived late to the party in the dorm, one of the first-year women said to me:

> It's too bad you weren't here earlier. [What happened?] Oh, some of the guys were doing a mock Communion, doing it all wrong. They used pretzels. It was really funny. (Field notes)

Students often made fun of outsiders' traditional expectations of ministers. For example, the following exchange I had with a second-year student alludes to parishioners' views of ministers as asexual:

> I was in Agnes' room. She said, "Do you mind if I change in front of you?" I said, "No." She said, "You can put it in your study—ministers *do* have breasts." (Field notes)

The students learn that becoming a minister at Midwest Seminary means they should act counter to traditional expectations. For example, one of the new students expressed some concern about taking the vocational tests required of all members in the first-year cohort:

> At breakfast Peter, the new student, said nervously, "Well, I'm off to be vocationally tested, to see that I'm not fit to be a minister." The other two second-year male students laughed. One of them said, "And that you *should* be here." (Field notes)

The new student was worried about not presenting himself as a traditional minister on the test. The veteran is telling him that he will fit in at the seminary to the extent that he doesn't fit the traditional image.

Although most of the jokes made fun of traditional religion, some of them also revealed students' skepticism about whether a humanistic seminary could really be a seminary. Some jokes suggested that the student was questioning the legitimacy of an organization that calls itself a seminary but doesn't seem religious. The students could accept their peers' remarks because they ostensibly made fun of traditional religion. But the joke may have carried another message; it also mocked the lack of religiosity. Students could question the lack of religiosity and make fun of parishioners' "misguided" expectations at the same time:

> A male seminary student walked into the cafeteria at lunch and neared our table. Ron, a first-year student, said to him, "Hi, Father. How are you doing?" The student he called Father said, "Fine, fine." I said to Ron, pretending to whisper, "Hmm, how come he's called Father?" Ron said, "Oh, I coined that because he's going to switch to an Anglican seminary and their priests are called Father. Also [smiling], he's High Church." I said, "I don't fully understand what that is." Ron said, "Oh, the service is full of liturgies, chants and praying—really structured: Not like here." I said, "You'd say this is Low Church?" Ron said, "Yeah." Eric, another first-year student, said smiling, "No. Basement Church." We laughed. (Field notes) . . .

In my interview a few months later with the student called "Father," he said, "My impression is that the school is about half liberal and half conservative. Yeah, half conservative and half . . . heretic. Yes," he said laughing, "half heretic." He then classified himself in the heretic category. The notion of heretic is not a humanistic, but a traditional word. Although this student disparaged the conservatives, his definition of the others as heretics suggests at least a slight put-down of those who are less conservative. Perhaps he used this strong language to show that he is not, as his High Church affiliation indicates to his peers, traditional. When I asked him in an interview about the High Church/Low Church distinction, he characterized his affiliation with the former as a preference or taste, rather than a matter of being essentially traditional.

> [What do people not like about High Church services?] Vestments, paraphernalia, the formalness. I do it because I like it. There's more of a celebration type atmosphere to it. Face it. We do things because we like to. And then we come up with some superstructure to back it up. And people are uncomfortable with that.

"Father," however, was not the only person who used the term "heretic" in a joking context to characterize many of the students. Other students also used the term "apostate" to describe themselves and their peers.

After two weeks in their first quarter of study, a few of the new students talked about their preconceptions of seminaries over lunch in the cafeteria:

> Others had left the cafeteria. Martin and I stayed to talk. He said, "You know what I worried the most about in coming here? What my roommate would be like. I figured I could get a really weird roommate in a seminary. I worried

> that I wouldn't be able to drink beer with him, in front of him. And my first night here, he not only brought in a case, but the *best*—Heineken. I'm not sure what to make of that! (Field notes)

Martin was laughing as he said this, but also fidgeted and looked a bit confused. Although questioning the legitimacy of the organization on the basis of the kind of beer students drink rather than the fact that they drink at all may seem ridiculous to an outsider, Martin is experiencing the dilemma which most students never resolve: which behavior and attitudes are definitely not "religious" and which are acceptable? Humanism does not provide the answers. . . . [T]his becomes particularly troublesome because socializers leave the question of goodness open but also lead students to expect homogeneity of "goodness" among their peers and teachers.

Students also joked and made cynical remarks about the humanistic role, and particularly the humanistic vocabulary, on occasion. For example, I was in Ellen's room (Ellen is a first-year student). Phil, a second-year student, came over. They were talking rather sarcastically about the argot of seminary students, such as "affirming" and "sharing." Ellen spoke "Another big one is 'community.' " Phil replied, "Yes, and that means everyone knows your business." Because humanistic expectations predominate in the seminary, students made such remarks more often in small groups of close friends and outside the classroom than in large groups. Moreover, in the company of close friends, students sometimes used traditional standards to evaluate others.

Students, then, dealt with their ambivalence about humanistic religion by expressing some of those feelings in jokes with double meanings. Also, although seldom in public, students did talk and think about their faith, whether they had been called to the ministry, and their conceptions of God. However, they tended to keep these matters to themselves or discussed them in private settings with a close friend or two or with me:

> I was waiting for a phone call in the dorm hallway. I heard two students talking in the room across from the phone. One of the women left. I said, "Gee, I thought I heard the word theology in there." Kathy said, "Yes, it does happen sometimes. You have to look hard for it, though. But sometimes during the noise at lunch two people will be off in a corner discussing . . . Tillich. Or in someone's room like this, it will be going on." (Field notes)

Some students who were quite adept at making religious jokes seemed to transform in the interview situation, suddenly showing a hidden, serious, religious side. Although I do not have distributions on how many people prayed privately, I do know that some fourteen students did, alone or with a friend. However, the norms prohibiting the public display of a serious attitude toward religion often made it difficult for them to find a prayer partner:

> I had to grope a lot the first term as to praying with other persons, I mean knowing which persons would be into that sort of thing and which wouldn't. [How do you go about finding out?] Well, I was in a class last term called "Theology of Prayer." Susan was in that, so we started praying together. . . . We talked and theologized more about prayer in that class than doing it, so you could find out how people felt about it. (Interview: female, first-year student)

It is likely that more students wanted someone to pray with them than looked for one. My data suggest that a situation of pluralistic ignorance may have existed: students wished at times to be "religious" with their peers but feared that they would disapprove.

IMPLICATIONS

The esteem accorded professional knowledge in a society is partly sustained by the profession's definition of it as esoteric, either technically, intellectually, or both. As a way of establishing their turf and excluding clients from decision making, professions usually develop sets of terms, or jargon, which only those who have had the training can understand.

Religious terminology, like any professional language, can be understood only by those who learn it. In the seminary, students do learn certain terms in their theology classes that outsiders probably would not understand. But this humanistic program's client-centered emphasis downplays the importance of theological terms. Hence, technical terminology and intellectual talks about theology rarely occur in students' conversations or even in their class discussions. In fact, professors who write books and articles on theology express their distance from the scholarly role when interacting with students.

Students at Midwest Seminary do learn an argot—that of psychologizing. Although not all outside audiences understand this, it is characteristically close to the contemporary language of everyday life. The language is more expressive than many parishioners might like, but it is nevertheless easier for them to comprehend than such terms as "hermeneutics." That is the problem; the language is so common that it does not distinguish religious knowledge from everyday information and talk. As a common language, it fails to provide a sense that the ministry is distinctive and esteemed.

• • •

REFERENCES

Bellah, Robert N.
1964 "Religious Evolution." *American Sociological Review* 29: 358–374.

Gilkey, Langdon.
1967 "Social and Intellectual Sources of Contemporary Protestant Theology in America." *Daedalus* 96: 69–98.

Hiller, Harry H.
1969 "The New Theology and the Sociology of Religion." *Canadian Review of Sociology and Anthropology* 6: 179–187.

Lemert, Charles.
1974a "Cultural Multiplexity and Religious Polytheism." *Social Compass* 21 (3): 241–253.
1974b "Sociological Theory and the Relativistic Paradigm." *Sociological Inquiry* 44: 93–104.

Luckmann, Thomas.
1967 *The Invisible Religion.* New York: Macmillan.

Miller, Donald E.
1975 "Religion, Social Change, and the Expansive Life Style." *International Yearbook for the Sociology of Knowledge and Religion* 9: 149–159.

Review Questions

1. The professors at Midwest Seminary emphasize the humanistic tenet of "world-openness." What does world-openness imply for the acceptable everyday behavior of ministers (and ministerial students)?

2. What would be the reaction of professors and seminarians to students who were anti-intellectual and deported themselves informally?

3. How did the students' expectations of the seminary mesh with what they found? How did they respond?

4. What role does "psychologizing" play in the seminary's philosophy?

PATRIARCHAL WOMEN: A CASE STUDY OF NEWLY ORTHODOX JEWISH WOMEN

Debra Renee Kaufman

THIS STUDY EXPLORES THE ATTITUDES, VALUES, EXPERIENCES, AND CONCERNS OF newly Orthodox Jewish women (called *baalot teshuva* in Hebrew) who have voluntarily entered a world many regard as patriarchal and oppressive to women. There is ample evidence attesting to women's second–class status within Jewish Orthodoxy. Feminists have emphasized the most blatant, and at times the not so obvious, areas of discrimination and oppression. They have asked for changes in divorce law (in Orthodoxy only a man can initiate and obtain a divorce), inclusion in the secular leadership of Jewish communal agencies and for concrete changes in the structure of the community (from day care centers to the acceptance of single mothers and homosexuals within the Jewish community). The inviolability of the Jewish code of laws in Orthodoxy prevents the possibility of women challenging a legal system created and continuously defined and redefined by males (Baskin 1985). Moreover, if women are not encouraged or given the opportunities to study the very texts from which the interpretations of those laws derive, they cannot challenge those laws in a manner that will be perceived by the community as authentic or legitimate. . . .

Rachel Adler, a leading feminist and critic of Orthodox Judaism, describes the Orthodox woman's ritual responsibilities in the following way:

> A woman keeps kosher because both she and her family must have kosher foods. She lights the *Shabbat* (Sabbath) candles so that there will be light, and, hence, peace, in the household. She goes to the *mikvah* (ritual bath) so that her husband can have intercourse with her and she bears children so that, through her, he can fulfill the exclusively male *mitzvah* (commandment) of increasing and multiplying (1983, p. 13).

Theology's role in transforming women within Judaism is paramount to feminist Suzannah Heschel:

SOURCE: Debra Renee Kaufman, "Patriarchal Women: A Case Study of Newly Orthodox Jewish Women," *Symbolic Interaction*, vol. 12, No.2 (1989) pp.299–314. Reprinted by permission of JAI Press.

> Questions of role and identity cannot be raised outside the larger context of the images which give rise to them and the theological positions which legitimate them. . . . Clearly, there is a need for theological reinterpretations to transform women in Judaism from object to subject (1983, p. xxxii).

However, the ways in which the *baalot teshuva* describe their experiences within patriarchal living suggest a range of feeling and experience many feminists might not expect. The data suggest that these women selectively adopt and even incorporate protofeminist attitudes and values into their familial lives. Most puzzling is the finding that although many *baalot teshuva* began their journeys toward Jewish Orthodoxy partly as a backlash against feminism and any "liberation" movement they perceived as placing individual freedom above social responsibility (see Tipton 1982 for similar findings among young Americans in movements in the seventies), they also maintain a gender identity deeply informed by and consonant with many values associated with some contemporary feminists, specifically those who celebrate the female, her life cycle experiences and feminine attributes (for a fuller discussion of second wave feminism and the *baalot teshuva* see Kaufman 1985a; 1985b; 1987).[1]

To understand these seeming paradoxes, it is important to understand the significance of Jewish Orthodoxy from these newly Orthodox women's perspectives and experiences. Beginning with the assumption that these women share in the construction of social reality and that their experiences are central to the construction of that reality, the focus of this study revolved around the following questions: How do these women react to the world of Jewish Orthodoxy, reflect upon the meanings of phenomena in that world, and wield symbols and communicate about those symbols? What do they incorporate, discard, and choose to ignore as they practice Orthodoxy? The answers to these questions help us address the paradox of how these women seem to make "feminist" sense out of patriarchal religion and social structure and how they seem simultaneously to accommodate and resist patriarchy.[2]

SAMPLE

The data consist of in-depth interviews conducted with 75 newly Orthodox Jewish women in the early 1980s[3] in five major urban areas across the United States.[4] Most women were between 16 and 34 years of age at the time of their Orthodox conversions and all had identified in some way with countercultural youth. One-third claim they had once identified with the women's movement.

Several methods were used to locate respondents. Interviews with leading rabbis, lay community leaders, and known *baalot teshuva* in each community helped to locate respondents according to three identifiable frameworks in Jewish Orthodoxy—modern, centrist, and ultra-Orthodox (Hasidic). Once within these settings, the referral method or snowball technique of sampling was employed, thereby identifying smaller interactive groups of *baalot teshuva* in each community.[5]

Of the seventy-five women reported on here, all are married, forty-five are Hasidic, twelve are centrist, and eighteen are modern. Almost all of them married men who were also *baalei teshuva* (plural of newly Orthodox Jews). The husbands were often as uneducated about Jewish Orthodoxy as their wives. In fact, the demographics suggest that if there were any differences in Judaic background between husbands and wives, the wives more often than the husbands were better educated (knew more Hebrew and/or had a better Jewish education). Almost all these women had become *baalot teshuva* before they were married and before they met their husbands.

METHODOLOGY

Focused and structured interviews were not useful in mapping the world of these newly Orthodox Jews. [I] began not with specific questions and probes, but with the women themselves, their concerns, their perspectives.[6] They spoke not as those nurtured, secluded and structurally dependent upon Orthodox communities or institutions all of their lives (and therefore easily marked as a byproduct of that particular environment), but as those who had at some time in their young adult lives made a choice to embrace the structural and theological conditions of traditional living. None had had any familiarity with Orthodox Judaism: Of the seventy-five women, only twenty had ever attended Sunday school and five had gone to a late-afternoon Hebrew-school program three times a week.

A number of predefined topics were covered in each interview. Such topics focused on the history of these women's embracing of Orthodoxy, their beliefs, practices, knowledge and feelings about Orthodoxy, their current familial and communal life-style, and their views about gender roles and feminism. The interviews lasted from two-and-one-half to five-and-one-half hours with an average of slightly over three hours each. A ten-page demographic questionnaire was left with each respondent along with a stamped envelope for its return.

To understand these women's links and ties to one another, families, community and to the theology they embraced, I spent many weeks in each community. . . . I used many [ethonographic and participant observation] techniques. I attended lectures, Sabbath services, classes, informal afternoon gatherings, sisterhood meetings, and coffee get togethers. I also found myself changing diapers, walking in parks, celebrating Jewish holidays, accompanying one woman to the hospital on the birth of her first baby, sharing La Leche and LaMaze notes from the days when my own children were that young. I visited wig shops (Orthodox Jewish women are required to cover their hair when in public), went to the *mikva* (ritual bath-house), sat behind a *mechitza* (partition between men and women in the synagogue), [and] ate meals in strictly kosher restaurants to put into a concrete context the experiences these women described (see Roberts 1981 for a detailed discussion of feminist methodology).

Refiguring Patriarchal Meaning: Celebrating the Feminine

As predominately middle-class, educated and somewhat liberal youths, these women struck out in many directions in their late teens and early adult years. Like countercultural youth (Wuthnow 1976; Glock and Bellah 1976; Tipton 1982; Breines 1982) who protested the Vietnam War, the amoral use of technology, the racial, ethnic and gender injustices and like those who moved in other religious directions, these women found the quality and focus of contemporary living deeply troubling.

Of the women studied, including those who came into their young adult years during the waning days of the counterculture, one out of three had had some experience with Oriental/mystic traditions (especially Zen, transcendental meditation, and yoga) and/or one of the personal growth movements such as EST or scientology. Twenty-five women claimed to have identified with and/or participated in the women's movement. Ten had been actively involved in feminist consciousness raising groups. Moreover, twelve women admitted to active involvement in the pro-abortion campaigns of the early seventies. All described themselves during their searching years as pro-choice and claimed that certainly in appearance they were "liberated" women.

In part, because many had personally experienced or feared the familial and economic instabilities of our times, these newly Orthodox women reject all secular liberation movements and quasi-religious communities, which, they feel, compromise responsibility to the family and community and promote individual autonomy and self-fulfillment (see Z. Eisenstein (1981) for a fine analysis of the links between individualism and the limitations of liberal feminism). For instance, many who had joined human-growth-potential movements found them to be a trap. One woman referred to her early seventies experiences with transcendental meditation as . . . "a great big organized be-in." "Something was missing," she continued, "I didn't want to be, I wanted to do. I wanted to feel I could make decisions that would lead to right actions." "Feeling good" and "actualizing oneself" through many of the human-growth-potential movements or Oriental/mystical traditions did not seem to provide for community and "right living on a here and now, day to day basis," as one woman phrased it.

All women expressed some concern about the loss of clear rules and expectations in marital, familial, and sexual relationships. Discussing their relationships prior to Orthodoxy, some emphasized their relationships with men who were unwilling or unable to make lasting commitments. One woman put it this way:

> There I was 25 years of age. I had had my fill of casual sexual relationships, drugs, communal living. I looked at myself and said: What will I be like at 40 years of age? An aging hippie with no roots and maybe just a history of bad relationships? I wanted something true and lasting.

For many the "dark side" of individualism had become a real, not merely abstract or theoretical, problem. Freedom at the expense of commitment was a theme prevalent in many of the interviews. Secular versions of liberal feminism were not satisfactory either. Several women compared their feminist experiences to the ways in which Jewish Orthodoxy spoke to them as women.

> You know, before I became *frum* (Orthodox) I was in a feminist consciousness raising group. We talked a good deal about our problems . . . about being women, students, lovers, and working women . . . we talked about whatever it was that was going on in our lives at that time, but we never really were able to formulate anything beyond or larger than ourselves. . . . We were good at defining the negatives. I needed something that spoke to me directly about being a woman.

Still another woman put it this way.

> In Judaism there is a positive assertion of who we are as women . . . the older I get the more I realize how good that is . . . I have found meaning in all this ritual . . . meaning I have never really had at any other time in my life. Torah [Five Books of Moses] has so much to say to me as a woman . . . My feelings about myself as a sexual person . . . the family purity laws[7] are so in line with me as a woman. . . . it is commanded that I not be sexually taken for granted, that I have two weeks each month for myself. . . . It is mind boggling to me to think that this wonderful Torah knows who I am as a woman for centuries.

The specialness of woman and the importance of her sphere of activity was stressed throughout the interviews and often juxtaposed to a rather rigid conception of . . . feminism. For these women, feminism represents the liberal tradition equated with the "early" Betty Friedan and the National Organization of Women. That is, . . . most of these women . . . [believe that feminism dismisses] differences between men and women and [focuses] on the world of work, where equal pay is the most important issue.[8]

By idealizing the feminine and emphasizing gender differences already present in this sex-segregated community, these women develop powerful images of themselves and their activities. Excerpts from conversations with three women illustrate their celebration of gender differences and how they make positive use of symbols and rituals within Jewish Orthodoxy.

Miriam, a thirty-six year old biologist with five children living in an ultra-Orthodox community, emphasizes the moral discipline women provide for the Orthodox community:

> The world needs more of what we do as women naturally. We must teach and guide men. You know in Orthodoxy women are not required to do any of the time-bound *mitzvot* [commandments].[9] Men need the discipline, we don't. We are closer to God—we are the *Shekhina* [in-dwelling of God]. We provide understanding—knowledge alone means nothing. We have a natural understanding of things. We don't need to go to *shule* [synagogue] three times a day or study regularly to fulfill our bond with God. Our discipline is in the everyday actions of our lives, in our intuitive understanding of what is right.

In response to my probing [into] what she meant by "intuitive" and "natural" understanding, Miriam responded with the following:

> Look, I don't mean that we should not take advantage of education and other opportunities. Chaim [husband] agrees with me when I say that Dvorah [daughter] should be afforded every opportunity to go to medical school. She is very good in science, like I was. This, of course, after she has had a good religious education and has her values straight. You know, there are Orthodox women doctors. There is nothing in Orthodoxy that prevents women from receiving advanced training or education. In that sense we can do everything a man can do . . . but we have a different understanding, you know, a different way of going about it.

The following excerpts are from a recently married childless twenty-four-year-old law student named Aliza. While she is not ultra-Orthodox, but self-identified as centrist, she had just told me of her fondness for Hasidut, the philosophy associated with Hasidism.

> There is no doubt that what I love about it is the way in which women are understood. The intensity of women's relationship to God is overwhelming. I think women are the collective unconscious way of safeguarding prayer in Judaism. Women in the Bible are known for their prayers—Sarah, Rachel, and Chana. They have such an intense relationship to God . . . it reminds men that what goes on in *shule* is not important but that the relationship to God is. We are the holders of the key for the most important aspect of inner life. The experience of being a woman in Judaism I would say is like Jungian "anima"—a profound introspection and inner intensity.
>
> I like the fact that the men and the women are expected to reach holiness through different means. I think it suits our personalities. Before I was married I tried *davaning* [praying] in an all woman's *minyan* (prayer quorum), but I always felt something was missing. I like being with men and being separated. It makes two statements simultaneously—that we are separate, different, yet together.

The following excerpts are from Debra, a thirty-year-old modern Orthodox mother of three and a journalist.

> I know this is going to sound strange to you but I feel like a spiritual feminist. Often when I awaken in the morning and I am saying my prayers I feel this profound spirituality, it's actually liberating. I go to this wonderful workshop once a week. It is offered by a *frum* woman who is a psychologist. There is music, meditation, group exercise, and, since most of us are vegetarians, some veggie snacks. We study the role of the feminine in Jewish thought. I feel so in touch with myself and the rhythms of my body. We've learned a lot about Jewish mystical thought, too. In the past I have taken a lot of courses—mostly having to do with ethics . . . but this workshop for women is the most important one. The others just make me know what good sense the Torah makes for personal living and mental hygiene, but my course on feminine spirituality relates the most to me as a woman. You know, I don't just feel good but I feel connected to a past and to a future.
>
> I think in a world that isn't *frum* most women are male-identified. I think before I became Orthodox I was like that. You know, what's male is better. Not in Judaism. If anything it is a bit reversed. Difference doesn't mean inferiority. In fact, only in Judaism have I found out who I really am. I am different, not just because I am Jewish, but, also because I am a woman. I have taken part in anti-nuclear demonstrations because I truly believe that women, more than men, understand those things which are life threatening. Those insights are all there in the Torah. I like being with other women a good part of the time, I like studying about myself and other women with other women, I like being separate with other women. It is a real sense of strength for me.

These women celebrate the feminine and the domain most associated with the female in religious Orthodoxy—the family. Marriage and family are key components in the structure of Orthodox Jewish women's everyday religious lives. One woman suggests that marriage is at once a personal and a sacred act. Through her familial practices as wife and mother she is able, she claims, to make a "dwelling place for God below." Another woman stated that marriage is the symbol of the highest relationship possible: "The day God gave Jewish people the Torah is called the day of his wedding." These *baalot teshuva* assert an unambiguous "pro–family" stance based on strong assertions that the family, like the spiritual, is essentially their realm. They take from Orthodoxy the religious values consonant with the "light" and nurturance they, and the tradition, define as essentially female.

The *baalot teshuva* focus on the most powerful and sacred images of themselves and their functions in this religious tradition. These women reclaim and emphasize classical theological sources to describe their roles as Orthodox Jewish women. Moreover, they make explicit the strong family-centered values that Orthodoxy prescribes for both men and women. For instance, the family, "their" domain, is described as "the sanctuary on earth." They often refer to the *Shabbat* (Sabbath) as "feminine" or as "a taste of the world to come." Among many of the Hasidic women there is an implicit belief that they "will prepare the world for the coming of the Messiah." Still others associate the female with the "in-dwelling" of God. These powerful images evoke for these women a sacred community of which they are a principal part, in direct contrast to the secular male culture that most have consciously rejected.

Practicing Jewish Orthodoxy: Making "Feminist" Sense of Patriarchal Social Structure

Perhaps, however, these *baalot teshuva's* discussion of the family purity laws are the most instructive of how these women seem to make "feminist" sense out of patriarchal religion and social structure. The laws of *nidda* and *mikva* as part of the family purity laws (one of the three most important social practices pertaining to Orthodox Jewish women) demand that there be a sexual and physical separation between husband and wife during her menstrual cycle. According to Talmudic law, separation between husband and wife should be maintained for at least twelve days, five for the actual period of flow and seven additional days during which no bleeding is visible (called clean or white days). On the evening of her seventh clean day, or any day thereafter upon her choosing, a woman goes to the *mikva* (a ritual bath).

"During *nidda*," explained one particularly articulate woman, "the woman falls between categories of life and death." She noted that when she teaches seminars, she often introduces non-legal, but traditional, sources of explanation to frame discussions of *nidda* and *mikva*.

She explains:

> For instance, when it is questioned why women and not men are still subject to impurity rituals I look to traditional explanations . . . you can find one that suggests that women are closer to God because of their ability to create life and that they are, therefore, subject to purity rituals . . . still another views the woman's body as the second temple. I like to think of a woman's cycle as part of all the sacred time rhythms in Judaism—the *Shabbat*, holidays . . .

All of the women rejected the term "unclean" as an uninformed and mistaken translation of *nidda*. Many explained that "impure" is a better translation, for it places the meaning of *nidda* and *mikva* in the sacred context in which it belongs. "Blood," argues one woman, "is the symbol of both birth and death. This is recognized in the balance between *nidda* and *mikva;* the first is the mourning of our temporarily lost capacity to give life, the other a celebration of our capacity to give life." Not one woman doubted the importance of the *mikva* to the community. As one woman put it: "There is no doubt about it . . . if a choice has to be made a community has to build a *mikva* before it can build a *shule* or even acquire a *Sefer* Torah (Five Books of Moses)." While not directly challenging the sacred status of the Torah in Orthodoxy, these women use the legal tradition to their own advantage. While these women may be making a virtue of their impurity (and in so doing accommodating themselves to patriarchal interpretation), they are simultaneously claiming strong traditional sources for normative and institutional support for women's sacred status within Judaism as well.

This same process is apparent in their discussion of the function of family purity laws. Almost all women noted the positive functions of such laws. Although newly married women were more likely to complain about the length of sexual separation, those married over longer periods of time and with more children emphasized the positive effects of those laws over the adult life-cycle. On woman notes: "When we were first married, I found it hard to consider sexual separation as a positive thing. In fact, during my menstrual cycle I felt I wanted to be held and loved more than at other times of the month. But I must admit over the years it truly serves as a renewal . . . it is really like being a bride again . . . well almost." Even among the newly married, many claimed that forced separation heightened desire. Referring to the sexual separation from her husband during *nidda*, one woman noted: "The separation restores our passion and places the control of it in my hands."

Many feminists have pointed to the way in which menstrual taboos have been a way to control and demean women and the insidious way such beliefs continue in our contemporary culture (see Douglas 1966; Culpepper 1974). Yet the *baalot teshuvas'* acclaim for the laws of *nidda* and *mikva* suggest a range of experience and meaning not anticipated by some feminists. Because these women have to attend intimately to their bodies to engage in sexual activity according to *halacha* (religious law), many speak of an increased awareness and harmony with their bodies they had never known before. Comparing their sexual lives prior to and after their embracing of Orthodoxy, these women claim a control not known before and a newfound respect for their bodies and their sexuality. They repeatedly reminded me that they cannot be "taken for granted."

In answering questions about abortion and contraception, these women were consistent in their belief that Orthodoxy gave them latitude in making reproductive decisions. None doubted that in Judaism the mother's health (mental and physical) takes precedence in matters concerning childbearing and rearing. Except for Hasidic women, most women readily distinguished between continual childbearing and the need for quality family relationships and a healthy family environment. Most of the centrist and modern Orthodox women, and even some among the ultra-Orthodox women currently use or have used contraception at some point in their marital life cycle.[10] As one woman put it: "Family planning does not necessarily mean small families."

Specific data on the frequency of sexual intercourse and sexual satisfaction and experimentation were not forthcoming. Modesty rules inhibit truly open discourse about such details. Therefore, the data on sexual practices are limited. However, it is quite clear that these women believe that the laws of *nidda* and *mikva* function positively for women within marriage.

Yet despite their pro-family stance and their emphasis on gender differences, these women are not restricted to practices traditionally associated with familial roles. Three-quarters of them currently work, and almost all intend to participate in the paid labor force at some time.[11] . . . The flexibility needed to maintain dietary laws, the many holidays, and the Sabbath encourages both men and women either to take part-time jobs or positions allowing great personal autonomy and decision making. Almost all of the women who did not have advanced degrees intended to retrain and/or obtain more education before returning to the labor force.

Whether they work or not, all of those women with children living at home use some form of child care or day care services regularly. Irrespective of their wives' work status, all husbands have some responsibility for the care of children. All husbands were responsible for some regular domestic activity as well—the most usual activity was weekly grocery and meat shopping. In addition to their husbands' help, one half of those women who work full-time have someone living in the household to help with the child care responsibilities and/or housekeeping. Many of the live-in help are young women who are in the process of converting to Orthodox Judaism. Of the remaining women, almost all have at least weekly help with housekeeping.[12]

Several reasons account for husbands' participation in household labor and their clear presence in the home. Men's religious obligation to pray three times a day and to study necessitates flexibility in their work patterns. This flexibility often allows them either to work at home or to be home during the day. Their presence in the home and the strict observance of holidays and the Sabbath as family-centered events structures frequent interaction among husbands, wives, and children. Moreover, men's frequent and consistent presence in the home fosters a strong family-centered orientation for them.

Finally, the data suggest that although most of these women do not focus on male privilege and authority in Jewish Orthodoxy, some maintain a strong belief that those areas that clearly mark women as second-class citizens will eventually change. For instance, fifteen women knew of and ten were actively involved in GET, an organization of Orthodox women designed to change the divorce laws which currently allow only men to initiate and obtain a divorce. It is interesting to note that such blatant inequalities in Orthodoxy were attributed to "poor" interpretation of *halacha* (Jewish code of law considered inviolable) not to Orthodox theology. Interestingly, when asked about what they might want to see changed in Orthodoxy, a few women talked of changes in the synagogue and *yeshiva.* "In time," said one woman, "women will be able to read from the Torah and study the *gemara.* It will take maybe another 300 years, but it will happen. I'm in no hurry." While one or two women could see the opening of men's roles to women, none wished dramatically to alter the practices associated with women in Jewish Orthodoxy.

DISCUSSION

Feminist sociology begins with the premise that women and their experiences are central to the construction of social reality. Loosely structured interviews allowed me to uncover the issues, concerns, and kinds of things that were of significance to these newly Orthodox women. . . .

These women claim that much of what attracts and holds them in this traditional life style is the nature and description of the feminine and the female in Orthodoxy. Both Hasidic and non-Hasidic women evoke classical Jewish sources to express their positive identification and participation in Orthodoxy and, consequently, in the world at large. The selected bits and pieces of tradition and theology they choose to relate strongly suggest that they consciously reformulate that Orthodoxy in their own image.

Ironically, it is through their "return" to a patriarchal tradition that many of these women claim they are in touch with their own bodies, and the so-called feminine virtues of nurturance, mutuality, family and motherhood. It is in the sex-segregated world of Jewish Orthodoxy that many of these women claim they have found their identities as women. They describe the Orthodox community as normatively organized around feminine principles and values, and correlate that which is associated with the female in Orthodoxy with the sacred and spiritual meaning of life.

Recognizing that social movements and/or ideologies which promise self-fulfillment and personal autonomy over familial and communal values almost always leave women at a distinct disadvantage (Ehrenreich 1983), these *baalot teshuva* negotiate their familial and personal status within Jewish Orthodoxy through the positive and sacred use of the symbols and structure associated with the female and the feminine. In so doing, they claim they hold men and the community accountable to them. For many, the formal world of patriarchy in Jewish Orthodoxy is preferable to the informal secular patriarchal [world] they have rejected. Concrete rules and expectations, especially about their lives as women in a community of believers, are an improvement, they claim, over the theoretical ideologies the political and social liberalism of the sixties and seventies advocated. They view themselves not merely as passive reflections of male imagery, but rather as moral agents for positive action. They not only believe in gender difference, they celebrate it.

... In the religious world, claim these women, femininity and that which is associated with it, is seen as a positive source of value, not only for the self but for the community as well. These *baalot teshuva* focus on "feminine" values which the community as a whole celebrates for both men and women. In this way, the *baalot teshuva* claim feminine qualities as normative for the community at large (see Handelman 1984). For instance, in Jewish Orthodoxy, passivity is equated with infinite capacity to receive divine understanding in the religious world. Both men and women are held to the practice of *tzniut* (modesty). That is, neither men nor women are to present themselves in an aggressive or self-important manner.

... [W]hile most of these women openly reject feminism or what they perceive feminism [to be], they also maintain a gender identity deeply informed by many protofeminist (although depoliticized) attitudes and practices. Like some second-wave feminists (Miller 1976; Rich 1976), the *baalot teshuva* celebrate the feminine not only by contrasting it with the masculine ethic of success, individualism and aggressive stances, but as a source of power and strength for themselves as well. They negotiate their familial and marital roles in ways, they claim, that help them maintain control over their bodies and their sexuality. They also claim strong family-centered values for the community at large and hold men accountable to them... on those grounds. They symbolically reconstruct the sex/gender system not only to enhance female status but also bring men's aspirations and value systems more in line with women's. In this sense, they are protofeminist.

However, although they [believe] they are theologically equal to men, they do not directly challenge the social structural sources of gender inequality. They do not challenge male hegemony in the public, legal community that is identified as Jewish Orthodoxy (the world of synagogue and study). They ignore the very premise of Orthodoxy which places men at the center of the religious community as rabbis, leaders and as those who study and interpret the heart of Orthodoxy—religious law. They do not explicitly acknowledge that the feminine virtues they celebrate also help to maintain a gendered religious division of labor. That division of labor helps to maintain their secondary status to men—in public religious ceremony and in religious law. In this sense, they are depoliticized.

• • •

Indeed, in the Orthodox Jewish community the shared belief system for both men and women is steeped in patriarchy. Feminists are not incorrect in their recognition that this serves as a powerful social control mechanism in maintaining male-dominance and in keeping women in their secondary place within the community of synagogue and study. Yet there is another set of belief systems that affects the everyday actions of men and women. . . . [Women] simultaneously ignore those institutions important to men and to what maintains male-dominance, while creating and/or maintaining their own more relevant systems of meaning. In turn, these systems help them negotiate their familial and marital roles.

CONCLUSION

Interpretive models of sociology encourage us, as Weber claimed, to give "an interpretive understanding of social action insofar as the acting individual attaches a subjective meaning to it" (1964, p. 88). Or as Blumer suggests to "get inside their worlds of meanings" (1969, p. 51). The epistemological and methodological basis of the majority of feminist and interpretive sociology calls for analytic categories as complex as the lives people actually live (see Cook 1983; Stacey and Thorne 1985; Farganis 1986; Kasper 1986; Cook and Fonow 1986; Grant, Ward and Rong, 1987; Stacey and Gerard 1988). . . . A feminist framework does not begin with the assumption that what goes on in the public world of men's relations is the most important focus in an analysis of female relationships or of community relations in general. Interactionist models highlight consciousness, language and agency. Together the two provide an analytic model capable of capturing the complexities and tensions that make up everyday behavior of any gendered subgroup. As "minded" social actors, women are capable of constructing their own systems of meaning and of negotiating their social reality; they are not simply or necessarily "robots," "victims," or "fools" (Stacey 1983).

However, a feminist model forces us to move beyond the value-neutral description of the actor's point of view to the consequences of action, behavior and belief in light of the larger social and historical relations in which they are embedded. These women selectively adopt and even incorporate protofeminist attitudes and values into their familial lives. However, their female consciousness (Kaplan 1982) is limited to Orthodox, heterosexual, Jewish women. Since the most important roles for these women surround their functions as wives and mothers, [women who are] unmarried, divorced, widowed, separated, and childless face clear problems within such communities. Moreover, although the *baalot teshuva* may reclaim or retrieve values attached to the women's community, those values are limited almost exclusively to the roles of motherhood and wifehood. . . . Furthermore, while they may claim positive values associated with the feminine, they do so without the mechanisms or legitimacy to reject what is still oppressive to them and others. Or, as Lipman-Blumen notes in her discussion of women who have [claimed] moral authority in the past, most "fail to extend moral authority so that it becomes part of social institutions beyond the family" (1984, p. 32).

The feminine principles, of which the *baalot teshuva* speak, are abstract qualities, giving, perhaps, an ideological cast to the community, but [lacking] the mechanisms to change or claim such practices for the community as a whole. In this sense the social practices from which the feminine principles are born still emanate from the world of women, not from the community of men and women. These women do not directly challenge a system of law defined and continually refined by men. At best, then, these women adopt short-term tactics which may provide a certain amount of psychic autonomy and space from men but are not capable, in the long run, of directly addressing and changing the politics of religious patriarchy or the division of labor that helps to maintain it.

NOTES

1. Some contemporary feminists believe that the female experience ought to be the source for dominant values for the culture as a whole (Miller 1976; Rich 1976); others argue that women are not only different from men but superior to them (Rich 1976; Daly 1978). Among both *baalot teshuva* and some contemporary feminists, there is a celebration of the feminine and the female, especially in light of her seemingly greater relational capacities.

2. In most social science studies, the Orthodox Jewish community is generally explored and then analyzed through the perspectives and experiences of men, especially through the male-oriented activities associated with synagogue and study. Even the two most recent books published on Jewish Orthodoxy, despite their rich detail and keen insights, fail to give us any compelling sociological explanation of Orthodoxy's potential appeal to women. In his book *From Suburb to Shtetl* (1979), Egon Myer cannot gain access, in that highly sex-segregated community, to the institutions relevant to Orthodox women's lives nor can he explore women's experiences within them. In *The World of the Yeshiva* (1982), William Helmreich confines his study to the all-male world of the *yeshiva*. Neither focuses exclusively on *baalei teshuva* (Hebrew plural for newly Orthodox Jews). Moreover, while the only full length book on *baalei teshuva, Return to Judaism: Religious Renewal in Israel* (1983), written by Janet Aviad, contributes much to defining some of the characteristics and properties of newly Orthodox Jews, it is limited to only those within *yeshivot* (schools of higher education) in Israel.

3. These data reflect one half of a larger sample of women (150) and are the basis for my book about feminism and the religious right (Kaufman 1990).

4. The five cities are: Boston, Cleveland, New York City and the Crown Heights section of Brooklyn, Los Angeles, and San Francisco. All five cities have among the largest recorded Orthodox Jewish populations in the country (from 5% to 13% claiming Orthodox affiliation).

5. There are no demographic portraits of *baalei teshuva* after they have committed themselves to marriage, family, and community. No claims are made that the *baalot teshuva* under study were randomly drawn as a sample of a defined universe, nor can the interviewed be considered statistically representative of those who return to Orthodoxy nor of Orthodoxy itself.

6. Since my interest was in the Orthodox world according to the women who had embraced patriarchal living, I did not interview men of the community. I did spend time talking with husbands and lay leaders in each of the communities.

7. The family purity laws require a two-week separation between husband and wife during menstruation.

8. As newly Orthodox women, only three remained active in any political feminist causes. Three had signed a petition for the Equal Rights Amendment.

9. In Orthodox Judaism women are exempt from commandments which are related to time and place. For example, men must pray at specific times during the day, women need not.

10. The custom, as opposed to legal tradition, in Orthodox communities, is to bear as many children as possible. Yet, despite this tradition, the average number of children for this population of women was 3.4.

11. Only forty percent (30) of these women had earned less than a bachelor's degree. Of these women, five worked. Of the forty-five who had earned more than a bachelor's degree, 20 had earned at least a master's degree, and 11 of these had professional degrees (four lawyers, two doctors, and five Ph.D.s). Of those who work, only those with advanced degrees work in what might be classified as male-dominated professions (e.g., law, university teaching, medicine, or executive positions). Except for several computer analysts, the remainder are in female-dominated semi-professional occupations (teachers, librarians, social workers, nurses). The higher her educational degree, the more likely the woman was to work full time. Similarly, the average number of children for those working was less (3.2) than for those who were not working (3.6).

12. These *baalot teshuva* are squarely within a middle-class socioeconomic category. The combined average income for this group was $37,000 a year.

REFERENCES

Adler, R.
1983 "The Jew Who Wasn't There: Halakhah and the Jewish Woman." Pp. 12–18 in *On Being a Jewish Feminist*, edited by S. Heschel. New York: Schocken Books.

Ammerman, N.
1987 *Bible Believers*. New Brunswick, NJ: Rutgers University Press.

Aviad, J.
1983 *Return to Judaism: Religious Renewal in Israel*. Chicago, IL: University of Chicago Press.

Baskin, J.
1985 "The Separation of Women in Rabbinic Judaism." Pp. 3–18 in *Women, Religion and Social Change,* edited by Y. Y. Haddad and E. B. Findly. Albany, NY: SUNY Press.

Blumer, H.
1969 *Symbolic Interactionism: Perspective and Method.* Englewood Cliffs, NJ: Prentice-Hall.

Breines, W.
1982 *Community and Organization in the New Left:* 1962–1968. New York: Praeger Publishers.

Cook, J.
1983 "An Interdisciplinary Look at Feminist Methodology: Ideas and Practice in Sociology, History and Anthropology." *Humbolt Journal of Social Relations* 10: 127–152.

———., and M. Fonow
1986 "Knowledge and Women's Interest: Issues of Epistemology and Methodology in Feminist Sociological Research." *Sociological Inquiry* 56: 2–29.

Culpepper, E.
1974 "Menstruation Mantra: Red, Crimson, Sienna, Scarlett." Dissertation, Harvard University.

Daly, M.
1978 *GYN/ECOLOGY: The Metaethics of Radical Feminism.* Boston, MA: Beacon Press.

Douglas. M.
1966 *Purity and Danger.* London: Routledge and Keegan Paul.

Ehrenreich, B.
1983 *The Hearts of Men: American Dreams and the Flight from Commitment.* New York: Anchor Press.

Eisenstein, Z.
1981 *The Radical Future of Liberal Feminism.* Boston: Northeastern University Press.

Farganis, S.
1986 "Social Theory and Feminist Theory: The Need for Dialogue." *Sociological Inquiry* 56: 49–68.

Glock, C. and R. Bellah
1976 *The New Religious Consciousness.* Berkeley and Los Angeles, CA: University of California Press.

Grant, L., K. Ward and X. L. Rong
1987 "Gender and Methods in Sociological Research." *American Sociological Review* 52: 856–862.

Handelman, S.
1984 "The Crown of Her Husband: The Image of the Feminine in Chassidic Philosophy." Unpublished paper available from the Department of English, University of Maryland, College Park, Maryland.

Helmreich, W.
1982 *The World of the Yeshiva*. New York: The Free Press.

Heschel, S.
1983 *On Being a Jewish Feminist*. New York: Schocken Books.

Kaplan, T.
1982 "Female Consciousness and Collective Action: The Case of Barcelona 1910–1918." *Signs* 7: 545–566.

Kasper, A.
1986 "Consciousness Re-evaluated: Interpretive Theory and Feminist Scholarship." *Sociological Inquiry* 56: 29–49.

Kaufman, D.
1985a "Women Who Return to Orthodox Judaism: A Feminist Analysis." *Journal of Marriage and the Family* 47: 543–555.
1985b "Feminism Reconstructed: Feminist Theories and Women Who Return to Orthodox Judaism." *Midwest Sociologists for Women in Society* 5: 45–55.
1987 "Coming Home to Jewish Orthodoxy: Reactionary or Radical Women?" *Tikkun* 2: 60–63 July–August.
1991 *Rachel's Daughters: Newly Orthodox Jewish Women*. New Brunswick, NJ: Rutgers University Press.

Lipman-Blumen, J.
1984 *Gender Roles and Power.* Englewood Cliffs, NJ: Prentice-Hall.

Meyer, E.
1979 *From Suburb to Shtetl*. Philadelphia: Temple University Press.

Miller, J.
1976 *Toward a New Psychology of Women*. Boston: Beacon Press.

Rich, A.
1976 *Of Women Born*. New York: W. W. Norton.

Roberts, H.
1981 *Doing Feminist Research*. London: Routledge and Kegan Paul.

Stacey, J.
1983 "The New Conservative Feminism." *Feminist Studies* 10, 4 (Fall): 559–583.

———., and B. Thorne
1985 "The Missing Feminist Revolution in Sociology." *Social Problems* 32: 301–316.

———., and S. Gerard
1988 "We Are Not Doormats: Post-Feminist Evangelicalism in the U.S." Unpublished Paper, Sociology Department, University of California, Davis, California.

Tipton, S.
1982 *Getting Saved From the Sixties.* Berkeley: University of California Press.

Weber, M.
1964 *The Theory of Social and Economic Organization.* Trans. A. M. Henderson and Talcott Parsons. New York: Free Press.

Wuthnow, R.
1976 *The Consciousness Reformation.* Berkeley, Los Angeles, CA: University of California Press.

Review Questions

1. What religious duties does Orthodox Judaism require? How are these duties "gendered"? What are the beliefs about men and women that underlie the rules?
2. What motivated the women in Kaufman's study to leave the larger society to convert to Orthodox Judaism?
3. What world view did the women create once they had converted? What were the "places" of men and women in their world view? What protofeminist values did they hold? How did the women go about creating this world view?
4. Kaufman contends that Orthodox Judaism in general does not grant women as much power and autonomy as men. Further, the particular women in the communites she studied were not as powerful as the men. Why and how did these women come to perceive themselves as powerful? What part did their earlier experiences in the larger American society play in shaping their perceptions?

Suggested Readings: Interaction in Institutional Contexts: Religion

Bell, Daniel. "The Return of the Sacred? The Argument on the Future of Religion." *British Journal of Sociology* 28 (1977): 419–448.
Bellah, Robert N. *Habits of the Heart.* New York: Harper & Row, 1985.

Berger, Peter. *The Sacred Canopy: Elements of a Sociological Theory of Religion.* Garden City, N.Y.: Doubleday, 1969.

Lofland, John, and Rodney Stark. "Becoming a World-Saver: A Theory of Conversion to a Deviant Perspective." *American Sociological Review* 30 (1965): 862–874.

Neitz, Mary. *Charisma and Community: A Study of Religious Committment within the Charismatic Renewal.* New Brunswick, N.J.: Transaction, 1987.

Slater, Philip. *The Wayward Gate: Science and the Supernatural.* Boston: Beacon Press, 1977.

Part IX. Social and Cultural Change

SOCIAL CHANGE IS A COMPLEX, ONGOING PROCESS. ANY OR ALL OF THE ELEMENTS of a culture may change—objects, ideas, beliefs, norms, roles, values, patterns of interaction. Change may be dramatic and sudden, as in the wake of a disaster or war. Or it can occur subtly and gradually over many decades.

Change may occur as the result of *formal* enactments, when those who are empowered to make laws for a nation, a state, or a company require new ways of doing things. Civil rights legislation, for example, led not only to changes in the procedures and policies of schools, businesses, hospitals, and unions, but to shifts in opinions and beliefs—some favorable to minorities and some which could be called "backlash." As the U. S. Food and Drug Administration determines which substances are dangerous to our health, even our eating habits may be altered by formal procedures.

More often, social change is not legislated or dictated but occurs *informally.* Examples of such change can be found in styles of dress, language, technological innovations, and the relative importance of religion in everyday life. The invention of the automobile has transformed our cities, our economy, and even our courtship practices. The microwave oven has changed the definition of cooking.

Informal change can also lead to formal change. This process can be seen with the gradual acceptance of marijuana smoking by middle-class society. When the editors of this book were attending college in the mid 1960s, few students were smoking marijuana at Oklahoma State University or Temple University. As marijuana smoking became part of the college experience, more and more young adults became users. Smoking soon spread to the high schools and then to the professions. As marijuana use became more extensive, the laws in many states were revised to focus on the major distributors rather than on individual smokers. Police, too, began looking the other way when college students and other adults were peacefully smoking in public.

Rarely does the alteration of one element in a culture leave the rest of the culture intact. Because social elements are intricately connected, change in one area usually affects many other areas, whether anyone intended for it to or not. Sociologists have long recognized that changes in one particular institution, the economy, rapidly ripple outward through other societal institutions.

The family is especially vulnerable to economic forces, because the family is, among other things, an economic unit. By law as well as custom, wives, husbands, and children share money, property, and each other's services. When transformations occur in our economic arrangements, families must often adjust to accommodate them.

In the last century, technological innovations led to the Industrial Revolution and spelled the end of the family farm, where all members had worked together on the homestead. Men left the home, first to work in factories, later to work in offices. The family unit was forever altered. The social role of "father" came to be associated with "breadwinner," the role of "mother" synonymous with "housewife."

In this century, women have increasingly left the home to work in the paid labor force. As we saw in Arlie Russell Hochschild's study of working parents, this economic fact has left its mark on the family. An unequal division of labor in the household has brought about tension and exhaustion for many working mothers, who commonly continue to do much more household labor than their husbands. Such hardship has no doubt contributed to the rising divorce rate.

In Hochschild's judgment, businesses and governments must eventually provide some relief for overburdened family members. Furthermore, men's roles must begin to change, making it acceptable for husbands to share in housework and child care. In the selection from Hochschild's work that begins this section, she describes some of the scarce "new men" on the forefront of gender-role change. It is likely that these men will be the role models for future generations.

The second article in this section focuses on the consequences of a medical innovation, the ventilator. A ventilator is a relatively simple, reliable machine that can be inserted in the tracheas of people who cannot breathe on their own. Biological death is thus avoided, but, as Howard Robboy and Bernard Goldstein discovered, "social death" may take its place. Since a ventilator-dependent person cannot speak or move around freely, and may in fact be housed in a hospital or nursing home, he or she can become socially isolated. Furthermore, medical personnel can offer ventilator patients no further assistance and therefore tend to wash their hands of them. Ventilator-dependent members may exhaust family resources of time, energy, and money. Spouses and children may begin to think of them as dead. No one, it seems, interacts with the ventilator-dependent as regular members of society.

This case provides an example of a particularly ghastly *unintended consequence* of an innovation that is serving its intended purposes well. Robboy and Goldstein wonder how many other "technological marvels" of biomedicine will turn out to be causes of social death.

THE SECOND SHIFT, PART TWO: THE NEW MAN

Arlie Russell Hochschild with Anne Machung

IN THE HISTORY OF AMERICAN FATHERHOOD, THERE HAVE BEEN THREE STAGES, EACH a response to economic change. In the first, agrarian stage, a father trained and disciplined his son for employment, and often offered him employment on the farm, while his wife brought up the girls. (For blacks, this stage began after slavery ended.) As economic life and vocational training moved out of the family in the early nineteenth century, fathers left more of the rearing of their children to their wives. According to the historian John Nash (1965), in both these stages of history, the father was often distant and stern. Not until the early twentieth century, when increasing numbers of women began to work outside the home, did the culture rediscover the father as an active presence at home, and establish the idea that "father was friendly." In the early 1950s, popular magazines began to offer articles with such titles as "Fathers Are Parents Too" and "It's Time Father Got Back into the Family." Today, most families are in the third stage of economic development but in the second stage of fatherhood. Mothers are in the labor force, but most fathers have yet to embrace a notion of themselves as equally important as their wives at home.

• • •

Eighty percent of the men in my study of two-job couples had one thing in common. They didn't share housework and child care. This introduced extra work for their wives and often tension in their marriages. The two men I describe in this chapter fully share the responsibility for and actual work around the house. They believe in sharing, and they take care of their children the way a "primary parent" does. Their starting points differ drastically, as do their means of arrival, but the influence on their marriage and children is the same.

MICHAEL SHERMAN

As the only son of an immigrant who began work at the age of twelve and rose to the top of the scrap-metal business in New Jersey, Michael Sherman became the repository of his father's ambitions. The reading of Michael's school report cards was a family event, while the cards his two older sisters brought home received little notice. From kindergarten through high school, he had always been first in his class. Now, as a man of thirty, he recalls still with a touch of bitterness how his father would dangle him on his lap, showing him off to admiring old men, and between report cards lose interest in him.

He grew up, therefore, more in the company of his mother, his two older sisters, and a maid. . . . Having been alternately idolized and neglected as a child, Michael early vowed that he would never treat his own children as his father had treated him. But, he told me, he initially expected his marriage to Adrienne to be like his father's marriage to his mother: he would get the "A's" for the household, he would earn the status. She would raise a lovely family.

He wanted Adrienne to be well educated and, in the phrase used in his parents' circle, a "brilliant mother." Unlike his own mother, though, she "might also work." When Michael was courting Adrienne, he made it clear: "It's fine if you work, but my career will come first." Michael planned a career in microbiology.

Adrienne had been the adored only daughter of older parents. Her father had walked her into the parlor after dinner—past the dinner dishes—to read together from the encyclopedia. A gifted student, she had intended to have "some sort" of career, perhaps as an anthropologist. Previous boyfriends had shown polite admiration for this plan; but by comparison, Michael seemed genuinely interested in it. . . . She agreed to put his career first. He agreed she should have a career of some sort, and they married.

Three years later, when he was finishing his last year of graduate school, Michael applied for all the best postdoctoral positions in the United States. He was accepted everywhere and chose one at Duke University. Adrienne quit her studies at New York University and applied to the Ph.D. program in anthropology at Duke; she was turned down. . . . So she arrived in Durham as Michael's wife, the rejected doctoral candidate. In New York, where she had done two years of graduate work already, she had been praised as an outstanding student in her department. Her mentor had invited her to lunch and discussed her work. She had close friends and colleagues. Now she sat alone every day in the library staring blankly at a cold stack of books, so miserable she could hardly read.

After a few months of this, something in Adrienne snapped. One evening, Michael came home at five o'clock from his "real" job as a postdoctoral fellow. Adrienne arranged to come home at the same time from her "unreal" job in the library as a would-be scholar trying to read. At 5:05, when Michael sat down as usual to read the paper and wait for her to prepare their dinner, Adrienne exploded in a burst of fury and tears. Why did *his* day entitle him to rest? Didn't *her* day count too? It was bad enough that the world was ignoring her career plans; did *he* have to ignore them too? She had been happy to follow him to Duke; that was fine. But she desperately needed his support for her own fragile career plans, and sharing the second shift was a symbol of that support. . . . If Michael couldn't bring himself to value her career ambitions as he valued his own, if he couldn't symbolically express this by sharing housework, she told him she would leave. Michael refused, and Adrienne left.

What *had* happened to Adrienne? After all, she had married Michael in good faith on terms they had agreed on. Only a year earlier, among supportive colleagues and planning a brilliant career, she could never have imagined leaving. There was also part of her that loved being a homemaker and a hostess. . . . She was not, it seemed, in flight from femininity or the domestic sphere.

But on the evening she had left Michael five years earlier, the idea of staying home felt intolerable. As Daddy's girl, the future scholar, she had done so very well. It had felt so good. As she sat alone in the library, rejected and isolated, staring blankly at her book, she wanted even more to do well again. She desperately needed Michael to back her up or she didn't want to be with him at all.

With Adrienne gone, Michael stopped to consider his choice. He felt that she knew and loved him far more deeply than any other woman could; and despite how impossible she'd been, he loved her. After two months, he woke up one morning with a decision: he could do without being waited on, could do without his career coming first. He'd rather have Adrienne back. He called to tell her he would share the second shift, and she quickly came back. Raised as a little king, Michael had never done housework before, but now in their modest apartment he did half. Adrienne felt much happier, and so now did Michael. Now on the new terms, Adrienne could brave it at the library.

Adrienne wanted Michael to share not only because it was fair to her but because she wanted equality to be just as important to him as it was to her. In truth, Michael shared the second shift because he loved Adrienne and knew how terribly important it was to her. At least that was Michael's main thought at first.

Adrienne applied to the graduate program in anthropology at Duke the next year, and this time she got in. After her first year there, Michael made another sacrifice in a spirit of genuine support. Although he had finished at Duke, he stayed on for an extra year so Adrienne could collect data for her thesis. For the first time, she applied for an instructorship. One day, her mother telephoned, trying perhaps to be supportive according to her own lights. She said to Adrienne, "You have so much to do, dear, I hope you *don't* get the job." Adrienne collapsed in tears. Michael picked up the phone, indignant at his mother-in-law. "What do you *mean* you hope Adrienne doesn't get the job? She *wants* the job!"

After Adrienne finished her thesis research, she followed Michael again to the best job he was offered. Miracle of miracles, she was offered an excellent job in a nearby city too. She spoke with quiet humor about a memo tacked on the anthropology department bulletin board listing all job applicants and the posts they had won: her name was at the top. "First I was seen as the tag-along wife with the chopped-up career. Then they saw that list and suddenly thought I was the hot stuff and Michael was following me!" Now the twists of fate could seem funny.

In the sixth year of marriage—three years after the showdown and one year after beginning teaching—Adrienne and Michael decided to have a child. When Adrienne got pregnant, Michael spoke proudly of "our pregnancy." Bedridden for the last two months, Adrienne taught seminars from their living-room couch. Michael did all the cooking and shopping and planning. When twin boys were born, Michael came home every day in time for the five-thirty feeding. As he recalled, "It was *very* important to me to be there for that feeding." Adrienne found it hard to handle both twins at the same time; for a while, before she finished breast-feeding one, the other was awake and ready. After six weeks they switched to the bottle. Michael fed one twin, Adrienne fed the other.

The twins grew into a rambunctious pair. One would climb on the other's back to try to scramble up the chimney. With conspiratorial giggles, they would push on the garden gate together, open it, and dash up the street. Once they took turns drenching each other in a bucket of motor oil. If Adrienne's showdown had at first forced Michael to "concede" to sharing, now Michael was beginning to have fun with it. As he reflected, "I'm amazed at myself. I hadn't imagined the extent of nurturing feelings I have that I had really played down." He began to feel proud: "I honestly think I'm the best father I know. I'm surprised at how patient I am, and also at how impatient." For their part, the twins responded appealingly to his attentions, and drew him into their play. Crossing the street, each reached up for "Daddy's hand." They alternated in the mornings, calling for Daddy or Mommy. In search of more time to spend with his sons, Michael asked for some leave time from his university. Part of the time, he had to travel to give papers, but that was fine with Adrienne.

But, increasingly, Adrienne was under more pressure at work. Now in her fourth year in the anthropology department, she found herself in fierce competition for tenure with six hard-working male assistant professors. How many articles had she published this year? How many more in the works? When was the "big" book due? Her department chairman took fiendish pride in telling junior colleagues how "tough it really was." He admitted that Adrienne put in far more time guiding student research than her male colleagues, but reminded her "as surely she knew" that teaching didn't matter in getting tenure.

When the twins were three, Adrienne was out of the house forty-five hours a week and worked all evening after they were in bed. Even with this effort, she was falling behind her male colleagues, whose wives took care of their second shift. As Adrienne explained:

> I realized I was going to sink in my mid-career review unless I published. So that fall when I was dashing around madly teaching and doing committee work during the week, I started working weekends. I worked through five weekends in a row, and I'll never do it again. It was a complete disaster. My kids regressed a hundred and one paces. They were upset about being separated from me, because Michael was out of town at a conference and couldn't take care of them. First I tried working in the study at home, but that was too hard. Then I went into my office, and that's where I got a surprise. One of my colleagues said, "What brings *you* in?" And another said, "We haven't seen you in all four years you've been here." These are the guys who've said to me—I must have heard it fifteen times in my four years here—"You've got your husband to support you." And when I meet them in the halls they always say, "How are the *twins*?"

During this period, the Shermans' baby-sitter grew depressed, began to drink heavily, and one day disappeared completely. Michael could do his share, but no more. For the first time in years, Michael yelled at Adrienne: "I'm happy you have a career, but I don't think you should have a career *like this*. There's an upper limit." She knew he was right. Adrienne asked her chairman to delay her tenure review but he refused ("If I did it for you, I'd have to do it for everyone."). She felt she'd reached a dead end; she thought of quitting. She could combine an old interest in sculpting with child therapy, a job outside a hierarchy. One comment by a rival faculty member, which she had suppressed to smooth her way before, rang in her head now: "Do you *really* feel like a mother to your children? Or is your housekeeper more of a mother to your children?" His tone said, "It must be hard on you," but he meant, she thought now, "It must be hard on *them*."

Adrienne spoke to a senior colleague about extending her tenure review deadline despite the chairman's veto. Out of sympathy, and perhaps guilt over their own struggling wives, the faculty granted her an extension. She asked for a half-time appointment and, with Michael's support, she fought for it. After more than a year of meetings; letters; calls; and long talks with deans, colleagues, and a network of feminists in other departments, Adrienne became the fifth faculty member on the entire campus to be granted a half-time tenure-track position.

Michael had yelled at Adrienne for withdrawing from the children, but had dissuaded her from falling into a swoon of maternal guilt and retreating into sculpture and flower arranging. He had hung in there. If a sharing showdown had shocked Michael into his egalitarianism, now he was discovering who he could be as a father and husband when he wasn't being the showcase kid. He was growing into it. Michael's salary was higher than Adrienne's salary, but this wage gap . . . didn't come up in the Sherman's interviews until I raised it, and then neither had much to say about it. Neither job came first; both came second.

Michael did not struggle with Adrienne; both now struggled against the pressures of their careers. Twins or no, their professional worlds spun on; colleagues wrote books, won prizes, got promotions. To reserve enough emotional time and energy for childrearing, they had to struggle with their ambitions at work. Both loved their work, and it took discipline to moderate their involvement in it. Adrienne was now also part of the tiny world of women professors busily scurrying from one committee ("It's an all-male committee, we really need a woman, could you . . . ?") to another, addressing the endless student demand for attention from "concerned" teachers, and finally settling down at night with a cup of tea to the "real" work of writing. Some of these women had children, many were waiting. All were overworked and many were workaholics who generated a workaholic sub-culture of their own which put pressure on all of them in turn.

If the Shermans had a "family myth," it was perhaps that Michael's transformation involved little sacrifice. The twins were one surprise after another. It was so much fun, he didn't want them growing up so fast. At the same time, it was hard for a straight-A showcase kid, carrier of the Sherman line, to back-pedal his scientific career while others around him were making a run for it. . . . Holding back at work was a sacrifice. Changing gender strategies midstream was a sacrifice. These were sacrifices other men . . . did not make, and in the eyes of women like Adrienne, this made Michael rare and precious. In the present-day relational marketplace, his market value was higher than hers. They were off the "marital market," because they couldn't imagine life apart; this shielded Adrienne from the unfavorable market realities. But she also felt deeply indebted to Michael for his sacrifices. If there was just a tiny bit of unresolved tension beneath their family myth, it centered on just how grateful Adrienne should feel to Michael for getting a "fair deal" in the second shift.

Meanwhile, both gave up the spectacular career success they might have had for the respectable careers their attention to family allowed. To some colleagues, Adrienne's half-time schedule made her seem like a dilettante. To half-disapproving, half-threatened neighboring housewives she was one of those briefcase-and-bow-tie women. By working short hours in a long-hours profession, by taking odd times of the day off to be with his children, Michael was even more anomalous. Both felt morally isolated from their conventional relatives in upstate New York, who continued to write letters reflecting puzzlement and disapproval, and from many of Michael's male colleagues, who ran through more wives but seemed to get more work done. Neither the old world of family nor their new world of work fit them easily. But they fit each other and pulled together against the social tide.

During my last meeting with the Shermans, they took turns laughing and telling me this story. The previous summer when they were visiting Michael's parents, Michael began clearing the dishes off the dining-room table. His mother, who now approved of their arrangement, remarked to his father, "Look how Michael clears the table. Why didn't *you* ever do anything like that?" Michael's father replied solemnly, "Adrienne is turning Michael into a homosexual." "Oh, Jacob," Mrs. Sherman cried, "don't be ridiculous!" Adrienne and Michael looked on, laughing and incredulous as Michael's mother began a sharing showdown of her own.

ART WINFIELD: NATURAL DRIFT

Art Winfield, a thirty-five-year-old laboratory assistant with a high school education, had only the barest acquaintance with the women's movement and his wife, unlike Adrienne Sherman, had never pressed him to do more at home. But Art has a natural interest in children and a passion for being with his five-year-old adopted son, Adam. Art was not the self-consciously celebrated New Man; he is a gentle, easygoing black man, the New Man disguised as an ordinary fellow.

He was taking night classes twice a week in lab technology mainly at his wife's urging; she had hoped these classes might motivate him to search out more interesting work. But as he drove to and from his lab, Art's mind would wander from his job to the bright smile that would light his son's face when he greeted him at the daycare-center door. "My son gets only three-and-a-half hours of my time a day," Art explained, "so the time I'm with him is very important to me." Sometimes when he came to fetch Adam at daycare, Art lingered for half an hour or so to see a secret hideout, climb a favorite tree, or organize a relay race. During several months when he was on leave from the lab, he stayed longer.

The Winfields needed two salaries to live, no question about it, so Adam had to be in daycare. But Art's feelings about it are mixed: "Adam's best buddy, his number-one main man is there [at the daycare center]. But sometimes he still gets tired of being there. It's real hard for a five-year-old kid to spend eight hours away from home. Sometimes I'll take the day off and take him out of daycare and spend a day at home with him."

• • •

Some fathers reach out more easily to a son than to a daughter, but this didn't seem true for Art. He and his wife, Julia, who is white, are trying to have a child of their own, and when I asked him how he felt about a daughter, he replied:

> I'd *love* to have a little girl. Yeah. I think little girls are precious. I'd like to have a father-daughter relationship, and I guess I'm sort of nontraditional when it comes to that. Regarding sports, or her basic outlook on life, I'd raise my daughter just as positively as a boy. My wife is a strong woman and I'd like to have a daughter like that too. Girls are very smart! They certainly learn a lot quicker than boys do. That's quite obvious. Plus it would be special for Adam to have a sister.

Art also enjoys children who are not his own, and they flock to him. Tough teen-age boys drop by the Winfields' home in a poor, rough neighborhood of East Oakland to show off their pit bull dogs, and talk. When there's trouble in the neighborhood, they protect the Winfields' home. One disturbed boy showed up regularly on Art's porch. As Art recalled:

> It was a challenge to me to get to know him, because I knew what he needed. His mother was raising five kids by herself, and he needed some attention. We worked together. He came around and got to be one heck of a kid. . . .

Art's wife, Julia, feels she lacks Art's gift with children:

> I love my own son, but I'm not good with everyone's kids, like Art is. I'm one of these people who doesn't know how old a child is. I'll ask, "How old are you?" And they'll say, "Why do you want to know, lady?" But Art knows what level to approach a child on. After a long day's work, it's hard for me to compliment all the little kids at daycare on their finger painting the way he does.

Art focuses on children. About tending house he simply feels that "sharing is fair." As he puts it:

> I went through a period where I wasn't really involving myself in a lot of housework—like most men, I have to admit. That's conditioning, too, because we're led to believe we're lords and masters of the household [laughs]—that there are certain things we're not supposed to do. Also, I'm kind of stubborn and it's wrong to be like that. Anyway, Julia works as hard as I do, probably a lot harder. She deserves to have me participate. So, for about ten months, since Julia's had to work overtime at her office, I've been doing half.

Art does the laundry, vacuuming, yard work, and half the cooking. Julia, a plump, good-natured woman of thirty, appreciates the help. But she also wishes that Art loved his work more. It seems to make her a bit anxious to be more engrossed in her own job (as a legal secretary) than Art is in his. She doesn't care about money; between them she feels they have plenty. It was more a matter of her wanting him to be more drawn to his job—because it is good for people to like their work, maybe especially if they are men.

For his part, Art feels that [he gets] pretty good pay, and that the center of a man's life ought to be his family. He wonders at Julia's ambitions for him. Does it mean there is something wrong with him? Does he seem inadequate? He explained to me in confidence, that he thought her anxiety might be due to her desire to please her older brother, a conventional man who had never approved of her interracial marriage, or their house in East Oakland. Art talked the matter over privately with his mother by phone, and finally agreed, without enthusiasm, to let Julia type out a resume for him and apply for an evening course in laboratory technology.

I asked Art why he thought his bond with his son was so warm, relaxed, and strong. He began his answer with his early childhood. His mother had raised his brother and himself by working as a cook in a childcare center. As he put it, "I could give you the whole black saga—living in a dingy apartment, sleeping in bed with my brother and my mother, rats jumping over it at night." From time to time, his father would appear at their apartment, argue bitterly with his mother, then disappear. "I think my father helped me know what kind of man I *didn't* want to be," Art said. He continued: "He was my biological father. And from the time I was born until I was nine, he was all I had as a father. We didn't really have the fatherly thing when I was coming up. Because my mother was a very strong force, I didn't realize I was missing a father."

When Art was nine, his mother married a longshoreman, a strong, gentle, kindly man with no children of his own. He worked the evening shift and was home days, waiting for Art when he came barreling in the door after school. Coming to trust and love this man was the most important event in Art's life:

> When he married my mother, he understood that it would take some time to interject himself into our family. I can recall that he took his time doing that. He got to understand us first. I was a sensitive kid, and the youngest, and it had to be explained to me that my mother was still going to be there, that he was joining the family to make it a little better. He was a *gentle* man, a *good* man.

Art spoke of his stepfather with great softness:

> I don't call him my stepfather. He's my *father*. He's everything a father ever could be. I love him as if I was the biological son. Because he's a good man. He's a gentle man. He's a very honest man. We were always together. I had a father that was always there to help me whenever I needed something. He wouldn't *give* me anything, but he made me realize I had to work for what I wanted. He really did teach us how to love. . . . Through him I learned

what I want to do with my own kid. I'm trying to form the same kind of relationship. I want Adam to know that I *really* care about him.

Vacations at his grandmother's farm in Arkansas were vacations "with my father." As he spoke about this his eyes dampened, as if it was *still* hard for him to believe his stepfather loved him. "I hate to keep saying this," he said, "but it's true, he's a *very* warm man."

Perhaps Art's double legacy—a father he did *not* want to be like and a stepfather he *did* want to be like—prompted his gift with children. In his bond with his own adopted son he may be consolidating his boyhood victory.

A THIRD STAGE OF FATHERHOOD

Both Michael Sherman and Art Winfield share the work at home. They didn't . . . wait to the end of a wail of a nine-month-old who's tumbled. They have their own styles of parenting, and it is primary parenting.

Michael Sherman and Art Winfield differ in how they arrived at their gender ideology; Michael backed in, starting with housework and moving to childrearing. Art stepped forward into it, starting with his feeling for Adam and quietly extending a principle of justice to housework. Egalitarianism also meant slightly different things to each; for Michael it was a way to "be fair to Adrienne," for Art it was a way of "being a number-one Dad to Adam." The results differ too: Michael is as much the primary parent to the twins as his wife, Art seems slightly more involved than his wife.

Certain motives forged in boyhood made them want to be the "New Man." Both had grown up in a largely female world; both had reacted against "bad" fathers, and neither had grown up as a typical male. Even as a teen-ager, Art had been unusually good with small kids, which past a certain age among teen-agers in East Oakland was unusual. Michael had never felt like a "typical boy." He didn't reject things masculine; he was always popular with the guys at school. But he didn't feel the most interesting things went on in the male world or that the most interesting people were there. In truth, Michael hadn't outgrown a traditional male identity; he'd never had one. In his high school gym class and later during basic training in the army, much of the time he felt he was acting the male role. It was as if he had grown up speaking a foreign language; he spoke it fluently and without a noticeable accent, but it remained a language not quite his own. As he put it, "I was always the guy hanging around the edge of the football field." Different private motives animate a gender strategy, and these private motives animated theirs. So when the door of history opened, when the culture lit the way, when the demands of two-job life called out, they wanted to walk in.

MEN WHO DO AND MEN WHO DON'T

In my study the men who shared the second shift had a happier family life, so I wanted to know what conditions tend to produce such men. How do men who share *differ* from other men?

The men in this study who shared the work at home were no more likely than other men to have "model" fathers who helped at home. Their parents were no more likely to have trained them to do chores when they were young. Michael Sherman and Seth Stein both had fathers who spent little time with them and did little work around the house. But Michael became extremely involved in raising his twin boys, whereas Seth said hello and good-bye to his children as he went to and from his absorbing law practice. Sharers were also as likely to have had mothers who were homemakers or who worked *and* tended the home as non-sharers.

Wives of men who shared eagerly offered complex psychological explanations for why their husbands were so "unusual." Yet each story differed totally from the next. . . . The "upbringing stories" of the wives of these unusual men often focused on the impact of their husband's mother. But the only recurring theme I could discover had to do with the son's disaffiliation from a detached, absent, or overbearing *father*. John Livingston's father, as he sadly described him, was a recluse who sat talking to no one most evenings. Michael Sherman's father praised him for getting good grades, then lost interest in him between report cards. Art Winfield's biological father disappeared entirely. Many men had bad memories of their fathers, but the men who ended up sharing childcare differentiated themselves from their fathers; seeing them as negative role models, they vowed *not* to be like them. The *most* involved father—Art Winfield, the father who played with the children at his adopted son's daycare class—was both disenchanted with his real father, a "bad" model of fatherhood, and ardently devoted to his kindly stepfather, a "good" model of fatherhood. What seemed important was the combination of how a man identified with his father and what that father was like—not how much the father had helped around the house.

But many people believed that it was "upbringing"—how much a man helped around the house as a boy—that made the difference. Evan Holt, who did his hobbies "downstairs" while his wife cared for the house "upstairs," said he was just acting the way he was "brought up" to act. Evan didn't do many other things he was brought up to do, like go to church, avoid using credit cards, or wait to have sex until after marriage. In these areas of life he was his own man. But around the house, he said he was just doing what his mother taught him. In other words, "upbringing" seemed to be a rationale to cover a strategy. In turn, strategies are propelled by motives that need explaining.

Apart from what a man wants for himself, apart from his will or strategy or notions of manhood, I would guess that men who shared at home shared a certain psychological predisposition. I would guess that men like Art Winfield and Michael Sherman have two characteristics in common: they are reacting against an absent or hostile father, and they generalize from this reaction to men's roles in general. At the same time, they have sufficiently identified with some male, and can thus feel *safe* empathizing with their mothers without fear of becoming "too feminine."

Did the men who shared the work at home love their wives more? Were they more considerate? It's true, egalitarian men had more harmonious marriages, but I would be reluctant to say that [other men] loved their wives less than men like Art Winfield or Michael Sherman, or were less considerate in other ways. . . . Two other, more external factors also did *not* distinguish men who did share from men who didn't: the number of hours they worked or how much they earned. Husbands usually work a longer "full-time" job than wives. But in the families I studied, men who worked fifty hours or more per week were just *slightly* less likely to share housework than men who worked forty-five, forty, or thirty-five hours a week. In addition, fifty-hour-a-week *women* did far *more* childcare and housework than men who worked the same hours. Other national studies also show that the number of hours a man works for pay has little to do with the number of hours he works at home.

Of all the factors that influence the relations between husbands and wives, I first assumed that money would loom the largest. The man who shared, I thought, would need his wife's salary more, would value her job more and as a result also her time.

American wives in two-job couples average one dollar for every three their husbands earn, and this average prevailed among the families I studied too.[1] Often, among the couples I studied, a man who works a job from the top rung of a "dual labor market" is married to a woman who does a job from the bottom of it—an executive married to a secretary, a dentist to a dental assistant, a doctor to a nurse, a pilot to a flight attendant. Economically speaking, most husbands have the more important job.

I assumed that the man who shares would not earn more, and that the wage gap between other husbands and wives might *cause* the leisure gap between them. Both spouses might agree that because his job came first, his leisure did too. Leaving childcare aside (since most men would want to do some of that), I assumed that men who earned *as much or less* than their wives would do *more* housework. I assumed that a woman who wanted fifty-fifty in the second shift but had married a high-earning man would reconcile herself to the family's greater need for her husband's work, set aside her desires, and work the extra month a year. By the same token, a traditional man married to a high-earning woman would swallow his traditional pride and pitch in at home. I assumed that money would talk louder than ideals, and invisibly shape each partner's gender strategy.

• • •

The Limits of Economic Logic

Money mattered in the marriages I studied, but it was not the powerful "invisible hand" behind men who shared. For one thing, this is clear from the family portraits. Michael Sherman earned much more than Adrienne but his job didn't matter more, and he shared the work at home. For years Ann Myerson earned more than her husband but put her husband's job first anyway. John Livingston valued his wife's job as he did his own, but she took more responsibility at home.

• • •

An intriguing clue appeared . . . when I divided all the men into three groups: men who earn more than their wives (most men), men who earn the same amount, and men who earn less. Of the men who earned more than their wives, 21 percent shared housework. Of the men who earned about the same, 30 percent shared. But among men who earned *less* than their wives, *none* shared.

• • •

The principle of "balancing" seems to be at work. According to this principle, if men lose power over women in one way, they make up for it in another way—by avoiding the second shift, for example. In this way, they can maintain dominance over women. How much responsibility these men assumed at home was thus related to the deeper issue of male power. Men who earn much more than their wives already have a power over their wives in that they control a scarce and important resource. The more severely a man's identity is financially threatened—by his wife's higher salary, for example—the less he can afford to threaten it further by doing "women's work" at home.

Men who shared the second shift weren't trying to make up for losing power in other realms of their marriage; they didn't feel the need to "balance." Michael Sherman had given up the *idea* that he should have more power than Adrienne. Art Winfield talked playfully about men being "brought up to be kings."

But Peter Tanagawa felt a man *should* have more power, and felt he'd given a lot of it up when Nina's career rose so dramatically. He'd adjusted himself to earning much less, but to a man of his ideas, this had been a sacrifice. By making up for his sacrifice by doing more at home, Nina engaged in "balancing." Among other couples, too, it's not only men who "balance"; women do too.

Thus, more crucial than cultural beliefs about men's and women's *spheres* were couples' beliefs about the right degree of men's and women's *power*. Women who "balanced" felt "too powerful." Sensing when their husbands got "touchy," sensing the fragility of their husbands' "male ego," not wanting them to get discouraged or depressed, such women restored their men's lost power by waiting on them at home.

• • •

Taken as a whole, one group of men—semi-unemployed, hanging back at work, or in training—neither earned the bread nor cooked it. And of all the wives, theirs were the least happy. Yet, either because they sympathized with their husbands, or expected their situation to improve, or because they felt there was no way to change it, and because they were, I believe, unconsciously maintaining the "right" balance of power in their marriage, such women worked the extra month a year. Meanwhile, their lower-earning husbands often saw their wives as intelligent, strong, "a rock"; at the same time these men could enjoy the idea that, though not a king at work, a man still had a warm throne at home.

• • •

Other evidence also points away from the logic of the pocketbook. In a 1985 report, Joseph Pleck found that over the last ten years, men married to *housewives* have increased their contributions to housework *nearly as much* as men whose wives do paid work, (p. 151). Housewives earned nothing ten years ago and they earn nothing now. Yet husbands of housewives now help their wives at home more. That isn't a matter of money talking, and not a matter of men "keeping the edge." They had the edge, and are giving some of it up.

These husbands of housewives may be helping more because of a rising standard of male consideration. Just as nonunion industries often try to avoid unionization by keeping wages in nonunion shops comparable to those in unionized shops, so husbands of housewives may be unconsciously responding to the women's movement by helping as much at home as husbands of working wives. Without quite knowing it, some "nonunion" (nonfeminist) women may be enjoying the gains won by "union" agitators. Again, the political struggle behind a cultural shift and not the timeless logic of the pocketbook seems to determine how much men help at home. To push the analogy further, the women who struggle to get their husbands to do more at home and whose husbands divorce them because of it may be like the workers who fight the company for better working conditions, win the point, but get fired.

The outrageous few improve things for the "good workers" who make no noise.

• • •

All in all, men who shared were similar to men who didn't in that their fathers were just as unlikely to have been model helpers at home, and just as unlikely to have done housework as boys themselves. But the men who shared at home seemed to have more distant ties with their fathers, and closer ones with their mothers. They were similar to non-sharing men in the hours they worked, but they tended not to earn a great deal more or less than their wives.

Sharing men seemed to be randomly distributed across the class hierarchy. There were the Michael Shermans and the Art Winfields. In the working class, more men shared without believing it corresponded to the kind of man they wanted to be. In the middle class, more men didn't share even though they believed in it. Men who both shared the work at home and believed in it seemed to come from every social class. Everything else equal, men whose wives had advanced degrees and professional careers—who had what the sociologist Pierre Bourdieu calls "cultural capital"—were more likely to share than men whose wives lacked such capital. Men with career wives were more likely to share than men with wives in "jobs." All these factors were part of the social backdrop to the working man's gender strategy at home.

• • •

The Idea of Fatherhood

Involved fathers had a much fuller, more elaborate notion of what a father was than uninvolved fathers did. Involved fathers talked about fathering much as mothers talked about mothering. Uninvolved fathers held to a far more restricted mission—to discipline the child or to teach him about sports. . . . When I asked uninvolved fathers to define a "good mother" and "good father," they gave elaborate and detailed answers for "good mother," and short, hazy answers for "good father," sometimes with a specific mission attached to it, like "teach him about cars."

I asked one man, "What's a good mother?" and he answered: "A good mother is patient. That's the first thing. Someone who is warm, caring, who can see what the child needs, physically, who stimulates the child intellectually, and helps the child meet his emotional challenges."

"What is a good father?" I asked. "A good father is a man who spends time with his children." Another man said, "A good father is a man who is around."

It is not that men have an elaborate idea of fatherhood and then don't live it up to it. Their idea of fatherhood is embryonic to begin with.

They often limit that idea by comparing themselves only to their own fathers, and not, as more involved men did, to their mothers, sisters, or other fathers. As a Salvadoran delivery man put it, "I give my children everything my father gave me." But Michael Sherman gave his twins what his *mother* gave him.

Men who are greatly involved with their children react against two cultural ideas: one idea removes the actual care of children from the definition of *manhood,* and one curtails the notion of how much care a child needs. As to the first idea, involved fathers' biggest struggle was against the doubts they felt about not "giving everything to get ahead" in their jobs. But even when they conquered this fear, another cultural idea stood in the way—the idea that their child is "already grown up," "advanced," and doesn't need much from him. A man's individual defense against seeing his children's need for him conspires with this larger social idea.

Just as the archetype of the supermom—the woman who can do it all—minimizes the real needs of women, so too the archetype of the "superkid" minimizes the real needs of children. It makes it all right to treat a young child as if he or she were older. Often uninvolved parents remarked with pride that their small children were "self-sufficient" or "very independent."

• • •

Involved fathers are aware that their children depend on them. Every afternoon Art Winfield knew Adam was waiting for him at daycare. Michael Sherman knew that around six A.M. one of his twins would call out "Daddy." . . . Such men were close enough to their children to know what they were and weren't getting from their mothers.

Uninvolved fathers were not. They *imagined* that their wives did more with the children than they did. For example, one thirty-two-year-old grocery clerk praised his wife for helping their daughter with reading on the weekends—something his wife complained he didn't make time for. But when I interviewed her, I discovered that her weekends were taken with housework, church, and visiting relatives.

• • •

In a time of stalled revolution—when women have gone to work, but the workplace, the culture, and most of all, the men, have not adjusted themselves to this new reality—children can be the victims. Most working mothers are already doing all they can, doing that extra month a year. It is men who can do more.

Fathers can make a difference that shows in the child. I didn't administer tests to the children in the homes I visited nor gather systematic information on child development. I did ask the babysitters and daycare workers for their general impressions of differences between the children of single parents, two-job families in which the father was uninvolved, and two-job families in which the father was actively involved. All of them said that the children of fathers who were actively involved seemed to them "more secure" and "less anxious." Their lives were less rushed. On Monday, they had more to report about Sunday's events: "Guess what I did with my dad. . . ."

• • •

In the end, caring for children is the most important part of the second shift, and the effects of a man's care or his neglect will show up again and again through time—in the child as a child, in the child as an adult, and probably also in the child's own approach to fatherhood, and in generations of fathers to come. Active fathers are often in reaction against a passive, detached father. . . . But an exceptionally warmhearted man, like the stepfather of Art Winfield, could light the way still better. In the last forty years, many women have made a historic shift, into the economy. Now its time for a whole generation of men to make a second historic shift—into work at home.

NOTES

1. More white women are entering formerly "male jobs." This may explain why white women just entering the job market in 1980 earned 83 percent of that earned by comparable white men. But the longer the two sexes stay on the job, the greater the wage gap. If the social class of each sex was determined solely on the basis of salary, benefits, and assets, the upper classes would be largely male and the lower classes largely female.

REFERENCES

Nash, John
1965 "The Father in Contemporary Culture and Current Psychological Literature," *Child Development* 36:261–297.

Pleck, Joseph H.
1985 *Working Wives, Working Husbands.* Beverly Hills, CA: Sage.

Review Questions

1. Among Hochschild's respondents, were men's relationships with their fathers or with their mothers more important in whether or not they shared housework and child care?

2. Which group of men were most likely to share household chores: men who earned less than their wives, the same as their wives, or more than their wives? How does the principle of "balancing" explain Hochschild's findings?

3. How did the "New Men" define and carry out the fatherhood role?

SOCIAL DEATH: SOME UNANTICIPATED CONSEQUENCES OF MEDICAL INNOVATIONS

Howard Robboy and Bernard Goldstein

In western societies, advancements in medical techonology are equated with support for belief in the possibility of prolonging life, progress in the treatment of illness and the continued evolution of modern society. In part, the effort to prolong life is based on the hope that further advances in science will ameliorate remaining medical problems and allow patients to resume a fuller life. However, in pursuing this hope, attention is focused more on celebrating the technology and prolonging the biological lives of these patients, rather than on the quality of their extended lives and the social costs endured by their medical caretakers and significant others. We contend that, paradoxically, in an attempt to prolong life, the employment of life-sustaining technology often prolongs death by extending patients' biological lives well beyond the end of their social lives. Thus, as implied by Illich (1976) in his discussion of treatment trajectories, with the employment of new medical technology, the manifest and latent functions of these innovations are often reversed.

Traditionally, prolonging life has meant maintaining both biological and social life. Now it is possible to sustain biological life with a complete absence of any social life. We define this situation as social death, the state in which chronically ill patients are perceived by their medical caretakers and/ or significant others as no longer being able to maintain a minimal amount of significant social interaction. Social death is not yet recognized as a basis for accepting biological death. Therefore, biological life is maintained despite the inability to prolong social life.

A prime example of such a medical innovation is the mechanical ventilator which evolved from the iron lung in the 1950s as a more mobile means for polio victims to sustain their breathing. Physicians soon

SOURCE: Howard Robboy and Bernard Goldstein, "Social Death: Some Unanticipated Consequences of Medical Innovations," prepared for this volume. Reprinted by permission of the authors.

began to employ ventilators for patients with other chronic lung diseases including lung cancer, amyotrophic lateral sclerosis (Lou Gehrig's disease), muscular dystrophy, emphysema, heart disease, AIDS, and in serious accident cases of upper-spinal-cord injuries and excessive amounts of water or smoke inhalation. It is estimated that there are over 6,000 adults on long-term ventilator use in the United States (American Association of Respiratory Therapists, 1984). Long-term ventilator dependence is defined here as the continuous use of ventilators for three months or more.

It has now become possible to maintain life, if only nominally. Some patients will be successfully weaned from ventilator dependence and will lead relatively normal lives. A very small number will return to a semblance of normal life, while remaining machine dependent. The majority, however, will remain hospitalized on ventilators, with a minimal and decreasing social life. To explain the disjunctions between the medical advances and the resulting arrangements by which individuals and groups attempt to cope with unanticipated social states such as social death, we employ Ogburn's thesis of cultural lag.[1] His central thesis is:

> that the parts of modern culture are not changing at the same rate, some parts are changing much more rapidly than others; and that since there is a correlation and interdependence of parts, a rapid change in one part of our culture requires re-adjustments through other changes in the various correlated parts of culture. . . . Where one part of culture changes first, through some discovery or invention, and occasions changes in some part of culture dependent upon it, there frequently is a delay in the changes occasioned in the dependent part of the culture. The extent of this lag will vary according to the nature of the cultural material, but may exist for a considerable number of years, during which time there may be said to be a maladjustment (Ogburn, 1964).

SOCIAL DEATH

Sudnow (1967) first introduced the term "social death" to mean, "that point at which socially relevant attributes of the patient begin to permanently cease to be operative as conditions for treating him, and when he is, essentially, regarded as already dead." He limits use of this term to situations related to the incipient death of acute-care patients. Our concern is the fate of chronically ill patients for whom the process of social death is both prolonged and continuous. Using Sudnow's terminology, the "decided phasing-out of attention given to 'dying' patients," is more complex as it involves patients' significant others as well as their medical caretakers (Sudnow 1967).

Thus, the concept of social death is more complex when applied to chronic-care, rather than acute-care, patients. For acute-care patients, death is imminent; for chronic-care patients, life goes on indefinitely. It is this indefiniteness that gradually helps to create a new definition of the situation—that patients are less (or no longer) able to meet minimal social obligations basic to human interaction. We use the term "social death" to label a status in the health-care trajectory where patients are legally and biologically alive, and their medical caretakers have little or no hope for their further recovery. This medical circumstance leaves medical caretakers and significant others with permanent obligations for patients' unfulfilled social roles and responsibilities. In turn, medical caretakers experience declining professional rewards while significant others suffer eroding emotional resources. On one end of the social death continuum are patients who are not able to be weaned or rehabilitated. On the other end lie comatose patients whose biological lives may be maintained with life-support systems.

Especially with chronic-care patients, the declaration of social death is only partially determined by their medical condition. The use of the label "socially dead" hinges upon the conflicting social obligations of patients' significant others as they are often caught between the illness demands of the patients and the normal demands of others in their paramount reality.

Lofland (1988) analyzes the bases of human relationships among primary group members in terms of the "threads of human connectedness" which are destroyed when loved ones experience loss and grief.[2] She notes that the death or loss of loved ones is often sudden, and grief and bereavement occur in a known societal context. In the case of long-term, ventilator-dependent patients, however, the sense of loss and feelings of grief and bereavement experienced by their close friends and family members are gradual and occur without benefit of appropriate guidelines. With social death, patients remain biologically alive, leaving their loved ones with mere memories of their former social selves and with cumbersome portions of the communication burden. The significant others who give must give and give again, without hope of reciprocity. Few relationships can survive over time under this strain. As Kalish (1983) states, "when a person perceives you, for all practical purposes, as dead or nonexistent, you are socially dead for that person." Once social death is declared by significant others, there are both quantitative and qualitative consequences for future interactions with these patients.

The concept of social death provides a framework for understanding the abandonment of these patients by their loved ones. Once they define patients as socially dead, they begin to mourn and to curtail their visits. Social relationships are also qualitatively reduced as expressions of grief enter the interactions. Ventilator-dependent patients who formerly were active spouses, parents, sons or daughters, come to be seen only as patients. To the extent that patterns of visitation are maintained, the social lives of family members must be reorganized to allow for the time and trauma involved. The nature of disruptions varies depending on whether patients are spouses, parents, siblings, or children; the size of the family; the amount of travel time involved; and the duration of the hospitalization. Since the concept of social death has yet to emerge as part of our consciousness, significant others must endure the burden of grief and mourning without the benefit of supporting ethics, norms and routines.[3] Traditional American norms provide that, after an appropriate period of mourning, widows and widowers are permitted to resume normal sexual relationships. But norms have yet to emerge to specify the appropriate behavior when the spouse is both legally and biologically alive, but socially dead. As indicated above, technology has prolonged the legal and biological life of these patients to a greater extent than their social lives.

The acceptance of social death in contemporary Western society is inhibited by broader social values, which Ernest Becker (1973) calls, "the denial of death." This denial requires that doctors and nurses prolong biological lives of patients, and that significant others perpetuate fictions of social relationships under pain of guilty consciences. Once the patients' loved ones declare social death, their burden is eased.

SOCIAL DEATH AND ITS IMPACT ON MEDICAL CARETAKERS

Many of the medical caretakers interviewed define ventilator-dependent patients as medical misfits, chronically ill, hospitalized patients who deviate from the model of the good patient: patients admitted acutely ill who respond to treatment in a few days and are soon discharged (Hughes [1956] 1971; Lorber 1975; Papper 1970). Medical caretakers are organized for this trajectory. However, when ventilator-dependent patients are housed in intensive-care units where the relevant equipment and trained staff are based, the rhythm of these units is disrupted. Such patients tend to be ostracized, sometimes even relocated physically "out of the way" as they come to be seen as socially dead.

As a result of the treatment trajectory, the burdens and frustrations of care increase as patients meet fewer and fewer of their social obligations. They need to be suctioned regularly, to be turned, and to be fed; they may be incontinent. As we noted earlier, the demand for traditional nursing care is incremented by excessive needs for companionship and reassurance. When this situation is compounded by the inability of patients to communicate verbally, friction and anxiety are likely to ensue.

The longer these patients are hospitalized, and the closer they are to being labeled as socially dead, the more likely it is that nurses will ignore their needs for attention. The absence of a quick recovery denies ICU staffs their usual professional rewards and results in a sense of guilt in the face of seeming failure. Nurses report becoming despondent, frustrated, discouraged, and burned out. Other staff report a lack of any sense of accomplishment.

The value of prolonged lives must be balanced against the personal, professional and bureaucratic costs to medical caretakers and institutions. Nurses report that they often cringe when they learn that emergency-room staffs have placed elderly patients with severe pulmonary disorders on ventilators and are in the process of transferring them to their units. They are familiar with the scenario which is about to unfold and express great compassion for the helpless patients. Given their values of patient-oriented care, the nurses are less concerned with the practice of defensive medicine and the employment of the latest technology to prolong life. Instead, they often feel that a natural death would be more appropriate.

> We have to carry out all of the measures that the physician orders. So they are not in there in the middle of the night giving them the antibiotics that burn their veins right out. And the patient cries. . . . The physician isn't sticking needles into an arm that's been stuck or a rear that's been stuck so many times that it's like hitting a board because the patient has lost all of their fat and lost everything and their skin is sloughing off. You're giving them more pain with everything you do. One I.V. fails and you have to put in another I.V. and that fails and you have to put in another. And their skin is terrible and the veins are gone completely. You have to stick them again. And the patients cry, they weep and they develop ulcers. You have to go again and do it. And you feel like a killer, you do. You feel so terrible to hurt these people again and again and again. You say, "I'm sorry, but I have to do this again. I'm sorry, but I have to give you another intravenous. I'm sorry, but I have to give you this medicine. Sorry, I have to put this tube back down your throat." (Interview #30)

Likewise, physicians report feeling helpless and perceive themselves to be professional failures. An intensive-care nurse comments on her experiences with the difficulties that physicians have dealing with death:

> Emotionally they are afraid. They can't seem to accept the patient as the dying patient. I know this might sound strange, but it is true. The nurses are much more accepting, much more able to step back and say, "This patient is dying, we should let this patient go." The physicians seem to . . . not be able to let go. . . . They are supposed to save lives and to give up and let the patient die, is a defeat for them. . . . Emotionally, they (the doctors) can't seem to deal with the patient. They get to the point where they don't want to look at the patient or touch the patient. They can't face the facts. . . . They feel

> like they lost. But they can't deal with the patient emotionally. They can't look the patient right in the eye and say, "How are you feeling and have you given up and what is your emotional state right now?" They can't do it. So they are no support to the patient. . . . The nurses get angry and they get angry at the physicians. They feel sorry for the patients. They want to help the patients.
>
> It is very frustrating, very frustrating. They're dealing with the family, they're dealing with the patients and they don't get the support from the physicians. . . . It's just the emotional aspect of death itself. They have trouble accepting that. You don't see a physician in a hospice unit. (Interview #30)

Unlike family members and friends who can declare social death and abandon patients, medical caretakers are obligated to continue to provide care, and hospitals then become dumping grounds. Discrepancies between physical and social life produce a status, social death, in which medical caretakers treat patients who are no longer socially alive, but whose bodies remain functioning. These discrepancies represent a cultural lag between traditional social meanings and the new social conditions created by technology. Society has yet to generate social processes or structures to correspond to this new treatment trajectory. Thus nurses, respiratory therapists, physicians, family members, and friends of ventilator-dependent patients often find that they too become victims of cultural lag.

Some hospitals are now developing step-down units to lower costs and to locate patients in units more appropriate to the expected trajectory. As Blau indicates in his discussion of "structural effects," changes in structure are likely to cause changes in expectations (Blau 1960). Where step-down units are established, additional staffing problems often emerge since these locations are usually not preferred choices in which to work. They are perhaps professional dumping grounds, places to which nurses drift because other options are not available. Hence, in such instances, higher turnover rates than usual are likely to develop.

SOCIAL DEATH AND ITS IMPACT ON PATIENTS

In contemporary Western society, we are socialized to accept the relevant therapeutic regimen when in the sick role and to return to normal responsibilities as soon as possible (Parsons 1951). However, these expectations must be redefined for chronically ill patients, especially those who are dependent on artificial hearts, dialysis machines, or ventilators. Dialysis patients are likely to be dependent on their machines for the rest of their lives, although transplantation is a possibility. Their machine dependency is not easily assimilated into daily routines and their goals are thus modified from recovery to the acceptance of long-term disability (Evans 1985).

Ventilator-dependent patients have an even greater adjustment to make than those on dialysis or artificial hearts. Being continuously machine dependent frequently leads to panic, so that they are often viewed by their significant others and medical caretakers as if they are living in constant states of medical emergencies (Robboy and Goldstein 1986).

Their quality of life is poor and they are denied the luxury enjoyed by dialysis patients of being able to spend some time away from their machines. This complete and constant dependence becomes the basis for a love/ hate relationship with the technology.

Although the machines have saved and are prolonging their lives, the constant sight of the wires and tubes, the frequent ringing of the alarms and the ever-present fear of possible machine malfunctions as well as possible power failures constantly hover on the edges of their consciousness. They are well aware that if the machines fail and caretakers do not come to their rescue, they will die. In this context, the dying process might be worse than death itself. Desperately gasping for breath is an inhumane, psychologically devastating, and torturously slow way to die. More so than other medical conditions or symptoms, suffocation is instantly associated with the onset of death. Ventilator-dependent patients probably flirted with suffocation either before they were placed on this life-sustaining equipment or while they were becoming acclimated to their machine dependency.

The experience of machine dependency creates inordinate demands for human contact. First, being connected to and dependent on machines for life leaves patients in states of interactional deprivation. Second, being immobile, these patients must entice others to come to them for human contact, often causing their medical caretakers to define them as excessively self-centered. In hospitals, nurses note that these patients regularly seek to get their attention—tapping on tables when they are unable to speak, deliberately setting off alarms, and so on. Family members report the same kind of tactics from ventilator-dependent patients receiving home care. This constant tapping or setting off of alarms may be viewed as efforts by patients to overcome feelings of powerlessness.

These panic reactions are parallel to the social phenomena of "new states of consciousness" in which individuals feel "out of control," lacking any social context to give meaning to their condition. For example, when marijuana and L.S.D. were first used by members of the general public, they often felt "out of control" and were labeled as having a marijuana or L.S.D. "psychosis" (Becker 1967). In American society, mental illness is frequently attributed to people who feel out of control and lack social reference points to give meaning to their conditions. Once these substances became more widely used and their effects became common knowledge in the drug subculture, getting "high" was no longer associated with being psychotic. As ventilator use becomes more common, we can expect that social frameworks will develop to provide meaning to this situation, thus lessening the panic.

Finally, to the extent that patients are located in acute-care institutions, expectations prevail that they will soon recover and leave. However only a minority of long-term, continuous-use, ventilator-dependent patients are weaned from their machines. Most become chronic-care patients misplaced in acute-care facilities where they cannot receive the required attention and emotional support.

SOCIAL DEATH AND ITS IMPACT ON SIGNIFICANT OTHERS

To sustain life mechanically without a traditional recuperation period creates an unfamiliar reality for the significant others of most ventilator-dependent patients. Once their other health conditions are stabilized, they may continue to be perceived by their significant others as acutely ill and socially dead. In this new reality, created by the status of social death in the treatment trajectory, these patients should be redefined as being chronically ill and/ or severely handicapped so that they can be relocated to more appropriate settings. Long-term residence in acute-care settings runs contrary to the expectations of hospital staffs and family members that patients will recuperate. Economically it violates the assumptions built into the DRGs (Diagnosis Related Groups) and reimbursement structures. It also contradicts the expectations patients have of themselves. Such disappointments often result in friction between patients, hospital staffs, and family members.

The impact of their chronic illness/ disability also varies with the nature of the pre-existing relations within families. There is evidence to suggest that well-integrated families will absorb additional responsibilities for a longer period of time. Loosely structured or malintegrated families are likely to relinquish their care responsibilities sooner (Sudnow 1967).

When family members maintain patterns of visiting, they develop relationships with hospital staffs. Our initial evidence suggests that these relationships may have varied forms and content depending, in part, on how family members feel about the continuing survival of the patients. In one case we observed, a patient's daughter took the initiative to learn the necessary nursing skills, to establish positive relationships with the hospital staff, and to become accepted as a help rather than a hindrance. Furthermore, from the staff's point of view, this woman was, "the ideal family member/ caretaker." She provided basic care for her mother and operated the various machines, relieving the nurses of some of their more burdensome duties. This was done diligently (fourteen hours a day, seven days a week, for over four years) and in a manner which fit the staff's definition of good patient care. We have other examples of heroic efforts by family members to maintain contact, to establish rapport with hospital staffs, to work out a modus vivendi that redounds to the benefit of patients.

In contrast, we have evidence of the washing-the-hands syndrome, in which the entire burden of maintaining the patient is put on the health care personnel.

Family time and space must be reorganized when patients remain hospitalized for extended periods of time. The social roles of patients in families are vacated, placed in limbo, and cannot be filled by others without serious repercussions. What do wives and husbands do about spouses who are not there to work, cook, take care of children, and make love? The patient is missing in action, socially dead, but biologically alive. Designated role players have yet to emerge who can make triage decisions in the best interests of patients, although the courts have occasionally appointed such persons. Family members often look to physicians for guidance without an awareness of the physicians' possible hidden agenda, to avoid litigation. Some hospitals have ethics committees, but they act only in an advisory capacity and may not always be readily convened. The belief in the potential of science to discover a cure or treatment and/or a hope for divine intervention act to deflect despair and permit a pseudo-hopefulness. At the same time, these traditional social beliefs direct the focus from the issue of social death and continue to focus the attention of medical caretakers on the biological or legal aspects of patient care.

SUMMARY AND CONCLUSIONS

Technological innovation in health care has unanticipated consequences well beyond medical practice or therapeutic regimens. The development of modern technology such as mechanical ventilators does more than save and prolong the lives of patients. It changes the conditions under which decisions are made concerning the maintenance of life. It causes family members of patients to take an active role in life-and-death decisions, a role for which they are ill-prepared. As Ogburn's theory of cultural lag would lead us to expect, we currently have neither the values, norms, routines, or institutions to cope with the social and cultural problems that have emerged. Patients, physicians, nurses, family members, and close friends struggle to develop adaptations to meet the unanticipated social consequences of new medical technology.

The concept of social death has begun to emerge to distinguish the state of existence lying between life and biological death. As a result, family members and close friends are abandoning chronically-ill patients as the social and emotional costs become too great to continue the traditional role relationships. Currently, such behavior draws forth a negative value judgment. Such behavior cannot be engaged in with grace, unlike the situation in traditional Eskimo society. There, it was socially acceptable to abandon individuals (particularly the infirm and aged) when the community determined that support for them was using up too large a portion of the community's emotional and economic resources.

NOTES

1. It is not necessary to accept a unidirectional change from material to nonmaterial culture to utilize Ogburn's thesis of cultural lag.

2. Lofland's (1988) seven "threads of human connectedness" are: role partners, mundane assistance, linkages to others, the creation and maintenance of self, support for comforting myths, reality maintenance, and the maintenance of possible futures.

3. This parallels experiences in which family members are in prisons, mental hospitals, prisoner-of-war camps, or are being held as political hostages.

REFERENCES

American Association of Respiratory Therapists
1984 "Chronic Ventilator Dependent Individuals: Results of Survey." February 2, 1984.

Becker, Ernest
1973 *The Denial of Death.* New York: The Free Press.

Becker, Howard
1967 "History, Culture and Subjective Experience: An Exploration of the Social Bases of Drug-Induced Experiences." *Journal of Health and Social Behavior* 8:163–176.

Blau, Peter
1960 "Structural Effects." *American Sociological Review* 21:178–193.

Evans, Roger
1985 "The Quality of Life of Patients with In-Stage Renal Disease." *New England Journal of Medicine* 312:553–559.

Hughes, Everett C.
[1956] 1971 "The Making of a Physician: General Statement of Ideas and Problems." Pp. 397–407 in Everett C. Hughes (Ed.), *The Sociological Eye.* Chicago: Aldine-Atherton.

Illich, Ivan
1976 *Medical Nemesis.* New York: Pantheon.

Kalish, Richard A.
1985 *Death, Grief and Caring Relationships.* 2nd Edition. Monterey: Brooks/Cole.

Lofland, Lyn H.
1988 "Loss and Human Connection: An Exploration into the Nature of the Social Bond." Pp. 155–171 in Candace Clark and Howard Robboy (Eds.), *Social Interaction.* 3rd Edition, New York: St. Martin's.

Lorber, Judith
1975 "Good Patients and Problem Patients: Conformity and Deviance in a General Hospital." *Journal of Health and Social Behavior* 16:213–225.

Ogburn, William
1964 *Social Change.* Gloucester, Massachusetts: Peter Smith.

Papper, Solomon
1970 "The Undesirable Patient." *Journal of Chronic Disease* 22:777–779.

Parsons, Talcott
1951 *The Social System.* Glencoe, Illinois: The Free Press.

Robboy, Howard and Bernard Goldstein
1986 "Continuous Emergencies." Presented at the Annual Meetings of the Society for the Study of Social Problems.

Sudnow, David
1967 *Passing On: The Social Organization of Dying.* Englewood Cliffs, N.J.: Prentice Hall.

Review Questions

1. What do Robboy and Goldstein mean by "social death"? How does it differ from physical death?
2. Americans generally view the ability to extend life as a great scientific accomplishment, but Robboy and Goldstein show that extending life may not be viewed this way by medical care givers, patients, and/or patients' significant others. Explain.
3. What other recent technological innovations have had unanticipated and unintended consequences for society and social interaction?

Suggested Readings: Social and Cultural Change

Atwater, Lynn. *The Extramarital Connection: Sex, Intimacy, and Identity.* New York: Irvington, 1982.

Berger, Peter, Brigitte Berger, and Hansfried Kellner. *The Homeless Mind.* New York: Vintage Books, 1974.

Erikson, Kai T. *Everything in Its Path.* New York: Simon & Schuster, 1976.

Lerner, David. *The Passing of Traditional Society.* New York: Free Press, 1958.

McAdam, Doug. *Freedom Summer.* New York: Oxford University Press, 1988.

Spicer, Edward H., ed. *Human Problems in Technological Change.* New York: John Wiley, 1952.

Zurcher, Louis, and George Kirkpatrick. *Citizens for Decency: Antipornography Crusades as Status Defense.* Austin: University of Texas Press, 1976.

ABOUT THE CONTRIBUTORS

Howard S. Becker (Ph.D., University of Chicago). He is currently Professor of Sociology at the University of Washington. His numerous publications include *The Outsiders, Sociological Work: Method and Substance, Making the Grade: The Academic Side of College Life* (with Blanche Geer and Everett C. Hughes), *Boys in White: Student Culture in Medical School* (with Geer, Hughes, and others), and *Art Worlds.*

Peter L. Berger (Ph.D., New School for Social Research). He is University Professor and Professor of the Sociology of Religion at Boston University. His books include *The Social Construction of Reality* (with Thomas Luckmann), *Rumour of Angels, The Sacred Canopy, Noise of Solemn Assemblies,* and *Invitation to Sociology,* from which the first article in this volume is taken.

Herbert Blumer (Ph.D., University of Chicago). He was a student of George Herbert Mead and is one of the major figures in micro-sociological theory. He taught at Chicago before starting the sociology department at the University of California at Berkeley. The selection included in this volume comes from his book, *Symbolic Interactionism.*

Spencer Cahill (Ph.D., University of California at Santa Barbara).He is Associate Professor of Sociology at Skidmore College. Much of his research has focused on the sociology of childhood and social life in public places.

William J. Chambliss (Ph.D., University of Indiana and holds a law degree). He is presently Professor and Chair of the Department of Sociology at George Washington University. His many books on the sociology of law and crime include *On the Take, Crime and the Legal Process,* and *Whose Law? What Order?*

Candace Clark (Ph.D., Columbia University). She is currently Associate Professor of Sociology and director of the graduate program at Montclair State College. Her present research in the sociology of emotions focuses on sympathy. She is an editor of *Social Interaction.*

Peter Conrad (Ph.D., Boston University). He is Professor of Sociology at Brandeis University and one of the leading sociologists in the sociology of health and illness. His books include *Deviance and Medicalization* (with Joseph Schneider) and *Sociology of Health and Illness* (edited with Rochelle Kern).

Kathleen Ferraro (Ph.D., Arizona State University). She is Associate Professor at the Center for the Study of Justice at Arizona State University and is involved in women's studies. Most of her research has focused on the lives of battered women.

Andrea Fontana (Ph.D., University of California at San Diego). He is Professor of Sociology at the University of Nevada at Las Vegas and President of the Society for the Study of Symbolic Interaction. His book *The Last Frontier* is excerpted here. In addition, he has co-authored *The Sociology of Everyday Life* and a book on social problems.

Donald Foster (B.A., Emporia State University). He is currently a case manager for the Four County Mental Health Service in Independence, Kansas.

Blanche Geer (Ph.D., Johns Hopkins University). She is Professor Emeritus at Northeastern University. Her long-term collaboration with Howard S. Becker and Everett C. Hughes has resulted in, among other publications, *Making the Grade: The Academic Side of College Life* and *Boys in White: Student Culture in Medical School.*

Erving Goffman (Ph.D., University of Chicago). At his death in 1982, he was Benjamin Franklin Professor at the University of Pennsylvania and also served as president of the American Sociological Association. Goffman's unique dramaturgical perspective is reflected in his many books, including *Behavior in Public Places, Stigma, Asylums, Interaction Ritual, Frame Analysis, Gender Advertisements,* and the early *Presentation of Self in Everyday Life,* from which our selection is taken.

Bernard Goldstein (Ph.D., University of Chicago). He is Professor Emeritus at Rutgers University. His research interests are in the fields of work and health.

Edward Gross (Ph.D., University of Chicago). He is now Professor of Sociology at the University of Washington. His books include *Industry and Social Life, Work and Society,* and *University Goals and Academic Power* (co-authored with Paul Grambsch). His most recent research is in the sociology of emotions, as is the selection on embarrassment included in this volume.

Joseph Hickey (Ph.D., University of New Mexico). He is Associate Professor of Anthropology at Emporia State University. His research has focused on pioneering communities and cowboys in the United States.

Arlie Russell Hochschild (Ph.D., University of California at Berkeley). She is Professor of Sociology at Berkeley, and since 1975, she has been writing about the sociology of feelings and emotion management. Her 1983 book, *The Managed Heart: Commercialization of Human Feeling,* won the Charles Cooley Award and a *New York Times* Book of the Year award. *The Second Shift,* excerpted here, has received acclaim in the United States and throughout Europe.

Ruth Horowitz (Ph.D., University of Chicago). She is Associate Professor of Sociology at the University of Delaware. Her research interests include deviance and delinquency.

Everett C. Hughes (Ph.D. in social anthropology, University of Chicago). At the time of his death, he was Professor Emeritus of Sociology at Boston College. Hughes was a major figure in the sociology of work and occupations and also served as president of the American Sociological Association. His many books include *Men and Their Work, The Sociological Eye, French Canada in Transition, Where People Meet: Racial and Ethnic Frontiers* (with Helen McGill Hughes), and *Making the Grade: The Academic Side of College Life* (co-authored with Howard S. Becker and Blanche Geer), which is the source of our selection in this volume.

Jennifer Hunt (Ph.D., City University of New York). She is currently Associate Professor of Sociology at Montclair State College as well as a Research Candidate at the Psychoanalytic Institute of New York University Medical Center. Her research and writing focus on the police, on qualitative research techniques, and on psychoanalysis.

John M. Johnson (Ph.D., University of California at San Diego). He is Professor of Sociology at the Center for the Study of Justice at Arizona State University. He is a former President of the Society for the Study of Symbolic Interaction and an editor of the journal, *Symbolic Interaction*. His research and publications have mostly centered on the field of social deviance.

David A. Karp (Ph.D., New York University). He is now Professor of Sociology at Boston College. He is a co-author of *Being Urban: A Social Psychological View of City Life* (with Gregory P. Stone and William C. Yoels), *The Research Craft* (with John B. Williamson, John R. Dalphin, and others), *Experiencing the Life Cycle* (with Yoels), and *The Sociology of Everyday Life* (with Yoels).

Debra Kaufman (Ph.D., Cornell University). She is Professor of Sociology at Northeastern University and the founder of their Woman's Study Program. She has co-authored *Achievement and Women* and, more recently, authored *Rachel's Daughters*.

Sherryl Kleinman (Ph.D., University of Minnesota). She is currently Associate Professor of Sociology at the University of North Carolina at Chapel Hill, and is the author of *Equals before God* (excerpted here) and many articles in the fields of symbolic interaction and the sociology of emotions.

Demie Kurz (Ph.D., Northwestern University). She is currently Co-Director of Women's Studies and a member of the sociology faculty at the University of Pennsylvania. Her present research interests include abused women and parents as agents of emotional socialization.

Janet Lever (Ph.D., Yale University). She is currently teaching Sociology at California State University—Los Angeles. She is a co-author of *Women at Yale: Liberating a College Campus* (with Pepper Schwartz) and author of *Soccer Madness*. She is also a research sociologist at the Rand Corporation and is currently at work on a study of HIV infection in female prostitutes.

Elliot Liebow (Ph.D., Catholic University of America). An anthropologist, his dissertation research resulted in the now-classic book *Tally's Corner*, from which our selection was drawn. Before becoming Professor of Anthropology at Catholic University, he served as a social anthropologist at the National Institutes of Mental Health of the federal government.

Donileen Loseke (Ph.D., University of California at Santa Barbara). She is Assistant Professor of Sociology at Skidmore College. Her work focuses on the social construction of social problems, and her book, *The Battered Woman and Shelters,* is forthcoming.

Lyn H. Lofland (Ph.D., University of California at San Francisco). She is currently Professor of Sociology at the University of California at Davis. Among her published works are *World of Strangers* and *Analyzing Social Settings* (with John Lofland).

Anne Machung (Ph.D. in Political Science, University of Wisconsin). She is Research Associate at the Institute for the Study of Social Change at the University of California at Berkeley and is studying women and work.

Marcia Millman (Ph.D., Brandeis University). She is Professor of Sociology at the University of California at Santa Cruz. Besides *Such a Pretty Face* (excerpted here), she is the author of *The Unkindest Cut: Life in the Backrooms of Medicine* and co-editor of *Another Voice.*

Horace Miner (Ph.D., University of Chicago). He was for many years Professor of Sociology and Anthropology at the University of Michigan.

Howard Robboy (Ph.D., Rutgers University). He is currently Associate Professor of Sociology at Trenton State College. He has written several articles on the sociology of work and the impact of medical technology on social relationships. He is also one of the editors of *Social Interaction.*

D. L. Rosenhan (Ph.D. in clinical psychology, Columbia University). He is Professor of Psychology and Law at Stanford University. He is the co-editor (with Perry London) of two books: *Foundations of Abnormal Psychology* and *Theory and Research in Abnormal Psychology.*

Barry Schwartz (Ph.D., University of Pennsylvania). He is Professor of Sociology at the University of Georgia. His many articles include sociological analyses of sleep and gift giving. He is the editor of *The Changing Face of the Suburbs* and the author of *Queuing and Waiting: Studies in the Social Organization of Access and Delay, Vertical Classification: A Study in Structuralism and the Sociology of Knowledge,* and a book about George Washington.

Carol B. Stack (Ph.D. in anthropology, University of Illinois). She is Professor of Social and Cultural Studies in Education and Women's Studies at the University of California at Berkeley. Her book, *All Our Kin: Strategies for Survival in a Black Community,* is a more detailed exposition of the article included here. Her current research is on African-Americans' reclaiming of the rural South.

Gregory P. Stone (Ph.D., University of Chicago). He was Professor of Sociology at the University of Minnesota until his death in 1981. His many articles deal with various aspects of the sociology of everyday life. He was a co-author of *Being Urban: A Social Psychological View of City Life* (with David A. Karp and William C. Yoels), co-editor and translator of *Herman Schmalenback on Society and Experience* (with Gunther Luschen), and co-editor of *Social Psychology Through Symbolic Interaction* (with Harvey Farberman).

Anselm Strauss (Ph.D., University of Chicago). He has been a leading figure in symbolic interaction for many decades and is Professor Emeritus of Sociology at the Medical School of the University of California at San Francisco. He is the author of *Mirrors and Masks* (excerpted here) and co-author (with Barney Glaser) of *The Discovery of Grounded Theory, Time for Dying,* and *Awareness of Dying.*

William E. Thompson (Ph.D., Oklahoma State University). He is Professor of Sociology and Anthropology at East Texas State University. His research is in the area of social deviance and juvenile delinquency.

Diane Vaughan (Ph.D., Ohio State University). She is currently Associate Professor of Sociology at Boston College. Her writings include *On the Social Control of Organizations* and *Uncoupling: The Social Construction of Divorce.*

Lenore J. Weitzman (Ph.D., Yale University). She taught at the University of California at Davis and Stanford University before moving to Harvard University where she is Professor of Sociology. Her book, *The Divorce Revolution,* is the most recent of her writings on the social roles of women.

William Foote Whyte (Ph.D., University of Chicago). Now Professor of Sociology at Cornell University, he has served as president of the American Sociological Association. His books include *Men at Work, Human Relations in the Restaurant Industry, Industry and Society,* and the classic *Street Corner Society.*

Charlotte Wolf (Ph.D., University of Minnesota). She is Professor at Memphis State University. Her research focuses on interaction between and within minority groups.

William Yoels (Ph.D., University of Minnesota). He is Professor of Sociology at the University of Alabama at Birmingham and has co-authored *Being Urban: A Social Psychological View of City Life* (with Gregory P. Stone and David A. Karp), *Experiencing the Life Cycle* (with Karp), and *Sociology of Everyday Life* (with Karp).